# AROUND THE WORLD
# IN 80 YEARS

# AROUND THE WORLD
# IN 80 YEARS

JAY J. STEMMER

authorHOUSE®

*AuthorHouse™ LLC*
*1663 Liberty Drive*
*Bloomington, IN 47403*
*www.authorhouse.com*
*Phone: 1-800-839-8640*

*Published by AuthorHouse  07/22/2014*

*ISBN: 978-1-4969-2538-1 (sc)*
*ISBN: 978-1-4969-2537-4 (e)*

*Library of Congress Control Number: 2014912244*

To Jacob Andrew Stemmer, my father


Who passed on the travel gene. May he rest
in peace with his final journey.

# Contents

# Captions of Pictures in the Front Cover

Glacier National Park, Montana - shot taken just before complete winter closing - parts of the Park were shut down and roads closed

Bayon Temple stone carving in Angkor Wat complex of Temples, Cambodia

Red Square, Moscow, Russia - taken with a long lens

Himalayas just north of Kathmandu, Nepal

Ta Prohn Temple site at Angkor Wat, Cambodia - the French cleaned up many of the temples and decided to leave one as is- known as the Jungle Temple

Hundertwasserhaus, Vienna, Austria - you eyesight is not going, it was designed this way

Note: some of the pictures inside were not taken at the exact location of the article they are displayed with - but, close by. Like horseshoes and hand grenades, close will have to do.

# INTRODUCTION

OK, I confess, I'm not 80 years old -yet. But I'm closing in and can't forecast the future. Some of my friends from college and the service haven't made it this far. So, I figured I should get my collection of articles together while I still can.

I remember when I was a kid and we all got in the car for a summer road trip. My father's two week summer vacation. Mom and Dad in the front seat and my younger brother and I fighting in the back. To Virginia and the Skyline Caverns and Williamsburg. Next year to Chicago and the stock yards, then Niagra Falls and Toronto. Two weeks to Miami Beach and back to New Jersey. I don't know if these trips gave me the bug to travel or it just fueled the existing one. Probably the latter. I went to a high school reunion a few years back and saw that the vast majority of the class still lived in New Jersey. I suppose they could have visited the Eiffel Tower and came home to live within 10 miles of where they grew up. But, somehow, I expect otherwise. Some of us seek adventure and others take comfort with seeing the same from day to day.

Modern America was founded by those going to a new land. New sights, new homes, new food and new people. Some didn't make it but most did and settled in for over 100 years. Then came the pioneers that wanted to go west. Most families played it safe and stayed on the east coast. The adventurers went onto unknown land and I expect the readers of this book are of a like kind. Over the years, I have preferred to use my vacation time to go to places I've never been. Every day then will be an adventure since I'll encounter something new. Naturally, there are risks. I had my pocket picked in the Madrid subway, I was mugged on the street in Chile, jailed in Norway, got into a fist fight in Greece and broke my leg in Moldova. None of these events are mentioned in the collection of articles to follow and there is a reason.

About 25 years ago I read an article that showed how I could help pay for my travel by writing articles and selling them to travel magazines and newspapers. I quickly learned that they published only upbeat stories. If I wrote that the place was boring and said, "Don't go there, it sucks", no one would buy the piece. So, when I was in El Salvador for 5 days, I wrote nothing. Why bother.

I broke the collection into 10 major headings instead of by Continent to try for a better balance in length. North America includes the Carribean, South America includes Central America. The Mid-East, Russia and China are all in Asia but the Asia segment is still the biggest with them removed. Africa is stand alone and Australia includes Tahiti because they're close. The northern most Pacific Islands sort of stand alone and Europe includes the Canary Islands even though they are off the coast of Morocco.

There are three ways to read the articles. One- pick a place you would like to visit and see if my words still make you want to go. Two- read about a place you have no interest in and see if I can change your mind. Three - read about a place you been to and compare your experience with mine.

I remember calling a hotel from the airport on Raiatia, Tahiti. The phone rang but no one answered. I continued calling for 15 minutes and a local Frenchman noticed my distress. I explained the problem and he told me that the hotel had burned to the ground 6 months ago and recommended another hotel. I ended up there and found it's kitchen building had burned out and I'd have to walk 20 minutes to town to get supper each night. But, it was a nice place and they were glad to have me. (Note- I was given fresh fruit for breakfast). That said, the information section with airfares and hotel prices is dated. You will pay much more than the price I show. Airlines and hotel chains merge, change names or go out of business. Still, if the price of the cheap hotel I mention has doubled over the years, then probably the price of nicer hotels up the street has doubled as well. It's to your benefit to use the internet to check the availability and price for everything. The Eiffel tower hasn't changed but the admission price has.

One of the problems of being a photo-journalist is in the selection of slides to submit for publication. It's a good thing for the magazine since they don't have to buy pictures elsewhere. For this book I have to select only a few from over 10,000 since the focus here is location, not photography. I have to leave out some beautiful pictures.

If you like to go to resorts and stay the week, this book is not for you. I believe you can only see Rome or Paris with feet on the pavement. Walk the streets, climb the hills, take the bus, ride the subway and take the train to the next town. I never rent a car overseas. Any accident will be your fault, the police will side with the local. I was about to punch out a Moroccan man who wouldn't leave me alone on the streets of Tangiers, Morocco. I stopped, thought, and took my own advice by envisioning the conditions in a Moroccan jail. I knew his story wouldn't match mine. I kept walking.

Much of my travel was independent and on a budget. Some was with tour companies and they would feature better hotels. There are destinations best seen with a tour company. They get better prices than you can for accommodation and make it much easier to get from here to there. Russia, India and China are good examples for tours. Most of the American pieces are from road trips. Like the early days but without my parents and no brother to fight with.

Note: I did sell one negative article to the Buffalo Sunday News. See if you can find it.

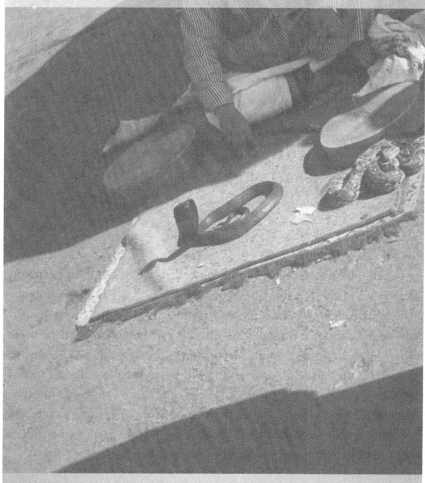

# I AFRICA

Casbah in Marrakech - live cobra

1

The very bottom of Africa, Cape Town

Capetown, So. Africa

CAPE TOWN, AFRICA has been called one of the most beautiful cities in the world. I'm not sure about that. It is clean and certainly the most attractive city in Africa. The city center has high-rise apartments, hotels and restaurants - much like all cities with a population of three million. And, most of the population lives in the suburbs. To the west of city center is the Atlantic Ocean and a series of bays that act like individual communities. To the southeast is the last of the Indian Ocean and one bay. A large one. Directly south, the Cape of Good Hope. The stormy tip where the cold waters of the Atlantic collide with the warm waters of the Indian Ocean. A sailboat crossing that cost many lives over the years.

After resting from the long series of flights (19 hours from JFK to Cape Town) we set off for the cities giant icon, Table Mountain. A rock, and nature reserve, that rises 1000 meters above the city. The cable car that goes to the top was designed by the same people that did the cable car in Palm Springs, California. It's round, holds 65 people and revolves 360 degrees on it's way up (and down). Two stations at the bottom, one for each car and only one station at the top. The ride is about five minutes. The cars are round because that offers excellent aerodynamics in high winds. There is a water tank built into the floor to act as ballast for moderate wind conditions. When the ride is wind free, the tank is emptied at the top and the water is supplied to the restaurant.

This mountain is six times older than the Himalayas and the weather seems just as bad at the top here, as it is in Nepal. We walked out of the cable building into rolling clouds and a gale force wind. Almost blew me back inside the building. The mountain is located at the bottom of Africa, in between Oceans of different temperatures and that creates high winds and blowing clouds. There are safety rails at the edges but they aren't very high and I was careful not to stand within five feet of any rail. A quick shift in the wind and one could be airborne for a 3000 foot fall. There is a restaurant and gift shop on top (the old stone building above the Twelve Apostles Terrace) and long lines outside both. The mountain is home to 110 invertebrates, including the ghost frog found nowhere else. It's a sanctuary for porcupines and mongooses. Birds too, black eagles, rock kestrels and red-winged starlings. No lions to worry about, the last one in the area was shot in 1802. There are over 1460 different species of vegetation. More here than in the entire British Isles. No wonder it has been designated as a World Heritage Site. The view is great when you get a break in the clouds and even with rough weather, this is a must see.

From there we took the scenic route, the toll road. It is a engineering masterpiece, cut into the mountainside from 1915-1922. That's back in the days of pick ax and dynamite. If you are in a car, you don't open the door or roll down the window. This is Baboon territory. One sat atop a parked car, waiting for an opening.

Dipping like a teet, at the very bottom of Africa, is the Cape of Good Hope National Park. We planned to take the tram to the lighthouse on the top of the hill, but, the tram was out of order. And it's a long walk. Forty five minutes up and, whatever, coming back down. We didn't have the time. Instead, you can stop for a quick lunch overlooking the Indian Ocean or visit the gift shop or grocery store. Missing the lighthouse, we drove around the hill and down to the beach. The end of the continent. The Cape. Next stop south is Antarctica.

The final stop was the African penguin colony around Boulder's Beach, part of Cape Peninsula National Park. They were named the Jackass Penguin, a name derived from the donkey-like braying sound they make, not their looks. They were renamed because they are the only species that breed in Africa. A series of long boardwalks brings you to the beach where most of the 3000 penguins seemed to be just hanging about. I saw a similar group of Jackass Penguins living by the Straits of Magellan in South America. Those penguins ran, as fast as their little legs would allow, from the water to their burrow since there were predators about. Slow ones were grabbed by a hawk or chased down by a fox. That didn't seem to be the case here. They were out in the open with no desire to hide. They do have enemies in the sea. Sharks, Cape fur seals and the occasional killer whale. There are land-based enemies as well. The mongoose, domestic dogs and cats and the Kelp Gulls which will steal their eggs. Maybe that's why they were out in the open. They are guarding. And such cute guards.

## THE END

## SIDEBAR FOR THE CAPE TOWN

GETTING THERE - Arranged through www.smarTours.com at 501 Fifth Ave, Ste. 1402, NYC, NY 10017, tel 800-337-7773. The basic tour of South Africa for 2 weeks is $2999 each for double occupancy. That's from JFK. Adding on the Victoria Falls extension, airfare from LAX to JFK, taxes, tips, meals, etc. the final cost was $5500.

Airfare JFK to Cape Town on South African Air (SAA) is roughly $1400 RT. The flight stops in Dakar to change crews and take on fuel. Change planes and airports (international to the next door domestic) in Johannesburg. Here, you take your own luggage from one terminal to the next.

WHEN TO GO - Seasons are the opposite to here. Spring and fall avoids the crowds and gives the best weather. December-January is the busiest at the Cape. Summer has warmer weather but also rain.

RESTAURANT - In Cape Town it's relatively safe to eat anywhere. Not so in other cities in South Africa. The hotel is the easiest bet elsewhere.

HEALTH - Malaria medication is a must if you're going into the interior. Not so for just Cape Town.

MISCELLANEOUS - Even though Cape Town is clean and looks safe, there are bad areas. Walking the streets alone, is foolish. South African Consulate, tel. 202-232-4400, safrica@southafrica.net. There are consulates in NYC, Wash DC, Chicago and Los Angeles. No VISA needed for USA citizens.

CARTHAGE, home of Hannibal who crossed the Alps
on the backs of elephants to beat the Romans.


CARTHAGE, TUNISIA - Hannibal the Great, Hannibal the magnificent, Hannibal the General who beat the Romans on their own grounds, in Italy. The greatest General in the world - he was at the top of his game but all good things come to an end.

Carthage was a great city of old. Located on Gulf of Tunis, North Africa it had two splendid harbors connected by a canal. Above, on a hill was the Byrsa, a walled fortress, protecting the city which was the center of an entire empire that stretched from the Atlantic Ocean to the borders of Egypt and north to include Sardinia, Malta, the Balearic Islands and part of Sicily. Their empire was built on comerce - mining of silver and lead, manufacturing, lumber, pottery, glassware and export of wild animals from the African jungles. Merchants but, and it's a big but, they were almost continually at war with Greece and Rome for 150 years. They produced little in the way of art or literature and their religion involved human sacrifice to the Gods, Baal and Tanit.

Hannibal was born in 247 BC and accompanied his father in the conquest of Spain when he was nine years old. Before starting, he vowed his eternal hatred of Rome, the bitter rival of Carthage. Hasdrubal, his brother-in-law, took over the war from his father and Hannibal was his chief assistant. When Hasdrubal was assassinated, the army chose Hannibal as Commander-in-Chief and he expanded their territory in Spain, such that Rome insisted on the surrender of Hannibal to them or war would be declared. It was declared in 218 BC.

He decided that since the Romans wanted him in Italy so badly, he would grant their wish and left Spain with 40,000 men, cavalry and elephants. He crossed the Pyrenees and then the Alps beset by blinding snowstorms, landslides and attacks of hostile mountain tribes. He entered Italy from the north, a complete surprise. He had lost 15,000 of his men in the dangerous passage but was able to recruit replacements from the friendly Insubres of Northern Italy. He won battle after battle marching south and then came the battle of Cannae. Rome had decided to put a stop to Hannibal and sent 50,000 men and a top General from Rome to crush him. It's a battle still taught in military schools today. Hannibal let the middle of his line collapse under the Roman onslaught. Sensing victory, they rushed ahead only to have the line come together behind them. The Roman army was annihilated.

Hannibal marched up and down Italy daring the Romans to sent legions after him but they wouldn't. He asked for reinforcements from Carthage but got none. Frustrated, he finally attacked Rome five years later but the city was too heavily fortified. He turned to his brother in Spain for help. Unfortunately, the Romans surprised the brother, killed him and defeated the army.

After 15 years on the road, Hannibal was recalled to defend Carthage from a Roman attack. They couldn't beat him in Italy so they went after him at home and there, they won. Peace was concluded in 201 BC.

## CARTHAGE

From the train station, I walked up the long hill to the Byrsa, the hill overlooking all the city. The Cathedral de St-Louis is a stunning sight seen long before you get to the top of the hill. It's a beautiful piece of gothic architecture. Inside, the church is quiet, solemn, dark and stone cold. Fitting oversight for the final destiny of Carthage (we haven't got to that part yet).

Adjacent the Cathedral is the what remains of the fortress and the few original remains of the city. You see, after the peace of 201 BC, Hannibal reduced corruption in the government and put Carthage's finances in order. The Romans charged him with working to break the peace and he fled to Syria. He joined their forces to fight the Romans but the Syrians lost and promised to turn him over to the Romans. He escaped to northern Asia Minor and the Romans, once more, demanded Hannibal be turned over to them. He took poison rather than surrender.

7

The third Punic war ended in 146 BC with the Romans destroying the city of Carthage and in a final gesture of contempt, they spread salt over the ruins and forbad occupancy for 25 years. So, very little of the original Carthage remains. But the grounds next to the Cathedral is the place to see original columns, stone blocks, art work and fortifications, all with a spectacular view of the city and harbor below. I was so impressed that within 10 minutes I had taken the one picture that would encapsulate all of Carthage. And five minutes later, I found another that better typified the entire ancient civilization. And ten minutes later yet another, better that the first two. If all you see of Carthage is the ruins on top of this hill, it's worth the trip.

I stopped at an intersection on route to the "Roman Amphitheatrum" when a passing cab driver spotted me and pulled over. I figured it was only two blocks away but my foot was giving me trouble and he only wanted $1. Easy prey. I was right about the distance and the driver waited patiently for me to look around and take pictures. On it's own, the amphitheater is nice, not great. My impression had to be diminished by the wonderful artifacts and view from atop the Byrsa. Then came the sales pitch and we bargained. On the map, the various sites are only a block or two apart. In reality, it would have taken hours to walk between them and this was the best deal I made on the entire trip. Aside from saving my foot for use another day.

Carthage remained in ruins, unoccupied, until 122 BC when a new city, Colonia Junonia was founded. But it only lasted 30 years. Then Julius Caesar visited in 46 BC and proclaimed that a new city should be built. And it was, in 29 BC and called Colonia Julia Carthago. This time it flourished and was second only to Rome in prosperity and eventually became a center of Christianity. Go figure.

Naturally, most of the ruins today are from the Roman time. Even though they were beaten and humiliated by Hannibal, they waited, and eventually got their revenge by destroying everything in sight and rebuilding in their own image.

We drove to the Roman baths on a site overlooking the beautiful Gulf of Tunis. The baths cover several city blocks of what had to be the best real estate in town. It's gorgeous. From there, inland to the Roman houses which must have looked like a condominium complex with units built into the hills. Then the baby cemetery, worth five minutes and finally Port Puniques on the end of a spit of land jutting out into the ocean. It offers a good view of the water front and the Cathedral, far far away.

Back at the train station (there are 6 Carthage stops, get off at Hannibal for the Byrsa), I continued on to Sidi Bou Said, three stops farther up the line. It's a pretty city, shown on postcards all over town. Clean white houses with light blue shutters. All the houses, white and blue. There is not much to do but it's worth picture taking.

Carthage fell to the vandals in 425 AD and remained their capital until 533. Then the Byzantines captured it and lost it to the Arabs in 697. In 698 it was again destroyed. Today Carthage is a wealthy suburb of Tunis the capital of Tunisia but what a story those old bones have to tell.

THE END

# CARTHAGE SIDEBAR

GETTING THERE - Airfare from Rome to Tunis is US$ 250 coach, $310 business class RT. Rome is serviced by Alitalia with excellent rates when booked with any of a large selection of tours. In my case, a week including hotel, meals and countrywide tours was $1300, including RT air. Rome is serviced by virtually all the major airlines in the world.

LAX-ROME economy RT is approximately $ 900. Consolidator fares run $ 500-700, check your newspaper. Carthage is ½ hour train ride from Tunis for 60 cents. Catch the train at the eastern end of Ave. Habib.

Remember, Tunisian dinars are worth nothing outside the country. If you want to change any left over dinars at the airport, you must have saved the original receipt from the first exchange.

WHEN TO GO - Tunisia is on the Mediterranean on the North African coast with hot, dry summers and mild, wet winters. The best time is spring followed by autumn. Tunis is in the north, the farther south you go, the closer to the Sahara desert you get.

WHERE TO STAY - Carthage is a day trip from the capital, so it's best to stay in Tunis. The finest in town is the L'Africa Meridien in the center of town at 50 Ave. Habib Bourguiba, Tunis, Tunisia tel. (01) 347-477 Fax (01) 347-432 Internet http://www.Forte-Hotels.com Singles/doubles start at US$ 130/140 and suites go to $425. Two blocks closer to the Medina is El Hana International, 49 Ave. Habib Bourguiba tel (01) 331-144. Fax (01) 341-199 Singles/doubles are US$ 85/115. Four blocks north of Ave. Habib Bourguiba is the old French colonial style 3 star Majestic Hotel, with large rooms for single/double for US$ 35/45. Tel. (01) 242-848. Add 10% tax to the rooms.

WHAT TO DO - If you are a real hiker, you can walk to the various sites armed with a map but you may spend more time walking between ruins than time at them. Any cab driver will negotiate a tour based on time. Figure on US$ 15 per hour as a good end price (see if you can beat it). Hint - walk to the Cathedral atop the hill first because it and the grounds next to it are worth 2 hours in themselves. Or end the tour there and walk downhill to the train station.

FOR MORE INFORMATION - Write to the Tunisian embassy at 1515 Massachusetts Ave. NW Washington DC 20005 tel. (202)862-1850

## Chobe - the best wildlife park in Botswana

CHOBE NATIONAL PARK has the largest variety of animals in the country. One might think that the best way to get there is to fly to Botswana. Not so. Lets look at the geography. The country is land locked with Namibia to the west, Zimbabwe to the east and South Africa just below. It's sort of round and Chobe sits at 1 o'clock. The capital, Gaborone, is at 5 o'clock. And, quite honestly, tourists don't come to Botswana to see this drab city. They come for the game reserves. You get the best bang for the buck if you fly to Victoria Falls in Zimbabwe and cross the border in the north. That's what we did.

After visiting Victoria Falls, we bought a day trip to Chobe. Up at 6:30 for a quick breakfast and 15 of us piled into the bus for an hours drive to the border. The tour costs $150US and includes all transport, the morning boat cruise, lunch and afternoon park tour and all park fees. You don't have to bring any money or change any. At the immigration check point we noticed dozens of dead dung beetles on the road. On their back, feet straight up in the air. Now, considering what they eat, what could have killed them? No one could figure it out.

First stop was the Chobe Marina Lodge in the heart of Kasane. reservations@chobe.botsnet.bw Rates are $158 S/ $219 D, with breakfast. It sits on the marshland section of the Chobe River that separates Botswana and Namibia. The boat cruise costs about $25. They have a nice gift shop and the prices here let you know that things are not cheap in Botswana. The shop takes credit cards (we were warned to not use credit cards at Victoria Falls in Zimbabwe - cash only, dollars or Rand). But, this is not Zimbabwe and the card worked out fine.

It's overcast and looks like it wants to rain, but the boat has a roof, so off we go. This huge delta is a sanctuary for birds and we saw a number of them perched on branches waiting for the sun. Then we spotted a collection of hippos wading around in the water. We got close but not too close. Hippos kill more Africans than crocodiles every year. An angry hippo is not to be messed with. The water was shallow enough that the top halves of the adults were out of the water.

And then it rained. Fortunately, the boat had raincoats which were needed to protect the cameras. After the rain stopped we came across a large black bird on a branch sticking out of the water. Wings spread in this minimum of daylight. He was trying to dry off. Then an eagle sitting at the waters edge. And a six foot crocodile on a patch of land in the middle of the river. He watched as we got closer and closer, and then ran for the safety of the water. We swung the boat around to give the hippos another shot. Seemed to be more of them this time and in deeper water. A large male swam towards us and it was time to leave. Back to the middle and we saw a bigger crocodile. We got within five feet of this eight footer and he didn't move a muscle. Just stared. We swung the boat around and saw some antelope grazing at the shore line.

Back at the hotel we had a marvelous buffet lunch and got aboard our jeeps for the land tour. A quick note about Botswana. This is one of Africa's success stories. They have had democratic elections since 1966 and since discovering three of the best diamond mines on the continent, they have a sound economy. Second only to South Africa. Fortunately they aren't cursed with corrupt and inept governments like in neighboring Zimbabwe and Zambia. This prosperity makes the country expensive to visit. The bulk of the population of 1.6 million live at the southern tip. Even though there is a vibrant economy the intra-structure is not suitable for land travel. To drive from south to north could take a land cruiser several weeks.

The jeeps - driver and one seat in the front and three rows of three seats behind with each row higher than the one in front. It's a short drive from the Marina to the park and we were on dirt roads in no time. As luck would have it we spotted one of the three lion prides that live in the park, right off the bat. Females and cubs. The male was somewhere, but we never did see him. The females looked over, then proceeded to ignore us. We aren't food, so they don't who care. A bit farther were some pretty ducks walking around a marsh. If the lions only knew. Only a snack, but then, a snack here, a snack there, it can add up. Then a group of Kudu's, the second largest and most attractive of all the antelope species in Africa. Light brown in color with very thin zebra type stripes. Later, a giraffe that walked in close to see what we were about. Adult giraffes have no enemies, they are too big. This one just looked and then waited for us to drive away.

It was a full day and time to return to Victoria Falls. I still don't know what could have killed the dung beetles.

## THE END

Kruger National Park is the best Africa has.

KRUGER NATIONAL PARK, SOUTH AFRICA is one of the biggest, oldest and best wildlife parks in the world. It has the greatest variety of animals in any park in South Africa and possibly the entire continent. This may be the sole destination that draws visitors to this country. It has the big five - lions, leopards, elephants, buffaloes and rhinos. It also has cheetahs, hippos, crocodiles, hyenas, giraffes, zebras and a variety of antelope. All together, the species include 147 mammals, 500 birds, 114 reptiles and 49 species of fish, although you're not apt to see the fish.

We came up from Swaziland, to the south and stopped at the Paul Kruger gate, one of the eight entrances. Half of the group piled into jeeps to cruise independently ($80 US). The rest of us stayed on the coach (bus). No matter which vehicle you're in, animal sighting is a crap shoot. The jeeps can go on trails the bus can't because of it's weight. But, I figured, the animals don't care about the size of the roads they cross and we're going to do a jeep tour tomorrow.

Our first sighting was a pair of giraffes. Mother and child. A big child too. Almost as tall as the mother but lighter skinned. A herd of grazing zebras, wandering gazelle and a male kudu. The kudu is the second largest antelope in this forest and considered the prettiest. We rounded off the early afternoon tour watching a mother zebra nursing her young.

At 3PM we checked into the Protea- Kruger Gate Hotel. Straight past the lobby and reception desk in the front, is the bar, then the enclosed dining room that seats 140. Farther on and down two flights of stairs is the open dining area that seats 220. From above it looks like a wood fence, enclosed, bull ring with a dirt floor. The rooms are in a number of single story wood buildings reached by boardwalk and stretch out into the jungle. Seemed like a half a mile walk to get to my very spacious room.

Dinner at 7, outdoors, in the bull ring. And what a buffet they have. The largest selection of food I've ever seen. Soups, salads, deserts, meat, sea food, vegetables - you name it, they had it. Sometimes mass cooking leads to bland taste. Not the case here and I was half through my first plate when a few drops of rain hit. Some of the tables emptied fast. Hand held plates of food were rushing to the steps. I was enjoying the roast beef too much and besides it was only a couple of drops. It could pass.

It didn't. It turned into lots of drops. Heavy ones. I grabbed what food I could carry and ran up the steps into the indoor dining area as the single drops turned into a torrent of rain. I joined some of our group at a window table and finished eating my wet food. Then there was crashing thunder and strong lightening. This was a violent storm and the skies were lighting up every few seconds. The staff was running back and forth between outside and in, trying to save what food they could. They were able to get 25% inside before giving up and then the lights went out. The dry, the wet and the very wet crowd ate what they could by candle light and light coming from the sky. Thunder punctuated all conversation.

I got six, silver dollar sized, candles from the front desk and slowly walked the half mile, on wet boardwalk, back to the room. Surprisingly, the electric lock on the door worked, but, the inside was pitch black. The candles gave enough light that the walls were the only things I bumped into.

The room lights popped back on at 2:30 AM. Good thing because it was up at 5 AM for the early morning jeep tour. Each jeep has a driver and one seat in the front. Then three rows of three seats behind with the seats being higher as you go back. Fortunately, the storm had passed. We had time for a quick cup of coffee, grab a box breakfast and jump into one of the jeeps. Off we went in a cool and overcast morning. Between six and eight o'clock we saw lots of gazelle and parked within five feet of a resting hyena. They are nasty animals with a bite strong enough to break bones. And like most of the animals, they saw us, and didn't care. We could have been a tree for all the attention they showed. Then a baboon mother moving through the tall grass with a baby hanging on her back.

Like a jockey on a horse. And then the road jam. The dirt roads are about 1 ½ lanes wide so passing is difficult if not impossible. But, the vehicles in front stopped for a reason. It took us twenty minutes to get to the spot and find out why. There was a pride of lions taking a morning snooze in an open, sandy beach, next to a stream. One male and a collection of females and cubs. The male watched us out of the corner of his eye. The rest were sound asleep.

Up the road were six vultures. Standing around. Waiting. Then it was time for breakfast in the park. A nice setting but then we opened the boxes. No one was overjoyed with the contents. Some eating, some trading and the rest went into the trash.

From 6-8 AM we saw a lot of big animals. From 9-11 AM, it was mostly lizards and birds. There was a lovely mongoose sitting atop a rock. Looking for a cobra, I'll bet. And a Nile crocodile, waiting for the sun to come out to warm him up.

They told us about the guide that got out of his jeep, on a bridge, to have a smoke. A nearby leopard came out of nowhere, leaped up and got him by the throat. The tourists in the jeep, terrified, drove off to get a park ranger. Rangers returned to find the guide and the leopard now under the bridge. Too late for the guide, he was as good as dead with the leopard's first bite. The rangers had to shoot the cat and the moral of the story is - smoking kills.

Lunch was at the golf club. A country club actually. A nice hot meal before touring to see more antelope. The buffet that night wasn't marred by rain. The Spring Bok is good but I didn't like the Ostrich. It tasted like salami and I don't like salami.

We were up early again because it's a long drive to Johannesburg. We went through the wild countryside of Eastern Transvaal (renamed Mpumalanga). The Bylde River Canyon has spectacular views, God's Window being one of them. Lunch was at the town of Pilgrim's Rest. Gold was discovered here in 1873 and, as you might guess, it eventually ran out and the money dried up. In 1972 the town sold itself to the government as a ready made historical village. It's now a quaint stop for tour busses. The Royal Hotel charges $55 single/$90 double. Two enterprising young men danced in the street wearing gray coveralls and boots. And no head. You make a buck however you can.

Downtown Johannesburg looks like a place where you would get mugged if you wore new shoes. So we stayed in the suburbs. Our bus rolled by Nelson Mandella's house - no parking allowed. The high walls were there for a reason. This town has no leopards but apparently the jungle is a safer place to be.

THE END

## SIDEBAR FOR KRUGER NATIONAL PARK

GETTING THERE - Arranged through www.smarTours.com at 501 Fifth Ave, Ste. 1402, NYC, NY 10017, tel 800-337-7773. The basic tour of South Africa for 2 weeks is $2999 each for double occupancy. That's from JFK. Adding on the Victoria Falls extension, airfare from LAX to JFK, taxes, tips, meals, etc. the final cost was $5500 (each).

Airfare JFK to Cape Town on South African Air (SAA) is roughly $1400 RT. The flight stops in Dakar to change crews and take on fuel. Change planes and airports (international to the next door domestic) in Johannesburg. Here, you take your own luggage from one terminal to the next. The flight from Cape Town to Durban is included in the tour price. From Durban, travel is by private coach (bus) to Zulu Land (overnight), through Swaziland (overnight) and into Kruger Park

WHEN TO GO - Seasons are the opposite to here. Spring and fall avoids the crowds and gives the best weather. December-January is the busiest. Summer has warmer weather but also rain.

RESTAURANT - Stops are made along the way and the good news is, people did not get sick. That said, it's still safe to bring Imodium. The hotel is the safest bet where ever you are.

HOTEL - We stayed at the four star Protea - Kruger Gate, modern, 96 good sized rooms. There is a large inside dining room, a larger outside dining area, a bar and swimming pool. The hotel is isolated so dinner and breakfast is included. www.proteahotels.com/krugergate

HEALTH - Malaria medication is a must for this area. Even though this group did not get GI disorders, that does not mean the next one won't. Bring appropriate medications.

MISCELLANEOUS - South African Consulate, tel. 202-232-4400, safrica@southafrica.net. There are consulates in NYC, Wash DC, Chicago and Los Angeles. No VISA needed for USA citizens.

Karnak, the killer donkey ride and cruising the Nile.

Oldest pyramid, Cairo

Balloon ride, Luxor

LUXOR, EGYPT - I remember Johnny Carson had a bit called "Karnak the Magnificent". And now thirteen of us on this tour were off to see the real thing. From hotel to site by horse drawn carriage. Seven carriages actually. It's a guided tour and, as is usually the case, the guide gives far more information than I could remember. I care but I don't care *that* much.

In short, if you could only see one temple in all of Egypt, this should be the one. The wall engravings are clear and intact. The Great Hypostyle hall with 134 papyrus shaped pillars is spectacular. The statues wonderful. And the remaining intact obelisk of Queen Hatshepsut is the tallest in all of Egypt. 80,000 people worked on this complex and it dates back to 1965 BC. They have their own lake and a statue the tourists walk around. Once or twice for something. Three times for luck. I think five times for marriage. I don't know how many times for divorce. Lots of people were walking around so I joined in. Three times and it must have worked. I didn't get Egyptian revenge from the food. Johnny Carson got it right, Karnak is magnificent.

The donkey ride to the Valley of the Kings seemed like a good idea at the time. Was I wrong. We got up at 5 AM to walk ½ an hour in the biting cold to get to the donkeys. Unlike a horse, the saddle has no stirrups for the feet and no horn to hold onto. Our guide said to hold onto the saddle with both hands since it's easy to slip off. A half hour later our donkeys left the paved road. With four layers of clothes on, I was shivering. Both hands were numb. What a mistake. I could have taken the taxi. Now we're headed up. Dirt and graveled path. The donkey seems to be doing fine, I'm not. And then the saddle starts to slip to the left with me on it. Fortunately, one of the donkey handlers is close and grabs me before I hit the dirt.

Then we hit a hill too steep for the donkeys and we have to get off. To climb up the hill, eight stories with frozen leg muscles that don't want to work. There are steps but it's a tough climb. Then we're at the top and back on the donkey with a shaky saddle. And a four hundred foot drop off the cliff to my right. Three feet to the right. Now the shivering isn't from the cold.

The donkey ride ends but we're still four hundred feet above the valley floor. We have to walk down the side of the hill. Dirt and gravel with some slopes at 45 degrees. It's slip and slide time. Fortunately, one of the handlers comes to my rescue and we slip and slide together.

The Valley of the Kings has 46 uncovered tombs. All robbed except King Tut's. Our tickets allow entrance in three tombs. No pictures allowed inside. Once inside, you walk through the tunnel with carvings on all sides, to the center, where the coffin was placed. Then the walkway on the other side of the same tunnel to get back out. Rames IV has 10,000 wall pictures and carvings. Stunning to see. 1100 BC and there is still some color left in many of the drawings. You can visit King Tut's tomb but that is an extra ticket.

On the other side of the mountain is the Temple of Queen Hatshepsut. Walk back over the mountain or cab. An easy choice for me. A tram takes us to the concession area of the Kings and a taxi to the concession area of Hatshepsut. From there, it's a tram to the temple. The Queen ruled for 15 peaceful years, 1473-1458 BC. It's the second level (there are three), where terrorists killed tourists a few years back. It took the police and hour to respond then. Not so now. There are armed tourist police at all the temples. This is an easy temple to walk through and is worthy of an hour.

Up at 5:30 AM for the balloon ride. Our group gets the first ride so we're airborne before sunrise. Not the best time for low speed film, but still the best time. After the safety briefing, we climb in and I mean climb. There are five compartments. One holds the pilot who controls the flame bursts (the middle) and the four corners are for us. Four or five per compartment. The basket naturally rotates so it makes no difference where you get in. Off we go and it's a beautiful sight. The countryside, Hatshepsut's temple from on high and several temples strewn about the valley. There must have been 10 balloons in the air at the same time but we were far enough apart that it added to experience rather than detract.

We landed on an open patch of desert and twelve guys immediately grabbed the sides to hold the basket on the ground. We got out, one compartment at a time. A second group was there, waiting. They boarded each compartment as it emptied. We gathered as a group after the balloons took off. They brought drums and we danced to the beat. Then the ceremony. Named certificates were handed out, one at a time and we each got a "balloon ride" t-shirt.

We were on the MS Doma now. The 28 passenger river boat owned by the tour group Explore! Nine of the original thirteen left for home and we four were joined by twenty coming down from Cairo for the river cruise. The Doma is a modest boat with a small pool and sun deck on top. The other half of the top deck is an enclosed meeting room and bar. The first level has the dining room and individual rooms. The remaining rooms are below deck. The bath has a combination shower (turned on from the sink) and a toilet and not much room to move around. The big cruise ships, and we passed a lot of them, have separate showers but you'll pay for it. There was time to just lay about and I was thankful.

Up at 6:15 AM for the Temple of Horus at Edfu. Just enough time for what might have been coffee in the dining room. We got there at first light and the timing was the best. This is the most preserved temple in Egypt, built between 237 and 57 BC. It's held up remarkably well.

A few hours upstream and we visited Kom-Ombo, a twin temple. Some say not as impressive as Edfu but I believe it's worth the walk. The left side is dedicated to the Falcon God, the right to the Crocodile God. It was finished in 217 AD.

In Aswan we checked into the Marhaba Hotel and from the roof you could see cruise boats lining the banks of the Nile. Some looked as big as our hotel. That night we walked to our restaurant the long way. Past the railroad station, past the spice sellers behind the hotel and along the waterfront to the Aswan Moon. Down stairs to one level, then down again and again. Our dining area floated on a barge on the Nile. Quite nice.

In the morning we piled into 5 taxis of indeterminate age to get to the Aswan Dam. Not the most picturesque place but who can go to Aswan without seeing the dam. Then our last temple, Isis on the island of Philae. That's where it was before the dam. UNESCO moved it to Agilkia island before it was submerged. By Roman times Isis was the greatest of all Egyptian Gods and this temple has had pilgrims for thousands of years. The next morning was the train ride to Luxor, an overnight, and fly home. Templed out.

# THE END

## SIDEBAR FOR THE NILE

GETTING THERE - Arranged through Adventure Center, 1311 63rd St., Ste. 200, Emeryville, CA 94608. tel 800-227-8747. www. adventurecenter.com They are a broker for hundreds of trips run by other tour operators. This tour was done by Explore!, a British company at www.explore.com.uk specializing in low cost, small group trips. The 17 days on the ground is a combination of two trips, Cairo to Sinai and a Nile River cruise. Tour cost of $1400, fees and visa are $85, meals about $300, optional side trips of $400, mandatory insurance of $120. Air fare is extra and prices depend on the time of the year. From the USA, prices range from $1000 to $2000 RT (over the holidays). Adventure Center will book the air fare for you. I went on line to find the best air fare and gave the flight numbers to A.C. to see if they could match the price. They were close enough. Air and tour were paid separately.

WHEN TO GO - Spring and fall avoids the crowds and gives the best weather. Winter is nippy enough to require four layers of clothing at night in the desert. Summer is an oven.

RESTAURANT - Aswan Moon restaurant, floats on a pontoon on the Nile in the middle of town. A popular hang out for locals and tourists. Large menu and reasonable prices. Recommended.

HEALTH - This is a third world country. See your doctor for shots. Egypt is well known for causing stomach problems. Bring Imodium.

MISCELLANEOUS - You will be hassled by people trying to sell you something from the time you arrive at the airport until you leave the country. Don't count on any of them telling you the truth.

Tired of Italian food during your visit to Rome? Take
a short hop south to Tunis in No. Africa

TUNIS, TUNISIA - I couldn't help but think of the lyrics, "Clowns to the left of me, jokers to the right, here I am stuck in the middle ....". Although I wouldn't exactly think of myself as stuck in Tunisia, it's location on the North African coast is enough to give me concern. Libya is to the right and Algeria, with weekly reports of massacres, is to the left. And then there's peaceful, tiny Tunisia stuck in the middle. This country is the home to the ancient city-state of Carthage, arch enemy of Rome and was a powerhouse in the world politics about the time of Christ. But that was a long time ago. Now they depend on European tourism and a modest oil export for their economy.

My introduction to Tunis, at the airport, didn't speak well for a first impression. The cambio (money changer) window was unattended so I couldn't get anything at duty free (not that I missed any real bargains), so I cleared customs. Walked out to the main terminal and was immediately hustled for a taxi. But I had things to do first. Reconfirm my flight out and change money at the cambio on the public side. Then I got hit for a taxi again and was taken out the right side of the terminal - he wanted 10 TD and I knew that was too much. Back in the terminal, I followed the signs and exited the other end of the building and was approached by a guy that looked like the taxi controller. I was at the right place, it was the taxi stand. At this point I didn't know the difference between the yellow metered cabs and all the other cabs, so I got burned for 10 TD anyway. Deceived by appearances.

My room at the Majestic was big and has a balcony, with French doors, overlooking the street. The atmosphere of the hotel is French colonial circa 1920's. TV shows on the 4 channels are in Arabic, Spanish, French and Italian. The special for dinner was Spaghetti Tunisian with chunks of beef and long green peppers. There is a little plate of what appears to be spaghetti sauce for bread dipping and it looks innocent enough but there is fire in that sauce. The meal was excellent but I paid for it in the morning and took an Imodium.

Breakfast is included and consists of coffee, rolls and a strange orange juice substitute. Finally I was off, south on the Avenue de Paris, a major street with modern triple car trolleys that go 15 blocks south to the train station. But I was only going 5 blocks. After passing 10 coffee and roll bars (they seem to be every seventh store), I turned east on Avenue Habib Bourguiba for the tourist office and shouldn't have bothered. They had no maps nor literature in English and didn't seem to care whether they did or not. However, back on the Ave. Habib, the L'Africa Meridian Hotel gift shop had a wonderful map. Pricey at US$ 7 but worth it. It shows northern Tunisia, all the streets of Tunis, a closeup of the streets of the Medina and the streets of Carthage. With map in hand, I headed west down the middle of Ave. Habib which is a pleasant, if narrow, park - towards the Casbah. I'd been in Medinas before and knew that the streets were like spider webs that had been stirred with a stick. That's good for self defense when invading armies attack but tough on tourists. It's easier to get lost than not and I'd been lost in the Casbah of Tangiers. But this time I had a map.

The Café de Paris is on the corner of Ave. de Paris and Habib and I mention it because it seems to be very popular at any time of the day or night and it has a prime location. There are tables and chairs on the sidewalk, like the streets of Paris but no evidence of waiters. Virtually all the customers are male and they sell beer. I don't know if they sell anything else because, inside and out, standing or sitting, beer is what everyone had. West of this busy intersection, the shops move up a notch, pricewise. This is a Muslim country and, surprisingly, the Catholic Church is right here on Ave. Habib. It's a grand old French Church that makes you think you're in Europe. Another block and the shops move up another notch and I'm in the high rent district and then I'm at the arch. The Place de la Victoire and entrance to the Medina. From here, it's three streets that lead inside. The guide book said to stay off R. Jamaa Ezzitouna because it's the most commercialized, so that's the one I took.

Ten feet inside and you're in another world. Busy, narrow streets, more like alleys or passageways. Shops on both sides with displays in front that further narrow the alley. People stop to window shop and some to barter, since almost all prices are negotiable. That constricts the passing room even more. In fact, no one seemed to mind when the bottle necked crowd had pass one at a time, alternating, one from each direction. I know how well that would work in New York. At first, I was annoyed but soon forgot about it and slowly pushed through each constriction like everyone else.

What ever your interest, there is a store here for you. I take that back, many stores. Ceramics, leather purses, pants, hats, shirts, embossed copper plates, fancy pottery, clothes, big paintings and small paintings, food stalls, swords, armor, shoes, more food and lets not forget those coffee and roll bars. I stopped at one of the few fixed price stores with blown glass ware and bought some perfume bottles. Just standing in the middle of the store is a delight to the eyes, sparkling colors glisten on every wall. Beautiful pieces of art in different sizes and shapes. And signs that say fixed price so there is no need to test your bargaining skills. Naturally, they sell perfume extract but I wasn't in the market - so I thought.

Finally, I got to the center (actually 2/3 through), the street dead ends at the Mosque Zitouna. That's where I met a fellow in front of a souvenir shop while reading my map. He was well groomed, soft spoken and wore a jacket (possibly the only one in the Casbah). He said the shop was his so I bought some t-shirts. He told where to go to get a good roof top view of the Medina and I was off. Two blocks later, I noticed he was at my elbow and willing to show me the way and frankly, I would have never found it otherwise. A right and left, and left and right and go straight and then left and into a carpet shop, up the stairs onto the shop roof. I knew this was going to cost me but the view is spectacular. From this vantage point you can see the Mosque tower, in close, and the tower of the Catholic Church in the distance. The roofs of the Medina shops blend together to form a unity of purpose.

I was able to get out without buying a carpet and he took me inside a Mosque and after a short tour ended up at a small perfume shop. Mind you, I had no interest in buying but this was a soft sell. There is a large selection of brand name women's perfumes and a lesser but significant selection of men's colognes. All the bottles are extracts and you add it to ½ liter of 90% alcohol when you get home. I would have never found the roof top, let alone had the chutzpah to go to a store's roof to take pictures and not buy anything, so I bargained. One men's and one woman's for US $ 10 each in a one ounce bottle with a cork in the top and well wrapped in paper. Thank goodness because three days later, in Italy, I opened my bag and was overcome with the smell of perfume. One of the corks came loose but the wrapping contained the liquid and nothing was damaged or had any residual smell. It turns out that the men's cologne survived.

I waited for him to ask for a tip after we got back to the main street, Ezzitouna. He was happy with $6 and, frankly, the tour was worth twice that. Mind you, he speaks very little English but that isn't really a problem. Just go to the Mosque turn right and look for the only guy in a jacket.

On the Ave. de Paris I was approached by a guy asking for a light. Even though I didn't have one, this was the only introduction he needed to show me he was studying English, showed me pieces of paper with English on them, asked to share a beer (no), coffee (no), then he lived way out of town and needed bus fare of 5 td (no), 3 td (no), 2 TD (no). He talked while we walked and didn't leave till I walked into my hotel.

I spent the next day at Carthage and decided to try Pizza Hot on the Ave. de Paris for supper. Yes, I spelled it correctly, Hot. Lasagna, why not, we're only a stones throw from Italy. But they were out of lasagna so I went to the small restaurant next to the beer palace, Café de Paris. They too were out of lasagne so I tried the acceptable medium pizza. It was only memorable because I had to take Imodium the next morning.

I had serious chaffing problems with my left foot and decided to buy a thick pair of sweat socks. So rather than my usual route down Ave. de Paris, I took the back streets towards the Casbah and found a clothing store used by the local people. Sign language is all that's needed and I got just what the doctor ordered. They were interested in my expensive Nikon camera and the young owner, ascerning that I was a photographer asked me to take his picture. Suddenly, he had an inspiration and picked up the 8 year old boy of the woman he was waiting on, to pose with. A pose, a smile, a flash and he was delighted.

This time I took the R. de la Kasbah into the Medina (middle one of the three) and it was completely different. This time the stores were assorted by wares. First, a whole collection of shoe stores, followed by clothing stores. No glitz, no glamour, just ordinary shopping for the local people and just as crowded as the other street. In the middle, I found the hat section and got a round red hat, made, oddly enough, from Australian wool and popular with the local men.

The following morning, the yellow metered cab ride to the airport was $3.25. Tunisian Air had a real breakfast waiting. An egg omelette, slices of orange, grapefruit, kiwi, coffee, yogurt, lots of bread and Cognac for the coffee. The Medina was great and I got some good stuff. All's well that ends well.

## THE END

## TUNIS SIDEBAR

GETTING THERE - Airfare from Rome to Tunis is US$ 250 coach, $310 business class RT. Rome is serviced by Alitalia with excellent rates when booked with any of a large selection of tours of Italy. In my case, a week including hotel, meals and countrywide tours was $1300, including RT air. Rome is serviced by virtually all the major airlines in the world. LAX-ROME economy RT is approximately $ 1000. JFK-ROME is $1000.

Remember, Tunisian dinars are worth nothing outside the country. If you want to change any left over dinars at the airport, you must have saved the original receipt from the first exchange.

WHEN TO GO - Tunisia is on the Mediterranean on the North African coast with hot, dry summers and mild, wet winters. The best time is spring followed by autumn. Tunis is in the north, the farther south you go, the closer to the Sahara desert you get.

WHERE TO STAY - The best in town is the L'Africa Meridien in the center of town at 50 Ave. Habib Bourguiba, Tunis, Tunisia tel. (01) 347-477 Fax (01) 347-432 Internet http://www.Forte-Hotels.com Singles/doubles start at US$ 180/190 and suites go to $425. Two blocks closer to the Medina is El Hana International, 49 Ave. Habib Bourguiba tel (01) 331-144 Fax (01) 341-199 Singles/doubles are US$ 115/135. Four blocks north of Ave. Habib Bourguiba is the old French colonial style 3 star Majestic Hotel, with large rooms for single/double for US$ 55/65. Tel. (01) 242-848. Add 10% tax to the rooms.

WHAT TO DO - Tunis is the capital and jumping off point for the beach resorts to the south. Tours are available from any hotel and there is good train and bus service to Hammamet, Port El Kantaqui, Sousse, and Montastir. It's a good base city to visit the ruins of Carthage, home to Hannibal who defeated the Romans by crossing the Alps on the backs of elephants. Carthage is in ruins because the Romans eventually got their revenge. And let's not forget the fascinating Medina at the end of Ave. Habib Bourguiba.

FOR MORE INFORMATION - Write to the Tunisian embassy at 1515 Massachusetts Ave. NW Washington DC 20005 tel. (202)862-1850

Victoria Falls, one of the seven wonders of the world

VICTORIA FALLS is on the Zambezi River and divides Zimbabwe, on the south, and Zambia, to the north. They are roughly 700 miles from the Atlantic Ocean to the west and the same from the Indian Ocean to the east. On the western tip of Zimbabwe, the southern tip of Zambia and the north-east corner of Botswana, this is not a place you're apt to get to by accident. Of these three countries, Botswana is the only one with an actual economy. A stable one, by the way. The other two have ben ruined by corrupt and inept governments. Unfortunately, that makes Zimbabwe and Zambia dangerous places to visit. That said, lets look at what's considered one of the seven natural wonders of the world.

The closest comparison is Niagara Falls, 1 km wide and 58 meters high. Victoria Falls is 1.7 km wide and 108 meters high. In defense, Niagara is easier to get to and easier to see - that is, a clear view of the entire falls. With Victoria, you can see the falls, but only in pieces, because of the jungle. Never- the- less, when David Livingstone saw the falls in 1855, he wrote in his journal, "on sights as beautiful as this, angels in their flight must have gazed".

We flew in from Johannesburg (one flight a day) and waited in one of two slow lines for Zimbabwe immigration and the issue of the mandatory visa. It was and hour and twenty minutes from the plane to the tour bus. Two minutes of that time was spent walking. Reports are that 1 million people have crossed the border from Zimbabwe to South Africa looking for work.

Miles from town, we saw the mist from the falls rising high in the air. We turned left in the town of 55,000 on what seemed to be the only other road and drove into the jungle. The town did not look like a place you would want to be in the daytime, let alone night. Atop a bluff, sits the Safari Lodge, voted the best of it's kind in Zimbabwe for the last 11 years. Built in 1994, it is on the Conde Nast Travelers Gold List. No doubt it's the best hotel in Zimbabwe and must be on the list of the best in Africa. But, the front entrance isn't all that impressive. It's an open air, three story high, thatched hut. All wood inside, all the buildings are wood. Reception desk to the right is bypassed and we went to the stairs in the center. One flight goes up, but, we took two flights down for the indoctrination meeting. Maps were passed out and warnings given. Don't go for a walk in the jungle below. You can see perfectly well from one of the viewing platforms. There are organized walks with armed guides for those who wish to venture out. All rooms have a balcony. Don't leave the sliding door open, or your front door, for that matter. Monkeys will come into the room wreak havoc. Oh yes, monkeys bite.

Rooms are in three separate buildings to the right and three to the left. All are two story and connected by covered walkways. The cover is necessary because it rains a lot here. The rooms are lined in dark wood. Desk, table, phone, A/C, bed with a mosquito net, bathroom with separate tub and shower. And a mosquito coil to be lit at night. No TV, no frig, no mini-bar.

There was time for lunch and drinks at the bar - open for animal viewing on one side. The lowest platform in the rear is at least 50 feet above the jungle. The animals aren't going to jump up. Birds, on the other hand, visited regularly.

Two of the group were without luggage which makes one wonder since it was a non-stop flight. But, it was time for our included boat cruise. We were met at the landing by tribal singers and dancers. It was a nice show and they welcomed the contributions. Tour groups are undoubtedly their only source of income. The boat went around the placid river above the falls. There are free drinks (including booze) and an egg roll and a meatball. We saw a few hippos at a distance, otherwise, if you missed this trip, you didn't miss much.

That night was dinner by candle light. All the food offerings were those you'd find at an expensive restaurant in New York City or Paris. Nothing plain and simple or inexpensive. And it turns out that the bar stops food service at 6 PM. So, it's slow service here (to help pass away the idle night hours, I guess) or nothing.

Except - in the front driveway, a van waits to take you to the Boma. For $40 you get entertainment from a local choir and a buffet. I later found a way to best both alternatives. Room service. A filet mignon sandwich with onion rings and very tasty french fries for $15.

Next morning is a visit to the falls. But first, a stop to see the 1,500 year old baobab tree just outside the entrance. It's a big, fat tree and very impressive. Then, inside the park. We started on the left side and worked our way around. The viewing areas have rails and most of the walkways are wet. You can get close enough to hear the roar of the water going over the edge. The power of the falls is underlined by the mist generated by the rocks below. Raincoats were passed out to protect us from the heavy, wet air. And then it rained. The raincoats are heavy ponchos with hoods and will keep you dry underneath. Until you sweat from the heat. The rain let up and the poncho's came off. From each of the dozen or so viewing platforms we can see a different section of the wide falls. Nowhere could we see them all. But, the power, the violence of the water roaring over the top and pounding into the rocks at the bottom - was scary. No way to go over these falls in a barrel and survive. And then it poured.

The rain stopped by the time we got to the curio market in town. One long collection of wood or stone, carved animals and locally made souvenirs. Ten feet in and I was approached after I pointed to a small wood elephant. He whispered in my ear as though it was a special price he wasn't willing to share with the others in our group. $60. I was shocked and insulted and said so. Loudly. And walked away as the price dropped to $10. I continued walking, he followed. $5. I walked another 30 feet and noticed that it was the same merchandise. And ahead, more of the same. I turned and went back. He said $4 as I passed him.

One block away is the Elephant's Walk Village, an indoor shopping center. There is good looking art work on the lawn in front - a good sign. Inside are some of the finest works of art I've ever seen. Beautiful statues, stunning pictures. Items that could be on display in art houses in New York City or Los Angeles. Naturally, we're not talking about bargain basement prices. But if you have the money to spend, this is the place to shop. The art work on display in the interior courtyard is worthy of museum display.

The afternoon was open to fill in with optional tours. Some played golf. It didn't rain but water collected on the course the players came back sopping wet. Others took the elephant ride and loved it. Why not, only the elephant's legs got wet. Others ate and drank at one of the viewing platforms watching the animals below. Antelopes, hyenas and birds. Didn't expect lions. Just more rain.

## THE END

## SIDEBAR FOR VICTORIA FALLS - ZIMBABWE

GETTING THERE - Arranged through www.smarTours.com at 501 Fifth Ave, Ste. 1402, NYC, NY 10017, tel 800-337-7773. The basic tour of South Africa for 2 weeks is $2999 each for double occupancy. That's from JFK. Adding on the Victoria Falls extension, airfare from LAX to JFK, taxes, tips, meals, etc. the final cost was $5500 (each).

Airfare JFK to Cape Town on South African Air (SAA) is roughly $1400 RT. The flight stops in Dakar to change crews and take on fuel. Change planes and airports (international to the next door domestic) in Johannesburg. Here, you take your own luggage from one terminal to the next. The flight from Cape Town to Durban is included in the tour price. From Durban, travel is by private coach (bus) to Zulu Land (overnight), through Swaziland (overnight) and into Kruger Park The flight (RT) from Johannesburg to Victoria Falls in Zimbabwe is included in the extension price. The flight from JFK to Victoria Falls (RT) should be roughly $1400.

WHEN TO GO - Seasons are the opposite to here. Spring and fall avoids the crowds and gives the best weather. December-January is the busiest. Summer has warmer weather but also rain.

RESTAURANT - Breakfasts are included. Lunch is at the hotel dining room or at the bar. Dinners are only in the dining room and all choices are fancy ones. The food is very good, the service slow and prices are what you would pay in a nice restaurant in the U.S. At night, the alternative is room service to get a hamburger ($15) and tomato soup ($6). Free transportation is available to go to a restaurant and show. $40 for the show and buffet.

HOTEL - We stayed at the five star Victoria Falls Safari Lodge in Zimbabwe. Voted best safari lodge in the country for the last 11 years. There is an inside dining area, an inside and outside bar dining and drinking area and a swimming pool. The hotel is isolated so breakfast is included. www.saflodge@saflodge.co.zw There are 72 very nice rooms, all with a porch (monkeys included). Rates are from $210-275 each for a double ($420-550) and $330-440 for a single. Cash only for meals and all purchases. Dollars or Rand. The hotel will accept credit cards but the group was warned against using them.

HEALTH - Malaria medication is a must for this area. Even though this group did not get GI disorders, that does not mean the next one won't. Bring appropriate medications. Beds have mosquito netting and the staff pulls it in place each night.

MISCELLANEOUS - Zimbabwe Consulate, tel. 202-332-7100, 1608 New Hampshire Ave NW. Washington DC 20009. VISA's are needed for everyone and can be bought at the airport for $30 US, cash for Americans. Canadians pay about twice that.

Victoria Falls, one of the seven wonders of
the world from the Zambia side

VICTORIA FALLS is on the Zambezi River and divides Zimbabwe,
on the south, and Zambia, to the north. They are roughly 700 miles from
the Atlantic Ocean to the west and the same from the Indian Ocean to
the east. On the western tip of Zimbabwe, the southern tip of Zambia and
the north-east corner of Botswana, this is not a place you're apt to get to by
accident. Of these three countries, Botswana is the only one with an actual
economy. A stable one, by the way. The other two have been ruined by
corrupt and inept governments. Unfortunately, that makes Zimbabwe and
Zambia dangerous places to visit. That said, lets look at what's considered
one of the seven natural wonders of the world.

The closest comparison is Niagara Falls, 1 km wide and 58 meters high.
Victoria Falls is 1.7 km wide and 108 meters high. In defense, Niagara is easier
to get to and easier to see - that is, a clear view of the entire falls. With Victoria,
you can see the falls, but only in pieces, because of the jungle. Never- the- less,
when David Livingstone saw the falls in 1855, he wrote in his journal, "on
sights as beautiful as this, angels in their flight must have gazed".

We flew in from Johannesburg (one flight a day) and waited in one of
two slow lines for Zimbabwe immigration and the issue of the mandatory
visa. I asked if I would need a multiple entry visa since I was going to visit
Zambia. No, the official said, "Not if you come back in the same day." It
was and hour and twenty minutes from the plane to the tour bus. Two
minutes of that time was spent walking. Reports are that 1 million people
have crossed the border from Zimbabwe to South Africa looking for work.

Miles from town, we saw the mist from the falls rising high in the
air. We turned left in the town of 55,000 on what seemed to be the only
other road and drove into the jungle. The town did not look like a place
you would want to be in the daytime, let alone night. Atop a bluff, sits the
Safari Lodge, voted the best of it's kind in Zimbabwe for the last 11 years.

Built in 1994, it is on the Conde Nast Travelers Gold List. No doubt it's the best hotel in Zimbabwe and must be on the list of the best in Africa. But, the front entrance isn't all that impressive. It's an open air, three story high, thatched hut. All wood inside. Reception desk to the right is bypassed and we went to the stairs in the center. One flight goes up, but, we took two flights down for the indoctrination meeting. Maps were passed out and warnings given. Don't go for a walk in the jungle below. You can see perfectly well from one of the viewing platforms. There are organized walks with armed guides for those who wish to venture out. All rooms have a balcony. Don't leave the door open, or your front door, for that matter. Monkeys will come into the room wreak havoc. Oh yes, monkeys bite.

Rooms are in three separate buildings to the right and three to the left. All are two story and connected by covered walkways. The cover is necessary because it rains a lot here. The rooms are very nice. Desk, table, phone, bed with a mosquito net, bathroom with separate tub and shower. And a mosquito coil to be lit at night. No TV, no frig, no mini-bar.

There was time for lunch and drinks at the bar - open for animal viewing on one side. The lowest platform in the rear is at least 50 feet above the jungle. The animals aren't going to jump up. Birds, on the other hand, visited regularly.

Two of the group were without luggage which makes one wonder since it was a non-stop flight. But, it was time for our included boat cruise. We were met at the landing by tribal singers and dancers. It was a nice show and they welcomed the contributions. Tour groups are undoubtedly their only source of income. The boat went around the placid river above the falls. There are free drinks (including booze) and an egg roll and a meatball. We saw a few hippos at a distance, otherwise, if you missed this trip, you didn't miss much.

Next morning is a visit to the falls. Zimbabwe side. But first, a stop to see the 1,500 year old baobab tree just outside the entrance. It's a big, fat tree and very impressive. Then inside.

Afterwards, we went to the curio market in town. One long collection of wood or stone, carved animals and locally made souvenirs. I walked in for thirty feet and noticed that every twenty feet, it was the same merchandise. Ahead, more of the same. I left.

One block away is the Elephant's Walk Village, an indoor shopping center. There is good looking art work on the lawn in front - a good sign. Inside are some of the finest works of art I've ever seen. Beautiful statues, stunning pictures. Items that could be on display in art houses in New York City or Los Angeles. Naturally, we're not talking about bargain basement prices. But if you have the money to spend, this is the place to shop. The art work on display in the interior courtyard is worthy of museum display.

The afternoon was open to fill in with optional tours. Some played golf. It didn't rain but water collected on the course they came back sopping wet. Others took the elephant ride and loved it. Why not, only the elephant's legs got wet.

Two of us wanted to go to Zambia to see the falls from that side. The guide book warned that if you walked across the border, you would likely get mugged before you got to the park entrance. So we arranged, from our appointed guide, an independent tour. $40 plus $10 for the Zambia visa and for that reasonable price, we got a van and two guides.

There were dozens of people just hanging around the border on both sides of the international bridge. One wonders what they were waiting for. We went into immigration on the Zimbabwe side, drove across the road/ railroad bridge and the guide took our passports (and $10 each) into immigration in Zambia. Now parked, people came to the van window trying to sell us small wood elephants. The park entrance is only a few yards from immigration.

From this side we were able to get upstream - before the falls. Then, there are railed clearings on the edges of various bluffs. As impressive as from Zimbabwe and some with less mist in the air. The roar of the water and the sheer power is still here, but we were used to it. At first it's scary, but now, we expect it. And a statue of Livingstone by a different artist than the one on the other side. And then it rained. Fortunately, our number two guide had been carrying four raincoats and on they went. Heavy

41

ponchos with hoods. Covered us to the knees. And we kept walking. The rain stopped, off came the sweat producing ponchos and we saw our first Victoria Falls rainbow. Beautiful.

Then across a narrow, 200 foot long, bridge over a deep gorge. The wind blew across as if trying to sweep us off and into the deadly waters below. Then it rained again.

The rain stopped just as we got to the cliffs edge overlooking the railroad bridge. Just then someone jumped. Although it was tough to see from a half mile away, he stopped before hitting bottom and bounced up a little. A bungee jumper. And then another man jumped, and came to rest along side him. As it turns out, the second one is there to help the both of them get hauled back up. That's how they do it here. And then it poured and we had to go back across that narrow passenger bridge. A torrent of rain and hurricane force winds.

This time the wind was so strong, the rain was coming at me sideways. My glasses were so wet, I was virtually blind and had to hang onto the guide (who weights more than me) with one hand and the rail with the other. Poncho flying in the wind.

Naturally, the rain let up when we got back to the van. This time, the Zambia immigration official wanted to see us in person. Our guide tried to do it alone, but it was no go. We had to present our wet, smiling faces. As though there is a big illegal immigration problem from high unemployment Zambia into high unemployment Zimbabwe. Who's kidding who here.

All in all, I think the views were better from Zambia and I'm glad we went. $50 and sopping wet pants (below the knees) shoes and socks. We got back in time to join the others eating and drinking at one of the viewing platforms watching the animals below. Antelopes, hyenas and birds. Didn't expect lions. Just more rain.

## THE END

## SIDEBAR FOR VICTORIA FALLS - ZAMBIA

GETTING THERE - Arranged through www.smarTours.com at 501 Fifth Ave, Ste. 1402, NYC, NY 10017, tel 800-337-7773. The basic tour of South Africa for 2 weeks is $2999 each for double occupancy. That's from JFK. Adding on the Victoria Falls extension, airfare from LAX to JFK, taxes, tips, meals, etc. the final cost was $5500 (each).

Airfare JFK to Cape Town on South African Air (SAA) is roughly $1400 RT. The flight stops in Dakar to change crews and take on fuel. Change planes and airports (international to the next door domestic) in Johannesburg. The flight from Cape Town to Durban is included in the tour price. From Durban, travel is by private coach (bus) to Zulu Land (overnight), through Swaziland (overnight) and into Kruger Park The flight (RT) from Johannesburg to Victoria Falls in Zimbabwe is included in the extension price. The flight from JFK to Victoria Falls (RT) should be roughly $1400.

WHEN TO GO - Seasons are the opposite to here. Spring and fall avoids the crowds and gives the best weather. December-January is the busiest. Summer has warmer weather but also rain.

RESTAURANT - Breakfasts are included. Lunch is at the hotel dining room or at the bar. The food is very good, the service slow and prices are what you would pay in a nice restaurant in the U.S. At night, the alternative is room service to get a hamburger ($15) and tomato soup ($6). Free transportation is available to go to a restaurant and show. $40 for the show and buffet.

HOTEL - We stayed at the five star Victoria Falls Safari Lodge in Zimbabwe. Voted best safari lodge in the country for the last 11 years. There is an inside dining area, an inside and outside bar dining and drinking area and a swimming pool. The hotel is isolated so breakfast is included. www.saflodge@saflodge.co.zw There are 72 very nice rooms, all with a porch (monkeys included). Rates are from $210-275 each for a double ($420-550) and $330-440 for a single. Cash only for meals and all purchases. Dollars or Rand. The hotel will accept credit cards but the group was warned against using them.

There are hotels in Livingstone, Zambia but the town is 11 KM from the falls. So most stay in Zimbabwe. The best place to stay on the Zambia side is actually inside the park. The Zambezi Sun. $160 S/ $170 D including breakfast.

HEALTH - Malaria medication is a must for this area. Even though this group did not get GI disorders, that does not mean the next one won't. Bring appropriate medications. Beds have mosquito netting and the staff pulls it in place each night.

MISCELLANEOUS - Zimbabwe Consulate, tel. 202-332-7100, 1608 New Hampshire Ave NW. Washington DC 20009. VISA's are needed for everyone and can be bought at the airport for $30 US, cash for Americans. Canadians pay about twice that. Zambia visas are $10.

## ZULU LAND

SOUTH AFRICA. To get a feel of where the Zulu are in this country of over 1.2 million square kilometers, lets say the country is round (it isn't because it's missing the north-west section). Swaziland (the independent country established for black people only) is at 3 o'clock. It shares it's Indian Ocean coast line with Mozambique, on the north. Directly north, is Kruger National Park which shares it's eastern border with Mozambique. The port city of Durban is below at 4 o'clock. The Zulu occupy the inland area between Durban and Swaziland. Just for reference, Cape Town is at 7 o'clock.

Early European settlers were the Dutch, the Germans and eventually, the British. They started in Cape Town and gradually moved up the coast to Durban. British influence increased and the Boers in Durban didn't like it. So they moved north onto land occupied by the Zulu's. The British agreed that the Boer encroachment was illegal but did nothing to stop it. Their plan was to kill two birds with one stone. The birds being the Zulu's and the Boers. Naturally, there was a war. The Boers won. A few years later, in 1879, the British invaded the Kingdom over a dispute about cattle and taxes. The British figured it would be easy going but it didn't start off that way. After initial losses, the British brought in their heavy equipment and in 1887 formally annexed Zululand and the Zulu King was exiled. All that is in the past and the Zulu are now part of the South African economy.

It's a full days drive from Durban to the Kingdom of Zulu. We had some time to relax at the hotel. Fed and rested, we set off the next morning for the Zulu market. An open market, with a canvas top for shade, that sells virtually everything. Colorful fruit next to wood carvings of elephants. Pineapples next to clay pots. Stone figures of rhinos next to straw bowls that are woven with swirling colors. And cold drinks in the back. If you wanted a wood water buffalo or stone turtle or a mango, this is the place to get it.

Then it was off to the DumaZulu village to see how the Zulu used to live. We are met at the gate by a warrior in skins and feathers. Thrusting his spear and threatening us in a language no one understood. It's a tourist trap, we know. The men and women are separated. Men go through all gates first. women follow. Men to the right, women to the left. OK, when in Rome.

The Zulu's inside are in costume. Men with skins around the middle and some with fur on their shins. The women in long black dresses or colorful, beaded, two piece outfits. No shoes. We saw how the men used rocks to flatten wood to make shields, the women stringing color beads for their dresses. One of the men was peeling something (using a steel knife) that looked like food. Maybe. I didn't ask if it was. I figured we would get, what we get, for lunch. He wore a gold colored superman's cape and a gold hat.

Then we sat on benches to watch the show. But first, Zulu beer. It came in a large clay cup and given to the person on the end of the row. Drink and pass on. Most of the people pretended to drink (cup to lip and pass on). Afraid of getting Zulu revenge. Hygiene and jungle usually don't mix. I figured they were going to feed us lunch, prepared here, and that was ample opportunity to poison. The beer was a bit sour, a mix between beer and wine. Not something I'd want seconds of.

First was the mock battle, two guys at a time. Spears and shields. They were, without question, energetic. Lots of wood on wood and no one got hurt. Then the girls danced. The guys danced. The guys fought. They all got together in a chorus line and it was time for lunch. An excellent buffet. The buffalo stew was good.

And no one got sick.

The Hluhluwe-Umfolozi Park is usually referred to as a single game preserve. Actually, it's two, separated by a thin corridor. Animals pass back and forth between the two so it doesn't matter what side you're on. The parks were set up in 1897 and are big enough to support 3 day tours. For us, three hours. We piled into three jeeps and were off. Each jeep has a driver (on the right side) and one seat to the left. Behind are three rows with three seats in each row. The seats are mounted higher as you go back. Instead of going in a single line, each jeep went it's own way. We know when it comes to seeing animals in the wild, it's a crap shoot. The driver knows where the animals were yesterday but that's of little help in knowing where they are today. Our first spotting was a group of zebras. The animals are so used to the jeeps, they ignore them. Usually. Some of the impalas get skittish but the large animals look at us like we're a tree. We got close to a group of water buffalos rolling around in a mud ditch. The mud helps them to cool off and may help with the flies. Hundreds of flies were hovering around each of their faces. We were careful to not make noise, water buffalo can be very dangerous. And then we faced down a rhino. He got close and we know that they are willing to charge almost anything. But, to our advantage, they have poor eyesight. We got a stare but no charge. There are lions in the park but we didn't see any. We did see lion food, impalas. Lots of them. One male in each small herd. Surrounded by females and their little ones. Didn't look like there was any preference to who crossed the road first for them. A custom clearly reserved for people.

THE END

## SIDEBAR FOR ZULU LAND

GETTING THERE - Arranged through www.smarTours.com at 501 Fifth Ave, Ste. 1402, NYC, NY 10017, tel 800-337-7773. The basic tour of South Africa for 2 weeks is $2999 each for double occupancy. That's from JFK. Adding on the Victoria Falls extension, airfare from LAX to JFK, taxes, tips, meals, etc. the final cost was $5500 (each).

Airfare JFK to Cape Town on South African Air (SAA) is roughly $1400 RT. The flight stops in Dakar to change crews and take on fuel. Change planes and airports (international to the next door domestic) in Johannesburg. Here, you take your own luggage from one terminal to the next. The flight from Cape Town to Durban is included in the tour price. From Durban, travel is by private coach (bus).

WHEN TO GO - Seasons are the opposite to here. Spring and fall avoids the crowds and gives the best weather. December-January is the busiest. Summer has warmer weather but also rain.

RESTAURANT - Stops are made along the way and people did not get sick. That said, it's still safe to bring Imodium. The hotel is the easiest bet where ever you are.

HOTEL - We stayed at the newly built Protea - Umfolozi River hotel. 4 star, modern, 68 (very nice) rooms. There is a large dining room, bar and swimming pool. The hotel is isolated so dinner and breakfast is included. www.proteahotels.com/umfoloziriver

HEALTH - Malaria medication is a must for this area. Even though this group did not get GI disorders, that does not mean the next one won't. Bring appropriate medications.

MISCELLANEOUS - South African Consulate, tel. 202-232-4400, safrica@southafrica.net. There are consulates in NYC, Wash DC, Chicago and Los Angeles. No VISA needed for USA citizens.

# II AMERICA

You want it, they got it - Skagway, Alaska

Grant & Lee, Jefferson & Washington and Walter S. Amos

Biltmore Mansion - 1887 - NC

Mt. Vernon - Washington's house - 1799

Appomattox was the name of the county not the town. The village was called Clover Hill and was a stopping off point for the Lynchburg-Richmond Stage Road. There was a tavern and a few houses. The county was formed in 1845 and the village picked as the county seat and renamed Appomattox County Court House. That's before they had a court house, they built that the following year. Slowly it grew and about the time of the Civil war the town had a population of 150 and the county 8,900. Fifty four percent of whom were black. Wilmer McLean and his family moved here from Manassas, VA to be near the railroad. He was a sugar speculator.

Robert E. Lee had Union troops on three sides of him and a river he couldn't cross on the fourth. His troops hadn't eaten for days, ammunition was low and desertions high. He could attack Grant, as was his wish, but to what end. He couldn't win and he knew it. The farmland of the south was already drenched in blood. Lee was an honorable man, he sent an envoy to Grant.

Lee arrived first, dressed to the nines. His best uniform, cleaned and pressed. Well groomed and looking every bit the General in charge. Grant came in from the west and looked like, well, Grant. He didn't dress up, he had his work uniform on, but then, the meeting wasn't for "best looking General". They met on April 9, 1865 in McLean's house, approximately 100 yards from the Court House building. Lee sat at the small white table, Grant the dark one, on opposite sides of the parlor fireplace. They engaged in small talk for about a half an hour and, finally, Lee brought up the topic of surrender. Grant was generous, and, didn't have to be. Officers could keep their side arms and men could keep the horses they owned. Three days later, Union troops lined the street as Confederate soldiers marched in, stacked their rifles, swore to keep the peace, picked up their passes (printed in the Clover Hill Tavern) and walk off.

Most consider Appomattox the end of the war but it wasn't really over until the surrender of Johnson's Army in North Carolina on April 26, Taylor's Army in Alabama on May 4 and Smith's Army in Texas on June the second. Appomattox may not have been the end but it was the beginning of it.

For whatever reason, the McLean house was razed in 1893 and the materials left on site to rot in the weather. The original Court House was burned to the ground in 1892. Both were reconstructed by the Park Service. Other original houses remain - Plunkett-Meeks Store, several law offices, the Jail, several individual homes and the Clover Hill Tavern (made of brick and the oldest). The National Park Service has done a good job in making the site as it was in April, 1865.

The Natural Bridge is 60 miles west of Appomattox, on the far side of the Blue Ridge Mountains. George Washington surveyed it and carved his initials on the wall. It's a limestone arch that spans the Cedar Creek and supports route US 11. It's 215 feet high, 90 feet long and varies in width from 50 feet to 150 feet. In 1774, Thomas Jefferson purchased the bridge from King George III for 20 shillings to preserve it as a mountain retreat. Jefferson built a 2 room log cabin to live in. The railroad came years later destroying the location's peace and quiet with thousands of visitors. I guess that includes me.

From the creek bed, it looks like a large oval was punched out of the rock to make way for the creek. It's a tranquil place, even with the tourists. There is a light show at night, nearby caverns to visit and a Natural Bridge Wax Museum, New Toy Museum and Haunted Monster Museum.

When I was a kid, we took road trips each summer. So, the Skyline Caverns were the first caves I ever visited. That was a while ago and I've been to a number of them since so I have a better data base for comparison. The caverns are at the northern entrance to Skyline Drive and the Shenandoah National Park. The park is a ridge top drive that goes from Front Royal in the north to Rockfish Gap, 105 miles south. The park is pretty, peaceful and has, literally, millions of trees. A great place for a walk in the woods or just sit, look and unwind.

Most caverns are discovered by accident, Skyline is different. It was discovered on purpose by Walter S. Amos. He studied the surface topography in 1937 and concluded there was a cave. He was right. The caves have the customary stalactites and stalagmites, crevices, pools and streams. In addition to the 37 foot Rainbow Waterfall there's the Capital Dome, Rainbow Trail, Painted Desert, Wishing Well, the Grotto of Nativity, Cathedral Hall, The Shrine and Fairy Tail Lake. This cave is unique in that it has Anthodites, tiny snow white crystals that grow in all directions. They grow one inch each 7,000 years and it's a mystery how they form. It's not the best caverns I've seen but the lighting is great. Later, I saw the lighting system is award winning. Figures, it's that good.

If you're going to do the Skyline Drive, the caverns is a good start or finish. How many caves are you going to see that were discovered on purpose, have rare Anthodites and the best underground lighting around.

THE END

## SIDEBAR FOR APPOMATTOX

GETTING THERE - Appomattox is about 25 miles east of Lynchburg, VA and about 90 miles west of Richmond, VA. Take US 460 east from Lynchburg and follow the signs on Route 24. The Natural Bridge is 60 miles west of Appomattox. Drive back to Lynchburg, north on US 29 and west on Route 130. It's a stones throw from I-81.

From the bridge, there's a choice for the Skyline Caverns. I-81 north (exit 175 to exit 300), east on I-66 to exit 6 (Front Royal) and follow the signs. About 140 miles. Or the scenic trail on the Blue Ridge Parkway. Go east on Rt.130 and look for the signs. The exit for this National Park is Front Royal.

WHEN TO GO - The best is spring and fall - less people. Appomattox is part of the National Park Service as is the Blue Ridge Parkway The customary fee is $10. The Natural Bridge has a combo ticket to include the museum for $17. Bridge only is $10. Skyline Caverns is $14 for adults with $2 discount for Auto Club and seniors. Pictures are allowed in all the attractions, only the caves are tricky - you need a flash or high speed film, maybe both.

If you need to find something to do in Little Rock

And who doesn't. Alright, to tell you the truth, I was in Arkansas on purpose. I wasn't early for a business meeting and needed to fill in the time. I'd driven above or below this State (through Missouri or Louisiana) on my previous cross country trips and I figured it was about time to see what was going on in Bill Clinton country.

From my base of operations in Little Rock, I drove north to Clinton, the town, with a population of 2,200. A mile past the Wal-Mart, turn right for Hwy. 9, the scenic route through the Arkansas back country. This road is lined with green. Light green from translucent new leaves alternating with the deep dark needles of the year round pines. The trees are spaced far enough apart that you can walk through the woods without a machete. A real forest, designed for a stroll. This is pretty country.

Most of the houses along the road are one story wood frame. A few are made of brick and others of rusted corrugated iron sheets. All the houses have at least 6 vehicles on the property, two of which have their wheels on the ground. The economy must be doing just fine here to have all those cars and pickups. Apparently no one trades in the old car when buying.

The countryside is a continuum of rolling hills and the highway has more curves than a sidewinder crossing hot sand. This is a road that cries for a sports car, but, it's a delightful drive no matter what you're in. I had been wondering how a small town like Clinton could support a Wal-Mart superstore and then I got to Shirley. Population 335 and another Wal-Mart. It's not hard to guess who the only employer in this town is.

## GREAT CAVES

I went through Mountain View, the only town of size this far north, and on for another 15 miles and more turns, of course. Fortunately, there are signs for Blanchard Springs Caverns and I just followed. It's located in the Ozark National Forest and is run by the USDA Forest Service.

People figure the limestone rock, from which the underground formations developed, came from an ancient sea some 350 million years ago. They don't know when the formations started, it's a guess, but, the stalagmites (ceiling down) and stalactites here (from the floor up), are older than the pyramids. The Dripstone trail opened in 1973 after 10 years of planning. It's an hour long, 4/10 of a mile in and covers the upper levels of the cave. The Discovery Trail opened 4 years later, covers the second level and has 700 stair steps. The Wild Cave Tour is invitation only, requires crawling and is strenuous. I took the Dripstone with only 50 steps. Temperature 58 degrees, humidity 100%. I've been in a lot of caves and for variety and presentation, this is one of the best in America. Columns and ice cycles (not real ice, of course) from two inches to twenty feet high. Some look like lava, others like vanilla ice cream was melted on them. And I swear I saw faces buried in the walls.

The Ozark Folk Center was on the way back to town so I stopped in. Crafts, music, dance and history of the Mountain folk culture. It was closed. The town of Mountain View was open. Population of 2,876 and home to the Annual Arkansas Folk Festival and the Arkansas Old-Time Fiddlers Assoc. State Championship Convention. Neither of which was on at the time, but, just as well. There would be no place to park. What a charming town. A veterans war memorial in the center of town and just to the right, a corner store with two guys on a bench outside. Just sitting there. That's the actual name of the store - Corner Store. Along the street there are well kept stores selling antique furniture (an oxymoron, I know) and a wrought iron store that will make furniture for you.. At the western edge of town sits the classic. An ice cream parlor, circa 1910, with electricity. Inside there is a long ice cream counter and a central staircase leading to the Doctors office on the second floor. How can anyone leave without an ice cream soda?

## AL CAPONE SLEPT HERE

Hot Springs is south of Little Rock and it used to be famous. Documents show that American Indians bathed in these waters in the 1700's. And drank the water. Since the average temperature is 143 degrees, they probably waited for it to cool down. Not a big deal since the water coming from the 47 natural springs is 4,000 years old. Legend has it that Spanish explorer Hernando de Soto and his troops saw the springs in 1541. The U.S. got title with the Louisiana Purchase from France in 1803. In 1832 the Federal Government set aside 4 sections of land as a natural resource.

The first bathhouses were canvas and lumber. No more that tents over the springs. That soon changed and Bathhouse Row was formed. By the 1920's, there was marble and tile for the floors and walls. Polished brass, murals, fountains, statues and stained glass. Some of this splendor was in the rooms. There were gymnasiums and beauty parlors and famous people. The hot springs have been visited by Sam Houston (therapy for skin disease), Bat Masterson, Cy Young, Babe Ruth, Jack Dempsey, President Herbert Hoover, President Jack Kennedy and, not in an order of significance, Jesse James.

While gambling, Wyatt Earp got drunk and became upset over his losses. He had to be de-armed and escorted out of town. Harry Truman didn't. It seems he played small stakes poker here and didn't carry a gun. During prohibition, Al Capone made deals with the local bootleggers to stock his clubs in Chicago. He shipped it north in railroad cars labeled "Mountain Valley Water". At one time, Al Capone and his gang occupied the 43nd floor of the Arlington Hotel while his enemy, Bugs Moran, stayed at the Majestic Hotel, one block away. There was no trouble, after all they were on vacation. The Arlington Hotel is still prominent on the strip and won't rent out room 442, the one that Capone liked.

That was then. People got around by horse and buggy and train and trolley car. After WWII emphasis moved away from water therapy and people took to the road in their cars. They preferred to move about rather than take a train to one place and stay for a week or two. One by one, the bathhouses on the row closed down. Now, only the Buckstaff remains open, but, there is current renovation at many of the hotels along Bathhouse Row. Some should be opening their doors soon with the opulence of the past - updated. There will be steam cabinets, hot tubs, massage tables, sitz tubs and hydrotherapy, surrounded by marble, tile, fountains and statues. Nothing like a hot bath to make the cares of the world disappear.

And if you need a spare part for your 1956 Chevy, I know where to go. Turn right just after Clinton.

## THE END

SIDEBAR FOR ARKANSAS


GETTING THERE - Figure on 2 hours to get to Mountain View and another ½ hour to get to the caverns. From Little Rock, go west on I-40 to exit 125 (30 miles), north on Route 65 to the town of Clinton. Just after the town, right on State 9 (east/north) to Mountain View. Then, go north on State 14 and follow the signs (left into the Ozark National Forest and right turn at the cavern entrance). For a different route back - take Route 66 west, which is the main street in Mountain View. It ends at Route 65, turn left (south) to I-40.

To get to Hot Springs - south on I-430 or I-440. They both intersect at I-30. South to exit 111, west on Route 70 for 25 miles. To return - at the south end of town, take Route 270 east to get back to I-30. Hour and a half to two hours, each way.

WHEN TO GO - The caverns are open year round, except holidays (870) 757-2211, the Ozark folk center from late spring to early fall (870) 269-3851, Hot Springs year round.

HOTELS - Little Rock has the gamut - the 4 * Capitol Hotel in downtown for $200/dbl 501-374-7474, to Ramada, Marriot, to Super 8 Motel, 501-562-9383. Mountain View has the Inn, $100/dbl, 870-269-4200 and the Ozark Folk Center Dry Creek Inn, $60/dbl, 870-269-3871. For Hot Springs the best bet is to call the visitors center - 800-772-2489 // www.hotsprings.org

If you thought Rhode Island was small, it has
an island off the coast - that's small.

Mother Goose Grave Stone in Boston graveyard

I grew up in New Jersey and never heard of Block Island. Long Island, sure, it was right next door and Martha's Vineyard and Nantucket are where the rich from Massachusetts go in the summer. I first learned of Block from the book "1,000 Places To See Before You Die", a New York Times best seller. I wasn't going to get to all 1,000, but, I was in Newport, Rhode Island, looked at the map and made up my mind the night before.

Rhode Island is officially, "State of Rhode Island and Providence Plantations", the longest name of any State. A population of about 1 million and, of course, the smallest State. It was established by Roger Williams after he was banished from Massachusetts. He bought the land from two Narragansett Indian Chiefs in 1836. It was the first State to declare it's independence from British rule (1776) and the last to ratify the Constitution (holding out for the addition of the Bill of Rights).

Block Island, unlike Rhode Island, is a real island, 12 miles from the mainland and known by ship's crews for it's treacherous shoals. The best way to get there is from Point Judith, a 45 minute drive south of Newport. It's not that far, as the crow flies, but there are bridges, traffic and low speed limits. Point Judith is the only place with ferries that take cars. Parking dockside is $10 a day and taking the car is $26. So I figured to take the car and I could see the entire island. Parking attendants at Pt. Judith told me that the officials are trying to raise the car fee on the ferry to $50 each way. At one hundred bucks versus twenty, I might have left the car. Anyway, this was spring, before the busy summer season, and I figured to have no trouble getting on board without making the suggested reservations before hand. I was wrong.

Spring is the season for renovation. There are 2 lines for vehicles to get on the ferry. One with reservations and the other without. Trucks with building materials, U.S. mail, contractor's trucks, trucks with food and beverage and a few cars all had reservations. I missed the 8 AM boat but got on the 10 AM. Note, you have to back your vehicle up the ramp and into the interior of the poorly lit ferry. I missed the sides of the boat and inside pillars, barely. Of course, it does make things faster at the other end

Two hundred feet from the ferry dock is the main street in town. The only own, Old Harbor. There are parking signs on the street and in the ferry lot, 2 hour limit. Some of the small shops have two or three spots in front of their stores, but, it's easy to see if you are in their store or not. I had a problem. The visitors center (by the boat dock) said they usually don't enforce the parking rules this early in the season. But, parking overnight, I couldn't be missed. A few hotels had on site parking (they gave me a list of hotels) and I could always drive out of town and park along the road and walk back. The car was becoming an albatross.

With a list of hotels in hand, I turned left and walked south to the Statue of Rebecca. A round-a –bout at the intersection of 4 roads. Rebecca was erected in 1896 by the Woman's Christian Temperance Movement to help lower alcohol consumption (recast in 2001). I walked up the hill to one of the most prominent and expensive hotels, the 1661. A beautiful old mansion with a terrific view and plush rooms. It had a parking lot. But the prices drove me back to the street. I stopped at several places on the way downhill and went into The Hotel Manisses (1870). Another beautifully restored mansion (with on site parking). The rate was better and I grabbed it. The room was smaller than the 1661 but just as nice. This is how the rich must have lived 100 years ago. Except for electricity and hot and cold running water, of course. On that note, I was startled with the flushing noise from the toilet. Gravity doesn't do it here. Lift the lid and there's a pressurized water unit.

The Manisses has a stained glass Victorian drawing room on the ground floor and an outdoor patio which is lit at night. First class. There is a free bottle of Brandy in the room. You can take it out to the patio at night. May as well, there's no TV.

## AROUND THE ISLAND

A short drive farther south is the Spring House. It's difficult to miss, sitting atop a hill overlooking the town and the sea with a huge front lawn. It boasts a gourmet restaurant and is one of the bigger hotels with 49 rooms. And one of the most expensive.

Block Island is about 11 square miles, has 17 miles of beaches although much of that is rock, 5 churches, 20 miles of nature trails, 851 year round residents and 2 lighthouses. The one on the southeast coast (1873) is the most accessible. It's a historic landmark and almost fell into the sea. The severe weather, which is common to this area, eroded the cliff it was on. They moved the beautiful red brick structure back in 1993. It's 240 feet above sea level and throws it's light out 35 miles. Swing around the bottom of the island and the Mohegan Bluffs, with 150 foot cliffs and there is a large fresh water pond. One of 365 on the island. Brick and wood houses dot the landscape - a picture postcard of early America. Stone walls cross the green meadows. There are 400 miles of stone walls. It looks more like a movie setting than real life.

Straight up the middle of the island is the cemetery. Atop a bluff overlooking the Great Salt Pond and New Harbor, a sheltered boat dock.

Headstones date back to the late 1600's. As you walk through the grounds, you see the same last names again and again - Ball, Rose, Champlin. The island was plundered four times by French pirates in the 1600's and 1700's. George Washington ordered them to move their livestock to the mainland during the Revolutionary War so the British wouldn't get the animals. Those were tough settlers.

The northern third of the island is essentially barren. The road ends 3/4 of a mile short of the Northern Lighthouse. Made of dark granite in 1867, it was restored in 1993. A black house on a dark beach with nothing around for miles, this is the setting for a horror movie. A third of the island is preserved open space. No wonder that 150 species of migratory birds stop here each year. Behind the bluffs, just north of town, is a beautiful long stretch of sandy beach. No hot dog stands but plenty of room.

## THE TOWN

That's where the action is. There are 39 restaurants - almost all close to the harbor. 50 gift shops, 12 art galleries, 2 movie theaters and a small gas station just north of town. The big hotels are next to the harbor or within a two block walk. You can get fast food, slow food, custom beer and a quiet peaceful time. Unless they pop the cork in the summer for local mayhem. But the Statue of Rebecca is there to prevent that.

## THE END

## SIDEBAR FOR BLOCK ISLAND

GETTING THERE - From Newport, RI - passenger ferries from mid-June to Labor Day. Takes 2 hours. tel 401-783-4613. High speed catamarans from the port of Galilee in Narragansett, RI from June 1 to Mid-October. $30 RT - tel toll free 877-733-9425. There are ferries from New London, CT (it would be faster to drive closer), tel 860-444-4624 and Montauk Point, Long Island. tel 631-668-5700.

The closest crossing is from Point Judith, RI. They have ferries that take people and cars (and big trucks). tel 401-783-4613 for reservations and, trust me, you'll need them. A same day round trip is $16. A car is $26 each way and there is a measure to raise it to $50 each way. If you are going to be in the car, you need a ticket as well. In May (before the season) there are 4 trips each way each day. During season, it goes up to seven a day. There are State run and private parking lots that charge the same rate - $10/day for cars. The private lots are closer.

There is an airport and you can fly there - a 15 min flight. From New England Airlines 1-800-243-2460 // e-mail FlyBi@bri.com. They will go to and from Block Isl. to Boston, Providence, Hartford, Albany, New Haven and East Hampton, Long Island..

WHEN TO GO - The best is spring and fall - less people and much lower prices. Using The Sheffield House Bed & Breakfast as an example. It's in Old Harbor and has 6 rooms. tel 1-866-466-2494 toll free // www. thesheffieldhouse.com. Room with a private bath, weekends - NOV 3-APR 29 = $95 // APR 30-MAY 20 = $135 // MAY 21- JUN 10 = $165 // JUN 11- JUN 30 = $185 // JUL 1- AUG 29 = $ 205 // AUG 30 - SEP 23 = $185 // SEP 24 - OCT 14 = $ 165 // OCT 15 - NOV 4 = $ 135. Assuming an average here of $135, for comparison purposes of the following sample (there are 55 places of lodging on the island). In town, The Atlantic Inn, tel 800-224-7422, 21 rooms, $130 // Harborside Inn, 800-825-6254, 36 rooms, $170 // Hotel Manisses, where I stayed, tel 800-626-4773, 17 rooms, $ 185 // Spring House Hotel, tel 800-234-9263, 49 rooms, $ 250 // The Adrianna, tel 800-992-7290, 10 rooms, $ 85 // Driftwood, tel 401-466-5548, 5 rooms, $ 60. Farthest from town is the Fagan Cottage, tel 401-466-5383, 1 room, $ 150. Closer to town are The Narragansett Inn, tel 401-466-2626, 51 rooms, $ 170 and Samuel Peckham Inn, tel 401-466-2439, 40 rooms, $ 145. Only some of these hotels have parking or TV's or food service. Best to ask. In season, reservations are a must. Out of season, half are closed.

RESTAURANTS - There are 16 places to eat around town. Off season, most are closed. 5 are in hotels and some are snack shops. If you're out of town, you're stuck. I had a great meal at Smuggler's Cove with reasonable prices. A short walk north of town.

## The Bourbon Trail

Somebody asked at the start of one of the distillery tours, "What is whiskey?". Sounds like a dumb question to ask at a brewery, but then, what better place. Think about it, there's Scotch whiskey, Irish whiskey, Canadian whiskey, rye whiskey, blended whiskey, sour mash whiskey, Bourbon whiskey, Kentucky whiskey and the Japanese even make a whiskey (probably from rice). Back in the old west, cowboys asked for straight whiskey and took whatever the bartender gave them. I guess the term whiskey is like car. You get the idea, it's just not specific.

Bourbon is specific, there are rules. First, it has to be manufactured in the United States. It has to be distilled at no more than 160 degrees from a fermented mash containing at least 51% corn and stored at no higher than 125 proof in new, charred, white oak barrels. It cannot be filtered and nothing can be added except distilled water. So, how did it get it's name, you ask. The whiskey came from the Reverend Elijah Craig who mixed corn, rye, barley malt and other grains to make this corn whiskey. It became popular and so much was produced around Bourbon County, Kentucky it was simply called bourbon. Today 90% of the world's bourbon is made in Kentucky at 12 operating distilleries. Bourbon can be made in other States but only Kentucky can use the State name on the bottle.

The official center of the Kentucky bourbon trail is Bardstown, KY, about 30 miles south of Louisville. Jim Beam is the closest, just off the Interstate. Heaven Hill is in Bardstown and Makers Mark to the south. There are four distilleries near Frankfort, the Capital of the State. Buffalo Trace, Labrot & Graham, Four Roses and Wild Turkey.

### THE TOUR

I decided to drive past Jim Beam and do Makers Mark first - it was the farthest. There was time, so I stopped in My Old Kentucky Home State Park in Bardstown. Reportedly, the house was the inspiration for the song and the grounds are quite pleasant. It was a nice break, then back to the car and after, heaven knows, how many turns, I got to Makers Mark whose grounds and buildings are so pretty the site is a National Historic Landmark. It was originally built in 1806 as a gristmill, but, as our tour guide said, "As you can see, we're in the middle of nowhere." They were so remote, the local farmers didn't want to go that far. The gristmill was going broke. Until they got the bright idea to use the grain and limestone stream water to make white lightening. They didn't call it that, of course, but we know better. They didn't sell bottles, people showed up with their own mason jars to get filled straight from the barrel. That business was a success making this site the world's oldest operating bourbon whiskey distillery. The property, with landscaped grounds and restored buildings (some date back to the early 1800's) is probably the prettiest of all manufacturers, but, it's also one of the smallest. It produces only 40 barrels a day with an industry average of 600 barrels. Makers Mark is the only distillery in Kentucky to replace rye with wheat in the formula. The yeast culture very important. They still use the original culture from 1842 when the distillery was founded. They kept it in storage at the local bakery during the 13 years of Prohibition.

How did they get the idea of the oak barrels you ask. Remember the Reverend Craig? Some of the barrels he was preparing for transport to New Orleans got charred in a fire. Being a good Scotsman, he didn't want to throw them away. He filled them with his white lightening and took them to market. Naturally, after all that sloshing around in the barrel, the whiskey picked up an amber color and a softer taste. The people loved it.

As an addendum, only Makers Mark and Wild Turkey rotate their barrels in storage to allow for a more even ageing process. Bourbon has to be aged two years although most do it for four. Another rule.

## THE BIGGEST GUY ON THE BLOCK

Once you drive onto the property, you can see it. Big grain silos, big distillers, big warehouses and a big parking lot filled with trailer trucks ready to deliver. The sign says, Jim Beam the world's top selling bourbon. Reading on, you see it's the number one whiskey in Germany and the number one spirit in Australia. They proudly just filled their nine-millionth barrel and that's only counting since the repeal of Prohibition in 1933. They started over 200 years ago and it's still a family run business. It started in 1795 but Jim Beam decided he didn't want to go to jail in 1920 because of warehouses filled with bourbon. He sold everything to a group of bootleggers. In 1933, at the age of 70, he started up again. Built it all from scratch in 100 days. The rest is history. And history is what you find on these premises. The house the Beam family lived in and an original barrel making workshop with original hand tools.

## WHEN IS BOURBON NOT BOURBON

Straight Rye Whiskeys are made of 51% rye. Canadian Whiskeys are made from corn, wheat, rye and barley malt with not one accounting for more than 50%. Tennessee Whiskey is filtered through a bed of sugar maple charcoal to remove impurities and give a smooth mellow taste. According to the rules, bourbon cannot be filtered, so Jack Daniel's, arguably the finest bourbon in the world, cannot be called a bourbon. It's a Tennessee Whiskey. And the making of charcoal is the first thing we saw on our tour in Lynchburg, TN, the only place Jack Daniels is made. It's the oldest registered national Distillery, 1866. There were 17 men and 3 women on this tour (there were 10 men and 8 women on the Makers Mark tour - I don't know if this is significant).

We went out back (after the introductory film) and saw them burning the sugar maple logs. They had to be careful. Not enough and they would have wood chips. Too much burning and it would be dust. Just right and they had the pebble size necessary to fill a 10 foot deep vat. The liquor drips on the top of the open vat and takes 10 days to filter down. Jack Daniels is a sour mash too. That means a portion of the previous mash is used to start the next mash. The main ingredient in all bourbons is the water - limestone water. There is a life sized bronze statue of Jack Daniels just outside the stream that flows from a cave. It's on a pedestal so we can look eye to eye. He wasn't a big man, 5'2" but apparently had a temper and it killed him. We'll get back to that.

All barrels are 55 gallons and made from American White Oak. But, they only put 53 gallons in each one to allow for contraction and expansion because of temperature. The barrels breath and lose 10% of the volume the first year. Then 5% each successive year. Distillers call it the "angels third". Oh yes, Jack Daniels had trouble opening his safe and kicked it. That broke his toe, it got infected and the infection killed him. At age 61.

Jack Daniels sells several labels - black label, green label, single barrel label and one that has been filtered twice. Naturally, the more handling, the higher the price. I asked our tour guide, a man of ample girth and 28 years with the company, if he could tell the difference between the standard bourbon and the premium priced ones. He said after two drinks, nobody could tell, it all tastes the same. I smiled - an honest response.

There is a small gift shop on the premises but the town, population 5,740, is one big gift store and is only a block away from the welcome center. If you can put the name Jack Daniels on anything - they have it.

Which is the best? They all claim they are and more than one claim to be the best selling. I drank Jim Beam when I was in the service. Later, when I had more money, I went to Jack Daniels. Both are 80 proof. Now, I like Wild Turkey. It's 101 proof. Costs more, but it's a good sippin' bourbon. As are the other two. Besides, I don't like Scotch and if you're a good American, you won't either.

## THE END

## SIDEBAR FOR THE BOURBON TRAIL

GETTING THERE - From Louisville, KY, take I-65 south to exit 112. On route 245, a short distance to the Jim Beam brewery on the left. Total of about 30 miles. Makers Mark is 35 miles south of here and count on an hour to get there. Continue south on Rt.245 until the US 150 intersection. Go right and through the middle of Bardstown (take care at the roundabout at the far end) go south on KY 49 to Loretto and KY 52 - go left (east) and it's out of town. Enough so you'll be sure you are lost, providing you didn't get lost getting to Loretto. Follow the Makers Mark road way signs starting in Bardstown. As far as getting back, you better have a good memory.

Jack Daniels is easy to get to. Take US 64 east from Memphis to Fayetteville. Lynchburg is 12 miles north off State 50. From Nashville, go south on I-24 to exit 81, south on US 231. About 12 miles before you get to Fayetteville, turn left on State 129.

WHEN TO GO - Anytime actually - depends more on the weather than anything else. The distilleries are closed for most major holidays but are open year round otherwise. Don't count on buying any product at cost or even getting a bargain. Unlike the beer breweries, no free samples. All three have gift shops. Jim Beam has the best on site selection. Makers mark is limited and Jack Daniels has a whole town as a gift shop.

From Crazy to Kiddy to Killer to some very Badlands
By

RAPID CITY, SOUTH DAKOTA - I had no idea there was so much to see and do in the Black Hills. Best to tackle it one day at a time and a good place to start is the Crazy Horse Memorial, 38 miles southwest of Rapid City. And talk about facilities. They have a three wing Indian Museum, education & conference center, twin theaters, Native American Cultural Center, sculptor's workshop, bronze showroom, mountain displays, a photo display room, snack shop, restaurant, gift shops, viewing veranda and a 16 ton, 1/34 scale model of the intended finished statue. You might expect all these supporting accommodations for the largest statue in the world, but, the only part finished is the head. They still have to do the body from the waist up and the front of the horse. Lets look back at the time table.

Lakota Chief Henry Standing Bear picked Korzak Ziolkowski as the sculptor. Korzak started in 1949 at the age of 39 with only $174 to his name. Korzak is no longer with us but his family continues with the project. Considering the pace, I wouldn't hold my breath waiting to see the finished statue. Never the less, the scale model is impressive and if you stand just right, you can get a picture of the model with the mountain face in the background. The project is non-profit and there has been no Federal financing. The shops and displays are worth the price of admission and it's easy to spend several hours here.

Local literature mentioned Dinosaur park so I went. The mountain top has a marvelous view of the city but the fake dinosaurs are for kids. For adults, check out the Minuteman II missals at the South Dakota Air & Space Museum at Ellsworth Air Force Base, east of Rapid City. They have real jet fighters and bombers parked on the lawn and there is a tour of a missel silo that leaves every hour. There are no secrets given away here since the Minuteman program has been scrapped. Back during the cold war, there were 15 launch centers here with 10 missals each. The silos were designed for one time use and one was saved (no explosives inside) to show visitors. The silos were not manned, just the launch centers. The tour goes down into the silo using stairs. The maintenance crew had to use a hatch and an iron ladder.

The Air & Space Museum is on the way to the Badlands National Park. But, all those road signs for the Wall Drug Store. And it's on the way as well, so I stopped. This could be the biggest drug store/restaurant/gift shop/clothing store/souvenir shop/snack shops in the world. One side of the street is the drug store and it's difficult to tell if it's one big store or a collection of many smaller ones. It has to be the size of a Wal-Mart and I never saw a place to fill a prescription. Still, if you need anything else, they probably have it here.

The Badlands. 75 million years ago, this was a shallow sea and the climate was warmer. Archeologists can determine what lived in this sea from the remains in the grayish-black sedimentary rock layer. As the plates moved under the west coast of America, forming the Rocky Mountains, the sea bed was lifted. Now, the layers from millions of years ago are exposed. The grayish rock called Pierre (peer) shows invertebrate fossils. Ones with no backbone. After the sea bed rose to the surface, the climate was warm and humid. Subtropical forest flourished for millions of years until the climate cooled. The forest was replaced by a savannah which turned into today's grassland. An array of now extinct animals lived here. They include relatives of deer, sheep, pigs, saber tooth cats, rabbits and rhinoceros'.

This is a forbidding landscape and it's difficult to imagine people living here, but they did. For 11,000 years. The earliest ones hunted the mammoth and later tribes, the bison. The Arikara were the first in the White River area and they were replaced by the Sioux. Then came the French fur trapper followed by troopers, miners and homesteaders. This is a bleak, harsh land.

THE END

## SIDEBAR FOR CRAZY

WHEN TO GO - The National parks are crowded during the summer especially during July and August. Spring and autumn are the best times for crowd avoidance and the best weather. Winter is not the time to visit South Dakota.

PLANNING - There are nominal fees for most attractions. Admission fee for Crazy Horse is $10. Dino Park is free. Guided tour of Ellsworth AFB is $5. Badlands National Park admission is $10. Crazy Horse memorial is 38 miles south of Rapid City, The Space Museum and the Badlands are east just off Interstate 90. They can all be visited in one day.

PLACES TO STAY - Road side rest stops and gas stations have hotel/motel booklets with discount coupons. Rapid City thrives on tourists and there are hundreds of hotels/motels in the area. Most all the major chains are here. Fall/spring rates are best, summer rates are 50 % more.

From Close Encounters of the Third Kind to
Custer's Last Encounter of the First Kind

Devil's Tower - First National Monument - 1906

RAPID CITY, SOUTH DAKOTA - I remember Richard Dreyfus
building something on his table with a mound of mashed potatoes in the
movie "Close Encounters of the Third Kind". I didn't know what it was.
Not until he went there and even then I'd only seen pictures. Never been

there and for good reason. Devils Tower isn't on the way to anything, so if you're traveling across the country it's easy to drive by. But, this time it's a destination and it's only 107 miles from Rapid City.

Stopped in Sundance, WY, where the Sundance Kid did get his name. They have an interesting Crook County Museum with old west artifacts, but, I was looking for remnants of the big film festival and there weren't any. Oh well, 28 miles to go.

Devils Tower can be seen from miles away. The surrounding land is relatively flat. President Teddy Roosevelt designated it as the nation's first national monument in 1906, so it's part of the National Park system. It looks like it just popped up out of the ground, but the reverse is true. This 865 foot high, flat topped butte, is actually the core of a volcano. About 60 million years ago, molten lava was forced upwards into the sedimentary rock where it cooled and hardened. Millions of years of erosion by wind and water, ate away the sedimentary rock leaving this core.

On July 4, 1983 William Rodgers and Willard Ripley made the first ascent in front of 1,000 spectators. Now 5,000 climbers come here from all over the world. About 220 routes have been used to get to the top. The closest walk around is the Tower Trail and it's 1.3 miles. The outer, Red Beds Trail, is 2.8 miles. More than 150 species of birds have been seen in the park. They include hawks, golden eagles, prairie falcons and turkey vultures.

I looked. Never could find Richard Dreyfus' hiding place.

Continuing west on I-90 will bring you to Custer's Last Stand, 78 miles east of Billings, Montana. But, for the sake of continuity, lets slip over a few hundred miles to Fort Abraham Lincoln State Park, an hours drive south of Bismark, North Dakota. This is where Custer lived. This is where he told his men to mount up on their fateful way to Little Big Horn.

This site is on the Lewis & Clark trail. It sits on the merging of the Missouri and Heart Rivers. The Mandan Indians lived here from 1575 to 1781. They didn't have horses to raid other Indian tribes. They were farmers. The women built good sized mud huts which would house 15 people. There was a hole in the roof for ventilation and a wind break inside the front door. The huts were so well built, they were 20 degrees cooler in the summer and warm in the winter. The larger, tribal meeting hut, was built by the men because the wood braces were heavier. Unfortunately, white settlers and traders brought smallpox with them and the Mandan were doomed. The land stood vacant for 100 years until the Army built a fort. Now, Park Rangers offer tours of the grounds and the guides are very informative.

Lt. General Armstrong Custer had a white, two story house which is nice even by today's standards. Now, it sits alone, surrounded by acres of grass. This is the house he left behind when he went off with the 7th Calvary in 1876. It's a full days drive on the Interstate to get to Little Bighorn. It took Custer months on horseback.

In 1868 it was believed that it was cheaper to feed than to fight the Indians. So, the U.S. signed a treaty at Fort Laramie, WY with the Lakota, Cheyenne and other tribes of the Great Plains giving them a large corner of Eastern Wyoming and promising to protect them. However, in 1874, gold was discovered in the Black Hills and prospectors swarmed into the area in violation of the treaty. The Army tried to keep them out and failed, so, they offered to buy the Black Hills from the Indians. The answer was no. The Lakota and Cheyenne left the reservation and resumed raids on the settlements. The Army ordered them to return by January 31, 1876 or they would use force.

There were three separate forces sent to find the raiders. Gen. George Crook from Ft. Fetterman in Wyoming, Col. John Gibbon from Ft. Ellis in Montana and Gen. Alfred Terry from Ft. Abraham Lincoln. Custer was attached to Terry. Crook's troops were knocked out of the campaign in mid-June by a large force of Lakota-Cheyenne. These Indians then moved west to the Little Bighorn River to camp. Terry ordered Custer and the 7th Cavalry to approach from the south, he would link up with Gibbons and approach from the north. Custer split his forces between Captain Benteen and Major Reno. Benteen was to scout to the south and Reno to cross the river and attack from the north. Reno was stopped by a large force of Lakota, outflanked, and forced to retreat. Benteen then joined him but neither knew where Custer was until they heard heavy gunfire to the north. They rushed to the rescue, but, by the time they could see Bighorn hill (they didn't see any soldiers), the firing had stopped, they were under attack and had to withdraw. They were too late to save Custer anyway. Reno and Benteen had seven companies, were now entrenched and under attack. The Lakota and Cheyenne had them surrounded and fighting for their lives for several days. The Indians finally withdrew when they saw the columns of Terry and Gibbons coming in from the north.

Custer had a Gatling machine gun but chose to leave it behind because it was heavy and would slow him down. He made another mistake when he split his forces so he was left with only 210 men on top of the hill. The attacking tribes had thousands. In all, Reno and Benteen lost 53 men in their various encounters. Custer lost all 210. The Indians lost no more than 100 in total.

The battlefields are well preserved. There is a monument atop Little Bighorn hill with the names of all Custer's fallen men and grave stones on the side of the hill showing where they fell. Custer died close to the monument. The National Park map shows the location of Custer's Battlefield and the Reno-Benteen Battlefield and the sites of the various Indian encampments. After this battle, most of the tribes scattered. Some went north, some south and most returned to the reservation. Custer was initially buried here in a shallow grave and later moved to West Point. This entire battlefield now lies within the Crow Indian Reservation. If Custer wasn't moved, he would be rolling in his grave.


THE END

## SIDEBAR FOR CUSTER

WHEN TO GO - The National parks are crowded during the summer especially during July and August. Spring and autumn are the best times for crowd avoidance and the best weather. Winter is not the time to visit Wyoming and North Dakota.

PLANNING - Admission fee for Devil's Tower and Little Bighorn is $10 each. Both are part of the National Park system, so with a National Park pass or Golden Age pass, they are free. Fort Lincoln is a State Park, so passes don't work. $10 entrance and the guided tours are included. Devil's Tower and Little Bighorn can all be visited in one day. Bismark, ND is a days drive away.

PLACES TO STAY - Road side rest stops and gas stations have hotel/ motel booklets with discount coupons. Rapid City thrives on tourists and there are hundreds of hotels/motels in the area. Most all the major chains are here. Fall/spring rates are best, summer rates are 50 % more. Billings, MT is the closest city of size to Little Bighorn. Neither Billings nor Bismark, ND have the quantity of motel rooms available in Rapid City, but, they both have most of the national chains.

## DEATH VALLEY

It's not easy to get green

Death Valley, California - Scotty's Castle

"You've got to be kidding," several friends said, "what's out there?" You could see it in their faces, endless sand dunes, cracked earth devoid of animals or plant life, the heat of a blast furnace, poisoned water holes, miles of featureless salt beds, the bleached bones of long gone prospectors and the remains of wagon trains abandoned to the desert inferno. They can't be blamed for those thoughts, since, to some extent, they are right. But there were no bleached bones or Conestoga wagon wheels - even the tracks have been blown away by the wind. Notwithstanding the dangerous history of Death Valley, there is a great deal to see in this rift between the Pantamint Mountain Range to the west and the Amargosa Range on the east. Death Valley Monument is a National Park with approximately 3,000 square miles within it's borders that cross the California-Nevada State line. Roughly 550 square miles are below sea level. t has the lowest point in the western hemisphere, 282 feet below sea level, and the hottest recorded air temperature in the U.S., 134 degrees Fahrenheit. Ground temperatures have reached 175 degrees. When they say, you can fry an egg, they mean it.

The most convenient way to get to the park is to drive 240 miles north east from Los Angeles. Through the Mojave desert, ascending the Inyo and Cottonwood Mountains with steep grades on both sides. Road signs warn you to turn off the car air conditioning when climbing the mountains because of the power drain on the engine. With the windows open, the night air of the summer, is hot.

## THE FIRST STOP

Gas, food and lodging are available at Stovepipe Wells, on the valley floor, six miles beyond the foot of the Cottonwoods. The general store and gas station on the left close at 6PM and open at 8AM. This is no place to run out of gas, so if you've traveled through the Mojave desert after sunset to avoid the heat, you spend the night here until the gas station opens in the morning. The village, on the right, is open year round, has 82 motel units, air conditioning, showers, a mineral pool and restaurant/bar. The water in the room is not recommended for drinking. The menu in the bar consists of a taco dinner with the salad bar or just the salad bar. Fresh fruit, lettuce, tomato and assorted condiments make the salad bar quite refreshing. The two tacos come with rice, beans and coffee. At $20 or $10, the prices aren't out of line, considering the location. The bar is very western, all wood, warm, clean and comfortable. It is 20 degrees cooler than the outside evening temperature which is in the 90's.

## THE BRIGHT LIGHT OF MORNING

After cold drinks, snacks and gas from the general store, the best time to see the length of the valley is in the morning from Dante's View. It's 50 miles from Stovepipe, past Furnace Creek, the parks center and another steep climb. At 5,475 feet, and virtually at the middle, you can almost see the 140 mile length of the valley. Directly below, are the salt flats, and Badwater - 282 feet below sea level. It appears to be an easy days walk from the foot of this mountain to the range directly opposite. An illusion that led some to their death. The view is inspiring and a bit scarey considering your life line is parked behind you. On the road back, the town of Ryan is to the right. It's private property and visitors are not welcome.

Twenty miles from Dante's view is Zabriskie Point (passed it on the way up) which is named after a borax mine superintendent. It's said to have inspired the movie of the same name, which can only make one wonder about the effects of prolonged exposure to the sun. A stunning array of streaked golden peaks, the eroded remains of a lake bed, five to ten million years old.

Turning south, just before Furnace Creek (an easy turn to miss) you drive 15 miles to Badwater, at the foot of Dante's view. Even in the desert heat, water is in the pool at roadside. Behind you, 282 feet above the pool, on the hillside is the sign - SEA LEVEL. The view, across the desert floor, with the rippling heat waves and obvious lack of life, is a lasting one. Six miles north (back towards the visitors center) on the left and off the main road, is Devil's Golf Course. The surface looks like severely cratered moon surface. The 200 square mile floor was formed by the evaporation of several ancient lakes that left alternating layers of salt and gravel. Moisture rises from the shallow water table with salt, in solution, to evaporate at the surface. Wind and rain carve the sharp edges of this hard brown crust that is 95% pure salt.

Two and a half miles north is the turnoff for Artists Palette, a ten mile, one way road through mountain cuts, gullies and dry river beds to see a mosaic of reds, pinks and yellows (produced by the iron salts), green from Mica and purple from Manganese. A half mile north of the exit is mushroom rock. Wind eroded basalt, that looks like a solitary black lava dropping, molded to the shape of a six foot mushroom statue.

## WATER, WATER

Furnace Creek is 6 miles north and a welcome stop for lunch. The Ranch is open year round with 225 units, a cafeteria, coffee shop, cocktail lounge, steak house (except summer), pizza parlor, Mexican Restaurant, swimming pool, tennis courts, golf and horseback riding. The cafeteria has a full selection of hot and cold food, beverages, ice cream and it all looks good. A favorite among the lunch crowd is watermelon.

Fifty miles north, at the tip of the valley, is Scotty's Castle. Construction of this Spanish style mansion began in1924 and it featured all the conveniences of it's time. Running water from a fresh stream a half mile north, indoor plumbing, electricity from the water wheel at the stream, a natural gas stove, and a working refrigerator hidden behind cabinet doors. A castle that Walter Scott, a con man and convincing storyteller, claimed as his own. In fact, Scotty had been a miner in the valley after running away from home at age 11 for Idaho where he worked at a timber operation. Stories of gold and silver deposits abounded in and around Death Valley's mine fields, and Scotty decided to cash in on the greed and hopes of investors. He talked people into a grub stake. They would put up the money and he would split the gold he found with them. Once staked, he spent the money on wine, women and song. Even if he couldn't sing well, he could weave a tale and ran into Albert Johnson, a Chicago insurance millionaire. Albert wanted a winter home and Scotty, now his friend, would look after it. Albert wanted a low profile and encouraged others to believe the mansion was Scotty's. The storytelling never stopped and was probably a source of great amusement to Mr. and Mrs. Johnson when they visited each winter. There was always a secret gold mine, the source of Scotty's apparent wealth. It must be under the house, the miners figured. They'd looked everywhere else. And Scotty never had to work another day in his life.

The inside of the house is seen by tour only. On the hour, given by the Park Service for $11. The house is kept in it's original state, by contract, when it was sold to the Government. Walking pads cover the carpet and the windows are covered to prevent the sun from bleaching the drapes. The furnishings are lavish, from the couches in the two story living room to the individual guest rooms which used to be rented to visitors, the sun room, and the music room with two working organs. The organ paper tape player is turned on at the end of the tour and the sound is deep, rich and overpowering. The moat in front of the castle was never finished and the park service must leave it that way.

Seven Miles from the Castle is Ubehebe Crater formed by a violent volcanic explosion. It's nearly a half a mile wide and 500 feet deep. The gas station attendant at the castle said, "Be sure to put your parking brake on if you leave the engine running." Seems some visitors didn't and their van rolled into the crater. The tow truck from Lone Pine wouldn't come to the rescue until $1000 was guaranteed up front. It's a long drive from Lone Pine.

The wind at the crater's edge was like being in a hurricane. Maybe it's like that only at the end of the day but it was strong enough to literally blow you off your feet. We had to lean towards the crater to keep our balance which kept us away from the craters edge. If the wind suddenly stopped...

From the crater, it's a three hour drive to Mammoth Lakes in the high sierras. Northeast from the castle over the Grapevine Mountains into Nevada, northwest for 16 miles and due west over the Sylvania Mountains back into California - horse shoe fashion. From the hottest place in America to pine trees and snow on the mountains (even in July) all in a weekend. What more could you want.

THE END

## SIDEBAR

GETTING THERE - From L.A. take US 5 north to CA 14, over the pass through the Angeles National Forest, past Palmdale, Mojave, to Olancha. Right on CA 190 for 66 miles to Stovepipe Wells. You can enter from the south end from US 15 at Baker, halfway between Las Vegas and Barstow. Turn north on CA 127. There are three entrances if traveling north on US 95 from Las Vegas. South on 127/373 at Amargosa Valley. South at Beatty on 90/374 (goes to Stovepipe Wells) and at 267 for Scotty's Castle.

PLACES TO STAY - Stovepipe Wells Village (619)786-2387, 83 units, AC, restaurant, bar, grocery store, pool, gas. Jun-Sept $90 double. $110 double otherwise. Open year round as is Furnace Creek Ranch (619)786-2345. The Ranch has 225 units, AC, several restaurants, cocktail lounge, TV in the room, general store, pool, gas. From $140 double summer to $190 otherwise. Furnace Creek Inn (619)786-2345 is open Oct 27-May 12 and rates run from $335 single standard room to $395 per night, double deluxe. Naturally, the Inn has all the amenities including evening entertainment. Jackets are required for men in the main dining room. The address is Death Valley, CA 92328.

WHAT TO BRING - Summer temperatures of 120 degrees are expected. Wear loose fitting, light colored, cotton clothes. Sun glasses, a hat, sunblock - even if it is overcast, the Ultra Violet rays can burn, plenty of liquids in a cooler in the car. Store photographic film in the cooler. Use a UV filter on the camera lens to get truer colors. It is allowed to take flash pictures inside Scotty's Castle even though you won't need the flash in the desert, you will inside the Castle. Temperatures from November through March are 60-70 in the day and 40's at night. There could be snow on the mountains in the winter.

OTHER INFORMATION - There are tours from the Fred Harvey Company at Furnace Creek for those tired of driving. Scotty's Castle, Titus

Canyon, Lower Valley Tour, Dante's View, Amargosa Opera, Charcoal Kilns, Aguereberry Point, and Casino/Gaming trips to Nevada. There is a minimum of 4 adult fares. Prices are $35-60. If your car breaks down - stay with it. The Park Service regularly patrols and will help. AAA emergency road service is available from Baker (619)733- 4339, Furnace Creek (619)786-2232, Lone Pine (619)876-4600, Northern Death Valley (619)938-2264, Ridgecrest (619)375- 3055. Death Valley may seem barren but it's not. The desert animals don't come out in the blazing heat, only people do.

There are a number of species of reptiles, birds and mammals well adapted to the desert. Various members of the pupfish family live in the saline waters. There are 1000 species of plants that live in the park and 21 of them live nowhere else in the world. There are spring wild flowers.

Interstate 15 - Mexico to Canada and
Some of America's finest National Parks

Bryce National Park, Utah

Grand Coulee Dam

SAN DIEGO, CA - Americans have a long history of taking road trips for summer vacation. More so since 9-11. When I was a kid my parents packed my brother and I into the back seat of the family car and off we went, in a different direction each year. I don't remember ever saying 'are we there yet' but my parents version may differ. US 1 runs up and down the east coast, 101 the west coast and I-15 goes through the Rocky Mountains which includes some of the most spectacular National Parks this country has to offer.

Forty five miles north of the Mexican border, just east of Escondido, is the San Diego Wild Animal Park. It can take much of a day to see the animals running loose in as close to a natural habitat as you can expect outside of Africa.

Continuing north, past Barstow, are the glittering lights of Las Vegas (even in the daytime). But this is a country trip and we're going to avoid big cities where ever we can. The overnight is in Mesquite, NV just this side of Utah. Rooms are incredibly cheap and the food abundant. After a full breakfast for $1.99 it's over the hill into Utah, turn right after St. George to Zion National Park. It's packed with tourists even in the fall. Too many people for me so I continue east on Route 9. For those who love mountain tunnels, this is heaven. Lights on and forge ahead through an engineering marvel. Once on the other side there is plenty to see - the park continues for miles. The top down, a bright sun, wind in my hair, a cup of coffee in hand and a ZZ Top tape playing as I fly along on a waving ribbon of asphalt - it doesn't get any better than this.

Twenty two miles north (towards Bryce National Park) is Route 14 which will connect back to I-15. It's the scenic drive I was looking for. Rolling hills, serpentine road and the trees are starting to change color. A dash of red, a background of green and the yellow leaves sparkle in the sun. Gorgeous. A few miles later and I turn north on Rt 143. Log cabins, Swiss Chalets, this is skiing country and it's beautiful even without the snow.

Back on I-15 I have to make up some time. I get past Salt Lake City just before dusk and stop in Ogden. Up early the next day, it's going to be a long one. Just north of Pocatello, Idaho and past the Blackfoot gas station/ restaurant/souvenir shop (with very good prices) I turn west on Rt. 26 for Craters of the Moon National Monument. It's 75 miles of desolate rolling brown hills without a tree in sight. The 1,100 square mile park has more basaltic volcanic features than any other area of it's size in the Continental US. It sits on a 6 million year old caldera (caldera's are formed when the cone of a volcano collapses). There is a 7 mile loop drive that makes it easy to see the highlights. The first sight is the most recent lava flow, 2,000 years old. Black crusted rock covered with cinder cones. Early observers thought it resembled the craters of the moon. Farther on is Big Cinder and at 700 feet is the worlds largest. These cones form when fountains of gas filled rock was shot into the air. The frothy lava cooled, hardened into cinders and fell to form symmetrical mounds.

It started to rain so I went straight to Idaho Falls and Rt. 20 north to West Yellowstone to get there just before dark. It's early October and off season rates apply. Most of the park's facilities are open from May 30 to October 15 (depending on the weather).

The next morning it's 14 miles to Madison, the first fork in the road inside the park. An easy 25 minute ride except for the buffalo. They live in the park and cross the road at less than a snails pace. I saw a male stand on the asphalt and stare at a car for 10 minutes. Posted signs warn visitors to stay in their cars and away from the wild animals. Buffalo can outrun a person and the males have sharp horns.

Old Faithful was on the way to Jackson Hole so I stopped. My timing couldn't have been better. Five minutes and there she went (intervals range from 40 to 126 minutes). Road construction stopped traffic just south of the park at the Snake River and I used the time to get a picture of 2 canoers on the winding river with the Grand Tetons in the background. There were road delays every day I was in the park - road construction, buffalo crossing, deer sighting, bear walking - and I learned to grab the camera and look around.

88

Fifty miles south of the park is Jackson, Wyoming an upscale town known as a ski center. The town also has a number of summer activities like, white water rafting, Grand Teton float trips, mountain bike tours, wagon train trips and even has a Ripley's Believe it or not museum. The city center park entrances are through a crescent of elk (or deer) horns. The Million Dollar bar has saddles for bar seats.

Heading back I took the turn left at Moose Junction for the 15 mile drive through Grand Teton National Park. The mountains are on the left, on the far side of Jackson Lake. Tall, ominous and rather scary looking with an overcast sky. I had the opposite feeling in Yellowstone. Each stop there was inviting. I wanted to walk into the woods, walk among the mud flats, wait for the small geysers to erupt, see more waterfalls, get in one of Mammoth Hot Springs pools (not smart, they really are hot). During the next few days, I had the top down, got inundated by a tree shedding it's seeds, got rained on, saw a beautiful rainbow on the far side of Yellowstone Lake, crossed the Continental divide eight times, saw a 12 point buck crossing a stream, a black bear and hundreds of Bison that challenged my use of the road. And then it snowed.

The roads were plowed but still wet. The scenic drive through Red Lodge at 11,000 feet didn't look as appealing as before. Wet at 7,000 feet can be ice at 11,000 feet. I went directly north through Gardiner at 5,300 feet to I-90 and back on I-15 north. From there it's a choice. North on I-15 to Shelby and west to East Glacier Park (238 miles total), or, just north of Helena, take Rts 287 and 89 and 2 through no mans land for 183 miles. I took the short cut. Two hours later it started to rain. That turned into a light snow and by the time I got to Browning it was a blizzard. Twelve miles to go, the road was clear so I forged ahead.

I awoke to find the car covered in snow. Two Medicine diner is across from the train station (and the tracks) and is the only place to eat. Fine with me. They had my exclusive business for the next few days.

I went north on Rt. 49 into the Two Medicine Entrance. Nine miles to the end. The snow capped mountains and white lined pine trees made for the most spectacular scenery I have ever seen. Then north to the Many Glacier Entrance. Twelve miles to the end with nary another car in sight. And scenery just as stunning.

Returning south, I stopped at St. Mary, The Resort at Glacier - The Great Bear Lodge. It was open as was the gas station (they are few and far between in this area), gift shops and restaurant. This is THE entrance for the east end of the park and where I was informed that the Going-to-the-Sun road was closed 14 miles in because of 4 foot snow drifts. The first 10 miles are along the shores of the beautiful St. Mary Lake. At Jackson Glacier Overlook, the road was blocked but the drive was well worth while. The next day I went the long way around, Rt. 2 along the south bank of the Flathead river, to the west entrance. West Glacier has accommodations and a train station but isn't really a town. The road was open to the top but I tried Camas road first. Five miles of trees (boring) and I turned back for Going-to-the-Sun road. Thirty two miles of curving roads, cutbacks, pull outs, terrific snow capped vistas and I got to the cloud covered top. Logan Pass and I couldn't see 20 feet in front of the car. Snow plows had cleared the road making it almost 2 lanes wide. Time to go back - carefully. Wet roads can turn to ice with a shift of the wind. I breathed a sigh of relief when I got back to Lake McDonald. You can see the glaciers from several roads but getting to one would be quite a hike. Summer would be the time for that. But now is the time for looking - it's breath taking.

## THE END

SIDEBAR FOR I-15


WHEN TO GO - The National parks are crowded during the summer especially during July and August. The colors come out in the northern parks in autumn which is the best time. Glacier is open from mid-June to mid-October depending on the weather. Yellowstone is open from May through October.

PLANNING - Park admissions are $10 for a 7 day pass. $20 for Yellowstone which includes Grand Teton just to the south. A Golden Pass for seniors can be purchased at any park entrance for $10. It gives unlimited entrance to all National Parks forever. If hiking and exploring is included, one would like a week for Yellowstone, five days for Glacier and two to three for Zion and nearby Bryce National Parks. Distances between the parks are roughly 450 miles and can be done in a casual driving day. Road side rest stops and gas stations have hotel/motel booklets with discount coupons. The lodges inside the National Parks are full service hotels. They are beautiful and not intended for those on a budget. They are also so popular that reservations are made a year in advance. Camping permits are available for all the parks. San Diego to Glacier National Park (which extends into Canada) and back is approximately 5,000 miles. Many elevations are 7,000 feet and can go as high as 11,000 feet. One should be in good health to go that high.

## RIVER RAFTING RECKLESSNESS

Why would anyone in their right mind sit on the front edge of a 12 foot long rubber boat and weave among sharp edged rocks with only a fraction of an inch of rubber between them and numbing cold, swirling water only to plunge head first over a sixteen foot waterfall into an angry, frothing, icy torrent? Knowing that a slip of the hand or a loss of balance could put them in the midst of an unforgiving undercurrent and make them yet another river statistic? But then, I'm getting ahead of myself.

It was a bright spring day, or soon would be, since I had to get up at 4:30 in the morning. Arrival time at Kernville was 8 AM and it was a 2 ½ hour drive from Los Angeles. I picked up my traveling companion, filled the trunk with gear (our STUFF, actually) and we were on our way. The last 48 miles was a challenging mountain run with S curves and blind turnabouts following the banks of the river. If only I had my old Alfa Romeo to do the mountain curves justice. Never the less, the adrenal gland got a warm up. There are road signs every few miles as a reminder - 141 people have drowned in the Kern. I wanted that number to stay at 141.

We met at a piece of vacant land next to the river's bridge and rented wet suits from the tour operators. Two types of boats are offered - paddle and oar. Paddle boats expect all occupants to paddle and work as a team to guide the boat. Simple enough - left, right, forwards and backwards. They hold 6 or 8 paying guests and a guide in the rear with a paddle and a loud voice to issue instructions. The oar boat will hold two guests in the front, the guide in the middle with long, row-boat type oars mounted on a metal frame strapped to the rubber boat, and two or three guests in the rear third unless the space is needed for supplies. Paddle boats usually don't carry supplies. The guides are supposed to be experienced, not just in river rafting, but specifically in the stretch of river they are guiding. Ours were, on both counts. How then does one get trained, you might ask? Trainees, follow experienced guides in supply boats. No paying guests are exposed to the dangers of inexperience. But our food is.

## THE QUALIFYING TESTS

Oar boat participants are subjected to tests before being allowed to continue. Overall good health is necessary and with wet suits, wind breakers and life vests on, the training begins. First the rules - if you're ejected from the boat #1 - Orient yourself # 2 - Get onto your back, the life vest will keep you afloat properly if it's pulled tight enough - if not, it will ride up over your face. The vest will be above the waterline, your mouth will not. #3 - Feet downstream #4 - Steer with your arms #5 - Use your legs to bounce off any rocks #6 - Head for the nearest boat to be pulled in OR grab the rope thrown in the water and be pulled BACKWARDS to the boat OR steer yourself to a slow moving section of the river and wait for a boat to come to you. Slow moving sections are the outside bends of the river. The inside bends move the fastest.

Then everyone got into the river (water from upstream snow melt) and floated downstream for practice. Following that, we hung from an overhead bar to insure there were no shoulder problems. Then a brief run back to the starting point, pack your bag and on the bus.

Our bus ride was 1 ½ hours with a mountain top stop to view the river, a half mile below. Beautiful and so far away. The bus eventually stopped in a clearing to unload and watch the mule train gather to start it's descent of the trail. The mules carried the boats, pumps and food for twenty of us on the three day trip.

## THE GRUELING WALK

We were each given a waterproof duffle bag in which we put our sleeping bag, personal gear, warm clothes for nighttime (at 7000 feet it gets nippy) and in my case, two cameras and lenses. The bag is loaded on our backs, not on the mules and we have to follow a narrow, curving, rock strewn trail, one thousand feet straight down to the river. This is the Forks of the Kern, a Class V and known to be one of the most challenging rivers in North America. The rubberized duffle bag was heavy when it was empty but loaded to the top with my stuff it weighted over 50 pounds.

Remember, the mules went first. Doesn't take long to pack a mule. A few hundred feet down the trail it was apparent the mules had a large breakfast. Now it's like walking in a mine field. I sweated a great deal for the next hour watching every step down the trail and the duffle bag must have absorbed every drop of perspiration. By the time I reached bottom, the bag must have weighted 150 pounds.

## FINALLY, THE BOTTOM

Lunch - a rest - and the guides drank stream water from a cup for luck. This area is so remote, the water is pure. Cold and clean. I had a cup, for luck. During the next few days I would be drinking a lot more stream water but not by design nor to celebrate good luck.

The afternoon was filled with Class III, IV and V rapids. My friend and I were in the front of an oar boat and we each had paddles in case help was needed (it wasn't). The air was crisp and clear and the river was running about 1750 cfs (cubic feet per second). The highest in three years. The river descends steeply on this section of the Kern and the guide has to make split second decisions on how to approach each rapids. Once the run has started, there is no turning back. The water is so powerful that the boat and its contents can be easily dashed against rocks as big as a house.

At water- flows this high, the guide must be familiar with each rapids. There often is a choice of paths, that is, which rocks to go between - one way is an exciting plunge over a five foot waterfall into a vortex of swirling white water. The other might be a header into a tooth shaped rock that would rip the boat to shreds and throw the us onto adjoining rocks. A good memory is essential. Within 15 minutes of the start we were soaked, head to toe, from crashing into waves. The wet suit was a blessing. The wind breaker was necessary because there is a constant, cold, head wind, streaming straight up the valley. One guy was thrown from his boat while going through rapids and we were waiting downstream to pull him into our boat. Changing boats is simple since all the boats collect, like wagon trains, before and after a run.

We camped before sunset to collect our gear, pitch tents and watch the guides prepare supper. Fresh salad was followed by T-bone steaks, baked potato and corn and capped off by chocolate brownies - all cooked on a wood campfire. The site is across the river from a beautiful mountain waterfall with a stream falling 200 feet over rock face made smooth by its passing. The night air was pure, the sky black and the stars too numerous to count. Bedtime came early.

## DAY 2

And so did the morning but the pace was leisurely. There is no rush to get ready as the guides made bacon, eggs, toast, juice and coffee. The sunrise made the waterfall across the way even more exquisite. Finally, out of the warm clothes and into the wet suit which had been hanging in a tree limb overnight to dry. Undo the tent, repack the bags, load up the boats and onwards.

We stopped at Ed's place along the south bank just before lunch. A mining company had abandoned several buildings a few years ago and Ed moved in. He does visit town on occasion and they say he doesn't mind visitors. His place is so remote, he doesn't get many but he was gone when we arrived. He has to walk to town across the mountain on the other side of the river. That's where the trail is. So, he built a hand operated aerial car to get across the river when the current is too strong for wading. He has a garden for vegetables in the summer, several flower gardens, a guard cat and a small, water powered, generator to provide electricity. Some empty shotgun shells in the yard shows that he hunts. Oh yes, least I forget, Ed has a wife.

A short run downstream and we park the boats for a hike. Fifteen minutes through a rugged tangle of trees and brush and we arrive at a stunning 100 foot high waterfall. Snow melt from another mountain cascading over lava formed granite to make its way to the sea.

The second night was much like the first with a good supper, some fireside stories and eventual sleep. So far, no boats had capsized. A second fellow had been thrown from his boat but there were no injuries. Surprising, since the powerful water had bounced several rafts from boulder to boulder like pin balls in a machine. The trick to staying in the oar boat is to hold onto a tie line inside the boat as it bounces through a water shoot. Boats plunge head first over a rapid and often the bow goes completely under water. You have to ride it like a horse except after the ride, the horse doesn't have to be bailed out. The water may be a foot and a half deep in the boat and it has to be removed or the boat isn't maneuverable. It's imperative to move quickly if the next rapids is a short distance ahead since the water inside can easily add a thousand pounds of dead weight. Each rapids is usually approached with the boat turned sideways to give the guide a better view. Then, at the last second, he leans hard on the oars to twist the boat forwards and aim at the open section. A heavy boat won't turn quickly enough and going through sideways is a sure way to capsize. The thought of being beneath an overturned boat bouncing among large rocks is not comforting. Your bottom will be doing the bouncing.

## THE WRONG WAY

We got caught by a surprising side current on a Class IV rapids. The boat would not turn because the current was stronger than the guides arms. He quickly realized the danger and, in a fraction of a second, reversed the oar from pull to push. If we couldn't go over forwards, we would go backwards. As long as it wasn't sideways, we had a chance. Just then, we hit the top and started the first of two, back to back, five foot waterfalls. The boat twisted and we dropped five feet - backwards. The second five foot waterfall was on us immediately and it was impossible to turn. We rode through the same way - backwards - expecting to capsize. It was disorienting, exciting and most importantly, we were stayed upright. We shouldn't be.

## KILLER CARSON

The trip was almost over. It was noon on the third day and the boats tied off at the bank, upstream from Carson falls. A Class V which becomes a Class VI at 2000 cfs. We are given the option of walking around and joining the boats downstream. Looking at it from the bank, it's a frightening, noisy, two step, curving, sixteen foot drop. Guides station themselves along the downstream banks with rescue ropes. The rafts are to go one at a time. Each has to wait until they receive word that the preceding raft was successful or the people who had been thrown out are rescued from the choppy water. Even these experienced guides had not all been successful in staying upright through this monster. No one takes the option of walking around. Which brings us back to the start of this story. Why am I here?

This was my sixth white water trip and third Class V. I'd seen several boats flipped over by powerful waves and a man thrown twenty feet in the air while going through a rapids - but never me and not my boat. But I had a strange feeling this time. I couldn't explain it. In the back of my mind, a warning said "Your luck can't hold out". But I wasn't here to watch the action from the shore.

We are still on point - the first boat out. We wish each other luck - I say a silent prayer - and we pull into the stream. Fifty feet from the falls, I can hear the thunder of the crashing water. As we draw closer, I know what raced through the minds of the people who went over Niagara Falls in a barrel.

There is a large rock blocking the best entrance - straight on - and we have to come from the center of the stream and make a right turn. The current, then turns us 90 degrees to the left and here we are. The sound of the crashing water is deafening. The boat is turning left and the front end is already perched in the air about to go over the top. We haven't completed our turn. Suddenly, we are falling headfirst and the boat is at a 30 degree tilt because we haven't completed the left turn. I'm on the downside and we crash into the first wave which curves backwards, straight into the boat. It hits me square in the face and chest and I'm thrown backwards. Both my hands have a death grip on the tie ropes in the front of the boat but I Find myself in the middle of the boat and my feet are straight up in the air. I try to right myself and my companion grabs my right leg to keep me inside the raft. Just as I struggle up, we hit the second falls. I see it coming, spit out a pint of water, and hang on. The second wave inundates the boat with water but it comes straight at us and crashes on top of our heads. We made it. The boat finally levels out and we hear the sounds of cheering from the shore. We calmly coast three hundred feet downstream and tie off. I walk back on unsure legs, to watch the other boats. Bailing could come later. And guess what, all the boats make it. What luck.

The next half hour of rafting is interesting but anti- climatic. The warnings of my mind had been in vain. My luck had held out. We say our goodbyes to the guides in the vacant lot where we left our cars. It's three in the afternoon and it will be a long drive home. I suppose the question still remains. Why? Is it the good food, the feeling of the great outdoors, the camaraderie we shared? Possibly. Mans' quest to conquer nature? The thrill of it all? Who knows! As for me, I have a passion for sitting in large rubber objects.

# THE END

## WHITE WATER CLASS SYSTEM

Rapids are graded in difficulty by Class. Usually the class of the stretch of the river is determined by the predominant class of the individual rapids with more weight given to the more difficult ones. Class I is moving water with small waves - you can take your rubber duck. Class II may have waves up to three feet and has wide channels. Class III has rapids with high and irregular waves, rocks and holes. The first Class III that I went on, a boat capsized the first morning out. Everyone, including the guide, was in the water. A downstream boat collected the survivors and the boat was right sided in the shallows. Nothing was lost, except the guides pride, because everything in the boat was tied down. Class III is a good place to start for adults - Class II for children. Class IV has turbulent rapids with powerful waves and numerous obstacles and requires expert maneuvering. Class V has violent rapids, unstable eddies, irregular currents and large holes. These rapids are always scouted and require experience and good physical condition. Scouting involves tying the boat upstream and walking to the rapids to determine the best possible way through. Class VI is suicide. It is only a number since people do not run a Class VI twice.

## SIDEBAR 2

GETTING THERE - A 2 ½ hour drive from Los Angeles. One hundred fifteen miles to Bakersfield, turn right on state hwy 178. Drive around Lake Isabella (left is shorter) and 50 miles later, Kernville. It's a six hour drive from San Francisco to Bakersfield.

TOUR OPERATORS - All trips have to be scheduled in advance. Contact - Outdoor Adventures, P.O. Box 1149, Pt. Reyes, CA 94956 tel. 1-800-323-4234 // South Bay River Rafters tel (310) 545-8572 or 1-800-655-RAFT. The Kern has a variety of white water offerings. Class II through V. One, two and three day trips. Upper, middle and lower sections of the river. The river is dam controlled which extends the rafting season for the lower stretches.

WHAT TO BRING - Wet suit, wind breaker (both can be rented), tie-on sneakers, sunglasses with tie-on strap, towel, dry clothes, shoes, socks, jacket for night time, waterproof sun screen, incidental cash. There is a dry bag for cigarettes, film, etc. - accessible at breaks. Waterproof camera for use in the boat, regular camera can be stashed for use on land. Fast film (ASA 400 or higher) for use in the boat. Normal film otherwise. Candy for snacks, if you are so inclined. Life vests are provided.

WHEN TO GO - White water is from snow melt and by definition will exist in the spring and into the summer depending on the winters snow fall. Usually, trips start in April and can last until June or July. The best water is April and May. The upper portion of the river drys up first and is the most challenging.

Monument Valley
John Wayne's favorite western setting
By

Headstone, Boot Hill, AZ

NORTHEAST CORNER OF ARIZONA - It was a dank, dreary morning. Dark clouds hung overhead. The rain was on and off again. The sun must have come up but the view of the horizon showed no sign. The northeast corner of Arizona is Indian land, a Navajo Reservation, a desert. A desert because it doesn't rain. Except for today. So much for my timing.

A small amount of light filtered through the openings between clouds and as I pulled into the Navajo Park Trading Post parking lot, the rain stopped. You actually have to drive into Utah on US 163 and take the diagonal road back into Arizona to get to the Monument Valley Tourist Center, which is the Trading Post. Now there were spots of light on the ground, surrounded by shadow. Now, it was a movie set for an ambush.

Monument Valley was the favorite setting for shooting Westerns by Director John Ford. The director's favorite western star was John Wayne and this is where they shot many of their movies. Familiar ground for those of us that have seen the black and white Westerns of the 30's and 40's. The grand Butte's still stand as silent witness to the gun fights captured on film. John Wayne made a lot of money fighting the Indians on these tribal lands but they are getting their share of it now. The Trading Post sells the likeness of John Wayne on posters, cups, saucers, shirts and what ever they can put his picture on. Naturally they sell garments, beads, arrow heads and blankets made by the Navajo's. But, if you want memorabilia of John Wayne, this is the place to be.

The valley is in the midst of several thousand miles of a Navajo Indian Reservation that overlaps Arizona, Utah, New Mexico and Colorado. The Navajo's are late comers to this arid land. Archaeologists have recorded more than 100 Anasazi Indian sites and ruins dating up to 1300 AD. It was the same climate then as now so it's a wonder they survived at all. The Anasazi planted crops and scattered them about to reduce crop failure. There are no streams in the area but there is some seepage from aquifers. The Anasazi hunted antelope and deer as witnessed by the drawings they left behind. Why they left is still a puzzle. It's not known exactly when the Navajo arrived but they did much the same with the crops and herded sheep.

There are guided tours that drive close to and around several of the Butte's and a good tour for those with a pocket sized 35mm camera. Rock climbing is not allowed nor is alcohol. I guess no one told John Wayne.

From here there are 2 ways to get to Four Corners. North on US 163 and turn right onto State 262 where I got lost because of the absence of road signs. I had to ask for directions. The other route is south on 163 (the way you came) and east on US 160 for about 80 miles. This is the only place in the USA where you can stand in four States at the same time. And it's on the same Navajo Reservation you have been driving on for hours. This land, like Monument Valley is not run by the National Park Service, it's Indian land. A Park Service Pass is no good. There is a $6 parking fee.

There is a concrete pad in the middle of the circular asphalt road with the four States names embossed in the concrete. In the center is a bronze medallion placed by the Department of the Interior with a cross hair to show the exact spot where the States meet. Step on the bronze and you're in all four States at the same time. There is an elevated viewing platform to take pictures of your friends standing in the middle. The circular drive has at least a dozen wood stands selling Ute, Hopi and Navajo wares.

Thirty five miles north of Four Corners is the town of Cortez, CO and a good place to stop before going east 16 miles on US 160 to Mesa Verde National Park. This site is known for the stone and brick homes left behind by the cliff dwellers. The Spruce Tree House Site is roughly 21 miles from the park entrance and should take 45 minutes on these curving mountain roads. No time to be in a hurry by squeezing this in at the end of the day.

The first Puebloans settled here in about 550 AD and lived inside the openings in the cliffs. Then they moved to the top and built houses above ground in 750 AD. Unlike Monument Valley, there were trees, water and abundant game. In 1190 AD they moved back into the cliffs and built the structures we see today. The Spruce Tree village was one of the largest and had 118 rooms in 8 structures. Approximately 125 people lived here. Crops where grown on the flat land above and they were known for their basket weaving and pottery skills. By 1300 AD the village was empty. They moved south to New Mexico and Arizona and we don't know why.

It's a two day trip from Flagstaff, AZ to Mesa Verde, CO. From movies about Cowboys and Indians made 60 years ago to the actual lives of Native Americans living 1000 years ago.

THE END

## SIDEBAR FOR MONUMENT VALLEY

WHEN TO GO - The National parks are crowded during the summer especially during July and August. Spring and autumn are the best times for crowd avoidance and the best weather.

PLANNING - There are nominal admissions for Monument valley and the Four Corners since they are both on Navajo Reservation land and not part of the National Park system. National Park admissions are $10 for a 7 day pass. A Golden Pass for seniors can be purchased at any National Park entrance for $10. It gives unlimited entrance to all National Parks forever. The trip from Flagstaff, AZ to Monument Valley, Four Corners and Cortez, CO can be made easily in one day. Mesa Verde should be done the following day.

PLACES TO STAY - Road side rest stops and gas stations have hotel/motel booklets with discount coupons. Flagstaff, AZ is 165 miles south of Monument Valley and there are dozens of hotels/motels. Most all the major chains are here since it is a stopping off point for visits to the Grand Canyon. Hilton Garden Inn, 1-800-333-0785, $90-150, Holiday Inn, 1-800-533-2754, $100-120, Comfort Inn, 1-800-228-5150, $60-120. Winter rates are cheapest, summer rates are double.

Close to Four Corners and Mesa Verde is Cortez, CO with Best Westerns, 1-800-547-3376, $75-130, Holiday Inn Express, 1-800-626-5652, $90-170, Days Inn, 1-800-AAA-Days, $70-100. Again, summer rates are the highest.

If you're on your way to New Orleans
stop by a plantation first

Statues - New Orleans café

The Nottoway Plantation house was custom built. John Randolph and his wife, Emily Jane Liddell Randolph commissioned a New Orleans architect to build the finest house on the Mississippi river. And indeed he did. The three story, 64-room mansion sat on a 7,000 acre plantation and was the largest house in Louisiana. John Randolph was a wealthy sugar cane planter and could afford it. The style is a mix of Greek and Italian and the 53,000 square foot mansion had all the modern conveniences of the time. Gas lamps, indoor plumbing and an intercom system in every room (using silver call bells).When it was finished in 1859, the couple had 10 children so they needed a lot of bedrooms. Unfortunately, their timing was bad. The Civil War was about to pay a visit.

It's easy to miss the small sign at the gate on State Highway 1. And the, "could use some sprucing up", driveway is a long one. There's a large house that sells tickets and souvenirs. You can probably book a room while you're here but it would have been easier to do it on line. That's right, the Nottoway is also a bed and breakfast. And that made me wonder since I just bought a ticket for the guided tour. Are they going to leave some rooms out because people are staying there?

Out the back door of the ticket house, down the path and there's the side of the house, one of the wings. It's impressive already. Follow the sign by turning right and you're on the front lawn. The house faces the Mississippi River. A stones throw from lawn down to the water. They say they've never been flooded (I asked during the tour).

Up the stairs to meet the front door greeters dressed for the 1860 ballroom dance. I joined the tour in progress. The house has been restored and furnished in period. Let's go back to the Civil War least one think the worst. The war tightened everyone's belt in the south. John Randolph took his slaves and went to Texas in 1862 to work on a cotton plantation and keep the family solvent. The Randolph's sent their teenage daughters away to a safer place. Emily stayed behind with the younger children, two visiting lady friends and a few slaves. One of the daughters kept a dairy which is the origin of the following.

In 1862 Union gun boats were sailing by the house and Union troops began to bivouac on the front lawn. Many of the houses on the river had been abandoned. Some were burned and others looted. Emily was determined to keep the troops out of her house so she went out to the front gallery, with a knife in her belt, and stood guard. As she stood there a group of Confederate soldiers opened fire on the Union troops. Naturally, the gun boats on the river returned fire. They weren't aiming at the house but the guns back then weren't all that accurate and rounds did hit the mansion. Emily quickly gathered everyone and ushered them to the ground floor basement where the walls were four feet thick. Fortunately the house suffered only minor damage. And later that year, she gave birth to child number 11, a girl. The Union army did camp on the lawn several times during the course of the war, but not inside, except to search for weapons.

Once inside the front door, you have to think of Gone With the Wind. On the ground floor is a beautiful, white ballroom. White floor, white walls, white ceiling, a fire place, a glass chandelier. A gorgeous room and it adjoins a white parlor with a brown piano.

Upstairs, the beds are custom made. I asked, why so short if John Randolph was over six feet tall. His feet would stick out the end. Turns out that they didn't sleep laying down. They believed that was unhealthy. They slept sitting up on pillows. The huge dining room table is set for twelve. Naturally, the room has a fireplace and a chandelier. The music room has pianos from 1830 and 1840, and a harp. The daughters were expected to play.

Then it was time to head south to New Orleans. Heaven knows, there's been a lot of print about the Big Easy. The French Quarter was largely untouched by the hurricane, it's on higher ground so the architectural charm remains. Bourbon street and the connecting streets still have the colorful two and three story buildings that give the district it's allure. Bourbon street is a collection of t-shirt shops with nasty sayings about Katrina, take out bars, a few hotels, more souvenir stores and more take out bars. You can walk the street here with drink in hand.

The St. Louis Cathedral is still gorgeous. There's a billboard on the side of a Canal Street building showing a bottle of Southern Comfort and the words, "nothing cancels Mardi Gras, NOTHING." One of the Bourbon Street restaurants has bronze statues in their front courtyard. "Fats" Domino, Al Hirt and Pete Fountain. New Orleans still has spirit - and jazz.

THE END

## SIDEBAR FOR NOTTOWAY

GETTING THERE - If you're driving in from Texas on I-10, get off just before the Mississippi River (on the other side of the river is Baton Rouge). Go south on L A 1 for 18 miles and Nottoway is on the left. From the Plantation to New Orleans, go south on L A 1, turn left on Highway 70 (goes north-east), right on a short stretch of Highway 22 to Exit 182 of I-10. Then east to N.O.

WHEN TO GO - The best is spring and fall - less people. Except during Mardi Gras when N. O. will be packed. Check for hurricanes first.

WHERE TO STAY - Nottoway is also a bed and breakfast. There are 17 rooms in the Mansion going for $210/D. 18 rooms in the Wings for $145 - 175/D. 34 rooms in the Overseer's cottage for $160/D and 3 Suites for $240-275/D. Reserve at www.nottoway.com New Orleans has far to many hotels to list. Visit www.neworleansinfo.com There is a visitor's center on the Interstate just inside the state line. They have brochures and hotel discount specials. I got a hotel in the middle of the French Quarter for $39/nite from info at the visitors center on I-10.

## POLO - HOLLYWOOD STYLE

Where do the Bold and Beautiful go at night? In Hollywood, people don't go to see but rather be seen at the polo matches. Many think that polo is only played outdoors on a large field. But you, being knowledgeable by reading this, will put the neophytes straight. Indoor polo is faster and a higher scoring game than it's outdoor counterpart. It's played on dirt the size of a football field (150 ft. X 300 ft.) rather than an outdoor, grass field, 10 times the size. That means, spectators here can follow the action. Indoor goal posts are 10 ft. X 12 ft. as opposed to 25 feet wide and up into the sky. Arena polo uses a larger ball made of yellow plastic which is easy to follow and it is played off the wall like in racket ball.

Indoor Professional Polo has three man teams instead of four. And six - five minute periods (chukkars) instead of six - seven minute periods. The outdoor game uses zone strategy because of the large playing field. Indoor, the players follow the ball or play man to man. In the arena, players must have quicker reflexes and stronger team work. And the yellow ball isn't the only thing to be bounced off the wall. The horses are different too. In outdoor polo, the horses are thoroughbreds. Meant for the long run. Indoor horses are a mix of thoroughbred and quarter horse. Cross breeding allows for the quick bursts of speed necessary to get to the ball. Fast.

The rich and famous file into the Los Angeles Equestrian Center about 7 PM. Celebrity polo starts at 7, although there is no guarantee that any of the celebrity team will be present during this workout. The members are Bill Devane, Alex Cord, Pamela Sue Martin, Doug Sheehan, Mickey Dolenz (the Monkees), and Jameson Parker.

The unfamous fill out a drawing ticket for a free Cadillac, or so it seems, and another ticket for a free trip to Hawaii. It turns out that the free Cadillac is actually a weeks use of a Cadillac, for free. Celebrities don't bother filling out the drawing tickets and make straight for the open air bar. They wouldn't dream of stepping down to a mere Cadillac and already have a condo on Maui. The actual match starts at 8 PM so there is an hour to drink and schmooze.

The really early arrivals have stopped at the Café Polo. An early dinner or drinks at the indoor bar or table hopping at the outdoor terrace facing the arena. There is an indoor buffet. Salad, rice, potatoes, broccoli, cauliflower and carrots before fish and roast beef (cut to your pleasure). Rolls and butter, of course. For desert there is, help yourself vanilla ice cream with several toppings and a variety of pies and cakes. Seconds or thirds on the food line and no supervision at the desert table. You can go from jockey size to Mr. Ed size in the space of an hour. The food is very good and the deserts, wonderful.

Polo has its roots in the tradition of the cavalry. It was necessary to develop riding skills and hand to eye coordination when charging into a field of battle with sword whistling at your side. That was naturally suited to the great outdoors. During the early 1900's, armories were built for the military and they proved easily adaptable to moving the sport indoors. A necessity for polo addicts who were unable to travel to West Palm Beach when the winter snows came.

Professional Arena Polo was started at the Los Angeles Equestrian Center in 1983 and that was the first time professional league teams were formed. The L.A. center is the only equestrian stadium where the fans can sit right on top of the action. Reportedly, the best seats are at the corners. Close to one goal and where much of the in fighting occurs. Reserved box seating is $50, reserved terrace tickets $25.00 and open terrace $17.50. We were in reserved terrace at about the fifty yard line and fifteen feet from an indoor bar. A natural collection point for those wishing to be seen.

The official program explains that every member of the United States Polo Association who officially participates in competition receives a handicap rating from minus one goal to plus ten goals. There are less than a dozen, ten goal players in the world. A player must have a five goal rating or better to play Pro Polo inside the equidome and less than 5% of the

USPA players meet this qualification. So, the play here, at 480 Riverside Drive, Burbank, CA 91506 tel (818)840- 9063, is the best in the country.

Tonight's match is between the LA Stars and the Miami Sharks. The Los Angeles team consists of Herman Louis DeCoite, a native of Maui and referred to as the "Hawaiian Hurricane", five goals handicap, "Smokin' Joe" Henderson, nine goals, a native of South Africa and may be the first player in America to be awarded a ten goal rating, Tom Goodspeed, team Captain, nine goals. A native of Wisconsin and husband of Juice Newton, the singing star.

Ceremonies begin with a selection of songs from the 18 piece Marine drum and bugle band. This precision team fills the air with music appropriate for the upcoming event. After all, what are horses without bugles. Then a young lady sings the National Anthem to a standing crowd. Each player is announced as he enters the arena. They gallop proudly back and forth hitting practice balls to warm up. Each player wears a rigid helmet and knee guards. Some have elbow guards. Referees wear baseball caps and the standard stripped shirts and they too are on horseback. It wouldn't be smart to be the victim of a stampede. The referees pick up the loose balls with a long stick that has a metal grabbers on the end and the game is about to begin. The teams line up in three pairs separating in a V and wait for the ball to be thrown into their midst. Denver Pyle has the honor of throwing out the first ball and the players scramble for possession. Movements are lightening quick and the action is much a blur. Bumping, pushing, flying mallets and a sudden rush to catch up with the flying ball. Meanwhile, back at the bar, the girls are schmoozing with the boys.

A goal is scored and then another. The partizan crowd cheers the L.A. team. A penalty is called and the fouled player gets a free shot at the goal posts. It's one on one as the ball is placed on the foul line. The player can shoot from a still position or get a running start for added speed.

The opposing player waits in front of the goal to block the shot. His mallet in front, between the horses legs hoping to deflect the speeding yellow bullet. The other players watch from both sides, behind the foul line.

The foul shooter is taking a standing shot. Swing. Bam. Another goal. The crowd cheers. The first of six chukkars is quickly over and the horses ride out of the arena for a short break. Field goal directions change after each chukkar so those sitting at the corners can watch their team shoot for goals for half the game. Like football at the end of each quarter. Meanwhile, back at the bar, the boys are schmoozing with the girls.

A tractor drives onto the field to smooth over any rough spots and erases all the foul line markings. The foul line marker comes on the field to lay new lines. The tractor drives over some of the new lines. The marker guy realizes that he shouldn't have extended the lines the entire width of the field and waits. The tractor obliterates some more lines to make it clear that he is driving the tractor and his tractor is bigger than the line making trolley.

Now that the field is smooth and the lines redrawn, the action resumes. Some of the fouls are obvious. Hitting an opposing team member on the head with your mallet causes a foul and a certain amount of ill will. Other fouls relate to the line of the ball. That is, the straight line the ball is following after it's hit. If riders are parallel, on either side of the moving ball, both players can go after it. However, if the ball is on a players right and the opposing team member on the left, he may not swing over the other players horse to get at the ball. That's an illegal hook. One player may not cut in front of another to get at the ball if he crosses the imaginary line the ball would have traveled, if it were left alone. That is an illegal bump. He may run up to, and run parallel, if he does not cross the line of the ball. If the horses are running parallel when they bump, it is not a foul. If a players horse hits another teams horse at too great an angle (determined by the referee), it's an illegal bump even if the offending player does not cross the line of the ball. The line of the ball is a straight line and if bounced off the wall, both straight lines.

Even though this is a gentlemen's game, it can get rough against the boards. Lots of bumping, shoving and mallets swinging. Fouls are almost always unintentional because approximately half the points scored in a game, are foul shots. In the heat of the battle it is easy to understand a player going after a ball that is rolling in front of him, only to realize that he is at 90 degrees to the balls natural line. Even if he gets there first, it's a crossing penalty. Clearly, these penalties exist for the safety of riders and horses. They are meant to prevent collisions. No one played chicken during this game and it's not apt to happen. Cars don't have eyes, horses do.

The L.A. Stars score another goal and the fans cheer. I'm cruising the crowd. Checking the metal name plates on the reserved seat boxes. Most are in company names and who knows who they gave the tickets to, for promotional purposes. Unlike some games, the people here LOOK at each other when passing. Some regulars recognize each other and embrace. Some show off their dates. Some scan the crowd.

10 PM and the game is over. L.A. wins 13 to 10. The crowd cheers again. Time to congregate around the entrance bar, have another drink and greet anyone you might have missed. After all, they could have been watching the game. Finally, to the Café Polo next to the exit. For some dancing. And a drink. And maybe just to schmooze.

THE END

Underground, Underwater, Underwhelmed and Overwhelmed
both sides of the Great Smoky Mountains

Graves at Graceland, TN

I suppose if you got an early start, you could visit all these places in a day, it's only 250 miles. I got to Chattanooga late, having spent the morning at the Jack Daniels distillery. There are no free samples at Jack's, in case you are wondering about me driving. Anyway, I made it to the ticket counter just as the guide at the elevator announced the last call for the tour. He saw me signal from the ticket counter and waited. The guy behind the counter was on the phone and apparently wasn't able to take my money, hand me a ticket and carry on a conversation at the same time. So we all waited for him to finish.

## Underground

Ruby Falls Caverns sits atop Lookout Mountain, a perfect place to put cannon to protect Chattanooga and the Tennessee River. It was an important Civil War battlefield and doesn't look like a likely place for caverns. But, they're there - 1,120 feet below ground. The caves have the customary stalactites and stalagmites, many at shoulder height in longitudinal crevices so it's easy to get a closeup look. There is a shallow pool and you can see the small, icicle shaped lime deposits growing towards each other. Pool reflections double the actual number and it's tough to tell which ones are real..

There's the Leaning Tower, millions of years older than it's namesake in Pisa. The big attraction is at the end of many long, narrow, winding corridors. The 145 foot waterfall. They switch on colored lights and you can walk behind it, through it and take a brief shower, if you have a mind to. I've been in a number of caverns and none had a waterfall as big as this.

Underwater

Ripley's Aquarium of the Smokies is in the middle of Gatlinburg, Tennessee. A land locked State and hundreds of miles from the nearest ocean. Go figure. 100,000 square feet, six galleries and thousands of fish. They have tropical fish and coral and a sting ray pool where you can touch the ray. They have jellyfish, sea dragons, a giant Pacific octopus with eight foot long tentacles and Japanese spider crabs with a leg spread of ten feet. They have the pretty fish and the nasty ones like the red billed piranha. They swim by and you can see the hundreds of tiny razor sharp teeth waiting for your finger. And the barracuda - they have in a shipwreck setting. Long, slender, steely eyed with a cold stare. Just looking for your arm. They have the ugly ones - the stonefish, and the deceivers. The ones that blend in so well you have to search the tank to find them. The camouflage grows from their skin.

The big feature is the submerged acrylic tunnel. Eleven foot sharks, four foot groupers and hundreds of fish from several feet long to under an inch are in a huge tank that's on your left, your right and overhead. The sharks glide within inches of an outstretched hand from one side, over your head and onto the other side. Close enough to look inside their mouths. And to top it off, there is an automatic walkway for 340 feet. You can stand still and it carries you the length of the tunnel. Naturally, you have to go back and do it again. Not that the walkway is fast, it isn't. But there is so much activity in the tank you couldn't see it in just one pass. I came here with low expectations and was I wrong. I was in Jacques Cousteau's aquarium in Monaco and few months ago, and frankly, this one is better. They boast that this is America's most visited aquarium and I can see why. It's world class.

## Underwhelmed

The Great Smoky Mountains national park is the most visited park in the Nation. I had high expectations here. There are trees, lots of trees. And hiking trails. And at the summit, the view is a sea of trees. All very pretty but not picturesque. And more miles of trees as I crossed from Tennessee to North Carolina. Along the way, there's a sign - The Most Photographed View in The Range. I pulled over - it was next to a souvenir store. It is a nice view. Six shades of green on the sides of a valley, a few farm houses and rolling hills in the background. I took the picture. The only one I took in the Great Smoky's. The most visited park? I wonder who does the counting.

## Overwhelmed

The Biltmore estate is in Asheville, North Carolina and if you want to see splendor, this is the place. The ticket isn't cheap at $40, but then, their hotel rooms aren't either. The estate is big - how big is it? It's so big, it has it's own Interstate highway. I-40 runs through the middle, overhead, of course. It's so big, it has two rivers running through it. The Swannanoa and the French Broad Rivers. It's so big, they have, in addition to the main mansion and adjacent gardens with 50,000 tulips, their own winery with a Bistro restaurant in the building. They are so big, the stables have a café. And there's the Deerpark Restaurant between the mansion and the winery. And a dining room at the Inn. What's Biltmore without a hotel. The Inn opened in 1913 and was proclaimed the finest resort in the world. Now, rooms are $120-180 double. Least I forget places to eat, there's a bake shop and ice cream parlor to the left of the mansion.

George Washington Vanderbilt II decided to build a country estate in 1887 and model it after a French Chateaux. He got Richard Morris Hunt for the house and Garden Conservatory and Frederick Law Olmsted, who did NYC's Central Park, to do the gardens. It took 1,000 men, 11 million bricks and who knows how many millions of dollars. The main mansion has 250 rooms, including 34 bedrooms, 43 bathrooms, a staff of 650, 10 telephones, elevators and refrigerators - remember, this was 1887. And I couldn't help but wonder - having a phone was fine but who could he call?

There are parking lots for each building - several for the mansion - and a bit of a walk. My first view of the mansion was from the far end of the 1,000 foot front lawn. It seemed that long anyway. I know what 10 of the staff has to do - cut grass. Walking the driveway gives ample time to view the front of the mansion and it's stunning. From the front, from the side, it's absolutely gorgeous. Inside to the right is the main dining room. It appeared that beams of light came in through the 70 foot high windows at a 45 degree angle to light the room, just enough. I could see, in my minds eye, a table with 64 people in colorful Medieval garb, drinking wine from silver chalices, pulling pieces from plates of roast duck and roast goose. I saw the remains of a roast pig, half full plates of mashed potatoes and green beans and heard the background noise of some people talking and others laughing. People smoking and the ceiling so high that no one complained. The dark wood of the walls, the huge table and it's the setting, the Hollywood lighting. I dare say, the most impressive dining room I have ever seen. The heartbreak is, no pictures inside the house. The estate has 1,600 prints and paintings, so it's easy to spend the day just for the art.

Attached to the mansion, to the right, are the stables. The courtyard tables were filled with people having ice cream and cake. It looked as they intended to spend the day. The walled garden is on the opposite side - to the left. A short drive or an easy walk and the tulips were in full bloom. Rows and rows of white, yellow and red.

Past the Bass Pond and the lagoon is the winery building. The Bistro here was doing a splendid business. The wine shop has a selection of Biltmore wines and accessories including gourmet cooking condiments.

Just outside the door there is a passageway, between the buildings with a clock tower at the far end. It felt as though I was back in Salzburg, Austria.

There are 8,000 acres here to walk and drive at will. Whether it's the art, the flowers, the wine, the ice cream, the half dozen restaurants or the pleasant drive around the grounds, take your time. Every one else is.

## THE END

## SIDEBAR FOR UNDER AND OVER - RUBY FALLS

GETTING THERE - Ruby Falls-Lookout Mountain Caverns is just outside Chattanooga, TN, close to the northern corner of Georgia and Alabama. Take exit 174 or 178 from Interstate 24 and follow the signs. Chattanooga is roughly 130 miles SE of Nashville, TN.

Ripley's Aquarium of the Smokies is in Gatlinburg, TN, the western gateway to the Great Smoky National Park. From Chattanooga, take I-75 north to Knoxville, I-40 east to exit 407, Route 66 south. It merges with US 441 south. A total of 155 miles. The aquarium is in the middle of town, off to the right (west) and there is a multi story parking building ½ a block farther. Street parking is difficult to find in town.

Its 87 miles from Gatlinburg to Ashville, NC. US 441 south goes right through the middle of the National Park. The choice is at the other side. Take US 19 east for the scenic drive or stay on US441 for 8 more miles and take US 74 to US 23 east - both routes merge before connecting to I-40 which goes to Ashville. Exit 50 north, look for the signs.

WHEN TO GO - The best is spring and fall - less people. Ruby Falls = $12 for adults, there is a combination ticket for the caverns, Rock City and the Incline RR - tel. 800-825-8366. The aquarium is $21 for adults, kids are less. 888-240-1358. The Biltmore is $40 for adults and it appears that people come to spend the day. 800-543-2961. No pictures allowed inside the main Biltmore Mansion. You need good weather for the mansion since the grounds are beautiful. For pictures, you need a flash or high speed film, maybe both.

From Stone Face to Stoned Wood
to Deadwood to Stone Dead if you're bitten

Mt. Rushmore, So. Dakota

RAPID CITY, SOUTH DAKOTA - I had no idea there was so much
to see and do in the Black Hills. I'd been here thirty years ago but didn't
take enough time. This time I did. First, a revisit to the Presidents on Mt.
Rushmore, just south of Rapid City. The idea of sculpting came from
South Dakota Historian Doane Robinson. But not of four Presidents and
it wasn't Mt. Rushmore. Let's back up a little.

Charles Rushmore, a New York lawyer came to Slaughterhouse rock in
1905 to inspect a clients tin mines. He asked what the mountain was called
and was told the name could be changed. So it was. Years later, he was so
embarrassed by reporters asking what he had done to deserve the honor, he
contributed $5,000 to the construction fund. Money sorely needed since
the initial financing was the nickels and dimes collected from the school

children of South Dakota. Historian Robinson's idea was to carve figures like Lewis and Clark, Buffalo Bill Cody and Chief Red Cloud.

Gutzom Borglum had other ideas and he was the sculptor. He picked Washington as father of the country, Jefferson because of his belief in the Declaration of Independence and the Louisiana Purchase, Lincoln for preserving the union and Teddy Roosevelt for linking the oceans with the Panama Canal. Southerners were violently against Lincoln but Roosevelt got the most ridicule. Borglum had been a leader in Roosevelt's Bull Moose Party and people claimed that Borglum and Roosevelt looked alike. But Borglum was the sculptor and could pick who he liked. Then came the financing and it was going nowhere. Until they got Calvin Coolidge to agree to vacation in the Black Hills. They renamed Hanging Squaw Creek to Grace Coolidge Creek and stocked it with trout and put in nets to make sure the fish couldn't swim away. Coolidge caught 10 trout in ten tries. Then the party. A barbeque with beef and buffalo, and moonshine, and music and dancing. The next morning an airplane dropped rose pedals over the Presidents residence and in a ceremony Coolidge watched Borglum lowered down the face of the mountain to drill four holes in the face of Washington. In 1929 Coolidge signed the Federal Assistance Bill and Borglum started his fourteen year task.

After Washington's face was done, they started Jefferson on Washington's right. Poorly placed dynamite ruined the rock so they moved to the left. That moved Roosevelt back towards the corner and a fault line moved it farther back. Those worry lines in Lincoln's face are veins of silver.

The total cost was almost one million dollars of which the Federal Government contributed 85%. Borglum intended to sculpt down to the waist but financing was always a problem. The work was done through the great depression and in 1941 we were facing a war. Borglum died after surgery in March, 1941 and the work was finalized in October, 1941. It is a stunning work of art and shouldn't be missed.

On the road between Mt. Rushmore and Rapid City are the Reptile Gardens where they claim to have the world's largest reptile collection.

After a visit, I don't doubt them. China is the only other country in the world to have alligators. Who knew? The Gardens have an Xanthic Prairie Rattler which is similar to an Albino, but rarer. And the top ten, most deadly snakes in the world, they have them all. Mambas, Puff Adder's, poisonous frogs, poisonous lizards, you name it. They have all the two step snakes. Once bitten, that's how many steps you get.

A short distance north of Rapid City is the Petrified Forest. After an informative video, you're free to walk the marked trail with a plastic coated, returnable, map. The site is high atop a cliff and stone logs sit amongst real trees. The rock logs are 120 million years old and used to sit on ground a lot lower. This was a sea bed, and as the land was forced upwards, a swamp and then a forest. The tallest stump is here 5'6" and there is a log pile claiming 931 pieces, all stacked. I didn't check the count.

Northwest is the town of Deadwood and the curving access road makes it a challenging drive. It must have been a rough trip in 1876. Gold and silver were found and the prospectors rushed in from all over the country. Rushed is a relative term considering the mountains and valleys. Naturally, gold and silver drew gamblers, hustlers and gunfighters. The famous ones include Wild Bill Hickok, Calamity Jane, Wyatt Earp and Doc Holiday. And this was where Wild Bill was shot in the back on August 2, 1876.

The town, with a permanent population of only 1603, has been renovated to look like it did in 1876 with the addition of modern gambling (slot machines). Saloons & hotels look like 1876 on the outside, even a Miss Kitty's restaurant (somebody must be rolling in her grave). OK, it's a tourist trap, but then, that's what we are. Right?

## THE END

## SIDEBAR FOR RUSHMORE

WHEN TO GO - The National parks are crowded during the summer especially during July and August. Spring and autumn are the best times for crowd avoidance and the best weather. Winter is not the time to visit South Dakota.

PLANNING - There are nominal fees for most attractions. Parking fee for Mt. Rushmore is $8. Admission fee for the Reptile Gardens is $11. Petrified Forest is $6. Deadwood is free if you don't gamble. Parking the car is $2-4 depending on how long you stay. The trip from Mt. Rushmore to Reptile Gardens to the Petrified Forest to Deadwood can be made in one day.

PLACES TO STAY - Road side rest stops and gas stations have hotel/ motel booklets with discount coupons. Rapid City thrives on tourists and there are hundreds of hotels/motels in the area. Most all the major chains are here. Fall/spring rates are best, summer rates are 50 % more.

## If it's Tuesday, it must be Tortola

SAN JUAN, PUERTO RICO - I can't say I'm all that thrilled with boats, I get seasick. But, I wanted to sample the islands of the Caribbean and this cruise seemed like an easy way to do it. An island a day. Island hopping by plane is a financial mugging. Seventy five to a hundred dollars for a ten minute flight to an island you can see from the shore of the one you're standing on. You could swim if it weren't for your suitcase. Anyway, the boat left Puerto Rico at 4 PM. Breakfast was served at our first stop.

### Saint Thomas, American Virgin Islands

The boat docked so far from town that we would need a cab, or walk for an hour in the hot sun. Fortunately, the Paradise Point Tramway was just up the street from the dock. $12 and you get a wonderful view of the capital and a free bird show. This turned out to be the high point of the island though I didn't know it then. A cab from the parking lot to town ($6) and I was looking forward to old memories. I spent my honeymoon in St. Thomas many years ago. But, things have changed. The local charm has been replaced by tourist shops. Well, the marriage was history so I shouldn't have expected much better. There were 12 trips offered by the boat, mostly snorkeling and diving and the same was offered on the other islands - there was plenty of time.

### Tortola, British Virgin Islands

The next morning there were seven tours to choose from. Three of us decided to get our own cab at half the tour price and set our own time table. To the west end of the island, north side - Long Bay Villas. Rates start at $90/nite and go to $855/nite depending on the season. After an hour of walking around $90 seemed excessive no matter what the season. Boring. Back to our cab and onto the south side of the west end - Pusser's Landing. This time we hit pay dirt. A terrific marina with a great bar, outdoor dining with a view and colorful shops. The conch fritters were just

OK at $7, crab cakes were good at $10 and Pussers painkiller quite nice at $5. Forget anyplace else, go to Pussers and spend the day.

## Dominica

Eleven trips to choose from on the most mountainous island in the Caribbean. Three in a cab for $100 and we could do two trips. On the way to Emerald Pool/falls we stopped to see the school bus pancaked by a tree fallen by high winds. On nice sunny days it's easy to forget that these islands are fodder for annual hurricanes. Any way, we pressed on. A bit of a walk to the pool but it's nice.

Trafalgar Falls is only 2 miles as the crow flies but not as the car drives. Like the spokes of a wheel, we had to go back to Roseau, the Capital, take two left turns and go back out. A $2 ticket and $2 for the guide we didn't need to see the twin falls. Emerald was better but on the way back we stopped at River Rock Café for lunch. Perched on a cliff and more food than a person should eat at one sitting, it made the trip to Trafalgar worthwhile. Try the Guaua shake.

## Martinique

The most populated island in the chain and the most civilized. It's French, draw your own conclusions. For $100 the three of us got an air conditioned Mercedes. First stop is the church on the mountain with a great view of the harbor below. Then north to the Rhum DepaZ Distillery a step back in time to the pirates of the Caribbean. Steam engines, water wheels (no longer used but interesting to see none the less). Naturally, free samples to induce you to buy. I had a shot and it tasted like kerosene. The distillery is within a stones throw of Mount Pelee an active volcano with smoke coming out of it now. It last erupted in 1902 with an explosion 40 times stronger than the nuclear blast over Hiroshima and laid waste to the nearby (then Capital of the island) town of Saint-Pierre killing all but 3 of the 30,000 inhabitants (one was in prison - in the dungeon and that's what saved him). By 1904, people began to resettle but the capital had moved to Fort-de-France, miles south. After the distillery we drove to Saint-Pierre. I had to take a picture of a stone ruins - a reminder of what was left after 1902. The volcano is due to erupt again, anytime. The cab dropped us off at the boat dock south of town for a quick ride across the bay to the marina at Pointe du Bout. Where the elite go to show off and home to the three classiest Hotels on the island - Le Meridian, Novotel Carayou and Bakoua. We had a late lunch at Le Meridian and spotted people from our boat laying about on the sand. A very pleasant place with a pretty view across the bay to the capital. Then, time to shop and naturally half the shops were closed for a long lunch even knowing that our boat only stops here once a week. Apparently the other half weren't French and wanted to sell their wares. I bought several shirts - reasonably priced. Onto the Carayou, walking in the blazing sun. Although not as flashy as the Meridian, we liked it better. It also has a great view across the bay. If you want to lounge around for the day, take the ferry to the Pointe. Eat, drink and shop till you drop.

## Barbados

A British colony - not that they didn't speak English on the other islands. The boat tour price for Harrison's Cave is $45. The three of us got a cab for $50. The cave is in the middle of the island and not easy to find. I saw rented cars take bad turns at ill marked intersections. So much for doing it yourself. First we sat through a video and then, en group, led to the tram. Lots of stalactites, stalagmites, subterranean streams and all the good stuff one expects in a cave. There are several stops so we could walk around underground but most of the viewing was done from the tram. For people with walking problems, this is a cave you can do.

Our cab dropped us off at a hotel for lunch and another cab brought us back. The hotel, beach, lunch and town were uneventful. I guess if you're from Liverpool the island would be a dream come true but, for Americans, I think Florida is a better bet.

## St. Kitts

Our last stop, a tiny island on the way back. The six tours looked boring so we went to town passing up on the large number of local display stands set up on the dock (first time they actually came to us). There is a town square (circle actually) and decent stores within one block of the square. After that it's run down shacks on route to the church and that's about it. Lunch at a second story restaurant overlooking the square is a pleasant way to kill time. Back to the boat and lots of time to look at the displays. As good, if not better selection as the stores in town. In essence, there is no real reason to go to town.

The following day we were back to San Juan where we could be herded like cattle off the boat, ever so slowly, to busses that drove us to the airport.

Summary

Granted, a few hours on each island is not enough time to get a real feel for the people or see all there is to see. Never-the-less, one does draw conclusions from what one did experience. I wanted to see which, if any, islands were worth spending a week without just laying around for seven days. I can lay around at home for free. The only one I feel is worth a re-visit is Martinique although I'm not willing to cross St. Thomas off the list since it's only a short ferry ride to St. John and St. Croix, the other two of the American Virgin Islands. I'm glad I did seven islands in seven days rather than commit to just one.

THE END

## SIDEBAR FOR TORTOLA

GETTING THERE - Carnival and other cruise lines run Carribean trips for a week, year round. My trip was $700 (per person/double occupancy) not including airfare. Boats run from San Juan, Puerto Rico and Miami, Florida. Miami is easier to get to and the airfare is cheaper ($400 verses $550 from the west coast). Carnival will arrange the air with one positive up side. If the plane is late Carnival will fly you to the next port so you can board. Otherwise, it's up to you. Boat prices are very dependant on season and what deck you book. The same trip at another time and another deck could run $2000. Check the travel section of your newspaper for specials.

TOURS - From four to a dozen depending on the island. Two people seems to be the breakeven point for tour vs. cab. You can try to bargain on the cab price but the drivers know the going rate and aren't very flexible.

MISCELLANEOUS - You don't need a passport but it's good to carry one just in case. Food on the islands is expensive because it's flown in. Food on the boat is good and plentiful. The ship supplies sea sick pills and you can buy wrist bands that do work (personal experience). If you want to compare several islands this is the only way to go unless you have money to burn.

# FLYING AN ULTRALIGHT

## Or Sixty seconds to Suicide

My friend and I were having a beer. "Lets teach a course." he said. "With our brains and organizational ability, we can't miss." Sounded good to me. He knew a little about Ultralights and had taken lessons on fixed wing aircraft. Unfortunately, I get airsick. Never the less, I was willing to give it a try. He would arrange the flying lessons and we would both be certified. Then, as Ultralight pilots, we would give courses at the local colleges, as experts. Make money, sell a book and write everything off on our taxes. The next day, I started to research the plane.

The Ultralight is an airplane that, by definition, is not an airplane. Since it's not an airplane, you don't have to licence it or be licensed to fly it. You can buy one for three to five thousand dollars, assemble it yourself, get in and fly it. Some people did just that and some of them died.

Of course, I'm not that dumb - I'm getting lessons.

You do need a license to teach someone to fly an Ultralight. Most of the Ultra's are single seaters but the teaching ones are two seaters. Designwise, there are hundreds of types and shapes. Some are enclosed but most are open to the wind. They come in kit form but the dealer who sold the plane will find someone to help with the assembly.

Basically, we are talking about a aluminum tube frame, enough cloth to cover the wings, a seat and a light weight, two stroke engine. And lots of nuts and bolts. Collapsed, it will fit into the back of a station wagon. An hour or so to put it together, if you're handy. The engine looks as if it were taken from a lawn mower and it's just as noisy.

For a craft to qualify as an Ultralight, the entire plane (empty) cannot exceed 254 pounds nor be able to carry more than 5 gallons of fuel. That takes care of hijacking to Cuba. It cannot be capable of exceeding 63.25 MPH airspeed and the stall speed must be less than 27.6 MPH airspeed.

Airspeed means, that when taxing on the runway into a 20 MPH headwind, with the tires going 10 MPH - just as you take off, the plane has 10 MPH ground speed and 30 MPH airspeed. The aircraft only recognizes the speed of the wind blowing over it. Stall speed, is the place where, if you go slower, there is insufficient lift to keep the plane in the air. You can also stall by pointing the aircraft upwards at too great an angle. The currents passing over the top of the wing surface become turbulent and no longer provide lift. In either case, when an aircraft stalls, the plane goes into a dive. Different airplanes will have different stall speeds because of different designs.

Even though Ultralight ownership is ungoverned, there are rules. The FAA passed regulation Part 103 on Sept. 2, 1982 that says, in part, that the Ultralight cannot be operated.

- in a manner that creates a hazard to other persons or property.
- no objects can be dropped that create a hazard to any other person or property.
- can only be operated between sunrise and sunset
- must have an anti collision light visible for 3 miles
- must be operated in uncontrolled airspace
- must yield the right of way to all aircraft. (remember, the Ultra is not considered an aircraft)
- must yield the right of way to all unpowered Ultralights
- must not be flown over any congested area.

My friend found a pilot with a shop at a small airfield in Lake Elsinore, CA. A licensed instructor of fixed wing and Ultras. Good looking, blond, thirty years old, physically fit. The kind of guy you would expect in a WW I movie with a scarf trailing in the wind. The kind of pilot you would send after the Red Baron.

My friend went up first. After all, it was his idea and if they didn't come back, I was off the hook. An hour later, they were back. We had explained to the pilot that we were interested in getting licensed and that meant lots of weekends with two paying customers. I had serious reservations about completing the entire course. I didn't share my concerns with the pilot for fear of getting an atypical ride.

He explained all the details about the plane and it was a simple matter to put on the crash helmet, jump into the left seat and buckle the safety belt. There is no parachute. We would be flying between 100 and 300 feet above the ground and there wouldn't be enough time for a chute to open if we did get into trouble. Our combined weight (the pilot and me) was more than the entire plane, so, if the engine quit, we would fall like an anvil. A characteristic of powered Ultralights is that they cannot glide. No coasting in for a safe landing on an empty country road. It's fly or die!

Off we went, into the wind for maximum lift with the lawn mower engine cranking away at full speed. The wheels lifted after 100 feet and we were doing 30 MPH airspeed. There is a small but effective tube with a floating ball inside that reads the airspeed (hollow end pointed forwards). The pilot held the control stick, placed midway between the two seats which points straight up and has a rubber hand grip for sure hold. Pull back for up and push forward and down for diving. To the right for right and to the left for left. Easy enough to remember. Gas is controlled by a foot petal much like a car. Keep the airspeed above 26 MPH to prevent a stall. You can push as hard as you like on the gas petal since the plane won't go faster than 35 MPH anyway. Piece of cake. We cruised away from the airfield and passed over a farmers house. He was in the yard with his dog and at 100 feet, he was easily recognizable. He was a person, not an ant on the ground as he would look from an airplane. I waved. He waved back. The dog barked.

Even with the helmet on, the noise from the engine was deafening and a conversation with the pilot was impossible. We could shout a few words back and forth but that was about all. Who cared, there was no need to talk, I was having a good time. The wind was buffing us about but the pilot always got us back on a straight and level course. I felt safe. We cruised over hills, past farm houses, across highways. I waved to the people in the fields, tracked the cars on the road, mentally gaging the right time to drop a water balloon if I had one. The first half hour went quickly and, even though I didn't like being thrown around by the constant wind bursts, I wasn't airsick. And then it hit the fan. "Alright," said the pilot, "it's your turn. Take her back." And he took his hand off the control stick.

We veered right and headed towards the ground and I was pulling the stick to the left when the pilot grabbed my hand, jerked the stick all the way to the left and jammed his foot on the gas petal (we each have a petal attached to a single control). "Keep the speed up," he shouted angrily, "or we'll go into a stall." The plane leveled and he pointed to the airspeed indicator. "Watch this, keep the speed up."

In no time, the plane nosed down to the left. This time I kept the speed up and pushed the control to the right. Nothing. More to the right. Again, nothing. I'm used to driving a car - rack and pinion steering. When you turned the wheel, the car turned - now. Not later. I'm figuring that if I push the stick too far to the right, the plane will turn 90 degrees or worse yet, flip completely over. Upside down lift is towards the ground. I'm turning a little at a time expecting something to happen and it's not. Suddenly, I feel the wind change. Instead of coming from the right, it's coming from the left and I reverse the right turn to a left turn just as the plane turns right and levels out. If this sounds confusing, imagine how I felt.

Then we hit an air pocket and the plane dropped five feet in a half second. The seat belt pulled at my waist. Thank God, it's working. Enough of this. I turned to the pilot and said, "You take over." But my right hand had a death grip on the stick and I would need the left to pry the fingers open. I was prying when, to my horror, he said, "NO", and kept his hands at his side. I didn't have time to argue because we were veering off to the right again. What a mistake I'd made telling him that I intended to get certified in this flying coffin. If I'd just said I'd wanted a ride, he would be glad to fly this thing. But, nooooooo. I wanted to get a license and he's determined to make me do the flying if it means the death of us both.

The pilot grabbed my hand, moving it to the left to correct for the latest wind change and stepped on the gas petal and pointed to the airspeed indicator again. I offered him the control again. He refused and I looked at my watch. I must have been flying for 25 minutes. The watch said one thirty seven. Thirty minutes out and only seven minutes into the return! Impossible! The watch is broken. This must be a dream. I'm flying with Freddy Kruger to the Elm Street Airport.

We suddenly went up ten feet, turned left only to then turn right and I hadn't moved the stick. A few seconds later we dropped ten feet. I was a few seconds behind every move. As soon as I got the plane straightened out, it went the other way. This didn't happen on the way out. I started to think back over my life. The sins in particular. I might have enough time to repent before the crash. Then, it looked like the airfield in the distance. I might make it. Five more agonizing minutes of being thrown about in the air with virtually no control over direction. Closer, we were getting closer. And I realized the spot I'd fixed on wasn't the airport at all. It was the feeling rowboat survivors get when they see the ocean freighter go by on the horizon. Never stopping. Not seeing them. The torture continued for what seemed like hours with each clear spot of grass looking like the airport. Finally, the pilot took control for the landing. It was smooth but who cared at this point. My right arm was numb and the fingers were curled into my palm. I had the death grip without the stick.

The pilot wanted us to sign a contract for future lessons. Fat chance. My friend was talking incessantly. He started talking after he landed and apparently hadn't stopped since. I had nothing to say other than we would get back to him. To myself - not in this lifetime.

On the road, I asked my friend about his flight. He moved the control stick too much, thus over compensating for each turn. The pilot was correcting his over turns as often as mine for lack of turning. Amazing, how fear causes opposite reactions and neither of us had any control over these reactions. I still remember the day I had two flights. My first and my last.

THE END

Take a widow from the west, an occultist from the east,
add some guilt, mix in lots of cash and you have

## THE WINCHESTER HOUSE

I heard about the house with stairways that went nowhere and doors that opened into space but I never knew where it was. Then one day I found myself in San Jose, California and on looking in a guide book, there it was. I couldn't resist.

Guided tours leave every half hour and tour is the only way to see the inside. Just as well, there are 160 rooms and it's such a maze the help used to carry maps to find their way around. The widow Winchester was young enough 44 to lead a full and productive life. Her only child passed away shortly after birth and with the passing of her husband, she was alone. Fortunately, she was well provided for as heir to the Winchester rifle fortune and received $1000 a day in royalties. That was a fortune back then; the going rate for servants was $1.50 a day. Then she had the occasion (as they would say in court) to run into an occultist from the east coast who told her that the lives of her husband and son were taken by spirits of those killed by the Winchester rifle, "The gun that won the west". She too would die unless she built a house for these spirits, work on which would never stop. So the Winchester house was built by teams of carpenters working 24 hours a day for almost 38 years. She lived in the house from 1884 to 1922. Work stopped the day after her death and according to her will, the furniture was sold or given to the staff and friends. Before the house opened as a tourist attraction, furnishings of the period were collected and the rooms appropriately decorated.

The tour starts at the side of the house and you get a feel for what's to come in the gathering alcove. A door on the right that opens to a wall. On the left, two doors, one normal sized and a child sized one right next to in. The Mrs. was well under 5 feet in height, this was her door. Around the corridor and through a doorway are a set of stairs. They go all the way to the underside of the ceiling. No trap door, no way out. They just stop at the ceiling.

Twenty four of the rooms are furnished. The sewing room with a wall of windows to provide ample natural light for the two foot petal operated machines. Mrs. Winchester's bedroom and the bed she died in at age 82 with antique furniture in prime condition. Then there are the low rider steps. She couldn't negotiate normal stairs so these were built. About two feet long and each step rises 1 inch so you have to walk an 18 foot corridor to go up 9 inches. Some low riders are in stairwells where you have to cross back and forth a dozen times to ascend to the next story.

Then the room with bare wood walls and matching wood ceiling and a single radiator for heat. Work stopped when she died. And the obsession with the number 13. A closet with 13 hooks to hang clothes. The beautiful Tiffany window (at $1500 the most expensive in the house) that would project a rainbow when the light shined through. But it was installed facing north and to make matters worse, a room was built behind it. Who was the blundering architect that did this? You guessed it, Mrs. Winchester and if any of the help questioned her about the plans, they were fired.

She had a staff of 40 including 10 full time carpenters and they were paid $3 a day, twice the going rate. If rooms were being added on without rhyme or reason, so be it. We visited several of the rooms damaged by the San Francisco earthquake of 1906. One had been her bedroom and she moved to another room and left it as it was. Must have been an omen. The laundry room with the clothes hand wringer, the pantry with rows of shelves to hold food for the large staff, the kitchen with wood burning ovens. Then there is the smallest pantry in the world. You open the door and it's one inch deep. Directly across is the largest. Open the door and it's a window to the next room.

The tour covers 110 of the 160 rooms. There are 2,000 doors, 13 bathrooms, 10,000 windows, 47 fireplaces, 40 staircases and secret passageways. Millions of dollars have been invested since 1973 by private investors to preserve this unique landmark. At the end of the guided tour you can take the garden walk on your own. It includes the 8 room farmhouse that functioned as the servants quarters, a coal- burning dehydrator that was used to dry the fruit grown on the estate, a water tower, plumbers shop, a pump house with a gas engine used to provide electricity, the garage that housed her cars, a greenhouse, the gas plant that manufactured gas before electricity was installed and the aviary where Mrs. Winchester kept several species of tropical birds.

The magnificent architecture is best appreciated from the gardens. And if you are into windows, WOW. This is your view. Inside, you can only see a few at a time. But outside! This is the best place to see the door that opens to nowhere. The second story sticks out from the first providing shade for those to walk under. On the second story just above the walk is the door to step out of. And fall to the walk below. Amazing what some people do with too much time on their hands.

## THE END

## WINCHESTER SIDEBAR

GETTING THERE - Winchester House is at 525 So. Winchester Blvd., San Jose, CA 95128-2588 tel. (408)247-2000. It's just north of I-280 before Stevens Creek Blvd. on the west side of the road next to movie complex.

WHEN TO GO - Opens at 9 AM every day except Christmas. Allow 2 hours for the house and gardens.

What do Monticello, Mount Vernon and Winterthur have in common?
Really old furniture.

I suppose if you got an early start, you could visit all three mansions in the same day. I didn't. Monticello is the farthest south, about the middle of Virginia. Mount Vernon is 115 miles north of that, just south of Washington DC. Winterthur is just north of Wilmington, Delaware about 110 miles north of the nation's Capitol. Even if you drove like lightening, there wouldn't be time to see the grounds and that's half the pleasure. And if you're into old furniture, there will be a lot of time spent indoors.

Jefferson was an architect among other things. He designed the 33 room house and lived in it from 1770 until his death in 1826. Aside from his time in the White House as President, of course. The first bricks were made in 1769 for the first design of 14 rooms. Additions and alterations were made over the years until it was complete in 1809. The finished house is about 11,000 square feet - including the cellars but not the pavilions and rooms under the terraces. This area of Virginia is noted for it's rolling hills and the house is on one giving it a wonderful view of the lush countryside.

The bus from the visitors center stops at the front yard and people collect for the guided tour. About 60% of the items on display are original. They include furniture, maps, books, scientific instruments and items from the Lewis and Clark expedition. There are thirteen skylights, eight fireplaces and five toilets. You don't see pictures of the "front" of the house because there are so many trees. The back is the classic view. Even Jefferson referred to two entrances, so, the back could be viewed as a "front" as well.

There is a gift store on the hill, next to the 1,000 foot long vegetable garden, one hundred feet from the house. It's a 5,000 acre plantation that's maintained by the Thomas Jefferson Foundation. The sad part is that Jefferson died more than $100,000 in debt and his daughter had to sell everything. Land, house, furnishings, slaves, animals and farm equipment. The man who bought it, went broke two years later. Uriah P. Levy, a naval officer then bought it and tried to bequeath it to the government without success. The Confederacy seized it during the Civil War. Uriah Levy's nephew finally got possession in 1879 and it was eventually sold to the Foundation in 1923. It's still a beautiful house and most of furnishings you see were Jefferson's.

Mount Vernon has a different setup. No busses, you just walk around the 200 acres. There is the main mansion and to the left, three museums and the upper garden. Then there are a half dozen small houses (on either side), a lower garden, a fruit garden, a wharf on the Potomac River, more gardens, George's family burial site and lots of walking trails. The first estate was granted to George's great grandfather, John Washington in 1674. Then it went to George's older half brother Lawrence. George got title when Lawrence's wife passed away in 1761. When he got the property, it had 2,000 acres and he expanded it to 8,000 over the years. He replaced the siding of the main house with pine blocks that were coated with paint and sand to give the appearance of stone. Today, the estate is owned by the Mount Vernon Ladies' Association, a not-for-profit organization and has been restored to appear as it did during the last year of Washington's life.

The house itself is not that impressive. It's a rectangular, two story with an attic, wood frame house with a back porch overlooking the Potomac. Having water close by makes it a step above Monticello. The grounds show that this was a working farm. Washington raised Ossabaw Island Hogs, Hog Island Sheep, Bronze Gobbler Turkeys, Dominique Chickens, Red Devon Cattle - all of these are rare breeds - horses, oxen and mules. The gardens are extensive. This was a working man's farm.

Winterthur isn't. Our tour guide considered buying furniture and overseeing the gardens as hard work. I don't. As far as I'm concerned, the man didn't work a day in his life. Henry Francis du Pont was born in 1880 to a family already rich. He decided to let the other family members run the business and he would spend his portion of the money on his estate (inherited family home). Winterthur is named after the town in Switzerland the du Pont's came from. Henry had a passion for early American life, or more so, the furnishings that came with that life. He proceeded to procure, legally of course, what ever he could find from America 1640 to 1860. Swap meets, attic sales, old furniture stores, other collectors, estate sales. He was very good at it. In fact too good. He and his family lived in a huge mansion, over 200 rooms. And he filled them with tables, chairs, beds, dinnerware, silver, needlework. textiles, paintings, prints, ceramics and glass ware. This house has a larger collection of George Washington's dinnerware than they have at Mt. Vernon. Not display dinnerware, these are plates that Washington and his family ate from. There are over 85,000 collection pieces on display. Like I said, he was too good. The mansion got full and Henry had to move the family to the 50 room guest house. What a trooper.

Considering that end tables of this period fetch $500,000, it would be impossible to put an accurate value on this collection. Possible a billion dollars. Anyone interested in old furniture of early America has to spend time here. I'm not a furniture guy, but, this collection is absolutely stunning. The next room as beautiful as the last. Guided tours are done in small groups and pictures are allowed inside.

There is a slow trolley that takes you through the gardens and afterwards, I felt it would have been better to walk. The entire estate is 979 acres so you won't see it all. There are 60 acres of flowers, the Enchanted Woods for children and lots of gardens close to the main house. With the flowers in bloom, the gardens are gorgeous. Henry du Pont did an outstanding job (alright, maybe some work).

The prettiest house - Monticello. The best working farm and the most comfortable place to live - Mount Vernon. The best old furniture - it's not even close. The best gardens -Winterthur again. A great place to visit, I'm not sure I'd want to live there.

THE END

## SIDEBAR FOR MONTICELLO, MT. VERNON & WINTERTHUR

GETTING THERE - Monticello is just south of Charlottesville, VA which is on I-64 that connects Richmond to the Blue Ridge Parkway in the west. There are signs on the Interstate- exit 121. The visitors center is first and on the right and you don't have to stop there. Next is the left turn that leads to the estate and buy your tickets there.

From I-64, exit 118, go north on US 29 to I-66. Right (east) to Washington DC. At exit 64, turn south on I-495 which circles the Capitol. Exit 177 south, the George Washington Memorial Parkway. The Parkway ends at the estate even though you can't see it. Take a sharp right (almost a U turn) for parking.

Get out of Washington DC headed north towards Baltimore on I-95 or US 295 - they eventually merge. I-95 north from Baltimore to Wilmington. Exit 7 (Penn Ave - Route 52) north - the street will change names. Follow the signs- it's on the right.

WHEN TO GO - The best is spring and fall - less people. Monticello = $12 for adults, a bus takes you to the house (up and back when you want to leave). A tour guide walks you through the house in groups. Outside you can spend as much time as you like. Mount Vernon = $12 for adults. You are on your own but there are informal groups that form (in line) for guided inside tours. No pictures allowed inside for either of these two. The grounds, you could spend hours. Winterthur = about $10 - there are combinations. Bus takes you from the center to the house (and back when you're done). Slow moving, open trolley tours the gardens. Garden walking is encouraged, and, weather permitting, a better choice. The house tour is structured. Tour guides take small groups through the upper floors and answer questions. Pictures are allowed inside the house. Recommended time for each of the mansions and grounds is 3 hours. If you pick a busy time, you could be in line for 3 hours.

# III ASIA

## The Pink City and The Amber Fort

JAIPUR, INDIA - Jaipur is called the Pink City because in 1876 the Maharaja Ram Singh had the entire, old city, painted pink, traditionally a color denoting hospitality, to welcome the Prince of Wales. It started a tradition maintained to this day. However, I won't lead you astray, the capital of Rajasthan with a population of 1.8 million, has little to see in just walking around town. As soon as you leave the front door of the hotel, you're met with squalor. Cows rambling along the street and leaving behind what cows leave. Poorly maintained streets and broken sidewalks. On the bad roads are camel carts, exhaust belching cars & motorcycles, some rickshaws, a number of bicycles and wary pedestrians trying to cross the street without being run over by any of the above. It's not a pretty sight, pink or not. I recommend you stay in the hotel and wait for your tour.

### THE TOUR

We boarded the bus at the Mansingh Towers in the center of town. I mention the Hotel because construction of the Amber Fort was begun in 1592 on the orders of the Maharaja Man Singh, but, our first stop was a drug store (chemist) up the street (1 block from the hotel) where antibiotics cost about the same as breath mints. Neither required a prescription.

The next stop was the Hawa Mahal, the Palace of Winds. The five story front, constructed in 1799, sports 500 windows overlooking the main street in the old city. It was originally built to enable the Royal Ladies to watch everyday life in the city. It's actually no more than a facade but a stunning one of honeycombed sandstone. Picture taking, for us tourists, is difficult since the street is active with traffic and a very wide angle lens is needed to capture the whole structure.

Eleven kilometers north of town is Amber, the ancient capital of the Jaipur State. People lived around the fort until they moved to the flat plains of Jaipur below. The fort sits high atop a mountain and we were in line for the elephant ride up. The ride goes for about $9 but was included in our tour and apparently included in others as well since there was a long line (half hour wait). Four people to an elephant and we got the oldest and slowest one. This elephant must have figured that the sooner he got to the top, the sooner he would be sent to the bottom to do it again. We were passed on the road up by 12 elephants that started after us. The first ones up passed us on their way back down.

From the main courtyard we started the tour. There's the Hall of Public Attendance with double rows of columns and latticed galleries overhead, the Hall of Victory with it's inlaid panels and mirrored ceiling, gardens, mosaics, sculptures, the Hall of Pleasure with an ivory-inlaid sandalwood door and a channel running through the room that carried water used to cool the room. Finely carved lattice windows and designed parapets that give a terrific view of the surrounding country. There is no doubt as to how well the Maharaja and his family lived. It's a magnificent palace.

We decided to forgo the elephants and chip in to take one of the many jeeps back down. Crammed in the back, eight per jeep and down we went, wide eyed, with screeching noises coming from the brakes, each of us wondering when we had been to church last.

A few miles down the road sits a vacant Palace in the middle of a lake. It appears that Maharaja's do that. Build one palace and move to another. We got off the bus and walked close enough for pictures but nobody wanted to get wet. This castle looked a whole lot bigger and nicer than where I live, but nobody's home here. What a waste.

Lunch was at the Rambagh Palace, once the home of the Maharaja of Jaipur but now an upscale Hotel. Great food, the best on the trip so far. At the front door, across the manicured lawn, framed by green trees, is the Amber Fort atop it's brown mountain. It's a postcard view and most people miss it. Oh yes, you can sit on the decorated camel in front of the hotel, for a fee.

Next stop, the astronomical observatory. The brainchild of the Maharaja Sawai Jai Singh who had it built in the 18th century. He was clever enough to send scholars abroad to study foreign observatories before construction began. At first glance it appears to be an odd collection of outdoor art. But they were used to calculate the positions of stars, altitudes and eclipses. Then there is the humongous 27 meter high sundial that almost blots out the sun. A good place to set your watch. There are small sculptures depicting each sign of the horoscope which are supposed to tell you something, I guess. I went to mine and learned nothing.

Maybe it's just me.


THE END

## SIDEBAR FOR THE AMBER FORT

GETTING THERE - There are a number of connecting flights to New Delhi from the west coast, usually through Bangkok, Hong Kong or Singapore. The low season (March to mid-May and September to November) has a discounted RT fare of $999 from the west coast with similar fares from the east coast (connecting through Europe). High season (June to August and December to January) fares are around $1500 RT.

The bus trip from New Delhi to Jaipur should run around 4 hours depending on the condition of the roads. The busses are first class, the roads aren't.

HOTELS - The Rambagh Palace was once the Maharaja of Jaipur's residence. Standard rooms are $185s/205d, superior $220s/240d, the Maharaja suite is $475, royal suite $675, tel. 381919, fax 381098. Raj Villas, also out of town, has 71 rooms, deluxe $260s/280d, luxury tents $300 and Villas with their own pool from $600-$1000. Tel. 640101, fax 640202, email =reservations@rajvilas.com. In the mid range is the Hotel Meghniwas, tel. 202034 for $44s/45d, with a/c, swimming pool and restaurant.

FOOD - Food poisoning is a danger throughout India. It would probably be safer to eat at the hotel.

HEALTH - Don't drink the water. That said, it is prudent to be up to date on Diphtheria, tetanus, polio, hepatitis A and typhoid. This is a third world country.

MISCELLANEOUS - Visas are required for USA citizens. For additional information contact the consulate at 3550 Wilshire Blvd., Suite 204, LA, CA 90010, tel. 213-380-8855, fax 380- 6111, OR, 1270 Avenue of the Americas, Suite 1808, NY, NY 10020, tel. 212-586-4901, fax. 582-3274, web site= www.tourindia.com

## ANGKOR WAT

Considered the most spectacular monument
ever conceived by the human mind.

Angkor Wat - rarely seen with the water reflection

ONCE UPON A TIME in a land far, far, away, there lived a great and powerful civilization. The people believed in Hindu and their capital centered on a temple mountain identified with Mt. Meru, the home of the gods. The first temple was built on the only natural hill in the area, Phnom Bakeng. It was 65 meters high and would give a commanding view of the countryside and the temples to come. The temple was built of stone during the rule of Yasovarman I, who reigned from 889 to 910 AD. This God-King lived in the temple and his sacred personality was viewed as the essence of the Kingdom. When he died, the temple became his mausoleum.

The kingdom covered the area from South Viet Nam northward to China and west to the Bay of Bengal, including much of Thailand and Burma. Of the 100 or so temples eventually built, Angkor Wat, with it's soaring towers is considered by some to be the most inspired monument ever conceived by man. It was built by Suryavarman II (reigned 1112-1152 AD) at virtually the foot of Phnom Bakheng. It's surrounded by a moat roughly 600 feet wide that forms a giant rectangle 1.5 km. by 1.3 km. Sole entrance is by stone causeway from the west to the enclosure wall that lines the moat. Beyond this wall is a paved 475 meter long avenue, 9.5 meters wide, lined with balustrades and flanked by the remains of a library on each side. The central temple from which the King held court has five towers topped with pointed cupolas. There are three interior levels and the towers add almost 100 feet to the total height of 170 feet.

Every day life is depicted in stone, alongside etchings of the conquering armies and the triumphant King. But the kingdom was not to be forever. Jayavarman VII's building campaign exhausted his kingdom financially and the Thai army to the west was growing stronger. In 1431, the Thai's, atop armored elephants, captured and sacked the kingdom. The Khmer fled and relocated the capital near Phnom Penh to the south. Angkor was abandoned to a few Buddhist monks who occupied and preserved the grounds until they died. The "lost city" and it's myriad of temples was then left to the vagaries of the jungle until a group of French archaeologists found the ruins and began a campaign of preservation in 1908. Their work, far from complete, has been interrupted by local and world wars.

## ANGKOR WAT

The work of the French is apparent when first crossing the moat. The left side of the causeway is untouched and the sandstone blocks are mis-aligned from centuries of settling. An etching of giant feet remains to represent foot prints of one of the original workers. Holes remain where wood pegs had been driven. Stone used in the temples construction, were quarried miles away and floated here on rafts. Ropes were tied to wood pegs driven into holes bored in the stone and the large blocks were moved with the help of 40,000 elephants. Wood roofs covered the buildings but, like the remains of the pegs left in place, have long since rotted away.

The inside of the moat wall is adorned with priceless statues and etchings. The walls are literally lined with carvings of life 45 generations ago, preserved in time on large stone tablets. The statues have fallen to a lesser fate. They have been the victim of thieves who decapitate the artwork and sell the heads on the black market. Remaining untouched is a ten foot high statue of Vishnu made from a single block of sandstone. The items held in its eight arms include a mace, a spear, a disc and a conch shell. Locks of hair are about as an offering by men and women about to get married and from those giving thanks for their good fortune.

Then you walk through the middle gateway of the wall and get first glimpse the central temple in all its glory. Fourteen hundred feet of stone path, 10 feet above the ground to either side, leads to a stone castle in the distance. It looks like a movie set rather than real life. It's the Land of Oz.

## ANGKOR THOM

Angkor Wat is the first temple you will see if you are on a tour. It's the closest to town (Siem Reap) and may be sufficient reason to make this long trip but there is much more to see. You will pass Wat again on the way to Angkor Thom which was built by Jayavarman VII (remember, the King that broke the Empire). Thom was a fortified city of 10 square kilometers meant to protect against the intruders from the west who were already coming closer. The walls were 25 feet high and circled by a 300 foot wide moat filled with crocodiles. In front of each of the five gates were giant statues of 54 Gods on the left of the bridge and 54 demons on the right. Alas, as history shows, neither the Gods nor the demons prevailed.

The most outstanding building, the Bayon, is in the exact center. A three story structure with 49 towers and 172 giant smiling faces of Avalokitesvara carved of stone. It is the face on book covers used to represent the area known as Angkor Wat and often, Cambodia itself. If not as awesome as Angkor Wat, it is to some, more interesting. There are 11,000 figures carved in the stone walls at ground level. People fishing, cooking, eating, building homes, giving birth. An extraordinary history book of pictures from the very people who lived the book.

Oh yes, the third story and the giant faces. The stone eyes do not follow you as you walk (as they do in some paintings) but dozens of eyes are always staring no matter where you are. It's eerie.

## MINEFIELD BAR

Just north of the town of Siem Reap, halfway to the entrance gate of Angkor Wat, on the right side of the road is the Minefield Bar. Or what's left of it after the fire. Graham, the owner, now sells hand painted t-shirts and towels depicting the local war and Cambodian history (the temples). Local t-shirts are made of polyester but his are all cotton with fabric imported from Thailand. The paint is from Germany. The art, and it could be framed as such, hangs in front of the bar to bake in the sun and set the colors. Color t-shirts are $15 and black and white is $10. Graham was an Aussie Army medic during the Viet Nam War and served in Laos. He ended up opening a bar here about the time United Nations troops took charge of Cambodia to ensure fair elections. The American Army officers, many of whom were actually CIA, liked to hang around with the Russians (KGB) and the British liked to drink with the Chinese. He has a scrap book to put faces on the colorful cast of characters that frequented the bar.

One episode involved a French officer who made a proposal to an attractive local girl. She turned him down and he became abusive. What he didn't know was that she was going with an American Colonel (CIA) who was close by. The American crossed the bar and calmly told the Frenchman that he could leave the bar of his own free will standing up or he could leave feet first.

The Frenchman left for the parking lot in front and, with several countrymen, proceeded to take automatic rifles from their truck and load them. Graham was watching the French and turned to get an RPG (shoulder held rocket) from behind the bar just as the local police pulled up to diffuse the situation. The rocket would have taken out the truck and anyone around it.

Graham has a collection of boobie traps. Claymores, shape charges, land mines for foot paths and hand grenades on a stick (one end of a string is tied to the pin and the other to a branch on the other side of the path). They were left in the jungle by the Khmer Rouge and are of American, Russian and Chinese origin. He's defused them so they would be safe and he's more than willing to show them. Unfortunately, there are no plans to reopen the bar. The UN troops are gone, tourism is down and the locals would never supply enough trade.

The bar is now gone, a piece of history and Graham is, who knows where.

## THE JUNGLE TEMPLE

Another must see is Ta Prohm. The French decided that one temple should be left as is, without restoration, and this is it.

## THE END

# SIDEBAR FOR ANGKOR WAT

GETTING THERE - The best way to get to Siem Reap is by air from Bangkok, Thailand to the west on Thai or Cambodia Air for approximately $250 RT. Service is also available from Saigon (Ho Chi Minh City) on Viet Nam Airlines, Aeroflot from Russia (via India) and Singapore Airlines from Singapore. Round trip to Bangkok or Singapore from the west coast of the USA is roughly $1200.

There are a number of tour companies that offer packages to Cambodia and Viet Nam for those not interested in independent travel. Most of the time in Cambodia is devoted to visiting the temples of Angkor Wat.

LOCAL ARRANGEMENT - Tours can be made at any number of travel agencies in Phnom Penh. They can be tailored to your needs (two, three or four nights and quality of hotel). Tours are all inclusive - round trip flight, drive to and from the airport, hotel, meals, daily entrance fees and guided tours. A tour is much easier than trying to visit the temples on your own. There are a string of 4 star hotels in Siem Reap.

ACCOMMODATIONS IN PHNOM PENH - The best in town is the Cambodiana Hotel on the Mekong River for $300 double. Certainly a 4 star hotel. The Diamond Hotel is deluxe as is the Allson only a block away. Both are in downtown and rates are $120 single, $160 double.

FOOD - First, don't drink the water. Eat at your hotel.

HEALTH - There are no vaccinations required for entry into Cambodia. However, it would be prudent to update your normal vaccinations including measles and polio and consider gamma globulin for infectious hepatitis. Even though Malarial mosquitos are more prevalent in the north, along the Thai border, it would be a good idea to protect yourself with Larium (once a week) or doxycycline (taken daily). Spray exposed skin with repellant containing DEET (at least 20%). Take Imodium and Pepto-Bismol for gastro intestinal problems. It is best to be in good health before entering Cambodia since the medical facilities will not match those Westerners are used to. Remember this is the third world.

MISCELLANEOUS - Visas are required and can be purchased at the newly renovated airport for $20 and a passport size picture. Money can be changed at the airport but it's not necessary to get Cambodian money since prices through out the country are also quoted in US dollars. Credit cards are widely accepted.

## WHITE WATER RAFTING IN BALI

The scenery is beautiful but it could be the death of you.

BALI, INDONESIA - I'd been to Bali 10 years ago and didn't see any white water rafting then. Maybe there wasn't any, but this time I saw the notice on the wall of a shop across the street from my hotel. I was actually on my way to look for another place to stay but the small notice on the wall of the shop caught my eye. I paused long enough for the owner/salesman to give a pitch and show me pictures from a three ring binder. I told him I was interested but first I had to find another place to stay. I took the first place I found after a long flight and, though inexpensive, it was a dump. Lo and behold he had a solution for that too. A really nice place for the same price I was paying and run by a friend of his. Next thing I know, I'm in a cab on my way north from downtown Kuta Beach with Kristan to meet his friend Tony, the owner of the Pelasa.

As it turns out, the place is gorgeous, the price the same as I was paying and downtown Kuta has expanded north to Legian so I'm not in the middle of nowhere. The three of us sat by the pool to shoot the bull and consume several large bottles of Bintang beer. Naturally, I signed up for the white water rafting. Oh yes, I moved in the next day.

### INTO THE MOUNTAINS

Pick up was at 8 AM and we stopped for four more people, then into the mountains. Halfway up we stopped for a picture break, a stunning view of the rolling terrain. Bali has active volcanos so there are hills and valleys galore. Back in the van to continue to the mountain top, well almost the top, 10,300 feet.

With helmets, paddles and life vests we walked down to the narrow but fast moving stream. Paddle boats, I dread paddle boats because it usually means beginners abound and you're in more danger of getting hit in the head from some one else's paddle than being thrown out of the boat. I've been on some of the most challenging rivers in the world, Class 5, and the danger there was the rapids, the undertows and capsizing at the wrong time (as if there was a good time). On the tough rivers, oar boats are the safest. That means the guide maneuvers from the middle of the boat with long oars and the passengers only pitch in when he needs help with a difficult current. Now, I had to worry about getting hit along the side the head by a paddle.

The self bailing boats went down a chute, we walked down a slippery slope. The water is fast moving but only ankle deep. No fear of drowning here unless you're face down. We were off and the scenery is just magnificent. The calm ripple of the shallow water, the chirp of birds in the air, one eye on the paddle of my partner in the front of the boat. And I almost missed the water pipe going across the river three feet above the water line. Fortunately my other eye was on the river and we all ducked into the bottom of the boat before being decapitated. This was the first but not the last of the, attention getting, pipe and log crossings that seemed to come out of nowhere. They tend to blend in with the scenery. But so will your head if you miss one.

I started to notice we were hitting the wall at every turn. Our guide warned us, "Bump" but we seemed unable to miss the collisions. Hummm, I started to wonder. Then we took several rapids backwards. That signifies loss of control by the guide and usually puts the boat in danger of overturning. Not that the water was deep enough to drown, but, like all white water rivers, rocks are everywhere and the danger of concussion is always present.

We pulled the five boats to the side for no apparent reason and then I looked ahead as the others got out of their boats. The river disappeared 10 feet away. I wasn't paying attention, we were at the top of a 15 foot waterfall. We walked around as the boats were pushed over and there is a second waterfall, 10 feet high. Two pushes. That would have been bumpy ride.

Back on the river again. Fast moving water, birds in the air, beautiful scenery, calm easy-to-take Class II rapids and I quickly threw myself to the bottom of the boat as a steel water pipe passed 18 inches above the rubber side rails. That one would have got me in the stomach.

I know that people live in these jungles, high up as it is, but we hadn't see any one. Then we pulled over for a break, I thought. Actually, 100 meters off the river is a stunning 100 foot waterfall. I saw a house off in the distance, somebody lives here. And this beautiful waterfall is right in their backyard.

Back in the water, things were going well even though this Class II was becoming a Class IV because we took 25% of the rapids backwards. I though at first it was because our guide didn't know what he was doing but I noticed the other boats had difficulty facing downstream too. None of the guides knew what they were doing. And there wasn't a rock ledge we didn't go right into. We always got a warning by the guide but the boat was taking a beating. All the boats were the modern self bailing ones (I started white water rafting on the ones where a bucket came with the paddle. You rarely needed the paddle but constantly needed the bucket), but ours had seen better days. Our guide had to reinflate the boat several times. And then we hit a bottleneck.

The river narrowed and there was only room for one boat at a time, going straight on that is. But our boat got stuck sideways in this funnel and the boat behind us came right on. Their front came over our side and we were taking water fast. Another five seconds and we would be completely full. I jumped to the side and threw both feet into the front of the other boat, pushing it back. Our under water side popped up just in time and we wiggled our way through the narrows. The boat was 3/4 full of water and if there were rapids ahead we'd be dead. Fortunately, it was a calm stretch.

A few miles later is a planned narrows, not that we didn't get bunched up anyway. This time, the narrows is just beneath a waterfall. No escaping a drenching here. We had a short waterfight with the next boat afterwards. Why not, we were all soaking wet anyway.

We got out at the bridge (and damn) by walking up a very slippery slope. A very narrow wet ledge that begged for shoes with cleats. Or they could have dug an adequate walk into the side. It would be a shame to survive the danger of paddle to head, capsizing from going backwards through rapids and being clothes lined by a water pipe only to break a leg climbing out at the end.

Some rafts from another company were being pushed over the dam beneath the bridge. Our guide told us that on that stretch, another company led 20 boats into a rapids and they all capsized. I can only wonder how small the brains were of the people in the last 10 boats. The guide added that there was a bad accident on that section of the river a short while back. Four deaths.

We hiked up 200 concrete steps with no hand rail to a building for a very nice buffet lunch, coffee and tea included, drinks extra. Then, what seemed like the remaining 10,000 feet of more steps, to get to the paved road. But then, I was lucky, I didn't get hit in the back of the head by a paddle.

## THE END

## SIDEBAR FOR BALI WWR

GETTING THERE - I got to Bali on the Cathay Pacific air pass. The price is $1399 for round trip from Los Angeles or San Francisco or New York to Hong Kong. It includes 21 days free travel from HKG to 15 cities Cathay Pacific flies to in South East Asia. All flights originate in and return to HKG and repeats are not allowed. The itinerary must be agreed on beforehand and tickets will be issued for each segment. Premium cities in India, Australia and New Zealand can be added from $ 200-500. Segment changes can be made afterwards for an additional fee.

Call Cathay Pacific 1-800-228-4297 or fax at 1-800-617- 9470 for free brochures. Book through a travel agent. There is one daily flight from HKG to Bali at 10 AM.

ACCOMMODATIONS - In Bali the choices are as varied as New York or Los Angeles, from 5 star to no star. I found a gem almost by accident, the Pelasa Hotel, Batu Pageh St., Legian- Kuta, Bali, Indonesia, tel 0361-753423, fax 62-361-753424, e- mail= cptour@yours.com. Beautiful grounds, pool, A/C rooms, bar, food for $30/person, breakfast included. 1 ½ blocks inland from The Bounty restaurant (burned down).

LOCAL ARRANGEMENT - The rafting trip can be booked at most any hotel. Or from Kristian, who can arrange other tours as well, tel 0812-3902590. His prices are as good or better than those quoted by the hotel for the same trip. The Ayung river is reported to be the better of the 2 rafting trips available. Bring a change of clothes and a towel, sun screen, camera (they will put in a waterproof bag for use at rest stops), rubber sole shoes, strong legs for lots of steps.

MISCELLANEOUS - No visas are required for USA citizens.

## THE BRITISH AND DUTCH WENT TO
## WAR OVER THE SPICES ISLANDS.

## NOW BANDA IS A PLACE TO DIVE AND EAT NUTMEG JAM.

BANDA NEIRA, INDONESIA - Is a charming little island and the only one of the Bandas with an airport. There are 7 main islands and 3 smaller ones that comprise the group.

Flying in, you can't see the town (there is only one) because a giant 2000 foot volcano (Gunung Api) is in the flight path. The pilot cruises around this awesome mound of lava 100 feet above the waves to the back side of Neira. Be sure to sit on the right side of the plane. The volcano is an active one, by the way, and is due to erupt soon.

Hawkers at the airport, restrained by the fence, hold cardboard signs for various hotels. The plane flies back to Ambon as soon as the new passengers board, so this is the time to fill the empty rooms. Transport is free, it's only a ten minute ride to town.

The couple seated in front of me on the airplane tried for weeks to make reservations for a flight and only succeeded at the last minute. They were trying from Bali, Indonesia. I tried to get a ticket in the Jakarta airport. They said the flight was full and finally agreed to make reservations when I wouldn't leave the counter but refused to issue a ticket. I got a ticket in Ujung Pandang (UPG), the next stop after Jakarta. They said the flight was full and I was on standby. I got the same story in Ambon when I confirmed the flight the next day. The 22 seat airplane left Ambon for Banda with 7 empty seats.

An Italian couple, at our guest house, tried for months to get reservations from Ambon to Banda. I ran across a Dutch couple in UPG that spent 2 weeks in Ambon and never tried for Banda because of the stories they heard about full flights.

The 22 seat plane had 12 empty seats on my flight back to Ambon (I was listed as standby #27). So much for, "You can't get there from here".

I could feel it the first day. People were saying hello to me as I walked the streets. Not just one or two people, virtually everyone. Old men and little kids were smiling and saying hello to me. I felt like a celebrity. We heard a cruise ship was expected in the afternoon and the entire town collected at the wharf. It was 2 hours late and the people were still there. Lining the street, sitting on walls, peering through the wire fence and some paid for tickets (10 cents) to be on the pier. The cruise ship was actually a small diving boat from Ambon with about 15 people on board but, hey, it was an event.

There aren't many tourists on Banda as you've probably guessed and very few of them are American. Just as well for us, the persistent. We had passed on the two real hotels on the water for a guest house in the middle of town (two blocks away). The staff went out of their way to be helpful. The manager drove to the airport every day to confirm the flight back. He also checked on outgoing boats from the other establishments to see if we wanted to go along. Trip price is by the boat not by the person.

The food is typical of island fare. Fresh fish and fruit every day. Indonesian revenge is a problem in the third world but not a problem here. Over eating could be since the meals were of good size and quite tasty.

## WALKING THE ISLAND

North of town, past the Laguna Hotel is the outdoor aquarium (for want of a better word). Two pools walled in from the ocean with an opening in the stone wall between the pools. There are little fish, good sized sharks and large turtles. Someone must feed them. Or replace the small fish on a regular basis. Farther north is the local beach and a dive site. Good for a half days walk and swim.

The more picturesque walk is through the waterfront street past the outdoor fresh food market and the various tourist shops. There are only 2 north-south streets so it's tough to get lost. The shops have necklaces and bracelets from local black coral and jewelry of all kinds made from nutmeg seeds. And the island specialty, jars of nutmeg jam. Nutmeg is what got most of the islanders killed years ago.

The Portuguese landed in the Bandas in 1512 and had the islands to themselves until the 1599. Then the Dutch arrived with orders to find source of the spices and cut the Portuguese out. And with a bigger fleet, that's exactly what they did. Not to be undone, the English set up a fort in 1601 on the island of Run (two islands west of the volcano). In 1619 the Dutch installed a new Governor General with grand plans. He got rid of the natives on Neira and imported slave laborers. In 1621 he attacked Besar, the largest island (just south on Neira) and virtually wiped out the native population. He then announced land grants for permanent settlers if they would produce spices for the Dutch. He would import food and slaves for the plantations and defend the islands. Those rules worked for almost 200 years. He ignored the British who stubbornly remained in the fort on Run.

Then the Napoleonic wars erupted and the English occupied all the Bandas. They replanted nutmeg seedlings on Sri Lanka, Sumatra and Penang. By 1860 they had no need of these islands and soon thereafter refrigeration was discovered. Meat no longer needed heavy doses of spice. The Bandas were obsolete, the fighting stopped. Until WWII.

## SOUTHERN WALK

Just south of the market and one block inland is an attractive Dutch church. It was built in 1852 to replace the stone one destroyed by an earthquake. The hands on the clock remain at 6:03 the moment of the Japanese invasion in 1942. Walk a block east and you are between the two forts. The most imposing is Benteng Belgica on the hilltop to the left. It was built by the Dutch in 1611 and was kept as a military headquarters until 1860. It's quite impressive.

The older is Fort Nassau to the right. It's not easy to find because the original stone walls date from 1529 and has been left to lapse into ruin since the mid 1800's. Three partial walls and a main gate are all that remain. There is a great view of Belgica from here.

Two school kids stopped to watch me snap a picture of the fort on the hill. When I pointed the camera at them, two others ran over to get in the shot. They're just friendly here. I continued to walk east and several men rushed to the windows of a stone building to wave and say hello. I returned their greeting and then saw the bars on the windows. It's the island jail.

Neira is a casual island so I kept east for a casual walk. Past a what could have been a plantation house with it's white columns and tile roof and around the corner, stone ruins reminiscent of early Rome right next to a collection of straw huts with a satellite dish in the midst. On to the southern shore and only 1000 feet away, the big island of Besar, the site of the massacre in 1621. But that was a long time ago. I walked back to town and smiled back at more strangers who said hello.

THE END

## BANDA SIDEBAR

GETTING THERE - From the west coast of the U.S., the most direct route is Hawaii - Bali - Ujung Pandang (UPG) - Ambon - Banda. You can only get to Banda from Ambon, $40 each way (flights on Monday, Wednesday, Friday). Daily service is available to Ambon from Biak on Irian Jaya (to the west), by Garuda Indonesian Airlines. However, I went from Singapore (to the east) which is serviced by Northwest, United, Garuda and Singapore Airlines (US $1300 RT from the USA west coast). Then to Jakarta and on to UPG (mandatory overnight). To Ambon in the morning (another mandatory overnight) and Banda the next morning. The return is much easier since all the flights connect and Banda to Singapore can be done in a single day.

Consolidator tickets from Los Angeles or New York to Singapore are available for around $700 RT. Consult the travel section adds in your newspaper. I bought an Indonesia air pass for $300 in the U.S. It's good for 3 segments and starts in Jakarta (gateway city). Additional segments are $100 each. My segments were JAK-UPG- AMB (#1). AMB-UPG (#2). UPG-JAK-BATAM (#3). The island of Batam is off the coast of Singapore. You don't have to finish in a gateway city. The air pass saved hundreds of dollars. Remember, this is Indonesia and flight schedules can change weekly.

WHEN TO GO - Indonesia has an Equatorial climate and is hot through out the year. The Moluccas (Maluku or Spice Islands) are the exception to normal Indonesian weather. There, the wet season is April through July. The best time to visit is September to March.

WHERE TO STAY - The best on Banda is the Hotel Maulana (tel. 0910-21022) for US$ 60 single/$75 double and $25 for 3 meals. Next door is the Laguna $20/35 and $17 for meals. The Delfika Guest House (tel. 0910-21027) is highly recommended with very basic rooms for $15/25 including meals. They will give you a box lunch if you go out for the day to fish or dive. There is little need to call ahead for reservations, you will be met at the airport by drivers holding signs of various lodgings.

WHAT TO DO - You can rent a bicycle for $3 a day but the island isn't that big and is easy to walk. There are 50 good dive sites around the outlying islands and there is an equipment shop across from the Hotel Maulana. Snorkeling gear can be rented from the hotels and you only have to ask around to find where a partially full boat of tourists are going. They charge by the boat, not the person. You can climb the 666 meter volcano in about 3 hours. A boat to and from and a guide should run about $10.

FOR MORE INFORMATION - Write to the Indonesian Tourist office, 3457 Wilshire Blvd., Suite 104, Los Angeles, CA 90010. tel. (213)387-2078. Write to the hotel by name, Banda Neira, Maluku Tengah 97593, Indonesia

# BORNEO FLOATING MARKET

## was there before the city, go figure

BANJARMASIN, KALIMANTAN, INDONESIA - The guide book said this was, far and away, the most interesting city in Kalimantan and the only one worth a few days. So, I had a week to kill before my flight to see the Komodo Dragons. Why not? Kalimantan is the southern two-thirds of the island of Borneo made famous for displays of shrunken heads outside warrior's huts, but, that's in the past. Head hunting is against the law now. Timber, mining and a trickle of tourists are the new interests.

They say timing is everything and mine wasn't very good. After finding several hotels completely full, I ended up with a suite at the Mentari. Standard and Deluxe rooms were taken. I had the feeling I was being taken but found out later that there was a convention of the largest of Borneo's lumber mills in town and they filled all the normal rooms.

Not knowing about the lumber people, I unpacked my bag and set out to scout the town for more reasonable quarters. And get tour information at the travel agent inside the Borneo Homestay. I looked at other hotels, nada. The unpaved, pot holed, narrow, ill lit street leading to the Homestay had "mug me" written all over it and twice I turned around ready to back track. But my search up to now had been fruitless and I needed something, even information, to make my walk through the city worth while. I stood in front of the unimpressive entrance and they came out to greet me.

I liked the prices on the city river and the floating market tours, left my first name, the name of my hotel, took their card and hit the road.

## THE WALKING TOUR OF THE CITY

The next morning, I was able to switch to a deluxe room and set out for a walk to the shopping district next to the river. For shopping purposes, the area has little to offer, but, shop owners and shoppers alike were asking me to take their picture. And no one put their hand out afterwards. Smiles were easy to come by and most posed as if it were a family portrait. I finally had to say no for fear of running out of film.

I figured the real shopping would be across the bridge, at the Mitra Plaza Shopping Centre. What I saw was a burned out shell of concrete. A few shops, with fresh paint, occupied the ground floor. There are good stores across the street. I was finding one surprise after the next.

On the map, Banjarmasin looks like a coastal city but it isn't. It's buffered from the Java Sea by miles of dense inhospitable wetlands and swamp. The Martapura river runs through town and is the connection to both sea going vessels on the nearby Barito river and the interior of southern Borneo. And the bridge over the Martapura, next to the Mitra, is a good place to watch produce coming in and going out. Commerce in action. Working boats and houses line the river on both sides. There are few paved roads in Borneo, the rivers are the highways.

## THE MUSEUM TOUR

When I got back to the hotel at noon I was greeted at the desk by a strange face, Mukani from Borneo Homestay. This country attracts few tourists during good times and this wasn't one of them. The Homestay caters to budget tourists (backpackers) and they only had one guest. My inquiry, yesterday, presented an opportunity not to be missed. I didn't ask how long he had waited at the desk for me to return from my morning walk. He offered a visit to a batik store and a tour to "the museum" for free. An obvious attempt to sign me up for other tours which I intended to take anyway. He is young, friendly, recently married, easy to talk to and admitted he would make a commission if I used his friend to change money. I admire honesty and off we went to the batik shop, a 20 minute bemo ride out of town towards the airport. The Citra Pasaraya has a good selection of merchandise (best I saw) and is worth a look even if you have no intention of buying. I had no intention and bought some shirts anyway. Then we squeezed back in another bemo (10 cents a ride) and went north for 1/2 an hour until the road stopped. From there it was an ironwood boardwalk next to the river. Wood houses with tin roofs in various states of repair line the banks of the river. And it was as though I was a celebrity. The kids all along the boardwalk waved, said hello, smiled, and yes, asked me to take their picture. Amid what an American could only consider squalid living conditions, there was a video game parlor building. Mukani told me of the current lumber convention and the local riots that torched the Mitra Plaza in 1997. Then we got to a fifty meter stretch of boardwalk that acted as a bridge over a side river. The lack of guard rail on either side wasn't as important as the fact that half the boards in the walk were missing or broken. This looked like an Indiana Jones movie without the hostile natives. The people here were overtly friendly, so I guessed they would pull me out of the river when the boardwalk collapsed under me.

We made it to the museum that no one visits because it's a half hour walk from where the road ends - without me getting wet. It has war swords, old guns, pictures from past wars and is interesting, sort of. The open welcome of the people that live here is the real treat.

## THE RIVER TOUR

We made it back to the Homestead to sign me up for today's river tour and tomorrow's floating market tour. Since the Homestead is located close to the river, that's where we got the boat. Banjarmasin has a population of 600,000 and most live on the dark brown river. We cruised the small streams off the side of the Martapura, south of town. The people bath in the river, brush their teeth in the river, take water for cooking from the river and build their outhouses over the river. I didn't put my hand over the side of the boat. The kids spotted us right off. They waved and cheered from their houses, from bridges, while swimming.

Banjarmasin is 95% Muslim, hence, there are 2,000 mosques, many of which line the river. And some of the houses look very upscale. There are a number of satellite dishes.

## THE FLOATING MARKET

The bad part is that you have to be up at 6 AM to get the boat to the big river, the Barito. We took the same boat as yesterday (I didn't ask if it was a relative) for the ½ hour ride upstream. The town of Banjarmasin rose to prominence in 1526 when one of the Kings won a war and moved the capital here. The floating market has been here longer but people aren't sure just how long. Boats come from as far away as four days upstream to sell their wares. Fruits, vegetables, produce of every size, shape and color imaginable are displayed in the various boats. We started at one end and drifted. Some bartered, some paid cash, everybody was here to deal. All you have to do is point, then come to a price. Then there was the restaurant ship with boats taking turns coming alongside. Hot coffee, tea, sweet rolls that you choose by spearing the bun with the nail on the end of a stick. The water is 25 meters deep here so the people are careful when walking from boat to boat. The market operates every day and it's an experience not to be missed. The fruit is good, just don't drink the water.

## THE END

## SIDEBAR FOR BANJARMASIN

GETTING THERE - I got to Banjarmasin from Bali on Bouraq Air, with a plane change in Surabaya, Java. Fifty minute flight, 3 1/2 hour wait and an hour flight for $100 each way. Flights to and from Bali are daily.

China Air had a special fare of $590 RT to Bali from California. Bali is serviced by Continental, Air France, JAL, KLM, Qantas, Singapore, Thai and others with coach fares of approximately $1000 RT.

ACCOMMODATIONS - In Bali the choices are as varied as New York or Los Angeles, from 5 star to no star. I found a gem almost by accident, the Pelasa Hotel, Batu Pageh St., Legian- Kuta, Bali, Indonesia, tel 0361-753423, fax 62-361-753424, e-mail= pelasa@indo.net.id Beautiful grounds, pool, A/C rooms, bar, for $20/person, breakfast included.

The best in Banjarmasin is the four star Hotel Arum Kalimantan (renamed with Arum added), JL.Lambung Mangkurat, Banjarmasin, 70111, Kalimantan, Indonesia, Tel. (062-0511)66818, Fax. (062-0511)67345, E-mail:arum@bjm.mega.net.id Rates are US$60/70 superior, US$260 junior suite. It's at the main intersection in town. Across the street is the second best, Hotel Mentari, tel (062-0511) 68944, fax. (062-0511)53350. Three stars starting at US$20 standard, US$40 suite. The Hotel Sabrina is a block east of the Arum with rooms for US$12.

LOCAL ARRANGEMENT - The best place in town to book tours is the Indo Kalimantan Tour, operated out of the Borneo Homestay. The prices are rock bottom and they are eager to accommodate because tourism is at an all time low. The address is JL. Simpang Hasanuddin 33 RT. 20 Banjarmasin 70111, Kalimantan, Indonesia. The Homestay is on a ratty road so you might want to call (062-0511)66545, Fax. (062-0511)57515, E-mail:Borneo@banjarmasin.wasantara.net.id Ask for Mukani, one of the most pleasant guides I've had the pleasure to meet.

MISCELLANEOUS - No visas are required for USA citizens.

## BALI'S BEMOS

The shortest distance between two points
isn't always a straight line

It seemed simple enough, Kuta Beach is on the west side of the Island and Sanur directly opposite at the eastern edge. Bali is not a large island and both towns are on the southern tip barely an inch apart on the map. Kuta is favored by vacationing Australians and is noted for its souvenir shops, restaurants, beer bars, singing, dancing, and general rowdyness. It also has gorgeous sunsets across white sands where the Bali Straights meet the Indian Ocean. Sanur has exclusive beaches, fine hotels (the jet set) and the American Express office on the Island. The dark overhead sky promised rain, so a guided tour looked unrewarding. It was a good day to visit the elite.

Bemos are a cross between a taxi and a public bus or public mini van. Taxis look like taxis - automobiles with a driver willing to take you anywhere on the island for a negotiable price. Bemos are usually vans but there is an occasional pickup truck. In Kuta, they line up on the north side of the street, one block east of the town square. Some have a scheduled route and others seem to have a route selected by a consensus of the passengers. There's no time table, they leave when there are enough people to make a profitable trip. If there is a final destination, it's not apparent to the casual traveler but the mention of a town name will evoke a yes or no. The guide book warned that there was no direct route between Kuta and Sanur. So what!

I went to the square and walked along the line of mini vans looking for a destination sign on any of the vehicles. I was approached by a dispatcher, or so it seemed, who asked where I wanted to go in perfectly good English (not all Balinese are English fluent). Knowing a connection had to be made (the guide book), I replied Denpasar. It's the Island Capital and roughly half way to Sanur. He said 500 rupiah and I turned to walk away. The price dropped to 300rp and I got into an empty van in the middle of the queue and waited. The van would comfortably hold eight and we pulled out after the ninth was shoe horned in. The ride was quiet, comfortable and afforded a wonderful view of the lush countryside. Twenty minutes later we stopped at a depot just short of Denpasar. Everyone erupted from the van into a slight drizzle. Lacking a plan, I walked towards the city center at a leisurely pace. Talk about gridlock, I was moving faster than the cars on the street. There are banks, department stores, printing shops but no t-shirt stores or native artifact shops that dot every corner in Kuta. It was a real city with major street congestion.

It started to rain and I started bemo hunting. The best price I could negotiate among the independent operators for Sanur was 5000rp and they had open sided pick up trucks. As if I wasn't wet enough. Quickly, I moved to share a space under a tree with ten local inhabitants when the rain turned into a torrent. Prospects looked dim. I was soaked and the rain continued to pour when, suddenly, a bemo van stopped in front of my tree (our tree, actually) and discharged a passenger from the front seat. I jumped at the chance. Holding the door open, I said, "Sanur?". He replied, "Kenesal", the name of a town I'd never heard of (it wasn't on the map I'd carefully memorized), but he said I could get to Sanur from there. It continued to pour. "How much?" 2000rp. I turned to leave (I was apparently soaked and in no position to bargain but this was only a ploy. I was getting in, regardless). He said, "How much?" I was caught off guard, expecting him to offer a lower price that I could counter with yet a lower one. I replied, "One thousand", he nodded and I leaped into the front. Principles are principles but wet was wet. I knew mine was the highest fare in the van but I was now out of the rain. He drove off and it continued to pour. I couldn't believe it, he'd turned the tables on me.

Twenty minutes later I was in a depot in the middle of nowhere. As the crow flies, the distance from Kuta to Sanur was no more than 10 miles and I'd traveled twice that and still wasn't there but at least the rain had stopped. The driver pointed me to another line of waiting bemos and I walked to the front one. A Sanur sign greeted me from the front of the bus and I was the first passenger. Amazingly, I'd received no strange looks from the Balinese even though I was the only foreigner in any of the vans and took much more room on the bench seats than they did. Tolerant people.

Now that I was alone in the Sanur van, there was time to think. The other passengers had paid the last driver when they got off. No one asked the price. They didn't negotiate. I was going to do the same with this driver.

This time they squeezed 12 people in. In the next half hour, the driver discharged and picked up several times in various small villages. We were down to eight when he stopped at the Bali Beach Hotel at the north end of Sanur. It had to be Sanur because I could finally see the beach.

The van turned around and drove back ½ mile to the main street and turned south, parallel to the beach. I waited for the semblance of a town but after a few miles figured that a collection of tourist stores was the best I could do. There wasn't any town center. Up to now, I'd paid no fare and sat silently watching. The last passenger gave the driver 300rp when he got off at the hotel. I stood to signal I wanted out and the van stopped in front of a variety store. Once outside, I offered the driver a 500rp note and stood waiting for change. He gave 200rp back. AH HA, I'd finally figured it out.

I went into the variety store and asked the location of the American Express office. The Bali Beach Hotel. Great. That was the last stop, a few miles back. I was on the street again, walking. A half mile on, a bemo driver was casually standing beside his vehicle on the other side of the road. I kept walking, waiting, and sure enough, he drove up and asked where I was going and quoted an outrageous price for the 3 mile trip. It started to rain again and I was obliged to bargain. 1000rp later and I was back to the front gate of the Bali Beach Hotel. He wasn't allowed to drive inside so I bid him adieu and walked past the gate guard as though I belonged. The rain had stopped. It took fifteen minutes to walk past the golf course on the right and manicured lawn to the left. The American Express office is in a small shopping plaza directly outside the hotel's front door. A first class inn, unlike anything I'd seen in Kuta Beach. Parachute sailing, 18 hole and miniature golf courses, a bowling alley, several stages for live entertainment, swimming pools, snorkeling, fishing, sail boats for hire and a heliport pad at the end of the fishing pier for those too busy to take a taxi. The white sand beach stretched north and south as far as the eye could see with no walls or fences. With all this openness, I had a feeling of isolation. Everything you could ask for was at the hotel but the inclement weather kept the guests off the beach and the golf courses. The Bali Beach hotel seemed to be an island on an island and therein, I felt confined. A beautiful prison with open doors and no where to go.

I bought travelers checks and it was time to return. I thought briefly of ordering a taxi from the front desk but dismissed the thought as quickly as it occurred. Ease and convenience wasn't the purpose of this trip. I walked out the front door to a line of vans and taxis. As expected, I was approached for a ride. Negotiations were tough this time. After all, I'd just walked out the front door of a 5 star hotel. I had decided to pick the airport as my destination because it would be a straight line trip on good roads that wouldn't weave through town after small town. He started with 20,000rp and I countered with 2,000. I thought we'd never get below the 15,000 mark (I walked away four times) until I gave in at 10,000. This ride was in a real taxi and the driver wasn't the fellow I'd bargained with. Another professional middleman. The driver was very friendly and in passable English told me about his family and his life on the Island. Suddenly, I spotted a Kuta sign on the express highway and asked the driver to turn. At this point, the distance to Kuta was the same as the airport and he complied. The roads changed from the smooth airport highway to narrow, bumpy asphalt. Lifestyles of the rich and famous would never be on this road but in no time, I was home.

From the airport, there are fixed price taxis to Kuta and Sanur. The airport would be located at the bottom of a large V. Kuta, at the top left of the V and Sanur the top right. I had cut across the top. The trip from Kuta to Sanur took me four hours. The return, a half an hour. I could have taken a taxi to the airport from Kuta and another taxi from the airport to Sanur for a total price of five dollars American. My excursion, paying more for the shortest rides and least amount for the longest rides came to a total of two dollars. But I saw the countryside and besides, if I took a taxi, there would have been no adventure.

## THE END

## TOURING BALI

GETTING THERE - Several major airlines Bali from America. Round trip coach fare is around $1300. Quantas flies from Australia and Singapore Airlines from Singapore. Tour packages are available from each airline.

ACCOMMODATIONS - Kuta now has 5 star hotels and is a modern city. I stayed in a modest thatch covered hut with twin beds and a bath. The grounds were beautiful - fallen flowers were collected daily. $50 a day. Sanur prices run from about $100 a day more than Kuta.

WEATHER - The rainy season on Bali is November to May but like all weather forecasts, the rain may start a little early or run a little late. Indonesia is on the Equator, it is hot year round.

FOR MORE INFORMATION - Indonesia Tourist Promotion Office, 3457 Wilshire Blvd., Suite 105, Los Angeles, CA 90010 tel (213) 387-2078.

## THE STREETS ARE PAVED WITH GOLD AND EVERYONE DRIVES A MERCEDES-BENZ. WHERE? BRUNEI, OF COURSE.

Brunei - President's Palace next to the river shacks

## BANDAR SERI BEGAWAN, NEGARA BRUNEI DARUSSALAM

- In short terms, BSB, the capital city of Brunei. As far as the streets of gold, that's what I envisioned for one of the richest and smallest countries on the planet. It's ruled by the Sultan, a benevolent despot and the richest or second richest man in the world depending on the current price of Bill Gates' Microsoft stock. The Sultans worth is around 37 billion or, given a modest investment return of 10% he would have a little over 71 million dollars a week to spend and not have to touch the principal.

The Sultan does share with his fellow citizens of which there aren't that many - 260,000. Free medical, free dental, no taxes, free schooling, free leisure centers, pensions for all, cheap loans, subsidies for cars and the best minimum wage in the area. All government workers get subsidized holidays and trips to Mecca (it's a very Muslim country).

Brunei dominated the island of Borneo, of which it's now only a small part, and much of the Philippines in the 15th and 16th centuries. That rule was broken by the British in the early 19th century and the country was eventually whittled down to 5765 square KM. They resisted becoming part of the Malaysian confederacy with the Malay state of Sarawak on all sides except for the South China Sea to the North, preferring to stay with the British. In 1929 oil was discovered offshore and the rest is history.

New oil fields have been discovered, so they are not about to run out of money and they are one of the world's largest exporters of liquefied natural gas. Cash is no problem which is fortunate since 80% of the countries food has to be imported. This is no surprise to the residents because most of the country is jungle, as is the rest of the island of Borneo.

I knew about the barrels of money flowing from the ground and a population that was well cared for before I set foot in the country. Not that I actually expected the streets to be paved with gold but I did expect to see the evidence of wealth oozing from the shops along the main streets and Rolex watches on every wrist. These expectations were soon dashed after I got off the bus at the terminal in the center of town. (see sidebar "You can't get there from here" to see why I was on a bus in the first place). I've been in seedy bus terminals before and this one fit right in. Small collections of poorly dressed people standing about either waiting for a bus or a job opportunity. It seemed to be the kind of place that a Timex watch would attract a thief's eyes. The Port Authority bus terminal in New York City has a much more upscale clientele.

The money changing stand on the second story of the terminal wouldn't take American Express Traveler's checks. "We only take money." he said looking at the travelers checks like Monopoly script I was trying to fool him with. The Standard and Charter bank, a block away, did take the travelers checks but after a sizeable 10% service charge. This country is expensive enough but getting burned on the exchange rate is like rubbing salt into a wound. Money in hand, we left the bank and it started to pour, so we caught a cab for the hotel eight blocks away.

## WALKING AROUND TOWN

Turning left from the Jubilee Hotel there is a tall modern office building and across the street a dilapidated wood shack that is reminiscent of pictures of the homes of share croppers living in dire straights in Mississippi. This was going to be a study in contrasts. A block closer to the waterfront is a beautiful Chinese Temple with colors inside so rich it almost burns your eyes.

A walk along the waterfront, Jalan McArthur, is uneventful, sightseeing wise, but we needed a boat ticket back (see sidebar one). At the end of McArthur is the edge of a huge shopping center complex but first, the Mosque. The Omar Ali Saifuddien Mosque stands high enough that it's gold center tower can be seen between buildings from various spots in town. Completed in 1958, it's named after the 28th Sultan and it's a sight to behold. White concrete walls with about a dozen tiny gold topped minarets circling a huge center gold topped dome. Real gold. The floors and walls inside are from the finest Italian marble, the stained glass windows hand made in England and the carpets flown in from Saudi Arabia. We're talking first class here. There are limited visiting hours for non-Muslims. If I though the view was stunning from the east, the main entrance, I had something to learn when I walked around to the south. A stone ceremonial boat sits next to the palace in a lagoon that circles this half of the property. This is the picture shown on postcards and in the guide book and it's difficult to walk away after only 10 minutes of picture taking. But there is something behind it that beckons.

The Explore Brunei guidebook, published by Brunei tourism, says that the Kampong Ayer or water village was described as the Venice of the East by the early European visitors. That may have been true in 1860 and it looks like that was the last time repairs were made to the wood houses and boardwalks. By reflex alone, it is depressing seeing these crudely patched, wood shacks with rusted corrugated iron roofs that look as if they would fall from atop their spindly wood stilts into the stagnant river heavy with garbage and excrement with the slightest breeze. The walkways between these houses would be condemned by the safety department in any U.S. city and the water, at low tide is no more than a cess pool. And standing at the very edge of the water village, you can turn around and see the gold topped palace.

The Sultan offered these people new homes and they refused, preferring to live on the river as they have for centuries. Just outside the village, on a badly paved road, are the Volvos and sports cars of the residents. Go figure. There are speed boats that cruise the river, easily seen from the bridge in the middle of the village. You only have to wave and one will stop to bargain for a trip up river to see the Sultans home palace. He doesn't live in town. Unfortunately, all you can see of the palace from the river is a tower and palm trees. And it's only a block back to the Yayasan shopping complex. So we walked back. These modern buildings contain stores with the same designer label merchandise sold at the finest stores in Paris, New York and Los Angeles. At designer label prices, of course. The buildings are connected underground by more upscale shops. Shop-a-holics could live inside with a credit card and a large bank balance. We looked for souvenirs and found nothing. As for t-shirts we found only "Brunei" and "I love Brunei". Forget it.

The down town area, east of the Yayasan, consists of mostly average looking shops not much different than the stores in any average downtown city. Neither fancy nor rundown. There is a Kentucky Fried Chicken and a Pizza Hut. We made it to the Brunei Hotel as the heavens opened with another monsoon.

There is no gift shop at the hotel - cigarettes, candy, toothpaste, souvenirs. None here. But ask at the desk and they have t-shirts. They do. Good ones.

There is no night life, so we walked the quiet streets after dinner. Quiet, because it oscillated between downpour and drizzle, but the Mosque is brightly lit with flood lights at night and it's prettier in the rain than in the sun.

The next morning was sunny and we retraced yesterdays path by the Legislative Assembly and the Ceremonial Hall on a stretch of land bigger than all of downtown. On the western side of this park is the Royal Regalia Museum that looks like the top of a large Tasty Freeze cone and contains the royal carriage, crown, costumes and pictures of the Sultan and his family. We grabbed a cab to visit the Sultan's palace 4 KM out of town.

It's closed to the public and all you can see is a tower and an armed guard at the gate. Undaunted, we went on to the Jame'Asr Hassanil Bolkiah Mosque, the largest in the country. Our timing wasn't right to enter the grounds but aside from being bigger, it's more impressive than the mosque in town.

A cab to the boat dock and wouldn't you know it, the same boat back for $2 more.


# THE END

## YOU CAN'T GET THERE FROM HERE

I was looking at the Malaysian airlines schedule to find the best flight from Miri to BSB and there were none. That's right, none. Malaysian airlines flies into every backwater town in Sarawak and Sabah but there were no flights to Brunei. Miri is the closest town, of any size, to the southern border of Brunei and it's the place the guide book said the oil riggers went for weekend fun. Wine, women, song and what have you, since Brunei is very Muslim. That means no booze in Brunei and it's even against the law to walk down the street holding hands. So forget wine and women and I wasn't sure if they frowned on singing as well. So if we are going to have any fun it's now, I figure, not in the near future. After a tour guide, cab driver and waitress gave puzzled looks to our questions, we concluded that if the riggers were having fun, they brought it with them. So now was out too.

I had ruled out taking the bus to Brunei since the connections didn't look promising. Changing busses at the border and unclear schedules made it look like a short ride could take the better part of a day. A flight would only take 20 minutes but there were none, at least to Brunei. Like it or not, we were left with a flight to Labuan Island, a free port just north of BSB with boat connections to Brunei's capital. Labuan is part of Sabah, a Malaysian province just north of Brunei. A 20 minute flight from Miri.

Leaving our luggage at the Labuan Hotel, at the waterfront, we promised to return and check in after a jaunt to Brunei. No problem. There are boat ticket offices along the coast street and it didn't dawn on me till later that each office only sold tickets for a specific boat company. You don't know the schedule of all the boat departures unless you visit all the ticket offices. They wouldn't sell a round trip ticket, we had to buy the return in Brunei. My first clue that the return ticket would cost more. $8 over and $10 back, as it turns out.

Fifty cents entrance fee for the terminal and we boarded a torpedo boat for the hours ride. The entrance door to the boat is a hatch that seals making the entire boat water tight. Long and trim, it rides on the surface like a German WWII torpedo honing in on a luxury liner.

On docking, we tight rope walked the 6 inch ledge on the outside of the boat, jumped and then climbed concrete steps lacking a hand rail to the outdoor customs queue. There are 3 booths - one for Brunei citizens, the other two for non-citizens - all clearly marked with overhead signs. And one customs guy, at the Brunei booth where four passengers lined up. The other 46 of us lined up at one of the empty booths and waited. Another customs fellow did finally appear but the message was clear about the disinterest in tourism. Fortunately, the Brunei only guy, got bored after his 4 passed through and he took some of us peasants.

The guide book showed the boat dock was about a block from the city and I was a little surprised when I walked around the terminal building and saw nothing but marshland. Not a tall building in sight but I had business to attend to. First, the money changer and then get a ticket back and this was the place to do it. All the service windows are outside since the terminal building is about the size of a three bedroom house. The money changer wouldn't take American Express travelers checks and didn't want American dollars either. He would take Malaysian Ringgits, which sort of figures since that's where we just came from, Malaysia. And took a hefty 20% commission in the bargain. The boat ticket office was open but the only person able to sell a ticket was at lunch. The job of the other guy was, I don't know what. Maybe tell people arriving that he couldn't sell tickets.

My companion now informed me that this port is not 1 block from the city but actually 27 KM north of town and the only way into town is the bus parked 100 feet away. I went back to the customs area and asked an agent if this was the only place to buy boat tickets and he said yes. No boat tickets in town. Back to the boat ticket window. The guy would finish lunch in ½ hour. My friend said the bus was leaving now and it was the last one of the day. One moment of quick thinking and we started to run as the bus pulled out. We made it, yelling helped. $1 each for a 35 minute ride to the bus terminal in the middle of town.

Later, we stopped in a travel agency in town to ask about boat tickets back and the Muslim girl behind the desk was extremely helpful. Not only with departure times but actually called a ticket guy for the boat. Now, we had to find that specific boat ticket office and it took 45 minutes because its hidden in an alley. Walking west along the waterfront, go past the main north-south street, Jalan Sultan, to the first alley, turn right and four shops in on the left hand side is a tiny office that sells boat tickets. I discovered later that Singapore dollars are interchangeable with Brunei dollars. You may even get Singapore dollars for change here. So, save enough Singapore dollars to spent and escape the 20% commission charge for changing money.

Not trusting the bus schedule we took a cab back to the boat terminal. It's a special cab, the ones around town aren't allowed to go out that far. I didn't ask why.

## BRUNEI SIDEBAR

GETTING THERE - From the west coast of the U.S., the most direct route is thru Manila or Hong Kong and continuing on Royal Brunei, Malaysian, Singapore, Thai or Philippines Airlines. However, I went from Singapore (to the east) which is serviced by Northwest, United, Garuda and Singapore Airlines (US $1300 RT from the USA west coast). Then from Johor Bahru airport just across the Singapore border, to Kuching, Sarawak ($60 US) to Miri, just up the coast ($55 US) and Labuan Island, Sabah ($20 US). From there it's an $ 8 boat trip to BSB and $10 to return.

WHEN TO GO - The heaviest rainfalls are from September to January. The country is next to the Equator so count on warm weather and high humidity, year round.

WHERE TO STAY - The best in the center of town is the Brunei Hotel, rooms US$ 150 single to $ 375 for a suite - 95 Jalan Pemancha, Bandar Seri Begawan 2085, Negara Brunei Darussalam tel. 673-02-242372-9, fax 673-02-226196. Several blocks in is the Jubilee Hotel ($120- $300), Jubilee Plaza, Jalan Kg Kianggeh, BSB. tel. 673-2-228070, fax 673-2-228080. A hefty walk from the waterfront is the Sheraton Utama Hotel ($280 US- $1000), Jalan Tasek, BSB. tel. 673-02-244272, fax 673-02-221579. There is a 10% service charge for all these hotels.

WHAT TO DO - If you like to shop, they've got everything Rodeo Drive in Beverly Hills has and then some. Most of the attractions are around the city center and easy to walk to. It's worth a few hours to walk around the Mosque and through the water village. Water taxis will take you upriver. The Brunei Museum and Malay Technological Museum are 7 KM out of town. The open air food market (fresh vegetables and seafood) is across the eastern river just across from the Chinese temple.

FOR MORE INFORMATION- Write to the Brunei Consulate at Watergate, Suite 300, 2600 Virginia Ave NW, Washington DC 20037. tel. (202)342-0159. Write to the hotel by name.

EVEREST

How to get to 25,000 feet on Mount Everest
without getting frostbite.

north of Kathmandu, Nepal

The HIMALAYAS, NEPAL - If you think this is an article about mountain climbing, you can stop reading here. The ice and snow covered trails and ravines have enough bodies to give me fair warning. There are those willing to endure three to six months of bone chilling wind, driving sleet and mountain sickness, and the very real chance of becoming another skeleton on the mountain, to say they climbed Mount Everest.

I got to 25,000 feet and that's good enough for me.

We were on a tour with a stop over in Singapore before a morning flight to Nepal's only international airport in Kathmandu. We were told to ask for window seats, right side, for the view. I was fortunate and got one and brought the right camera equipment. There is a wonderful view of the Himalayas in the distance during the last fifteen minutes of the flight.

What they didn't tell people is that the mountain range isn't close enough to get a respectable picture with a pocket camera and it's 35mm lens. I shot most of a roll at 200mm. Beautiful to see, even through plexiglass.

Our carry-on bags were X-rayed in the Kathmandu airport after arrival. That was a first. With bags in hand, we followed our guide, out the front door and down the middle of the road in front of the terminal amidst the smell of fertilizer and underarms and boarded our bus for the hours ride into the mountains. That is, once we got out of the constant traffic jam within the city limits. It's a winding single lane road that snakes it's way up, always up, leading to Club Himalaya Resort, Nagarkot. This 42 room hotel was built so every room has a view from it's own balcony. And a stunning view it is. Just to the left is a dark brown and green, terraced hill dotted with red brick and white stucco farm houses, a five story red pagoda and the snow capped jagged Annapurna range in the background. Picture taking starts here.

Then there are two viewing platforms outside the room but within the hotel (stories two and three) and a large patio at ground level just outside the hotel. There is a good view of the entrance road's ribbon of ascent from the level two platform and the surrounding rich multi-level fields. The sunset was hampered by an overhanging cloud but the white mountain tops had a pick hue as the sun went down.

The main dining room is a magnificent atrium with glass walls and a map showing the name of each peak in the distance. The wall murals here are nature itself. There is a cozy bar at the rear of the main level and swimming pool, Jacuzzi, sauna and saloon, just beneath the dining room. Supper buffet was chicken imperial, fish, fried cottage cheese tubes, spaghetti with meat sauce, rice and green beans. Soda is a buck. Considering we're in the middle of nowhere, the food is quite good. The hotel puts on a slide/information show with free drinks (the best part).

Don't anticipate good photography but the local concoction does pack a punch.

Sunrise is picture taking time again and we're up at 5:45 AM, like it or not with the sounds of horns, dogs and chickens drifting into the room.

But the mountain peaks aren't as colorful as the day before. We were spoiled. Mt. Everest is 70 miles northeast as the crow flies and a mere spot on the horizon from where we stand. And that was the closest I was to get to the King of Mountains with my feet on the ground. Breakfast is hot dogs, omelette, broccoli, shoe leather tough pancakes and coffee. There's no time to use the hotel pool and we're off for a day in Kathmandu.

Buddha Air flights leave on the half hour from the international airport starting at 6 AM, weather permitting. We were up at 5:45 to catch the 7 AM flight 100. Kathmandu is at 7,000 feet and the flight is under an hour. All seats have a window and assignments are by chance and made on the tarmac next to the plane. I lucked out with 8C, in the rear, right side. The best seats are 7,8,9 C. In the middle (4,5,6), you're over a wing. The stewardess (that's right, just like a real airline) gave each of us a map showing the mountain names and heights. The left side has the view on the way out.

As we got close to Everest, the passengers are invited into the cockpit, one at a time, to take pictures. My turn was when we were directly in front of the world's tallest mountain. With a long lens, I was close enough to see trees if there were any. All of this at 25,000 feet. The plane doesn't dare go higher because of the winds. Small planes don't fly directly over Everest because the severe downdraft on the back side would literally pull it into the mountain.

There is plenty of time to take pictures on the way in or out and it's common to trade seats across the aisle after the person has a few shots. So, there is no need to panic if you get a poor seat assignment. Make some friends before you board.

So, I've been to Everest, at 25,000 feet (5 nautical miles away - a mere technicality). No three months of hiking, no frostbite, no gasping for air and no $50,000 fee. I can still lie to strangers and say I climbed to the top. How would they know otherwise.

## THE END

## SIDEBAR FOR MT. EVEREST

GETTING THERE - There are a number of connecting flights to Kathmandu from the west coast, usually through Bangkok, Hong Kong or Singapore. We had a stop over in Singapore. Nepal is serviced with a discounted RT of $1059 from the west coast with similar fares from the east coast (connecting through Europe). The airline may arrange a nights lodging for you in the connecting city.

Buddha Air reservations tel.542494, e-mail: buddhaair@buddhaair. com, website: www.buddhaair.com They operate five, brand new, state of the art, Beech 1900D aircraft each worth US $5 million. Everest RT is US $125 with a guaranteed window seat.

HOTELS - The Nagarkot Resort/Club Himalaya rooms are only $75s/90d. Add $23/person for 2 meals, $38/person for 3 meals. They have a 1 night/2 day package with meals and hotel pickup in Kathmandu for $140s/200d. The hotel has 42 rooms, is an hours drive from Kathmandu and is 7,200 feet above sea level.

Write: Club Himalaya Nagarkot Resort, P.O. Box 2769, Kathmandu, Nepal. tel:977-1-413632, fax:977-1-417133, e-mail:clubhim@mos.com.np, website:www.nepal-hotel.com

FOOD - There is no other real option at Nagarkot. The hotel breakfast is $8, lunch/dinner $18.

HEALTH - Don't drink the water. Yellow fever immunization is only required if coming from infected parts of Africa or South America. That said, it is prudent to be up to date on Diphtheria, tetanus, polio, hepatitis A and typhoid. This is a third world country.

MISCELLANEOUS - Visas are required for USA citizens. For additional information contact the consulate at Suite 400, 909 Montgomery St, San Francisco, CA 94133 tel.(202)667-4550, e-mail:nepali@erols.com. Or 2131 Leroy Place NW, Washington DC 20008

Hanoi to Halong Bay

A slow bus on a fast road

Ho Chi Minh Grave

HANOI, Northern Viet Nam - It's been ten years. Doesn't seem that long ago, but it was. Back then, the airport terminal was wood and plaster, in need of a coat of paint and better maintenance. It could have been a copy of what you might expect at a small Mexican town in the 1930's. The van taking us from the airport to town was slowed down by ox carts on the 2 lane road. Passing was easy enough since there were few cars. Providing there wasn't an ox cart coming the other way, of course. There was one 5 star hotel in town, the Sofitel Metropole. Hanoi was the Capital but German and Japanese money was being invested in Saigon, not here. Things have changed. Well, some things.

Now the airport terminal is a modern building of steel, concrete and glass. The road to town is improved and there are more vehicles and few ox carts. The view is much the same, rice fields and old wood buildings. Now there are five, 5 star, hotels including a real Hilton (not located in the same place as the notorious Hanoi Hilton, the prison for the American POW's) and another Sofitel, the Plaza, located 3 miles north of the first one. The city roads are now congested with motor bikes. One million of them for a population of 3 million. The other 2 million are either on a bicycle or on a bus.

The city tour is much the same. That means little has changed it what to see, but, it's a must tour for first time visitors. Ngoc Son Temple (and pagoda) is on an island in Hoan Kiem lake. This sizable lake is in the middle of the city, 2 blocks east the Sofitel Metro and you can walk out onto the island. Then a drive to the Temple of Literature, dedicated to Confucius (Khong Tu) in 1070. Both sites are just beautiful and will eat up a lot of film. Just as well because next is Ho Chi Minh's mausoleum where you don't need a camera. It's a gray concrete bunker with some pillars on top and an armed guard in front. There is still a line drawn on the street over which you must not cross. Heaven only knows why since Ho's been dead for years. Anyway, he wasn't there at the time. Every year, from Sept. to Dec., his corpse is sent back to Moscow for maintenance. Change the embalming fluid or whatever. The twist is that Ho asked to be cremated after death and the powers to be decided otherwise when he couldn't object.

The house Ho lived in during the war is next. It's plain, simple and attractive. The grounds are very pleasant. Around the corner is the 1 pillar pagoda, 1050 AD. Delightful, particularly in mind of what comes next, Hoa Lo - the Hanoi Hilton prison. Ten years ago, pictures from the street were forbidden and armed guards patrolled the sidewalks. Now it's part of the city tour and there's a free brochure, with pictures, of the prison.

The prison was opened by the French in 1896. According to the brochure, "thousands of brave patriots endured savage treatment by the prison guards during the French Colonial period. Despite the torture, they made frequent ingenious attempts to escape from the clutches of their oppressors". There are black and white pictures on the wall and shackles in the cells to attest to the torture and atrocious conditions while the French were in charge. That was until October, 1954 when the French left. It was a State prison from then until 5 AUG 1964 when it was made a prison for American prisoners of war. That lasted until 31 MAR 1973. Absent from the walls are any torture pictures taken from 5 AUG 1964 to 31 MAR 1973. There is a posted letter stating that the American POW's were, "well treated with adequate food, clothing and shelter". Thirty years later and they still can't be truthful. Anyway, 2/3 of the old prison was demolished to make way for what is now an apartment and office complex called the Somerset Grand Hanoi.

We made an unscheduled (not part of the normal tour) stop at the studio of Anh Khanh. The studio is actually his house. It's 2.5 KM from the Long Bien Bridge and off the main road so it's not easy to find. Anh is a retired policeman and full time, sort of (that means when he feels like it) artist. The house is a 2 story, plank and log structure with the first story mostly open. His art adorns both floors and the large gardens on sides of the house. Several us commented that the art reminded them of Salvador Dali. Paintings are inside but many of the statues and, for lack of another word, structures, are outside in the garden. This is a side trip to ask for.

We walked through the old section of town. Where the local people shop. Except for the advent of electricity, we just stepped back 200 years. The Vietnamese love the outside. Their merchandise extends to the sidewalk as though it's part of the store. Families eat on the sidewalk. They socialize, play cards, sew dresses and ask customers to take a look - all on the sidewalk. If it rains, they have umbrellas.

That night we went to the famous Thang Long Water Puppet Theatre for the show. The stage is a large pool of murky water with a curtain in back. String band off to the left side. Two to three foot high wood and metal puppets come from cuts in the curtain and move around the water surface. Some may be on underwater tracks, others moved by long, hand held bars by behind the curtain. The puppets will have 1 or 2 movements, a swinging head or arm as they move back and forth across the water. It's a musical show, sung in Vietnamese. If you like music that is shrill and irritating, it could be the show for you.

The trip to Halong Bay is an all day affair. Each way is four hours because the powers to be decided the speed limit for busses is 35 MPH. Cars on this expressway can go 50 MPH. A highway and we're getting passed by motorbikes. Roughly halfway is the pit stop at an art center for crippled people. There is no social net for these poor souls and this center gives them a job. They hand embroider replicas of famous paintings, tigers, family portraits or any picture you give them to copy. It's the finest sewing I have ever seen. It's so good that from 15 feet away, it looks like a photograph.

Halong Harbor is on the Gulf of Tonkin in the South China Sea. It's a UNESCO World Heritage site with more than 3,000 islands. Ha Long means, "where the dragon descends into the sea". Legend has it that areas dug out by the dragon's tail filled with water leaving only the rocks. Fishing boats, pirate boats - they are all cruise boats now - take you for a 4 hour tour of the bay. Lunch is included and you can buy drinks at the bar. It's unique, it's beautiful and it's worth the 8 hours on a bus. For those who might want to spend more than one day in Halong, there are a half dozen modern hotels for $100/double.

Hanoi is in transition. Some in the 21$^{st}$ Century, some in the 19$^{th}$. The good thing is, you can see both.

## THE END

## SIDEBAR FOR HANOI TO HALONG

GETTING THERE - There are no direct flights from the USA. From the west coast, there is one stop service from Korean Air for $2015 RT, regular coach fare. There is also 1 stop service through Seoul on Asiana Air for a discounted fare of $1222. Thai Air has service through Bangkok for a discounted fare of $1147. You need a visa for Viet Nam. It can be obtained in Bangkok or the application form can be obtained in the USA and presented, at the Hanoi airport, with 2 passport sized pictures and $25 USA.

We took a 16 day tour with SmarTours - Hanoi- Hue - Hoi An - Danang- Saigon - Ankor Wat - Bangkok - Los Angeles, for $2600 each. They sent us the paperwork for the visas.

WHEN TO GO - Halong Bay is cold and drizzly from February to March. Northern Viet Nam is hot and dry March to September. After September it cools down and chances of rain increase.

HOTELS - The Sofitel Plaza Hanoi is just north of town but is the newer and nicer of the 2 Sofitel Hotels, both are 5 star. The Plaza rates are - US $ 192.50 s/ $212.50 double. email: sofitel@sofitelplazahn.com.vn tel (84.4) 823 888. Rates are much the same for the new Hanoi Hilton Opera, located downtown next to the Opera House. Plus 10% tax and 5% service charges. The Spring Hotel has rooms for $100s/$190d, email: springhotel@ fpt.vn tel 825 2219. The New Tong Dan Hotel is close to Hoan Kiem Lake with similar rates. email: tongdanhotel@hn.vnn.vn

HEALTH - No shots necessary.

MISCELLANEOUS - For additional information contact the Vietnamese Embassy at www.vietnamembassy-usa.org tel. 202.861.0737. Anh Khanh studio tel.84-4-8271216 email:khanhartvn@yahoo.com

## The Greatest Headhunter
## in Borneo

SABAH, BORNEO - We are at the Monsopiad Cultural Village, a half hours drive from Kota Kinabalu, the Capital of Sabah. The village is named after the famed headhunter and is run by 6th and 7th generation descendants. The purpose is to honor Monsopiad and show how the native tribes lived hundreds of years ago. And, as a tourist attraction it's also a way to make a living. The village sits on the same ground the long dead warrior lived.

Lets get some background. Borneo is an island, almost pie shaped and borders the South China Sea. It's due east of Singapore and north of the island of Java. If you took a bite from the north west section, about 1/3 the area, you would have Sarawak in the south, Sabah in the north and Brunei in between the two. The remaining 2/3 is Kalamantan and belongs to Indonesia. Hundreds of years ago, the entire north west section was ruled by the Sultan of Brunei. He was having trouble with insurrections from the native tribes and the British were able to help. The British also had a presence on main land Malaysia. Skipping ahead, the Japanese occupied all of Borneo during the second war. When the war was over, these states were on their own for a while. After the Dutch pulled out of Indonesia an eye was cast to assimilate all of Borneo. Sarawak and Sabah decided to join Singapore and become part of Malaysia rather than Indonesia. Brunei had oil and wanted no part of joining anyone. Singapore later pulled out to form it's own country but Sarawak and Sabah stayed the course to become semi-autonomous States. Their citizens are free to travel to peninsular Malaysia but the reverse is not so. There are 200 Dayak tribes in Borneo. Dayak is the term for non-Muslim tribes of Borneo (most of Malaysia is Muslim). The dominant tribe in Sabah is the Kadazan.

The history of when tribes first formed in Borneo is, at best, hazy. Tribal warfare goes back to the time there were two tribes. It was common for neighboring tribes to rob and pillage whoever they could. And for the offended tribe to exact revenge, when they could - much like what went on in the rest of the world. It was the custom to come home with the head of your enemy. Absolute proof that you actually got him. And therein lies the story of Monsopiad.

He was the grandson of the village headman and so was given special training. Turns out he was very good at it. He vowed to bring back the heads of the people who had ransacked his village over the years. He wanted no other reward than the respect of the tribe as a great warrior. Three boys went with him as witnesses and over the years he was successful. He hung the severed heads from the rafters of his house. His reputation spread and the robberies stopped. He gained such a reputation that no one dared challenge him. The village was now safe. Unfortunately, he had become addicted to the blood letting. He would pick fights to have an excuse to kill and behead yet another man. The tribe had a problem and selected a group of warriors to solve it the only way they could. Monsopiad fought back fiercely but, in the end, he was doomed. The tribe still honors his good deeds while they regret they were left with no choice. Monsopiad collected 42 heads and they are on display, hanging from the rafters, at the village.

On entry to the village, you notice the single family houses on stilts. Not the long houses used by other tribes. All wood, about eight feet above the ground and roughly 400 square feet. Being this high protects from flooding and critters crawling into your bed at night. Then we were collected as a group to listen to the band play a few numbers. Wood sticks hitting metal pots and sticks hitting hollow logs. Pleasant enough but I won't be buying the album. Then we went to an open sided shed to see how the ancients processed grains - stone grinding wheels, woven baskets, wood utensils and plates. Then across the road to the house on the hill. The memorial to Monsopiad. There are black and white pictures of the High Priestess Bianti, the 5th descendant line from the headhunter. And, hanging from the rafters, out of our reach, are the 42 heads saved over the centuries.

Back across the road to the auditorium for the stage show. Normally I don't like these shows because they are poorly done. But not this one. Men and women dancing with fluid movements to the equivalent to our waltz - beautifully dressed, by the way. Then the star of the show - the headhunter with the glassy, drug induced stare intended to frighten his opposition. He loads his blow pipe and shoots 50 feet, to one of the balloons tied to the ceiling. A hit and a round of applause. Then he, slowly (and I mean slowly) walks among us, glaring and staring. In Hollywood, this is over acting, but here it's a photo opportunity.

After walking the aisles, he picks the prettiest girl and brings her on stage Apparently he had good reason for taking his time. He shows her how to hold the blow pipe and loads a dart. She blows and fifty feet away another balloon breaks. He's not happy but the audience erupts with applause.

Then the bamboo stick dance. Two pairs of ten foot long sticks are held four inches from the floor and each pair is snapped together with a loud crack as dancing girls jump from one to the other. Foot co-ordination much like skipping rope. However, a mistake here could cause a broken ankle bone. The audience is invited on stage to join in. This time the men holding the sticks are very careful. The snap of the sticks doesn't sound as loud as before.

Later, I saw the imprint of a large leaf in the concrete walk way. A little thing. But it shows the detail these members of the Kadazan tribe went to. There is a swinging wood and rope bridge crossing the river. Only four people at a time. The bridge moved with each of my steps. I wonder if Monsopiad walked across a bridge like this one.

THE END

## SIDEBAR FOR BORNEO

GETTING THERE - The most economical way to visit Borneo is with a tour company. If you choose to go on your own, the airfare from LAX or JFK is approx. $2300 RT to Kota Kinabalu. Two stops and two changes of planes. Roughly 24 hours from the U.S. airport to the destination hotel. I used smarTours for a two week tour that included Sarawak, Sabah and Kuala Lumpur. All air (9 flights), four star hotels, guided tours and half the meals for $2500. 1-800-337-7773 or www.smarTours.com

WHEN TO GO - Monsoon season is November to February - but it will rain year round. Borneo is close to the Equator and it's hot and humid all the time. Dress accordingly and bring a poncho.

HOTELS - There are hundreds of hotels to choose from, most all the high end chains. Check their web sites for prices. There are local hotels in the $30 range like the Kinabalu Daya Hotel - www.kkdayahotel.com.

HEALTH - No shots necessary.

MISCELLANEOUS - For additional information contact the Malaysian Embassy at 2401 Massachusetts Ave NW, Washington DC 20008 or 1-202-328-2700.

Forget Bruce Lee - The Komodo is the REAL Dragon

Deadly Komodo Dragon walking towards me

LABUANBAJO, FLORES, INDONESIA - I know you've heard it before "You can't get there from here", but, that's how it seemed to me when I tried to get to Komodo Island 10 years ago. Booked a tour in Bali, 3 nights, four days. We'd fly east over Lombok to Sumbawa, two islands over. Then take a van to Sape on the eastern end of the island where we'd catch a boat for the six hour ride to Komodo. Camp out, pay the guide to buy a goat and, with the goat as bait, we would wait for the fiercest, man eating (and goat eating), ferocious, nine foot long, 400 pound Dragon to rip the poor goat to shreds with it's enormous claws and fearfully sharp teeth, while we took pictures. I know it sounds cruel but Dragons have to eat too. Anyway, four guys got Balinese revenge and the trip was cancelled.

I tried again last year. The tour company in Bali said their boat was broken, so I worked out a plan of my own. Fly to Labuanbajo on the western end of Flores and hire a boat going west for the three hour ride to

Komodo. Flores is closer than Sumbawa. Less boat time and LBJ is bigger than Sape, so the town will be more interesting. Turns out I could book a flight into LBJ but the return flight was full.

There are only two flights a week from Bali and I only had a week. Two for two. They say third time's a charm, so it was back to Bali to try again. I went to the Merpati Airlines office at the airport. They would only sell me the ticket to LBJ. The return I'd have to buy in Labuanbajo. Hummm, I'd have to take my chances on how many people wanted to come back on the same flight as me. At least they took my Visa card.

There were rumors of these monsters by fishermen working in the area long before their existence was confirmed by the west. The Dutch visited Komodo in 1910, shot two of the dragons and brought the skins to Java as proof. Actually, the Komodo Dragon is a monitor lizard, the biggest. Powerful jaws, massive bodies, strong legs with the ability to outrun a man for short distances. Like all monitors, they eat other animals. The Dragon normally eats deer, wild pig and water buffalo which inhabit the islands. The latest estimate is 1600 on Komodo and 800 on the neighboring island of Rinca.

There have been some reported on the island of Flores (they are good swimmers) but they would be difficult to find. The farmers kill the Dragons when they find them eating their live stock. Why only on these islands? No one knows.

Being a large reptile, they rarely move until warmed by the sun. They seem to be stone deaf but have a keen sense of smell. They have sharp teeth, dagger like claws on each foot and a tail strong enough to knock a man over. The real killer, however, is the bacteria laced saliva. They bite a prey and wait for the infection to kill it in a day or two. They have an immunity for the bacteria and eat without worry. Except for other Dragons that might want a piece of the action. But then they will eat other Dragons too, if they can.

Reportedly, an older German man stayed behind from his group to change the film in his camera. When the group went back for him, all they found was his hat.

Our flight was on a 52 seat Fokker 27. The overhead bin doors opened on takeoff. We got a green donut, green egg roll, fried banana and rice and a really good chocolate and vanilla flan. More than I expected.

There are five times more tour guides waiting at the airport than tourists arriving. When I exited the arrivals door it was like a piece of bacon dropped into a piranha pool. After 30 seconds of feverish simultaneous pitches and pleads, I ended it all by selecting one guy. The other 19 guides rushed back to the door to get the next brave soul. The Merpati office is at a house close to the airport and it was the first stop. Return ticket in hand, it was time to go to Agusto's office for the mandatory sales pitch. Here's where I made a mistake, I didn't wait to shop around. After 10 years of waiting, I took the first deal for the next day. Tourism is at such a low ebb, I checked into the Wisata Hotel without actually signing in. Cheap price quoted, pick a room and that was it. Later, I walked to the most expensive hotel, south of town. A long walk in the sweltering heat, it turned out. They had air conditioning but the rooms weren't much nicer and it was miles from town. And it was empty. Not a guest in sight.

The town of Labuan Bajo is virtually one street wide along the harbor. I was at the southern end and walked to the port at the northern end, passing the only sanctioned Komodo Dragon souvenir store on the left. It's run by the National Park service with fixed prices. It is the only game in town for Komodo t-shirts, hats, etc. I would soon find out that things had changed since the guide books of old. Komodo Dragons are now protected and the islands they live on are National Parks and administered by the government.

## THE OVERPRICED TOUR

Agusto met me at the hotel first thing and watched me eat breakfast. Coffee, a banana and rolled pancake. We took one of the constantly roaming bemos to the harbor and waited for the boat to arrive. My boat.

A guy and girl came up and asked if I wanted to join them on their boat to cut the costs. Agusto panicked and insisted we go for bottled water. I knew why but went anyway.

My boat had a large deck and that's where the Captain laid out the blanket. He was using the only chair on the vessel. The water was calm which was a pleasant surprise, the channels between islands is known for being rough. Flying fish were too fast to get a picture.

We were the third boat to put to dock at Rinca. A twenty minute walk through a desert devoid of life, to park headquarters and I met the others. A South African guy, Swiss girl (the ones that asked me to join them) and a Swedish guy. Four people, three boats. US$4 entrance fee, sign in, and they assigned two guides.

The viewing platform is atop the hill and the Swedish guy yelled to me in time. I almost stepped on a Dragon. They blend in very well with the ground. That would have been the end of me. One bite. No hospital in LBJ, 2 ½ hours away, and the next flight to Bali was 4 days away. The infection would kill me in two days. About 8 Dragons were literally just hanging around, waiting. The biggest was 9 feet long, probably 400-500 pounds and clearly master of his domain. I started taking his picture when he was 10 feet away and he walked right at me. Cold steel eyes, flicking tongue and drool coming from each side of his mouth. Males outnumber females 3.4 to 1, so I figured it was a male. When he got close, I backed up. The Dragons did not hang together like I've seen alligators do at a farm. They keep their distance. But the big guy had taken a liking to me, so I jumped onto the platform. We had an hour to shoot and the guide gathered us for the jungle walk. I discovered, twenty minutes later, that it was a walk to nowhere in particular. Maybe some Dragons in the wild, maybe a Water Buffalo. I figured, maybe nothing. One guide led two of us back.

Indonesia is on the equator. Temperature and humidity both push 100 and the concession stand was what the doctor ordered. So the soda was luke cold, it was a breath of life. I changed film, went back up the hill for more pictures and almost stepped on another dragon. And this time

I was looking down. Dragons will attack larger foes when cornered and threaten by hissing. I got one hiss from an eight footer who decided I was close enough. I took his word for it.

The frozen milk shakes at the Borobudur are to die for on a sweltering day. But if you hear a hiss, back up fast.

## THE END

## SIDEBAR FOR KOMODO

GETTING THERE - I got to Labuanbajo from Bali on Merpati Air, with a stop in Sumbawa. One hour twenty minute fight, ½ hour wait and a half hour flight for $100 each way. Flights to and from Bali are twice a week, days change. China Air had a special fare of $590 RT to Bali from California. Bali is serviced by Continental, Air France, JAL, KLM, Qantas, Singapore, Thai and others with coach fares of approximately $1000 RT.

ACCOMMODATIONS - In Bali the choices are as varied as New York or Los Angeles, from 5 star to no star. I found a gem almost by accident, the Pelasa Hotel, Batu Pageh St., Legian- Kuta, Bali, Indonesia, tel 0361-753423, fax 62-361-753424, e- mail= pelasa@indo.net.id Beautiful grounds, pool, A/C rooms, bar, for $20/person, breakfast included. 1 ½ blocks inland from The Bounty restaurant.

The best in Labunbajo is the New Bajo Beach Hotel, south of town and isolated. Rooms with A/C start at US$11. The second best is the Hotel Wisata with a ceiling fan for US$3 single. Both have food and drinks. The best restaurant is the Borobudur on the hill overlooking the harbor, in the center of town.

LOCAL ARRANGEMENT - There is no best place in town to book tours although there are plenty of agencies. You have to shop around and bargain, bargain, bargain. Even if you pay twice the going rate like I did, it's still cheap. US$20 should get you RT to Rinca, $30 to Komodo, $40 for a package deal of both with overnight on the boat. Labuanbajo has caves just out of town and it makes for a good ½ day trip for US$7. Trips to the interior are 1 to 4 days, forget about airplane connections. The 4 day trip should go for about $150 with very modest accommodations (that's all they have).

MISCELLANEOUS - No visas are required for USA citizens.

Kota Kinabalu, the starting point for the treasures of Sabah

KK, SABAH, MALAYSIA - Kota Kinabalu was razed during WWII to prevent it from being used as a port by the Japanese. At the time, Sandakan on the east coast was the capital but it was bombed into ashes by the allied forces in 1945. The capital was moved to Jesselton in 1946 and the town was renamed Kota Kinabalu in 1963, the same year Malaysia gained their independence from the British.

Sabah is the poorest of the Malaysian provinces, probably because they have been so troublesome to the central government in Kuala Lampur. Their independence was disputed by both Indonesia and the Philippines. Sabah and Sarawak, with tiny (and very rich) Brunei in the middle, occupy a small portion of the island of Borneo. The rest of the island belongs to Indonesia. The present population of Sabah is 3.1 million of which 1 million are from the Philippines. To this day there is an active smuggling trade between Sabah and the province of Mindanao in the Philippines. Some of Mindanao's pirates seek refuge in Sabah when the Philippine government tries to clamp down on them.

The province is semi-autonomous, like Sarawak to the south. Geography helps, they are separated from Peninsular Malaysia by the South China Sea. They presently feel that they are under populated, so they have decreed that families with 5 or more children pay no taxes.

Most visitors use KK as a jumping off place for climbing Mount Kinabalu or diving at Sipadan or a visit to the Orang-Utan rehabilitation center on the outskirts of Sandakan but, KK the city, is worth a look.

KK is a few miles long, and it's only four blocks deep - in from the harbor. North of the centrally located Post Office is most of the action. The P.O is on the main drag, which changes names every few blocks and runs parallel to the waterfront. Just across the street from the P.O. is the narrow but interesting war memorial park. A block north is the cinema.

Not many movie theaters for a population of 300,000. Facing the movie theater is a huge supermarket.

A block father and turn left. A Burger King across the street from the best hotel in town, the Hyatt. Their bar, Shenanigans, is THE place to be at night. Behind the Hyatt is the boat dock and my first venture to the offshore islands.

## TAKE MY BOAT MISTER

I got within a block of the waterfront and I was approached for a boat tour. You name it and they'll take you for $30. I did wonder, to myself, how much it would cost to get back. At the official dock, with published schedules and rates, I got a round trip ticket to Manukan Island for $3. It was a 20 minute ride on a small boat that bounced between three foot swells and I was down wind from a guy badly in need of Right Guard. I jumped off at the first stop in need of nose plugs and Dramamine. It's a long pier and the boat was gone before I got to the ticket booth and saw the "Welcome to Sapi Island" sign. Oh well, 75 cents admission and I might as well make the most of it. Sapi is a darling little island and the one most visited. It has a fine beach, good snorkeling, picnic benches and a good nature trail if you want to venture into the jungle. There is little in the way of facilities. I learned the boats aren't well marked and schedules not necessarily adhered to. The ride back, on a private boat was $3. I got tired of waiting for the public boat.

Right next to (just north and the reason the Hyatt doesn't have a gift shop) is the Wisma Merdeka a huge modern shopping center. There is a supermarket, Kentucky Fried Chicken, several excellent gift shops with local wares, clothing, electronic stores and a store of Famous Amos cookies. Even if you are not a shopper, it's easy to spend several enjoyable hours looking in the various shops.

Just north, and across the street, is the Wisma Sabah which houses the two travel agencies I used to book tours. Both Discovery and Sabah Holiday go out of their way to be helpful. Further north and another block in, is Rocky's Fun Pub and the LA Pub but they are not open in the daytime. This section of town is not as prosperous and it may be ill advised to walk these streets at night. Shenanigans is bustling after 8 PM and the crowd is a mixture of the upscale and those who want to be.

## MOUNT KINABALU

This huge piece of rock is only 9 million years old. It came to be after a core of solid volcanic rock pushed up from the depths, broke through the ground and grew to it's present 4101 meters. It' still growing, 5 mm a year. It's the highest mountain between the Himalayas and New Guinea and it's an odd sight - a bald topped rock sticking out of the jungle. The climb is a two day affair and it's supposed to be easy enough for children and senior citizens to climb, so they say. Frankly, I know how thin the air is at over 12,000 feet and I didn't buy the easy bit. The kick is that you need a guide, it's not optional, and you have to get up at 3 AM, from the nights stop on the mountain, to climb in the dark and reach the summit for sunrise. Three in the morning, climbing on jagged rock in the dark, in bitter cold, with enough oxygen for a chipmunk. I took the surface tour of the jungle around the Park Headquarters where we almost saw the mountain top in the distance (cloud cover). The package includes a tour of the orchid garden with a variety of beautiful flowers.

With some time to kill, I walked to the other shopping center at the south end of town, Center Point. It's more upscale than the Merdeka with designer labels known the world over. It's a beautiful mall that seems more likely to be in Beverly Hills than on the island of Borneo. Well worth a visit, in fact, if you are just passing through KK and only have time for one stop, this should be it.

## I'LL MAKE IT TO THE RIGHT ISLAND YET

This time I had my wits about me and asked before I got off the boat. Manukan Island is the most developed and just as pretty as Sapi. They have a gift shop, chalets for overnight stay (modern and attractive for $75 weekdays and $100 weekends), swimming pool, tennis court, full size restaurant, two places to rent snorkeling equipment and a small display of bombs left over from WWII just sitting on a bench. The beach is long, white, clean and uncrowded. I don't know what more you could ask for. I had an ice cream cone on my way out and wasn't paying attention. I thought it was vanilla. It was Durian, the Asian delicacy fruit that smells worse than week old garbage. The smell is so bad, the fruit is banned from hotels. You are not allowed to bring the fruit to your room and, believe me, they can quickly tell if you did.

At least the ice cream was cold. I went to Shenanigans and washed my mouth out with a beer.

## THE END

## KOTA KINABALU SIDEBAR

GETTING THERE - I came from Singapore (to the east) which is serviced by Northwest, United, Garuda and Singapore Airlines (US $1300 RT from the USA west coast). Then from Johor Bahru airport (JHB) just across the Singapore border since it's 50% cheaper than flying out of Singapore to Malaysian Borneo. From JHB to Kota Kinabalu, on Malaysian airlines, it's US$150 economy, $200 business class each way.

The tour of Mt. Kinabalu can be made with Discovery Tours, Locked Bag 23, 88992 Kota Kinabalu, Sabah, Malaysia. e-mail:DISTOUR@ PO.JARING.MY internet: http://www. infosabah.com.my/discovery tel. (6) 088-221244. Fax (6) 088-221600. They are the American Express representative in Sabah.

If Discovery tours are full, try Sabah Holiday, Lot G31, Ground Floor, Wisma Sabah, 88000 Kota Kinabalu, Sabah, Malaysia. tel (6) 088-222708 Fax (6) 088-221751 Email:pooi@pop.jaring.my I found them very helpful. Both Discovery and Sabah Holiday are in the Wisma Sabah building on the first floor.

WHEN TO GO - The heaviest rainfalls are from October to March with the heaviest in December and January. Sabah is virtually on the equator so count on warm weather and high humidity, year round. Bring an umbrella, no matter.

WHERE TO STAY - The best in the center of town is the Hyatt Kinabalu, tel. (6) 088-221234 Fax (6) 088-218909. It's right on the waterfront with rooms from US$ 120. The winner for colonial charm is also the oldest, the Jesselton, with rooms from $90. tel. (6) 088-223333 Fax. (6) 088-241401. Out of town, closer to the airport, is the Shangri-La Tanjung Aru Resort, tel (6) 088-225800, with rooms from $140/180 for singles/doubles. All rooms have 10% service and 5% govt. tax added on.

WHAT TO DO - Visits to the islands just offshore can be made from the boat dock. Snorkeling equipment is available on the islands. The tour companies listed above can arrange trips to a Borneo fishing village, city tour, Kota Belud Sunday market, a Longhouse visit, white water rafting on the Kiulu or Padas rivers and overnight trips to Sandakan, Turtle Island and Mt. Kinabalu climb.

FOR MORE INFORMATION- Write to the Malaysian Tourist office at 818 West 7th St, Suite 804, Los Angeles, CA 90017 Tel. (213) 689-9702 or 595 Madison Ave., Suite 1800, New York, NY 10022 Tel (212)754-1113.

## LAHU TRIBE OF NORTHERN THAILAND

### Visit the golden triangle by elephant

CHAING RAI, THAILAND - One hundred feet down the bank, the long boat was waiting to take us up the Kok River. Seven of us scramble in, one abreast. The boat is about fifty feet long and wide enough for one person to sit sideways. With the motor in the rear, there is no problem slicing a path through the water but with that slice comes a spray that drenches those in the middle.

Two hours up the Kok and not a soul in sight. Jungle to the left, jungle to the right, the buzz of the motor from the rear and water spray from the front. There was time to reflect on how we got here. An early morning start in the back of a covered pick up truck in Chaing Mai. Seven tourists on wood benches with our gear beneath and a pint of rough Thai whiskey supplied by the guide. A quick stop at the natural hot springs for pictures and refreshments. Then we stopped in the middle of nowhere at a road side barbecued corn stand. One native, fresh corn and no village in sight. The corn was delicious and with a fresh pint of whiskey to wash it down we continued north to Chaing Rai. Three and a half hours from the start we were walking around the shopping area while Ben, our guide, bought fresh chicken and vegetables for later. Then on to the river.

We left the boat on the shore at the Karen tribe village. A quiet place except for the children playing at waters edge with the elephants. A quick walk through and out the back end into the Thai section of the golden triangle. Twenty minutes later, our first surprise - the stream. It was too wide to jump and a foot deep. Off came the sneakers and socks and I made first use of my bottled water to wash the mud from my feet on the other side.

## THE MOST INCREDIBLE ELEPHANT RIDE IN THE WORLD

Ben decided to get the elephants now even though they were scheduled for the next day. We waited while working on the third pint. It was going down smoother than a few hours before. Finally, we lined up on top a 10 foot cliff next to the stream and one at a time, stepped onto the elephants head, walked across his neck and into the basket tied to his middle. Elephants for the paying guests, handlers walked. Our elephant let us know right off who was in charge. He moved directly down a 45 degree embankment that would have thrown us off if it weren't for the hand rails we clung to for dear life, and then he stepped into three feet of sucking mud. We went up stream, over five foot boulders, up 60 degree rock slides and were literally thrown from side to side with enough force to eject us from our lofty perch had we not had a death grip on the bamboo rail. The beast knew we were there but couldn't care less if we stayed there. We were 300 insignificant pounds on his back. No roller coaster ride has more sudden drops or violent turns than this ride.

Our elephant was hungry and paused every minute to rip branches and leaves from the passing bush. Each time, the handler responded with a whack to his rear end with a stick. All of which had no effect what so ever on the number of times he paused for food. When his mouth was empty, he stopped. Eat, smack, eat, smack. We were the last ones in line and he would break into a trot to catch up after a particularly tough bush but it was clearly his idea, not the handlers. Occasionally, the handler would yell commands in elephant talk. Whey or ughhh or whooo or ho ho. If our beast understood the commands, he didn't let on.

Just as we settled into a leisurely pace up a three foot wide mountain trail with no brush and a 200 foot drop to the left, came the unexpected. Another elephant coming down. There was no room to pass and I couldn't believe the casual way it was handled. With rider on top, the elephant coming down stepped a few feet off the trail, down the 45 degree slope, dug his feet in for a firm hold and waited for us to pass. It was loose ground and if one foot had slipped, there would be no stopping the plunge of elephant and rider.

211

Then we hit level ground and our guy decided he was tired of being in last place. Without warning, he kicked in passing gear, trotted to the right and slipped past the elephant ahead. It's possible he would have tried for lead elephant in the next open stretch but it was not to be. One minute the sun was setting, a deep crimson hanging on the tree tops, and as suddenly as someone shuts the blinds, it was dark. The night jungle was still except for the soft thump of our elephant's padded foot hitting the soft earth and the intermittent shrill cry of a bird looking for a companion. It was so dark, the green of the jungle had turned to black.

Someone yelled to Ben, "Can elephants see in the dark?"

"I don't know," he replied, "we've never done this in the dark before."

We must have looked at each other, but it was too dark to tell.

## THE VILLAGE

Two and a half bone jarring hours from the river and we arrived at the village, saddle sore, with arms that ached from the strain of holding onto the bamboo rail. What a relief! What a ride!

We gathered in the big room of Ben's family hut. Floor mats lined one half of the long room and we stretched out while the family set about to cook supper in the front room. Kerosene lamps provided low, but adequate light, and there was a large ice filled bucket of beer in the middle of the floor. I have no idea where the ice came from but the beer hit the spot.

The cooking was done in a wok over firewood in the middle of the floor of the entrance room. There are only two rooms. The toilet is around the back. We had rice, chicken, tomato and cauliflower and ate like the famished. As much as we liked, the family joined us afterwards. Beer was $2 a bottle but country whiskey was passed around for free. Opium was 80 cents a hit and family members showed how it was done. Lying on your side, struggling to keep the pipe lit. I counted 8 adults and an undetermined number of kids in the extended family. Ben, our guide, is the only one of four brothers to remain single. In this tribe, the male must live with the future in-laws for three years before marriage.

That lack of freedom is too high a price to pay for Ben. At least for now.

One becomes aware of the village chickens at 4 AM. Even in the middle of a sound sleep - what other kind of sleep could one have after last nights' indulgences. I hit the porch at first light to see not only chickens but pigs, ducks, cats, dogs, cows and water buffalo. Don't forget the elephants from last night, this was a very tricky place to walk around and keep your shoes clean.

The early morning jungle mist was soon replaced by the golden glow of sunrise. A thin pipe ran down the slope to provide water to the porch where dishes were washed and, presumably, bathes were taken. The animals were still and a quiet filled the air. Ben's tribe, the Lahu, is originally from Burma and they prefer to live at 3000 feet on the side of a hill. The slope is barren and rutted from rain. Grain was being crushed the old fashioned way. They step on the end of a plank to raise the mallet on the other end and step off to let it fall onto the grain which is held in a small stone container. All the huts are built above ground with the downside poles as much as ten feet longer than those on the entrance side.

Breakfast was served on the porch. Toast, coffee, tea, pineapple and a hard boiled egg. And we were off for a sweat inducing downhill walk to the falls, on a dry trail. If wet, it would have been a mud slide. Not a safe slide, mind you, for there were several sections with a 100 foot cliff to one side. I ducked by a four foot web with beautiful sunlit concentric circles. In the middle was the spider with a leg spread as big as my hand.

Twenty minutes before the falls is the trading store that looks like it was taken from a western movie. The wild flowers around the store are too gorgeous to miss. Across the rope and plank bridge, down the path and up the rocks to a peaceful natural stone pool in the middle of the rain forest.

There was more jungle ahead and another days walk but I'll always remember the first day. No amusement park will ever match that elephant ride. Who says you can't get away from it all.

## THE END

## SIDEBAR FOR THE HILL TRIBES

GETTING THERE - Bangkok is serviced from the USA by United, Northwest, Delta, Air France, British Airways, Canadian Airlines, Cathay Pacific, China Airlines, Singapore Air, Swissair and Thai Airlines. The lowest fare from Los Angeles is $1200 RT on China Airlines. Bangkok to Chaing Mai is $66 RT on Thai Airlines. Overnight trains (10 to 12 hours) go from Bangkok to Chaing Mai for less than half the air price but are usually booked in advance.

LOCAL TOUR ARRANGEMENT - Can be made at virtually any hotel in Chaing Mai or any of the numerous travel agencies. There seem to be more travel agencies than tourists, so some agencies may be less than honest in their promises. The going rate is about $70 per night per person which includes transportation, lodging and meals. The range is from one to four nights. Virtually all of the agencies, in the hotels or on the street, have photo books showing the sights, itineraries and maps. There are variations, so it would be best to look at several. It may be safer to book from one of the better hotels, in case you aren't satisfied, and use a credit card even though they will ask for three percent more to cover the credit card charge. I bargained the three percent away, after all this is Thailand where you bargain for everything.

HEALTH - Malaria and dysentery are two major concerns in the back country of Thailand. I learned later that the high country doesn't have a problem with mosquitos, hence virtually no malaria. But I was eaten alive by mosquitos in Chaing Mai in the few spots I missed with insect spray. Bring Imodium or pepto bismo for your stomach, just in case. None of us had a problem.

PACKING - I was given a small knapsack for the trip. Bring extra socks, underwear, toilet kit, towel, insect repellant (just in case), at least 2 liters of water (buy in town), rain coat (a large plastic garbage bag with a small hole cut in the bottom will double for one and is very light weight), sunglasses, hat and plenty of film for the camera. Bring some high speed film to use when you are bouncing around on the elephant. Pack light, you will be carrying your kit for some very long walks.

FOR MORE INFORMATION - Contact The Thailand Tourism Authority 5 World Trade Center, #3443, New York, NY 10048 tel. (212)-432-0433 //or //303 E. Wacker Dr., #400, Chicago, IL 60601 tel. (312) 819-3990 //or //3440 Wilshire Blvd., #1100, Los Angeles, CA 90010 tel. (213) 382-2353

## LANGKAWI ISLAND

*The roads weren't made of gold, they were made of marble*

We were having lunch on the terrace of the country club. The bright tropical sun lit the manicured greens in the distance and it was too hot to play golf. The waiter brought iced tea, steamed rice and huge prawns. I noticed the rectangular man-made pools a few hundred yards from the terrace and asked. Yes, they raised these monster shrimp right there, a stones throw from our elevated view. In the distance, across the bay, is a section carved out of the mountain. A white patch punctuating the stretch of green trees. Not a landslide but the result of blasting, it's the home of the marble company we were to visit later.

Next came the mixed vegetable soup with translucent noodles, a large plate of vegetables and a large three pound fish for each of us. Enough food for two days. And all the time in the world to eat. There was no hurry, it was all a part of a very relaxed tour.

We had left Georgetown, Penang on a beautiful boat, the Selesa Exspres, for a comfortable two and a half ride straight north through the eastern Indian Ocean along the west coast of Malaysia. We were met at the boat dock and dropped off in town to cruise the stores and shop to our hearts content. Langkawi is a free port and many of the Malaysians take the trip to stock up on cigarettes and liquor at a fraction of the price from the mainland.

Kuah is the only real town on this sparsely populated island of 48,000. A main road and three streets running to the side like a large capital E. There is major renovation underway with a large shopping center being built along the waterfront to eventually replace the existing town. Langkawi has big plans according to our young tour guide. Hong Kong was be taken over by the Chinese in 1997 and businesses would eventually flee. Langkawi plans to fill that void. There is plenty of land and 1/3 of the island has been designated for business and industrial development. In 1987, there were 10 cars on the island. Now there are 9,000 and he is convinced that development will come and thankful that 2/3 of the island is to remain a tropical jungle. Untouched and unspoiled. It reminded me of the voices in "Field of Dreams" - build it and they will come.

## THE MARBLE ROADS

On the way to the Kedah Marble Company we got the story. In 1962 an Italian tourist took a look at the gravel used on the roads. Who better to spot marble. He was shocked, the people were using local rock to pave the roads and had no idea of it's worth. Since then, Langkawi has become one of the major suppliers of marble all over the world and is said to be the only quarry with pure white. The yard is filled with tons of white cubes and huge pieces of marble recently blown out of the mountain. The gift shop is a collectors delight. Red, white, black, pink, stripped, solid. Statues, paperweights, knives, chess sets, beads, you name it. I bought a pure black egg. Shiny and smooth, the same size as a real egg for $1. The down side of marble shopping is the weight. A good size piece would need a fork lift to get it on the plane home. But, if you are in the market for quality marble, the prices here are so good, you will feel that you're stealing. During the island tour, the guide took us to the only remaining asphalt road with white marble used as aggregate. Six feet of black tar and white marble in the center of a fourteen foot road.

## THE ISLAND TOUR

Back in the van for a ride to the public beach on the north of the island, Tanjong Rhu. Sun bathers have to come self contained since there are no public bathrooms or dressing facilities. There are stands for hot food, beer, soda, souvenirs and boat rentals. The imaginary line that crosses the sea between Malaysia and Thailand is just off shore and there has been talk of building a casino on one of the little islands on the Thai side. And boat connections from Langkawi and mainland Thailand. It may be awhile.

There are three first class hotels and we visited them all. The Burau Bay Beach Resort, with 80 rooms, has a kidney shaped pool and is on the beach. Cottages are available for about US $150. Close by is the Langkawi Island Resort with 220 rooms and a wide range of prices, US $80-320. The most impressive is the Pelangi Beach Resort, with 300 rooms, and rates from US $150-425. A beautiful structure whose lawn chess set has pieces three feet high and a masseuse for your back after a strenuous game. There are concrete seats for the bar in the pool. No need to climb out when you are in the need for refreshment. If you're going to relax, relax. The Pelangi even has its own jet airplane parked at the Langkawi airport. It seems, the guests need not worry about transportation either.

Then back to town. We used the morning to sight see and compare prices. No reason to carry things in the van. There was plenty of time and we knew where to go. Prices are reasonable since this quiet island is off the beaten track. We didn't see more than a hand full of non Asian faces all day. Of course, Hong Kong is still going strong and even if the local chamber of commerce is right, it may take years for the tourist trade or industry to discover this undeveloped piece of land. And then, Macao is a lot closer and Singapore is another option. The competition will be strong. Until then, which ever way it goes, this will remain a quiet island, in the Indian Ocean, off the west coast of Malaysia. Undiscovered by the madding crowds.

We returned to the boat dock in time to view the harbor filled with sail boats and pulled out just as the sun was setting. A softly diffused ball of fire that shed an orange glow to the blue sea and the green mountains of the background. We got back to Penang at 10 PM and grabbed a rickshaw bicycle taxi back to the hotel. I'll have to come back and see what happened with their grand plans.

THE END

## LANGKAWI SIDEBAR

GETTING THERE - The easiest route is from Kuala Lumpur (KL), via Penang on daily flights on Malaysia Airlines (US $150 RT). Price from Los Angeles to KL is around $1300 RT advance purchase. However, I went from Singapore which is serviced by Northwest and Singapore Airlines (US $1300 RT) to Penang. Round trip airfare from Singapore to Penang with a stopover at KL or Medan, Sumatra is $322. Purchase in Singapore at any travel agency. From Penang to Langkawi by air is US $50 RT and by catamaran US $ 40 RT.

In short, the fastest and most direct route is LAX - KL - Penang - Langkawi by air. The more casual route is LAX - Singapore - Penang (by air) - Langkawi (by boat).

WHEN TO GO - Langkawi has an Equatorial climate and is hot through out the year. The wettest months are September to November. Loose fitting cotton clothes are best.

WHERE TO STAY - There are a selection of first class hotels. The Pelangi Beach Resort has 300 rooms, has it's own airplane and is the islands best. Rates from US $ 150-425 per night. Tel. 04-911001. Then there is the Langkawi Island Resort (220 rooms) from US $ 60-425. Tel. 04-788209. The Burau Bay Beach Resort (80 rooms) for US $ 150. In the main town of Kuah, there is the Captain Resort (45 rooms) and the Langkawi Chalet (36 rooms) for US $ 40 and $ 30 respectively.

WHERE TO EAT - The are a number of restaurants in town but the best food is at the better hotels. Seafood is featured.

WHAT TO DO - A tour package is available in Penang which includes all transportation, a tour of the island, lunch at the country club and visits to the best hotels with plenty of time to shop for US $60 RT.

This is a Malaysian free port and many people load up on tax free items. Local tours can be arranged at the hotels.

MORE INFORMATION - Write to the Malaysian Tourist Board, 818 West 7th St., Los Angeles, CA 90017. Tel. (213)689-9702

Laid Back in Laos

LUANG PRABANG, LAOS - This was a 4 day add on to a 12 day tour of Thailand. The Visa for Laos takes a couple of days to process and we would be on the road to Chaing Rai during that time. The travel agent said the capital, Vientiane, was boring and the Thai people preferred to vacation in Luang Prabang. It was small town and charming. Good enough. The Hotel Phousy was our first choice but it was full. So we took the New Luang Prabang assuming "New" was descriptive. Fortunately, we stayed at 5 star hotels in Thailand. Unfortunately, we got used to it..

Laos has been Communist since the end of the Viet Nam war. The country is bordered on the north by China and Burma, on the east by Viet Nam, the south by Cambodia and the west by Thailand.

Luang Prabang is in the north, at the juncture of the Mekong and Nam Khan rivers and has a population of 16,000. Over the four days we probably saw every one of them. At the airport, we were met with unsmiling officials that did a stamp, stamp on the passports, just like in the movies. I changed $100 into kips (a mistake) and got stacks of money. After filling four pockets with kips, I put the rest into the suitcase. We got a fixed price van to town.

The asphalt road turned to dirt. Then potholes and a construction zone that may have been there for 10 days or 10 years. Considering the ramshackle houses at roadside, we were in the low rent section of town - we hoped. The New Luang Prabang is 50 feet from the main intersection in town. We looked out the van window and assumed it was "new" inside.

Three girls were waiting at the counter eager to check us in. One carried my heavy bag up two flights of stairs faster than I could have. Twin beds, window view of a building, no TV and a combo bath. That means no tub and a shower hose that sprays water throughout the entire room.

Adequate, not as fancy as a Motel 6. It became very clear how nice our hotels were in Thailand.

Out the front door and left, that's where the rest of the town is. Within fifty feet we met a middle aged German woman traveling through Laos to Thailand at a leisurely pace. Six months on the road to go from Viet Nam to India. Over the next several days we met a dozen or so travelers hitting the small towns in Laos on route from Viet Nam and on the way to Chaing Khong, Thailand (the golden triangle town in northern Thailand close to Burma and China). Some planned to go to Burma, others Thailand. The rest were headed east. No one was headed north into China or south into Cambodia.

There is no lack of tourist agencies on the main drag, but the one next to the hotel was slow to respond and we walked out. Two blocks later we were at the Royal Palace or what used to be the Royal Palace. In the 1975 revolution, the Royal family was exiled to the north and never heard from again. The grounds, on the Mekong River, are now a museum and art school with Buddha sculptures. Two blocks later we bought our first tour for US$ 5. A river tour to the Pak Ou Caves. We decided to look at other hotels. After several blocks along the main street, we found none. There are hostels off the main drag where the travelers we met were staying for US$ 3-5/nite. They were on the road for months, we weren't.

Diagonally from the "New" is the Hotel Phousy. Our first choice, but they confirmed it was full. It's a nice looking hotel and the desk was helpful in showing us, on the wall map, where the other upscale hotels were. After miles of walking and tuk-tuks (a 3 wheel motorcycle that carries 2 passengers) we ended up at the Mouang Luang Hotel. Nice rooms, nice grounds, a swimming pool and only US$ 50/nite. Unfortunately, it's blocks from the main street and that's the only action in town. It would be a cab ride back and forth several times a day.

We got back to our hotel to find the street blocked off. We only had to walk fifty feet to the front door so it was no big deal. The market sets up in the street every night. From the main intersection for 3 blocks, to the

Royal Palace. Food, souvenirs, clothes, shoes, art work, you name it. Not just the sidewalks, they use the street too.

After freshening up, we hit the tuk-tuk waiting area at the intersection, bargained for a one way trip to the Grand and waited. The guy couldn't get the engine to start. After 20 tries, the kick start finally caught and we were on our way - sort of. Two miles later the engine coughed and died. Fortunately, in front of a gas station. The driver removed the gas tank, filled it at the pump, put in back on and away we went - sort of. Now the engine was over revving and the ride was getting slower. And we were out of town, in the middle of nowhere. He kicked it, coached it, made a right turn, slipped a gear and the engine died at the main gate to the Grand. We paid him and walked in.

We bargained at the front desk (for informational purposes) and got the normal room rate dropped from US$ 150 to $120/ double. The hostess walked us to the bar which is in a separate building. Cable TV, plush furniture and empty. A waiter appeared and we had a beer - US $ 2. Afterwards, we were escorted to the outdoor dining terrace along the Mekong. The main indoor dining room was taken by a Laos Government conference. We were the only ones on the terrace. I had chicken stuffed with salmon and very good french onion soup for US$ 8. We met the cab back at the main gate. US$ 2 to get back.

Breakfast is on the roof of the New LP. Two fried eggs, ham, french roll, OJ and coffee (included). We joined 7 others in the long boat for the cruise down the Mekong and stopped at the paper artwork village and the liquor village (they distill here and it tastes like gasoline). They sell the same nice silk clothing and accessories as in town. There are steep banks to each village and you have to be careful. There was a cute four year girl on one bank, all dressed up, looking for tips. I couldn't resist.

Two hours downstream we got to the temple. There are actual steps here and above are 2 caves built into a limestone cliff and crammed with Buddha images. It's unique and well worth visiting. Why it's 25 KM downstream from town, I don't know. A four hour tour for US$ 5. Can't beat it. We met a couple from Tennessee that had 4 months to go before running out of money. Fortunately, one can live on the cheap here. They showed us the Ole Ole restaurant in town. The claim to fame here is a big TV with cable and CNN in English. A large beer is 80 cents. Vegetable soup with chicken = 90 cents. Below average salad is 80 cents. That night we were back at the Ole Ole for supper. Spaghetti napoleon, coffee and ice cream = US$ 2.80.

The Kuang Si waterfall trip is also US$ 5 and we took it the next afternoon. It's 29 KM south of town and features several levels of falls over limestone and beautiful turquoise pools on both sides of the wooden bridge at the base. It's a perfect place for a picnic. The water is chilly but swimable. There are lots of vendors on the road leading up to the falls so you don't have to bring any food or water if you're looking to picnic.

We met Ari the day before at the permanent market across the street from our hotel and ran across him again. A 28 year old writer/producer that dropped out. The career wasn't going anywhere so he sold everything and left a few months ago. Started in Viet Nam and stayed in a lot of small towns between there and here. Next is Thailand and on to India if the money holds out. There's no hurry. His room is $3 a day, meals about the same. Met a cute girl from Israel on the road. Things could be worse. He figures they were in Hollywood.

The good thing here is - no hurry. If you don't do it today, you can do it tomorrow. A days living expenses is less than the price of a drink in Los Angeles so what's the rush. I'm back in the land of swimming pools and six dollar beers but it was nice to be laid back for a while. I wonder if Ari ever made it to India.

THE END

SIDEBAR FOR LAOS

GETTING THERE - There are no direct flights from the USA. Besides you need a visa and that may take a few days. Best to fly to Bangkok and make arrangements there. Bangkok is served by most major airlines with consolidator prices of $600 RT from the west coast and $800 from the east coast depending on season.

You can make the arrangements yourself but it will probably cost more and you may get caught up in red tape. Laotian officials may respond better to a Travel Agency. We stayed at a 5 star hotel in Bangkok and they could not book the trip but called a travel agency that could. We took a cab to the other agency and made arrangements there. You have to leave your passport with the agency for a few days so it's best to set it up at the beginning of the trip and tour Thailand for several days first. There are adds in the local newspaper for weekend trips to Luang Prabang, 2 nights-3 days and those agencies can be contacted directly. A three day visa is approx. US$ 100. One week $115.

WHEN TO GO - The best time is between November and April. It rains the least and is not too hot.

HOTELS - The tour price includes air (RT) and hotel. US$540 for 3 nights at The New Luang Prabang, 3 star, private bath, double. It's at the main intersection in town and the nightly market starts right outside the front door. For US$580, 3 nights at the Hotel Phousy, 3 star, private bath, double. It's next to the main intersection, across from the night market. It is nicer looking than the New Luang Prabang. The Mouang Luang Hotel, 4 star, private bath, double is 6 blocks from the main street and requires a cab to get back and forth. US$590. Cab fares are cheap but the location is inconvenient. The most inconvenient and most luxurious is the Grand Luang Prabang. The above 3 and 4 stars are not equivalent to USA 3 and 4 stars, but, the Grand deserves it's 5 star rating. It's 20 minutes south of town, in the middle of nowhere. It has 80 rooms and suites, marble bathrooms, beautiful grounds and is along the Mekong River. US$ 140s/150d, suites are $250-300. Tel (856-71)253-851-7, fax (856-71)253-027-8. E-mail: info@grandluangprabang.com. Website: www.grandluangprabang.com. Plus 10% tax and 10% service charges at the Grand.

HEALTH - No shots necessary. Liver flukes (opisthorchiasis) is a danger from undercooked fish.

MISCELLANEOUS - For additional information contact the Laos Embassy at 2222 'S' St. NW, Washington DC 20006, tel. 212-667-0058

## It's tough to see a longhouse
in Borneo

KUCHING is the capital of Sarawak, one of the two Malaysian states on the island of Borneo. Lets get some background to see where we are. Borneo is an island, almost pie shaped and borders the South China Sea. It's due east of Singapore and north of the island of Java. If you took a bite from the north west section, about 1/3 the area, you would have Sarawak in the south, Sabah in the north and Brunei in between the two. The remaining 2/3 is Kalamantan and belongs to Indonesia. Hundreds of years ago, this entire north west section was ruled by the Sultan of Brunei. He was having trouble with insurrections from the native tribes in Sarawak and the British were able to help. The British also had a presence on main land Malaysia. Skipping ahead, the Japanese occupied all of Borneo during the second war. When the war was over, these states were on their own for a while. After the Dutch pulled out of Indonesia an eye was cast to assimilate all of Borneo. Sarawak and Sabah decided to join Singapore and become part of Malaysia rather than Indonesia. Brunei had oil and wanted no part of joining anyone. Singapore later pulled out to form it's own country but Sarawak and Sabah stayed the course to become semi-autonomous States. Their citizens are free to travel to peninsular Malaysia but the reverse is not so. There are 200 Dayak tribes in Borneo. Dayak is the term for non-Muslim tribes of Borneo (most of Malaysia is Muslim). The dominant tribes in Sarawak are the Iban and Bidayuh.

Tribes that still live in the jungle usually stay in a longhouse. It is, like the name, a long house. Thirty or forty people sleeping under one roof. Years ago, I stayed in a longhouse in northern Thailand. An all wood structure, on stilts. Two rooms. About 25 feet deep and 100 feet wide. At the top of the steps there was the kitchen, about 100 square feet and a dividing wall separating it from the other room. The large bedroom/living room had mats on the floor against one long wall. The other half was bare. A wood outhouse was out back on an outcropped rock. I was there as part of a tour of the area that borders Burma. This house belonged to relatives of our guide so we were expected.

The Lonely Planet guide book says you can't just go back country in Borneo and see a longhouse. First of all you need a permit from the National Park service to go back country. That done, you can't walk onto a tribe's land and expect to be invited into their house. After all, they live there and who are you barging in? Officially, headhunting has been outlawed but it was a long tradition for the people that live here, if you catch the drift. Pay the money and take a tour.

A visit to a longhouse was included on this tour. Accommodations and meals were to be first class. We were headed for the Hilton Batang Ai Longhouse Resort. Thirty one tourists piled onto the bus for a six and a half hour trip (only four hours if you drive straight through). An hour in, we stopped at the local, open stall, food market. Fruits and vegetables in shapes and colors you probably haven't seen before and sweet drinks, in a variety of colors, made with the local water. Reportedly, the water in Borneo is safe to drink but I wasn't going to take the chance.

A half hour later we pulled to the side of the road. A section that looked no different than the jungle we'd already passed. But here, there are pitcher plants that eat the bugs that fly in to get a taste of the sweet nectar at the bottom. And beautiful, tiny, wild orchids. Next stop was at a farm that makes pepper. Must be a secret process, no pictures were allowed. We passed a river dam that supplies electricity for Kuching and stopped in a small town for lunch. Family style - fried rice, sweet chicken and a banana for desert. And back to the bus.

We waited for a half hour at the rest stop building. A place to sit down and there are bathroom facilities. Finally we walked down the hill to meet the boat, off loading those headed back to the city. A small boat with 2 decks but we had to shoe horn thirty three people into the bottom deck. People on top would cause the boat to roll over. Twenty minutes, pier to pier, and a eight flights of steps to walk up to the reception area. You can take the stairs or the steep, paved road. An ATV was there to cart the bags. To the left of the reception area and lounge, is the bar (in the rear) adjacent the large dining room with the buffet table in the middle. All plush, finished with native wood. Out the back door is a huge swimming pool. Town houses on the hill overlook the pool.

On each side of the main building are there long houses. They contain the rooms. I mean really looong houses. Must have taken me twenty minutes to walk to my room but what a gorgeous room it was. A large bed, TV, refrigerator, coffee maker, air conditioning, and a full, large bathroom. The room oozed warmth and luxury. There is a sliding glass, back door to let in light and allow an easy exit into the jungle. If one had a mind to do so.

There are balconies on the main building for those who prefer outside dining and drinking. Cocktails are about $5 and meals range from $10 to $20. The Batang Ai has 100 rooms and suites (town houses atop the hill by the pool). There is a tennis court and ping pong table. To occupy the days, they offer a trip to some of the local forts (hour and a half drive), a visit to the Hydro-electric plant and fish hatchery, visits to some of the local towns, a river safari and a visit to a real (occupied by a local tribe) longhouse.

The next morning we collected by the dock for our trip to the real longhouse. Four of us had umbrellas, twenty two wore ponchos and four had nothing - and it was pouring rain. I looked over at the open boat and asked the guide if this was going to be our boat, just to be sure. Two hours each way in a boat with no cover in the pouring rain. Not a drizzle, a tropical downpour. Nine of us walked back up the hill.

I had coffee, read my book, had a very nice lunch. It poured for the next four hours. Fortunately, the sun came out in mid afternoon for those coming back on the boat. That night some that went said the trip was very interesting. I'm sure it was but getting soaked in a two hour boat ride made the comfort price way too high. I would spend hours in the pouring rain, getting soaked to the skin in an open boat, if my cruise boat sank. Otherwise, forget it.

Sunset over the lake is pretty. Soft, subtle reds hung over the lake. The dining area is comfortable, an easy place to while away the hours. The staff behaved as if they were thankful to have their jobs and went out of their way to be helpful. And the longhouse room is so nice you can't help but go to sleep with a smile on your face. So, I didn't see a longhouse lived in by a native tribe. But, I slept in a really nice one.

## THE END

## SIDEBAR FOR BORNEO

GETTING THERE - The most economical way to visit Borneo is with a tour company. If you choose to go on your own, the airfare from LAX or JFK is approx. $2400 RT to Kuching. Two stops and changes of planes. Roughly 24 hours from the U.S. airport to the destination hotel. I used smarTours for a two week tour that included Sarawak, Sabah and Kuala Lumpur. All air (9 flights), four star hotels, guided tours and half the meals for $2500. 1-800-337-7773 or www.smarTours.com

WHEN TO GO - Monsoon season is November to February - but it will rain year round. Borneo is close to the Equator and it's hot and humid all the time. Dress accordingly and bring a poncho.

HOTELS - There are hundreds of hotels to choose from, most all the high end chains. Check their web sites for prices. There are local hotels in the $30 range like the Telang Usan Hotel - www.telangusan.com.

Arrangements can be made to visit the Hilton Longhouse through the Hilton Kuching, Jalan Tunku Abdul Rahman, P.O. Box 2396, 93748 Sarawak, East Malaysia. tel. 60-(0)82-248200 or e-mail = sales_kuching@ hilton.com There is daily shuttle service from the Kuching Hilton to the resort - 4 hours for about $40 RT.

HEALTH - No shots necessary.

MISCELLANEOUS - For additional information contact the Malaysian Embassy at 2401 Massachusetts Ave NW, Washington DC 20008 or 1-202-328-2700.

## ON THE ROAD TO MANDALAY

This is not a trip for mom and the kids!

Boy washing family's prize possession at sunrise
-shot from overnight moving train going
from Mandalay to Rangoon (Yangon)

MYANMAR (BURMA) - I couldn't help but think of the road pictures. Bob Hope, Bing Crosby and Dorothy Lamour traipsing through the Asian country side, trying to stay out of trouble and avoid the bad guys lurking in the bushes. So innocent and such fun. I had to see for myself.

You can get to Mandalay by train or plane from Rangoon (officially renamed Yangon as Burma was renamed Myanmar). Mandalay, for no apparent reason, kept its name. I arrived in Rangoon on Thai Airlines and boarded the airstrip bus for a 100 meter ride to the terminal. When the Army is standing around with automatic weapons in plain view, you board the bus even if it's quicker to walk. Just beyond immigration is the mandatory money changing desk where a minimum of US $200 (or the equivalent in travelers checks or pound sterling) is exchanged for 200 FEC. Anything over $200 is refundable when you leave if you have saved your receipts. Customs is a simple nod, more of a check that you've changed money.

First things first. I went to the departure section of the terminal to confirm my return flight on Thai (everybody overbooks) and returned to the transportation desk to get a taxi ticket for MTT in town (6 FEC). Myanmar Tours and Travel (MTT), is the government agency that controls all transportation. Trains, tours, flights and hotels are booked here for foreigners. It's a drab office with a counter, no furniture and schedules of tours and trains posted on the wall. There are two daily trains to Mandalay, the snazzy express train with a "dining car" (which was full) and the slow one for 30 FEC. I took what I could get. Voucher in hand, I ventured into the other room to pay the cashier. Four Frenchmen that had just booked the same train were conferring in the corner almost out of earshot. The cashier glanced from side to side after collecting my money and whispered for me to come closer. The official exchange rate is 6 Kyat (pronounced chat) to US $1 as he pointed to the official sign. "I will give you 110" and he glanced from side to side again as though looking for spies. I knew there was a black market in currency because I ran the money changing gauntlet from the taxi to the front door of MTT. But I couldn't tell counterfeit money from real Kyat - what better place to get the genuine thing. The government had voided 50's and 100's in 1991. Here, inside the room, I could check to make sure none were slipped in. I changed US $50 and got a roll of Kyat that would choke a horse.

Naturally, the French guys got the same deal. With time to kill, we compared notes on the tax free cigarettes we bought at the airport for resale in Burma for which we expected to profit handsomely on the black market. I asked at the front desk about a flight back from Mandalay since I didn't relish another 14 hour train ride. "Inquire at the Mandalay Hotel. MTT desk." I asked if I could purchase it now only to get the same response. Maybe it wasn't meant to be.

You can fly from Rangoon to Bangkok or Mandalay on Myanmar airlines, if you have the courage and advance reservations. Twenty four notice is needed to make a flight reservation. Courage, since the airline fleet is shrinking because of plane crashes. The price one pays for being a military dictatorship cut off from the rest of the world. Burma is ranked one of the 10 poorest countries. Lack of spare parts - planes fall.

The five of us hit the street at the same time and it was like dragging a carcass through African vultures. We were the only game in town and the hawkers wanted to change our money or book a hotel or get a taxi or sell us anything at all. The RR station was a 20 minute ride in the back of a pickup truck that had bench seats on either side. The Burmese public bus system and prices are negotiated before hand.

The RR terminal is a throw back to WW II with very little maintenance happening since. Literally thousands of people were about. Standing around, sitting or sleeping on benches or the concrete floor. Some watching Government programs on TV and the rest watching the strange white faces. They couldn't have all been waiting for a train. The xenophobic government has only recently opened the country to tourists and we must have looked odd indeed.

The MTT representative at the train station found us and led the way to the correct car after we had time to purchase bottled water and snacks. There are two coaches specifically reserved for tourists. The air was filled with mosquito repellant sprayed on all exposed skin. French and American anti-diarrhea pills were safely stashed in the luggage. And the train pulled out on time leaving thousands of sarong clad men and women still at the station. "Not a pair of pants in sight", a French fellow noted.

It is a comfortable train with one seat on the right and two on the left. Well cushioned with generous leg room and the ability to really recline. All the windows were open and there was a refreshing night breeze. Later, the outside shades came down. Metal panels with slits to allow some air. Finally the inside glass windows were lowered when the night became cool.

The vendors began to canvas the aisles with an assortment of meat kabobs. It could have been chicken, goat, fish. I understand that grasshopper kabob is popular. Mystery meat on a stick. A variety of liquids in plastic bags are offered throughout the night but dire warnings of dysentery keeps me to the water and cookies I bought at the station. The native passengers take out curry and rice and fish they brought with them and the car is filled with exotic aromas. I leaned the seat all the way back, stretched out and dozed off.

The morning came quietly. Muted yellow rays of the sun brighten the lush green fields long before the air becomes warm. Noise from the train startles a flock of resting white egrets in the distance and they fly as one over the empty rice fields. Miles and miles of farm land without a soul in sight until we reach the next town. Houses alongside the track are made of woven straw. Some punctuated with red and aqua marine patches of color. Local tradesmen quickly board the train for a few minutes and children wait for coins tossed from the train. There is no mad scramble for money that misses the mark. Collection is orderly, as if it was going to be shared.

## MANDALAY

English speaking hawkers waited five feet from the coach steps in Mandalay. There are few tourists and the opportunity to sell a taxi ride is not to be missed. I went to the Mandalay Hotel, the city's finest to get a room and book the flight back. Unfortunately, the train took 17 hours and left me 2 hours short of the required 24 necessary to book the next days flight. The hotel was filled with visiting dignitaries, hence, no available rooms. All of this explained at the MTT desk in the lobby of the hotel. I cast my problems back to Aung Zaw Ming, the government representative, for a solution. His English is excellent and the solution was straight forward. The MTT desk has no phone, so he used the hotels' across the lobby to reserve a room in town at the Sapphire (recently approved by the government for tourists) and booked me on the deluxe train in place of the air flight. I bought a city map for less than 50 cents and he volunteered to help with a city tour. The snazzy train back was the express with a dining car. Something to look forward to.

The Sapphire Hotel is in the middle of town, a far more desirable location as far as I was concerned. Two blocks from the market and three from the restaurants recommended in my guide book. The large lobby had a check-in desk, a couch, a small refrigerator for bottled water and lots of open space. They were openly glad to see me and I had the feeling I was the only guest in the hotel. Not so, but I was the only tourist. A 12 year old boy carried my case on his shoulder to the 3rd floor and with bottle of water in hand from the front desk, I was on my own. It's a good sized room with two double beds, private bath and a view of the city through barred windows. Perfectly satisfactory for 20 FEC.

Distances are deceiving in Mandalay. The three block walk to the restaurants took 20 minutes and I got a rude awakening. The MTT map is in English, the street signs in Burmese. Myanmar is one of countries least influenced by the west and I did not expect to find a Burger King or Sizzler. I picked the Mann Restaurant which would have been closed by the health authorities anywhere in America. The sweet and sour chicken came in a mild red sauce with cauliflower and onions. Fride beans (that's how it was spelled) are peas in the pod. A coke and enough rice to feed four, came in just shy of US $2. The menu includes the following categories (in English), pork, fish, eels, prawn, frog, sparrow, brain, egg, duck, liver, vegetables and salad. I got two cold Tiger beers to go for under a dollar each and went to the market.

The inside section sells small electrical appliances and clothing and is uneventful. The surrounding area, which goes on for blocks, is far more interesting. Food stands galore, with sales to the occasional orange clad Buddhist monk. A complete array of fruits and vegetables and an eclectic array of hardware stores with items to repair anything from horse and buggy to pipes and roofs. The shops are rich in softened color and texture and looked like a still life photo. Mine was the only white face among thousands and unlike other countries in Southeast Asia, I didn't draw stares. The people noticed and then went about their business. The camera drew an atypical response as well. There was no objection to picture taking but more one of curiosity or amusement. Some figured it was a hoot that I would want to take their picture at all. They wouldn't pose but they couldn't suppress the smile. Food is plentiful in this agricultural economy and one can absorb a feeling of the culture from an hour in the Zegyo market.

There is no night life in Mandalay, just the sounds and feel of the city. Breakfast was served with ceremony in the second floor lounge of the hotel. On the coffee tables by each couch. Coffee from a large thermos, milk, two fried eggs, 3 pieces of toast, butter, strawberry preserve and bananas. Each plate individually served as though it deserved a dignity of it's own. I felt safe since there were no ill effects from yesterdays supper. A good breakfast for 1 FEC and no problems later.

## PAGODAS

I arranged for a driver and tour at the front desk for 1600 Kyat. Since the driver didn't speak English, we headed for Mr. Ming at MTT in the Mandalay hotel. Ever helpful, he outlined the route for the driver and we were off for some of the most stunning sights in all of Asia. The Shwenandaw Monastery was moved from the Mandalay Palace to the present site in 1880. An all wood building, intricately carved, a surprising survivor WW II when most buildings were burned to the ground. Next door is the Atumashi Monastery looking like a Roman ruin with only the walls and interior pillars remaining. Then, the Kuthodaw Pagoda, 1857, some stunning architecture adorned with aqua and gold paint and white tile. This is the home of the worlds largest book, 729 stone slabs on which are inscribed all the Buddhist scriptures.

The bottom of Mandalay Hill is guarded by two huge concrete lions. From here it's 1700 steps to the top or a fifteen minute serpentine drive. An elevator completes the last 100 feet and a few steps later, I entered another world. A world of glitter and light. Pieces of reflective glass are imbedded in the columns and walls. Not aligned to give a proper reflective image but sufficient to dance the light from surface to surface. Each face of the center square has a separate statue of Buddha in it's own alter. The large outer square is tiled and lined with columns. Worshipers are quietly sleeping on straw mats in random corners. There is an open air restaurant and a variety of gift shops specializing in various depictions of Buddha. And a stunning view of the countryside. Little pagodas on the surrounding hills and green fields as far as the eye can see.

From here we went into the walled grounds of the Mandalay Palace. The buildings are under construction and several are no more than movie prop fronts painted flat red with white and gold trim. These buildings were burned during WW II and the government charges 5 FEC to help restore the site to the old designs.

I ran into the French guys at the Embroidery center, a tourist trap that sells over priced iron work (opium weights and such). They thought they had a buyer for their cigarettes and would find out that night. I told them about the German couple I'd run into that sold their's for no profit at all and wished them well.

Then to the Mahamundi Pagoda, the only one with an entrance fee. All of the monasteries and pagodas up to now were different and the architecture of each unique. This was no exception. A young Buddhist monk trainee practiced ringing a bell several times his size by hitting it with a large wood bat. He looked surprised that I took his picture. I've been through a bit of Southeast Asia and never seen anything as quietly beautiful as the pagodas of Mandalay.

We went to see marble carving which is done on the front lawns of a cluster of single family homes. All statues of Buddha: huge ones, life size ones, small ones, either sitting or lying down. I simply walked by the fence and among the carvers and took pictures at will. They looked up in turn and went back to hammer and chisel as though I was paint on the wall. Wood working is the same, in the front yard of another section of town and they specialized in elephants. Each carved from a single tree trunk and most the size of a pony. Nothing to take home here.

When I returned to the hotel for my bag, they offered the use of my old room for a shower and gave me a fresh liter of bottled water for the train. Gracious indeed. This train ride was shorter, 14 hours. "Dining car" meant that you could order food and eat in your seat. They passed out a menu in English with the following : cheese sandwich, chicken sandwich, hamburger, cheese burger, fried egg, scrambled egg, toast, french toast, tea, Nescafe, coffee mix, maltova, black coffee, orange squash, ice tea. I didn't have the courage to try. Back to cookies and water.

The sunset was breath taking. Miles of bright crimson that silhouetted the trees and contrasted with the green of the fields. I stared at the colors until darkness set in and went to sleep. Sunrise was slow. The mood was set when I saw a single file of eight workers walking through waist high grain fields colored gold by the mornings sun. Bob. Bing. Dorothy. Things have changed.

THE END

## SIDEBAR FOR MANDALAY

GETTING THERE - Bangkok is serviced from the USA by United, Northwest, Delta, Air France, British Airways, Canadian Airlines, Cathay Pacific, China Airlines, Singapore Air, Swissair and Thai Airlines. The lowest fare of $1200 RT is on China. The American carriers charge $1680 RT coach. Bangkok to Rangoon (Yangon) is $234 RT on Thai Airlines and a few dollars less on Myanmar Air which is not recommended because of a bad safety record. A visa can be obtained in Bangkok for $33 and 3 passport photos with a two day waiting period.

A flight from Yangon to Mandalay is a little over an hour. Trains depart daily in both directions and tourists can only buy upper-class tickets (first class). The normal train takes 17 hours and costs 30 FEC. The express "with dining car" takes 14 hours for 38 FEC.

LOCAL ARRANGEMENTS - All transportation, hotels and tours must be booked with the local Myanmar Tours and Travel (MTT) office. In Yangon, it's in the middle of downtown at the corner of Sule Pagoda Rd. and Maha Bandoola St. In Mandalay it's at the Mandalay Hotel. They will book trains, planes, hotels and have a variety of tours. Hotels and tours can be arranged with any taxi driver that meets you at the train or plane station and what you get is up to you.

CAUTIONS AND REQUIREMENTS - The government is paranoid about journalists or anyone that appears to work for the media. Take care when filing in the visa application. I left a substantial amount of camera equipment behind in Bangkok. You are required to exchange US $200 or the equivalent in travelers checks or pound sterling upon arrival for 200 FEC. They recognize the need for hard currency. Money in excess of $200 can be exchanged back if you keep your receipts.

HEALTH - Burma defines third world. There is definite exposure to basilic and amoebic dysentery so bring a supply of Imodium and Pepto

241

Bismol or Kaopectate. Although Malaria is not reported to be a problem in the major tourist areas, it can't hurt to bring repellant with DEET. Don't drink the water. Hotels will supply bottled water for the room. Bottled coke, water and beer are easy to find. I did not get sick in Mandalay.

THE BLACK MARKET - You need two pockets to carry separate money. One for FEC which is the hard currency equivalent of US dollars and needed for taxi rides from the airport and all MTT booked travel and hotels. The official exchange rate is $1 = 6 Kyat but dollars can be exchanged for 110 Kyat and travelers checks for 120 virtually anywhere. If you don't use the black market Kyat, a simple meal will cost $35 instead of $2. Do not accept 50 or 100 Kyat notes, they are worthless. At black market exchange rates for dollars, Burma is a bargain.

FOR MORE INFORMATION - Write: Myanmar National Tourist Office, 2514 University Dr., Durham, NC 27707. tel. (919)- 493-7500. Or The Embassy of Myanmar, 2300 S St. N.W., Washington DC 20008. tel. (202)332-9044

These men risk their lives to bring you Birds Nest Soup!

NIAH NATIONAL PARK - I'd heard about the guys that climb rock walls to get nests for the Chinese delicacy, "Birds Nest soup", but I'd never seen the place where, each year, several of them fall to their death. It's not a sport, these chaps expose themselves to a 100 foot fall for one reason only - money. They are just trying to make a living.

We were picked up at the Miri airport by Engu, our English speaking guide. Two tourists in the back of a van that seats nine for a two hour ride on a paved but bumpy road, south to the town of Niah. It's a small village of 19,000 with no mall, no small shopping arcade, not even a McDonalds. In fact, the most modern building in town was our hotel, the Niah Cave Inn. It's the best in town and modest by USA standards. A quick in and out and it was time for lunch. Our guide drove us (three blocks) to a restaurant, on the far side of town, that looked like it needed a visit from the public health department. I watched as we drove through the town and I didn't see anyplace that looked better.

Engu interpreted, and we had the special. Beef, chicken, vegetables, rice and cans of soda. It was tasty and I had Imodium close at hand just in case - this is the third world and dysentery is always on one's mind.

Back in the van for a couple of miles and we were at the National park center, entrance is by permit only. Normally you would have had to arrange for a permit in advance but this is a tour so fees are paid and paperwork already done. A ten minute walk through the park grounds ends at the Niah River boat dock. Reportedly, the river has crocodiles and snakes but we didn't see any and we were there for 20 minutes. Not that the river is that wide but the motor boat that was going to take us across was drifting downstream while the boatman kept trying to start the outboard engine. Finally, a boat from the far side of the river came to his rescue before he drifted the 17 KM downstream to the South China Sea.

The trip across took less than a minute, the walk ahead was something else. There is a boardwalk for the next several miles and it can be a pleasant stroll through the jungle. The planks are Belian wood which are so heavy they don't float in water but they are durable. I was wearing a photo jacket to help carry extra lenses, a flash, film and assorted stuff that go with a heavy professional camera. All of this equipment didn't weigh very much at the beginning of the walk even though it was 100 degrees with 100% humidity. Several miles later I felt as if I was carrying a Buick.

Just at the fork in the road - left to the Rumah Chang longhouses and right to the caves - are two women, senior citizens, selling fruit and soda, bottled water and beer. Most disheartening is the fact that they carry all their wares in and out on the same boardwalk we're on. My clothes are sopping wet with perspiration. Any self respect I had is now gone.

Right around the corner is a large, open, iron gate which seems completely out of place in the middle of the jungle. Actually, it's there to keep out poachers. You see, the collection of the birds nests is government regulated. Only the local Penan tribe have the concession and collection time is limited to two seasons - May to June, after the breeding season and in October when new nests are made. The men collect the nests before eggs are laid so the Swiftlets just make new nests. The nests sell for US$ 200 a kilo and the tribe keeps close watch on who enters the caves.

A little farther is a steep indent on the rock as though a pie slice has been taken out of the hill. Bamboo poles line the inside walls, a frame, lacking the connecting shelves. At one time this was a trading center for the area. As a matter of fact, evidence has been found that this area has been occupied by humans for 40,000 years. At the far end, the floor changes to that of a moon surface with subdued lighting, filtered, by both the jungle trees outside and the vines dangling from the caves edge. It's a setting for a Steven King movie and if there were monsters, there are enough rock outcroppings inside for them to hide behind.

We climb out of the far end of the cave, walk along the narrow rock ledge, turn the corner and there it is - Kuala Besar, the Great cave.

Standing outside in the light, looking in, it's huge and it's dark. I can't see the roof of the cave itself and 300 feet ahead is a split level wood house inside the cave. I'm delighted, a concession stand with food, drink, a rest room and comfortable chairs. Up to now there has been no place to sit. There are 4 million swiftlets and several million bats that live in these caves. It figures that all of their guano is not confined to the outside of the cave, if you catch my drift. Any rock you sit on has a layer of, guess what.

We cross a small wood bridge to enter the cave and walk along a dome shaped, pock marked, enormous rock floor that ends in a ledge at the far side. At the back of the cave, to my left, are long flights of wood stairs that lead up to tunnels that connect to interior caves. The ones that are pitch black. The cave of bones to the left, Burnt cave straight ahead and Moon cave and Sleeping Place to the right. But the Great cave is fascinating and this is as far as I go. My friend and Engu, flashlight in hand, climb the stairs and disappear into the darkness. I go to the concession stand to break out all this camera equipment I lugged in. A quick look and I realize that the concession building is actually the home base for the birds nest collectors. They live here. They're cooking a meal, clothes are hung out to dry. But there's a bench on the porch to sit on, to hell with the guano, I sat.

Bamboo poles hang from the ceiling and that's what the men shimmy up to get to the roof. They reach out with hands and sticks to knock the nests loose and their partner on the ground collects them. No safety net, no tie lines. A slipped hand and it's death 100 feet below. The cave is far too big to effectively use the camera flash, so I resorted to time exposure photography. Fortunately, there are flat sections of rock that will hold the camera steady for pictures of the roof. Pictures that can see, with time exposure, what the eye can't in real time. I spotted a large mushroom shaped rock 30 feet high, close to the cave entrance, with a guide sitting on top. It reminded me of Alice in Wonderland. There was no ladder, I don't know how he got up there. The swiftlets are day flyers and the bats nocturnal, so if you have the inclination, you can wait till dusk and watch the changing of the guard.

# THE BEST MEAL IN BORNEO

That night it was back to the same no name restaurant with no menu. But it seemed to be the hot spot in town since it was full with young guys drinking beer and swapping lies. So far we Americans didn't get sick so we figured to try something different - wild boar, jungle ferns, green leaves, prawn, rice and a quart size bottle of Tiger beer. It was absolutely wonderful. Ask for it, wild boar and jungle ferns.

# ON THE ROAD AGAIN

Breakfast was different. The restaurant with no menu found an egg and toast to go with a glass of coffee and a can of orange juice. The more adventuresome had fried noodles. Just out of town, we stopped at a roadside produce stand. They have red and green colored fruit that looks like spiny sea urchins. Hidden beneath that formidable skin is a translucent white, mildly sweet fruit and it's very good. Fresh cucumbers with salt is good too.

An hour up the road is Lambir Hills National Park. The walk is a gradual climb, slippery in spots but relatively easy to negotiate. The first falls are pretty but continue on, cross the bridge to Latak falls. There are picnic benches and a beautiful waterfall. Sit for a while and if you are quiet enough, the sounds the birds and monkeys will return. If you have the time, the park encompasses 6952 hectares of land and miles and miles of trails. Or you can wade into the pool at the base of the waterfall and wash the guano from the seat of your pants.

# THE END

## NIAH SIDEBAR

GETTING THERE - We came from Singapore (to the east) which is serviced by Northwest, United, Garuda and Singapore Airlines (US $1300 RT from the USA west coast). Then from Johor Bahru airport just across the Singapore border, to Kuching, Sarawak ($60 US) where we bought a tour for $200 (per person) from Tropical Adventure Tours, Ground Floor, Mega Hotel, Lot 907, Jalan Merbau, 98000 Miri, you can also write to them at P.O. Box 2197, 98008 Miri, Sarawak, Malaysia. tel. 60-85-419337 or 414553 Fax 60-85-414503, internet= http://www.jaring. my/sebweb/tropical/main.html The tour included air from Kuching to Miri, pickup at the airport, all transport thereafter, the best hotel in Batu Niah, all fees, all meals and a tour guide throughout. I considered doing the trip independently but at this price, it wasn't worth the effort. We made the mistake of booking through Borneo Excursion Travel, who is not recommended, but the tour was done by Tropical Adventure, who is recommended.

WHEN TO GO - The rainy season is from October to March with the heaviest in December and January. Sarawak is virtually on the equator so count on warm weather and high humidity, year round. Bring an umbrella, no matter.

WHERE TO STAY - The best is in the center of town the Niah Cave Inn, Lot 621, Batu Niah Bazaar, 98200 Miri, Sarawak, Malaysia. Tel. (6) 085-737333 or 737999 Fax (6) 085-737332. US $ 40 for a double room. If they are full, there is the Park View Hotel, tel (6) 085-737021. There are chalets at the park center which are nice but very lonely at night. They have to be booked with the National Park Service and you can do that with Tropical Adventure Tours.

In Miri, there is the 4 star Mega Hotel, Lot 907, Jalan Merbau, 98000 Miri or write to P.O. Box 1165, 98008 Miri, Sarawak, Malaysia. Tel. (6) 085-432432, Fax (6) 085-433433 email: megahot@po.jaring.my Singles from US $100 to $1000, double from $150 - 1000. The 3 star Dynasty Hotel, Lot 683, Block 9, Jalan Pujut-Lutong, CDT 20, 98009 Miri, Sarawak, Malaysia. email: dyhlmyy@po.jaring.my has doubles from US $ 80. All rooms have 10% service and 5% govt. tax added on.

WHAT TO DO - If you stay in the park there is nothing to do at night. The town is not a hotbed of activity either but there are people in restaurants and on the street. After a full day of hiking, you may want a good nights sleep and it doesn't matter.

FOR MORE INFORMATION- Write to the Malaysian Tourist office at 818 West 7th St, Suite 804, Los Angeles, CA 90017 Tel. (213) 689-9702 or 595 Madison Ave., Suite 1800, New York, NY 10022 Tel (212)754-1113.

PENANG ISLAND, lots to see other than the
Pit Vipers in the Temple

James Bond Island - renamed after the film

GEORGETOWN, PENANG - Youseff hustled us as we walked by. Not a hard hustle - he would stay with us for the next hour and keep asking until we finally gave in. Ten ringggits an hour for a city tour on his bicycle rickshaw was a better price than the drivers on the main street but at 120 pounds, wringing wet, I wondered how long he could last in this heat.

## CITY TOUR

After brief stops at a few temples, we went to the grave of Francis Light, the founder of Penang. This island is the oldest British settlement in Malaysia and even predates Singapore. Captain Light took over this virtually uninhabited island in 1786 and Georgetown went on to become a prosperous trade center. The cemetery is well shaded and only occasional beams of light penetrated the trees. Combined with the dark, well aged head stones, this scene was like a setting from the Twilight Zone. Just the three of us, the quiet, the eerie lighting and only the sound of our footsteps to indicate life. The street was more comfortable.

On to the bustle of the waterfront and the boat people. Not immigrants but a small segment of the population that live on ramshackle floating houses that would never make it if put to sea. Then we went past the colonial homes facing the coast with a warm sea breeze in our face. Beautiful mansions befitting the splendor of the past.

Finally, the delightful WAT CHAYKALARAM, home of the 100 foot Reclining Buddha, third longest in the world. The major Thai temple in town, with green and brown serpent dragons, red, white and glittering gold houses, ornately designed grill gates in red and the female like Buddha taking a nap with her eyes open.

Two and a half hours later we were back at the hotel. Youseff had held up quite well. Next on the agenda was Penang hill (2500 feet) for sunset. This time we got Danny from a taxi queue a few blocks from our hotel. He had our undivided attention for the 20 minute drive and had a deal to offer. He would come back to the cable car station at 9 PM (since we could never find a taxi at that hour) and had a good price for the island tour. We

intended to use public busses but, after some negotiation, the convenience
of having transportation on demand was too good to pass up.

The cable car trip is in two sections of 15 minutes each, changing cars
at mid point. As forbidding as the hill is, the cable car dropped passengers
off along the way. There are houses hidden among the trees. One is among
three huge boulders. Big enough to crush the house if any of them toppled.
I wouldn't be able to sleep at night.

The top affords a stunning view of Georgetown at night but the
restaurant is a dump. I had an A&W RUT BIR, locally canned and
watched Wheel of Fortune on TV in English. Sure enough, Danny was
waiting at the bottom of the hill. And he was right on time the following
morning in his Volvo. A car that goes for about US $80,000 in Malaysia.
Hummm.

## THE ISLAND TOUR

First stop was the Botanical Gardens, for the monkeys not the flowers.
It's against the rules to feed the monkeys in the park, so the monkeys
simply moved outside the gate to beg. Clever little fellows that will take
food right from your hand. Males, females, babies hanging onto their
mothers backs. It's a living.

The KEK LOK SI is the largest Buddhist Temple in Malaysia,
constructed between 1890 and 1910. Tour busses cannot negotiate the
narrow winding road into the mountains, so it's a half hour uphill walk
for those folks. Danny found a spot inside the gate. The beautifully colored
buildings are of Chinese design at the bottom, Burmese at the top and
Thai in the middle. A dozen levels contoured into the mountain side with
a courtyard, plazas and various viewing towers. A must see. There were
firecrackers lying about and I lit one. A screaming rocket went into the
air with more sound than fury. Unfortunately, the noise drew an angered
monk in orange robes. He chased us to the car. While the monk vented
his spleen at Danny in Malaysian, we drove off.

I had heard about the temple with pit vipers hanging from the chandeliers. Reportedly, they didn't bite tourists but I had to see for myself. The entrance is announced with a collection of huge red, green and yellow smoking candles that are a sight unto themselves. I entered the small temple careful where I stepped. A few feet away, I saw the alter with vined sticks planted in the top of a vase at either end. Candles provided light and smoke filled the air. I looked up, no chandelier. As I got closer, I saw a collection of eggs just beneath the snakes twirled among the sticks and the sign on the wall, "All visitors touching or handling the snakes do so at their own risk". Wagler's Pit Vipers, three feet long within easy reach were comfortably curled on the collection of sticks at each end of the alter. They remained undisturbed by the visitors. In the adjacent room are photographers anxious to take your picture with a de-fanged snake wrapped around your neck. The harmless ones have a red paint spot on the top of their head. The photography business was not good that day.

Where do the local people go to get away from it all? Kerawang Waterfall, in the middle of the island. A fresh mountain stream meanders through the jungle, over rocks and under a bridge to the sea. The narrow road next to the entrance is lined with shops. My first experience with the renown durian fruit. Durian is banned from hotels and airports because of it's foul odor. They say that once you get by the ugly smell, the fruit is delicious. So we gave it a try. They lie, it tastes just as bad as it smells. I needed mouthwash, a drink, a towel for my tongue, anything. As we left for the butterfly farm, Danny told us a story. He was on his way home, off duty, with some durian in the trunk of the cab when he was stopped by two Australians for a ride to the airport. He reluctantly agreed to take them and watched the rear view mirror as he drove. Ten minutes later he could see them sniff the air and look at each other, puzzled. They couldn't place the smell and looked about the cab to determine the origin of the stench that continued even with the windows open. Danny said nothing for the ½ hour ride and the two literally fell from the cab in their haste to exit. A smell that defies description and can permeate metal. Be warned.

The Butterfly farm is fascinating. They fly about freely from flower to leaf in a large enclosure and might land on your shoulder if you remained still. Red, indigo, brown, white, yellow. Butterflies with one color on the top of their wings and another on the bottom. Ones that disappear on a leaf when they close their wings. Absolutely stunning.

A stop at the north shore for sunset and a cold coconut drink and back to town. Danny was never without a story, didn't ask for more money and was more companion than guide. A people person who didn't make enough money on us for his car payment. We left a few days later. Guess who took us to the airport?

THE END

## PENANG SIDEBAR

GETTING THERE - The easiest route is through Kuala Lumpur (KL) on Malaysia Airlines. Price from Los Angeles is around $1300 RT advance purchase. However, I went from Singapore which is serviced by Northwest and Singapore Airlines from LA for the same price. Consolidator tickets from LAX to Singapore are available for around $800 RT. Consult the travel section adds in your newspaper. Round trip airfare from Singapore to Penang with a stopover at KL or Medan, Sumatra is $300. Purchase in Singapore at any travel agency.

WHEN TO GO - Penang has an Equatorial climate and is hot through out the year. The wettest months are September to November.

WHERE TO STAY - The nicest hotels are on the north side of the island at Batu Ferringhi Beach. Golden Sands Resort tel. 011-60-4-811911. Rasa Sayang Resort tel. 011-60-4-811811 for $250 double. Holiday Inn tel. 011-60-4-811601 for $150 double. Modest accommodations are available in Georgetown, the capital. The Waldorf Hotel tel. 011-60-4-626140 is $45 for a double.

WHERE TO EAT - the strongest influences here are Chinese and Indian there are restaurants within a block of anywhere you stay. Western food is available when you tire of Chinese and curry. It's safest to eat at the hotels and even the modest ones have restaurants.

WHAT TO DO - There are, in essence, two tours. The city tour of Georgetown which should be done by bicycle rickshaw at about $6 per hour (depending on your bargaining skills). The island tour can be done by cab, by arrangement of course, for about $70 for the whole day. That doesn't include meals and any park fees but you can stay as long as you want, where you want. Ours was with Danny Lim, Cosmos Tours, 1-A, 1st Floor, Hotel Oriental, Penang Road, 10000 Penang, Malaysia. Tel.

04- 631-011, fax 04-636567, home phone tel. 04-688392. He is a real character and added to the whole trip.

MORE INFORMATION - Write to the Malaysian Tourist Board, 818 West 7th St., Los Angeles, CA 90017. Tel. (213)689-9702

## THE KILLING FIELDS OF CAMBODIA

PHNOM PENH, CAMBODIA - Legend has it that four statues of Buddha were deposited here by the waters of the Mekong river and discovered by a woman named Penh. A pagoda, Wat Phnom, was erected at the site atop a 27 meter knoll. Hence, the name Phnom Penh, the hill of Penh.

Many of us were introduced to Cambodia by the academy award winning film "The Killing Fields". A grim and realistic portrayal of the torture and extermination of tens of thousands of innocent men, women and children at the hands of the Khmer Rouge. Pol Pot was determine to keep control by exterminating the educated members of the populace and turning the rest into farmers. The insanity of Cambodians killing Cambodians started in 1975 and continued until the Vietnamese Army occupied the city in 1979. Viet Nam finally withdrew in 1991 to allow the United Nations to install a transitional government and have fair elections. An election was held, the UN withdrew and the Khmer Rouge moved back into some of the rural areas. Phnom Penh, the capital, is safe from the rebels but the Cambodian army has not rid the countryside of routine terrorism.

There are no burned out buildings in downtown to indicate the effects of artillery shells. Most of the population is under 20 and the exterminations are only a note in history to them, but the effects of Pol Pot and the Vietnamese occupation are apparent in the dire economic conditions that still exist. Few streets, even in downtown, are paved. There is a lack of street lights and intersections are a confusion of cars, motorcycles and tricycle taxis trying to weave their way through. Eventually they all get across but pedestrians have to be on their toes when crossing. The key is to walk slowly and they will drive around you.

All is not grim even though this is the third world. There are three deluxe hotels with excellent restaurants. Even the moderate hotels have reasonable accommodations and restaurants with food that is safe to eat. The No Problem Café is a must visit, if just to relax in the comfortable lounge with a gin and tonic. The Central Market, a block west of the Diamond Hotel, is worth a visit. As is the Hotel Le Royal, seven blocks north of the Diamond. Most journalists stayed here between 1970 and 1975 and scenes from "The Killing Fields" were set here (filmed in Thailand). The Royal is undergoing renovation and should be a first class hotel when it reopens. Automobile taxis are available by phone and tricycle, single seat taxis are on every block. A dollar will get you across town on a cyclo but you had better know where you are going. The drivers (peddlers) don't speak English nor read maps.

Celebrations are held throughout the country at the end of the monsoon season, mid-November. In Phnom Penh, boat races take place on the Mekong and are best seen from the grounds of the Cambodian Hotel. It's the best hotel in town and the races can be viewed while having lunch.

Tuol Svay Prey High School was take over by Pol Pot's security forces in 1975 and turned into Security Prison 21 (S-21). It is now a museum giving testament to the brutality of the Khmer Rouge. Turning left from the entrance (small fee) there are gravestones in the central courtyard to mark those who died under torture. The 25 X 25 foot rooms that used to hold students are starkly bare except that each has a single steel frame bed, with springs, sitting alone in the center. No mattress, no chair, only a picture on the wall showing a victim on that bed in 1975. Light shines through bars, now rusting, on the large windows. It is quiet, eerie. The next building has 5 x 10 foot holding cells, without doors or beds. Just bars on the windows and an empty pot on the floor. The next building has a sign to explain the barbed wire on the second and third floors was to prevent suicides. Prison rules are posted and they send chills up your spine. The last building on the right shows a collection of torture boxes constructed by the Khmer to extract confessions. Each has a painting on the wall showing the device in use. The final display is a map of Cambodia made from human skulls. The Khmer Rouge were meticulous in keeping records, like the Nazis, and over 17,000 people were taken from here to the "killing fields" south of town.

After this gruesome museum, it's best to see the Royal Palace. Although 60% of the contents were destroyed by Pol Pot, what remains is stunning to behold. The center piece and largest building is the Throne Hall. The present structure is 100 by 30 meters and built in 1919 to replace the wooden structure erected in 1869. The columns and stairs are Italian marble and the 59 meter high tower was inspired by the Bayon Temple at Angkor Wat. Inside is the silver Pagoda, so named because of the 5000 silver tiles that line the floor. On a pedestal atop the dais is a 200 pound gold Buddha decorated with 9584 diamonds. Cameras are not permitted inside.

The Killing Fields, Choeung Ek, are located 15 KM south of town. Reached by a pothole strewn dirt road with narrow bridges that appear barely able to bear the weight of a car let alone a tour bus. It is best visited on a day following S-21. At the center of the entrance is a multi-level glass stupa filled with the skulls of 8000 victims. They are arranged on the shelves by sex and age. The sole guide of this memorial site shows one of the hooked steel crowbars used to crush the heads of many that were thrown into mass graves. The Khmer Rouge wanted to spare the expense of bullets. Eighty six of the one hundred twenty nine communal graves have been unearthed as the depressions in the surrounding ground attest. Some no bigger than 30 x 30 feet with the remains of 400 people. Each hole has a sign indicating the number of victims buried. Pieces of bone punctuate the ground no matter where you walk. Least we forget, it is a clear reminder that evil continues in this world.

After this gruesome piece of history, a brief respite can be had at the elegant bar of the No Problem Café. Perhaps some shopping at the stores on either side or a walk east towards the Mekong. On the corner, on the second story, is the Foreign Correspondents Club (open to the public). A drink, some lunch, while watching the water flow by. The Mekong is the life blood to millions of survivors.

# THE END

## SIDEBAR FOR PHNOM PENH

GETTING THERE - The usual entry to Phnom Penh is from Bangkok, Thailand to the west on Thai or Cambodia Air for approximately $250 RT. Service is also available from Saigon (Ho Chi Minh City) on Viet Nam Airlines, Aeroflot from Russia (via India) and Singapore Airlines from Singapore. There is no other practical way to get to Phnom Penh except by air. Round trip to Bangkok or Singapore from the west coast of the USA is roughly $1200.

There are a number of tour companies that offer packages to Cambodia, Laos and Viet Nam for those not interested in independent travel. Most of the time in Cambodia is devoted to visiting the temples of Angkor Wat. Prices start at approximately $1000 from Bangkok for 7 days. A 17 day tour including Singapore and Viet Nam is approximately $4600, including air fare from Los Angeles. Call the following companies for their brochures: Advantage Travel (800)882-2098, Wings of the World (416)482-1223, Adventure Center (800)227-8747.

ACCOMMODATIONS - The best in town is the Cambodian Hotel on the Mekong River for $200 double. Certainly a 4 star hotel. The Diamond Hotel is deluxe as is the Allson only a block away. Both are in downtown and rates are $90 single, $130 double. The quality falls off sharply to 2 stars, at best, for the Asie across the street from the Diamond and the Pailin and the Paradis two blocks south and the Hotel Renakse across from the Royal Palace. All are about $35 for a double. The Hawaii Hotel, east of the central market, is new and has singles for $35.

FOOD - First, don't drink the water. Each of the afore mentioned hotels have ground floor restaurants. They cater to tourists and the food is safe to eat. Available are Thai, French and Western style. The best restaurant in town is the No Problem Café, No. 55, Street 178. It's about 1 KM north of the Hotel Cambodian and managed by Thierry Dauptain, an ex-patriot Frenchman who has managed first class restaurants through

259

out south-east Asia. The guarded grounds are open every day and the food is excellent.

LOCAL ARRANGEMENT - Local tours can be made at the better hotels. A personal city tour by taxi can be arranged at any hotel. Three hours for $10. Especially helpful was Mr. Prayut Voeung, Checkpoint, Lobby Floor, Diamond Hotel, 172-184 Monivong Blvd, Phnom Penh, Cambodia. tel. (855)23-26635, fax (855)23-16637. He is a bright young man, English fluent and was able to put together a tour of Angkor Wat when local travel agents could not.

HEALTH - There are no vaccinations required for entry into Cambodia. However, it would be prudent to update your normal vaccinations including measles and polio and consider gamma globulin for infectious hepatitis. Even though Malarial mosquitos are more prevalent in the north, along the Thai border, it would be a good idea to protect yourself with Larium (once a week) or doxycycline (taken daily). Spray exposed skin with repellant containing DEET (at least 20%) since Larium and the other medicines do not prevent malaria but mearly suppress the symptoms. Take Imodium and Pepto- Bismol for gastro intestinal problems. It is best to be in good health before entering Cambodia since the medical facilities will not match those Westerners are used to. Remember this is the third world.

MISCELLANEOUS - Visas are required and can be purchased at the newly renovated airport for $20 and a passport size picture. Money can be changed at the airport but it's not necessary to get Cambodian money since prices through out the country are also quoted in US dollars. Riels only come in small denominations so US $100 would yield enough stacks of riels to fill a briefcase. Credit cards are accepted. The Cyclo bar at the Cambodian and the No Problem Café are the only two places for night life.

You want to buy a used camel? The PUSHKAR
Fair is the place for you.

PUSHKAR, INDIA - New camels, slightly used camels, camels driven by an old lady on holy days. That's the theme for the fair even though I didn't personally witness any of the camel transactions. Transportation sales are the same the world over. But, I'm getting ahead of myself.

We started at Le Meridien Hotel in New Delhi, a five star establishment known for it's beautiful atrium, headed for tents inside the "world famous Pushkar Fair". I'd never heard of Pushkar before this trip. but, what did I know. The schedule said a seven hour bus trip to our overnight at a Maharaja's Palace, then on to Pushkar. The bus stopped on the outskirts of town to view a statue of Shiva, a local custom meant to give us luck in our travels. Shiva the destroyer, has 1008 names, and takes many forms. The Champion of animals, Lord of the dance, the entity without which creation could not have occurred. All very confusing to me, but there's no reason to turn down good luck.

261

In no time we hit road construction which slowed things down but not nearly as much as the news that there was a demonstration in the town ahead. Our modern, air-conditioned bus took to the side roads. Apparently in an area our driver wasn't familiar with since he stopped to ask directions four times. We got to the Castle Mandawa Hotel (12 hours elapsed time) at eight o'clock, just in time for supper. A marvelous outdoor buffet in the courtyard. The castle, built in 1775, consists of several buildings. Some connect, some don't and finding your way around is a challenge at night. Narrow doors, narrower stairs and twisting corridors made me wish I had chalk to mark the way. My room was cluster of several small rooms. I entered to a waiting room with a couch. To the left is another furnished room (no door) with no apparent use. Straight ahead and up two steps to the bedroom, big enough for two beds. The good sized bathroom (with door) is attached to the bedroom. It's all quite nicely done and would qualify as a suite on a square foot basis.

Narrow stairwells and twisting corridors are done on purpose in castles. It's much easier to defend if the bad guys have to come at you one at a time. There isn't much to see in the town but the castle is worth a roll of film.

Fortunately, we got to the fair by the next afternoon to check into "best available Swiss tents" at the Raj Resorts. Time for some clarification here. The town has a normal population of 13,000. During fair time, it's close to 250,000 and all the hotels are booked well in advance. And at ten times their normal price. Hence, a number of tent cities are constructed just for the weeks of the fair. Next, don't take the word 'resort' literally. Mind you it was a spacious tent with an attached bath (porcelain to sit on and a tiny sink) but not one of our group had the courage to test the make-shift shower. It looked like the runoff water would drain out under the beds. That's if you could figure out how to work the shower at all.

I got a map of the area and noticed that the Raj was off the map. However, camel driven carts were at the entrance to take us to the area of festivities (about 1 ½ miles). The carts aren't faster than walking but it's easier. The fair is an annual event with the exact date set by the Hindu lunar calendar whereby the devotees can cleanse away their sins by bathing in the holy lake. We were warned that cameras weren't welcome at the lake. Photographers have been attacked in the past for taking pictures in this area.

In addition to the mass of people, there are 50,000 camels and cattle for livestock trading, horse and camel races, street theater, musicians, mystics, a Ferris wheel and shops galore. If you want to buy anything in India, you can buy it here.

We just touched on the main street shops the first night. There is a huge tent with over 100 stalls inside selling everything from gold earrings to shoes.

Since this is a holy site, there is no alcohol, no meat, no eggs and lots of potatoes. Over the next several meals, I was presented with 15 ways to do potatoes. At first, it's a novelty but after a while one longs for a beer and a hard boiled egg.

The following day we walked the fairgrounds. Tourists on camels, Hindus on the ferris wheel, women wearing the brightest of silks. Translucent yellow, orange, red, green flowing in the sun as the women moved through aisles. And the smells, every fifty feet there was a barbecue (no meat but lots of spices). Colorful necklaces, silk scarfs and gowns, kitchen ware, carefully crafted metal bracelets that sparkled in the light, flowers for sale, leather bags for your money and leather jackets for the cold nights. And a man making knives the old fashioned way, with a forge, anvil and hammer.

For you shoppers out there, yes, they do bargain.

Least you get the wrong impression of our tent city accommodations, we had real plates and silverware, cloth covered tables, plenty of vegetables to eat and a live band. They did a good job considering what they had to work with (and I like potatoes).

This collection of Indian religion, festival and commerce is unique. It's an experience unknown to 99.9% of the world's population. Oh, I found that I am allergic to camels, go figure.

## THE END

## SIDEBAR FOR THE PUSHKAR FAIR

GETTING THERE - There are a number of connecting flights to New Delhi from the west coast, usually through Bangkok, Hong Kong or Singapore. The low season (March to mid-May and September to November) has a discounted RT fare of $999 from the west coast with similar fares from the east coast (connecting through Europe). High season (June to August and December to January) fares are around $1500 RT.

The bus trip from New Delhi to Pushkar will probably require an overnight stay in the middle. It's best to get a package including lodgings at Pushkar since they are at a premium during the fair.

HOTELS - The Hotel Castle Mandawa is a popular overnight stay on the way to the fair. Rooms are $28-44 single, $35-88 double. tel. 01592-23124, fax 23171. Hotels at Pushkar have rates ranging from $10-45 but are booked a year in advance for the fair. Even the tent accommodations are booked well in advance but they are inside the grounds and provide meals. RTDC's Tourist Village has standard tents for $70s/85d, attached bath tents for $105s/120d and deluxe huts for $120s/135d all include meals. tel.0141-202586, fax.201045. Royal Tents are $175s/225d with private bath and meals. tel. 0291-433316, fax. 635373. Royal Desert Camp is $90s/100d with bath and meals and free shuttle service. tel.72001,fax72226.

FOOD - Food poisoning is a danger throughout India. It would probably be safer to eat at the hotel/tent keeping in mind the limited selection no matter where you eat (no meat, fish, eggs, alcohol).

HEALTH - Don't drink the water. That said, it is prudent to be up to date on Diphtheria, tetanus, polio, hepatitis A and typhoid. This is a third world country.

MISCELLANEOUS - Visas are required for USA citizens. For additional information contact the consulate at 3550 Wilshire Blvd., Suite 204, LA, CA 90010, tel. 213-380-8855, fax 380-6111, OR, 1270 Avenue of the Americas, Suite 1808, NY, NY 10020, tel. 212-586-4901, fax. 582-3274, web site= www.tourindia.com

## HO CHI MINH CITY

Still called Saigon by most, it's ready for business and
welcomes tourists with open arms.

TAN SON NHAT AIRPORT, SAIGON - I never figured to get
thrown out of the country just after getting there. Well, maybe a fleeting
thought. I had a letter from a visa service explaining that I was allowed
to fly into Ho Chi Minh City. The letter went on to say, in English and
Vietnamese, that I would be met at the airport by a representative with my
visa. I was assured things would be fine. Yeah, right.

The rep never showed but there is a visa application counter in the
small waiting area. I don't know if our letter was any help since the official
barely gave it a glance but in 15 minutes and several forms later, there were
the visas. The same forms we filled out for the visa service n the U.S., by
the way. I must admit to some trepidation at being an American in Viet
Nam, the reception could be hostile. Nothing could have been further
from the truth. The custom officials were courteous, the cab driver went
out of his way to find a hotel in our price range and the people at the hotel
were happy to have us. I had a sense of too much friendliness, which tends
to make me suspicious. It took a few days, but I got over it and found the
people to be genuinely warm and helpful. Aside from the ever present street
hustlers, but that I expected.

## THE WALKING TOUR

The best way to see any city is with your feet on the pavement. So
I worked out a circular walk and you can really start anywhere on the
circle. We began on Le Loi Blvd. close to the Ben Thanh market where the
locals shop for fresh fish and vegetables. It was built in 1914 of reinforced
concrete and covers 11 square kilometers. In front is a belfry and clock,
a symbol of Saigon. We didn't go in but walked the boulevard east and
window shopped the hundreds of stores making mental notes on route to

the Rex Hotel. We would return later to the Rex which served as the hotel of choice for Military Officers during the war. The lobby/lounge is warm, rich, comfortable and a great place to watch French, German and Japanese businessmen run up their expense accounts. A good place for an afternoon drink. Rooms start at US$ 190 and go to $1500 a night. We continued a block further to the Caravelle Hotel for a sumptuous breakfast on the 9th floor for six bucks. From the table you overlook the length of Le Loi Blvd., the Rex, miles of stores and the Continental Hotel across the street. One of the best views in town and good food to boot.

From there, you backtrack to the Rex and turn right to the stunning Hotel de Ville (town hall) built by the French in 1908. It houses the City People's Committee and isn't open to the public. Least I forget, blocking the view is a statue of Ho Chi Minh, compassionately holding a child. Around the corner is the Saigon tourist office which has no free literature. Don't bother.

Nguyen Hue Blvd. starts at the Hotel de Ville and runs SE to the Saigon River. It's as good a street for shopping as Le Loi and you can always come back later. Instead, go east two blocks to Hai Ba Trung Street and turn right towards the river. By now you will have caught on that there is no end to jewelry, clothing and souvenir stores. Two blocks SE and you are on the corner of Dong Du St. and the center of Saigon's nightlife. Turn right. Saigon Light is upscale and like the Hard Rock Café, is open during the day for drinks and meals. The Apocalypse Now is only open during the evening and it's not a place I'd care to eat at. Next to the Apocalypse is the Saigon Hotel, which attracts a rather diverse crowd. That means some clean cut and some sleazy (rooms vary from $70 to $190). Back to the main street, it's only two blocks to the river and the most expensive hotel in town, the five star Saigon Floating Hotel. It was towed up the Saigon river from the Great Barrier Reef in 1989. Mind you, it's a boat so the rooms are small, but it is first class.

As you exit the boat, there is a statue of Tran Hung Dao the war hero that defeated Kublai Khan in 1287. Along the river are scores of floating restaurants and tour boats. On the right is the newly refurbished Riverside Hotel, quite nice. Around the next corner is Maxim's restaurant, the best in the city. It's a must for supper. They put on a stage show reminiscent of Ted Mack's amateur hour, a little of this and a little of that, and the show is worth the price of the meal in itself. As for food, I had vegetable soup, filet mignon, fries, lettuce and tomato, coffee and crepe suzettes for $22.

Now you can continue along the waterfront (road bends to the right) to the Vietcombank, on the corner of Pasteur Street, to get a cash advance on your MasterCard. With pockets full of money, its back to Pasteur for two blocks (away from the river), turn left on Ham Nghi Blvd. and in two blocks, it's back to the Ben Thanh Market. The start of Le Loi Boulevard, remember, shopping. And three blocks to a drink at the Rex Hotel.

## THE DRIVING TOUR

You can rent a taxi for eight hour or four hour, city tours or visit the Cu Chi tunnels, 30 miles out of town (about six hours). They were unwilling to combine the tunnel visit with the half-day city drive to make one long day, so we had to choose. A friend of mine just returned from Saigon and had taken the tunnel trip. He found himself on hands and knees crawling through an endless array of claustrophobic mole sized holes in the ground that left him crippled for the next two days. He forgot that the average North Vietnamese soldier has a significantly smaller frame than the average adult American male. I figured that twenty minutes crawling on my hands and knees could seem like days and the time wouldn't pass any faster when my only point of reference was the backside of the guy in front. We opted for the half day drive in the city for $25.

The name of the Museum of American War Crimes has been changed to the War Crimes Exhibition and is the most popular attraction for Westerners. It's mostly a collection of American guns, rockets, tank turrets and even a fighter plane left behind. These were obviously the weapons used in the crimes, whereas the Russian and Chinese weapons shown were used in peaceful ventures. It's worth a visit to look at the hardware but don't expect to see much crime.

On the outskirts of town, half way back to the airport, is the Giac Lam Pagoda which is the cities oldest, 1744. Peaceful, quiet and not on the tourist track, it is a welcome respite from the busy downtown streets. The inside is purposefully underlit and commands respect. The altars are adorned with gold statues amid dark wood and soft lights. A bell and muted stick hang in a corner adjacent a wall board on which believers hang the handwritten names of sick family members. The sound of the bell is meant to carry to the heavens and bring relief for the ill. There are variations of the same theme, some with wallet sized pictures, in several rooms. It is all like a quiet prayer.

We drove through the large section of Chinatown but it is mostly stores for the local inhabitants and there was no reason to stop. Then the American Embassy and I remembered the last pictures of evacuations by helicopter from the roof. It's been returned to the United States and will be reopened as our embassy. Twenty years of clutter and neglect will have to be cleaned up. There is a soda cart on wheels at the corner for the few that stop and look. White clad young Vietnamese girls cycle past without a sideways glance. A large portion of the population wasn't born until after 1975, so it wasn't their war.

Then we stopped at the Notre Dame Cathedral built by the French in 1883. A beautiful structure with a large square in front. Saigon is filled with independent entrepreneurs operating from push carts loaded with fresh fruit, vegetables, soda, cigarettes, you name it. Try the green dragon fruit with a bright red skin and white insides speckled with black seeds. It's very good.

The last stop is the Presidential Palace or Independence Hall which was renamed the Reunification Hall on April 30, 1975 after the Viet Cong ran their flag from the forth floor balcony. It's a modern building designed by a Paris trained Vietnamese architect and completed in 1966. It has been preserved as it was the day power changed hands. English speaking tours are provided for a nominal charge. The rooms are tastefully decorated, some flamboyantly, and the layout is one of openness and space. The rooms have character. It feels like a Presidential Palace.

It is interesting to note that men and women gather at separate tables to eat lunch on the sidewalk. I don't know what it means.


THE END

SIDEBAR FOR SAIGON (Ho Chi Minh City)


GETTING THERE - The two main routes are through Hong Kong or Bangkok, Thailand where connections are made for Viet Nam Airlines (daily flights). Round trip to Bangkok from the west coast of the USA is roughly $1200. Bangkok to Saigon is $350 RT. Bangkok - Saigon - Hanoi - Bangkok is $450. Northwest, Delta and United are the American carriers serving Bangkok.

There are a number of tour companies that offer packages to Viet Nam for those not interested in independent travel. A 17 day tour including Singapore, Cambodia and Viet Nam is approximately $4600, including air fare from Los Angeles. Call the following companies for their brochures: Vayatour (800)999-8292, Asia Pacific Adventures (213)935-3156, Advantage Travel (800)882-2098, Wings of the World (416)482- 1223, Adventure Center (800)227-8747.

VISAS - Visas are required and can be bought at the airport. Visas can be obtained from a visa service in the larger US cities, look in the yellow pages of the phone directory. Allow for AT LEAST 2 weeks lead time (US $130). Visas can be purchased in Bangkok or Hong Kong through the travel agency you use to buy the tickets on Viet Nam Airlines at half the US cost. However, it takes 5 business days for processing. It's not inconvenient if you plan to spend a week in Bangkok.

ACCOMMODATIONS - The best in town is the five star Saigon Floating Hotel which was towed to the Saigon river from Australia's Great Barrier Reef in 1989. The small shipboard rooms cost US $275-$575. tel. (84-8)290783, FAX (84-8) 290784. The following is only a partial list of good hotels: The Rex, formally the favorite of US military officers, US $190-$1500, tel. (84-8) 292186, FAX (84-8)291469, The Riverside Hotel (close to the Floating Hotel), US $159-300, tel. (84-8)224038, Hotel Continental, US $190-$300, tel. (84-8)294456, FAX (84-8)290936 and the always popular Saigon Hotel, close to the night spots, US $90-$200.

There are at least 10 hotels in the $100 price range within two blocks of the Saigon Hotel.

HEALTH - There are no vaccinations required for entry unless you are leaving a yellow fever infected area. Customs officials will check your immunization card on arrival. The entry form has a series of health questions. It would be prudent to update your normal vaccinations including measles, polio, tuberculosis, hepatitis A and B, typhoid, tetanus and diphtheria. Bring Imodium and Pepto-Bismol for gastro intestinal problems. It is best to be in good health before entering Viet Nam since the medical facilities will not match those Westerners are used to.

WHERE TO EAT - A list of nice restaurants would go on for several pages since there isn't a block in the city without an eating establishment of some sort. All of the better hotels have restaurants that serve Western and a variety of Oriental food at reasonable prices and the food is safe to eat. Safe, is a very important issue in all of Southeast Asia. That said, here are some recommendations - the Caravelle Hotel, 9th floor, for an excellent breakfast ($6) and a view of the city to boot (look down on the Continental Hotel) - Le P'Tit Bistro, 58 Le Thanh Ton Street, tel. 230219 for wonderful French food (the pork chops are to kill for) all for $20 - an absolute must is Maxim's, tel. 296676, next to the Majestic Hotel at 13 Dong Khoi Street, the best in town. Filet Mignon dinner and desert for $22 and you get a stage show for free. A variety show of local talent and is worth the price of dinner in itself.

WHEN TO GO - Late January and early February is Tet, the Vietnamese New Years celebration. Flights and hotels will be booked solid. The wet season is May to November with daily but short lived downpours. Otherwise, the best time to go is now, before other American tourists catch on that the country is open for visitors.

North and South of Saigon

Escaping the chaos

Ho Chi Minh City, Viet Nam or Saigon, as we know it, has a growing population of just over 5 million. Actually, most of them call it Saigon too, but not in front of a government official. Five million may seem like a lot of people but the country has 80 million (#13 in the world) and the economy is still largely agricultural. They need foreign investment to develop and many countries are understandably uncomfortable with a Communist regime. Japanese and German money have been invested in Saigon making it the financial engine for the entire country. It's a big city that's getting both bigger and taller. Construction cranes are all over the city. The sidewalks are busy, the streets are busier - some may say chaotic is a better word. The city attracts people from the farmland looking for a better life. Can't blame them, but, there seems to be just too many people. So, we took two tours outside the city. South to the Mekong Delta and north to the Cu Chi Tunnels.

The Mekong delta was the rice basket for Viet Nam when our troops were there some 30 years ago and it still is. The Mekong River starts in Tibet and runs through China, Laos and Cambodia before entering Viet Nam around the bottom, close to Saigon. The 6 th longest river in the world. It spreads out as it dumps the soil carried from upstream forming thousands of tributaries and islands. We went to My Tho at the top of the delta and an easy day trip from the city.

My Tho has about 170,000 people but we weren't there for the city. About 35 of us piled onto a big boat to cross 3 kilometers of muddy water. The river is about 15 meters deep at this point which is 15 kilometers from the South China Sea. We transferred into 5 small motorized boats to weave through a series of canals. The first island stop was for honey and lime tea and pictures for those who would put the boa constrictor around their neck. They make coconut candy in this village. Naturally, there are free samples and boy are they sweet. And inexpensive for those who need a sugar rush. Then there was tasting of honey from a comb taken from a bees nest. Apparently, the bees don't mind since no one was stung. Back to the boat where there was coconut milk directly from the coconut.

The second island had the mid morning snack. Passion fruit, pineapple, chili dip, some sort of brown fruit, banana and dragon fruit. The fruit is really good but one must be careful with what you drink. They make their own moonshine here and it's for sale. It ain't smooth. Then lunch at a permanently anchored boat in My Tho dockside.

It can't come as a surprise that, along the river, people eat a lot of fish. One of the three types given for lunch (served family style with bowls of rice) is the elephant fish. One of the ugliest looking species I've ever seen. Looks shouldn't count when it comes to eating and, just a taste, shouldn't kill you. If you like fried fish, you can gain weight here. Some did.

We stopped at China town on the way back to the city. A couple of hundred years ago, the Vietnamese lived only in the North. A group of Chinese were having trouble with an oppressive government (some things never change) and asked permission to move to Viet Nam. The locals didn't want too many Chinese to move among them for fear they would eventually take control so they gave them permission to move into the unoccupied south. The Chinese started Saigon and after a while, it became quite prosperous. The Vietnamese up north said we would like to send some of our people to join you. The Chinese said no thanks. The Vietnamese said we'll send the Army first if need be, but, we will be coming down. The Chinese moved, lock, stock and barrel, to an open area south of the city. The north Vietnamese moved into the established, and empty, city of Saigon and the rest is history.

The next day was the visit to Ben Duoc Tunnel, part of the Cu Chi Tunnel network, 70 KM north west of Saigon. During the war, the allied forces had a terrible time with this area. In this section alone, there were over 200 km of tunnels. We sent guys into the tunnels - there were booby traps. We tried to flood them - they used water proof doors. We tried gas - didn't work either. In desperation, we carpet bombed the area. That worked, when all the vegetation was gone. What was moonscape then is now back to jungle.

But first, there was the pit stop. A home business, the making of edible rice paper used to wrap egg rolls and other food items. The rice is mixed into a broth, cooked over wood and spooned onto a hot skillet. Five inch circles are cooked and carefully placed onto mat trays. They are covered with an open weave mat and put in the sun for drying. These are farm people and can make an additional $4 a day from the paper.

The tunnels have been preserved for tourists. A few of the sections closest to the surface, that is. Keep in mind, these tunnels were the home base for thousands of the Viet Cong. There were kitchens, sleeping quarters, planning rooms and hospitals. There were several levels that could be reached through trap doors and ladders and holes that are above floor level. One of the guides demonstrated the disguise of the entrances by brushing aside leaves on the ground to reveal a square wood door. He pulled it open and proceeded to climb in. It couldn't have been more that 14 inches on a side. I couldn't have gotten two legs in. He pulled the top closed and 30 seconds later, he popped a cover 25 feet away. We didn't see that coming.

There are several sections with stairs leading to good sized rooms. Twenty by thirty feet. From there the guide lead, those willing, through sections of tunnel crawling on hands and knees. It doesn't take long to realize that there is a significant difference in size between the Vietnamese and the Americans. There is a display of American rockets (the launchers, actually) and some unexploded small bombs. There is a display of locally made whiskey for sale ranging in price from $1.00 to $10 a bottle. Close by are 2 large bird like cages that are empty. They used to hold monkeys for the visitors, but no more. I wondered what they held years ago and then, moved on to the gift shop. It's a nice shop with a good selection of shirts, hats and other souvenirs at very reasonable prices.

In Viet Nam the youngest son inherits the house. Not the first born as we're used to seeing. And there's a good reason. The youngest son stays in the house and has to take care of the parents when they get old. By then, the older children have families of their own to take care of. The youngest becomes the caretaker, and, as his reward, he gets the house. Anyway, we were on our way back to town for dinner at the roof garden of the Rex Hotel. I was the first born and I didn't get the house. Just as well.

THE END

## SIDEBAR FOR SAIGON N&S

GETTING THERE - There are no direct flights from the USA. From the west coast, there is one stop service from China Southern Air, through Guangzhou, China, for $929 RT, regular coach fare. There is also 1 stop service through Taipei on China Air for $1013. Direct service should start from San Francisco in the near future. You need a visa for Viet Nam. The application can be obtained in the USA and presented, at the Saigon airport, with 2 passport sized pictures and $25 USA.

We took a 16 day tour with SmarTours - Hanoi- Hue - Hoi An - Danang- Saigon - Ankor Wat - Bangkok - Los Angeles, for $2600 each. They sent us the paperwork for the visas.

WHEN TO GO - Saigon is hot and rainy from April to September. Hot and dry for the other months.

HOTELS - There are hundreds of hotels to choose from, virtually all the major chains. The Hotel Equatorial, tel. 84 8 839 7777, email= info@ hcm.equatorial.com, is just off the city center and has rooms for US $150-$230/single or double..The Rex Hotel is in city center. tel. 829 6043. email, rexhotel@hcm.vnn.vn, with rooms from US $100-$550.

HEALTH - No shots necessary.

MISCELLANEOUS - For additional information contact the Vietnamese Embassy at www.vietnamembassy-usa.org tel. 202.861.0737.

SENGGIGI BEACH, the best of LOMBOK ISLAND
Where's that you say?

Next Island over from the hustle and bustle of Bali.

SENGGIGI BEACH, INDONESIA - I didn't come here on purpose. Well that's not exactly true, I did intend to stop here on my way back from the island of Flores after a visit to Komodo Island to see the man eating dragons. I expected to fly from Flores to Lombok and spend whatever time I had left in Indonesia on this beach before my flight back home from Bali. It didn't work out that way.

To make a long story short, I checked on flights to Flores at the Bali airport and with 2 travel agencies. I had a week to make it and it turns out that I could get there but couldn't get back for my flight out. So, Plan "B", get a seat on one of the several daily flights from Bali to Lombok. All full. Plan "C". There's the slow boat from a port half the way up the coast or the more expensive catamaran from Benoa port next to the airport. I went for speed.

The Mabua Express is a big ship, clean and sleek. Sea sick pills are on the bar for one and all. There are TV monitors mounted overhead and time enough to show a movie. They give you a box lunch, a roll and cup of water. The gesture is admirable. The ride was comfortable, didn't need the pill.

There's a stand in the middle of the aisle at the Lombok boat terminal, taxi for $6 or bus for $2. A full size bus with comfortable seating but not much room for luggage. It's a one hour drive to Senggigi and they will drop you off at the hotel of your choice. Oddly enough, the thirty people on the bus wanted to be dropped off in the center and figure out accommodations later. An indication of the casual or budget traveler that you're apt to find here.

After checking in at the Mascot, with well groomed grounds, no need for a pool since the ocean is at the rear, A/C room (looks like a native hut), TV (two stations, both Indonesian), I walked to the main road (there is only one paved road) and stopped at the first building that had a travel agency sign. Round trip, guided tour of Gili Trawangan for $20. Why not?

Granted there are some that come here because it's the most developed area on Lombok. There are four and five star hotels on the beach, snorkeling, boating, fishing or just laying about doing nothing. It's a small town catering to the well to do at the Sheraton to the north end and backpackers at the south end. Something for everyone. Then there are the Gili islands. Gili Air, the closest and the most suitable for families. Gili Meno, the middle one with the fewest people and Gili Trawangan with the most facilities and reported to be the party island (my choice).

I walked north to the only modern shopping center in town. Spaghetti and ice coffee at the Café Enak for $3. Two blocks north, beach side, is a local shopping center, grass huts and all. They sell touristy stuff at good prices (you have to bargain) and there are several restaurants right next to the sand. The view is wonderful and it's a nice place to relax with a cold one.

## GILI HERE I COME

Much to my surprise, the tour guide was the same guy that sold me the ticket. A van, a driver, him and me and we drove towards the beach for 100 meters. Road construction blocked the way so we walked the remaining 100 meters. He went to a stand on the beach and talked to a fellow with a uniform. None of my business, so I looked around. There were a number of beached boats and local people either grabbing a few rays or just milling about.

Business done, we walked to the beach and the captain was pulling his boat close enough for boarding. I had one pair of wet shoes outside my door and they were taking their time drying. I wasn't about to get my last pair wet so I timed the waves. Successfully.

The boat has bench seating but is so narrow that two people can't sit across from one another. There's an outboard motor so we didn't have to depend on the wind. Outriggers on both sides so we wouldn't have to swim ashore and an overhead canopy. The coast line north of the town center is rugged and scenic and if you're not interested in visiting the Gili islands (and you may not be after reading the rest of this story), hire a boat and cruise the coast line, it's very pretty.

The village center on Trawangan starts at the pier but we kept going. Past the pier, past literally dozens of grass huts (independent businesses) towards the north end. On a vacant stretch, the captain and his helper beached the boat. There are no motor vehicles on the island and in no time we were approached by a horse drawn taxi trying to sell an island tour. Unsuccessfully.

This is the area for snorkeling and there were several people in the water. There is a shopping center just north of the pier and it was as quiet as our walk to the center of town. Very few tourists. We stopped at the snazziest restaurant in town, the Borobudur, just south of the pier. It's far from fancy and after walking past the hotels, I got a feel of the island. It's a good place to play Robinson Crusoe. I can see an active night life if you're in, or close to, a place with a lively crowd. Otherwise, this could be like a cemetery at night. Accommodations are rustic. Swim with the fish during the day and read a good book at night.

We took a horse cart back. The guide went to find the captain and I sat in an idle rattan chair and it disintegrated beneath me. No, I'm not that fat. The next chair held and I got a soda at a nearby hut. The captain and guide joined me for a chat. A sales pitch actually. The captain offered to sell me his boat for the equivalent of $2,000 US and he would send me a check every year from the profits. Naturally, I'd get free trips each year when I visited. But storm clouds were brewing and it was time to go, the currents can get nasty between here and the mainland.

That night I had an excellent German snitzel, potatoes, green something and coffee for $4 at the first class Café Lombok. The Hotel Intan Laguna, the Senggigi Beach Hotel and the Sheridan are as nice as you will find in Hawaii and at a fraction of the price. And the bus company that took us to town will pick up at your hotel and take you to the boat. If you want to escape the frantic pace of Bali, first class or as a beach bum, go to Senggigi. By the way I didn't buy the boat.

## THE END

## SIDEBAR FOR SENGGIGI

GETTING THERE - I got to Bali on the Cathay Pacific air pass The price is $ 999 US for round trip from Los Angeles or San Francisco or New York to Hong Kong. It includes 21 days free travel (unless you register online at www.cathay-usa.com as a CyberTraveler to get a total of 31 travel days) from HKG to 15 cities Cathay Pacific flies to in South East Asia. All flights originate in and return to HKG and repeats are not allowed. The itinerary must be agreed on beforehand and tickets will be issued for each segment. Summer departures (May 8 to Aug 21) are $ 200 extra. Upgrades to 1 st class are about twice the price. Segment changes can be made afterwards for an additional fee. Call Cathay Pacific 800-228-4297 or fax at 1-800-617-9470 There is one daily flight from HKG to Bali on Cathay.

There are several flights a day from Bali to Lombok, $60 RT. Apparently booked well in advance since I couldn't get a seat. The fastest catamaran (2 1/2 hours) is $25 each way, the Mabua Express, leaving Benoa (next to the airport) at 8 AM.

ACCOMMODATIONS - In Bali the choices are as varied as New York or Los Angeles, from 5 star to no star. I found a gem almost by accident, the Pelasa Hotel, Batu Pageh St., LegianKuta, Bali, Indonesia, tel 0361-753423, fax 62-361-753424. Beautiful grounds, pool, A/C rooms, bar, food for $20/person breakfast included.

In Senggigi the choices aren't as many but the range is the same. There's the Sheraton Senggigi Beach, five stars, just north of town, the Lombok Intan Laguna, 4 stars, center of town, the Hotel Senggigi, 4 stars, town center with single /doubles from $130-$550, tel 62-370-93210, fax 62-370-93200, email= senggigi@lombokisland.com Next door to the Hotel Senggigi is the Mascot, 3 stars, with single/doubles at $40. tel 62-370-93365, fax 62-370-93236. All the above have 21% service and tax added to the bill. There were 30 people on the bus from the boat to the hotel strip, no one had room reservations.

MISCELLANEOUS - No visas are required for USA citizens.

What has red hair, long arms and is smarter than the
people you don't like?

SANDAKAN, SABAH, MALAYSIA - This former capital of Sabah is
the home to one of four Orang-Utan sanctuaries in the world. The others
are: Medan, Sumatra - Semenggok, close to Kuching, Sarawak - Tanjung
National Park, Kalimantan.

I almost missed this tour altogether. I was ready to check out of my
hotel in Kota Kinababu, the capitol of Sabah after trying, unsuccessfully,
to book the tour with two travel agencies when the call came. I already
had the airline ticket to Sandakan in hand.

Sandakan was a booming harbor in the late 1800's and became the
capital of British North Borneo. It remained the capital until the Japanese
invasion in WWII. Allied bombing in 1945 leveled the city and the capital
was moved to Jesselton, now renamed Kota Kinabalu, on the other coast.
The town may have been a bed of activity 100 years ago but it's sedate
now. There is an active waterfront but no evidence the town is geared for
tourists.

I was picked up at my hotel, 8 AM sharp. Sepilok is the first stop,
23 KM from town. Feeding times are at 10 AM and 3 PM and we had a
brief visit to the small gift shop before a half mile walk into the jungle on
a well maintained boardwalk. Orang-Utan means "man of the forest" in
Malay and their populations have decreased because of forest clearing and
capture for pets. They are now protected by law and this center provides a
safe haven for babies abandoned by the mother and those made orphans.
The rules are posted, no feeding, no touching. Orang-Utans are susceptible
to human diseases and they don't want a flu epidemic spreading through
man's closest relative.

The viewing station is fifty feet away from the feeding platform which
is 20 feet above the ground. It's circular and attached to a tree trunk.

Ropes connect the tree to adjoining ones and that's the popular route for those looking for a free meal. All of the apes in the preserve don't show up but those that do, get bananas and milk. Every day, all the time in hope that they will get bored with the never changing menu and learn to forage for themselves. Two little ones arrived first and they are adorable. They have the table manners of a two year old. That means, none. Then, slowly, hand over foot on the rope, an adult male arrived and the two little ones moved as far away as they could. One went so far as to hang off the edge by one hand. Not that the big male showed the little ones any signs of aggression, in fact he ignored them. However, a 100 pound Orang-Utan is a lot stronger than a 200 pound human and is nobody to mess with. They all ate bananas and slobbered milk towards their mouth and down their chests. And then ate more bananas. There were at least fifty people in the viewing area and camera shutters clicking like mad. A mother with her baby firmly holding on to her chest hair, came over to join us on the viewing platform. She watched us. After the feeding, several with now full stomachs wandered close. They had no fear and were completely indifferent to picture taking. Not posing but not shying away either.

We had lunch at the center, chicken, rice, something that may have been a salad and coffee before we set off on the 114 KM drive to the jungle lodge on the banks of the Xinabatangan river, the longest in Sabah. The lodge is run by Discovery tours and we were the only guests. It's private land and is rented to the tour company. There are several individual wood chalets with beds and running water and toilets. Electricity shuts down at midnight.

The river cruise was scheduled for the late afternoon but it was raining and by supper time it turned into a monsoon. Last year, the rain was so heavy, the banks of the river rose 10 feet to the level of the porch which collapsed beneath the surprised Chinese tourists standing there watching the river. Dinner was an absolute delight. Sweet and sour fish, rice, very tasty beef, boney chicken, mixed vegetables with carrots, string beans, some green leafy stuff. All by candle light in the middle of the jungle in the middle of nowhere in the pouring rain. Plenty of free coffee and ½ liter bottles of cold Anchor beer for $3.50. And enough food left over to feed a family.

Then came the dreaded slide show and we were a captive audience. But the projector wasn't working. We smiled and had another beer. Fate was not on our side. Our guide fixed the projector and we watched bad slides of the area taken with a point and shoot camera. Oh well!

Up at 5:45 AM to get the river cruise we missed yesterday. There was a low fog on the river but no rain. There are tribes living upriver so there is a cholera risk to the water on the main river but not on the tributaries. No tribes live upstream on the feeding streams. There are crocodiles but we didn't see any. We motored up one of the branches to see the Probosis monkey who only lives in Borneo. The male has a harem of eight females and a nose the size of a zucchini. It's so big that he often has to lift it to get food into his mouth. We are fortune, there are several sitting in the trees only 100 feet away. By the way, the females don't have a big nose.

Breakfast is a fried egg, a muffin, two pieces of toast, lime juice and coffee. And we're off for ½ hours drive to the Gomantong caves where Swiftlets nests are harvested for the Chinese delicacy "birds nest soup". Here my luck ran out. The largest, knee high, waterproof boots are size 7 so I'm left to walk in my sneakers. Through the mud, across algae covered rocks (the path across the stream) and to the cave entrance. The mammoth Simud Hitam cave with a roof 90 meters high. Millions of Swiftlets build their nests inside the cave where they are collected twice a year. Just after they have been made (between February and April) whereupon the birds just build another and after the breeding season (July to September). The men climb to the roof to dislodge the nests hoping they don't lose their grasp. Each year several fall to their death but it's a risk they take. The nests can go for as much as $500 a kilo and in this part of the world, that's big money.

Workers are in the process of building an elevated walkway to enter the cave but for now, it's the ground or nothing. There is a reason for the boots, all the guano is not confined to the back recesses of the cave. Our walkway is two pieces of round bamboo sitting on black guano. One slip from the well oiled (it's not oil) bamboo surface and I'm ankle deep (or even higher) in bat and Swiftlet guano. This is not a walk to lose your balance on. A fall forward or backward would surely be an experience long remembered and would be not be soon forgotten by those riding in the van back to town afterwards. Fortunately, I have a long lens for the camera. Even getting this close, the sneakers are now a write off but the cave is impressive.

Our timing was right for the way out. Workers are finishing a new elevated walk out and we are the first tourists to use it. We should have been the first ones to use it going in but who knew?

## THE BLACK SPITTING COBRA

Camera and lenses safely packed away, we're on the long bumpy road back to town when we spot an Hawk in the middle of the dirt road. The van stopped thirty feet away and the hawk stared at us for a good twenty seconds before flying off. A hundred feet and he perched on a branch. Then we saw it. An 18 inch, black Cobra in the road. He spotted us too, recognized a threat and rose to full threatening height for a strike. The guide said it's a spitting cobra and I knew what that meant. The only camera handy was my point and shoot and I'd have to get within five feet to get a meaningful shot. For a regular Cobra, I could do it, but a spitting Cobra can shoot his venom more than five feet. They aim for the eyes and even baby cobras have enough poison to kill. I stayed in the van. After a long minute, the Cobra realized we were no threat and quickly slithered into the brush at the side of the road. But the Hawk was not to be denied his lunch, he flew into the brush, groped around and finally got his prey. He flew back to his perch on the other side of the road with the Cobra in his claws and waited for us to drive off before eating.

Lunch was at the 5 star Renaissance Hotel, one KM up the hill from Sandakan. It's a beautiful place. Then the town tour. I did see a real birds nest (not for sale). It's about the size of a small ash tray. Four KM west of town, along the coast is the magnificent Puu Jih Shih Buddhist Temple with a terrific view of the harbor. This temple cost millions to build, so there are some very wealthy people that live in Sandakan.

The Fokker 50 was full on the way back. A Discovery van was there at the Kota Kinabalu airport to drive me to my hotel. That night, I went to the Burger King around the corner for supper. Ah, good to be home again.

# THE END

## SEPILOK SIDEBAR

GETTING THERE - I came from Singapore (to the west) which is serviced by Northwest, United, Garuda and Singapore Airlines (US $1300 RT from the USA west coast). Then from Johor Bahru airport (JHB) just across the Singapore border since it's 50% cheaper than flying out of Singapore to Malaysian Borneo. From JHB to Kota Kinabalu, on Malaysian airlines, it's US$130 economy, $180 business class each way. From KK to Sandakan, the airfare is US$ 100 round trip.

The tour of Sepilok, the jungle lodging and cruise, Gomantong caves, town tour, all meals and transportation except air is $130. All arrangements, including air and hotel can be made with Discovery Tours, Locked Bag 23, 88992 Kota Kinabalu, Sabah, Malaysia. e-mail: DISTOUR@PO.JARING.MY internet: http://www.infosabah.com.my/discovery tel. (088) 221244. Fax (088)221600. They are the American Express representative in Sabah.

If Discovery tours are full, try Sabah Holiday, Lot G31, Ground Floor, Wisma Sabah, 88000 Kota Kinabalu, Sabah, Malaysia. tel (6) 088-222708 Fax (6)088-221751 Email:pooi@pop.jaring.my I found them very helpful. Both Discovery and Sabah Holiday are in the Wisma Sabah building on the first floor.

WHEN TO GO - The heaviest rainfalls are from October to March with the heaviest in December and January. Sabah is virtually on the equator so count on warm weather and high humidity, year round. Bring an umbrella, no matter.

WHERE TO STAY - The best in the center of town is the Hotel Nak, P.O. Box No. 761, 90708 Sandakan, Sabah, Malaysia. tel. (6) 089-272988 Fax (6) 089-272879. It's showing signs of wear and tear but rooms facing the sea are US$ 35. Five star accommodations are a KM out of town, up the hill at the Renaissance Sandakan Hotel. Rooms start at US$ 120, suites are $500. It's a beautiful facility. Write to: KM1, Jalan Utara, P.O. Box 275, 90703 Sandakan, Sabah, Malaysia. tel.(6) 089-213299 Fax:(6) 089-271271 Internet:http://www.renaissance-intl.com All rooms have 10% service and 5% govt. tax added on.

WHAT TO DO - If you're on the two day tour, it includes the Orang Utan center, overnight at the jungle lodge, river cruise, Gomantong caves, city tour of Sandakan. If you have an interest in seeing Turtle Island this is the time to add on since the boats leave from Sandakan for an overnight on the island. It's an hour and a half boat ride each way to see the 200 pound Green turtles lay their eggs in the sand. US$ 160 for Turtle Island per person.

FOR MORE INFORMATION- Write to the Malaysian Tourist office at 818 West 7th St, Suite 804, Los Angeles, CA 90017 Tel. (213) 689-9702 or 595 Madison Ave., Suite 1800, New York, NY 10022

## KANDY
### Without the calories


SRI LANKA - Let's say you finished your business in Colombo, the capital of Sri Lanka and you had a day to kill. Moreover, the downtown area is rundown and depressing. Add to that, there are Army road blocks at most major intersections with troops armed with machine guns behind sand bag emplacements. And Hotel entrances are protected with armed guards. You could stay inside the modern Hilton, the large Galadari Hotel or the older (and reminiscent of the British Colonial days) Galle Face Hotel. Or take a day trip to the city Sri Lanka citizens consider their finest - Kandy. That's what I decided to do.

## THE TRAIN

The express train leaves the Fort Railway Station at 7 AM so I was out the door early expecting to be accosted by tuk- tuk (the 3 wheel motorcycles) drivers immediately, just like always. Not a one in sight, so I walked, missing the 6:30 AM deadline for a round trip ticket. First class one way, in the observation car was $2.10. The train station is one, long block, east of the Hilton and set back from the road. It's an unimpressive building, so my late arrival was more of a blessing. The observation car is in the rear with assigned seats facing backwards so you can see what the train just passed. I figured to read or make up for the sleep I missed by getting up so early. Instead I got one of the most bone jarring rides of my life. The train rocked from side to side and up and down with an intensity that would loosen the filings in your teeth. Sleep was out. I quickly gave up an attempt to read and watched the jungle pass by. There is a fold down table, overhead fans and window drapes that have been in place for a while. The seats are cushioned and comfortable. The best description of the interior decor is drab. The 2 ½ hour trip took 3 hours and the Kandy station was a welcome sight. The return ticket, now bought in advance before leaving the station, was $4. There were touts outside the station (as expected), for taxis, tours, places to stay, places to eat, places to stand around, or whatever. I walked straight out, uphill, past the crowded street flea market selling clothes, food and other consumer items, past the myriad of large busses parked on and across the street and saw the clock.

## THE TOWN

The Clock Tower marks the west side of town and is a good sign post if you get lost. Kandy is only 115 KM inland from Colombo but is 500 meters above sea level and far more pleasant, climate wise. With 100,000 people it's the second biggest city and was the last hold out from the invading Europeans. It defied the Portuguese and Dutch for three centuries and finally fell to the British in 1815. It was the last capital of the Sinhalese kingdom. The focus of Kandy is the lake but first, I had to find breakfast. I went to the Queens Hotel, the best in town and facing the north side of the lake. The dining room was empty and breakfast time was over but I got bacon and eggs anyway.

## THE LAKE

The lake is artificial. It was created by the last ruler of the kingdom of Kandy, Sri Wickrama Rajasinha, in 1807. It was dug by hand and the local chiefs that protested for their people were put to death on stakes in the lake bed. So much for dissent. The island in the center was used to hold the Sultans harem. He crossed by barge to visit, assuming his subjects were all poor swimmers. After the unromantic British took over, the island was used to store ammunition.

The town itself is very busy. The streets are crowded with people and there's plenty of traffic. That means no sand bags and machine guns. Until you get to the walk along the north side of the lake where there are road barricades. Two blocks farther, close to the Temple of the Tooth, I saw the first troops. Oddly enough, one soldier walked up to me and asked if I were British. I told him I was American and he asked where I lived and my name. He was friendly and I figured he was just looking for conversation but I was taken back at first. There are precautions here but Kandy may be less of a target for the Tamil Tigers, the people who live in the northeast of Sri Lanka and want independence and figure planting bombs is the way to get it. It's much more casual here. More comfortable, more like a real city. The Temple of the Tooth houses Sri Lanka's most important Buddhist relic, the sacred tooth of Buddha. It is said to have been snatched from the flames of his cremation pyre in 543 BC and smuggled here in the 4th century AD. It was moved from town to town, captured by an invading army and taken back to India in 1283 AD but eventually brought back. The present Temple started construction in 1687 and it's been in Kandy ever since. No cameras allowed inside. It would take the better part of the day to walk around the lake, if you are inclined. It is very pretty. Cross to the other side and the view is one deserving of a postcard. There are lakeside benches to sit on and watch the boats pass leisurely by. This is the place to mediate. Perhaps to wonder how to tell one persons tooth from another.

On the western side of the lake, close to the clock tower is another flee market with consumer items. And a block east is Cargills 1844, the touch of the British remains. Another block and I was at the Queens pub, separate entrance from the hotel. An ex-pat American from Eugene, Oregon asked me about my camera at the bar. He said he had a less expensive Nikon and was afraid to carry it around for fear of thieves. He was living in Kandy and said, "I know it's a rat hole here but it's my rat hole."

I thought about that a while later and I suppose it is a rat hole compared to Eugene, Oregon but I found Kandy comfortable and refreshing compared to Colombo. I felt no threat here, my only dread was the train ride back.


THE END


293

## SIDEBAR FOR SRI LANKA

GETTING THERE - I got to Sri Lanka on the Cathay Pacific air pass. It includes 21 days free travel (unless you register online at www.cathay-usa.com as a CyberTraveler to get a total of 31 travel days) from HKG to 15 cities Cathay Pacific flies to in South East Asia. All flights originate in and return to HKG and repeats are not allowed. The itinerary must be agreed on beforehand and tickets will be issued for each segment. Premium cities in India, Australia and New Zealand can be added from $ 200-500. Segment changes can be made afterwards for an additional fee.

There is no question that this is a great deal and Cathay Pacific words their agreement very precisely. No departure from the approved plan or the entire trip ticket is void. It's smart to work out the schedule (which will take several hours) in advance to allow time to catch the next flight. Also, be flexible since some flights are full and you won't know until after you submit your plan. Once approved, you're OK. Call Cathay Pacific 1-800-228-4297 or fax at 1-800-617-9470 for free brochures. Book through a travel agent.

The downside is - arrival time in Sri Lanka is 1 AM and departure is 2:30 AM on Cathay Pacific flights.

ACCOMMODATIONS - The Hilton (387 rooms)is the best in Colombo, $ 185+ US, tel 544-644, fax 544-657. The Galadari (446 rooms), just south, $ 130, tel 544-544, fax 449-875. The 1864 Galle Face (77 rooms), $ 90, suites to $ 190, tel 541- 010, fax 541-072. And the older but spacious Grand Oriental, $ 75, tel 320-391, fax 447-640.

FOOD - Stick to the hotels.

LOCAL ARRANGEMENT - The train station in Colombo is 1 block from the Hilton, 2 from the Galadari, 10 from the Galle Face, 4 from the Grand Oriental. A first class ticket on the observation car is $ 4.00, one way. Don't expect luxury.

MISCELLANEOUS - No visas are required for USA citizens.

Visiting the Taj Mahal

The good, the bad and the annoying

Taj Mahal

AGRA, INDIA - We were on our way to Agra, home of the Taj Mahal but stopped the tour bus at Fatehpur Sikri, the fortified ghost city that was once the capital of the Mughal empire (1571-1585). It's forty KM west of Agra and a good place for a break. Legend says that the Emperor Akbar was without a male heir when he visited Sikri to see a Muslim saint. The saint predicted three sons and after the first son arrived in 1569, Akbar built the city to honor the prophecy. It's said that Sikri was later abandoned because of lack of water but Akbar spent most of his time away, waging war, and simply moved his capital to another town. Never the less, red sandstone is durable and the impressive buildings are well preserved. Ghost towns are a bit eerie, I get the feeling I'm walking amongst the dead.

The Taj Mahal was scheduled for late the next day so we would be there at sunset. Someone in the group got the bright idea that sunrise would be better and asked our tour guide if the places we were to visit tomorrow could be switched around. He put it to a vote and the change didn't take. That led to tour bus miles of bickering and some independent planning.

We checked into our hotel and the desk clerk said that sun rise was at 6:30 AM. Since I was willing to do both sunrise and sunset I was asked to split a cab to do an early morning run. Naturally, the cab and extra admission fee would be on us. And we would miss breakfast since the bus would leave with or without us for a full day of scheduled events. Some of the sun risers asked the others if they would be willing to hold the bus a half hour just in case they were late. The answer, in a word, was no. More bickering. I was willing to leave at 6 AM for the short ride to the Taj but my cab partner insisted on 5:30 AM. I saw no reason to get there in the dark and wait for 45 minutes until there was enough light to take a picture. So, I withdrew.

## THE TOUR

We boarded the bus (with all hands on board) for the Itimad-ud-daulah, the baby Taj. This is the tomb of the Emperor Shah Jahan's Chief Minister and was designed by his daughter who later married the Emperor. I know, this is starting to sound like a soap opera. The daughter, Nur Jahan, built it in a style she used for a similar tomb she built in Pakistan. She began in 1622 and finished four years later. It was the first Mughal structure built entirely from marble and the first to make extensive use of marble inlay. At first sighting, if I was told this was the Taj Mahal, I would have believed it. It's beautiful after lunch, we visited a marble sales shop (tour operators tend to do that). End tables (marble top with wood base) were going for US$ 2000. Dining room tables went for the price of a good used car. Having all the marble I need, I ventured into the gift shop and got caught anyway. For US$ 18, I got a small replica of the Taj in a sturdy travel box.

Now it was time for the big event and what a song and dance that turned out to be. First of all, the bus can't drive to the entrance. It must park at an off site lot where we all board electric trolleys after shedding the forbidden items. Those not allowed inside the monument grounds. No candy, cigarettes, lighters, matches, throat lozenges, mints, soda, coffee, tea, anything to eat, and, apparently, tripods (one of our people had his taken at the gate). Denuded of creature comforts we disembarked fifty feet from the entrance and were besieged by vendors selling tourist stuff. We noticed that the entrance fee for us was 500 rupees and only 50 for Indians.

Once past the ticket taker, it's a short walk to the dark, dome shaped entrance gate that frames the brightly lit Taj Mahal in the distance. And the view is breathtaking. Even with the maddening crowd pushing us back and forth, it's a stunning sight.

They say the Taj Mahal is the most extravagant monument ever built for love. Indeed, but it's not a temple, it's a mausoleum. The Emperor Shah Jahan was so heartbroken over the death in childbirth of his second wife, he ordered this magnificent crypt be built. Work started in 1651 using 20,000 craftsmen and it took 22 years. Some of the workers had their hands or thumbs amputated afterwards to ensure the perfection of the building could never be repeated. Supposedly, after 22 years of waiting, the Emperor was told the work was finally done. Only the scaffolding had to be removed. He asked how long that would take and was told several months. He decreed that anyone who helped untie the scaffolding could keep the pieces. The building materials were gone in a day.

From the entrance, walk down a few steps and you are at the beginning of a long waterway which shows the perfectly symmetrical building and it's reflection in the water. The various watercourses and viewing platforms are punctuated by women in colorful sarongs that contrast with the white marble background. A photographers delight.

The main structure is on a platform about 12 feet above the garden level, but you can't just walk up. You have to check your shoes at the collection stand to the right. Considering the stairs and the surrounding platform is in the open air subject to wind, rain and blowing dust, one can only wonder about the purpose of the shoe collection.

It is possible to get inside an interior chamber through the front door but the crowd pushing in and out is worse than that on a subway train at rush hour. And, it's the perfect place for pick pockets. We decided to walk around. In a separate building to the left is a sandstone structure that looks like a mosque and is one. Just walking the exterior of the main building is a delight in itself. Semiprecious stones are inlaid into the marble. Walls are engraved marble and done with meticulous care. Each of the four sides is balanced. On reaching the right side there is a duplicate of the sandstone mosque on the left, it was added for balance. It cannot be a mosque since it faces in the wrong direction.

Sunset was approaching and we stopped along a watercourse for a picture. Local guides/touts were ever present to tell us the best place to stand, looking for a tip. It's helpful the first or second time but after the tenth helpful hint, well, you know. Sunset came with a light pink hue.

We were attacked by the vendors who were patiently waiting outside, just beyond the ticket booth. It was not unlike a shark frenzy. Only moments before we boarded the electric trolleys and would be gone forever. Prices dropped quickly. I got a good deal on four t-shirts.

It is said the Taj Mahal is the most beautiful building in the world. That's subjective, of course, but if it isn't, it's right up there near the top. And I have a little duplicate at home to remind me of just how beautiful it is.

THE END

## SIDEBAR FOR THE TAJ MAHAL

GETTING THERE - There are a number of connecting flights to New Delhi from the west coast, usually through Bangkok, Hong Kong or Singapore. The low season (March to mid-May and September to November) has a discounted RT fare of $999 from the west coast with similar fares from the east coast (connecting through Europe). High season (June to August and December to January) fares are around $1500 RT.

The public bus trip from New Delhi to Agra should run around 5 hours depending on the condition of the roads. US$2, one way. Flights take an hour for US$100 but domestic air in India has a bad reputation for delays and safety.

HOTELS - We stayed at The Trident (best food on the entire trip). Rooms are $90s/120d, but go up to $110s/130d, plus 10%, for their high season - October to April. tel. 331818, fax 331827. The Taj View is five stars, tel. 331841, fax 331860 with rooms for $185s/200d. The best is the Mughal Sheraton, tel. 331701, fax 331730 with standard rooms for $230s/240d and with view $275s/300d. Mid range is the Hotel Atithi, tel. 330879, fax 330878, rooms $50s/60d, with a/c, swimming pool and restaurant.

FOOD - Food poisoning is a danger throughout India. It would be safer to eat at the hotel.

HEALTH - Don't drink the water. That said, it is prudent to be up to date on diphtheria, tetanus, polio, hepatitis A and typhoid. This is a third world country.

MISCELLANEOUS - Visas are required for USA citizens. For additional information contact the consulate at 3550 Wilshire Blvd., Suite 204, LA, CA 90010, tel. 213-380-8855, fax 380-6111, OR, 1270 Avenue of the Americas, Suite 1808, NY, NY 10020, tel. 212-586-4901, fax. 582-3274, web site= www.tourindia.com

## TEMPLE TIGER RESORT
Yes, I wanted to see a tiger in the wild.

Royal Chitwan National Park, NEPAL - We got up at 6:30 AM for what we knew was going to be a long day. We were in Kathmandu at 7,200 feet above sea level with a view of the Himalayas north of town and on our way south to the flat lands at 200 feet above sea level. Hard to believe in a country that seemed to consist of nothing but mountains. The world's tallest to boot.

It all started 60 million years ago when the Indian sub-continent detached from Africa for a collision with the Eurasian continent. The Indian plate jammed into and under the Eurasian plate causing the top crust to buckle and fold. This upheaval created the Himalayas, blocked old rivers and formed new ones. Nepal, in the shape of a hot dog, now sits atop the land mass of India. The capital, Kathmandu, is approximately in the middle, the national park we're headed for is south. The Royal Chitwan Park is bordered on the north by the connecting Rapti and Narayani rivers and on the south by India. Clearly, heavy rains in the mountains will eventually end up in these low land rivers.

Our bus started down the one and a half lane Mughling Highway (two lanes if you count the shoulders) that follows the Trisuli river. The river having carved out a twisting path through the mountains. The view is terrific along the winding road and we had hours to enjoy it. Our bus was new and well maintained but the same can't be said for the public transport busses using the only road south from Kathmandu. I counted three dead busses (one overturned) and a number of stalled trucks. Some were pushed to the side but others just sat and created a temporary road block and minor traffic jam as vehicles had to take turns getting around. There are no gas stations on this road and there were quite a few people left stranded. A word of warning for budget travelers taking a public bus.

We stopped at a cliff side restaurant at about the half way point. Sodas, coffee, snacks and an outhouse that protrudes over the cliff for those that trusted the supports.

The road going south stops at Narayanghat where it meets the east-west highway. This town exists because it is at the intersection of the two main roads and is a trading center for the whole district. Nothing to see here, so we turned right and quickly encountered the first of two washed out bridges. Fortunately, the river bed was dry and that's how we drove across.

After a few miles, we turned south, off the asphalt road and zig zagged for a few miles before our second rest stop. One of our party handed out miniature candies to the kids that collected around the bus. A small boy ripped open the foil, took a bite of Snickers, made a face and spit it out. The only time I've ever seen a kid not like candy.

We got off the bus at the Narayani River with our hand carry luggage to board row boats with no oars. The guy in each boat used a pole and must be paid by the hour since the boat speed never exceeded that of the natural river flow. A half mile across and we must have drifted a mile downstream. Then, six in the back end of each truck, we had a bumpy twenty minute ride to the camp's entrance.

There was no time to unpack since it was closing in on 4 PM and we had to get on the elephants for our first ride/search mission. The Indian elephant is a little smaller than it's African counterpart but still the biggest thing in the jungle. We went directly into the overgrowth and in ten minutes we spotted a black Rhino and her baby. The elephant driver sits on the animal's head and he whistled to the others. Soon, four elephants were converging on the Rhino that was getting increasingly nervous at being cornered. Rhinos have notoriously bad eyesight but elephants are hard to miss. A cornered Rhino charges, except in the case of an elephant who is considerably larger. We were sitting on a wood platform strapped atop the elephants back, four, five or six to a platform (depends on the size of the tourist's bottom) all jockeying for a picture taking view. After a hundred or so flash pops, we continued crashing our way through the underbrush and, at dusk, we spotted a leopard high in a tree. Barely visible in the dim light. He tried hiding at a large fork fifty feet up and gave up when we didn't leave. He leapt to the ground and disappeared. We saw the dead monkey he stashed in the next tree, high above the ground. He would be back after we left. The elephants knew the way back in the dark.

The evening slide show has bad pictures (crocodiles shown in the shade and birds no larger than specks) but there's no TV. Supper buffet was elegantly done on tables with linen and cloth napkins and good food. And a well stocked bar for those needing a cocktail. Early to bed since we had to be up at 5:30 AM.

## THE NEXT MORNING

I guess the early tourist gets to see the bird. And before breakfast to boot. This time in 15 foot high grass and through marshland in a strong morning mist. Dew was dropping hard enough to sound like rain. We saw another black Rhino and two types of deer. There are several benefits to being on an elephant. 1- He does the walking for you, not much faster mind you, but still. 2- He walks through mud and marsh without complaint. 3- He wades through water five foot deep and you stay dry. 4- In the tall grass, poisonous snakes are at his feet, not yours. 5- A confronted animal won't charge an elephant. 6- A Tiger will only stare at an elephant, they are too big to eat, you aren't.

For breakfast, there was oatmeal and raisins, banana, omelettes, really good potatoes, fried tomatoes, hot dogs, toast and coffee.

There was time to walk around, nap and go to a "meet the elephants" presentation. Lunch was chicken, pork, rice, potatoes, bread and coffee.

After lunch there was a one and a half hour jungle walk where we saw no animals. The saying here is that there are more people sightings by tigers than tiger sightings by people. Stands to reason since the Tiger is a night hunter and is very territorial. He marks his ground and heaven help the invader who ventures in. An adult male requires about 60 square kilometers and the Chitwan has a total of 50 adult males. In essence then, no matter which camp you go to, there will be only one Tiger to see. And he can hear you crashing through the jungle from a long way off.

That evening, we took a jeep ride for 1 ½ hours and saw deer and pigs. We stopped at the river for a boat ride at sunset. A beautiful collection of red and pink colors hung on the surrounding mountains. It was just stunning. And not a crocodile in sight, they heard us coming too.

An elephant ride was not scheduled for the next morning, but, faced with an unarmed uprising, they gave in. It was only 45 minutes but we took a different route since we were to end up at the river. Up a small stream flanked by tall grass and, leaving the jungle, across what can only be described as desert. I felt like Lawrence of Arabia on the wrong animal.

We flew back on Cosmic Air. The airport is next to that town at the intersection of the two main roads. Since we had enough people to fill the plane, they left early. A half hour later, we were back in Kathmandu. OK, I didn't see a Tiger. It was a long shot and I knew it. The lodge book said one was seen three months before. Somebody else got lucky.

THE END

## SIDEBAR FOR TEMPLE TIGER

GETTING THERE - There are a number of connecting flights to Kathmandu from the west coast, usually through Hong Kong or Singapore. We had a stop over in Singapore. Nepal is serviced with a discounted RT of $1100 from the west coast with similar fares from the east coast (connecting through Europe). The airline may arrange a nights lodging for you in the connecting city. Cosmic Air, Royal Nepal Airlines, Buddha Air, Necon Air and Gorkha Air fly to a number of towns in the region. Kathmandu to Bharatpur is $75 one way. A half hour flight. Visitors are usually part of a tour and transport to and from the park is arranged and included in the price (bus).

HOTELS - Temple Tiger is at the west end of the park. Rates are $400s/500d a day including meals. tel.01-221585, fax.01- 220178. Write to P.O. Box 3968, Kantipath, Kathmandu, Nepal. Going east is Tiger Tops, the best known and most expensive. They offer three lodges varying in price. The Jungle Lodge is $550s/700d a night, The Tented Camp $325s/400d and the Tharu Village Safari Resort $250s/300d. tel.01-411225, fax:977-01- 414075, e-mail: info@tigermountain.com. Write P.O. Box 242, Durbar Marg, Kathmandu, Nepal.

There is also the Island Jungle Resort, P.O. Box 2154, Durbar Marg, Kathmandu for $260s/320d cottages, $230s/300d tents and the Gaida Wildlife Camp, P.O. Box 2056, Durbar Marg, Kathmandu for $270s/320d huts, $220s/260d tents.

FOOD - Included. They frown on hunting the wildlife.

HEALTH - Don't drink the water. Yellow fever immunization is only required if coming from infected parts of Africa or South America. That said, it is prudent to be up to date on Diphtheria, tetanus, polio, hepatitis A and typhoid. This is a third world country.

MISCELLANEOUS - Visas are required for USA citizens. For additional information contact the consulate at Suite 400, 909 Montgomery St, San Francisco, CA 94133 tel.(202)667-4550, e-mail:nepali@erols.com. Or 2131 Leroy Place NW, Washington DC 20008.

## TUK-TUK, SAMOSIR ISLAND IN LAKE TOBA
## IN THE MIDDLE OF SUMATRA

### Getting there is half the fun

We were besieged by self assigned tour guides, taxi drivers, helpers and hustlers as soon as we stepped out the front door of the airport. It was Medan, the capitol of Sumatra with, as one might guess, very few flights to deliver prey. We were two blades of grass in a swarm of locust. Medan? Hotel? Taxi? Lake Toba? Change money? Where do you want to go? Do you want a tour?

The terminal facilities are accessed from outside so we were obliged to endure the gauntlet. One of the fellows attached himself to us as I spotted two money changers. "The second one gives better rates" he volunteered. I checked both and he was right. Then I went into the tourist bureau as my partner watched the bags. We were going to Lake Toba and I knew there was a bus. It turns out that the bus stop is seven kilometers from the airport, the price to Lake Toba is 20,000 rupiah (RP) each and might take five to six hours. A taxi would cost around 80,000 RP, depending on our bargaining skills and would take four hours. The Malaysian Airlines office is one kilometer from the airport and the return flight had to be confirmed.

Armed with a map and the appropriate X's noting the bus stop and hotel with the airline office, I found my partner still listening to our new found friend. Clearly, politeness was mistaken for kinship. Logically, we would need a taxi to get to the airline office and again to get us to the bus stop. We only had one bag each but who knows how many people would pack into the public bus. Time to bargain, with occasional glances at the hustlers lurking in the background just waiting for negotiations to fail. And making sure our guy saw me look at the competition.

The whole deal for 70,000 RP (US $35). We followed him to his taxi and got in the back. He got in next to the driver and gave directions to the hotel. We looked at each other, it wasn't his cab at all. And a beat up piece of junk, to boot. Humm. We all - the extended family - parked in the hotel lot and I went into the office to confirm our flight departure. Without a confirmation, they would give away our seats even though we had reservations. When I returned to our guarded baggage there was another deal. We were to change cabs - to a much nicer one - and the new driver would take us the rest of the way. The hook was that these two would get 40,000 RP now and we pay the remaining 30,000 RP to the new driver after we get there. Oh well, in for a penny, in for a pound.

The new driver and the new cab went to the dispatchers office in town. An attractive English speaking woman came out of the office and asked if we would be willing to take a passenger along for the ride. The driver spoke no English and seeing the passenger was a young lady, we agreed. We figured it was the driver's girlfriend. Finally, we were on our way and out on the open road, into the hill country and through the jungle. Until he stopped at a road side store to get some snacks. And later stopped for gas. And later stopped for cigarettes. We were still making good time over rickety bridges and through small town after small town when a policeman stepped into the middle of the road and flagged us down. No one in the front seat spoke English and no one in the back spoke anything else.

The driver showed his papers and then his frustration when the cop started writing a ticket. We were going slowly through town, so it couldn't be for speeding. The driver stamped his feet and leaned into the cab to explain the situation to us in Indonesian. He reached out his hand for money, expecting us contribute to the fine. This was no time to indicate any comprehension of the scene and we returned blank stares. He became more frustrated. The policeman finished the ticket and our driver followed him into the police station to complete the transaction. It was the first day of the month and we concluded that his registration had just expired.

We asked him to turn down the radio earlier and he was satisfied to drive and brood. It was a cassette of Indonesian bells and drums played loud enough to entertain the entire car and any shop we drove by. An hour of drums and bells was enough. We enjoyed a modicum of peace and quiet.

An hour later, in the midst of a snaking mountain road, he pulled in a small car park on the edge of a cliff. A comfort stop, we expected, and got out to stretch our legs. There was a wonderful view of the lake to the left and right, as far as we could see. Directly in front of us was a mountain extending from the far side of the lake. Far too big to be our island (it was) but impressive and no way to tell if it was an island or an extension of the far shore.

Then a man appeared from nowhere. No houses or structures in sight and yet, there he was. With faulting English, he had a deal. He would take us across the lake on his boat to his hotel and he wanted to negotiate the price. There was no boat in view let alone a hotel so we weren't going anywhere sight unseen. We stretched, he talked. We got back in the cab. Now the twists and turns of the mountain were negotiated with drums and bells at full volume.

We stopped at the entrance gate twenty minutes later with hearing impairments. The guard was very polite, took 500 RP (25 cents) for the two of us and volunteered the going rate for the ferry boat. The driver took the near empty streets at Indianapolis 500 speed, serenading the whole town with his radio. After a screeching halt at the ferry terminal, he waited while our bags got out first and I counted the 30,000 RP into his out stretched hand. He continued to wait while we walked into the run down terminal and he stayed an additional 20 minutes. Guess he figured we would change our mind about a tip.

The terminal, for want of a better name, is a bar/restaurant with a ticket counter. The fellow in charge speaks very good English and since the next boat would leave in a half an hour, that's how much time he had to make a deal. The boat ticket price was as quoted by the gate guard, so far so good. Then the hotel and the buttering up. He didn't use the term rich but clearly dignified people like us wouldn't want to stay in a dump. We would obviously want a hotel suited to our station in life. A full bathroom in the room, hot and cold water, the best restaurant and on and on.

We changed the subject to transportation back to Medan. The price was 85,000 and we needed a reservation. Politely refused. He continued, "Medan has 1,000 cabs. We have only three. If you don't reserve, there may be no cab when you want to leave." The point was well taken. After driving through town, even at breakneck speed, it was apparent we didn't want to be stuck in Parapat for even one night. Money up front, of course. I've been to Indonesia before and found, unlike China, they stick to their word once the agreement is reached. He gave a receipt without us asking.

Now back to the hotel, he still had time. We planed to visit several and select on the spot but, "The boat will drop you off at any hotel but you must select one." Humm. Then, for the first time, he talked rates. The best hotel on the island, Toledo I, is 60,000 RP a night for two. That's US $30 total. Sold. He called them and made the reservation and didn't balk when informed we would pay at the hotel.

The Captain of the boat looked fifteen years old and had an assistant who looked younger. The boat was older than the two combined. A half an hour trip and after dropping off two passengers, the first mate had a deal for us. The walkways to the front of the boat were 18 inches wide and there was no guardrail. Easy to slip into the water, so he would carry our bags onto the dock. Eventually, the Captain joined in while the boat ran unattended. After grueling negotiations, assisted by the fact that we were perfectly capable of carrying our own bags, we settled at 200 RP each (10 cents).

Unfortunately, the boat left us at Toledo II and after looking at the rooms, we walked ½ mile to Toledo I. The staff carried our bags.

Stairs and more stairs. Stairs up from Toledo I and back down to II. Then, more stairs down from the lobby to the lake and up to the room. The architecture is Batak and stunning to look at. A nicely appointed room with a beautiful view of the lake. No phone, no TV, no radio but there is hot water. Several boat docks, jet skis to rent, a large restaurant with inside and patio dining, a SMALL concession shop and an auditorium for evenings entertainment. There was a Japanese tour group a few Europeans and us. A hundred people - 1/3 capacity. My first meal was sweet and sour chicken, rice and coffee (US $4). Very good. My friend had fried chicken (not good). One of the biggest dangers in Indonesia is from the food. Simple to pick up a bug that confines you to the room for days. Neither of us had that problem here. The next few days were spent relaxing. Eating, laying about and watching the hotel staff put on variety shows in the evening. Singing, dancing, juggling, magic, whatever.

We rented a cab to take us to town. A twenty minute drive or an hours walk on a much abused road. A few dollars well spent. There are no souvenir shops at the hotel and an abundance in the town of Tomok. You name it, they've got it and the Tomb of King Sidabatu. Off the main drag, up a side street lined with shops (good bargains). He was one of the last animist kings before the arrival of Christianity. He is inside an above ground, weathered, sculptured, stone crypt that faces three rows of engraved grey stone benches. Directly behind the benches is huge tree with above ground roots that grow to and under the benches. An eerie monochromic scene with the only color coming from the surrounding jungle and the green mold on the stone crypt. A setting for the Twilight Zone. Save some time to look at the merchandise in the stands. Remember, they're willing to deal.

Peaceful, relaxing and a joy to the eyes. The third world at it's best and all in the middle of nowhere. When we returned to Parapat, a new van was waiting for us. The driver recognized us immediately. Plenty of room to move about and four hours later he dropped us at the hotel of our choice. Who could ask for anything more.

THE END

311

## TOBA SIDEBAR

GETTING THERE - From the west coast, the most direct connections are from Kuala Lumpur (KL), via Penang on daily flights on Malaysia Airlines. Price from Los Angeles to KL is around $1300 RT advance purchase. However, we went from Singapore which is serviced by Northwest and Singapore Airlines (US $1300 RT). Then to Penang and on to Medan on Malaysian Air. Round trip airfare from Singapore to Penang (including Medan, Sumatra) is $222. Purchase in Singapore at any travel agency. Consolidator tickets from LAX to Singapore are available for around $700 RT. Consult the travel section adds in your newspaper.

WHEN TO GO - Indonesia has an Equatorial climate and is hot through out the year. The wettest months in Sumatra are September to March. Loose fitting cotton clothes are best. Lake Toba is in the mountains, it can get chilly at night.

WHERE TO STAY - TOLEDO I is the best and equivalent to a Travelodge or Days Inn. US $27 for singles and $30 for a double. Meals are $3-4. TOLEDO II, down the road has doubles for $20. At the south end of Tuk-Tuk is Carolinas, one of the oldest and most popular with rooms from US $5 to $20. There are at least 40 places in between and some as low as $2 a night. Draw your own conclusions.

WHERE TO EAT - The best food is at the better hotels. And the safest from Indonesian revenge. We ate at TOLEDO I and had no problems.

WHAT TO DO - You can rent a car to go around the island but there isn't much to see. Mind you, it's a big island with a bigger mountain in the middle. You can also hire a jet ski, or a boat for a water tour or a taxi for a trip to town (shopping, shopping). Otherwise, bring books.

FOR MORE INFORMATION -Write to the Indonesian Tourist office, 3457 Wilshire Blvd., Suite 104, Los Angeles, CA 90010. tel. (213)387-2078. Or the Toledo Inn, Tuk-Tuk, Samosir Island, North Sumatra, Indonesia. tel (0625)41181 fax. (0625)41174.

# THEY SAY WHEN YOU DIE YOU CAN'T TAKE IT WITH YOU.

# IN TORAJA, THEY DO.

Sulawesi, Indonesia - Toraja Houses modeled after
the boats that brought them there

RANTEPAO, SULIWESI, INDONESIA - In some cultures, if a young girl doesn't have a big enough dowry, she can't get married. In America, a great deal of money is spent on showcase weddings. In Toraja, it's different. Grandma can sit on the porch, stone dead, until the family comes up with the rupiah to bury her properly. Not that the undertaker gets the money, it's all for appearance. I heard about "sending the dearly departed out in style while delivering the family into poverty", and that's what brought me to the middle of the Island of Suliwesi.

Suliwesi is roughly in the middle of the Indonesian chain of Islands that stretch 3000 miles from east to west. Borneo is to the left and the Spice Islands to the right. The island, in the shape of an inverted "U" with a tail hanging in the wind from the top, looks more like a badly shaped ink blot than an island. Strange shape, strange customs. There are 12 million residents and dozens of dialects, two of which are spoken nowhere else in the world.

I was approached on the bus to Rantepao to buy a tour package. An easy mark since I was the only white face on the bus. It was a soft sell with a reasonable price. I went for it because it included a funeral ceremony. He knew where one was and I didn't.

## THE TOUR - DAY 1

The first scheduled stop was the village of Bori, 6 kilometers north of town on a dirt and gravel, pot holed filled, excuse for a road and I was out of the van taking pictures before we got there. It was just me, the driver and the English speaking guide. I could stop when I wanted and there was a small community of traditional houses along the road crying out for my camera.

The roof of each house is shaped like a long boat rearing high in the front and in the rear. All the houses are above the ground on poles and the roof sticks into the air twice as high as the house proper. The exterior walls have geometric designs and renderings of the Buffalo painted in red. Red is to symbolize life, the color of blood. They all face north to pay homage to their ancestors who came to this land by boat. Numerous buffalo horns are attached to the front pole which supports the high gable. The buffalo is a sign of wealth. The more horns, the higher the status. Rice barns have the same shape but no horns.

The first official stop was the Bori cemetery (for lack of a better word). There's a small ceremonial site alongside the road with tall slender stone monuments (megaliths) used for festivities following a burial. The wealthy use it for free having paid for the monuments. Others can rent the site. Adjacent, is a large rock in which stone cutters have carved crypts for the rich. Family members are buried in the stone tomb and the opening is closed with steel plate or concrete after each use. The wealthy are buried with many of their possessions, like the ancient Egyptians, and grave robbers abound.

Between the megaliths and the large burial rock, is a stone path leading up into the jungle. At the top is a banyan tree. The poor carve a small hole in the tree to bury a still born with its placenta. The hole is sealed with wood and the babies soul is believed to grow with the tree.

The next stop was Palawa, a traditional village with a dog that took a dislike to me. Fortunately, it was all snarl and no bite. Then, Sadan the weaving center of the region and Nanggala a wealthy village. The fascinating spot, Marante, came at the end of the day. The rich have caves dug into the rocky hillside. The deceased is entombed with his gold, jewelry and other worldly possessions and the entrance is sealed. Then a wooden platform is mounted outside to hold life sized wood statues depicting the family. They stand guard at the grave. Keep in mind, these crypts are halfway up the side of sheer rock and aren't that easy to get to.

On the other side of the shear face is a gentle climb and caves have been dug into soft earth. The less prosperous use these openings. A decaying coffin had four skulls sitting on top and four damaged skulls and bones lying in front. Nothing to take here except the half empty plastic bottle of drinking water left for the dead should they become thirsty in the afterlife. Around the corner is "the swinging bridge" that leads over the river to the village. It didn't look too sturdy to me. I stayed on my side.

## DAY 2

The first stop was the village of Lemo, the most impressive burial site of all. It's the one featured in postcards. We walked past the longest array of tourist shops to the edge of the plateau. One hundred feet below is a green valley of rice with a shear rock face on the other side, 500 feet away. At this distance it looks like a village built into the rock. On closer inspection, however, the face is pockmarked with square openings (sealed, of course) denoting crypts chiseled into the rock but more impressive is the rectangular cuts just below that hold 10 life sized mannequins dressed in white. A wood bannister is installed and the standing models are resting their hands on the rail, looking down at us. There are 12 such stone platforms all lined with replicas of family members.

Directly across, on the hillside from whence we came is the model maker. An elderly gentleman hard at work carving each new model by hand. An American tourist left a Polaroid picture and will be back in a year to pick up a life size model of herself. It takes all kinds.

Next stop was Kambira, the site of a Banyon tree grave for the young. Then Lobe, where the orphans put on a flute serenade. The little ones are so cute and played their little hearts out. Donations are accepted and not included in the tour price. I mention this because many of the sites have token fees and the funeral ceremony expects a gift (usually a carton of cigarettes). These are included in the tour price.

## THE FUNERAL

Ceremonies are held in the village of the deceased and can be miles back in the jungle. I lucked out with one held close to a paved road. The access, however, was on a steep downhill path turned to mud from yesterday's late rain. One false step and I would slide to the bottom, on my bottom. How then, to take this treacherous path and keep camera, lens, flash and film from harm's way. Very, very, slowly. And an ample use of the guides shoulder. Several slips but no falls; past the villagers lining the path waiting to pay their respects.

Just inside the large tent were 5 empty plastic chairs. We sat to be served cookies and coffee and chat with one of the sons. An educated man with perfect English who welcomed me as if I was a member of the family. My guide handed the carton of cigarettes in a brown paper bag to one of the attendants while the son and I made small talk. Diagonally across were two of the grand daughters in red ceremonial dress. They smiled at all who entered and then, to my surprise, took my picture with a small Kodak. Clearly I wasn't a member of the family but I was being treated as an honored guest. Frankly, I felt a little guilty. Still, I returned the favor and took their picture. They were all smiles.

317

I've never taken pictures at a funeral before but after such a gracious welcome I was more at ease. We moved to one of the bull pens along the left side and sat on the ground to wait. There are three cordoned off areas and we advanced as the closest was emptied into the largest area at the rear. That section had chairs and the men and women sat on either side. Prayer was made over the loud speaker system to each new group in the chaired section. Pigs were carried past strung upside down on sticks by teams of men. Some were alive, some had been cooked over an open fire. This was the second of a four day ceremony and the feast of pigs and buffalo would take place over the next two days.

The deceased was a grandmother and died 10 days ago. As is the custom, she is considered among the living until the ceremony is finished. Her soul will ride the souls of the pigs and buffalo to the afterlife. Her status will be the same there as in this life, so the number of animals slaughtered is important and the entire village will witness the ceremony. And feast on the kill.

It is possible to "borrow" animals from others in the village for the ceremony. But, like all debts, they must be repaid in kind and one or two buffalo could represent an entire family's net worth. Sons and daughters inherit the parents property equally. That is, what remains of it. It's sad to think of so many animals being sacrificed but in this case the meat is eaten by the attendees. It does not go to waste. But, thinking ahead to the next funeral, how long must Grandpa sit in the living room, hard as a carp, before the family can afford to bury him.

## THE END

## TORAJA SIDEBAR

GETTING THERE - From the west coast of the U.S., the most direct route is Hawaii - Bali - Ujung Pandang (UPG), Suliwesi, Indonesia. Then fly north from the UPG airport to the airport just north of Makale - $60 each way (if the airplane isn't grounded for maintenance). An airport bus or taxi to Makale is about $10 and twice that to Rantepao. Rantepao is in the center of Toraja, Makale is on the southern edge.

There are connecting flights from the USA thru Tokyo or Hong Kong and onto Jakarta and back to UPG. I went from Singapore (to the east) which is serviced by Northwest, United, Garuda and Singapore Airlines (US $1300 RT from the USA west coast). Then east to Jakarta and UPG.

If the airplane is not flying north from UPG to Toraja, there is a 10 hour bus trip. The outdoor bus terminal is east of town, half way back to the airport. The bus costs $10 (one way) for non air conditioned and $15 a/c. Tickets are bought at the bus. There are several busses to choose from and the a/c ones run infrequently (inquire ahead of time).

WHEN TO GO - Indonesia has an Equatorial climate and is hot through out the year. The dry season is from May to October plus or minus a month at either end.

WHERE TO STAY - The best in Rantepao is the 4 star Marante Highland Resort, five miles north of town. Rates run from $120 single/$150 double to $190 for a suite, plus 21% service charge and tax. tel. 0423-21616 fax. 0423-21122 or write P.O Box 52, Rantepao, Suliwesi Selatan, Indonesia. The best in the middle of town is the Hotel Indra II for $55/65. tel. 0423-21442. It has a beautiful interior garden and the dining room overlooks the river. Across the street is the Indra I for $25/30 including tax and breakfast. tel. 0423-21163. Next door is Indra City (all owned by the same people) for twice the rate of Indra I. All the Indras take Visa and MC. There are a number of $20 a night hotels just around

319

the corner from the Indras, it's a small town. In Makale, the best is the Marannu city Hotel for $70/90. tel. 0423-22028.

WHERE TO EAT - The hotels are the safest bet and offer the best food. Indonesian revenge is always a problem in the third world so be sure to take Imodium and Pepto Bismol. I did not get sick. Just south of Indra II is Kiosk Mambo with good Indonesian and Torajan food.

WHAT TO DO - You will be approached (this is Indonesia) at the airport or the bus stop to arrange a tour package for the area. Doing it by yourself with public transportation will be very time consuming and is not recommended. There is a tourist service in Rantepao but everyone is selecting from the same menu and all prices are negotiable. I was nabbed at the bus stop in Makale and driven by private van to Rantepao on the pretext that this was normal bus service.

My two day tour was slightly less than $75 a day and included the guide, the van, a driver, gas, parking and entrance fees and donations (except the Lobe orphans, which was up to me). It included 5 sites the first day and 6 the second, including a funeral ceremony. The itinerary was laid out on paper on the back of a map of the area. The guide was Yohanis Kiding, c/o Hotel Indra I, Jl. Landorundun 63, Rantepao, Suliwesi Selatan, Indonesia and is recommended. tel. 0423-21163

FOR MORE INFORMATION- Write to the Indonesian Tourist office, 3457 Wilshire Blvd., Suite 104, Los Angeles, CA 90010. tel. (213)387-2078. Or write to the hotel by name.

# IV AUSTRALIA

## BATHURST and MELVILLE ISLANDS

### Home of the Tiwi Aborigines

Melville Island, north of Darwin, Australia
- Catholic church - time exposure

NORTHERN TERRITORY, AUSTRALIA - There are a couple of reasons very few outsiders have ever been to Bathurst Island. First, its 80 kilometers north of Darwin, Australia and Darwin isn't on the way to anyplace in particular. Second, The Darwin area is virtually closed during the yearly monsoons (wet season) from October to March. Third, most tourists go to Darwin to visit Kakadu National Park, one of the natural wonders of Australia. It's a huge rain forest, 100 KM by 200 KM, and can eat up a two week vacation by itself. Lastly, Bathurst and the neighboring Melville are privately owned by the Aborigines and access is by permit only. Private ownership is the result of the Aboriginal Land (NT) Act of 1976 which allowed groups to claim land with which they have traditional ties.

It's about a half hour trip from the Darwin airport over the Beagle Gulf of the Timor sea to the small airport outside Nguiu, the main settlement on Bathurst. An uneventful flight in a single engine Cherokee that would be death defying in poor weather. The plane carries tourists and much needed supplies for the market in town. The Tiwi's don't farm and subsisted in the past as hunters and gatherers. They didn't trade and there was no money, so if they wanted something they made it themselves.

The first street lights were installed in 1976 and the first phones in 1980. In order to generate capital, the Tiwi Land Council formed a joint venture with a Darwin tour company. Trips are managed by the tour company for a fee and the council gets hard cash to finance the tribes needs. The permit fee is included in the tour price.

## THE CATHOLIC PRIEST WITH 150 WIVES

The Australian guide met the plane and, after a brief trip through town, stopped at the Catholic Church. Nguiu was formed as a mission in 1911 and has since become an important part of the Tiwi peoples lives. The customs of the church and this ancient tribe were hardly alike in the early years and after more than 80 years, many of the old customs remain. The Aborigine women are engaged at birth and usually married between years 10 and 13. Men usually first married at 35 and had the most wives just before death. The husband not only had a wife but was responsible for all her sisters. When he died, she married the next relative. So, some husbands not only had their own wives, but also inherited others after a brother died. This gives new dimension to the term "enlarged family". The women had no say in the matter.

One of the wives-to-be took exception to her betrothed and ran away. The island is of good size but not large enough to hide on for very long. So she ended up at the Catholic church and threw herself at the mercy of the priest. In a creative moment he approached the council with a proposition. Keep in mind, there had to be face saving on both the sides of this conflict. The groom would be publicly spurned and have no woman. The girls family would be publicly humiliated for raising such an outlaw. The priest

323

offered to take the girl as his own and compensate the grooms family. The council agreed and both sides saved face. Unfortunately for the priest, this set a precedent and shortly thereafter another young girl didn't want her husband to be. In a few years, the priest had accumulated 150 wives. And then the Bishop found out.

Fortunately, the church was unusually tolerant or possibly the priest had a way with words. After all, he did convince the Aborigine council to go against thousands of years of tradition. He was allowed to remain but no more wives, please.

## THE JAPANESE PRISONER OF WAR

Darwin was bombed by the Japanese during WW II in an attempt to gain a foothold in Australia. On February 19, 1942 a Japanese pilot crashed on the island on route to Darwin. Shortly afterward, Matthais Ulungura, a Tiwi, captured the terrified pilot who expected to be eaten by the cannibals that inhabited the island. So he was told. To his surprise, he was turned over to the authorities and put in prison. The bent propeller from that airplane leans on a building next to the church. The church itself is a marvelous wooden structure on stilts with an altar rich in aborigine custom.

The town, population 1300, is ruled by the council in which men and women vote. It is freely elected and the decisions are final. Beer can be bought only at the market and is rationed. There is one place in town to drink beer and it's open six days a week from 4:30 to 7 PM. If anyone gets drunk, everyone in town knows about it. If a husband and wife argue, everyone knows the next day. There is a policeman with two assistants but not much in the way of real crime. Nguiu has a school, market, post office, bank, museum for tourists, restaurant, housing association, Tiwi design screen printing workshop, Tiwi pottery and Bima wear clothing. All jobs on the island are filled.

Morning tea and biscuits are taken at the park where local women make original art designs on sea shells and flat rocks. Pretty and colorful with pigments made from local ingredients. Among the guard dogs, hovering around for leftovers, is a tame dingo. They are not tame in the outback on the mainland. The art is for sale here and in Darwin.

Then a quick tour of the single story pre-fab housing section. The Tiwi's decided that they wanted homes just like those on the mainland. They can't be owned, for good reason as we shall see later, and the rent is $8 per month for each family member than works. Unemployment is high since there are more people than jobs and a Tiwi's first obligation is to the family. Hence, rent applies only to working members. Unless an item is specifically designated as personal property it belongs to all family members. Like the television or the refrigerator or the food therein. One cannot say no to an uncle or sister-in-law since all is family owned. Individual property is allowed but all personal property goes into the grave when the person dies. If a man wants to watch his shows on his TV, he can, but if he doesn't bequeath it to the family in time, it goes in the grave with him. Neither husbands nor wives tell family members how much they make. Nor each other for that matter since that would solicit a request for money.

## NEPOTISM RULES

Which brings us to the Bima Wear Clothing manufacturing company. A group of about 40 formed a collective to make a line of designer wear. Original aborigine patterns of dresses and assorted women's wear. A successful collection of colorful clothing that is sold at selective boutiques on the mainland. All 40 workers are equal partners and are paid wages from the profits. The trouble was at the start. First obligations are to the family and the original members had to hire relatives who couldn't be fired without the family losing face. And there was more family than jobs. The solution was to hire a white lady from the mainland as manager. An adjacent business takes Tiwi designs and screen prints them on bolts of cloth for use in Bima's sewing operation. A short distance away is Tiwi pottery, manufacturing vases and assorted kitchen wear for sale.

## MELVILLE ISLAND

The guides' wife met us at the beach with her jeep and a towed boat. It was backed into the water not 50 yards from a recent tragedy. A Tiwi woman had left her baby for a moment and returned to see a crocodile eating her child. The child died after she shoed the creature off. These waters are infested with crocodiles and this story is not unique. The Tiwi's believe that during creation, the aborigine was made first and animals were made from people. A man killed with a spear comes back in another life as a crocodile.

A jeep was waiting on he other side for the half hour jungle trip to Taracumbie Falls, in the middle of the sister island. Lunch is buffet style with cold cuts, corn, salad, cantaloupe, oranges and apples. The base of the falls is at the bottom of a tricky thirty foot ladder hidden by untamed rain forest. But that adds to the charm as does the rope swing. A beautiful, peaceful waterfall in the middle of the jungle in the center of nowhere. Just the birds, the water and you.

## THE GRAVEYARD

Death is a ceremony not unlike other cultures. The family gathers at the grave posted with six foot totem poles to commemorate the deceased. If he or she owned a house, it must be burned to the ground. All personal possessions go into the grave. They cannot speak the first name of the deceased again for fear that it will recall his spirit from the dead and anyone in the tribe with the same first name, changes it.

Most of the tribe has lunged into the 20th century although some continue to live as hunters and gatherers. They no longer take a boat to the mainland to abduct women from the other tribes. The Tiwi's never used a boomerang. They were willing to steal women from the mainland but not the customs.

## THE END

## SIDEBAR FOR THE BATHURST

GETTING THERE - Sydney, Australia is serviced by Northwest, United, Quantas, Air New Zealand and others. Normal coach fare is around $1200 RT from Los Angeles but there are frequent discounts offered by the airlines and bargain tickets advertised in the travel section of the newspaper for around $800 RT. There is service to Darwin on Australian Airlines from eastern Australia.

LOCAL TOUR ARRANGEMENT - Can be made at the Darwin Airport at the Tiwi Tour Airline counter. Advance bookings can be made at Tiwi Tours, GPO Box 1397, Darwin, Northern Territory, Australia 0801. tel. (089) 815144. After hours tel. (089) 816528. Fax. (089) 815391. Reservations can also be made toll free in Australia at tel. (008) 891121.

CHOICE OF TOURS - All the following include transportation - Half day Bathurst for a tour of Nguiu = US $120. Day tour of Bathurst includes lunch = US $150. Full day tour of Bathurst and Melville islands including lunch (the best deal) = US $180. Available are 2 and 3 day tours for US $ 420 and US $ 540. Overnight accommodations are in a twin share fabric cabin with electricity till 11 PM. Showers are toilets are communal and meals are barbecued. Extra days are US $190 each per person.

FOR MORE INFORMATION - Write: The Western Australian Tourist Commission, 2121 Avenue of the Stars, Suite 1210, Los Angeles, CA 90067 (213)557-1987 or the Australian Tourist Information Office in New York (212)944-6880, Chicago (312)644-8029, Los Angeles (310)477-3332.

## BORA BORA ON A BUDGET

### or Stretching your dollar in French Polynesia

Budget, like good looks, is a relative term. Bora Bora and the rest of the Society Islands are known for their beauty and their high costs. Guide books state it directly - there are two prices here, expensive and very expensive. That said, there are ways to cut costs dramatically and still enjoy one of the most beautiful islands in the world. This is not a rock bottom guide for those willing to sleep under a tree and eat coconuts but for those on a modest budget who choose to spend their money on the experience rather than hotels and fine dining.

### GETTING THERE

All international flights land at Papeete, Tahiti. Connecting service to Bora Bora is provided from there. More on that later. The busiest months are July and August, so the chances of finding a bargain are close to zero. The low season is from 25 DEC to 15 JUN and that's when you are in the best position to choose. The islands are close to the equator and there is little difference in temperature during the year. The rainy season (intermittent) is between November and April. Dry season (still a chance of short rains) is from May to October. Departure cities from the mainland USA are San Francisco and Los Angeles and the scheduled airlines are Air France/UTA, Air New Zealand, Quantas and Hawaiian Air. The normal coach fare from Los Angeles is around $1100 but during the low season, there are specials.

Specials are offered by consolidators in the travel sections of the major newspapers. Here are some samples of the round trip fares from Los Angeles to Papeete during the low season-Corsair = $509, AOM = $530, both French airlines, Air France = $530, Quantas = $660. There are restrictions, Corsair leaves Monday night only and none of the airlines fly every day. I got an AF ticket for $550 leaving on the weekend and returning mid week. Once you're in Papeete, there are two ways to get to Bora Bora, boat or plane. Three boats service the islands. The Taporo IV leaves Monday, Wednesday and Friday at 5 PM and arrives 11 AM the following morning. The Temehani II on Wednesday and the Raromatai on Tuesday and Friday with similar departures and arrivals. A cabin goes for $30 and sleeping on the deck overnight about half that. These boats are freighters and haul cargo, the cabins are very basic and arrival times vary. Schedules in the islands are more flexible than in the USA.

Flying time to Bora Bora is 45 minutes and there is no choice of airlines. Air Tahiti has a monopoly and the fare is $130 US one way on a twin prop 40 seater. There are four flights a day and they will charge you overweight for anything over 30 pounds. A hand carry purse or a camera bag is allowed. Leave the hair dryers, radios and electric shavers at home or you will pay more than they are worth. I took the boat from Raiatea for $10 US and arrived 3 hours later. Flew back and made the weight.

Flying is convenient because it's from Faa'a, the airport serving Papeete. Make a right turn after departing customs and walk to the end of the terminal for reservations and the flight gate. Your flight to Bora Bora may leave you some idle time and you may as well spend it in Papeete. If you are going by boat, you must go into the town. There are two ways to get to town. The 15 minute taxi ride is $17 US during the day. 50% more at night and double on holidays and Sundays. However, there is a baggage check in at the airport a few steps past the Air Tahiti office where a medium sized bag can be stored for $3 a day. Then walk to the center of the terminal, turn right and walk thru the parking lot, up the double set of stairs and carefully cross the road. On the airport side is a bus stop but there isn't one on this side. Never the less, Le Truck will stop at the slightest signal since they are independently owned. A sign in front will say Papeete and the fare is $1 to the center of town. Take care where you depart. Walk back one half block along the waterfront and turn inland for 2 blocks, left turn to the off road waiting area for Le Truck back to the airport. If you stay on board Le Truck at the center of town, for another fare, you can go the additional 5 blocks to the boat terminal.

## AT FAA'A AIRPORT

Papeete is the only real town in the islands but you may wish an island tour instead. There is a money changer at the airport that opens for all international flights and it's a good place to change your money. Information on touring companies can be obtained from the tourist information counter at the airport but they won't call for you. A 50 CFP coin into the phone and wait for the dial tone. Alternatively, the Avis and Hertz car rental concessions are owned by touring companies and will help if you look lost. An island tour costs $ 44 US, runs from 9 AM to 3:30 PM and they will pick up and drop off at the airport.

## ARRIVING IN BORA BORA

If you come by boat it will be next to Faanui Bay, the bay north of the capital and only town, Vaitape. If by air, the boat will take you from Motu Mote, the island with the airport, to Vaitape. In both cases you will be met by taxis and Bora Bora's Le Truck. Bora Bora's population is about 2600, so there is less business for Le Truck, hence, higher prices than Tahiti. Vaitape is located at about 9 O'clock and the best beaches and accommodation deals at about 6 O'clock. Le Truck will cost from $3 to $5. When coming from the boat, the driver automatically stops at the only grocery store in town for the passengers to stock up. From the plane, you're on your own.

## LODGING

Even in low season it's best to have reservations since the bargain places go first. On the high end there's the Yacht Club (10 o'clock), a Japanese resort on Motu Toopua directly across from Vaitape (9 o'clock), Hotel Bora Bora (7 o'clock) and the Hotel Matira, the Park Royal and the Marara (6 o'clock). Their prices begin at $250 for a room on land and $550 US for one over water. The only beach on the island is in the south west corner (7 o'clock to 6 o'clock) and that's also where the best budget accommodations are. Closest to the road on a peninsula jutting into the lagoon is Chez Nono Levard (pronounced Noel), a friendly and comfortable place on the beach with a beautiful view. Singles for $44, doubles $55 and a bungalow (up to four people) $148/day. Kitchen facilities are provided and that will be important after you see the cost of meals. Breakfast and dinner are available for $9 and $20. They can take 20 people and this is probably the best deal on the island.

A few minutes walk on the peninsula is Chez Robert an adequate facility with room for about 14. Prices are about the same and kitchen facilities are available. Robert is not particularly friendly but the house is on the beach facing the lagoon. A 10 minute walk past the peninsula is the recommended Chez Pauline. On the beach with bungalows, a view and kitchen facilities for prices similar to the above. They also have camping for $16 (bring your own equipment) and new, up scale bungalows with kitchens for about $100. They have room for about 48, plus campers.

## TRANSPORTATION

Considering that taxi rides go for about $20 a pop, getting around can be an important consideration. The Hotel Bora Bora is a 20 minute walk from the peninsula and a ride to town is 20 minutes on Le Truck which runs, at best, sporadically. They have good rates but you may kill several hours waiting. Bikes can be rented at the Chez's for $5 a half day and $9 a full day but they aren't good for carrying groceries. Le Truck is the best bet for carrying large supplies of liquid refreshment. There are car rental places in town (they will deliver) for $83/day and scooters for $40/day.

## FOOD

By now you have a rough idea of the cost of eating out. Breakfast is $10 and lunch and dinner $20 - $50 per person without alcoholic beverages. Breakfast at the Hotel Bora Bora is $21 US. There is an alternative if you choose to not cook - snack stands. Within a 10 minute walk of the peninsula, towards the Hotel Bora Bora, is Snack Matira on the beach side and Ben's, on the inland side. Matira has the juiciest hamburgers for $3.50, milk shake ($3.50) and an egg hamburger for $4. An omelette with everything in it and a beer at Ben's for $12, lasagna for $10, and a pizza with bacon, mushrooms, olives and pineapple for $10. Soda is $2.20 a can. Mrs. Ben is an ex-pat from Costa Mesa, CA. Married Ben from BB and moved here 10 years ago. Both shops are open from 11 AM to 8 PM and are recommended.

## WHAT TO DO

Much of the beach at the 3 Chez's is shaded by palm trees and the are tables and chairs for lounging around. Much of the pale blue lagoon is shallow and you can swim or snorkel to your hearts content without ever leaving the grounds. However there are two tours that shouldn't be missed. A half day inland tour of the island with Danny for $37. He makes 4 excursions from the main road to mountain tops on roads that are often too treacherous to walk. Included is the spectacular view of the Hotel Bora Bora and the surrounding lagoon from the TV tower. Breathtaking. Then the view of the guns installed during WW II to protect the harbor from the Japanese. Guns which now overlook the new Japanese Hotel across from Vaitape.

The second is a lagoon tour. Chez Nono will collect you from other accommodations for a full day of lagoon cruising, snorkeling (literally thousands of types of colorful fish and coral) and Polynesian lunch for $48. The best place is the second stop, just before lunch, where the current slowly pulls you over a mile of coral, some of which is inches from the surface. Shouldn't be missed.

For night life there are few choices. On TV, I saw some of Doogie Howser dubbed in French. There is the Hotel Bora Bora bar, a 20 minute walk and Bloody Mary's, hangout for the stars, 10 minutes farther. Bloody Mary's has a pick up and return from the Hotel BB and the Yacht club. The celebrities, listed in front, include Dudley Moore, Prince Rainer, Jimmy Buffett, Marilyn Chambers, Jane Fonda, Marlon Brando and lots more. It's not cheap but you can nurse a beer. Then there's Le Recif, close to the Yacht Club, a late night club. For a quiet evening there's the Chez Christian restaurant at the Revatua Hotel (2 o'clock) and they will pick you up. Meals in the $40 range.

The Chez's will arrange for Le Truck to take you back to the airplane or the boat. There are custom boutiques along the road between the peninsula and the Hotel BB. Their souvenirs are unique and higher priced than those in town but it's free to look. In town, t-shirts are $15-20, hand painted ones $30, shell necklaces $11-16, small stone figures and ash trays $20. The necklaces, etc. can be bought from the shop in the parking lot at Faa'a airport for the same price or better. Remember the weight, if you're flying.

## THE END

## SAVINGS IN A NUTSHELL

GETTING THERE - Coach price from Los Angeles to Papeete is $1100 RT. Specials offered by consolidators in the major newspapers go for $550 RT. Don't go in July or August, the busy months. Plan for May, June, September, October to miss the rainy season. Savings $550 per person. At the airport in Papeete. Take a tour of the island from the airport if there is time to kill. The cost is about the same as you would drink at the airport lounge. If you go to town, use Le Truck for $1 instead of the $20 taxi each way. Savings $36 for two.

There are 4 flights a day on Air Tahiti, USA tel. (800)5533477 to Bora Bora. Forty five minutes, one way for $130. They charge for weight over 30 pounds so travel with a light weight bag like the type that fits into the overhead compartment of a regular airplane and a camera bag or purse that can hold the heavy items (cameras, etc.). Savings $40 each.

Spend a very basic night (18 hours) on a freighter. Taporo IV, Compagnie Francaise Maritime de Tahiti, BP 368, Papeete, Tahiti (tel.42-63-93) - Temehani II, Societe de Navigation Temehani, BP 9015, Papeete, Tahiti (tel. 42-98-83) Raromatai, BP 9012, Papeete, Tahiti (tel. 43-90-42) for $30. Savings $100 per person each way.

When arriving in Bora Bora, stock up on liquids at the store before taking Le Truck to your place instead of the taxi. Savings $20 plus an extra trip for the heavy items.

LODGING - Chez Nono Levard, BP 12, Vaitape, Bora Bora (tel. (689) 67-71-38/67-74-27). Chez Pauline, BP 215 (tel. (689) 67-72-16). Chez Robert, (tel. (689) 67-72-92). Singles $44, doubles $55, bungalows (up to 4 people) $148, all with kitchen facilities. Savings $200-400 a day.

FOOD - Three meals a day at the Chez's are around $50 per person and twice that at the hotels. The three Chez's have kitchen facilities and refrigerators. Savings $30 a day per person by using the kitchen. Two snack shops are within easy walking distance. They aren't open at breakfast time but will serve omelettes anytime and even grill steaks. Average meal is $10. Savings $20 a day per person.

Bruny Island

There are rough waters in Southern Tasmania

Hobart, Tasmania - Bruny Island is advertised as a "Wilderness and Wildlife Adventure" tour, south of Hobart, off the coast and essentially in the middle of nowhere. That was for tomorrow. Today we'd take a stroll around Hobart, the capital. Tasmania is Australia's only island state and two hours south, by air, from Sydney. Directly south of Tasmania is Antarctica and this isolation made it the perfect place for British Penal colonies, but, that's a thing of the past. Now it's a modern State with fashionable cities and vast areas of wilderness including 19 national parks. And, some of the cleanest air in the world.

Sydney is Australia's oldest city, Hobart the second oldest. We started the 2 ½ hour walking tour in one of the oldest sections of town, Salamanca Place. The sandstone Georgian warehouses replaced wood ones in 1835 and are recently restored. At the street level are craft shops, cafes and bars. All upscale and very touristy. Three blocks east we turned south on Runnymeade St. for a steep uphill climb to Arthur's Circus, a circle of quaint houses (postcard shot). Another block and west on Hampton Road which is lined with pretty cottages and boutique shops one would expect in a classy (expensive) district. A chocolate shop caught our eyes. The store window is filled with glass jars of candy. So high you can't see inside the shop. Who could resist?

The Tasmanian Island fudge is US $1.50 a piece. It's mild, smooth and not overly sweet. Now the walk is downhill, past St. David's park and Parliament Square to the Elizabeth St. pier. This is the current waterfront and the place to book a myriad of boat tours. Just past the pier are several dark iron statues depicting Louis Bernacchi and his dog Joe posing for a camera on a tripod. Louis was the first Tasmanian to winter in Antarctica. We continued to Hunter street and back uphill to our hotel. Had to burn off the fudge.

Next morning, the bus picked us up at the Tasmanian Visitors center and south we went to the ferry at Kettering. The ferry has 2 decks. Trucks on the bottom, cars on top and a capacity of 28 cars per level. It makes 10 trips a day and costs US $20 for a car. Bruny Island looks like two islands but is connected by an isthmus that looks like it would disappear at high tide. It doesn't but bad weather is not uncommon in this area and I have no doubt that there are times when part of the connecting road disappears and the ferry stays in port.

The island was sighted by Abel Tasman in 1642 and was later visited by the infamous Capt. Bligh. It was named after Rear Admiral Bruni D'Entrecasteaux who explored the area in 1792. Initially, the aborigines and the newcomers got along well. Then the sealers arrived. Then alcohol, then violence. The aborigines moved to other islands. Now there is a population of 642.

We stopped at the Adventure Bay shop for coffee and cake and to pick up the people who got there on their own and would do the boat trip only. A half mile walk to the boat and we were off. The boat is a 44 foot eco-cruiser and the Capt. said it was meant to handle rough waters. He repeated that later when we were being thrown out of our seats and across the aisle. The boat has a rounded hull so it rolls with the waves and is not apt to capsize. That means it pops about like a cork in rough water. The first 1/3 is the bow, the next 1/3 is interior seating with plastic sheet on the left side and open ports on the right. The last 1/3 is open sides and row seating. There were about 40 people and some chose to stand outside the middle third and hang onto the rail. We were given life vests and a full rain poncho with a hood. The Capt. said that 30 knot winds were normal for this area but currently some of the winds were up to 55 knots. I get sea sick and that's not what I wanted to hear. They handed out cinnamon tablets for those with motion sickness. I took four. Twenty minutes out and we hit some 10 foot swells and the boat literally left the water and crashed down on the other side. Half of us were thrown out of our seats onto the other half. I was convinced that the people outside on the rail had a death wish. The Capt. repeated that the boat was able to handle this kind of punishment. I wondered if my body was and hung onto the seat so I wouldn't be playing bumper car with the other people.

Adventure Bay, the starting point, is half way down the east side of the southern island and we were going down the east side towards the bottom. That's towards Antarctica. The Capt. explained that the waters were rough because this is the spot where the Antarctica current meets another and they clash. He hoped to get to the very bottom and the seal haulout (island loaded with seals) but he wouldn't know until he got close.

Hundreds of feet of shear cliff face go right to the sea. There are collections of sea kelp that grow 4 feet a day. The water is calmer close to shore and many times we were able to get within 10 feet of the stone face. Cliff edges stick out like tall walls, into the sea, and the waves have eaten holes into them at the waterline. Naturally, the boat went through. Pinnacles stick out of the water waiting for the waves to slowly eat them away and there is a blowhole that sprays the dark green water out 100 feet. We got close enough to wet down everyone in the rear of the boat

As we got closer to the seals, we hit 15 foot swells and the Capt. said no. He apologized and said safety first and gave everyone $10 credit at the gift shop. As badly as we were bounced around, oddly enough, I felt safe on board. This is the only way to see this rugged wilderness at the ends of the earth and if you don't get sea sick you'll have the time of your life.

Back to dry land and the Adventure Bay shop for lunch (included with the full day tour). A bowl of pumpkin soup and a great ham sandwich with vegetables. For the $10 credit I got two jars of Tasmanian mustard.

On the way back we stopped at the isthmus. One chap was surf sailing on the bay side. Calmer waters. There are stairs to a high point where one can see both islands. From here, on a clear day, you could almost see Antarctica.

## THE END

## SIDEBAR FOR BRUNY ISLAND

GETTING THERE - There are no direct flights from the USA. From the west coast, there is one stop service from Sydney, Australia to Hobart (change planes). Quantas has specials, depending on the season, for LAX-SYD, round trip, for $999 including 2 internal flights. Normal fares are LAX-SYD for $1800, consolidator fares are $1100. Quantas and Virgin Blue fly SYD-HOB. Virgin Blue is US $ 80 one way, Quantas $100. The full day tour is US $ 115, including lunch and pick up from your hotel. If you rent a car and drive to the tour office on Bruny, the boat cruise only is US $ 58. Remember, the ferry ride is US $ 20 each way.

WHEN TO GO - The seasons are reversed in Australia. Our winter is their summer. Summers are warm, not hot. Autumn is cool with frosty nights. Winter is cold, the State has 2 ski resorts. Spring is windy. Hobart is on the southern coast of Australia. The summer is best but the total air fares are approx. $300 more than winter.

HOTELS - There are hundreds of hotels to choose from in Hobart, virtually all the major chains. The Tasmanian Visitors center is very helpful - tasbookings@tavisinfo.com.au - and www.tasmaniasouth.com for both Hobart and booking this cruise.

HEALTH - No shots necessary.

MISCELLANEOUS - For additional information contact the Australian Tourist Commission - www.australia.com. All visitors need a visa and the only reasonable way to get it is on line - www.immi.gov.au

Kakadu

and the land of the Aborigines

Darwin, Australia - It was the end of the wet season but that doesn't mean it's dry. In a morning walk along the Esplanade I found the palms of my hands sweating. A combined temperature and humidity of 200. Still better than the monsoon season when Darwin becomes a virtual island surrounded by flood water. With a population of 71,000 it's a modern, cosmopolitan town and the capital of the Northern Territory. Roughly 1/3 of the territories people are Aboriginal and Darwin is a good starting place to investigate that culture.

Kakadu National Park starts 153 KM east of Darwin and much of it is Aboriginal land leased back to the government to be used as a park. It's roughly 200 KM north to south and 100 KM east to west and is Australia's richest and most accessible areas of Aboriginal rock art. The oldest paintings date back 6000 years and the new go back only 50 years. Keep in mind, the Aborigines still live here.

Our second stop (first is a coffee break at a road side store) is Nourlangie rock for the Anbangbang paintings which are 1000 years old. The cliff side has a rock overhang which protects the wall paintings and served as shelter for the people for 20,000 years. The red sandstone cliff side is accessed by wood steps and a walking platform. One of the recent paintings (1964), and one of the most famous, is Namarrgon, stick figures depicting Aboriginal dancing. Farther on is Nabulwinjbulwinj a bulky skeletal figure, a dangerous spirit that eats females.

Included on the tour is the Yellow Water Billabong cruise, an hour and a half boat trip through the mangrove swamps. There are some birds but the crocodiles kept away. Twenty minutes downstream we see the dock used during the dry season. The road to get there is underwater now. There are large sections of what looks like grassland. The shoreline. But, it isn't. It's a floating mat.

Lunch is served inside a double trailer next to a hotel with a nice pool and very nice bathrooms. Little things mean a lot in the middle of nowhere. Lettuce, tomato, cucumber, lunch meat, roll and butter, pasta noodles, sliced potatoes with sauce and coffee. Outside it's 110 degrees.

Jabiru (population 1780) is the only real town in the area and we get a short tour including the Crocodile Holiday Inn which is in the shape of a crocodile. Enter at the mouth. Six of the 20 people are dropped off at the Kakadu Lodge for the overnight stay. The rest will change busses and return to Darwin. The lodge is a deluxe back packer accommodation. Rooms are plain but have a coffee maker, air conditioning and a refrigerator. Individual units are in a circle with shower/toilet facilities towards the middle. The reception center has a small grocery store but closes before 8 PM. There's a large pool right next to the bar and only restaurant for miles around. A beer is US $ 3.20 and the cheapest item on the meal menu is a hamburger for US $ 12. It took almost an hour, after the order, to get the burger.

Day 2 - Today we start off with a boat tour that wasn't on the schedule. The paved road is still flooded so our bus isn't going to the other side. We board a boat run by an Aborigine. He carries spears in the overhead and gives a demonstration of how to get fish. The wood spear floats. He cruises up and snatches it from the water. Fishing is allowed in these waters but only with lures - no bait. And on that note, no pet cats are allowed in Jabiru. Dogs yes, cats no.

Our guide Tim gets out of the boat with 2 gas cans. In two feet of water, he walks the flooded road to a bus hidden around the bend and drives it backwards to the boat for us to transfer. And off to the Uranium mines. Uranium was discovered in Jabiluka in 1971 and an agreement to mine was reached with the Aboriginal people of the area. Mine development was delayed by the "three mines policy" which was scrapped in 1996. Then it was alleged that the Aboriginal elders were coerced and there were demonstrations and court battles. By this time, mine #1 was depleted and closed. Finally, mine #2 was deemed a religious site and mine #3 was started and is still operating. The government has an agreement with those it sells the uranium to - it's only for medical and non-military use. The mine has a large Aboriginal staff and provides jobs in an area where there are very few.

From here we go to Ubirr, on the Arnhem escarpment. Aborigine land. The first painting on the walk is 1400 years old. Dark red on red sandstone. Then, the story of Mayubu. He had his fish stolen and followed the men back to their camp. At night, he rolled a large rock over the entrance to the cave, sealing them in. A traditional story warning against stealing. Then the painting of the Rainbow Serpent. This story varies from tribe to tribe, but here, the serpent is a woman named Kurangali. She painted her image on the rock showing her journey through various places in Arnhem. Usually resting, she can be destructive if disturbed, causing floods, earthquakes and eating people.

The last significant painting is a warning on this sacred site. If you disturb the stones you will get a sickness that swells the bones (Miyamiya). The skeletal drawing shows swollen joints. This area is close to the Uranium mine. The elders might have not known why their people were getting sick but they knew to stay away.

THE END

## SIDEBAR FOR KAKADU

GETTING THERE - There are no direct flights from the USA. From the west coast, there is one stop service through Sydney, Australia to Darwin (change planes). Qantas has specials, depending on the season, for LAX-SYD, round trip, for $999 including 2 short internal flights. SYD-Darwin is a 4 ½ hour flight and may not be included. Normal fares are LAX-SYD for $1800, consolidator fares are $1100. Qantas and Virgin Blue fly SYD-Darwin. Both have a complicated fare schedule with a wide range of prices within the same day. SYD-Darwin on Virgin Blue (Blue Saver fare) is US $ 111, one way, non-stop. The highest price on the same day, on Virgin Blue, is US $ 450. Qantas has a Red-e-deal for US $190, one way, non stop and it's highest price on the same day is US $ 650. The special fares can be found and booked on line - www.quantas.com.au and www.virginblue.com.au.

The tour was booked at the AAT Kings office, darwin.daytours@ aatkings.com.au. tel. (08) 8923 6555. Tours can also be booked from your hotel for the same price. This 2 day tour was US $ 292 per person and included 2 lunches and a private room without a private bath. The same tour is US $ 425 per person with private room & bath at the Crocodile Holiday Inn. A one day tour is US $ 124, if a fifty minute flight is included, the one day tour is US $ 270 per person.

WHEN TO GO - The seasons are reversed in Australia. Darwin has 2 seasons, wet and dry. Monsoons hit from October to March. Dry season is April to September. The rain is not predictable and the wet season does not always start or stop on schedule. The total air fares to get there are approx. $300 more in summer than winter.

HOTELS - Centrally located are the Crowne Plaza Darwin, US $ 120 double, Novotel Atrium US $ 180 D, sales@novoteldarwin.com.au, Saville, US $ 190 D, www.savillesuites.com.au. Palms City Resort, US $ 110 D, www.citypalms.com, Value Inn, US $ 65 D, www.valueinn.com.au

HEALTH - No shots necessary.

MISCELLANEOUS - Don't be fooled by the exchange rate. For comparable goods and services Australia is approximately 20% more expensive than America. For additional information contact the Australian Tourist Commission - www.australia.com. All visitors need a visa and the only reasonable way to get it is on line - www.immi.gov.au

KATHERINE GORGE

NORTHERN TERRITORY, AUSTRALIA - The first Australian city the Japanese bombed at the start of WWII was Darwin and the first casualties were the Post Master and his staff. The lovely park and cemetery commemorating their death is the tour's first stop.

The van continued south from the temperate rain forest of north central Australia towards the vast interior desert. The day would log in 750 kilometers, round trip, not nearly far enough to leave the rain forest but if one were there during the yearly monsoon and could navigate the flooded roads and head straight south, the air would eventually become bone dry.

A road train passed going north. A truck with enough trailers to stretch for 150 feet with 60 tires on the road. It would have to start slowing miles before Darwin.

We stop for a lunch at a quiet off road stream. The birds are chirping in the trees and the water bubbles by. On the other bank, quiet as can be, are 500 bats hanging upside down from the branches of the trees. Fruit bats resting from last nights meal. On our side, a picnic buffet is set up. Salad, bologna and chicken. No fruit. Why invite trouble?

The Gorge is 300KM south of Darwin and was created by the Katherine river much like the Grand Canyon was created by the Colorado. One of the major differences is that fresh water crocodiles live in the Katherine. The river trip is taken in two steps. A modern 67 passenger boat casually takes you to the mid point rapids. There is bug juice to drink (something like kool aid) and the boat Captain says, "sit down" to those by the rail. It's a large, open sided, shallow draft boat with good views no matter where you sit or momentarily stand. On the left, a crow stands high on his legs on top a jutting rock, flaps his wings and cries out. Master of his domain. The river twists like a snake and twenty minutes from the start, it docks at the rocks. They would be rapids if the water level were higher but this is the season just before the monsoons.

During the twenty minute walk around the rapids you can see aborigine drawings on the cliff face. Pictures of animals and a self portrait of an early family. From the boat at the second dock you see the sheer cliffs that time and water have etched. A lone white birch that found a crevice one foot above the water line. A two man canoe passes our boat and continues downstream. Small boats can be rented but some campers bring their own boat. Twenty minutes downstream and our boat turns back.

Ten minutes later it stops at what can only be called a beach. A natural curve in the river has collected pulverized rock that is not much different than sand anywhere else. It's time for a swim and not a crocodile in sight. Frankly, none were seen during the whole trip. But there was a lizard. Two feet long, half of which was tail. He scampered along the sunny rocks and found a water filled depression in one of them. He took time for a bath and went on his way.

The walk back around the rapids seemed shorter this time but you still had to take care stepping over the rocks so as not to sprain an ankle. The road trip back is a long one but there were no bat bites, no falls or broken bones and no one was eaten by a crocodile. A good trip you might say. Katherine Gorge would be a nice place to camp out for a few days.

THE END

## SIDEBAR FOR THE KATHERINE

GETTING THERE - Sydney, Australia is serviced by Northwest, United, Quantas, Air New Zealand and others. Normal coach fare is around $1200 RT from Los Angeles but there are frequent discounts offered by the airlines and bargain tickets advertised in the travel section of the newspaper for around $800 RT. There is service to Darwin on Australian Airlines from eastern Australia. A one way economy ticket from Sydney is about $490 and about $260 from Cairns.

ACCOMMODATIONS - On the medium side, there is The Airraid City Lodge, 35 Cavenagh St, Darwin NT, phone number (089)81214 and the Larrakeyah Lodge, 50 Mitchell St. phone (089)817550, both for about US$75 double and centrally located just north of the Smith St. Mall. Just west of the mall is the ITT Sheraton at US$200 double, phone toll free from the US and Canada (800)325-3535. Similarly priced, at the upper end are the Atrium, the Beaufort and the Travelodge.

FOOD - There is s wide variety - Thai, Chinese, Mexican, vegetarian, Indian, French, Greek, Italian and American. Try the Buffalo and Barracuda combination at the Steakout on Daly St for under US$25.

LOCAL TOUR ARRANGEMENT - Can be made from any hotel by phone. Approximately US$120 at Tour North, 60 Mitchell St., Darwin 0800, phone 41 1656 or AAT Kings, 10 Daly St., Darwin (089)47 1207. It's recommended to bring good walking shoes, a shady hat, sunscreen, insect repellant and a bathing suit. Monsoon season is from October to March and Darwin virtually closes down. There are no tours.

FOR MORE INFORMATION Write: The Western Australian Tourist Commission, 2121 Avenue of the Stars, Suite 1210, Los Angeles, CA 90067 (213)557-1987 or the Australian Tourist Information Office in New York (212)944-6880, Chicago (312)644-8029, Los Angeles (310)477-3332.

# KINGS CANYON

Australia's answer to the Grand Canyon

IN THE MIDDLE OF THE DESERT, AUSTRALIA - I was a victim of circumstance. Some might say, fate. I'd booked four days worth of tours of "the Rock" and the Olgas when I landed at Connell Airport just outside the park boundary at Ayers Rock. The only other town for 1000 miles in any direction was Alice Springs. Everything else was desert. This wasn't a surprise, mind you, and I did fly above a half continent of barren land to get there. But it was to see Ayers Rock and the Olgas. There didn't seem to be any simple way to get to Kings Canyon. There was a brief sentence on the canyon in each of the guide books, "Beautiful to see," they said, "but you need time and special arrangements to get there." I'd never heard of the canyon before this trip, let alone met anyone who had been there.

The package of tours to Ayers Rock and the Olgas was a bargain. Multiple trips to both attractions (there are only two) for half price. They were selling like hot cakes and I bought a package. And took the airport bus to my hotel for a good nights sleep. Unbeknownst to me, the tour company went into receivership, at midnight, while I was fast asleep.

## THE RUDE AWAKENING

In the morning, I innocently boarded the bus for the first tour - Ayers Rock. The name on the bus was not Deluxe Tours and the driver was not in a good mood but I figured there must be reciprocal agreements between the touring companies and the driver must have had a bad night. Not so. This was the last trip for this bus. It was going into the impound yard at noon and the driver had no way home. He lived in Alice Springs, 445 Kilometers to the north east. I felt sorry for him but this ship was sinking and I had to find my own lifeboat when the bus dropped us back at the village.

Deluxe was a large tour company and the middle of the night seizure came as a surprise to travelers and employees alike. The village at Ayers Rock has a travel agency and I made a straight line for it. Word was out but the crowd hadn't arrived - yet. Shock, I suppose. The travel agent was extremely helpful and after a few phone calls, my flight plans were changed and I was booked on the last day of a three day trip originating from and ending in, Alice Springs.

The next morning I boarded the large, air-conditioned touring bus on the way back to the Springs via Kings Canyon. I was the only American and joined thirty one Australians on board. They ranged in age from teenage to retired. The first part of the trip was approximately 100 KM due east, 100 KM north and 100 KM west to arrive at the canyon. The seats were comfortable, it was a bright day and the whole crowd was in a good mood.

Regular stops are planned for those who want to stretch their legs and those who want a cigarette. Mount Connor was the first stop. Just before the northern turnoff. South of the road, it looked like a mountain that had been sawed off close to the base. It rose from the distant desert floor and stopped as though God wanted a table top for giants.

Mid way on the northern road, we stopped at a hundred year old oak tree to catch a glimpse of the resident falcon and continued to the Wallara Ranch. The ranch, located at the juncture of the north and west roads, was started in 1960 and offered the only accommodations to travelers in this remote area. A rustic bar and restaurant with incredible back woods charm and a few mobile homes which serve as motel rooms. Unfortunately, the Wallara has fallen on bad times and was going into bankruptcy the following day. Waiting outside, I was waving the back of my right hand from the chest past my face to keep away the flies when a fellow traveler said, "I see you've learned the Australian salute." I was about to explain the misunderstanding when he continued, "All the politicians you see on television, do the same thing when they are being interviewed outdoors." He moved his hand to brush the flies away from his face, "See, the Australian salute." We had our late morning beer, boarded the bus and turned west.

## SELL CAMELS TO THE ARABS ?

Just short of the canyon, after a bumpy ride on a corrugated dirt road, we stopped at the Kings Creek Station. No one bothered to look for the creek or the water. The station does have food, gas, toilets and showers but no beds. To supplement their income, they catch wild camels and sell them to the Arab countries. Years ago, camels were imported to help miners in the desert. When the mines folded, the camels were turned loose and now run free in the desert like the kangaroos and dingos (wild dogs). Lunch was soup, salad, bread, lunch meat, pasta, coffee and incredibly good chocolate cake.

From here, the bus ride was a short fifteen minutes to the canyon. We were warned the initial climb was strenuous and some opted to walk the canyon creek bed instead. The canyon creek is at the same level as the parking area, the view is from up above. The entire walk over the top was scheduled for three and a half hours but the first 45 minutes was the killer. From the bottom, you can't see the top but there are natural steps since the rocks are aligned in layers. The steps vary from three inches to three feet high. The first half hour went fairly quickly and I stopped for a break. I was drenched with sweat. The top was still nowhere in sight. I turned to look down and got vertigo. The real ground, the desert floor, was too far down to think about going back. Maybe the top is just a few more feet, I told myself. Hand over fist over foot, holding onto rocks and pieces of brush, I pulled myself even higher. It was like climbing a ladder. Forty five minutes from the bottom, I finally hauled myself to the top. Exhausted, I waited for the other half of the party to catch up.

## THE LONG VIEW

From the cliffs edge, I looked down to our bus. A speck of white on the red desert floor. It appeared no bigger than a carelessly discarded golf ball. In 1872, Ernest Giles, one of Australia's last great explorers, was the first European to see this canyon. He was then trying to cross 1800 kilometers of trackless desert to the Western Australian coast.

The horse shoe shaped walk across the top is tricky but not physically demanding. Mostly level rock with good traction for rubber soled sneakers. We saw a white Ghost Gum tree perched on a cliffs edge, scrub brush and small trees in areas where rock has been pulverized by wind erosion into soil. Cycads (sigh-cads) which were one of the common plants when dinosaurs walked here. The climate is no longer wet but hearty generations of cycads have survived almost unchanged. We walked over rippled rock, around boulders, across rock ledges, gently ascending and descending a few feet at a time.

Suddenly there was a bee hive of solid rock. A rust red dome brightly lit by the sun contrasted by the deep blue of the background sky. As large as a building and one expected it to have a purpose. Hollowed out for cave dwellers, perhaps. But the land is too harsh, it was just there. We saw the green leaves of tree sprigs that gained a foothold in the rock crevices high above the ground and lo and behold, a mistletoe tree. Couples took turns standing beneath for the free kiss. As we jaunted across the tiered rock, we occasioned patches of earth with wild grass, some shells of trees, some trees bent from the wind, a large cliffside with hundreds of layers of rock speckled with green leaves from single branch plants whose seeds took refuge in the cracks. At the half way point, we came to the edge of a chasm. Five hundred feet down from the sharp edge and five hundred feet across. A spectacular and dangerous view which stopped no one from standing at the brink. We could see some of our party walking along the creek bed at the bottom of the ravine. Elfs, too far away to hear our cries of recognition.

A little further was an outcrop of rocks severed from the main surface body. A single log had functioned as the bridge but noone seemed willing to take the chance of a fatal fall from a misstep. A wooden plank bridge with handrails was built alongside and was the crossing of choice. From the outcrop, we could look down the ravine and see the edge we so carelessly approached only minutes before. Returning to the main body of the rock we encountered the highest level section. There were trees. Small ones, of course, because of the limited rain and harsh winds. One tree had found a natural depression in the rocks and was growing over the water in the hole to protect it from the evaporating rays of the sun. It goes years between rains in this part of the desert and the tree was protecting it's life saving water.

## THE OASIS

At the very back end of the walk, wood stairs have been built into the cliff side to allow descent and cross over to the other side. At the bottom of the ravine, far from our reach, was an oasis of black water and palm trees. The sides of the cliffs shielded this small area from the sun. The other side of the canyon had much less vegetation but there was a collection of fifty bee hives of rock. A town hall meeting with each member standing to vote. And around the corner a large tabletop like protrusion of rock with a mushroom shaped stool of rock sticking up from the center. It only lacked the Mayor of the desert, sitting on the stool, to convene the meeting. The back-side walk was brisk and we only stopped to catch the view of the sun on the opposite side. It looked like a sheared cliff of caramel colored marble.

The walk down was far more gradual than the one up but it's ease is deceptive. There are many sections of loose rock and we all lost our footing several times. But, no accidents and no falls. The bus was a welcome sight because the water coolers were brought out.

## THE LAST SUPPER

One hundred kilometers later we were back at the Wallara Ranch for the last supper. Ours and theirs. Grilled steaks, baked potatoes, salad, thick bread and apple crumble for desert. Washed down by a hearty Fosters beer, of course. A wonderful meal consumed by a ravenous bunch. Fat and full, we were on our way just before sunset. Two hundred and sixty six KM to Alice Springs. The road from the canyon continues due east to connect with the paved road that runs north to the Springs. Along the road, we saw a single dingo, watching. His eyes glared yellow in the fading light.

A few hours later, the driver dropped me off at my hotel in Alice Springs. It had been a long, tiring and exhilarating day. My Australian travelers were a happy and friendly group eager to talk about their home towns, World War II, the ranches they live on, how to make kangaroo stew and American and Australian politics. As the bus pulled away, I waved with the Australian salute even though there weren't any flies about.

THE END

## SIDEBAR

GETTING THERE - Ayers Rock is serviced directly by Australian Airlines.

LOCAL TRANSPORTATION - Cars can be rented at the Airport - Avis, Thrifty, Budget, Hertz (all very expensive). The Northern Territory Government Tourist Bureau has a great deal of information about tours available in the area. Tours do not run every day and it is wise to plan ahead.

PLACES TO STAY - Sheraton Ayers Rock tel 089-562200, rooms about $290. Four Seasons Ayers Rock tel 089-562100, rooms about $200. Yulara Maisonettes tel 089-562131, rooms $125 with shared bath. Youth Hostel dorm beds for $20. Ayers Rock Campground tel 089-562055 for $75 for an on-site van. Accommodations in Alice Springs are numerous with prices about 25% less than Ayers Rock.

FOR MORE INFORMATION - Write: Northern Territory Tourism Commission, 2121 Avenue of the Stars, Suite 1210, Los Angeles, CA 90067 tel (213)277-7877

## Launceston, Tasmania
## and the Cataract Gorge

Hobart, Tasmania - Although there are direct flights to Launceston, we flew from Sydney to Hobart, the capital. It's Australia's only island state and two hours, by air, from Sydney. Directly south of Tasmania is Antarctica and this isolation made it the perfect place for British Penal colonies, but, that's a thing of the past. Now it's a modern State with fashionable cities and vast areas of wilderness including 19 national parks. And, some of the cleanest air in the world.

Sydney is Australia's oldest city, Hobart the second. We had a few extra days in Hobart and decided to visit Launceston, the third oldest. It was founded by Lieutenant Colonel William Paterson in 1805 and called Patersonia. It was their third attempt to establish a permanent settlement on the Tamar River and the northern coast of the island. In 1907 it was renamed in honor of Governor King who was born in Launceston, England. Today it's a cosmopolitan city of 68,000 and home to Boag's Brewery (self proclaimed as the best beer in the world).

The visitor's center has a map showing the driving route for the Tamar valley wine country, just north of town. As a matter of fact we were staying at a motor lodge even though we arrived by bus (3 hours each way - US $ 45 RT). Most of the cars in the parking lot were from Tasmania although there were a few from the mainland. The brewery has tours, there's a planetarium, the National Automobile Museum of Tasmania has classic cars, the Old Umbrella Shop with a selection of old umbrellas and a 90 minute ghost tour departing from the Royal Oak pub. One must wonder if there is a correlation between the number of ghosts you see and the number of drinks you had at the pub before the tour. If you don't have a car, there's a half day tour of the Tamar Valley for US $ 40. And, there are four parks in town for leisurely walks. But, we didn't have the time and wanted to see the Cataract Gorge.

We did have time to walk the town and find Home Point, the dock for the Cataract Gorge 50 minute boat tour. There was a light rain as we walked down Charles Street and I saw my first double rainbow. The lower one had the brightest colors of any rainbow I'd ever seen and directly above it, like a mirror image, was a second. The higher one was a bit washed out but the colors were clear. Absolutely stunning and my camera was back at the motel.

We wanted the 9:30 AM boat ride the following morning and it's a good thing we reconnoitered the dock area first. The entrance is at the top of Royal Park, west of downtown and at the intersection of several streets. Easy enough to make a wrong turn at 8:30 in the morning. They do have four hour cruises for about US $ 65 but that seemed like overkill.

The boat is a modern one with a unique silent drive system and the first half of the trip is to the east. Up the South Esk river looking at the cliff side homes to the left and the dock facilities on the right. Some of the homes are supported by posts but I was told that there are no earthquakes here so that isn't a problem. The boat turns around & meets the juncture of the Esk and the Tamar, under the double bridge and down the gorge. It is wilderness and there are beautiful rock formations but it won't impress those who have seen the Grand Canyon. Of course, that comparison isn't fair, this is the best Tasmania has and one should take in that light.

Since we alighted at the top of Royal Park, we decided to walk south, through Royal and Kings parks, to the main road. We came out at Penny Royal, Gunpowder Mills. They have exhibits of water mills, windmills, gunpowder mills and a 45 minute cruise up the gorge on a paddle-steamer. There is a gorgeous waterfall springing from the mountain on the other side of the river but the entrance price of $20 seemed steep, so we moved on. Under the bridge overpass is a huge, boldly colored painting (graffiti). I had to take a picture. It's as good as some of the work I've seen in art galleries.

There are two walks available. The south side is considered difficult so we crossed the Tamar to the north side. The paved walk goes on for miles and the views are much the same as from the boat (only half as many, of course, since you can only see the far side). There was an artist at one of the rest pavilions making a drawing. Naturally, I took the picture even though the drawing will be more dramatic. He can leave out what he doesn't like.

Walking back through town, I couldn't help but notice the 1906 clock on top of the tower of the stone and brick Post Office. But if I thought this building was nice I got a surprise a block away at Cameron & George streets. The Holy Trinity Anglican Church. Turrets and arches made from brick. Some of the congregation was outside and asked us to go in. We did and got a friendly guided tour. The inside is more impressive than the outside. The original church was built in 1842 but an earth tremor made it unsafe. The new building was completed in 1902 and some additions were made in 1986. Arches and turrets made of brick was especially challenging since light weight metal supports weren't available at the time. Imported English oak is used behind the altar and there are mosaic panels and wood carvings along the walls. Gargoyles at the ceiling, kings and queens beheaded up on the arches and the crests of the Bishops who had jurisdiction. The organ was brought from London in 1854 and incorporated into a replacement in 1887. There's a rose window on the eastern wall and a chimney built into a pinnacle on the choir vestry. The church isn't always open (insurance requirements) but if you find the door open, the inside will take your breath away.

THE END

## SIDEBAR FOR LAUNCESTON

GETTING THERE - There are no direct flights from the USA. From the west coast, there is one stop service from Sydney, Australia to Hobart (change planes). Quantas has specials, depending on the season, for LAX-SYD, round trip, for $999 including 2 internal flights. Normal fares are LAX-SYD for $1800, consolidator fares are $1100. Quantas and Virgin Blue fly SYD-HOB. Virgin Blue is US $ 80 one way, Quantas $100. The bus from Hobart to Launceston takes 3 hours each way for US $ 45 RT.

WHEN TO GO - The seasons are reversed in Australia. Our winter is their summer. Summers are warm, not hot. Autumn is cool with frosty nights. Winter is cold, the State has 2 ski resorts. Spring is windy. Hobart is on the southern coast of Australia, Launceston the north. The summer is best but the total air fares are approx. $300 more than winter.

HOTELS - There are hundreds of hotels to choose from in Hobart, virtually all the major chains. The Tasmanian Visitors center is very helpful - tasbookings@tavisinfo.com.au - and www.tasmaniasouth.com for both Hobart and Launceston.

HEALTH - No shots necessary.

MISCELLANEOUS - For additional information contact the Australian Tourist Commission - www.australia.com. All visitors need a visa and the only reasonable way to get it is on line - www.immi.gov.au

The MacDonnell Range
West of Alice Springs, bordered by Aboriginal land


Alice Springs, Australia - In it's 125 year history, the Alice, has gone from a telegraph station to a modern city. An oasis in the middle of Australia without the fig trees, camels and water hole. OK, there are some camels just out of town and reportedly millions of gallons of fresh water in an underground lake collected over 10,000 years but you can't see it and there aren't any fig trees. With a population of 25,000 it's the biggest town for roughly 1000 miles in any direction. Alice Springs acts as a connecting point for those visiting Ayers Rock on a two or three day tour. Prices here are far better than at the rock and the Alice airport has much better connections to other points in Australia.

There are a number of day trips into the outback and the West MacDonnell range is one of them. The east and west ranges stretch like a spine on both sides of Alice Springs and are loaded with gorges, water holes and walking tracks. Twenty two KM west of town is Simpson's Gap in a mountain range 400 to 800 million years old. This is a cut through solid rock made by a river that barely ever runs. It took 60 million years. And the opening at the bottom is only wide enough to fit a car through. Trees grow in the middle of the dry river bed. Rock wallabies can be seen living in the jumble of rocks but they blend in well and stay away from people.

Stanley Chasm is on Aboriginal land and is 51 KM west of Alice. It's a half hour walk over and around large rocks but it's worth the tricky path. The sides of this narrow opening are nearly vertical. The floor is not sand as it was at Simpson's gap. Here it's pebbles and at the far end, boulders that block the opening. Flood waters have clogged it with rocks too big to pass through and now time will take over. Mother nature will open it again. There is a store at this stop and we take time for tea and cake (included).

The Ochre Pits are 117 KM west of Alice. Next to, but not on, Aboriginal land. The sides of an ancient river bed have various shades of red. The colors in this weathered limestone were used by the natives for their wall paintings and to color themselves. The colors are actually iron oxide stains. Next is the Ormison Waterhole for lunch. Ham & cheese sandwich, good selection of cut fruit, granola bar and an apple (included). There is a small lake here and time for a swim. For those that brought a suit and wanted a swim right after lunch. There is a life preserver hanging on a tree for anyone in trouble.

We went to the lookout station for Mount Sonder (1380 Meters). It's not the highest mountain in the area but is a favorite for local artists to paint. The last stop is the Glen Helen Resort. Keep in mind, when you get this far out, this is it or sleep on the ground. Even though you might not think "resort", they can call themselves whatever they want. They have rooms, a friendly bar, a restaurant and live music five nights a week. Breakfast is US $9, lunch about the same and supper US $22. It's a good home for a dozen different bush walks in the area.

We got back to Alice Springs in time for a drink at Bojangles and a walk on the new mall.

THE END

## SIDEBAR FOR MacDonnell RANGE

GETTING THERE - There are no direct flights from the USA. From the west coast, there is one stop service through Sydney, Australia to Perth (change planes). Quantas has specials, depending on the season, for LAX-SYD, round trip, for $999 including 2 short internal flights. SYD-Alice Springs is a 3 ½ hour flight and may not be included. Normal fares are LAX-SYD for $1800, consolidator fares are $1100. Quantas and Virgin Blue fly SYD-Alice. Both have a complicated fare schedule with a wide range of prices within the same day. SYD-Alice on Virgin Blue (Blue Saver fare) is US $ 120, one way, non-stop. The highest price on the same day, on Virgin Blue, is US $ 370. Quantas has a Red-e-deal for US $190, one way, non stop and it's highest price on the same day is US $ 540. The special fares can be found and booked on line - www.quantas.com.au and www.virginblue.com.au.

The tour was booked at the Central Australia Tourism Assoc., Gregory Tce & Todd Street. Tours can also be booked from your hotel for the same price. This full day tour was US $ 80 per person and included lunch and snacks.

WHEN TO GO - The seasons are reversed in Australia. Our winter is their summer. Summers are warm, not hot. Autumn is cool with frosty nights. Winter is cold at night. Spring is windy. The desert is hot in the day and cool at night. The spring and fall are best but the total air fares to get there are approx. $300 more in summer than winter.

HOTELS - Centrally located are the Aurora Alice Springs, US $ 120 double, www.tti@aurora-resorts.com.au, The Desert Rose Inn, US $ 85 D, tel. 8952-1411, the Todd Tavern, US $ 40 D, tel. 8952-1255.

The Glen Helen Resort, US $ 55-120 double. www.glenhelen.com.au.

HEALTH - No shots necessary.

MISCELLANEOUS - Don't be fooled by the exchange rate. For comparable goods and services Australia is approximately 20% more expensive than America. For additional information contact the Australian Tourist Commission - www.australia.com. All visitors need a visa and the only reasonable way to get it is on line - www.immi.gov.au

Monkey Mia, Australia
No monkeys, but there are dolphins

Prince Leonard (self appointed) - Hutt River Province

Perth, Australia - It was a four day trip up the barren western coast of Australia.. The Indian Ocean to the left and thousands of miles of red dirt and dust to the right. A map of Australia overlays nicely on one of the

363

continental United States. Perth lines up with Los Angeles and Monkey Mia would be in the middle of the wine country, north of San Francisco.

Our first stop is the Pinnacles Desert in Nambung National Park, four hours away. The vehicle is a 4 wheel drive, 20 seat van, pulling a trailer with our food and luggage. Six guys, five girls and Mike, the young tour guide. The pinnacles is unique in that jagged, pointed rocks stick straight out of the golden sand, some to 12 feet. All of this within sight of white sands on the beach of the Indian Ocean. Logically one wonders how these rocks could grow out of the sand - that's what it looks like. In fact, millions of years ago this was a thick bed of limestone. Plant roots exploited the cracks in the weaker sections allowing the water in. The plants died and the channels filled with sand. Erosion and wind cleared these channels out leaving the peaks. The rocks didn't come up, the desert went down.

After sandwiches for lunch at a roadside picnic table (lunch meat, tomatoes, lettuce, green peppers, grated cheese, cucumbers, mustard, ketchup and mayo - slice and make your own) we stopped for sand surfing. Eight hours and 420 KM north of Perth. White sand dunes right next to the ocean. A waxed board to stand or sit on and 150 foot slide down the dune. But then, the walk back up. Two steps up, slide back one. Three steps up and slide back two.

It was almost dusk when we hit the fork in the road, turned inland to climb uphill towards Kalbarri and our dorm rooms for the night and the overheat buzzer in the van went off. Mike took the turn and stopped. The paved road showed a trail of water drippings. Mike, with help, went into the engine compartment, found a leaky radiator hose and wrapped it with a rag and duct tape. There is a town 5 KM north on the other fork according to the road sign. There are no cars in sight, we're in the middle of nowhere. Cell phones don't work here. The van is not equipped with a radio. An hour has passed, Mike finally decides to try for the town. We all get in, he turns the van around, takes the turn north and the buzzer goes off again. He stops, we get out and wait. Mike doesn't know what to do. We wait, the sun sets. We get back in, turn around, start uphill on the original road and the buzzer brings us to a stop. While waiting in the dark, we see lights on top of the hill, 1 kilometer away. Mike collects everyone's water bottles to fill the radiator and we get in for our last chance. Just as the van pulls off the road, at the top, the buzzer goes off and we coast into the parking lot of a red algae plant. The night shift is on in this 24 hour a day plant that grows and harvests red algae, here in the middle of the desert. The night shift workers are gracious. Mike uses the phone and says a replacement van will be coming south from Kalbarri only 60 KM away (about 37 miles). It'll be here in an hour. We drank the plant's coffee, ate their cookies, used the rest room, learned about the processing of algae and an hour and a half later, Mike brought in sandwich food from the trailer. Three hours later we had eaten, ran out of small talk and asked where the "one hour away" van was. Our van had time to cool down and with fresh water from the station, it was time to leave. Mike figured we could make it and would probably cross the van coming south to get us. Both predictions came thru.

At the hostel, it took ½ an hour for them to figure out which rooms to put us in and hand out bed sheets. Like they didn't know we were coming three hours ago.

DAY 2 - A replacement van took us to the Kalbarri National Park, 1000 square KM of bush land. The road was so rutted, Mike stopped the van and let air out of the tires. The Murchison Gorge is worth seeing. The river, which runs infrequently in the desert, took millions of years to carve through this rock and there is a spectacular view by lookout window.

We stopped at Chinaman's Beach for lunch. Even with the high winds, we used the beach barbeque grill to cook hamburgers. The few trees/shrubs in the area are 5 to 10 feet high and don't offer much of a wind break. We finished the day at a hostel in Denham, 26 KM from Monkey Mia. Like most back packer places, they have cooking facilities and we made our own supper.

DAY 3 - Monkey Mia started when a fisherman gave a dolphin some fish and it came back the next day for more. That was 40 years ago and now the Indio-Pacific (bottlenose) dolphins show up every morning for free fish and this site has become an industry. There are camel rides for US$8, sailboat rides for US$20, the catamaran is US$32, but, feeding the dolphins is free. The crowd of 50 to 100 take off shoes, roll up their pant legs and wade out to knee depth. The permanent staff feed the dolphins first to break the ice and then hand out fish to the onlookers so they can have a turn. Seven dolphins showed up and took turns at the free food. The down side is, no touching the dolphins because they can catch human viruses. There is a good sized restaurant, overnight lodging, a gift shop, a grocery store, a museum and a video show. The dolphins can live up to forty years, weigh 120 KG (average man weights 80 KG) and will eat small sharks. Sharks will, in turn, eat small dolphins.

From there we drove to Shark Bay at Eagle Bluff to see the off shore islands. They are not land but made of bird guano that used to be harvested for fertilizer. Next stop is Shell Beach for a swim. There is no sand. The beach is entirely pinky-nail sized cockleshells - billions of them. One hundred feet out the water is only knee deep. In the past, the shells were ground up and used as building materials. Nearby is the Hamlin Pool, a marine reserve with the world's best known colony of Stromatolites. The microbes that collect on the rocks in these shallow waters are almost identical to organisms that existed 1900 million years ago and evolved into more complex life.

This time we went to a farm house for the night. Close to the barn is the facility for toilets and showers. Five hundred feet away are motel room sized dorm rooms that take four to a room. Electricity but no running water. One of the stews for supper (put over rice) had kangaroo meat which must be an acquired taste.

DAY 4 - We switched vans and tour guides yesterday. Our original van continued north to Exmouth for the 7 day trip and we took the van coming back from Exmouth. The new leader, Drasco, was a guide in Croatia and immigrated here after their war. Bright, energetic, experienced and the one to look for when taking this trip.

First stop is the Hutt River Province Principality. A self proclaimed independent country of 18,500 acres created on 21 APR 1970 when farmer Len Casley, disgusted with government quotas on wheat, seceded from the Commonwealth under a legal loophole which was quickly closed thereafter. Despite the governments efforts to overturn the secession, HRH Prince Leonard and Princess Shirley remain the Monarchs of the only Principality in the world declared without bloodshed. The Princess gave us the guided tour. They have a post office, their own stamps, a church, a gift shop and their own flag and constitution. There are 13,000 citizens world wide and the Princess stamped our passports at the post office. Apparently several countries recognize their claim since they have diplomatic offices overseas. Their income comes from farming and there are no facilities for overnight stays. There is a huge statue of the Prince's head and another of what might be considered art. Those who have preconceived ideas of what a Prince and Princess should look like should stay in the van.

Back in the Commonwealth, we stopped at Greenough Animal Park to feed the goats, kangaroos and sheep. They gave each of us a bag of animal feed nuggets. But first we got to handle a python or two. The southwest carpet python gets to 9 feet and the one we got to drape around our neck is half grown. We made Perth at suppertime. Wonder what the Princess is making for supper.

THE END

## SIDEBAR FOR MONKEY MIA

GETTING THERE - There are no direct flights from the USA. From the west coast, there is one stop service through Sydney, Australia to Perth (change planes). Quantas has specials, depending on the season, for LAX-SYD, round trip, for $999 including 2 short internal flights. SYD-PER is a five hour flight and may not be included. Normal fares are LAX-SYD for $1800, consolidator fares are $1100. Quantas and Virgin Blue fly SYD-PER. Both have a complicated fare schedule with a wide range of prices within the same day. SYD-PER on Virgin Blue (Blue Saver fare) is US $ 192, one way, non-stop. The highest price on the same day, on Virgin Blue, is US $455. Quantas has a Red-e-deal for US $151, one way, non stop and it's highest price on the same day is US $ 610. The special fares can be found and booked on line - www.quantas.com.au and www.virginblue.com.au.

The tour was booked at the Western Australia Visitors Center, www. westernaustralia.net, which is across the street from the Perth train station. The tour company is www.travelabout.com.au. To be fair, as disorganized as they were on this tour, we took another, far more difficult tour, and that trip ran smooth as silk. The 4 day trip to Monkey Mia is US $ 388, including meals, back packer accommodations and pick up from your hotel. They have 7 day trips that go to Exmouth and return to Perth for US $ 600, 10 days to Broome with no return for US $ 1200 and Broome with return, 15 days for US $ 1520. You can customize a trip since vans cross going up and down.

WHEN TO GO - The seasons are reversed in Australia. Our winter is their summer. Summers are warm, not hot. Autumn is cool with frosty nights. Winter is cold at night. Spring is windy. The area north of Perth is desert country. The spring and fall are best but the total air fares are approx. $300 more than winter.

HOTELS - There are hundreds of hotels to choose from in Perth, virtually all the major chains. The Visitors center is very helpful (e-mail is above).

HEALTH - No shots necessary.

MISCELLANEOUS - Don't be fooled by the exchange rate. For comparable goods and services Australia is approximately 20% more expensive than America. For additional information contact the Australian Tourist Commission - www.australia.com. All visitors need a visa and the only reasonable way to get it is on line - www.immi.gov.au

## THE OLGAS

What's a big girl like you doing in a place like this?

ULURU NATIONAL PARK, AUSTRALIA - To get to the Olgas, you must first get to the middle of nowhere. Australia is roughly the size and shape of the continental USA and Uluru National Park is approximately where Kansas City is if the park were in America. In the middle. With a major exception. This park is surrounded for 1000 miles in all directions by a desert with the exception of the town of Alice Springs, 445 KM to the Northeast (280 miles) and the tourist facilities at Yulara Resort, two miles north of the park boundary. The park has two attractions - the most well known is Ayers Rock or Uluru, to the Aborigines and the second, the Olgas, is called Kata Tjuta which means many heads. The Olgas can be seen over the ever flat ground from Ayers Rock but distances can be deceiving. They are 40 KM away and would be a trying walk in 120 degree desert heat.

## BACKGROUND

Archaeological evidence shows that the Aborigines have lived in this area for at least 10,000 years. Uluru National Park was handed back to the Aboriginal people (who call themselves Anangu) in 1985 and was leased back to the Australian Government. The park is jointly managed by the National Parks and Wildlife Service and the Uluru/Kata Tjuta Land Trust (represents the Aborigines). The entire park area is of cultural and spiritual significance to the Anangu since they believe it plays an important part in their Dreamtime.

## BRING WATER

The two hour plane trip from Sydney lands at Connellan Airport, 4 Kilometers north of the Lasseter Highway, the only paved road that connects to the rest of the world. The highway, naturally, ends here. A

$6 bus ride goes south to Yulara Resort or "the village. Accommodations range from the four star Sheraton to a campsite, a half mile away. The bus will stop anywhere in the village. Tour tickets for the Olgas can be purchased at the airport or from the hotels or the travel agency in the village center. Busses run mornings and afternoons, timing themselves to return at either lunchtime or after sunset. Stay with the bus for a morning or sunset guided tour or get off the morning bus and spend the day. There are ample warnings in the literature for those who decide to spend the day. Temperatures can reach 120 degrees and sun stroke is a definite risk. There is no snack bar, no latrines, no water. In fact, there is absolutely nothing. If you spend the day hiking and miss the afternoon bus when it makes its two stops, you are on your own. The desert gets very chilly at night. But the desert heat is the most dangerous. Two German hikers got lost a while back and one of them died from dehydration. There are cautions to bring a liter of water for each hour walked.

The bus picks up at all accommodations and, a half hour later, stops at the park entrance. The ranger collects $4.25 entrance fee which is good for one day. Two trips into the park on the same ticket are OK, if they are in the same day. Busses used to turn west on the Docker River Road. A pot holed, dirt road of 32 KM that was so corrugated it reportedly could shake the fillings from your teeth. The new Kata Tjuta road is complete and the turnoff is 3 KM south of the old road. It runs roughly parallel and is a few miles longer but is completely paved all the way to the Olga Gorge Walk, on the west side of the Olga range.

Geologically, the Olgas are the remains of an immense bed of sedimentary rock which is now almost entirely covered by the debris from erosion and wind blown sand. There are 36 individual domes which may have once been a single rock several times the size of Ayers Rock, the areas main attraction. Australia is the oldest stationary continent and this collection of impressive rocks is the result of millions of years of weather. It has gone as long as eleven years between rain falls in this region and the plants and animals have to be very hearty.

# THE TOUR

As luck would have it, it rained the night before and dark clouds threatened throughout the day. The bus drove past the Olga Gorge walk and turned east onto the old dirt road. The road is four lanes wide and can easily accommodate passing busses but the major obstacle was the cloud of red dust created by the jeep in front. Not to be left blind or kept from his appointed rounds, the bus driver put the petal to the metal and passed the jeep - people doing an independent tour. Our dust cloud was now their problem. The first stop was the Kata Tjuta Lookout Walk, seven KM east of the Gorge. This northern walk (2 hours return) is straight between several massive domes and connects with the Link Track (one hour each way), approximately in the middle of the entire range. The Link Track runs westward and connects with the circular, Valley of the Winds walk (2 hours return). That is, a complete walk of the Valley of the Winds will return to the west end of the Link Track. The Valley of the Winds walk can also be reached from the north by 20 KM of dirt road that circles all the Olgas from the east. Our half day sunset tour had no time for either the 20 KM road trip or the interior walk. Twenty minutes of viewing the massive, sand blasted domes and the bus was ready to go. The dust clouds had settled and the jeep was nowhere in sight. Perhaps it had filled with sand and was along side the road, camouflaged as a red dune. We returned to the Olga Gorge just as the overhead clouds lifted and the suns rays poured through. The Gorge is a one hour return walk depending on how far in you wish to go. It is flanked by cliffs on the right and left that come together at the very end, so you can't get lost by walking too far. But you can miss the bus. A rather dreadful consequence that made everyone careful of the time. Camping out was not on the agenda.

The enormous rock to the right is the tallest of all of the domes - 1785 feet above the desert floor. While looking at these intersecting monoliths, you are walking on a floor of both smooth and pockmarked, partially submerged boulders. Some as small as a house and others larger than a city block above the desert floor. As though walking on the tip of an iceberg. There are cracks in the rocks, loose bits of stone chipped away from millions of visiting feet, steep climbs and rippled surfaces that appear to be cooled lava flow.

## OLGA IS ALIVE

The area is not as void of life as one thinks it should be. In fact, 150 kinds of birds, 22 mammals and nearly 400 plant species have been found in the park. It had rained the night before and there was a pool caught in a crease where boulders intersected. The water couldn't seep away, so Eucalyptus trees and brush found the a place to nourish. Some pools collected in depressions of open rock with no cracks for roots to take hold and there was no vegetation. The blazing sun would evaporate the water before a plant could get a foothold. The luck of the wind would tell which seed would survive.

The walk is an easy one with shoes equipped with gripping soles. An eighty year woman was doing quite well with her sneakers, taking care to watch her steps. The massive size of these domes of rock is difficult to grasp until you see people framed against them in the distance. The people look no bigger than ants.

The bus waited for all to return and continued to the final stop - the sunset viewing site. Patiently, with cameras poised, we waited for the sun to peek through the over hanging clouds. Light aircraft circled overhead to give their passengers a view of red and orange rock warmed by the setting sun. The deserts' colors change throughout the day, from the warmth of sunrise to the intense, mid day, overhead glare and finally, the reddish glow of sunset. But it was not to be on this day. The clouds blanketed the sun until the desert was dark. But the sun was bright during the gorge walk and that was the best part. An awesome spectacle rising from the desert floor with no apparent purpose. The domes are grand and stately. Perhaps the Aborigines are right, the reason is spiritual.

## THE END

SIDEBAR

GETTING THERE - Ayers Rock is serviced directly by Quantas Airlines from Sydney and Cairns, with connecting flights to all major Australian cities.

LOCAL TRANSPORTATION - Cars can be rented at the Airport Avis, Thrifty, Budget, Hertz (all very expensive) and mopeds from the Mobil gas station in the village for $30 a day. Australian Pacific Tours (800)821-9513 USA and others run busses to the Olgas daily and can be booked from any village hotel or the village travel agency. Trips are $25 return.

PLACES TO STAY - Sheraton Ayers Rock tel 089-562200, rooms about $200. Four Seasons Ayers Rock tel 089-562100, rooms about $200. Yulara Maisonettes tel 089-562131, rooms $100 with shared bath. Youth Hostel dorm beds for $10. Ayers Rock Campground tel 089-562055 for $50 for an on-site van.

FOR MORE INFORMATION - Write: Northern Territory Tourism Commission, 2121 Avenue of the Stars, Suite 1210, Los Angeles, CA 90067 tel (213)277-7877

Perth To Alice Springs - the hard way
Across the Great Victoria Desert

Perth, Australia - Our guide, Geoff Kennedy, said only 2000 people have ever made this trip. Naturally, that doesn't include the Aborigines, but then they had to walk the 2700 kilometers and that could have taken over a year. We were driving. Six days, five nights. Across some of the land given back to the Aborigines and those sections required a permit to cross.

At 9 AM we stopped at York for tea and biscuits. It's a charming little town and our first chance to talk with each other. There are 6 Swiss (3 girls and three guys), one Japanese girl and two Americans. One of the Swiss guys is over 55 and joins the two Americans in the "old enough to be your grandfather" club since the other six people are 20 years old. From York, it's on to the Kalgoorlie gold mine, the super pit, and it's huge. Gold was first discovered here in 1893 and a frontier town soon emerged. They're still mining gold here (Australia's largest) and the town has that wild west feel. This is the last real town we'll see for a while and we all hit the Woolworth's. We got a small pillow (important), insect repellant (essential), sun screen (never used), bottled water and a case of beer. Beer is not sold in or allowed on Aborigine land but we don't intend it for resale and will drink it at night by the campfire. The onboard cooler will hold 2 beers per person.

We cover 750 KM (465 miles) on paved roads and pull 1/4 of a mile off road for the night. The vehicle is a 4 wheel drive made for off road travel. The front seat has Geoff driving on the right side and room for 2 passengers but only 1 ever joins him up front. Behind is a bench seat for three. The main body is connected with the front by an open porthole, 18 inches high by 5 feet wide. Easy enough to crawl through. The main passenger compartment has 2 seats on the right and one on the left. Directly behind is the same 2 + 1 and the rear bench has room for four. The seats are padded and recline a bit. Seat belts are installed and wearing them is mandatory. We found later, on rough road, that the belts are a very good idea. The van pulls a trailer that has our food and utensils. A portable propane tank is stored on it's roof. The back of the van opens for a compartment holding an ice cooler and a freezer connected to the electrical system of the van. Luggage and the SWAG's are stored on the roof and covered with a tarp. A SWAG is a canvas bedroll with a foam pad sewn inside. A sleeping bag is inserted and both have zippers.

We are in the middle of nowhere, not even any animal sounds. The sun is setting and we have to work fast. This is a working trip. The men gather firewood, light the fire and set up folding seats around the blaze. The girls set up the big folding table, Geoff gets the propane tank, connects it to the grill and fills the pot with water stored in the vehicle water tank. The girls cook and the guys clean up. These duties will alternate each night. A flourescent light is clipped to the battery so the girls can see. Supper is spaghetti boulanaise by the campfire.

Day 2 - There is coffee, and bread and jam, and cereal with milk for breakfast. A shovel and roll of toilet paper for those in need. We collect all our garbage in a plastic bag and off we go to the town of Menzies, 132 KM north of Kalgoorlie. The town hall went 100 years without a clock so on their 100 year celebration, they had one installed. There is little else to see but it's a welcome break. Then comes the ghost town of Gwalia. Herbert Hoover managed the gold mine here at the end of the 19th century. There are 3 occupied houses but you'd never know to look. The gold dried up and the beautiful, New Orleans style, two story, State Hotel sits empty. A burned out car shell, a repair shop with rusted tools. Eerie.

We turn east and the paved road stops but the flies don't. Thousands are waiting each time we get out of the van. We have to spray full face and neck, front and back to keep away 99% of them. Our shoes are covered with red dust. There are a few trees here and they're only to 10 feet and they look more like shrubs. Lunch will be the same every day. Bread, lunch meat, fresh tomatoes, peppers, cucumbers, grated cheese, onions, lettuce, mayo, ketchup and mustard. Supply your own water or soda which you bought at the store. There is plenty of beer and some wine but that is saved for the night. And then we hit the Tjukayirla roadhouse, 1000 KM from the Indian Ocean and the Timor Sea. An oasis without palm trees. They have a store with cold drinks, snacks & real food, a shower and a sit down toilet. What a treat. To top it off, they have a classy shirt with their sewn in logo (US$ 28). Not a t-shirt, a dress shirt. The gas pumps outside are enclosed in meshed iron grate and so is the front door and windows. They tell Geoff about a new campground behind the roadhouse. So, we go. Past the dump and 18 KM off the road. It doesn't look much different than the place at 5 KM in or 10 KM in. But here we are. The guys cook - chicken, fresh onions and pepper on boiled rice. Emu egg for desert. That is, a peach half floating in vanilla custard (quite good). All by the bonfire. We sleep under the stars again.

Day 3 - We stop at a roadside Aborigine waterhole. About 4 feet deep with sheer sides. Unfortunately, birds get in but they can't get out. They rot and that spoils the water. The road is so rutted that the van is in a constant state of vibration. My nose hurts from the light weight sunglasses bouncing and I have to take them off. Geoff says that his forearms and hands become numb from holding onto the steering wheel during each trip. Supper is spaghetti with chunks of beef, fresh sliced onions, broccoli and carrots with bonfire cooked bush bread (heavy like short bread).

Day 4 - There is a metal plaque nailed to the inside of a dead tree commemorating this route traveled by Ernest Giles in 1874. This is the Sandy Blight Junction road, a section of the great Central road that crosses the Victoria Desert. So far we've seen a wild dingo, a number of camels and a couple of kangaroos. None of them paid us any mind. The flies still do.

Geoff stops the van so we can walk 1/4 mile from the Western Territory sign to the Northern Territory sign. Red dirt, red dust and a couple of shrubs baking in the desert. It's over 100 degrees in the sun but the walk is a relaxing escape from the bone jarring vibrations of the van. The air conditioner keeps the temperature in the mid-eighties inside the vehicle and it feels cool when we get back in. Next stop is the Docker River store, one of the few Aborigine towns that allow outsiders to stop. And for good reason, they've gotten bad press. One of the human rights groups visited this town a while back and said the government checks every fortnight wasn't enough. The government had to build houses for the aborigines. So they did but the front yards and the streets are strewn with trash. It looks like a dump. Aborigines drop candy wrappers, empty cans and bottles where ever they happen to be. Pictures hit the newspapers and the Aboriginal communities responded by banned visitors and photography. The gas pumps at the store are in iron cages, the front door and windows are protected with bars and the outside public phone has been smashed and burned. The community gets a percentage of the profits from the store which is run by white people. I got a warm hard boiled egg for 50 cents. Little things mean a lot when you're in the desert.

Louis Lasseter was stranded without food when his camels bolted. He walked 15 KM and found a cave for shelter and we stopped for a look. The cave overlooks a dry creek bed with green trees on the banks, so there is water here if you dig deep enough. He lived here for 25 days and set out to walk 140 KM to Mount Olga on 25 January, 1931 carrying just under 2 liters of water. He was assisted by a friendly aborigine family and made it to Irving Creek a distance of 55 KM. He said he'd found gold. They figured the summer sun had fried his brain and he was crazy. He died on 28 January, 1931. Naturally, we walked the creek bed, overturning rocks. Always a chance he wasn't crazy. We don't stand too close to one another. Not because the other person smells but because of the way we know we smell.

We stop for lunch within sight of the Olgas, a massive collection of rounded rocks 30 KM west of Ayers rock. Grilled hamburgers with all the trimmings and off we go. Just 7 more KM of alternately sliding back and forth on the red dust and vibrating over the hard ruts. Paved road, thank God. The aborigines call the Olgas, Kata Tjuta, which means many heads. Several independent hikers have died here from lack of water. Not a problem as we walk up Walpa Gorge and back to the van loaded with water bottles. Mt. Olga is actually 200 meters higher than Ayers Rock but never got the press.

We check into the Ayers Rock campground. They have showers, a sit down toilet, grocery store and an actual bar. But first, back to the van so we join the hundreds of visitors at the road side parking place for sunset pictures of Ayers rock. Supper is chili. Another nite under the stars is cut short by a 4:30 AM wake up call.

Day 5 - We drive to another road side spot for sunrise at Ayres. We have breakfast there as the other vans, busses and cars pull away. The group splits. Some to walk around the base of the rock, others to the concession building. Climbing the rock is allowed but the aborigines discourage it. The rock is so big that the hundreds that are climbing look like ants. The concession area has a wonderful museum of Aboriginal art and history, a gift shop and a full cafeteria. We're on the road by noon and stop 100 KM away at a café to make our own sandwiches.

We hit Kings Cross Station at 4:30. They have gas, cooked food, snacks, beer, wine, ice cream, showers, sit down toilets, a pool, ATV's for rent and helicopter rides for $40-100-190 (price depends on the air time). Supper is steak, sausage and zucchini cooked over a wood campfire + a cooked slice of pumpkin and fresh lettuce, tomato, pepper, carrots, broccoli and cabbage with a choice of french or Italian dressing + pappadams (fried, curled and like potato chips without the salt). A traveler panicked here (on a previous trip) after being bitten by a scorpion. She was screaming and convinced she was going to die. After a few minutes, Geoff pointed out that she was still alive and things calmed down. She put her sleeping bag on top of a scorpion hole and he was just trying to get out. We all check the ground under our bags.

Day 6 - The group splits at Kings Canyon. Some to the top for a 2 ½ hour climb and walk, others at canyon level for a 1 hour walk and no climbing. It's a beautiful place, top and bottom. Unfortunately, it's back to the rutted dirt road for a couple of hours to connect to the highway. The outback's last chance to loosen the fillings in our teeth. Sandwiches for lunch and onto a road side café with a sign "don't pet the dingo". Time for a beer and watch the dingo play the piano. For this, he gets a small tub of ice cream and licks it clean.

Finally, it's Anzac Hill overlooking Alice Springs. 2700 KM. Geoff says the vans are usually good for 30 trips and have to be sold. This van is due for the auction block. Drop off at the various hotels and we get together at Bojangles for supper. It's a great place. There is so much stuff hanging from the ceiling and walls it would hours to list it all. Not an inexpensive place, but not to be missed and we can all have too many beers. No one is driving tonight.

Ayers Rock draws millions every year. Some of them venture to the Olgas. Fewer get to Kings Canyon. Only 2000 have gone across the Great Victoria desert and now I'm one of them.


# THE END

## SIDEBAR FOR PERTH TO ALICE

GETTING THERE - There are no direct flights from the USA. From the west coast, there is one stop service through Sydney, Australia to Perth (change planes). Quantas has specials, depending on the season, for LAX-SYD, round trip, for $999 including 2 short internal flights. SYD-PER is a five hour flight and may not be included. Normal fares are LAX-SYD for $1800, consolidator fares are $1100. Quantas and Virgin Blue fly SYD-PER. Both have a complicated fare schedule with a wide range of prices within the same day. SYD-PER on Virgin Blue (Blue Saver fare) is US $ 192, one way, non-stop. The highest price on the same day, on Virgin Blue, is US $455. Quantas has a Red-e-deal for US $151, one way, non stop and it's highest price on the same day is US $ 610. The special fares can be found and booked on line - www.quantas.com.au and www.virginblue.com.au.

The tour was booked at the Western Australia Visitors Center, www.westernaustralia.net, which is across the street from the Perth train station. The tour company is www.travelabout.com.au.

The 6 day, 5 night trip costs US$ 720 per person including pickup at your hotel, transport, all meals and a SWAG. Sleeping bag insert rental for the SWAG is US$ 12 to pay for the cleaning. They have a 3 day express trip back, Alice Springs to Perth for US$ 360. No meals and no sight seeing. On both trips bring your own drinking water, pillow and insect spray to keep the flies off.

WHEN TO GO - The seasons are reversed in Australia. Our winter is their summer. Summers are warm, not hot. Autumn is cool with frosty nights. Winter is cold at night. Spring is windy. The desert is hot in the day and cool at night. The spring and fall are best but the total air fares to get there are approx. $300 more in summer than winter.

HOTELS - There are hundreds of hotels to choose from in Perth, virtually all the major chains. The Visitors center is very helpful (e-mail is above).

HEALTH - No shots necessary.

MISCELLANEOUS - Don't be fooled by the exchange rate. For comparable goods and services Australia is approximately 20% more expensive than America. For additional information contact the Australian Tourist Commission - www.australia.com. All visitors need a visa and the only reasonable way to get it is on line - www.immi.gov.au

Quicksilver

Top notch way to the Great Barrier Reef

Cairns, Australia - Is the connecting point for the Great Barrier Reef. People don't come here for the beach, there isn't one, it's a mud flat. But the tourists flock here in droves. In response, the city has spent a couple of hundred million to upgrade the international airport and the port marina and terminals. Every third shop on the main streets offers tours. To Green Island, to Fitzroy Island, a tour to both Green and Fitzroy, a visit to Franklin Islands National Park and a selection of trips to atolls or shallow waters where the boat sits as the people dive or snorkel. The town (population 99,000) is one big tourist trap, but then, that's why they come. The upside is, the town has a wide selection of accommodations and food and so many tour companies that they compete for your dollar.

We looked at most of the deals on the signs all over town and decided on Quicksilver for a trip to the reef. Maybe it was good marketing, but it looked to be the best. Early morning hotel pickup for delivery to the port terminal and board the Quicksilver VII for the hour's ride north to Port Douglas. Here we switched to the Quicksilver VIII for an hour and a half ride to the reef. The VIII is a Wavepiercing Catamaran, approx. 140 feet long, 50 feet wide with a cruising speed of 35 knots and finished in April 1995. An aluminum boat meant to be able to take rough water. A good thing since the water was not smooth. There's free coffee and tea and free Dramamine. The seats are comfortable, a video of the reef plays on the TV and the crew has done this trip so many times that everything runs as smooth as clockwork.

We paid for the Ocean Walker Dive in advance and they now collected the medical forms we had to hand in. My partner mentioned glaucoma drops on the form and was told, "no go". The money would be returned at the point of ticket purchase. I went out on deck for some fresh air and the strong winds sucked the boat ticket from my breast pocket and it flew overboard. Fortunately, one of the crew gave me another. The divers are called to a meeting upstairs to explain the procedures and give groups of six a dive time.

Thirty nine nautical miles out (about 45 miles) we arrive at the Quicksilver platform built at the edge of the reef. The ocean floor drops suddenly from here and there is no more reef. The good thing is, it's pristine. Unfortunately, in rough weather, the ocean floor gets churned and the water is cloudy. The boat docks at the platform and stays so you can leave whatever you want on the boat and can go back and forth. The aluminum platform sits on the ocean floor and does not move with the waves. The platform is roughly 150 feet long, 72 feet wide, weighs 230 tons, has a capacity of 500 and was completed in September, 1994.

We exit at the top level of the platform which has tables and chairs. The level below has two entrance areas on the ocean side. To the right are grated steps to the area for divers. Certified and otherwise. Bins hold purple wet suits, fins and gear. Help yourself. Tables and chairs on this level too and most of this space is used for people changing clothes. There are stalls for changing. A matter of choice. To the left of the diving area is a similar one for snorkeling and similar bins. Directly behind is the cafeteria line and more tables and chairs already filled with clothes and bags. You have to move fast to get a spot at a table. Those not needing a wet suit have grabbed fins and a mask and are already in the water. Staff members are in the water and close by, watching. People are in line for the cafeteria. What to do first.

I have the first dive time but it's not for a half and hour so I go to the underwater viewing, one level below. Portholes give a good view of the bottom and the abundance of fish looking for free food. Some must empty their cafeteria plates into the water. Unfortunately, the water is a bit cloudy making everything black and white.

Our group of six has collected. My wet suit fits tighter than my skin but at least I don't need those awkward fins. It's ocean walk, not swim. We strap on weight belts and walk down the grated steps on the snorkeling side to an area where the water is chest high. They lower the heavy glass Helmut onto my shoulders and I practice breathing the supplied air. So far, so good. Then I'm escorted by a staff member down the metal grate stairs which one would expect to have good grip for the rubber boots. Unfortunately, the steps are under water and a collecting point for algae. Feet slip from the stairs that's probably why each of us has an escort down to the final viewing platform. The stairs and platform have metal rails to hold onto and for me, it's a must. Weights and all, the water is moving me up and the current is moving me sideways. I have to hang onto the rail just to stay in place. The water is not crystal clear but the staff divers offer food to the fish and they swarm around us. The staff takes pictures of us and we of them and the fish - as best we can since the Helmut is in the way. Point and shoot means just that. Even those with a fear of drowning should be OK with this dive. The surface is 15 feet above and always within view. Should the supplied air malfunction, it's simple enough to bend over to drop the Helmut (it stays in place by gravity alone), unhook the weights and float up. One of the four divers (never more that 5 feet away) would get to you first anyway.

Getting up is easier than down and I made it just in time for the next free submarine trip. The sub makes an extensive sweep of the area and you get a good view of the ocean bottom. My friend tried to get a ride on the helicopter which flies from a pad 200 meters north of the platform. Booked solid.

For those who don't want to get wet, there's the free underwater viewing, the free submarine and the US $ 112 helicopter ride. You can wear your glasses and not get your hair wet on the Ocean Walk. The buffet has a wide selection of food and that's part of the problem. Someone who stands there pondering holds up the line for all. Easy enough to can gain five pounds here so swim first.

Back at Port Douglas we had the option of boat or bus back to Cairns. The Dramamine was wearing off, the bus looked good.

## THE END

## SIDEBAR FOR QUICKSILVER

GETTING THERE - There are no direct flights from the USA. From the west coast, there is one stop service through Sydney, Australia to Darwin (change planes). Quantas has specials, depending on the season, for LAX-SYD, round trip, for $999 including 2 short internal flights. SYD-Cairns is a 3 hour flight and may not be included. Normal fares are LAX-SYD for $1800, consolidator fares are $1100. Quantas and Virgin Blue fly SYD-Cairns. Both have a complicated fare schedule with a wide range of prices within the same day. SYD-Cairns on Virgin Blue (Blue Saver fare) is US $ 160, one way, non-stop. The highest price on the same day, on Virgin Blue, is US $ 407. Quantas has a Red-e-deal for US $150, one way, non stop and it's highest price on the same day is US $ 580. The special fares can be found and booked on line - www.quantas.com.au and www.virginblue.com.au.

The tour was booked at an agency along the esplanade. Tours can also be booked from your hotel for the same price. From Cairns and back it's US $ 160 ($8 cheaper from Port Douglas). By boat to Port Douglas with an option of boat or bus to return to Cairns. Lunch and on board coffee is included. Also included are fins and masks for snorkeling, underwater viewing through platform windows and the submarine ride with underwater viewing. On platform options include - guided snorkeling tour with Marine Biologist = US $ 46, introductory dive including the equipment = US $ 108, certified dive including equipment = US $ 74, ocean walk with supplied air glass Helmut = US $ 108, ten minute helicopter ride = US $ 112, helicopter from Port Douglas to platform = US $ 23. www.quicksilver-cruises.com

WHEN TO GO - The seasons are reversed in Australia. Cairns is in the northern part of Australia and close to the equator. It will be hot. The wet season is January through March and is the season for cyclones. Rain can be expected from November through May. The total air fares to get there are approx. $300 more in summer than winter.

386

HOTELS - We booked at the Accommodation Centre, 36 Aplin St. www.accomcentre.com.au They have a 3 ring binder with hotels arranged by price and show amenities and pictures. Most of the major chains have hotels here.

HEALTH - No shots necessary.

MISCELLANEOUS - Don't be fooled by the exchange rate. For comparable goods and services Australia is approximately 20% more expensive than America. For additional information contact the Australian Tourist Commission - www.australia.com. All visitors need a visa and the only reasonable way to get it is on line - www.immi.gov.au

RAIATEA, the perfect island to do
absolutely nothing.


RAIATEA, FRENCH POLYNESIA - The small airport on Raiatea
has a nice welcome sign and provides shelter from the sun and that's all
you really need. On the far wall is a large map of the island that shows
Le Motu Hotel in Uturoa, the only real city. Even though the hotel was
destroyed by a cyclone, their phone line rings busy. So then, the first thing
you must decide is how much nothing you want to do, since that will
establish where you stay.

Looking at the map, the airport is on the NE corner of the island and
about 5 Kilometers south is the Bali Hai Hotel. The islands best. It has
attractive bungalows both on land and over the sea - with a glass pane
in the floor to watch the water beneath. The seaside rooms are large and
have long windows. A terrific view to watch the sunrise from your bed.
Even though the sun sets on the other side of the island, light plays over
the mountains adjacent the lagoon on which the Bali Hai sits and it's a
wonderful sight.. You will not be distracted by a television, radio or phone
in your room (there aren't any). Just the sound of the wind and the waves.
A Polynesian breakfast can be arranged. Bread, coffee and fruit. The hotel
is one KM south of Uturoa, the capital. A casual 20 minute walk north
will access the restaurants in town. About 15 minutes south is Pension
Marie-France which specializes in accommodations for divers. They serve
food and you can undoubtedly buy a meal and listen to the fish stories of
the guests.

On the NW corner of the island is the Sunset Beach Motel which
has bungalows with kitchens. It's a very good deal for families since the
kitchen offers a considerable cost saving. They have a large compound
with palm trees and grass, wonderful for picnics. The sun sets over Bora
Bora on this side of the island and one can spend hours delighting in the
spectacle. To the right, a 10 minute walk back towards the airport is the
yacht club, known as the Moorings. The boats are in view across the lagoon

and are a must see. Arrangements can be made at the Moorings for an airplane ride over the island, sailing, diving and other water sports. And a trip to the sister island of Tahaa. A twenty minute water taxi trip north of the Moorings is the Marina Iti on the southern tip of Tahaa. The finest facility on this island. There is a large open area with a bar, lounge and dining area that faces the lagoon and Raiatea. One can spend an entire day sitting about and punctuating the eating and drinking with an occasional walk around the pleasant grounds. It is a captivating place that beckons another visit.

If the boat trip isn't to your liking, it's easy enough to show up at the Moorings at about noon with a six pack or two and talk with yacht owners from all over the world. It would help if you had some stories about the one that got away but if not, they will. The Moorings has very little in the way of facilities so refreshments should be a guarantee of acceptance. Both the Bali Hai and Sunset Beach Motel require a trip to town for food. There is a full supermarket and the Le Gourmet snack shop, both open during the day. Other island snack shops are much like a 7-11 but not as reasonably priced and without hot food. The one in town, however, does have a menu and serves food until they run out (about supper time). In the eastern section of Uturoa, next to the water, is the Quai Des Pecheurs. A very nice French restaurant with a great view and a bar. It is upscale although the surroundings are decidedly waterfront down-scale. Across from Le Gourmet snack shop, on the second story, is Le Jade Garden. A good Chinese restaurant with dancing on the weekends. They also have a nice bar. One of the owners spent 15 years in America and is an interesting fellow to talk to.

## FOR THE HERMITS

On the east coast, eleven KM south of the airport is the Hotel Raiatea Village and a mile farther, the Pension Greenhill. Both serve meals and face Faaroa Bay. Both are close enough to town for a $40 taxi ride but are removed enough from the center of things to offer seclusion. For those needing the ultimate in seclusion, there is the Hotel Te Moana Iti on the south east corner of the island. The gravel road serving the southern half of the island is pitted with large pot holes making the trip slow and a bit bumpy. All in your favor if you want to be left alone. They have meals and well manicured grounds. There is no walk by or drive by traffic since Te Moana isn't on the way to anything and the bungalows are well off the road. AND a short distance away is the most spectacular view on the island - seen from the roadside, atop a cliff. The aqua colored lagoon and the white caps of deep blue water crashing over the barrier reef. Framed by the island of Huahine in the background. Fabulous!

Transportation should be considered along with the availability of food in selecting a place to rest. The shortest trip by taxi - Bali Hai to town - is $20 each way. If you plan to lay about, then the distant hotels are the best bet since they have restaurants. The Sunset Beach and Bali Hai require trips to town. There is a way to kill two birds with one stone if you wish to rent a car and circle the island. Autos rent for about $140 a day and the full circle is 96 KM or about 60 miles. It will take the better part of a day because of the rough roads in the southern half. Get the shopping done first thing and drive clockwise, planning to be at Sunset Beach for the sun setting over Bora Bora. There are no beaches on Raiatea, nothing to climb, no temples to walk through and a population of only 8,600. There are few people to see on the island drive except those inside the snack shops alongside the road but there are some very pretty churches. Each town has it's own and each design is unique. There is very little traffic and you should virtually have the road to yourself. The circle trip is not much more strenuous than a casual walk to town.

If you can't rest here, you can't rest anywhere.


THE END

## RAIATEA IN A NUTSHELL

GETTING THERE - Coach price from Los Angeles to Papeete is $1100 RT on Air France/UTA, Air New Zealand, Quantas and Hawaiian Air. Don't go in July or August, the busy months. The annual October festival features fire walking. There are 2 to 4 flights a day on Air Tahiti, USA tel. (800)553-3477 from Papeete to Raiatea. Forty minutes, one way for $165. They charge for weight over 30 pounds so travel with a light bag like the type that fits into the overhead compartment and a camera bag or purse that can hold the heavy items (cameras, etc.).

LODGING - One KM south of Uturoa, the capital, is the Bali Hai, the island's best, starting at $210 (tel 689-66-31-49). Five KM north of town is the Sunset Beach Motel and the bungalows have kitchens for about $100 (tel 689-66-33-47). The Sunset is probably the best bet for a stay of a few days. The Hotel Raiatea Village is 11 KM south of town for $85 and meals are available for $45/day (tel 689-66-31-62). A mile farther is Pension Greenhill for $100 including meals (tel 689-66-37-64).

RESTAURANTS - Not much of a choice here. The Bali Hai's burned down and Le Motu was destroyed by a cyclone. There are two in Uturoa - Le Jade Garden for Chinese food and Quai Des Pecheurs at the waterfront for French food. Breakfast is about $20 and dinners about $45 without alcohol. Double that if you like to like to have a drink before and after a meal. There is a snack shop in town for lunch or early supper. They close at 6 PM. The food is good, by the way.

WHAT TO DO - There is no beach and swimming isn't recommended. However there is a marina and the following can be arranged - small boat tours for $75 and large boat rentals for $1000, snorkeling, diving, water skiing, sailing and fishing. Airplane rides are available (Charles Higgins 689- 66-32-44) and island tours from Paradise Tours (tel 689-66-23-64) and Havai'i Tours (tel 689-66-27-98). Any of the lodgings can arrange for a car or Vespa rental ($120 and $60).

# ROTTNEST ISLAND - DUTCH FOR RAT'S NEST

Who in their right mind would want to go there?

PERTH, AUSTRALIA - First of all they're not rats. The island was discovered by the Dutch explorer Willem de Vlamingh in 1696 and he mistook the furry creatures scurrying around. They were, in fact, Quokkas, a friendly little marsupial about the size of a ground hog or a fat hamster. Second, the island is THE popular day trip for the people of Perth.

Perth is the only city of size (population 810,000) in Western Australia and is located approximately where Los Angeles is in the United States. From the map it appears to be on the on the coast but it's actually 12 miles up the Swan River. Rottnest is 12 miles into the Indian Ocean and has beautiful white sand beaches not available on the banks of the Swan. The island was a prison from 1838 to 1903 and thereafter a meeting place for Perth society until the recent improvements made to attract a larger audience. Now it's a favorite holiday spot for relaxing on the beach or cruising the countryside by bicycle.

There are tours offered in Perth that include the boat trip, lunch and a bus tour of the island but the price isn't less than if you did the same on your own. From Perth, you take a bus to the pier for the 9 AM daily departure. There is an hour and a half ride on a comfortable, air conditioned boat with a bar (should you wish a morning adult beverage). When you approach the Rottnest pier you will see light, aqua blue water flowing on white sand contrasted by the orange brick arcade.

## THE FIRST STOP

Virtually at the foot of the pier is the tourist center and the line from the off loading boat. There are two tours to choose from. A one hour tour of the south-east third of the island leaving at 13:45 for $8 and two hour tours that cover the rest of the island leaving at 10:45 and 13:30 for $11.00.

There are maps of the island and a time schedule for the public bus. More on the bus later.

Straight ahead is the circular Bistro, specializing in fish and chips. There are beverages and a shaded patio overlooking Thompson Bay and the white crescent shaped beach. To the north of the Bistro is the shopping center with a general store, boutique, laundry, bakery and assorted gift shops. There is a museum, hospital, police station, tennis courts, playground and the office to rent tents for overnight camping. The bakery makes fresh bread, rolls, pies and pastries that are not on anyone's diet but it's pleasant to sit in the open patio, eat and listen to the birds sing and beg for crumbs.

The island is 6.9 miles long and 2.8 miles at its widest point and there are two ways to see it (other than the bus, of course). Rent a bike, the smart way - the rental shop is south of the center - and walk. If you're a hiker, walk from the center, inland to Rottnest Lodge, next to the chapel, through the welcome gate, the lobby, past one and two story accommodation buildings, the Governor's Bar and to the rim of Garden Lake in the rear. The first of several salt lakes that dot the island low lands. It's a pretty view that highlights the low rolling hills.

## THE FORK IN THE ROAD

Circle the lake along the paved road and on the far side is the first fork in the road. To the right is Geordie and Longreach Bay, straight ahead is the center of the island. Towards the center, you pass Hershell lake on the right, a large expanse of shallow, light blue and 2 kilometers later, the second fork in the road. There are few roads and one wrong turn will set you on a path for hours. Turn right towards Pine Lake (north). On the overlooking hills are electric windmills waiting for gusts from the west. There are no wind breaks between Rottnest and Africa. Six thousand miles of Indian Ocean to Durban, South Africa. When the windmills are silent, you can feel a slight breeze while being enveloped in quiet. The hills have no trees, hence no birds. If you stand still, there are virtually no sounds at all. Just a quiet light wind and the beating of your heart.

Pine Lake, like all the lakes, are in the low spots. Collecting points between the gentle hills and there you find trees. And shade. And a spot to rest. Around the curve in the road is Bulldozer Swamp and Baghdad Lake with ducks cruising the red shore line. Over the top of the hill, 1.4 kilometers from the last fork, is another lake at the north coast. Long, wind swept grass, lines the lake and 1.3 kilometers ahead is a spectacular sight.

## IF YOU WANT TO HIDE FROM THE LAW, THIS IS THE PLACE

Suddenly, Geordie appears on the left at the bottom of the cliff. From green shrubs to white sand to a sliver of aqua and finally, the deep blue of the bay. On the far side are a double row of apartments, facing west just up from the beach. A stunning bay peppered with a few anchored boats and a near empty beach. This little peninsula has Longreach Bay on the other side with 36 apartments facing east. There are 49 lower units on Geordie Bay and 16 in single row that circle the peninsula top. Walk between the 49 units of Geordie to the jetty, turn right to the Geordie/Longreach Village Shop, in the center. It's the General store/restaurant/bar/snack shop/patio eating place. It's the only game in town.

Behind you, at the bottom of a long flight of steps is the pier, a clean white beach and a quiet harbor. All the units look alike and a stranger in town is easy to spot. A quick dash to the boat and thousands of miles of ocean to the north and west to get lost in. This is as close to the edge of the earth as one is apt to get.

## THE BEST BARGAIN ON THE ISLAND

The path back to the center is simple. Continue along the road you just left for 1.3 kilometers, past Garden Lake (remember, the first fork in the road) to the rear of Rottnest Lodge. Then catch the public bus ($3.50) for an hours tour of the periphery of the entire island. The south coast, the school class touring the island on bikes, the west coast with its gorgeous views of the reef shores, backtrack through the narrow neck, past Rocky Bay, Ricey Beach, City of York Bay, Catherine Beach and Geordie Bay. The bus makes the circle every hour and you can get off where ever you like and get back on an hour later. The best buy in town and you can spend an hour at a reef and a beach and a bay. Back at the Bistro, you can eat and drink beneath a patio umbrella overlooking the beach. Or hire a boat for snorkeling or scuba diving among the offshore wrecks, cruise the reefs in the submarine or lay on the white sand and soak up some rays. This is an island for unwinding. A beautiful place to take time out.

THE END

## SIDEBAR FOR ROTTNEST ISLAND

GETTING THERE - Sydney, Australia is serviced by Northwest, United, Quantas, Air New Zealand and others. Normal coach fare is around $1200 RT from Los Angeles but there are frequent discounts offered by the airlines and bargain tickets advertised in the travel section of the newspaper for around $800 RT. There is service to Perth on Australian Airlines from eastern Australia and Darwin. A one way economy ticket from Sydney is about $375 (it's 2041 miles).

Boats leave the Perth ferry terminal daily at 9 AM and depart Rottnest at 4:30 PM for $50 RT. You can fly (11 minutes air time verses 1 ½ hours on the boat) if you are in a hurry for around $100 RT.

LOCAL TRANSPORTATION - Busses within the city limits of Perth are free. On Rottnest it's best to rent a bike for $12 a day. There are two bus tours offered - one hour for the south- east section and a two hour for the remainder of the island at $10 and $15 respectively. The best bet is to take the one hour public bus ride for $3.50 which circles the whole island and then rent a bike to pedal where you like.

PLACES TO STAY - The Rottnest Lodge Resort (tel. 292 5026) in the rear of the village for $50 to $100 double. A short walk south is The Hotel Rottnest (tel. 292 5011) for $50/100 including breakfast. You can camp in rented tents for two for $10 at Tent-Land (tel. 292 5033).

FOR MORE INFORMATION - Write: The Western Australian Tourist Commission, 2121 Avenue of the Stars, Suite 1210, Los Angeles, CA 90067 (213)557-1987 or the Australian Tourist Information Office in New York (212)944-6880, Chicago (312)644-8029, Los Angeles (310)477-3332.

## SARAH ISLAND - REMINDERS OF A PRISON IN THE MIDDLE OF A RIVER IN REMOTE WESTERN TASMANIA

HOBART, TASMANIA - You can't get there from here. At least that's what it seemed like at the Tasmanian Government Tourist Bureau at 12 noon on Saturday. They had just locked the doors since the Bureau closes at noon but the fellow behind the counter was trying his best to help me. I wanted to take the cruise up the Gordon River from Strahan, population 600. It's the only town on the rugged and treacherous west coast of Tasmania. There are no trains so I considered the bus but it didn't leave Hobart, the Capitol of Tasmania, until Monday. Early in the morning and would get me there at suppertime. That would eat up three days so I asked about renting a car. He said the drive would take about 5 hours because much of it was over rough mountain roads. The cruise was an all day affair and I would have to drive back at night if I was to cut 3 days to 2. Should the car break down, I would be stranded in the middle of nowhere, in the mountains with little prospect of help until the morning. Didn't look good until I asked about flying. Turns out this little town has an airport and that's when things started to click. He called the cruise service to book me and asked if they could pick me up and deliver me to the local airport. They would. Then, he booked with the Airlines of Tasmania for Monday morning with an evening return. There are no weekend flights into Strahan. I booked a hotel room for the next three nights in Hobart and for Sunday, a tour of Port Arthur. I'll remember the help and courtesy of this office for some time. It was above and beyond the call of duty for a Government official.

### THE FLIGHT

I'm a nervous flyer and I didn't expect a 747 for a 55 minute flight but I didn't expect a commuter airplane either. Twin props with four seats on each side of a center aisle. Thank God there were two propellers, just in case. We flew over cloud cover until hitting the Indian Ocean when the sky suddenly cleared and on circling north I saw Macquarie Harbour and the narrow entrance at Hells Gate. The sand bar and treacherous tides only allow shallow draft boats.

Strahan was the first stop. The other two passengers stayed on board as the plane continued on to Queenstown, Smithton and ended in Melbourne. A station wagon was waiting and it was my ride. "How did you know when I'd get here?" I asked. "Heard the plane" he replied, "and drove up here."

I was on the small boat, the Wilderness Seeker (forty five tons) and regretted not being on the large cruise boat, the Gordon Explorer which held 250 passengers. The Explorer is beautiful and big but only does half day cruises. I was soon to find I was on the right boat after all. There were about 20 of us on a forty passenger boat with a full bar and meal/snack stand. We cruised for 14 miles through the black waters of Macquarie Harbour. The water is clean even though it's as dark as tea. The color comes from rain water washing tannen from the shore plants.

## SARAH ISLAND

Our first sighting was a long patch of green, Sarah Island, with a speck of green to the left, Grummet Island. Both were used for prisoners during the years 1821-33 but Grummet originally held women convicts. They were eventually removed for moral reasons, it is said, and replaced by the worst men as a punishment. These men had to work in wet clothes because they had to wade ashore and work in chains all day.

The boat docked at the end of a planked pier and we were on our own for the next hour or so. At the far end of the island is the new penitentiary - 1828. A three story structure built to house 30 men on each floor. Aborigines were held on the first floor for a brief time but the convicts objected by banging on the floor boards and urinating through the cracks. So much for tolerance. Each man was given a daily ration of 1 kilo of bread which was baked in the earth covered oven. It was heaped with fuel, the ashes removed and the bread placed inside to bake on the hot bricks.

There is a beautiful view point at the islands end showing its proximity to the mainland. An easy swim and two convicts tried it. They made it to freedom but several days later were starving after thrashing about in the dense growth. The two city thieves had no food, no shelter, no farm house to break into, no anything. The leader wanted to return to the jail but his partner said no. They fought, the partner was killed and the leader returned to food and shelter. Unfortunately, he was sent to Hobart for trial for murder and hung. There were no more swimming escapes.

Convicts were trained as blacksmiths, shipwrights, sawers, cooks and whatever was needed to be self sustaining. They built ships (the largest a 250 ton barque) and furniture for the compound and for use in Hobart. The ships were of particular value since this area had a supply of the prized Huron Pine whose oil content caused it to float high on the water. It would seem then that escape by ship was the logical way out. It was but not the way you might think. A group of prisoners overpowered the guards and the crew of a supply ship and sailed away. They were soon given up for lost since none of the hijackers were sailors and the seas in this area were known to be rough. One way was north towards Australia where they would soon be apprehended, the other Antarctica where they would surely die and the others, thousands of miles of Pacific Ocean to the east and Indian Ocean to the west.

As fate would have it, nine months later they landed in Chile with a cock and bull story the Chilean police believed. Not that anyone would have believed the truth. They were welcomed in town and became part of the community. Some got jobs, some married but most returned to their old ways. The police noticed a significant increase in crime and checked with England. Soon, the British sent a boat and returned all of the convicts to Tasmania.

It's a pretty but primitive island. Made a national park in 1954 not that it would be overrun by local inhabitants - there are none. The native aborigines were killed off years ago. On the way back to the boat I paused for another look at Grummet Island famous for the murder of Constable George Rex. He was tied, gagged and held under water until he drowned. Nine convicts were hanged in 1827 for participation in the murder. This was not a nice place to be.

## TEMPERATE RAIN FOREST

We continued up the Gordon to see a gnarled Huron Pine at waters edge and docked at the Franklin-Gordon Wild Rivers National Park where we could get a closer look at this famous species of tree. The Huron Pine (Lagarostrobos franklinii) grows naturally only in Tasmania and only in the remote wilderness of the western section of the island. In fact, it was one of the reasons Sarah Island was selected for a prison. It requires a cool, wet climate, is shade tolerant and can survive year round swampy conditions. If a branch touches the ground, it forms roots and another tree begins. The uniqueness is from an oil, methyl eugenol, which can be up to 7 % of the weight and causes even green timber to float. Its affinity for water makes it float high and resistant to rot (often lasting centuries on the ground) or marine organisms. A natural for ship building.

The park has an elevated walkway since most of the ground is wet and one of the first sights is a 120 foot tall Huron. Not an attractive tree, covered with lichens and more knots than one would care to count. It is not a tree that can be grown commercially because it takes 100 years to grow a foot in height. A little farther is a twin-trunked Huron probably 2000 years old. The Huron is the second longest living species on earth after the Bristlecone Pine of North America. This tree was growing about the time of Christ. There is a similarity to the rain forests we are familiar with in Africa and the Amazon. This one lacks the heat but the vegetation is just as lush.

We finished 20 miles from Strahan, 7 miles up the Gordon, named after Magistrate James Gordon who lent his boat to James Kelly in 1815. Mr. Kelly found Macquarie harbor and the river that empties into it. A gutsy guy - if he got into trouble here that would have been the end of him.

On the way back we paused at a fish farm in the harbor to watch the fisherman tending his crop. There was some time before the return flight and the town of Strahan starts at the boat booking office. King Billy Teas gift shop for local wares, the Happy Hamer's Hotel (only place to stay in town), the Strahan news agency and the Fabulous Foodmarket. I returned to the booking building and this time I didn't ask how he knew the right time to drive to the airport.

THE END

## SIDEBAR FOR SARAH ISLAND

GETTING THERE - Sydney, Australia is serviced by Northwest, United, Quantas, Air New Zealand and others. Normal coach fare is around $1200 RT from Los Angeles but there are frequent discounts offered by the airlines and bargain tickets advertised in the travel section of the newspaper for around $800 RT. There is service from Sydney to Hobart on Quantas.

Strahan can be reached from Hobart, Monday through Friday on the 7:45 AM flight on Airlines of Tasmania tel.(003) 918422 or toll free inside Australia (008) 030 550. The return flight is at 4:45 PM. Ticket price $138 RT. There is a one stop flight from Melbourne to Strahan leaving at 2:25 PM, and the return is at 8:50 AM, Monday through Friday. The price from Melbourne is $252 RT.

LOCAL TRANSPORTATION - Cars can be rented in Hobart and several companies will deliver to the airport. Advance Car Rentals tel (002) 31 1566 are among the most reasonable at $50 a day. Others include Annie's tel. 28 0252, Curnow's tel. 23 7336, and Drive Away tel. 31 2222. Busses are available, if you have the time. A bus pass is about $50 for a 7 day pass. World Heritage Cruises will pick you up at the Strahan Airport (which has no facilities whatsoever) if they know you are coming tel. (004) 71 7174. Otherwise, you walk to town.

PLACES TO STAY - In Hobart they are too numerous to mention and can be booked at the Tasmanian Tourist Bureau, 80 Elizabeth St. from 8:45 AM to 5:30 Monday through Friday and mornings till noon on weekends tel. 30 0211. The choice in Strahan is limited to Happy Hamer's Hotel for $25/50 tel. 717191, the Strahan Lodge a mile out of town for $25/30 tel. 71 7142 and Strahanberry Cottage, a bed and breakfast a half mile out of town for $35/50 tel. 71 7141. They all include breakfast.

TOURS - The big boats, Gordon Explorer and the James Kelly II offer half day tours and the Wilderness Seeker 9-3:30 and is the only one able to stop at Sarah Island. All prices are $30 US tel. (004) 71 7187 at the wharf.

FOR MORE INFORMATION - Write: The Tasmanian Government Tourist Bureau (TGTB), 80 Elizabeth St., Hobart, Australia. tel. (002) 30 0211 or the Australian Tourist Information Office in New York (212)944-6880, Chicago (312)644-8029, Los Angeles (310)477-3332

## TAHAA an undiscovered island in French Polynesia

"Most people don't come over to visit because they don't know how to get here." said Philippe Robin as we bounced over the choppy waters between Raiatea and the Marina Iti on Tahaa. "It's really very easy," he went on as the little boat leaped again into the air, "they can come directly from the airport and if they call ahead, I can meet them with the boat." Water sprayed over the windshield and I was grateful for the enclosed cabin, small as it was. There were two of us inside with Philippe and room for one more - two, if they were friendly. There was space on the deck but no way to stay dry. The other passenger, for this 20 minute ride, was an attractive French girl who disappeared after we got to the other side. I still wonder where she went since there is no town - only the Marina - and jungle for miles around.

Tahaa is the sister island just north of the larger Raiatea, flanked on the east by Huahine and on the west by Bora Bora. All three can be seen from Tahaa (pronounced Ta-ha-a). It shares a lagoon encircled by a reef in the shape of an open figure eight with Raiatea inside the bottom loop and the sister inside the top. Tahaa (54 square miles) is undeveloped, has little in the way of paved roads, no airport, no public transportation and just got electricity in 1992. The Marina Iti, on the other hand, is quite modern, has a computer for reservations and billing and is able to generate it's own electricity.

I enjoyed one of the first real breakfasts in French Polynesia. Eggs over easy, bacon, toast, butter, jam and coffee. Salt and pepper were in little open bowls. All served on the quiet patio overlooking the lagoon as the early morning sun started to warm nearby Raiatea. The French prefer croissants and coffee and the Polynesians, fruit and coffee. Finding eggs in the morning is a real treat.

I rented the Renault and Philippe gave me a map of the island, pointing out the best route. The roads are mostly gravel and sea shell and some exist only on the map. After a few miles I learned the two major driving hazards. Coconuts in the road and crossing chickens. Like most islands, the roads circle the perimeter but on this island they are also within inches of the sea. Close enough to get salt spray on the windshield. The first town, Haamene, is at the base of a long, long bay. Natives were fishing the shallow water close to town for their lunch. Farming and fishing are for local consumption, the main export is vanilla. The town consists of a few houses, some storage sheds and a church in the center. Each town has its own church and each with a different design.

I continued counter clockwise to Hipu opposite the motu containing L'ile, a tiny resort with three bungalows. An upscale pension with advance reservations required and the ultimate in privacy. Too far from the shore to see and this is one place where you really can't get there from here. Finally the Capitol city, Patio, and I was almost through it before I realized I was in it. It was time to stop at "the store" for refreshments. They sell tires, clothes, food and cold drinks. The sun was overhead at this junction and my desire for a cold soda overweighted the need for new tires.

The journey had been a quiet one. Very few cars on the road and no other tourists. None. Just a few of the locals clearing brush or fishing. The population is 4000 and most seemed to be inside. Onward, on the single lane road with sea shells crunching under the tires and a slight ocean breeze carrying freshly salted air over the path. A few children curiously stare at a strange face passing and the occasional chicken playing chicken with the car. The route was much like tracing a star. Going out one side of a lagoon and rounding the corner to come back inside another. The water covered the color spectrum from light blue and translucent blue-green to deep blue. All punctuated by the white of the waves crashing through the coral reef.

Patio is at 12 o'clock and the best views of Bora Bora are between here and Tapuamu at 9 o'clock. Past the lagoon and the reef and the motus stands the island with razor sharp peaks pointed straight towards the sky as if in defiance. Bora Bora at a distance is a stunning sight to behold.

There are no real restaurants on the island so I stopped at a snack shop close to Tiva. It is reported that a Chilean slave ship was wrecked near here and some of the crew vanished. They say their descendants, the Spanish clan, remain in Tiva. I had a Pepsi, an ice cream bar and a mystery pie. It could have been banana or mince. I'll never know.

The only section of paved road is the mandatory "short cut" over the narrow section in the middle of the island. Undoubtedly, it's paved because of the steep grades on both sides. The gorgeous sight at the crest is unlike any other. Viewed over the lush flora, on the west side from whence we came, is Hurepiti Bay and just across the road the view of Haamene Bay and two tall sail boats nestled safely. Both are deep bays and virtually cut the island in two with Mt Taira in the middle. A double view that shouldn't be missed.

## VANILLA

On the recommendation of Philippe, I stopped at Gustave Matimo's Vanilla plantation in the midst of the next mountain pass. He was working in the fields and kindly took the time to show off his farm. The vanilla flower must be hand pollinated and nine months later the bud has created a collection of what looks like green string beans. They are dried for 3 months in the sun and another 2 months inside before banding. The bands are collected in burlap sacks and sold for $100 a kilo. The sun dries the bean black but there's no mistaking the strong vanilla smell. Normal bananas grow downwards when ripe but Gustave's ripen up. All we needed was ice cream for a sundae.

It was a short distance back to the Marina for a cold drink. Philippe had to return to Raiatea to pick up his two boys from school and I decided to take the 3 o'clock ride since the water was calm. He keeps a car on the other side and offered a ride back to the Bali Hai. You bet, the fifteen minute taxi ride would cost more than the boat ride.

Philippe was right, it is easy to get to Tahaa but it's a path seldom taken by travelers. To an undeveloped, unspoiled, little known piece of French Polynesia.

## THE END

TAHAA IN A NUTSHELL


GETTING THERE - Coach price from Los Angeles to Papeete is $1100 RT on Air France/UTA, Air New Zealand, Quantas and Hawaiian Air. Don't go in July or August, the busy months. The annual October festival features fire walking. There are 2 to 4 flights a day on Air Tahiti, USA tel. (800)553-3477 from Papeete to Raiatea. Forty minutes, one way for $105. They charge for weight over 30 pounds so travel with a light bag like the type that fits into the overhead compartment and a camera bag or purse that can hold the heavy items (cameras, etc.). The boat Taxi from the Raiatea marina to Marina Iti is $11 each way.

LODGING - If you wish to stay on Tahaa, make reservations with Philippe Robin, Marina Iti (tel. 689-65-61-01). Bungalows for $120/person/nite including breakfast and dinner. Whatever you need in the way of a tour can be arranged here. Then there is L'ile on the motu north east of the island (tel. 689- 65-64-80). $165 for the first person and $135 for each additional person and that includes meals. Pension Hibiscus (tel. 689-65-61-06) is on Haamene Bay. Bungalows are $120/person/nite, including meals.

WHAT TO DO - The Marina has a Renault (2 people) and a Mazda (1-9 people) for $85 and $95 a day, respectively, including everything (tax, insurance, gas) for independent touring. Airplane rides are available for ½ hour for $85 and an hour for $127. Small boat tours for $50 and large boat rentals for $1000. Also available are snorkeling, diving, water skiing, sailing, fishing, guided mountain walks, vanilla plantation tour and trips to various places on the adjacent island, Raiatea. There are other tour operators but many of their tours start at the Marina Iti.

Tasmanian Booze

Downunder, they make a unique brand of spirits

Hobart, Tasmania - We had been standing in line inside the Tasmanian Visitors Center for a half an hour to book some tours and change our hotel room. It was a busy morning and after a dozen phone calls, and another half hour, the sales rep finally got what we were looking for. I made an off handed comment that I could use a drink. She replied that we were in the right place since there was a distillery only 30 meters away. Really?

Alright, it was still morning. Late morning and it couldn't hurt to look. Out the door onto Davey Street and walk right for a half a block. At first, we walked by and then backed up to look. It was just a bar. The sign overhead read The Lark Distillery and café. So we looked in the window. Open space for tables in the front and the bar at the back end. No customers but it was open. With a shrug of the shoulders and a look of - we're here anyway and if we don't like it, we'll leave. We walked in.

Immediately to the left is a large copper barrel. It takes up that corner and has a fence to keep out the unwanted (perhaps those looking for a free drink). There are signs and plaques on the wall attesting to the fact that this is a real distillery. Award winning news clippings and the such. We made it to the back and one of the owners figured we could use the guided tour. After all, we were the only customers. She took us back to the front to see the 1800 liter wash still. It wasn't working at the moment but if fact produced all the unique liqueurs they make. The copper barrel has a porthole on it's upward sloping top and an inverted copper funnel pipe extending from the top center. The funnel turns about 100 degrees after 3 feet to coils and the rest of the apparatus which we didn't pay too much attention to. As it turns out, the Lark was established in 1992 to produce single malt whiskey & premium (their word not mine) Tasmanian Spirits. That was 153 years after the last licensed colonial distillery closed it's doors.

Naturally, there is free tasting, but first, the secret ingredient. The Lark became locally known for it's unique Bush Liqueur using the native Pepperberry. They even had a live plant in a pot. The fruit, if that's what you call it, is the size and shape of a blueberry. It's ground into a powder and added to many of the liqueurs and does have a unique taste. Slightly peppery with a sweet back taste. The samples would be in a shot glass with enough to barely fill the bottom. Clearly, a taste did not mean a drink. The Bush Liqueur would come last because of it's strong taste and no free sample of the Single Malt Whiskey (in other words, Scotch). They have a price list order form and I took notes on one of them.

First is the Tasmanian Sweet Apple Schnapps. 25% alcohol (50 proof) and it's very smooth. Top notch. It's made from apple cider brewed by Natural Fruit Beverages Tasmania from Sturmer cider apples grown in the heart of the State. The cider is distilled on the premises and the strength cut to 40% alcohol. Apple flavor is typically difficult to retain during the distilling process but by using the sharp Sturmer apple, they are able to keep the flavor without adding any artificial ingredients. The Schnapps is then cut to 25% with filtered water and sweetened. Next is the Tasmanian Apple Schnapps (40%). Not cut and not sweetened. It's dry with a light taste of apple. My partner liked this one, I preferred the sweet apple.

Next is the Pepperberry Vodka (37%). It's double distilled and uses the pepperberry. It's very nice and quite smooth. Then the Pepperberry Gin (37%), double distilled with the pepperberry. It's the best gin I've ever had. In fact, the success of the Bush Liqueur prompted them to make Gin and then Vodka.

Cherry Max came from an original Cherry wine produced in the Coal River Valley of Southern Tasmania. They experimented by adding dark cherries and letting them soak in the spirit. The dark ones are removed after 3 months, sweetener added and enough filtered water to get to 17% alcohol, much like port wine. The name says otherwise, but it's a light liqueur. Last is the Bush Liqueur made from the native pepperberry. The berries are crushed, steeped in neutral alcohol and distilled. Filtered water

409

brings it to 32% and it's slightly sweetened. The taste is unique, not hot with a sweet back taste.

Suddenly other customers came in and were offered free samples. For some reason she decided to give us a small sample of the Scotch. Maybe guilt over the divided attention. I don't particularly like Scotch so I'm not the best judge. That said, I found it light and smooth. It's distilled from Franklin Barley (malted at the Cascade Brewery), yeast and water. They brew their own "whiskey wash" to a strength of 7 %. Whiskey wash is beer without hops. Then peat 20% of the malt like some Scottish Whiskeys. They do not use new oak barrels but old wine/port/sherry ones cut down to make smaller barrels. The smaller barrels give a higher rate of evaporation so they only have to mature for 3-5 years.

Now for the prices. Not cheap, mind you. All the following are for 500ml (½ a liter). Bush = US $ 35, Apple Schnapps = US $ 34.50, Sweet Apple = US $ 31.50, Cherry Max = US $ 25, Vodka = US $ 27.50, Gin = US $ 27.50, Single Malt - US $ 65. They have a web site for orders but there's a catch. They can't send to an individual, only establishments licensed to sell alcohol.

So, have it shipped to your favorite bar or restaurant. You have to try the gin, and, how many people have a bottle of Tasmanian Bush Liqueur in their cupboard?

THE END

## SIDEBAR FOR TASMANIAN BOOZE

GETTING THERE - There are no direct flights from the USA. From the west coast, there is one stop service from Sydney, Australia to Hobart (change planes). Quantas has specials, depending on the season, for LAX-SYD, round trip, for $999 including 2 internal flights. Normal fares are LAX-SYD for $1800, consolidator fares are $1100. Quantas and Virgin Blue fly SYD-HOB - Virgin Blue is US $ 100, one way.

WHEN TO GO - The seasons are reversed in Australia. Our winter is their summer. Hobart is off the southern coast of Australia. Hobart summer is best but the total air fares are approx. $300 more than winter.

HOTELS - There are hundreds of hotels to choose from, virtually all the major chains. The Tasmanian Visitors center is very helpful - tasbookings@tavisinfo.com.au - and www.tasmaniasouth.com

HEALTH - No shots necessary.

MISCELLANEOUS - For additional information contact the Australian Tourist Commission - www.australia.com. All visitors need a visa and the only reasonable way to get it is on line - www.immi.gov.au

The Lark Distillery email - info@larkdistillery.com.au - web - www.larkdistillery.com.au

## RAFTING IN THE RAIN FOREST

There are some tough rivers in the jungles of Australia

TULLY, AUSTRALIA - I was pushing my luck and I knew it. I'd been white water rafting on some of the most challenging rivers in the world and never been thrown out of the raft. I witnessed an entire boat capsize on the morning of the first trip I'd ever taken. A huge wave that we had successfully broken through, flipped the boat behind us upside down as easily as you could flip a coin. The river guide took a great deal of ribbing from the other guides during lunch.

And this was only Class III.

Then there was the fellow thrown 20 feet into the air from the back of a boat I was in. Looking around, I saw the stunned look of disbelief on his face as he hung in the air for a brief moment, awaiting the inevitable fall back into the river. I'd taken a friends advice, always sit in the front of the boat. That's where the action is. The first into a wave and a good sight line on which way to move. In the front, you sit on a corner formed by the outside edge and an interior supporting rib that goes across the boat. Both have ropes attached and a two hand hold is invaluable during a rough ride. I'd been bounced around by the turbulence of several rivers, but my hands never let go of the ropes.

On the Tully, I made two mistakes. Well, one, actually. I didn't move fast enough to get in the front and ended up in the middle of the boat. That means one rope to hold on to. All the boats were paddle boats. A mistake I couldn't control. I've always chosen oar boats where the guide steers from the middle with two long oars. Professional guides know the river, the currents, the rapids. They know which way to point the boat. The powerful currents do the rest. Paddle boats ... well. Everyone has a paddle and they think they are helping to guide the boat. As often as not, they paddle in different directions at the same time. I was trapped.

Guides were assigned to groups of six or seven and we received our instructions in the boat - on the water. Paddle left, paddle right, forward, back, over right and over left.

Speed was important. "Over right", and the three people on the left threw themselves across four feet of slippery rubber to careen into those of us trying to find space for them and still stay in the boat. It was a tangle of arms and legs and life preservers and helmets. "Over left", and faces met knees, arms met stomachs and fingers groped at helmets to maintain balance. Speed and grace were mutually exclusive during this maneuver. And then there were the paddles. They had to stay in one hand while feet were sliding across the inch of water that was always in the bottom of the boat. I asked the guide about the helmets and he confided that they were protection from the paddles not from the river rocks.

And we were off. The area was beautiful. Lush tropical jungle on both sides. This area has the highest annual rain fall in Australia - 11 feet. Rocks as big as a desk. Some as big as a room. The sun was bright. The gently flowing water was cool-not cold. It was winter in Australia but we were in the rain forest and the air temperature was 80 degrees. The order "Forward" came from the back of the raft and we obeyed. There was the soft swish of six plastic paddles in the water. On command, we stopped after a few seconds. The tropical birds resumed their chatter. Approaching a huge rock from the left, the water seemed to slope downwards and then we could hear it. You can always hear rapids approaching. The current quickly carried us around the boulder and into a fast moving, wide, two foot drop. The crash into the swirling eddy at the bottom caused a wave to climb over the front of the raft, soaking us all.

Finally wet, the subsequent waves would have little effect. Onward we charged, with an occasional "Paddle left" or "Paddle right" and half the times we did it correctly.

We took shelter by a large rock to let the video guy in the pontoon boat pass. An odd looking boat with a large waterproof, white box to keep the video camera dry. The boat looked like two large, upcurved, black bananas attached in the center with a seat for the driver. He moved quicker and much easier than we did. Then we came to a section with too many rocks. The waterflow is controlled by the upstream dam and there may have been a clear way through with a higher water flow but there didn't appear to be one now. The river was too wide and the water stretched too thin and the rocks were too big and the spaces between were too small. But we trusted our guide and made for the fast flow between two four foot boulders.

"Over right", he yelled as we entered the space. The three on the left leaped on the three of us on the right and the boat tilted. We were trying to go through on the side and we almost made it. On shear reflex, we started to rock from side to side as the bottom skidded along the rock to the left. We rocked, we slipped some. We rocked some more and the boat, helped by the fast current beneath, started to slip and suddenly we were free. Into the frothing white water on the other side. "Back", the guide yelled, but the command wasn't necessary. We were half tipped over coming out of this crevice and everyone knew the boat was dangerously close to capsizing. And the video guy was on the next rock, taping the whole thing.

Over the next quarter mile there were the normal three and four foot drops over waterfalls, the churning currents and sliding over smooth rock face with barely two inches of water cover and several sections with too many rocks and too few spaces between. By now, we were experts at "Over right" or "Over left" but still couldn't find enough space for all the arms and legs to fit. The guide had to get out of the boat twice, to help. One thousand pounds of raft jammed into a five hundred pound space between two boulders. A delicate balancing act - six of us rocking back and forth while the guide is standing on the rock, lifting up one side of the raft - and then (the tricky part) the guide jumping back in and us lurching back to the proper side just as the raft breaks free so we don't tip over when we hit the rapids at the bottom of each escape. So far, so good. We were good, we were perfect, we were upright and everyone was in the boat. And then came the big one.

I heard it before I could see it. We were coming in from the left and I could hear the roar. The boulder blocked my view until we were at the top of the crest but I knew that threatening sound and braced myself. Right hand grabbed the rope along the outside of the raft. I sat facing forwards, put my left hand out for balance, still holding the paddle, and dug my right foot beneath the inflated rubber cross brace in front of me. The boat crossed the crown and tilted down and I saw it. A six foot drop into a hole whose exit was blocked by a vicious, back curling, white capped wave of solid water. We shot down still slightly turned since we entered from the left and crashed into tons of water. The raft shuddered and came to a momentary halt as the weight of the craft tried to punch a hole in the wave. The boat buckled in the middle and the back end came forward. The fellow behind me was now pressed to my back and suddenly, the wave opened and the front end was released. The wave crashed over us and the pressure that bent the boat in half was released. The boat straightened out with a snap.

There are times in life when we can relive events in slow motion. Our memories allow us to see what happened, a frame at a time. This wasn't one of them. I was in the boat and in less than the blink of an eye, my fully extended body hit the top of the water with a slap. The right hand still had its death grip on the rope. I was an appendage to the raft as a whirlpool spun us 180 degrees and I was now downstream. In reconstructing, I must have cartwheeled straight up into the air and pivoted around the rope. Whipped in a circle, until, upside down, I slapped flat on the top of the water. Quickly turning over, I pulled myself in as the raft continued downstream. Now I wondered if there was a boulder behind me and I would be crushed if the raft collided. People were not helping pull me back in and I yelled. They turned around and snatched me from harms way. Only then did I realize why they were distracted. The fellow behind me was also thrown out but he hadn't been able to hold on to the rope. He was drifting upstream and they were trying to rescue him.

Unscathed, the magnificent seven continued. Virtually out of nowhere, a waterfall appeared. It cascaded over a fifteen foot, sheer rock face to our left and the boat went directly under it. The water was cold and we stopped, suspended. Then I saw the guide was paddling backwards to hold our position and I opened my mouth to protest. That was a mistake. My mouth immediately filled with water. None too soon we escaped the waterfall, which was a sight worth seeing from a distance. We beached the boats for lunch.

There is a permanent tent site with a grill for hamburgers. Several types of salad, bread, coffee and Kool Aid. Seconds were encouraged. The food is transported down to the site by metal basket along cables running down the side of the mountain. Very professional setup. Then the after lunch, entertainment. A rope swing over the river. The water is deep enough for the five to ten foot fall (depending on when you let go of the rope).

Back to the river to make the most of our run. The hydro electric dam allows water to run from 10AM to 2PM and we wanted to see how far we could get. The fellow diagonally across from me in the middle, lost his balance on a rapid and fell backwards into the water. The retrieval was easy. By now the crew was experienced at rescue. Then the guide said, "Everyone in the front" and six of us crowded into a space designed for two and we slid down a six foot water slide and buried the front of the boat in the waiting water. A few more rapids and it was time to leave. We had come fourteen kilometers in four hours. We changed into dry clothes and drove to spaghetti, rice, roast beef and salad at a rustic bar. After dinner, we watched the video and could purchase copies.

Aside from my trip straight up - I guess it was only a matter of time - the trip was an excellent one. Unique from other rafting trips, professionally organized and smoothly run. It's on my list to do again. Wonder if they have any oar boats?

THE END

SIDEBAR 1

WHITE WATER CLASSIFICATIONS

Class I - Moving water with small waves. It is acceptable to bring a rubber duck.

Class II - May have waves up to three feet and has wide channels. Good for beginners and children.

Class III- Rapids with high and irregular waves and rocks and holes. Boats can capsize. Good for adults.

Class IV - Has turbulent rapids with powerful waves and numerous obstacles and requires expert maneuvering.

Class V - Has violent rapids, unstable eddies, irregular currents and large holes. These rapids are always scouted and require experience and good physical condition. Scouting involves tying the boat upstream and walking to the rapids to determine the best possible way through.

Class VI - Suicide. It is only a number since people do not run a Class VI twice. When a VI rapids is encountered on a river, the crew carries the boat around it.

## SIDEBAR 2

GETTING THERE - The Tully river is 150 KM (93 miles) south of Cairns, Queensland, Australia - in the north east corner. Cairns Airport is serviced directly from the USA by Quantas, United, Continental and others and locally serviced from Brisbane, Sydney, Alice Springs and Darwin.

LOCAL TRANSPORTATION - Tour companies pick up at local hotels free of charge at approximately 7 AM. The tour operators are very accommodating and will pick up at any local street corner or on route to the river. Drop off is approximately 6 PM. Total cost is approximately $85 US from Cairns and a few dollars less from Innisfail, Mission Beach, Ingham or Tully. A few dollars more from Townsville, to the south of Tully.

WHAT TO BRING - Bathing suit, tie-on sneakers (no socks), sunglasses with tie on strap, towel, dry set of clothes, dry shoes (wet ones not allowed on the bus), waterproof sun screen, incidental cash. There is a dry bag for cigarettes, film, etc. - accessible only at lunch. Waterproof camera. Helmets and life vests are provided. Class IV river.

FOR MORE INFORMATION - Trips are run by two local companies. Raging Thunder, 111 Spence, Cairns (tel 51 4911) and R 'n R, 49 Abbott St., Cairns (tel 51 7777). Tully trips are run daily-year round and can be booked from any local hotel at no extra charge. Lunch and supper are included.

THE WAVE - This one you can't surf because it doesn't move an inch.

WESTERN AUSTRALIA - First stop is York, a quiet picturesque town of only 1100. It became a settlement in 1830 and grew to support a farm based community but the population soon leveled off and the town now gives a sense of being fixed in the late eighteen hundreds. Carefully preserved colonial buildings like Williamsburg Virginia. The Settler's House with accommodations for "Respectable Couples". The Old York Police station made of brick and stone, the Castle Hotel built in 1853 with its white veranda overlooking the quiet street, a holdover from the coaching days. The mustard colored Town Hall across from the Imperial Inn with a red frame British phone booth marking the corner. Most of the people from the tour went to Grandmas Kitchen for Country Fair at its best. Morning tea actually. The bus started inland from Perth at eight sharp after collecting passengers from around town. This, like most Australian touring buses, was air conditioned, high off the ground and spacious inside with comfortable seats. More room than one gets on most airplanes.

Morning tea and biscuits actually means cakes, pastry, rolls, butter, jam or whatever your diet can withstand. A brief walk around town brings you back to a more tranquil time. Soon, its back on the road to the flat plains and a sparsity of livestock that attest to the difficult living conditions on the edge of the outback. Just when the monotony of the landscape turns your head to a magazine, the bus stops alongside the pet cemetery. In the middle of nowhere, without a house in sight. On the horizon is a dirt cross road with concrete tombstones and flowers. For Shep, Joshua, Kelly and others. A small line of trees and brush are planted to protect the graves from the wind.

## WAVE ROCK

Two tours arrive at the rock at the same time and alternate between the rock and the restaurant adjacent the park. At one o'clock the rock is in half shade, curled at the top like a wave about to crash. It's a granite cliff,

49 feet high and 361 feet long formed by weathering and water erosion that undercut the base and left the smooth overhang. The dark vertical lines are formed by spring water that seeps through from above. People walk up the curved face until gravity forces them back. The rock has been dated to be 2,700 million years old. It was here long before people could walk up its side. At the far end are steps to the top and a view of the flat expanse of the land surrounding Hyden, the closest town. Small depressions in the granite are water holes and rugged Australian brush has taken hold. A small dam was built on the edge of the rock in 1928 to provide water for the settlers. This is the very edge of civilization since the middle of Australia is a vast desert.

After lunch, the bus drives around the park to Hippo's Yawn an immense boulder that looks like the top of a hippo's head sticking from the ground in mid yawn. The mouth is hollow and must have provided shelter for the Aborigines that used to inhabit the area. They have stayed away for the last few centuries. Maybe because of Mulka.

## MULKA THE TERRIBLE

The next stop is the cave of Mulka. The entrance is low to the ground even though the inside is spacious enough. Aboriginal legend has it that Mulka was the son of a woman who fell in love with a man forbidden to marry. Her penalty was to bear a child with crossed eyes. Even though Mulka was tall and strong, his crossed eyes prevented him from accurately throwing a spear and becoming a successful hunter.

Frustrated, he resorted to catching and eating aborigine children. He lived in this cave where the imprints of his hands can be seen on the walls. His hand marks are high on the ceiling attesting to his great height. When his mother scolded him for becoming the terror of the district, he turned on her and killed her. All the more disgraced, he fled south into the desert. The rest of the Aborigines were outraged and set to track him down. They caught him 156 KM south-west of Hyden and speared him to death. Not deserving a proper burial, they left his body to the ants as a warning to those who break the law.

The inside of the cave is dark but a flashlight clearly shows drawings and hand prints preserved from the elements. Hand prints higher on the ceiling than the reach of an ordinary man.

The next stop is an immense, flat granite surface larger than several football fields. Cracks in the granite lead to holes in the rock. Rain water would collect in the holes and the aborigines would cover them with brush to prevent evaporation. They didn't carry water with them and would stop at holes carefully covered through out the country side during their travels. On the far side of the rock is a large field of light orange, button sized flowers, fresh from the recent rain. A delightful array of life.

Half way back is the last stop. Babakin for afternoon tea. The town's auxiliary, four delightful women, prepared tea, coffee and a buffet table of home baked cakes, cookies and assorted treats. Diets go on hold for the next half hour. The town is small enough to have "Welcome" and "Sorry to see you go" on reverse sides of the same sign. A tiny community not unlike many in the Midwest with the same friendliness and willingness to talk to strangers.

A twelve hour day and it's back to Perth but when football fans talk of the wave, to some it will have another meaning and a flashing reminder of Mulka the Terrible.

THE END

## SIDEBAR FOR THE WAVE

GETTING THERE - Sydney, Australia is serviced by Continental, Northwest, United, Quantas, Air New Zealand and others. Normal coach fare is around $1200 RT from Los Angeles but there are frequent discounts offered by the airlines and bargain tickets advertised in the travel section of the newspaper for around $800 RT. There is service to Perth on Quantas from eastern Australia. A one way economy ticket from Sydney is about $375 (it's 2041 miles).

LOCAL TOUR ARRANGEMENT - Wave Rock and three other one day tours can be arranged through Pinnacle Travel, corner Hay and Irwin Streets, Perth, Western Australia, 6000. Local toll free Tel. 008-999-069 or Australia Tel. (09)325-9455 or International Tel. 61-9-325-9455. Tours can also be booked by Western Australia Tourist Centers, Forrest Place (corner Wellington Street), Perth. Toll free Tel. 008-993-333 or Tel. (09)483-1111. Tour is approximately US$54 with lunch and US$44 without.

PLACES TO STAY - The Western Accommodation Center, Tel 277-9199 has desks at the domestic and international airport terminals and can book rooms free of charge. There are any number of nicer hotels in the US$ 100-150 range including the Hilton International, Hyatt Regency and Sheraton Hotel. On the budget end, there's the Savoy Plaza, Tel 325-9588 for US$80 double with breakfast, the Grand Central, Tel. 325-5638 for US$60 double, the Royal on Wellington across from the bus station for US$60 double - they are basic rooms with bath down the hall and centrally located but you might want to look first.

FOR MORE INFORMATION - Write: The Western Australian Tourist Commission, 2121 Avenue of the Stars, Suite 1210, Los Angeles, CA 90067 (213)557-1987 or the Australian Tourist Information Office in New York (212)944-6880, Chicago (312)644-8029, Los Angeles (310)477-3332

# V CENTRAL +
# SO. AMERICA

ANGEL FALLS - in the middle of Venezuela's Amazon.

Impossible to get to? Not so, it was a piece of cake!

Angel Falls - world's tallest falls -
shot from a plane in the Amazon, Venezuela

CANAIMA, VENEZUELA - I was with a tour group visiting Caracas, staying at the Macuto Sheraton which isn't in Caracas at all. It's on the Caribbean as is the capitol's airport. From the airport, continue eastward along the Caribbean coast, instead of turning inland for Caracas, for about

½ hour to the nicer hotels. You'll pass the 1 and 2 star accommodations along the way. Caracas is a city many like to get away from and the northern shore is where they come.

I didn't imagine I'd be able to visit the falls for several reasons. The closest town is Canaima, if you can call it a town. More like an airstrip and a tourist camp. Two hours from the coast on a plane that turns around to fly back. The flight has to be expensive. Then the food and lodging for a captive audience. The prices must be like hot dogs at the ball park. Then the logistics. Canaima is 50 KM from the falls. Walking is out, so it's by boat or air. The boat trip is 3 days in and 1 day out and only during the rainy season (June to November) when the water is high enough. Flying is faster and cheaper. But that doesn't mean cheap since we're still in the ball park and they set the prices.

Oh, one more thing, the weather. Angel Falls, at 979 meters, is the highest waterfall in the world. Sixteen times the height of Niagara. Water plunges from the edge of a tepui, a flat topped plateau or island rising from the jungle floor with vertical walls. The area around Canaima is endemic with these sandstone and quartz walled tabletops formed by millions of years of erosion. Each tepui is an ecosystem unique from the jungle below. They are high enough to be in and above the clouds, the source of the water for the falls. All this means that you may not see the falls for the clouds.

Still, we saw an advertisement for the falls at the Sheraton travel office and were determined to go. USA $360 for round trip air, double occupancy room (one night), all meals (4), boat trip on the lake and plane trip past the falls. All my objections evaporated, I was in.

## THE CAMP

We were met at the airport and driven to the jungle lodge check in. About 300 yards actually. Room assignments, meal vouchers and a pitch for the afternoon boat trip down river which wasn't included. USA $30, why not? I was expecting tents and outhouses. Was I wrong. We had duplex bungalows in the shape of a figure 8 with a pair of us on each side. Two beds, a dresser, closet and indoor plumbing. Cold water, but then we are 1000 miles into the Amazon, not at the Waldorf. The center of activities is the dining area, bar, collection point, etc. An open sided, three level wood pavilion with thatched roof built into the side of the hill overlooking Canaima lake. On the right are waterfalls cascading into the lake and tepeys fill the background. Up close is a small white sand beach. It's a beautiful view for dining or just sitting around shooting the breeze.

We had lunch, cafeteria style, before the canoe trip on the lake. The food is plentiful and tasty with enough choices to tempt anyone's pallet. For desert, I had a piece of cake.

The canoes are long and trim with a motor at the back and shallow draft. On a calm lake one might not give the last item much thought but the canoes came very close to the waterfalls. The sound of the water pounding into the lake make conversation impossible and the waters choppy. No life jackets and ten pounds of camera, lenses and film tend to make one anxious when the boat rocks and there is only two inches between the lip of the boat and the water. Never the less, a good short trip, don't miss it.

## THE $30 BOAT TRIP

This one you could miss. We got into the back of a truck and listened to our kidneys clang together over 5 miles of bad road and I'm being generous with the word road. Then a half mile walk downhill on a road too rough for the truck and into the canoes. Twenty minutes later we pulled ashore 100 feet shy of the waterfalls (we heard them). A 10 minute jungle walk to a waterfall as interesting as the shower in my room and another 10 minute walk to a nice white sand beach at the foot of the aforementioned falls. Take the high path down, less hopping over rocks. The water only drops 10 feet but the falls are pretty and the beach is deserted, except for us. But there is a nice beach back at the lodge and far more impressive falls on the lake.

## THE FLIGHT PAST THE FALLS

Servivensa supplies the flights to and from Canaima and past the falls. This tour was so well organized that I suspect they also own the lodge and concessions as well. All to our benefit, by the way. They use a specially equipped DC-3 with panoramic windows on both sides. The seats are two wide on one side and single on the other with plenty of space to move around. We got an early morning time and were glad of it. The clouds move in by noon.

In no time we were over the lake with an aerial view of the waterfalls we could taste during yesterdays canoe ride. People were glued to the windows as we cruised over more lakes, jungle, waterfalls and tepeys. One tepui after another with thousand foot vertical walls shooting straight through the mat of green below. As though a giant hand reached beneath the earth and pushed a square kilometer of jungle floor up towards the sky and ordered it to stay. The clouds were out and covered many of the table top tepuys. But they supplied the water for the falls on our left and right.

Then we got to the big one. There was no announcement, we just knew. The top 1500 feet was clear. A cloud hung below the half way point and it's shadow darkened the trees below. A single strand of water falling three thousand feet over the edge of one of the world's natural wonders. The plane flew by several times, reversing directions to accommodate each side. The pilot knew what he was doing.

Speaking of pilots, the falls are named after Jimmy Angel, an American bush pilot who crash landed on the top of the tepui in 1937 while looking for gold. The amazing part is that Angel, his wife and two companions cut a trail through the jungle to the edge and managed to descend the vertical cliff and return to civilization eleven days later.

After the flight, there was plenty of time to hit both souvenir shops located between the airstrip and the pavilion. A lacquered piranha, with all his sharp little teeth, sits in my bookcase. And a picture of the falls on my wall.

THE END

## SIDEBAR FOR ANGEL FALLS

GETTING THERE - First you have to get to Caracas. American Airlines has the most extensive air routing to South America for USA carriers and it's domestic flights connect in Miami. Caracas is also served by United, Viasa and a host of International carriers. Our all inclusive tour was purchased at the travel agency in the Macuto Sheraton tel. 944300 but is available from any other local hotel like the Melia Caribe tel. 945555. Servivensa, the local provider, is an offshoot of Avensa, the local Venezuelan airline (also International). The cost was $360 for RT air from Caracas, one nights room (double occupancy), all meals, boat trip around the lake and flight to Angel Falls.

VISAS - Visas are not required for US citizens.

HEALTH - There are no vaccinations required and no one got sick at the camp. Bring mosquito repellant.

WHEN TO GO - The rainy season is June to November. The water for the falls depends on the rain so the falls might be small after January. However, this is the Amazon and there is no real dry season. The biggest obstacle may be the clouds and there is no way to forecast cloud cover (early morning flights to the falls are better).

FOR MORE INFORMATION - Contact the Venezuela embassy, Tourist information, 1099 30th St. N.W., Washington DC 20007, tel. (202)342-6847, fax (202)342-6827

Arica - on the edge of the perfect desert

Arica, Chile - designed by Eiffel while visiting from Paris

ARICA, CHILE - This has to be the skinniest country on earth. 2666 miles long and, on average, 124 miles wide. It's a buffer zone between the Pacific Ocean and the formidable Andes. Chile extends from the Antarctic in the south to Peru in the north and Arica is so close that you could throw a stone from it's airport into Peru. Not to long ago you didn't have to throw a stone since Arica was in Peru. And Bolivia had a coastline.

I just spent a week at the southern end of the Andes. Overcast skies, chilling winds, a formidable landscape devoid of trees and sunlight. I needed to get back in the sun and what better place than the northern edge of the Atacama - called the most perfect of deserts because some costal stations have never recorded measurable rainfall. And Chile went to war over this desolate place. It was called The War of the Pacific (1879-1893). Nitrates, important in the manufacture of gunpowder, were being mined in this 400 mile stretch of emptiness. The mine workers were largely Chilean but the operations were on Bolivian land. The Bolivian Government thought that the Chilean shipping ports were making to much money and added a ten percent tax. Chile took offense and dispatched gunboats.

Peru wanted no part of this conflict but had signed a pact with Bolivia and had to side with them. Chile asked Peru to back off. They couldn't and Chile declared war on Peru. It was a naval war. Bolivia had virtually no navy and Peru didn't have much better. Peru cried uncle when Chilean troops marched into their capitol, Lima. Chile took all of Bolivia's coastline and part of lower Peru. Later they discovered copper in the Atacama and prosperity for Chile continued.

## GOING NORTH

I got a seat on the right side of the plane. Over one thousand miles of beautiful snow capped Andes, the backdrop to one thousand miles of uninhabitable desert. One thousand miles of sun baked brown. At the airport I caught a taxi colectivos to town. Four in a cab that could comfortably hold two, but, for $3 I didn't complain. From my cheap hotel two blocks north of the mall (that I didn't know of at the time), I went out for supper. I saw six blocks of weather beaten buildings with bars on the windows. What a town, what a dump. It reminded me of the back streets of Tijuana twenty years ago. The only thing missing were the hookers.

The following morning I went to Geotours, right off the mall and my perception changed. The buildings on the mall are new and the people up scale. The Rodeo Drive of Arica. The side street (Bolognesi) with Geotours, has independent vendors and bargains galore. The best shopping in town. Anyway, I booked a day tour to Lago Chungara 14,000 feet up into the Andes (US$18). The guide suggested I don't book the town tour, I could walk that on my own. An honest man. Take no booze or milk products the night before. I knew the dangers of high altitude sickness since I'd spent some time in Bolivia. I followed his advice.

## AROUND TOWN

I walked south to the base of El Morro, the 1000 foot flat topped mountain that overlooks the town. The fort on top offered protection for the town during the War of the Pacific. It is too high to walk up so I headed back towards the mall and spotted the chocolate shop. For research purposes, I bought 12 pieces for US$1.50. Now I could grab a cab for the long drive to the top.

There is a flag rustling in the wind on the edge overlooking the town, flanked by artillery pieces. A stunning view that extends along the curved coastline into Peru. The town looks bigger from up here and the harbor is filled with small boats. There's no longer a fortress but it's clear where cannons were located to fire on the ships close to shore. There is a stone plaque commemorating the site and a large statue of Jesus. The statue is a resting place for birds tired of fighting the strong headwind. The small museum (75 cents) shows details of the battle to take the town. To the south is a coastline devoid of people. I decided to walk down. Half way, I decided it was a smart move to have taken a taxi up.

The Plaza Colon, at the base of El Morro, is a beautiful park. It's punctuated by the church San Marcos designed by Alexandre Eiffel in 1875. Yes, the same guy that did the tower in Paris. A block west is the former custom house, Andula de Arica, also designed by Eiffel in 1874. There is time to shop, eat and get to bed early.

# INTO THE ANDES

The van was prompt at 7:15 AM and we stopped at a store at the edge of town for supplies. Then north to the Y in the road. Straight ahead is Peru, so we went right following the RR tracks. Trains are scheduled to go to La Paz, Bolivia but only for cargo.

At km 37 (kilometers from the Pacific Ocean) we stopped at the church at Pocochile. The graveyard behind shows the vast barren landscape. Miles of brown earth. Nothing green. Back to the van. The driver popped in a cassette of pan flute music and just as I was about to commit suicide, we stopped for the first sighting of plant growth. A cactus at 2000 meters in elevation. This area gets a little rain in January and February. The higher you go the greener it gets.

We stopped for breakfast/lunch at 10:30 AM. A sandwich with cheese virtually painted onto the bread and tea that tasted like spinach. I talked to our driver and he confirmed my assessment. There are Germans on his tours, and French, even some Canadians, but, almost no Americans.

A roadside stand had llamas walking about looking for food. And blankets for sale. The snow capped mountains in the background are volcanos. Some active, some not but this is the Andes and no matter which way you look there is a potential active volcano, snow cap or not. We stopped at a gorgeous collection of lakes and islands at km 170, elevation 13,500 feet. The air is thin and we are all breathing faster to get enough oxygen. Pilots put on oxygen masks at 10,000 feet and we are well above that.

We finally hit the small Lake Chungara park headquarters building/restaurant/grocery store. The local Indians have makeshift stands in front. Blankets, ponchos, artifacts. At 14,820 feet in elevation it's one of the highest lakes in the world and in the distance are the twin Pallachata snow capped volcanos. Dormant, they say. A beautiful sight and we're walking slower now. Vicunas are grazing on the thin grass next to the station. They must be used to people since the sound of camera shutters never made them look up.

One of the three backpackers hanging around said they should camp out here for the night, But, one was sitting on the ground, leaning against the Headquarters building wall, head in his hands with a splitting headache. It didn't look good.

Back in the van we headed back to km 145, the town of Putre for late lunch. Rice, a small potato, 2 slices of tomato, a chicken leg and coffee. We got back to town and real air at 8 PM. I walked to McDonald's and wondered what happened to the backpackers while munching on a couple of hamburgers.

The next morning I checked into the Best Western (now called the Volapuk), located on the mall. The best part of town was now at my doorstep. After breakfast I walked north to the casino. It was closed for repairs. Further north is the Hotel El Paso. They have a nice garden, plain lobby, comfortable pool area, a tiny gift shop and virtually no guests. It was time to go back to the mall where there are always lots of people. Window shopping is always a pleasant way to pass time and there are plenty of sidewalk eateries to sit and people watch.

THE END

SIDEBAR FOR ARICA


GETTING THERE - From Santiago the airfare to Arica is approx. $250 RT on Lan Chile. Santiago, the Capitol, is serviced by American, Continental, Northwest, United and most foreign carriers. RT fare from the USA is $800-1200 depending on season and departure city.

ACCOMMODATIONS - The best in town is the Hotel Arica, south of town. Rooms are US$ 110/130 singles/doubles. Tel. (058)254-540/fax 231-133. On the north side of town is the Hotel El Paso at US$ 100/120 (tel. (058)231-041, fax 231-965). Newly renovated and most convenient is the Hotel Best Western, right on the mall. Rooms for US$ 55/65. Tel. (058)252-575.

TOURS - Geotours at Bolognesi 421 is on a side street ½ block north of the mall. I appreciated their honesty. They can arrange 1, 2 and 3 day tours into the Andes for about US$ 60/day per person. Tel. (058) 253-927/fax (058)251-675. Next door is Ecotours at Bolognesi 460. There are two large parks on the Chilean side of the Andes for hiking and camping. Parque National Lauca which I visited and south of that is Reserva National Las Vicunas.

MISCELLANEOUS - There aren't a lot of fancy places to eat in Arica. Better stick to the mall or one of the better hotels. There is a $61 entrance fee at the Santiago Airport in response to the U.S. charging a similar fee for Chileans getting a USA visa. WARNING - there is an exposure to high altitude sickness in the Andes. It can be fatal, consult with your doctor - there are medications that can be taken.

# MOST PEOPLE GO TO BELIZE FOR THE CORAL REEFS, BUT THERE IS
# A TROPICAL JUNGLE TO THE WEST AND NO SHARKS.

SAN IGNACIO, BELIZE. You know you've reached town when you cross the single lane, all steel, Hawkesworth Bridge that spans the Macal River. The towns on neither side of the bridge look snazzy, more like two Mexican villages that have fallen on hard times. But then again, we didn't come to Belize to see a modern city. We're here for the jungle.

We didn't get off to an auspicious start anyway. The plane from Houston was supposed to arrive at 2:30 and didn't get in till 7:10PM. We climbed into the van for a 2 hour drive due west to the landmark suspension bridge that separates Santa Elena on the east from San Ignacio on the west side of the river. Combined population of 8,000. We turned left, went up the hill for a long block to our Hotel, the San Ignacio. The rooms are plain despite the add that the Queen of England stayed here. There is a fan, a full bath and a balcony with a view that is easily ignored. At the bar we had a view of a very nice adjoining dining room that was closed because it was 10PM. Who cares, the bar is open. A bottle of beer is just under $3 and rum and coke is $1.50. Besides, it's too late to eat at 10PM anyway. And, there was entertainment. A gigantic 5 inch tarantula was resting in the middle of the barroom wall not 10 feet from our table. Sometime, between rum and cokes, he moved and all 7 of us looked under our feet. They are very strong on ecology in this part of the jungle and we didn't want to mistakenly step on him. Right.

Breakfast was very good, befitting the warm comfortable dining room we were glad to be able to finally use. No orange juice and they were out of grapefruit juice. But the banana juice is wonderful, trust me.

So there was no hot water in the room. There were no scorpions in our shoes either, so you take the good with the bad. We boarded the van for a bone jarring 2 hour ride over bad dirt roads to the 1000 foot falls in the middle of the Mountain Pine Ridge Forest Reserve, 800 square Kilometers of National park. And just in time, the fog was rolling in. It's a beautiful waterfall erupting from the midst of the jungle to cascade over rock to the ravine below. We walked down to the viewing platform and got our pictures before the fog made the hillside and valley invisible. On our way out, a van was driving in with another group. No one said a word. Those people would have to buy a postcard.

We were supposed to see Xunantunich, a Mayan ruins abandoned in 900 AD after a devastating earthquake. But the road was washed out, a common occurrence in this neck of the woods. So we headed for the 5 Sisters, a resort in the area, for an early lunch. It's just past the Francis Ford Coppola resort (Blancaneaux Lodge) which is open to the public most of the year. He likes to have a retreat with some of his cronies each year and flies in from the Belize airport to the makeshift airstrip next to his lodge. During those times, it's closed.

The 5 Sisters is a gem in the middle of the jungle. Guests have individual thatch roofed wood cottages built into the side of the hill overlooking the waterfalls below. The office/ lounge/ bar/ dining building has a small gift shop, a charming indoor restaurant and a balcony in back for outdoor dining. Lunch was a ham sandwich, an orange, a sliced banana and grapefruit juice and a great view of the waterfalls, natural swimming pools and river 200 steps below. T-shirts are $13.50 in the lobby. This is a first class resort (eco conscious) in a great location but you better bring your entertainment with you. There is no walking to town from here.

Then on to the Rio Frio caves. All the tours follow much the same pattern so those entering this reserve will probably see the same things. In a different order perhaps, to prevent all the vans arriving at the same location at the same time. Each van has radio contact with a central base so things can be co-ordinated. The cave has a 65 foot mouth that's entered from a tricky hillside climb that gets you to a rocky ledge 45 feet from the bottom. The rock surfaces are uneven and sometimes slippery. Caution is the apt word here. Oh yes, even the strongest flash will not light up the inside of the cave for a usable picture. Save your film for the outside.

The cave is open at both ends so some of the group walked around the outside to the other end. But some of us discovered some little bitty, walking leaves and, upon investigation, found army ants beneath each little piece of green. There were thousands of them walking past each other over a set trail. Down the length of a branch 8" from the ground, across the dirt, over fallen branches and into the dense jungle. Towards the right with pieces of leaves the size of a fingernail and to the left empty handed (so to speak). The jungle is filled with leaves but these determined fellows wanted this particular brand and none of them ventured off the trail.

Then back into the van for The Rio on Pools, the designated swimming opportunity. 500 feet down, on rickety steps, to the river. It wasn't appealing, so we passed on the swim. The river runs over rock and it would be a good place for a dip but none of us thought to bring a swim suit.

We were close to the Guatemalan border so we went through the customs check point and drove around the adjoining town. Not much to see here, so it was back to the hotel, have a drink and hit the town at the bottom of the hill for shopping. There is a vast collection of t-shirts and miscellaneous trinkets in the stores. Prices are not as low as one might expect in a third world country so the store keepers didn't make much on us. We were headed for Ambergris Caye (the upscale section next to the barrier reef) the following day and figured the selection would be better there. (P.S., the prices weren't) Anyway, there were lots of $1.50 rum and cokes waiting for us back at the hotel.

## THE END

## SAN IGNACIO SIDEBAR

GETTING THERE - Continental Airlines serves Belize through Houston and American Air through Miami and Chicago. Fares from the west coast start around $800 RT.

WHEN TO GO - The dry season is from October to May and the busiest time is mid-December to April. Hurricane season is June to November and Belize got hit hard in 1931, 1961 and 1978. The airport is only about 2 feet above sea level, so if a storm is coming - get out. The interior is humid year round.

WHERE TO STAY - A Good place is the San Ignacio Resort Hotel, 18 Buena Vista St., P.O. Box 33, San Ignacio, Belize tel. 011-501-92-2034, fax 011-501-92-2134, E-Mail: sanighot@blt.net. $50 double + $25 for A/C + 7% room tax + 10% service charge. In the jungle is The Five Sisters Lodge, Mountain Pine Ridge, Belize tel/fax 011-501-91-2005, doubles for $95. On the road to the 5 sisters is Blancaneaux Lodge owned by Francis Ford Coppola, P.O. Box B, Central Farm, Cayo, Belize tel/fax 011-501-92-3878, doubles $160.

WHERE TO EAT - Eat at your hotel unless you're staying at a guest house in town ($15). Then go to Eva's for meals at $5.

TOURS - Maya Tours, 20423 State Rd.7, Suite 6000, Boca Raton, FL 33498 tel. 800-392-6292; Tropical Travel Representatives, 5 Grogans Park, Suite 102, The Woodlands, TX 77380-2190 tel. 800-451-8017; International Expeditions, 1 Environs Park, Helena, AL 35080 tel. 800-633-4734. All hotels in Belize will offer tours, they need not be arranged beforehand. Tours of all the sites in and around San Ignacio can be booked and run from Belize City. The only difference is 2 hours travel each way.

If you choose to stay first class in Belize City, there is the Ramada Royal Reef Resort and Marina, P.O Box 1758, Belize City, Belize tel.011-501-2-32670, fax 011-52-2-32660, approx $100 double and the Radisson Fort George Hotel, P.O. Box 321, Belize City, Belize tel. 011-52-2-77400, fax 011-501-2-73820. approx $120 double. Both are just outside the city proper. The next level of hotels is a sharp drop from 4 stars to 2 and brings you close to the city. Walking the city streets at night is dangerous.

FOR MORE INFORMATION - Write to the Consulate General of Belize, 5825 Sunset Blvd., Suite 203, Hollywood, CA 90028 tel. 213-469-7343 fax 213-468-7346

# CONTADORA ISLAND RESORT

## The best in all of Panama

ARCHIPIELAGO DE LAS PERLAS, off the coast of PANAMA - We could tell this was upscale the moment we stepped into the terminal. It was clean, well lit and had ticket counters like those back home. We had arrived at the San Blas islands terminal, 200 feet away, only a few hours ago. Not clean, shadowy and unorganized. A lot of backpackers and a building in need of renovation, paint and seats for the waiting room. These two terminals are back to back and use the same airfield (and the same airplanes, it turns out). It's the city airport, only 5 minutes from the nicer hotels. The 25 pound baggage limit for small aircraft is ignored. Designer suitcases are meant to hold nice clothes, lots of them.

But then, nice, that was the point. We wanted to end our stay in Panama at a nice place. Isla Contadora is about 70 KM into the Pacific and only one of the 140 islands in the chain named for the large pearls that were once found in their waters. It's the only island with a hotel and we found out later that it's the only hotel on the island.

The 3 PM flight left full at 3:15 for the ½ hour flight. The landing plane stopped at the control tower at the runway end, 200 feet more and we'd be swimming. We asked which way to go and followed the pointed finger downhill, around the end of the runway and back uphill to the other side of the runway. Still no signs, so we asked at what looked like a motel (condos). We followed the asphalt road towards the beach avoiding the ATV's coming uphill and there it was. Two big smiles walked into the large, wood warm, multi-story lobby and checked in.

First impressions are meaningful. We walked through the arch to the center compound circled by attractive two and three story wood buildings. To the right is a below ground bar serving those standing in the pool. A sign showing the activities is in front of your face, there's a large grass lawn, real trees (not jungle), a large cage with macaws, and another with monkeys. We got lost, but eventually found our place across from the tennis courts. A/C, cable TV, frig, modern bathroom and sliding doors in the rear that lead to a nearby bar. The drinks are free, so much for the two bottles of rum we brought.

The hotel is in the middle of a semi-circular bay, protected by peninsulas at both ends. It's a long beach with condos overlooking one end. Relaxing and beautiful. The reception building has the main dining room and an attached bar. There are 2 other restaurants, Seafood and Italian in other buildings, reservation only. Free, as was the buffet in the main room. For supper, I had roast beef, scalloped potatoes, spaghetti, tomatoes, cucumber and three deserts from the buffet. Quite possibly the best food I've ever eaten at a buffet. Afterwards, we thought we could run them out of rum and coke. We couldn't.

Breakfast was delicious too. OK, the OJ was a little bit off but they had the little sections cut out of the grapefruit and on a plate. No squirts in the eye. After checking out the nudist beach, over the hill and around the corner, to find it empty, we rented ATV's. You know, the little vehicle with three big wheels that is supposed drive up hills and over valleys. Mine worked fine but my partners started and croaked three times before the owner led the way on his motorcycle. We hadn't planned on "follow the leader" but then I figured my partners crummy ATV was going to die again and the owner is coming along to fix it. The island is a lot bigger than the map we got at the desk led us to believe.

And lots of hills, so forget walking. There are some very nice homes both on the coast and in the interior. Our "guide" pointed out the Christian Dior house, five stories, overlooking the sea. Business must be good, this modern house would cost big bucks anywhere in America. And then my ATV sprung a chain, go figure. Fortunately, the repair man was close at hand. There are two lakes in the interior, a grocery store, police station, medical clinic, restaurant, fenced in manicured lawns and a church. We got our $20 worth for the hour and my friends ATV never stalled again.

Lunch was sliced pork, beans, Spanish rice, iced rice pudding with raisins, topped with cinnamon. I'm not a gourmet but I was starting to look forward to the meals.

The glass bottom boat runs twice a day and it's done by a husband and wife team. She's Canadian, he's Panamanian. There are some colorful fish and turtles but it's not as good as going over a coral reef. But the couple was a wealth of information. Contadora has one hotel now, but there are plans to build an inexpensive one on the island next to the resort, 50 rooms and no meals. And, there are plans to build a very expensive resort on the next island over. Competition is on it's way. Fishing is excellent in almost any direction and that includes the big ones, like sailfish. There are white tip and reef sharks in the water but they don't bother people. Why is there a restaurant when the food at the hotel is free and very good by the way? The island residents like to go out to eat every once and a while.

The hotel workers don't live on this island, it's too expensive. They live on the next island over and that's where the boat's headed (only to look). And on the left, with it's own impressive pier, is the Christian Dior Southern Rep's house. Talk about nice.

The hotel workers get back and forth by water taxi and the population of the small island is 400. The main reason the population is sparse on all the islands is the scarcity of fresh water. The channel between these two islands is calm but not so for the stretch between the islands and the mainland. Those waters can be rough. And that's where the whales pass by each year for southern mating. The entire boat ride is two hours and worth taking even though there aren't a lot of fish to see close to shore.

There is a 9 hole golf course. And a ping pong table next to the sunken bar, free drinks for the loser. And another pool by the tennis court. Roast turkey and mashed potatoes for supper, ohhhh. Now I have to go on a diet.

THE END

442

## SIDEBAR FOR CONTADORA ISLAND

GETTING THERE - Gateway cities in the U.S. are Miami, Houston, NY, Washington DC, Dallas and Los Angeles - Miami being the principal one. RT airfares from Miami or L.A. are around $750. Continental and American Air offers frequent service and Copa is the Panamanian national airline. I flew Eva Air from L.A. for $740 RT in deluxe class. Copa connects to all the major cities in Central America, if you're thinking of a side trip.

ACCOMMODATIONS - In Panama City, the best is the Miramar, $295 double, tel (507)214-1000, overlooking the canal. Caesar Park, $225 dbl, tel (507)226-4077, the Radisson, $265 dbl, tel (507)265-3636, in the middle of the nicest shopping area. All the above are 4 star and the Caesar has a casino. The El Panama, $225 dbl, tel 269-5000, Plaza Paitilla Inn, $180 dbl, tel 269-1122 and Riande Continental, $165 dbl, tel 263-9999 are 3 star and have casinos. The California is a 2 star hotel, $55 dbl, tel 263-7736, fax 264-6144.

LOCAL ARRANGEMENT - There are literally hundreds of tour operators in the city. After a bad experience with a recommended one I found a good one, Por El Mundo, Calle 45-E No 4, Bella Vista, tel (507)264-6766, fax (507)264-6436, e- mail: mundo@sinfo.net They helped with an assortment of tours run by others, one stop shopping so to speak. Available are - City tour, shopping in duty free Colon, Panama Canal, Barro Colorado Island Tour, El Valle de Anton Canopy Tour, San Blas Islands, Hotel Contadora Resort.

For the Panama Canal, Argo Tours, tel (507)228-4348, from the USA tel 1-888-Panama 1, fax (507)228-1234, half day transit $115, Ocean to Ocean $175. San Blas Island special offer from Viajes Versalles S.A., tel (507)263-4085.

MISCELLANEOUS - Visas or tourist cards are required for all. U.S. citizens are issued a tourist card for $5 at the ticket counter in the US.

## If you liked TIKAL, you will love COPAN

COPAN, HONDURAS. Monster pyramids and huge temples are a sight to behold and in some perverse way, the stones and alters upon which virgins were sacrificed to the Gods, do grab my attention.

I'm not an archaeological buff of the Mayan civilization or any other for that matter. I say this as a matter of fact not pride. When the guide points to individual stone inscriptions and explains each is a month on the Mayan calendar, my mind wanders. I'm not a barbarian, it's just that the details don't hold my attention. Although much is known of the ancient Mayan civilization, much is not. The guides often admit that some of their explanations are guesswork. And after a while, some etchings do all look alike.

### BACKGROUND

The small town of Copan Ruinas, usually called Copan has a population of 23,000 and is a stones throw from Guatemala, to the north. It's a 3 ½ hour drive from the nearest big city, San Pedro Sula (close to, but not quite on, the Caribbean Sea). Honduras was named by Columbus who landed here on his forth and last voyage. It means "depths" in Spanish after the deep waters off the north coast. It's a rugged country with 75% of the total land area comprised of mountains. It's also poor, with severe unemployment and the largest exports are coffee and bananas.

### MAYAN COPAN

It is guessed that the first Mayan settlement in Copan was around 1000 BC. The culture collapsed in 900 AD with the rest of the Central American Mayans. The early years are still being pieced together but around 435 AD, the King was Great Sun Lord Quetzal Macaw. His family continued to rule through a succession of Kings till 900 AD. One of the greatest Kings was Smoke Imix (Smoke Jaguar) who ruled from 628 to 695 AD. He built the tribe into a major military and commercial power in the region. He was succeeded by 18 Rabbit (695-738 AD), the 13th King. 18 Rabbit took the tribe to war, was captured and beheaded. He was succeeded by Smoke Monkey (738-49 AD) who was followed by his son Smoke Shell (749-763 AD), one of Copan's greatest builders. Smoke Shell was responsible for the most important monument, the Hieroglyphic Stairway which depicts the achievements of the dynasty from it's inception to 755 AD. Building continued under the Yax Pac (Rising Sun) reign from 763-820 AD. The great temples and buildings are more a part of the later Kings than the earlier ones.

## THE TOUR

The ride from the San Pedro Sula airport was smooth along a four lane highway until we hit the city line and then everything came to a stop. They still have turnabouts, a leftover from the British. Instead of a traffic light, there is a circle that vehicles enter from all four directions. They work well with light traffic but jam up, in all directions, at the slightest overload.

Finally, we drove through the gate (with armed guard) at the Copantl Hotel, an older but posh establishment. A virtual island encircled with trees and an iron fence. After getting settled and checking out the impressive artwork displayed throughout the large lobby, we took the elevator to the top. There is a warm, comfortable, Old English style bar with an adjoining patio for outdoor dining. They were firing up the large outside grill for steaks and chops and my mouth started to water and it wasn't even dinner time. A beautiful view of the city lights, the smoke of the grill and we agreed, we're coming back here to eat. Little did we know.

We found out that drinks were half price in the ground floor bar and down we went. A double rum and coke for $2.75 and this bar is five times as big as the one upstairs. Not as cozy, but comfortable enough to stay too long. By the time we left, the roof restaurant was full, we were lightheaded and made due with the coffee shop instead of the second, and snazzy, dining room on the ground level. I had excellent grilled pork chops, a full meal, for $6 plus 10% tax + 10% added tip. A bargain even with the added 20%.

There is a casino, so we headed out the front door, turned right and right again to the building next to the hotel. Past the recessed door to the obvious entrance and into a room of slot machines and bingo. This is the casino? It took less than a minute and we were back outside. Only by chance did we stumble into the entrance we casually went past, the real casino. With blackjack and roulette but no crap table. We lost less money at the first place.

## ON THE ROAD AGAIN

In the morning we boarded the van for a 3 ½ hour drive through curving mountain passes and green jungle valleys to our new abode, a Best Western Hotel, just on the outskirts of Copan.

The ruins are only a few minutes from town and the visitors center has a very nice relief map of the grounds. A quarter of a mile past the center is the official entrance, marked by two affectionate (or fighting), brightly colored macaws. A little farther and we entered the West Plaza with the five story, stepped, Acropolis and several carved stelas (stone artifacts). The tablets, tables and statues are wonderfully preserved and absolutely beautiful to see. We weaved our way through to the south end of the site, Structure 16, atop the cliff overlooking the remains of the Nobel's houses 50 feet below. A thatch house holds miscellaneous original stones that will be used to reconstruct the homes in the near future.

Structure 16, like the Acropolis is built of small stones roughly the size of a cinder block. Climbing is not allowed except where the guide climbs. We followed him up the back of 16, viewed wonderful carvings in the stone columns and entered the east plaza at the top of the arena. It's ringed with stone seats much like the Roman coliseum, though not as tall. There were no lions but the games were just as lethal. Competing teams played a game similar to soccer and the winning team was sacrificed to the gods. That's right, the winning team. So much for being champions two years running.

Then across the top of the Temple of Inscriptions, next to and higher than, the Acropolis, and saw several huge carvings in the brick walls and columns. Not even the guide is allowed to touch the stones, he points with a stick with a feather attached to the end. From here there is a beautiful view of the great plaza below.

Upon descending the tricky stairs, there are mysterious faces carved in the stones among a huge tree's roots. At the southern end of the great Plaza is the famous Hieroglyphic Stairway (743 AD) protected from the elements by a long awning. 63 steps of carved hieroglyphics, thousands of them, describing the history of the tribe. It's still being deciphered since some the steps have been damaged and others jumbled. It's the longest inscribed text in the new world. Stunning.

We wandered through the plaza looking at the inscribed tablets and small pyramid altars and were drawn to a large mushroom top shaped rock. Upon closer inspection we saw a spiral grove cut into the rock from the top to the bottom. The guide explained it was for the flow of blood from sacrifices made right here.

Copan is smaller the Tikal but better organized. It stands out because the statues, etchings, pyramids and buildings are better preserved. We went to the museum the following morning (300 feet from the visitors center) and it is astonishing. You walk through a tunnel to the inside of a pyramid to see treasures protected from the elements. It's the most impressive third world exhibit I've ever seem and is not to be missed.

## THE END

## COPAN SIDEBAR

GETTING THERE - Continental Airlines serves San Pedro Sula, Honduras through Houston and American Air through Miami and Chicago. There are direct flights from New Orleans, New York, Los Angeles and San Francisco. Fares from the west coast start around $750 RT. San Pedro Sula is also served by TACA (El Salvador's airline) and Tan/ Sahsa (Honduras airline) from other Central American countries. Airport exit tax is US$ 20.

WHEN TO GO - The dry season is from November to April and the rainy season is May to October. Copan is inland and may get less rain then San Pedro Sula which is close to the coast. The interior is humid year round.

WHERE TO STAY - The best in San Pedro Sula is the older but posh Copantl Hotel and Club, P.O. Box 1060, San Pedro Sula, Honduras, C.A. tel. 504-56-8900, fax 504-56-7890. 5 stars with a casino on the premises. It's gated and has armed guards. In Copan, the newest is a Best Western, the Posada Real de Copan, Km 164, Carretera de San Pedro Sula a Copan Ruinas, Honduras, tel. 504-98-3480, fax 504-98-3498.

TOURS - Maya Tours, 20423 State Rd.7, Suite 6000, Boca Raton, FL 33498 tel. 800-392-6292; Tropical Travel Representatives, 5 Grogans Park, Suite 102, The Woodlands, TX 77380-2190 tel. 800-451-8017; International Expeditions, 1 Environs Park, Helena, AL 35080 tel. 800-633-4734. Tour arrangements can be made at the Copantl Hotel in San Pedro Sula.

FOR MORE INFORMATION - Write to the Consulate General of Honduras, 3007 Tilden St., NW, Washington DC, 20008 tel. 202-966-7702 or Honduras Consulate, Tourist Section, 3450 Wilshire Blvd., Suite 230, L.A., CA 90010, tel. 213-383-9244, fax 213-383-9306

## COPPER CANYON

A train ride through Mexico's answer to the Grand Canyon

MEXICALI, MEXICO - Do you like Alfred Hitchcock movies of the 1940's? People talking, planning, keeping a clandestine rendezvous to the click clack of train wheels on steel tracks. Meals in the dining car with the scenery swishing by in the background while the table moves to and fro and the actors never spill a drop from their coffee cup. The forced intimacy of close sleeping quarters with a loved one or meeting new people in the lounge car where the sudden movements of the train forces physical familiarity. Or, if you just like roughing it without showers - this is the trip for you. A four day and four night excursion from Mexicali to Creel by train through the Copper Canyon.

The continental divide runs atop the Rocky Mountains from Montana through New Mexico and continues south through the Sierra Madres in Mexico. It passes just east of the logging town of Creel, in the State of Chihuahua, our journeys end. Creel is in the Central time zone, two hours later than Pacific time or California time (where the trip starts). Copper canyon can be seen by train traveling north from Sufragio to Creel or the reverse but the northern one is preferred. There are no roads through this collection of canyons and the Chihuahua al Pacifico, or mountain train, was completed in 1961. A paved road has been completed from El Paso through Chihuahua to Creel. So those who are only interested in the mountain train ride can drive to Creel and take the train south and then north on separate days.

## THE FIRST NIGHT

Reservations were already made at the Hotel Lucerna in Mexicali and those who chose, could drive across the border and park for free at the Hotel. It is important to stop at the border and buy Mexican car insurance for the days you will be driving in Mexico. The risk of driving without it (American insurance is no good in Mexico) is unthinkable. They will impound your car for the smallest accident and wait for the courts to settle the matter. Your car is collateral. We chose in AA Parking in Calexico on the California side for $30. The lot is fenced and the car was untouched during the trip. The tour company provided a school bus for transport to the Hotel in Mexico for no charge. Most took this option. The twenty minute bus ride got us to our rooms at 9:30 PM.

The Hotel Lucerna caters to businessmen and is clean, modern and not inexpensive for Mexico. The room was large enough for two double beds, a dresser, table, TV and space to walk around. On a par with Holiday Inn except for the bottle of water for drinking. The Hotel has restaurants, a bar and a disco but our morning call was 6 AM and there was only time for a club sandwich ($15 US).

## DAY 1

The phone rang and a knock came on the door five minutes later. Time to walk around the empty pool, check the fountain in the next courtyard and catch a cup of coffee before boarding the school bus for the ride to the train station for an immigration check. The station is nothing to look at but my partner had reasonably priced bacon and eggs with no after effects. Bananafish tours owns the three Pullman cars and the dining car that were being connected to the main passenger train. 1940's cars that would have otherwise been destroyed. Promptly at 8:20 AM we were on our way for the trip across the Sonoran Desert. My 8 foot long and 5 foot wide compartment had a padded bench seat that could handle three, a toilet with a padded cover and a sink that folded out from the wall over the toilet with a small medicine compartment above and a vanity mirror. There was a mirror on the wall facing the bed and one on the back of the door which helped to make the quarters look larger. And a roll of toilet paper and a gallon of drinking water. There was space under the bench seat/bed to store luggage. Two Pullman cars were in front of the lounge car and one behind. Our four cars were at the rear of the train with normal passengers in the front cars. Each Pullman had a permanent porter and assistant and they introduced themselves to each compartment. One would stay on duty in the corridor at all times. He would sit on a stool at aisles end and watch the traffic. Security as well as help. They come from a pool of Mexican railroad workers who take this work on a rotating basis. It is good duty since they made several times their normal salary.

The rooms emptied quickly with people congregating in the dining portion or the lounge portion of the meeting car. Some stood between cars to have a smoke. There were three sittings for meals, one for each Pullman. The dining room occupied half the car with linen covered tables and the lounge section had a sofa and several padded chairs. There is a collection of magazines and books from previous travelers at one end and the tour desk at the other end with a large ice chest filled with soft drinks and beer. A small bar is next to the chest for those who want mixed drinks. A tab is kept for all customers and business started within the hour.

Just after lunch, we went through the Alter Desert at Puerto Penasco and stopped to stretch our legs for about 20 min. After we were on our way again, I noticed the train was moving very slowly. A blessing of sorts since normal balance is a challenge with the train at 55 MPH. You feel like a bumper car bouncing from wall to wall when walking down the corridor. The real trick is to make it across the lounge car without ending up in someone's lap. Of course, there is a plus side to that, if you plan it right. Going to the rear of the train, I saw the reason. Workers were installing new concrete ties beneath the track. It hadn't been straightened yet and the track line we had traveled, curved like a snake. I was surprised we were able to stay on the track at all. Apparently, business as usual for the Mexican train system.

The Benjamin Hill stop came about supper time. We have to hook up to the Nogales train and the wait can be as long as one hour. We had an hour and those who looked, found the liquor store close to the station. Our food was purchased in America and cooked in the small kitchen in the lounge car.

Depending on the traffic or the weather, the Sonora-Baja train arrives at Sufragio, about 20 miles inland from Los Mochis, at anytime between

2 AM and 6 AM. There are several passenger stops along the way but I learned to sleep through them. The porter had made the berth into a bed with a foam mattress, sheets, a pillow and blankets.

## DAY 2

I awoke to the sounds of silence. No clickety clack, no banging of cars, no bouncing back and forth. I closed my eyes. But I'd grown used to the movement, like a baby being rocked in the cradle. Unable to sleep, I lifted the window shade. Sunlight.

I joined the early risers in the train yard and watched the hook up of the gondola. An open topped, steel shell with four foot walls on all sides. After breakfast, we were hooked to the mountain train and were under way. It is about and hour and a half to the first (Rio Fuerte) of 36 bridges and an impressive view of the canyon river. The scenery is uneventful until just before lunch when we enter the town of Temoris. A large sign to commemorate the completion of the railroad is perched high against the mountain overlooking the town. Next to the sign is a waterfall. Both can be seen after crossing the curved Santa Barbara Bridge as the train quickly gains 1,100 feet in altitude. Looking backwards, its an inspiring view across the canyon. This is the spot where the train turns 180 degrees inside a tunnel and comes out going the other way. As the train climbs, there are pines to the left and right and the river that follows the train, changes from side to side. The track curves one way and then the other, following the curves of each mountain. Sheer rock face to the right is quickly transplanted by rock face to the left. And then there are the tunnels. Eighty six in all, at irregular intervals. Some for a few seconds and others long enough to let everyone in the gondola know the diesel engines are burning a lot of fuel. We saw mountain goats roaming the hillside. Two passenger cars at the bottom of a ravine. Abandoned. In several small towns, families were seen living in old RR cars, left along side the tracks.

We passed farms and ranches in the flatlands and rolling hills. Quiet and peaceful. Corn and cattle but no people. Stately pines and beautiful rock formations and the river that always stays close to the tracks. We continued to climb.

At 5:30 the train reached Divisidero. A mandatory stop since this is where the northbound and southbound trains pass. The downhill walk from the station to the overlook is 300 feet and is lined with vendors. Souvenirs, hot food cooked over wood or charcoal atop 55 gallon drums, baskets from the size of a babies shoe to that of a large flower pot. Sold without hassle by natives too shy to meet your eye. The food smelled very, very good.

The overlook is the most impressive of the trip. From the cliffs' edge you can look into Urique Canyon and Copper Canyon. Clouds blocked the sun which would have brightened the colors, never the less, the view was absorbing. Over in the corner, at the edge of the cliff, is the Hotel Cabanas. A clean, warm, romantic hideaway of dark wood and light stone with a dining room that overlooks the canyon through large plate glass windows. The perfect place for a night, for lovers.

An hour and a half later we arrived at Creel. Hotel Nuevo is across the tracks from the train station and the Parador de la Montana is at the other end of this small town. At 8,000 feet above sea level, the air was nippy but it was good to get our feet on solid ground. Both hotels have restaurants and suppers are about $20 US. After checking into our room at the Nuevo and a low pressure water shower, we walked through the town. Next to the station is the town square. Virtually empty at 8 PM on Friday night. Classical music serenaded the square from loud speakers within the church. Interesting. We walked the only street in town to the Parador but another tour group had occupied the dining room. La Lupita's restaurant, across the street, is a family run establishment with no menu and no English. Four chicken enchiladas, beer and coffee came to $15 US. The Parador has the only bar and we returned after dinner. Drinks are just under $5 US at the small, informal and friendly room at the lobby's rear.

The main street was still quiet at ten and we returned to the Nuevo. A pretty hotel made from wood logs with large rooms and double beds. The only station on the TV had a Jerry Lewis movie. Early to bed seemed easy.

## DAY 3

Seven thirty and the air was brisk. A mist hung over the low lands as the sun sent its first rays over the mountains to the east. A horse, just outside the door, was having dew covered grass for breakfast. It was quiet. It was beautiful.

After breakfast, we collected inside the school bus for a short drive to the Tarahumara Indian caves. Most of the road was not meant for vehicles and the ride not meant for human kidneys. This Indian tribe depends on agriculture and the making of pottery and hand crafts for its livelihood. They are independent, shy and abjectly poor. The cave we visited is only two miles from town. Dug from the hillside, it has a dirt floor, twenty foot high domed ceiling and wood fence covering the front. Belongings are meager except for the goat pen built into the back wall. There appeared to be ten goats inside the dark, four foot high mini cave with its own wood fence. The women dress colorfully and the children seem unusually quiet. Undoubtedly, due to our presence, which, although announced, is tolerated because of the money we leave. They are a peaceful tribe and as such get little support from their government. It was very interesting and a little sad.

The bus carried us another mile to the middle of a rock field. There was a huge rock shaped like a frog. Another looked like a mushroom. One, like a tear perched atop a stone base. Boulders that seemed to sit, unattached, on others. Women sat with baskets for sale and the children posed around the strange rock collection.

The train was to pick us up at noon so there was time to shop at the stores around the square. Wood carvings, baskets of any size, art work, beautiful blankets. A couple bought matching drums, four feet in diameter and six inches deep. We were ready at twelve. The train wasn't. There had been a derailment on the track and we had to wait.

The ride to Divisidero was two hours, since the tracks hadn't been fully cleared. Only thirty minutes to enjoy the hotel and the grand view. It was comfortable. It was peaceful. It was time to get back on the train.

We were retracing our steps through the canyon but now the views were behind us. A few hearty souls spent some time in the gondola car, the rest in the lounge.

## DAY 4

The train from Guadalajara picked us up at 3 AM. The gondola was left behind and we traveled north through the night and the following day. The longest day. People talked in the lounge, walking the corridors or rested in their compartments. Due to the vagaries of the train system, we arrived in Mexicali at midnight. Paired off in groups of fours, we took cabs to the American side after a routine customs check at the border. Then to one of the gas stations in town, and into the night. The desert air on the way home was refreshing.

If you love trains or tunnels (86 on the way up) or bridges (36) or remote, pristine, high mountain country, then this is the trip for you.

## THE END

## SIDEBAR 1 - THE DINING CAR MENU

### DAY 1

Lunch - Ham & Cheese sandwich, carrot sticks, chips

Supper - Turkey, mashed potatoes, beans, tortillas, apricot surprise

### DAY 2

Breakfast - Bagels, cream cheese, jam, fruit, coffee

Lunch - BBQ Chicken, beans, salsa, tortillas

### DAY 3

Dinner - Spaghetti, rolls, cherry surprise

### DAY 4

Breakfast - Scrambled eggs, rolls, fruit, coffee

Lunch - Tuna sandwich, banana & pineapple salad, chips, cookies

Supper - Cold cuts, salads, left overs

Meals can be purchased separately or in a package for $35. It is advised to bring snacks since there is no food available between meals. Food available at the hotels at each end of the trip fills in the missing blanks above.

SIDEBAR 2

GETTING TO MEXICALI - From San Diego, drive east on Interstate 8 and south on 111 which turns into Imperial Ave in the town of Calexico. Turn right on 2nd St, just before the border to AA Parking & Trucking, 201 W. Second St., Calexico, CA tel (619) 357-3213/ 24 hrs. Or, after buying Mexican Insurance for the days you will be driving, go across the border and turn left (east) on Avenida Madero, right (south) on Calzado Justo Sierra to the Y in the road and bear left to Blvd. Benito Juarez. A half mile further, on the left is the Hotel Lucerna, 2151 Blvd. Benito Juarez, Mexicali, Mexico / direct dial from the US 011-52-656-61-000. From Yuma, drive west on Interstate 8 to 111 and then south.

DRIVING - From El Paso, Texas, go South through Ciudad Juariz and continue on Route 45 south to Chihuahua. The train goes from Chihuahua through Creel and the Copper Canyon to the coast. Or drive west on route 16 from Chihuahua, approximately 100 miles and turn south on the Creel road.

CLIMATE - Creel has warm, rainy summers and cool, dry winters. Days are warm especially in the summer and nights can be very cool in the winter with the possibility of snow.

WHAT TO BRING - Passport, Flashlight, medication, snacks, clothing that can be put on in layers, binoculars or camera with a telephoto lens, film of various speeds. High speed film (ASA 400 or above) may be needed if the sky is overcast. Remember you are shooting from a moving train and fast shutter speeds are necessary to prevent the pictures from blurring.

FOR MORE INFORMATION - Tours of four and five days are run by Bananafish Tours, 707 30th Street #6, San Pedro, CA 90731 tel. (213) 548-6841. Longer tours are available from Adobe Tours, P.O. Box 12334, Albuquerque, NM 87195 tel. (800) 852-2054 and Tour-Masters, Inc., 3350 Wilshire Blvd., Suite 580, Los Angeles, CA 90010 tel. (800)992-8877 or (213)386-1698

## YOU SAY IGUACU AND I SAY IGUAZU,
## LETS CALL THE WHOLE THING HOT

The bus ride from the airport to The Hotel Bourbon, the only five star hotel on the Brazilian side, was only fifteen minutes and since the air conditioning wasn't working, we pretended we were in a sauna.

There were a few hours to kill before our afternoon tour of the falls and I looked around the hotel. Adjacent the attractive, lobby is a nicely appointed, vacant bar, lounge and coffee shop. The large outdoor pool is in the rear with the jungle as the outside border. A church is outside in a separate building with only the top portion above ground. The hotel is air conditioned but the church is kept cool by being beneath the ground.

The falls are on the Rio Iguacu, as they say in Portuguese, the language of Brazil. Iguazu (EE-gwa-sue) in Argentine Spanish. This river divides the two countries and joins the Rio Parana 12 miles downstream. The Rio Parana divides Paraguay from Brazil and Argentina. Fifteen miles from this river junction, upstream on the Rio Parana is the massive Itaipu dam which supplies hydroelectric power to all three countries. One third of the dam's output is sufficient to supply the electrical needs for the entire country of Paraguay.

Most of the 275 falls are on the Argentine side so the best viewing is from Brazil. The falls are higher than Niagara and twice as wide. The waters collect from the Amazon rains (from October through April) and the muddy water flows over soft, red sandstone and hard, black basalt to make an incredible display over several miles of eroding cliffs.

Our non-air conditioned bus picks us up at 4 PM. Ten miles later, the bus driver pays the park entrance fee and we began our descending walk from the front of the Hotel das Cataratas, a four star hotel and the only one inside the park. From the very beginning, the view is impressive. Gently flowing water, cascading over sheer cliffs surrounded by thick jungle growth, a half mile in the distance. The view gets better as the walk winds down the Brazilian cliff side formed by the rivers erosion. The river separates us from the multiple falls that stretch for two miles on the other side.

The walk is a challenge in itself. Partially paved, there are frequent stone steps, many of which have been loosened by the tourist traffic. There is a distinct absence of handrails by many of the stairs and it is prudent to walk on the inside. Far better to fall towards the cliff than towards the river. I saw the results in an elderly woman who wasn't fortunate. Her group flew on the same plane as ours. Her face was filled with scratch marks and her broken right leg was in a full cast. She was continuing her tour. What a trooper! The park entrance fee is apparently not used to maintain the tourist walkway.

Taking pictures along the walk is complicated by the constant flow of perspiration into my eyes. I hadn't thought to bring a sweat band and my eyebrows kept filling to capacity. No wonder, since the temperature and humidity adds to 200. No matter how you divide this number, it comes to a considerable loss of body fluid and my clothes are wringing wet, well before I reach the bottom. My handkerchief is drenched after a few passes over my face. Of course, there are independent entrepreneurs selling plastic bottles of water along the way. The views continue to be spectacular until the paths end at the elevator station and the formal refreshment stand. This is a two story, open structure that allows you to get within twenty feet of a powerful Brazilian side waterfall. The roar is such that conversations cannot be held close the platform edge. A truly impressive sight. And frightening with all its power.

There is a modest fee for the elevator (9 cents) and the only other alternative is to walk back the same path. The elevator is the size of the average broom closet and could comfortably hold four plus the elevator operator. We squeezed nine sweaty bodies in for my trip. It was so crowded that the operator had to ask one of the passengers to press the button for the top. He couldn't raise his arms. Since it was a button operated elevator,

I was puzzled at the need for an operator, in this rising cupboard. I suppose there should be jobs for those whose olfactory nerves have been severed.

That night we decided to go across the border. One group wanted to eat in Paraguay and the other seven wanted a meal AND a visit to the casino. We negotiated our transportation separately in a bargaining procedure that took a half hour. Our group was too big for a taxi and we ended up in a van. Both drivers were uniform in their opinion that Paraguay was not a place to eat. Brazilians went there to shop, but there were better restaurants on this side of the border. But we insisted. For $9 US each, we got round trip transportation with a driver who would wait. I was hoping to eat at the casino. Little did I know.

With passports in hand we were waived through the Ponte Internacional da Amizade, the international bridge over the Rio Parana that connects Foz de Iguacu with Cidade Puerto Pres. Stroessner. The Paraguayan city looked like the poorer section of Tijuana. We ended up at the best hotel in town, probably one star. One of our seven spoke fluent Spanish and handled the ordering in the comfortable, but plain, dining room. There were only two other people eating here, so we didn't lack for service. My steak with eggs, french fries, rice, lettuce, ripe tomatoes, coffee and Pepsi cost $6 US, including a generous tip. It was a good meal. We paid in Brazilian money and the hotel was delighted to have us.

On to the casino, which the guide book had warned was not up to Las Vegas standards. The entrance is guarded by two uniformed militia, armed with automatic weapons. There weren't going to be any robberies tonight. Just inside, we are confronted by slot machines and video games which line the twelve foot wide by fifty foot long room. In the rear are closed double white doors. That's where the action is! The room beyond is forty by fifty feet and populated by an upscale crowd, compared to the people in the front. Two crowded roulette tables, three empty black jack stands and an empty crap table. Five of us got chips and decided to try the roulette. Not my choice of games but, like the saying goes, it's the only game in town. One of our girls starts to win. Like many beginners, she is not only winning but letting go with shrieks of joy each time her numbers hit. A custom the Paraguayans haven't adopted, but, like all joy, it was contagious. Although the other winners remain quiet, they smile and the croupiers are having a delightful time. She wins a modest amount and the rest of us are modest losers.

On the return trip we are determined to get our passports stamped. Customs was again non existent and we parked the van and go inside the small building. Our politeness and enthusiasm convinces the local official to accommodate this group of grown children. We get a Paraguayan stamp. The other group, who we never saw across the border, didn't. We told the driver it would be a two hour trip but actually got back four hours later.

Morning came early but the buffet breakfast had everything. Ten types of breads, scrambled eggs, fried eggs, bacon 1/4 of an inch thick, sausage, cereal, orange juice, tomato juice, a mystery juice, coffee, four kinds of lunch meat and enough fresh fruit to feed a zoo. We rent the same driver and van to go to the Argentine side of the falls. The driver is delighted since this is extra money and he has a wife and three kids. After breakfast, the van sat lower. The trip is $10 US each. This time, passports are stamped at the Ponte Internacional Tancredo Neves, the bridge over the Rio Iguacu. Lacking Argentine Australis for the park entrance fee, our first stop is Cidade Puerto Iguazu, the city right across the border.

This is Sunday and the banks are closed. Cambios (money exchanges) are closed. The town has a center and the stores and bars are open so we change our money in a department store. Fifteen minutes later we are at the Marco Argentino, the obelisk shaped marker on the Argentine side of the intersection of the Rio Parana and the Rio Iguacu. Where Paraguay, Argentina and Brazil meet. The boundary is actually in the middle of the water of the intersecting rivers and we are on the tallest overlooking hill. We take pictures of each other in front of the monument.

The park entrance fee is the equivalent of $1.40. The paved road soon turns to gravel but the ride is comfortable. The boat trips to Devils Throat, that I'd read about, are not available. Too dangerous, the boatmen said. I didn't believe them, the water looked too calm.

The walkway has an unusual Z pattern. It is a mile long and some sections are obviously new. Twisted steel is sticking from the water where old sections used to be. Powerful currents must have ripped the wood over structure from its pinnings. The air is full of mist, 100 feet from the walkway end. Water flows under the entire length of the walk but it is placid and slow moving. Not the case at Devil's Throat, at the very end. The roar of the water, close enough jump into, is deafening. The drops of mist drench everyone on the platform. The violence of the sound is awesome and at the same time, riveting. From the falls edge we can look down, through the mist shrouded valley, towards the Brazilian footpath we walked the day before. Then, we were 1/4 mile downstream from this incredible giant. I couldn't imagine anyone surviving this falls in a barrel, there are too many rocks at the bottom.

Wet but inspired, we drive to the Hotel Internacional Iguazu, on the Argentine side. A five star hotel with a view of the falls from the second story lobby and outside patio. And from the bar and dining room beneath the lobby. The front entrance is at lobby level. This is the only hotel with a view of the falls FROM the hotel.

The road inside the park is flanked by jungle. Thick and green. We are not tempted to take a stroll, clearly a machete is needed. On our trip back, we drive through thousands of butterflies. They are as thick as locust but far more colorful as they fly carelessly, in clouds, across the road.

The tour took four hours and we are back to pack for the late afternoon flight to Buenos Aires. We moan in chorus as the non-air conditioned bus parks in front of the hotel.

THE END

## SIDEBAR


GETTING THERE - Iguacu is serviced by Varig through Rio and Sao Paulo tel. 800-GO-VARIG. Rio de Janeiro is served by American Air, and Avianca. Local Brazilian flights connect Rio and Sao Paulo to Iguacu at the Brazilian side airport. Aerolineas Argentinas tel. 800-327-0276 fly to Iguazu on the Argentine side airport from Buenos Aires.

WHERE TO STAY - In Foz de Iguacu, Brazil - Hotel das Cataratas, the only hotel inside the park. Hotel Bourbon. Both have doubles for $250. On the Argentine side, Hotel International Foz, Rua Almte. Barroso, 345.

THE CLIMATE - The falls are in the Amazon so it is hot and humid year round. Summer temperatures (Dec-Mar) are around 100 degrees with winters (Jun-Sep) about 10 degrees less. There are 80 inches of annual rain and it can rain at anytime. Dress accordingly.

FOR MORE INFORMATION - Brazilian tourist office, 551 Fifth Ave., #519, New York, NY 10176 tel. 212-286-9600. Argentine tourist office, 12 W. 56th Street, New York, NY 10019 tel. 212-603-0443.

# LA PAZ, BOLIVIA IS THE HIGHEST CAPITAL IN THE WORLD. YOU CAN BARELY CATCH YOUR BREATH.

La Paz, Bolivia - President's stone face in market square

We landed where the air is thin. 13,500 feet, at the top edge of the fish bowl crater that holds La Paz. Pilots are required to put on an oxygen mask when flying over 10,000 feet. That's in an open cockpit, of course, not inside a commercial airline. So we all stepped out of a pressurized cabin into a little bit of outer space. And nobody noticed the difference. Until later.

We zig zagged our way down from the rim past the shanties of one of the several distressed sections of town. Bolivia is one of the poorest Latin American Countries.

After the hotel check-in, our first hike was two blocks uphill to the cathedral on Plaza Murillo and we had to stop halfway up to catch our breath. This was our first opportunity to see the Aymara and Quechua women and their distinctive bowler hats, two sizes too small. This is the most Indian country in South America, 50% of the population is of pure American Indian blood (another 35% is Spanish and Indian mix). Most of the women wear a ahuayo, slung across the back and tied at the neck. The brilliantly decorated cloth is used to carry everything from babies to coca leaves. The cathedral, on top of the hill, is not the most famous in the city but it's the prettiest.

Four blocks south (downhill, something we all started to appreciate) is the Iglesia de San Francisco (started in1549), the largest and most important church. The large plaza in front is a major hangout for the younger set and the pickpockets that prey on tourists. We were out of breath, it was time for a rest. That night, those who didn't take pills for altitude sickness got their first headaches.

## SOME BACKGROUND

La Paz is the center of this landlocked countries government but it wasn't always landlocked. At one time, Bolivia stretched all the way west to the Pacific Ocean thru the Atacama region, a barren desert. In the mid 19th century, rich deposits of guano and nitrates were discovered and Bolivia, lacking the money to develop the area, hired Chilean companies to do the mining. When Bolivia imposed a tax on the minerals in 1879 they ended up shooting themselves in the foot. Chile declared war and took 350 KM of the coast. Their next dispute was with Brazil in 1903 wherein they lost 100,000 square KM of their northern territory. This time the fight was over rubber. This was not to be the end of their troubles. Between 1932 and 1935 they went to war with Paraguay, a country on the south eastern border. The trouble started when oil companies began to investigate the Chaco area for potential deposits. Standard Oil sided with Bolivia and Shell supported Paraguay. The Bolivians had more troops and still lost the war, and another 225,000 square KM of it's territory. They are still rich in minerals but the metals must be freighted over long distances. Combine this with lack of capital, corruption, internal strife between the miners' union and the state and you have a high cost mineral producer. In agriculture, they grow enough for internal consumption but little to export.

## WITCHES MARKET

Two blocks behind the San Francisco church is the market to visit. Fresh fruit, yellow, red and green vegetables, snow white potatoes unlike any you've seen in the U.S. and the flavor and brilliant colors of the indigenous people that match their wares. The Indians are camera shy, however, and look away or cover their face when they see a lens. You can buy herbs, seeds, magical ingredients that will cure any ailment you have or be stricken with in the future or just protect you from bad spirits. Also for sale are fake fossil imprints taken from the high desert (just out of town) which used to be at the bottom of the sea. The story about the bottom of the ocean is true it's just that the imprint is on plaster of paris and made last week in someone's garage. For the macabre, the street vendors sell llama fetuses in water in a jar. I don't know if they are real or not, or very much care.

The area from the church to the market has stores filled with local wares - silver, jewelry and hand made clothing in the brightest colors the eye can handle. This is a third world economy, the prices are very good. You have to ask on the street for coca leaves. They are dirt cheap (10 cents) but don't get conned into buying dry ones. You also have to get some black tar looking stuff to chew along with the leaves or they don't work. Frankly, it didn't do much for me in either case. Virtually all the local population chews coca leaves and it's reported to be good for altitude sickness.

Coca tea is served at all restaurants and given to incoming tour groups at the hotel. It's refreshing but if you're looking for a buzz, forget it. You probably have to drink five gallons before you feel anything. The local alcoholic drink for the masses is made from fermented corn. It's inexpensive but tastes like gasoline.

## OUTSIDE OF TOWN

Our first trip, 10 KM out, was to the Valley of the Moon which isn't a valley at all. It's a hillside of strange looking miniature pinnacles and canyons formed by erosion of the wind and occasional rain. Within sight, is a beautifully manicured golf course. It's close to the "Beverly Hills" area of greater La Paz. The average factory worker makes about $70/month, executives $2000/month. The well to do live here in walled communities with a guard at the gate.

The homes in the area are nice, not spectacular, and look like those in upper middle neighborhoods in the USA. The renting procedures are quite different, however. Cash is given up front, anywhere from $500 to $30,000, for a 1 or 2 year lease and the money is returned when you move out. The nicer the house, the more the cash, but you get it all back. The owner keeps what he made on the money during that time.

We took a break at the small town of Laja. The 16-18th century, brown sandstone church in the town square is the center attraction. It's a simple, symmetrical and attractive structure with a plain cross over the central dome and has towers at each side with three openings in each tower to hold bells. Each tower has a simple cross on top. Religion is a linchpin in Bolivian society.

From there it was to the high plains with not a tree in sight. We passed small clay and straw farm houses on acres and acres of land. And almost nothing green growing. A desert of monochromic brown. No electricity, virtually no water (it seldom rains) and animal dung provides the fuel for heat and cooking. Any wood in the area was burned years ago. We drove to the mountains for a stunning view of the barren plains below and the snow covered mountains in the distance. These Andean peaks are at 14,000 feet. Beautiful. Quiet.

## THE END

## LA PAZ SIDEBAR

GETTING THERE - American Airlines serves La Paz through Miami. Fares from the west coast start around $1200 RT. La Paz is also served by Aerolinas Argentinas, AeroPeru, British Air, KLM and Varig.

WHEN TO GO - Bolivia is close to the Equator but it's 11,500 feet above sea level, so warm clothing is needed at night. The rainy season is November to March.

WHERE TO STAY - The two best are the Hotel Presidente for $180 double tel. 011-591-2-368-601 fax 011-591-2-354-013 and the Radisson Plaza Hotel, $200 double, tel. 011-591-2-316-161 fax 011-591-2-316-302. The Presidente is downtown and the Radisson is about a mile away. Prices include tax and breakfast. Others include the Sucre Palace Hotel, $75, tel 011-591-2-390-251 and the Hotel Alem, under $60 tel. 011-591-2-367-400.

WHERE TO EAT - The restaurant atop the Hotel Presidente, the Belle Vista, has a great view, entrees $20. Then there is Italian food at Pronto Ristorante, Calle Jauregui and Avenida 6 de Agosto and La Casa de los Pacenos at Calle Sucre 856 near Pichincha for local dishes.

HEALTH - La Paz is the highest capital in the world and altitude sickness is a real threat. Typical symptoms include loss of appetite, headache, nausea and shortness of breath. There are pills to take to relieve the symptoms, consult your Doctor. This is not something to be dismissed, mountain climbers have died from altitude sickness. I took the pills and had no problem. It's best to eat lightly and exercise sparingly at first.

FOR MORE INFORMATION - Write to the Bolivian Tourist Information Office, 97-45 Queens Blvd., Rego Park, NY 11374 tel. 800-BOLIVIA.

## PANAMA CANAL

American influence is going, going, gone.


PANAMA CITY, PANAMA - Most people know of the unsuccessful attempt of the French to build the canal but there is a lot more to this story. Political intrigue, bickering, back stabbing, civil war and that's before thousands of construction workers died in the disease ridden jungles.

The French weren't the first. In 1524, King Charles V of Spain ordered a survey made to determine the feasibility of building a canal. Nothing happened. In 1878, the Columbian Government, who owned Panama at the time, awarded a contract to build a canal to Lucien Wyse. He in turn, sold the contract to Ferdinand De Lesseps, the French diplomat and contractor, proud of his success as builder of the Suez Canal. De Lesseps began work in 1880 to build a sea level canal alongside the existing railway. A task more difficult than he thought. In the process, 22,000 workers died from Yellow fever and Malaria. And there were construction problems and financial mismanagement. The company went bankrupt in 1889.

Meanwhile, the US was considering building a canal through Nicaragua or Panama and one of De Lesseps chief engineers, Philippe Bunau-Varilla, formed a new canal company. He agreed to sell it to the USA in 1903 but the Columbian government nixed the sale.

While all this bargaining and non-bargaining was going on, revolutionary sentiments had been brewing in Panama to break away from Columbia. In 1903, a civil war erupted. Bunau-Varilla had a lot to gain financially if the sale went through, so he approached the US Government to back the Panamanians if they declared independence. And that's what happened. The USA immediately recognized the new government of Panama on 3 NOV 1903. Columbia sent in troops but it was too late.

Two weeks later, Bunau-Varilla, now Panamanian Ambassador to the USA, signed a treaty giving America far more than the deal Columbia turned down. It gave the USA sovereign rights for an area 8 KM on either side of the canal in perpetuity and the right of intervention in Panamanian affairs. A delegation from Panama was on their way to Washington DC but they got there too late. The treaty was signed over their protest. There have been bad feelings between Panama and the U.S. ever since.

As a footnote, Columbia didn't recognize Panama as a separate nation until 1921. The USA did sign a new treaty with Panama in 1977, phasing out ownership by December 31, 1999. There is a clause that we have the right to defend the canal beyond 1999.

## THRU THE CANAL

One company runs partial transits on Saturday and full, ocean to ocean transits, once a month. Pacific to Atlantic, south-east to north-west. Panama City sits on the Bay of Panama and that's where the vessels line up waiting their turn for passage (average wait is 24 hours). From the bay, they pass under the Bridge of the Americas to the dredged channel, 7 miles long. On the right is the port of Balboa where our ship joins in at 7:30 AM.

Boats (the big ones) are not allowed to go through the locks under their own power. A tug boat follows the ship to the Miraflores locks, a two step lift of 54 feet. We hang in close to the tug. This system is slightly over a mile in length. Each lock is 1000 feet long and 110 feet wide. The lock gates here are the tallest in the system because of the extreme tidal variations of the Pacific. Once you enter the first lock, you're in fresh water.

## HOW IT ALL WORKS

One of the early French engineers considered locks but that idea was dismissed for a sea level trench which the USA also considered. Our engineers finally decided on locks. They would build a dam upstream on the Chagres River (Madden Dam) which runs perpendicular to the canal and roughly halfway between Panama City and the Caribbean port of Colon. Gatun Dam, close to Colon, would stop the river from emptying into the Atlantic. The locks at both ends would allow fresh water to escape as needed for the boats to pass. The center of the country would be flooded to form a large lake.

It makes sense. It's 50 miles between Colon and Panama City. Jungle on both sides of the continental divide. Ships are raised 85 feet and the canal width is 500 feet. As difficult as it was to build, that's 85 feet times 500 feet times 50 miles of dirt and rock they didn't have to remove.

## THE PASSAGE

On approaching the lock, the vessel is taken in tow by six electric locomotives, three on each side, that run on tracks on the edge of the lock. The ship is secured in place as the rear door closes and the fresh water flows in from Miraflores lake. The tow boat is close by and we are tied to it. It usually takes 9 hours from ocean to ocean so there is lots of time to walk around our ship, the Fantasia del Mar. There are plenty of tables and chairs inside but the bow gets the most attention. There is free coffee and soda and plenty of room to move around, except in the front of the ship where 90 of the 100 passengers are standing. Two lifts and a short cruise across Miraflores lake and we enter the Pedro Miquel locks, the last one on the Pacific side. The huge steel doors at each end are double doors for a better seal.

Now we enter the famous Galliard cut, 8 miles of rock and shale. This is the continental divide and the deadliest cut of all. There were devastating slides during and even after final construction. The sides are now reinforced with concrete to prevent more slides. In the channel there are floating, green, solar powered, buoys with lights atop. The canal is open 24 hours a day, every day. Oddly enough, they only pass ships in one direction at a time. On the hillsides are large white signs with an "X" cut out. The floating buoys are electric now but you can imagine the difficulty in keeping the lanterns lit in 1920. The ships are on their own power now. At the end of the Gaillard cut, you turn left, then right into the huge Gatun Lake. Twenty three miles across and it's time for a, very nice, buffet lunch.

We don't follow the slow moving freighter we've been tailing. Our small boat jumps ahead and tailgates another ship on the way down to sea level. The Gatun locks are three steps at a time and when we enter the first lock, the view from the bow is spectacular. You can see the 2 locks ahead, stepping down to Limon Bay and the Caribbean in the distance. This is the view not to be missed.

We go from boat to bus at the port of Cristobal, next to Colon, for the 1 ½ hour ride back. The funny thing is that the USA paid $40 million for the rights in 1903, $387 million to build and $3 billion dollars since to maintain the canal. We've only recovered 2/3 of that money. Why didn't someone think about raising the transit fee?

THE END

## SIDEBAR FOR PANAMA CANAL

GETTING THERE - Gateway cities in the U.S. are Miami, Houston, NY, Washington DC, Dallas and Los Angeles - Miami being the principal one. RT airfares from Miami or L.A. are around $750. Continental and American Air offers frequent service and Copa is the Panamanian national airline. I flew Eva Air from L.A. for $740 RT in deluxe class. Copa Air connects to all the major cities in Central America, if you're thinking of a side trip.

ACCOMMODATIONS - In Panama City, the best is the Miramar, $250 double, tel (507)214-1000, overlooking the canal. Caesar Park, $195 dbl, tel (507)226-4077, the Radisson, $195 dbl, tel (507)265-3636, in the middle of the nicest shopping area. All the above are 4 star and the Caesar has a casino. The El Panama, $175 dbl, tel 269-5000, Plaza Paitilla Inn, $140 dbl, tel 269-1122 and Riande Continental, $105 dbl, tel 263-9999 are 3 star and have casinos. The California is a 2 star hotel, $50 dbl, tel 263-7736, fax 264-6144.

LOCAL ARRANGEMENT - There are literally hundreds of tour operators in the city. After a bad experience with a recommended one I found a good one, Por El Mundo, Calle 45-E No 4, Bella Vista, tel (507)264-6766, fax (507)264-6436, e-mail: mundo@sinfo.net They helped with an assortment of tours run by others, one stop shopping so to speak. Available are - City tour, shopping in duty free Colon, Panama Canal, Barro Colorado Island Tour, El Valle de Anton Canopy Tour, San Blas Islands, Hotel Contadora Resort.

For the Panama Canal, Argo Tours, tel (507)228-4348, from the USA tel 1-888-Panama 1, fax (507)228-1234, half day transit $95, Ocean to Ocean $155.

MISCELLANEOUS - Visas or tourist cards are required for all. U.S. citizens are issued a tourist card for $5 at the ticket counter in the US. Local currency is the US dollar.

## THE BEAUTY, THE THIEF AND THE
## BIGGEST PARTY IN THE WORLD

Rio, shot from the Botanical Gardens

RIO DE JANEIRO, BRAZIL - Have you ever been to a big New Years Eve party? Maybe a friends house with fifty people. Or a club function with a thousand people. No, no, I mean really big. A stadium with fireworks and almost 100,000 people? Afraid not, I mean really big. I'm talking about three million in a continuous crowd, on one night, shouting and drinking and celebrating the coming of the new year. That big. Well, I wanted to be in that party and got to Rio a few days early.

We checked into the Copacabana Palace, a Rio landmark on the Av. Atlantica, facing the beach of the same name. Guide books give ample warning that passports, airline tickets, jewelry and excess cash should not be carried on the street, hence, the safe in the room, in the closet rear.

Rio is a dangerous city. Foreign debt was among the highest in the world and unemployment over 25%. Underemployment affects another 20% and inflation has been up and down. If you wear gold chains on the street, they may be grabbed from your neck, emerald earrings pulled from your ear, watches slipped off your wrist and purses slit open from behind. The unemployed are trying to feed their families.

## THE BEAUTY

Our first outing was to Corcovado mountain and the Monument of Christ the Redeemer. From the mountain base, we took the new Swiss built train installed in 1979. They make the 30% grade in 17 minutes at 9 miles per hour. Back down is 22 minutes since they slow to 7 MPH. Taxis are available but the train ride is pleasant and scenic. Once you get off the train, the walk begins. Two hundred twenty seven steps to the top and cameras and lenses become heavy. The walk, baggage or not, is well worth it. The view from 2800 feet above the city is fantastic on all sides. The Atlantic ocean and the beach of Copacabana and south to Ipanema and Leblon. The Jocuei Club racetrack, the botanical gardens, the Maracana soccer stadium (holding 200,000 people, it's the worlds largest), and Sugar Loaf just this side of city center. Most of the crowd stares in awe at the 120 foot high statue of Christ. The monument is of reinforced concrete and weighs 1,145 tons. The distance between the outstretched arms is 92 feet and each arm weighs 88 tons. The head alone weighs 60,000 pounds. Being dwarfed by this colossus is inspiring and at the same time, humbling.

We then drove south of Copacabana through Ipanema and Leblon. The farther south, the more exclusive and the more expensive the real estate became. The beaches are uniformly white, clean and at least a football field

475

wide between the waters edge and the road. All the beaches are public and are used year round by every class of society. Brazilians love the sun but the days of the dental floss bikini seem to have passed. Suits are small but not unlike those on American beaches.

Lunch was at one of the many restaurants sharing space with the Copacabana hotels on the Av. Atlantica. Sidewalks are fifty to one hundred feet wide and restaurants that have inside seating have twice as many tables outside. I put my camera on the table and the first thing the waiter did was tie the strap to the center umbrella post. They didn't have cigarettes but the waiter sent a 12 year old shoe shine boy to the table. He had me watch his kit while he went for the smokes. The beer and cigarettes arrived at the same time from different directions. The boy gave me a 100,000 cruzeiro bill for change. It was an old cruzeiro which was replaced by new cruzados (worth 1000 times more) but both are still in circulation. In celebration of this new found wealth, I had a shoe shine for a dollar and we bought the boy a coke. He didn't speak English but knew a few key words. After lunch we browsed the beachfront sidewalk market. Reasonably priced bathing suits, jewelry, t-shirts and various types of artwork. A great place to gift shop for those back home.

## THE NEVER ENDING SHOW

Local tour operators offer a Samba show for $50, including round trip transportation and two free drinks. One of the people in our group asked around and booked the same show, without the middle man, for $25. After a short bus trip we took the long stairs to the second story night club. Seating was tiered, so you could see above the row two feet in front but from side to side, we were packed in like sardines. Good thing I was with friends because we were going to have an intimate evening whether we liked it or not. There is no going to the bathroom. Once you are seated, that's it. The waitress took our order and the two drinks arrived quickly. Then the show started with music the decibel level of a jet engine. I felt pinned to my seat. I looked at the two drinks on the table as though I was in a Memorex commercial, waiting for the glass to shatter.

Then the girls came out. Tall, leggy and dark (all Brazilians aren't dark) and beautifully costumed. Sequins and feathers and hats that could have made Carmen Miranda quiver. The girls pranced and strutted to the music for a few minutes and on leaving the stage, were quickly replaced by similar girls beautifully dressed in different costumes. They pranced and strutted for a few minutes and were replaced by the first set of girls who had now changed costumes. This continued, to ear splitting Samba music, for the next agonizing hour. Suddenly the music stopped. The silence was startling. An emcee stepped on stage to ask the audience to applaud when he called out the name of their country. He started with Afghanistan and proceeded to mention every country in alphabetical order. Even though their was no applause for Kenya, he continued with Korea and Kuwait. When he got to Togo, I tried to borrow a knife from the guy behind me to cut my wrists. After what seemed like hours, he reached Zanzibar. Finally, the show continued with more costumes and more prancing and for a change of pace they pumped smoke onto the stage for effect. Now, we could only see the top half of the girls. The smoke, as is it's wont to do, started to rise. The next three, costume changed, strutting, prancing numbers became a blur. As in a London fog. Time stood still. I tried to sleep but the music volume prevented that. Finally, after what could have been weeks, the show ended. A thousand hearing impaired people slowly filed down the single staircase to the outside. We were shell shocked and we must have looked like people from the Night of the Living Dead to those passing by on the sidewalk.

## THE THIEF

Eventually, we talked. It turns out that each of us thought the others enjoyed the show and suffered through. Then I knew why the music was so loud. No one could talk. We were back on the Av. Atlantica discussing our options for drinks and food. Dan was standing five feet to the side, letting us decide, so it might have appeared that he was alone. A heavyset woman, thirtyish, came from nowhere and gave him a big hug. I didn't react until I saw her hands move quickly from the hug into his pockets. The group saw it too and yelled in alarm. I was closest and moved towards her but, like lightening, she was gone. He carried no wallet and his back pockets were empty, so nothing was missing, but we were stunned. He had been frisked, picked and tossed back in less than two seconds by a pro. Wham, bam, thank you sir.

We talked about the speed and audacity of it all, at the restaurant. The waiters speak Portuguese and no English. Spanish didn't help much either but my spaghetti dinner was wonderful. All the meals in Rio are large and very, very good. And cost $10 plus or minus two Bucks.

Unbeknownst to us, another robbery was about happen the same night at about the same place. Mark is 30, 6'2", 220 pounds, athletic looking and likes to jog. He was alone on the brightly lit main street, a block from the hotel, when two men held him up at knife point. He lost money and some pride. The real money and important documents were in his safe.

## THE CITY TOUR

The next day, four of us rented a cab for the day for $50. Our first stop, the Botanical Gardens, is large and pretty but not special. President Vargas' Palace has a fine art collection and gorgeous furnishings. Then, lunch at La Tour in downtown. It's atop the 34 story office building at Santa Luzia 651 and revolves 360 degrees each hour. The head waiter grew up in Riverside, CA and moved to Rio with a Brazilian wife. No need to guess at the menu here. Great views of downtown, the domestic airport, Llha Fiscal in the bay, Sugar Loaf and Corcovado. The food is terrific and the view unsurpassed.

We walked along the Avenida Rio Branca, the main commercial heartline, flanked with modern buildings until we reached the Convent of Santo Antonio. Built in the early 1600's, it sits on a hillside overlooking downtown. Along side, is the richest church in Rio, the Sao Francisco da Penetencia with a hand sculptured interior covered in gold foil. It is impressive and there is an elevator to the top.

Next, was Sugar Loaf, which is actually two mountains. The first cable car takes you 700 feet to the top of Urca and you must walk through the shops and restaurant to reach the second cable car. Both trips are similar.

The cars are the size of a living room and carry 75 people. They bump their way into the dock much the way a boat does between a narrow space. You get close and then, bump, bump, bump from side to side. Swiss ingenuity at work again. The views at 1,230 feet are spectacular. As good as the Corcovado but a different part of the city. The domestic and international airports on one side and Copacabana beach and the hotels on the other and a hidden beach and hotel sandwiched between two mountains close to Urca's base. We stayed on top for sunset and returned to the lower level for drinks and to watch the city lights. Absolutely wonderful. Multi-colored gems shining in the night below us and Sugar Loaf, spot lighted to the rear.

## FLEES ARE GOOD FOR YOU

A taxi took us to the flee market in Ipanema the next morning. Hats, shirts, paintings, leather goods, artwork, luggage, furniture, you name it. They say, the same jewelry from the same stores in town but at half the price. The place was mobbed. A bean bag chair of leather the size of a Hugo was on sale. You could hold a party on the bean bag. I was imagining having it fork lifted into the cargo hold of the airplane. Only later did it dawn on me, you buy the bag and fill it up with your own beans when you get home.

The turkey lunch was great. Enough on the plate to feed a family but the custom in Brazil is, no doggie bags. People were singing in the restaurant in anticipation of the New Year. We walked outside to a parade led by a sound truck trumpeting music. Behind it, there were men dressed as women, women dressed as women. Women drinking beer in the street, or were they men? Thousands and thousands parading down the beachfront, singing and drinking. The parade got longer as restaurants emptied and people joined in. PAAARRRTY!

## THE BIGGEST PARTY IN THE WORLD

New Years eve is celebrated by young and old, rich and poor. The shops closed early and the Av. Atlantica was closed to traffic. People poured in from the suburbs to join the throngs filling the beaches. By eight o'clock the wide sidewalks were filled with people, Av. Atlantica was filled, and the

300 feet of beach between the street and the ocean was solid party goers. The custom is to wear white and since it's the beach, there doesn't have to be a lot of white. Flood lights illuminated the beach in all directions. Band stands were built every 1000 feet and live music filled the air. We had a birds eye view from the hotels third story balcony and then from upper story rooms facing the front. There were fireworks from the city center, way off to the left, fireworks from Ipanema to the right and then, fireworks over the heads of those in front of us. I suppose no one caught fire because they were only half dressed and too drunk to notice, if they did. The drunks were held upright by the crowd. Yachts came into the harbor with lights strung from their rigging. It rained and the band played on. It was a madhouse and we went down to join them. The beach air would have flunked a breathalizer test. It was solid party from the city center beaches to Copacabana, Ipanema, Leblon. The population from Rio and the surrounding cities emptied on to the beach that night. Three million happy, dancing people. What ever their cares were, they were forgotten that night.

The hotel gave free champagne with breakfast the next morning. The clean up crews had already begun and the street and beach were nearly clean. What a great city. Oh yes, that 100,000 cruzeiro bill I got in change from the shoe shine boy, I tried to spend it later and found it was worth absolutely nothing. I wasn't surprised.

## THE END

SIDEBAR

GETTING THERE - Rio is served by the national Airline, Varig, tel. 800-GO-VARIG, and Aerolineas Argentinas, tel. 800-327-0276, American and United.

WHERE TO STAY - Most of the deluxe hotels ($300 for a double) face the beach but there are some moderate priced ones ($150 double) among them. In Copacabana, on the Av. Atlantica, are the Meridien-Rio at 1020 (tel. 275-9922), Copacabana Palace at 1702 (tel. 255-7070), Rio Othon at 3264 (tel. 255-8812) for deluxe and Excelsior at 1800 (tel. 257-1950) and Olinda at 2230 (tel. 257-1890) for the modest prices. Hotels less than $150 are available downtown -Argentina, tel. 225-7233, Florida, tel. 245-8160, Paissandu, tel. 225-7270. Busses to the beach are frequent and cheap.

WHAT TO BRING - The seasons are reversed. Summer is Dec-Mar and temperatures can reach 105 degrees. Winter (Jun-Sep) the temperatures are 20 degrees less but Rio is tropical. Casual clothes go a long way and you can buy bathing suits at local street markets at reasonable prices.

MONEY - Taxis are cheap and public transportation prices are next to free. Good, large meals are in the $10 range and the very best are a bargain compared to equivalent restaurants in the U.S. Current cost information should be obtained from the airlines or associated tour groups.

FOR MORE INFORMATION - The Brazilian tourist office is at 551 Fifth Ave., #519, New York, NY 10176 tel. 212-286-9600. The airlines serving the city have connections with local touring companies and can give information on discount package rates for airfares, hotels and local tours.

## SAN BLAS ISLANDS

On the edge of the Caribbean, the Kuna Indians are a tribe
unto themselves and the women are dressed to the nines.

SAN BLAS ISLANDS, off the coast of PANAMA - The canal runs
from Panama City, north-west to the port of Colon, cutting the country
roughly in half. Approximately 100 Kilometers east of Colon, on the
Caribbean, is the city of El Porvenir and from there to Columbia in South
America is the province of San Blas. A thin coastal strip of land 200 KM
long inhabited by the Kuna Indians. The large Darian province covers the
rest of the eastern half of the country. It's all jungle, Darien and San Blas.

The Kuna's cultivate coconut (their main staple) and corn, rice, cocoa
and yucca on the mainland. They choose to live on the islands. Of course,
they're also fisherman. There seems to be some debate about the number
of islands. One source says there are 365 islands, one for each day of the
year, another 378 islands. Our organizer, a Kuna himself, said there are
49 islands with a Chief on each. The others must be uninhabited, however
many there are.

The Kuna remind me of the Amish. They are peaceful, mind their
own business, take care of their own problems and want to be left alone.
After all the bad press the USA military gets for interfering in the sovereign
affairs of other nations, it was good to hear a story from the other side. In
1925 the government of Panama tried to exterminate the Indians and the
USA sent a Battleship to the area to stop it. The Kunas like Americans to
this day.

The Indians believe no one owns the land but they do own the coconut
trees and crops that grow there. They are short in stature, broad backs,
big heads, strong chest, short legs and small feet. The men wear shorts.
The women, in contrast, are all dolled up. They wear hand stitched, short
sleeved, red patterned molas, a red and yellow printed scarf on the head,

a colorful long skirt, dozens of bracelets on both arms and legs and gold nose rings, ear rings and sometimes necklaces. The women cut their hair short and often have a black line tattooed down the center of the nose.

On a casual day, they may leave off some of the jewelry. But the colorful clothes, that's the daily garb.

## OUR TOUR

We went to the Viajes Versalles travel agency to book for the $135 trip advertized in the newspaper. That Island has toilets where you squat over a hole, however, for a few dollars more, there's a brand new place with real porcelain fixtures, a shower and free transport to the other islands for $185. Keep in mind we have no idea what any of these places are like, so it's all a shot in the dark. A warning the agent gave us, the natives have recognized the value of money. They will pose for and even ask you to take their picture, then ask for a dollar afterwards.

We arrived at 7 AM for the 8 AM flight that left at 9 AM for a short ½ hour ride. A brand new, 12 seat Cessna that ran on auto pilot till we circled the islands. The airstrip at the mouth of the Sidra River is so concealed by jungle that we were almost on it before I saw the asphalt. There is a 25# limit on baggage so it was easy to deplane. The terminal, so to speak, is a small platform, with a roof, attached to the pier. We didn't know where we were going so we showed our ticket to the fellow asking, followed directions and got into a long, narrow, dugout canoe with 4 others and off we went, parallel to the shore heading west.

We were given rain coats, the bags went into the front and were covered. The swells hit us broadside and we almost tipped several times. The sea water spray was constant and we were soaked from the waist down by the time we got to this beautiful island. It looked like the picture of Kwadule.

Gorgeous, clean white sand, native grass huts, palm trees, emerald green water and people jumping up and down on the pier to welcome us. That's when I figured something was amiss. They were greeting the people in the back of the boat and we were at the wrong island. The guy on the pier said we passed ours 15 minutes back.

Alright, so there was no jumping up and down, but the owner, Simon, was glad to see us. We get the hut on the right of the pier. Apparently he built two as an independent enterprise and is the bartender/cook/handyman. The hut is really big inside, two single beds, a table, 2 chairs and a dirt floor. Back on the pier is the dining room/bar/meeting room with attached kitchen. In a separate "building" at the end of the pier is the bathroom with a real toilet that flushes into the water and a shower next door.

We ask Simon for a beer and he takes us to the kitchen to show us his large deep freeze. He opens the lid and it's empty. Beer and soda later. Right.

In the next two hours, a gasoline powered generator, cases of Pepsi and cases of Old Milwaukee beer arrived in separate canoes. He wanted to be sure the guests arrived before stocking up. With time to kill and no beer, we took a tour of the island we shared with several Kuna Indian families. We had the beach front property, they had the middle. The clean beach, swaying palms, gentle warm breeze gives one a feeling of peace with the world. The views on and from the island are nothing short of spectacular. It's a quiet paradise and if we didn't know better it could be the south seas of the Pacific.

Lunch is rice, potatoes and something that looks like spam. And warm Pepsi. A young couple arrives to take the other hut. Afternoon is nap time. Supper is potatoes, small lobsters, crab, beer and Pepsi. The other couple, newlyweds? Don't seem to be getting along. They leave first thing in the morning.

Breakfast is one egg with onions, 2 pieces of bread, coffee, sugar, milk and a jar of mayonnaise. Simon's son has taken a liking to us and showed us his little ball-of-white- fuzz dog, a new mother and his miniature racing cars. We walked through the village and the kids pose for a picture without asking for money. Time to read, lay about, take a swim and drink beer.

A heavy set middle age German couple takes the hut of the newlyweds who must be on route to a divorce lawyer by now.

Lunch is lobster, potato, tomato, lettuce and beer. The rain stops by 4 PM and we ask for a trip to the big island. The 4 of us, German couple included, take a 20 minute ride to Nargana. The boat goes slowly because we're getting broadsided with 4 foot swells and lots of sea spray.

However, we're wrapped in plastic tablecloths to stay dry.

The island is actually two islands in one. Each island has a separate tribe, 400 on the left and 800 on the right joined in the middle by a poured concrete basketball court. The grammar school is here and even a pay phone. We meet Nikki, the organizer of San Blas trips and get the background on the area. 49 islands each with their own chief and one big chief for all islands. They can, thanks to the Americans, vote for the president of Panama but Panama can't run their government. Kids get school to 6th grade for free, it's private school afterwards (for $$). There are government scholarships for the gifted and they usually don't return.

The women are selling molas, a napkin size one is $15. They are unique. T-shirts are $15 and several women ask for their picture to be taken. The huts are much like ours but here they are crowded together here. There is a real store, in case you need film or whatever.

Supper is lobster tail (Simon posed with the live lobsters earlier), potato, lettuce, tomato and Old Milwaukee. We got up at 5:30 AM the next morning for coffee and ½ hour boat trip in the rain to the airport. This time we are covered by two plastic tablecloths. We arrived at 6:30 AM for the 7 AM flight and joined 26 others under the roofed platform at the end of the pier. It was like being in a Japanese subway at rush hour. It poured and stopped only to pour again. At 10 AM, Nikki arrived to tell us the plane was delayed because of the rain. No kidding. The plane finally arrived at 11 AM and there was a dash for the 12 seats.

Our island is named "Naranja Chico", little orange. There is good swimming, a little bit of coral, a lot of peace and quiet and lobster up the wazoo. Simon is accommodating, we could have gone fishing, or to Kwadule island but the rain put us off. It's a good place for a honeymoon or just laying in the hammock between two palm trees and destroying a case of Old Milwaukee.

## THE END

## SIDEBAR FOR SAN BLAS

GETTING THERE - Gateway cities in the U.S. are Miami, Houston, NY, Washington DC, Dallas and Los Angeles - Miami being the principal one. RT airfares from Miami or L.A. are around $750. Continental and American Air offers frequent service and Copa is the Panamanian national airline. I flew Eva Air from L.A. for $740 RT in deluxe class. Copa connects to the major cities in Central America, if you're thinking of a side trip.

ACCOMMODATIONS - In Panama City, the best is the Miramar, $235 double, tel (507)214-1000, overlooking the canal. Caesar Park, $165 dbl, tel (507)226-4077, the Radisson, $165 dbl, tel (507)265-3636, in the middle of the nicest shopping area. All the above are 4 star and the Caesar has a casino.

The El Panama, $155 dbl, tel 269-5000, Plaza Paitilla Inn, $120 dbl, tel 269-1122 and Riande Continental, $105 dbl, tel 263-9999 are 3 star and have casinos. The California is a 2 star hotel, $33 dbl, tel 263-7736, fax 264-6144.

LOCAL ARRANGEMENT - There are literally hundreds of tour operators in the city. After a bad experience with a recommended one I found a good one, Por El Mundo, Calle 45-E No 4, Bella Vista, tel (507)264-6766, fax (507)264-6436, e- mail: mundo@sinfo.net They helped with an assortment of tours run by others, one stop shopping so to speak.

SAN BLAS ARRANGEMENTS - It was impossible to get good information on where to go. I got a brochure from the tourist bureau at the Atlapa Convention Center (rear of the building, second story). El Pornenir has an airport and probably the snazziest accommodations, Hotel Porvenir, 23 rooms, tel (507)270-1448. Then there is the Anai Lodge, 14 rooms on Wichubwala Island, $65 per person, tel (507)239- 3025. Nalunega Island with 10 cabins. Carti-Sugtupu with 4 rooms, tel (507)228-8917. Ailigandi with 5 rooms, (507)224- 9694. The Kuannidup with 10 cabins on the Sidra River, $65 per, tel (507)227-7661. El Porvenir I could find on the map but where the other islands are or how to get there remained a mystery. Then I saw 2 adds in the tourist book, Iskardup Ecoresort, Jungle Adventures, tel (507)269-6017 and Kwadule Eco Lodge, Green World Eco Tours, tel (507)269-6313, $150 single/$220 double. Then I saw a newspaper add for an unspecified island for 3 days, 2 nights, from $135, including airfare. All of the above include meals since there's no place to go to eat out. San Blas special offer from Viajes Versalles S.A., tel (507)263-4085.

MISCELLANEOUS - Visas or tourist cards are required for all. U.S. citizens are issued a tourist card for $5 at the ticket counter in the US.

## TABOGA ISLAND

There's pirates treasure buried somewhere.

ISLA TABOGA, off the coast of PANAMA - It's called the island of flowers because at certain times of the year it's covered with luscious smelling oleander and jasmine. It's history is not so sweet. It was settled by the Spanish in 1515 just two years after Balboa first sighted the Pacific Ocean. It pre-dates Panama City, the countries capital. It has a sheltered deep water port that was used while the port was being built on the mainland. The problem in Panama City was the large tidal variations and the ships couldn't anchor close to shore.

It was from Taboga that Pizarro set off to conquer the Incas of Peru in 1524 and was the main port for ships coming from South America. Henry Morgan, the famous pirate visited the island after sacking Panama City in 1671 and it's said he left some buried treasure behind.

Now it's a year round resort for the local people escaping the dismal areas of the capital city. The boat leaves the Balboa pier every day except Tuesday and Wednesday. It's not a fancy boat, there are two levels and a good view from the open top deck. You go under the Bridge of the Americas, across the mouth of the canal, past the ships waiting at anchor to transit and through the Bay. The 11 mile trip takes a pleasant hour.

At the end of the island pier, there's a fork in the road. To the left is the footpath to the small town and another fork in the road. You can walk low and come back high. Coming back is where you see the Church said to be the second oldest in the Western Hemisphere. The road continues back to the pier and it's time to go right. There is an attractive sea side bar with cold drinks and music loud enough to be heard on the mainland. Twenty feet farther is a gate and guard. $5 gets you $5 worth of script to be used at the Hotel beyond. It's not optional to purchase and keeps the freeloaders out.

The hotel has a beach on both sides of an inlet connecting to the small island of El Morro. An inlet which disappears at high tide. In the 1860's El Morro was the headquarters of the Pacific Steamship Navigation Company and there are some ruins of what remains of the walls. And a small cemetery hidden in the dense jungle.

This is one of the snorkeling areas. On weekends there are boats to take you around the island to other snorkeling areas of even the caves on the backside (the perfect place to hide ill gotten treasure). An abandoned hotel in the distance looks interesting. Reportedly used by Manuel Noriega for weekend trysts. But it's fenced and the gate is locked.

The Hotel Taboga has a pool and comfortable open air dining room to spend your script. That's easy enough to do since a plate of Spaghetti and a soft drink costs $5. The grounds are pleasant and it's a comfortable place to spend a day. The small stand next to the pier sells T-shirts, fixed price. If you've got a day to kill in Panama City, this is a good alternative. And if you've a mind, bring a shovel, there's treasure out there - somewhere.

THE END

## SIDEBAR FOR TABOGA ISLAND

GETTING THERE - Gateway cities in the U.S. are Miami, Houston, NY, Washington DC, Dallas and Los Angeles - Miami being the principal one. RT airfares from Miami or L.A. are around $750. Continental and American Air offers frequent service and Copa is the Panamanian national airline. I flew Eva Air from L.A. for $740 RT in deluxe class. Copa connects to all the major cities in Central America, if you're thinking of a side trip.

ACCOMMODATIONS - In Panama City, the best is the Miramar, $275 double, tel (507)214-1000, overlooking the canal. Caesar Park, $195 dbl, tel (507)226-4077, the Radisson, $195 dbl, tel (507)265-3636, in the middle of the nicest shopping area. All the above are 4 star and the Caesar has a casino. The El Panama, $185 dbl, tel 269-5000, Plaza Paitilla Inn, $150 dbl, tel 269-1122 and Riande Continental, $135 dbl, tel 263-9999 are 3 star and have casinos. The California is a 2 star hotel, $50 dbl, tel 263-7736, fax 264-6144.

LOCAL ARRANGEMENT - There are literally hundreds of tour operators in the city. After a bad experience with a recommended one, I found a good one, Por El Mundo, Calle 45-E No 4, Bella Vista, tel (507)264-6766, fax (507)264-6436, e-mail: mundo@sinfo.net They helped with an assortment of tours run by others, one stop shopping so to speak. Available are - City tour, shopping in duty free Colon, Panama Canal, Barro Colorado Island Tour, El Valle de Anton Canopy Tour, San Blas Islands, Hotel Contadora Resort.

For the Panama Canal, Argo Tours, tel (507)228-4348, from the USA tel 1-888-Panama 1, fax (507)228-1234, half day transit $100, Ocean to Ocean $155. For Taboga Island, just show up for the boat, 8:30 AM everyday except Tuesday and Wednesday, call Argo to be sure of times.

MISCELLANEOUS - Visas or tourist cards are required for all. U.S. citizens are issued a tourist card for $5 at the ticket counter in the US.

## ON THE ROAD TO LAKE TITICACA

## WITH A LOOK AT A CIVILIZATION
## THAT PRE-DATES THE INCAS

We landed where the air is thin. 13,500 feet, at the top edge of the fishbowl crater that holds La Paz. Pilots are required to put on an oxygen mask when flying over 10,000 feet. That's in an open cockpit, of course, not inside a commercial airline. So we all stepped out of a pressurized cabin into a little bit of outer space. And nobody noticed the difference. Until later.

After the hotel check-in, our first hike was two blocks uphill to the cathedral on Plaza Murillo and we had to stop halfway up to catch our breath. This was the first opportunity to see the Aymara and Quechua women in their distinctive bowler hats, two sizes too small. This is the most Indian country in South America, 50% of the population is of pure American Indian blood (another 35% is Spanish and Indian mix). Most of the women also wear a ahuayo, slung across the back and tied at the neck. The brilliantly decorated cloth is used to carry everything from babies to coca leaves. The cathedral is not the most famous in the city but it's the prettiest.

Four blocks south (downhill, something we all started to make note of) is the Iglesia de San Francisco (started in1549), the largest and most important church. The large plaza in front is a major hangout for the younger set and the pickpockets that prey on tourists. We were out of breath, it was time for a rest. That night, those who didn't take pills for altitude sickness got their first headaches.

### SOME BACKGROUND

La Paz is the center of this landlocked countries government but it wasn't always landlocked. At one time, Bolivia stretched all the way west to the Pacific Ocean thru the Atacama region, a barren desert. In the mid 19th century, rich deposits of guano and nitrates were discovered and Bolivia, lacking the money to develop the area, hired Chilean companies. When Bolivia imposed a tax on the minerals in 1879 they ended up shooting themselves in the foot. Chile declared war and took all of the coast (350 KM). Their next dispute was with Brazil in 1903 wherein they lost 100,000 square KM of their northern territory. This time the fight was over rubber. This was not to be the end of their troubles. Between 1932 and 1935 they went to war with Paraguay, a country on the south eastern border. The trouble started when oil companies began to investigate the Chaco area for potential deposits. Standard Oil sided with Bolivia and Shell supported Paraguay. The Bolivians had more troops and still lost the war, and another 225,000 square KM of it's territory. They are still rich in minerals but the metals must be freighted over long distances. Combine this with lack of capital, corruption, internal strife between the miners' union and the state and you have a high cost mineral producer. In agriculture, they grow enough for internal consumption but little to export.

## ON THE ROAD

Tiahuanaco (or Tiwanaku) is Bolivia's most important archaeological site. It's 72 KM due west of La Paz, roughly half way to the Peruvian border on the south side of Lake Titicaca. The lake is almost rectangular shaped, 170 KM long by 97 KM wide with the top tilted 45 degrees to the left. Tiwanaku is close to the southern tip but not close enough to benefit from the water.

It's a desert, a high one, but a desert none the less and one wonders why anyone chose to live here in the first place. General agreement is that the civilization started here about 600 BC but the ceremonial sites (ruins) date from 700 AD. There is an order in which to tour the various spots with numbered signs showing the way. There are piles of sandstone rocks (rubble) that mark what used to be a home, cleverly engineered trenches to move water, a below ground pit the size of an empty Olympic swimming pool with faces carved on individual stones. They have been saved from some of the ravages of the wind by being below ground level. The most impressive "building" is saved till last. It's a ritual platform the size of a football field with most of the walls crumpled and it's surrounded by a dry moat. Steps at the far end lead up to a ten foot stone statue set back from and framed by a rectangular stone arch. As though God was looking down, watching. The steps are barricaded, so we circled to the right to find an opening. In the corner of the interior is a huge, hand carved, stone arch weighting about 500 tons, sitting on flat land in the midst of nothing. Thru the open center you can see the vast plains of the desert and hear the solitary wind blowing. Earthquakes, malice from the invading Spanish Armies and pilferage from the local people have left permanent scars to these once magnificent buildings. The largest of the stone slabs remain (175 tons). How they were transported here, no one knows. The people vanished into obscurity after 1200 AD but they had a profound effect on the area. Evidence of their religious culture have been found in the Inca society to the north which didn't begin until 1440 AD.

After a box lunch (brought the food with us), we back tracked to the fork in the road and turned north to the Inca Utama Hotel, right on the lake in town of Huatajata. Still in Bolivia, on the south-east corner of the highest navigable lake in the world. The hotel has a museum, a lifesized reed galley boat like the natives of old used to fish in the lake, a bar and the only restaurant for miles around. There was red trout from the lake for supper which was quite good and an evening of local entertainment. They featured a four piece band with a guitar, a ukulele, a Llama skin covered drum and a pan flute. Instruments changed from time to time but there was always a wood flute. There was singing and lots of dancing and the brightest of costumes.

## ON THE LAKE

The hotel is the port for hydrofoil tours of the lake and as we pulled out, one of the local men paddled alongside in a reed canoe. The hydrofoil is first class and designed to skim these cold waters at 12,500 feet. The water is clear and clean and ranges from 40 degrees F. in the winter to 64 in the summer. The lake is the survivor of an ancient inland sea and has 36 islands. We stopped at Isla del Sol which is believed to be the birthplace of the sun. There are some ruins on the island if you wish to climb 200 steps to see them. The local children are out in force to make some money and I couldn't resist a cute little girl in her bowler hat two sizes too small. But not a smile on her face, this is business.

We left the boat in Copacabana, still in Bolivia, for lunch. Miracles began to happen here in the 16th century after the town was presented with a statue of the Virgin of Candelaria. It's now a pilgrimage for people from all over the country. It's a border town and the last chance to shop in Bolivia. Prices jump up in Peru.

After we crossed the border, the terrain changed dramatically; there was green grass, trees and fields of crops. It was amazing because we had only gone a few miles.

We drove through Puno to the Hotel Esteves on the northwest corner of the lake. Sunset was approaching and the view through the giant plate glass window in the lounge is nothing short of spectacular. The beautiful colors of sunset over miles and miles of sky high fresh water.

## THE END

## TITICACA SIDEBAR

GETTING THERE - American Airlines serves La Paz through Miami. Fares from the west coast start around $1200 RT. La Paz is also served by Aerolinas Argentinas, AeroPeru, British Air, KLM and Varig.

WHEN TO GO - Bolivia is close to the Equator but the lake is 12,500 feet above sea level, so warm clothing is needed at night. The rainy season is November to March.

WHERE TO STAY - The two best in La Paz are the Hotel Presidente for $160 double tel. 011-591-2-368-601 fax 011-591-2-354-013 and the Radisson Plaza Hotel, $190 double, tel. 011-591-2-316-161 fax 011-591-2-316-302. The Presidente is downtown and the Radisson is about a mile away. Prices include tax and breakfast. Others include the Sucre Palace Hotel, $65, tel 011-591-2-390-251 and the Hotel Alem, under $60, tel. 011-591-2-367-400.

On Lake Titicaca, the Inca Utama Hotel, $120 double, (owned by Crillion Tours) write c/o 1450 S. Bayshore Drive, Suite 815, Miami, FL 33131: tel. 305-358-5353, fax 305-372-0054.

The Hotel Esteves has first class facilities and was built by the Peruvian government in 1977. It's been private since 1995 and one would expect the service to be first rate as well. Unfortunately, it's not the case and it's a shame. This management doesn't know how to run a hotel. Rates are $120/double.

WHERE TO EAT - In La Paz, the restaurant atop the Hotel Presidente, the Belle Vista, has a great view, entrees $15- 25. Then there is Italian food at Pronto Ristorante, Calle Jauregui and Avenida 6 de Agosto and La Casa de los Pacenos at Calle Sucre 856 near Pichincha for local dishes. Eat at the Hotel Inca Utama and Esteves.

HEALTH - La Paz is the highest capital in the world and altitude sickness is a real threat. Typical symptoms include loss of appetite, headache, nausea and shortness of breath. There are pills to take to relieve the symptoms, consult your Doctor. This is not something to be dismissed, mountain climbers have died from altitude sickness. I took the pills and had no problem. It's best to eat lightly and exercise sparingly at first.

FOR MORE INFORMATION - Write to the Bolivian Tourist Information Office, 97-45 Queens Blvd., Rego Park, NY 11374 tel. 800-BOLIVIA.

Torres del Paine - the pride of Patagonia

PUNTA ARENAS, CHILE - This may not be the end of the earth but it's awfully close. You could probably walk there if you had a mind to. This used to be the jumping off point for ships to Antarctica. We had flown south from Santiago for 3 ½ hours (one stop) to get to the largest city in the south (pop. 113,000). I looked around while waiting for my bag. 100 tough looking guys and 4 women. I made a mental note to stay away from dark alleys while I was here.

I figured there isn't a lot to see in Punta Arenas. I confirmed that while walking the town searching for the tour agencies listed in my travel book.. Two no longer exist and the 3rd was closed. So much for the north end of town. Turismo Pali Aike, two blocks south of the square, had the full range of tours but the travel desk at the Hostal Califante had better prices so I booked there. Lomits restaurant, one block north of the square, was the busiest place in town so I went in. Hamburger, coffee and a beer was $4.50.

The bus left at noon the following day so I had time for an early morning walk. Chubby kids with pink cheeks and everybody has dark hair. Alaska popped into the back of my mind. The air is brisk, the sun hidden behind a fully clouded sky. No bright lights, little color. This is a monochromic town. People are wearing coats even though this is summer.

I boarded the public bus at 1 PM for the 3 1/4 hour ride north to Puerto Natales. I was so far south I had to go north to get to the bottom of the Andes. The land is flat as a pancake. No crops, no trees, no sign of life for miles and yet the Army has several check points.

Puerto Natales

I checked into the Milodon Hotel (friendly, quiet and virtually empty) and went across the street for supper. The Cristol Restaurant has pizza with lots of cheese.

Pick up was 7:30 AM and they were on time. 9 people in the van. First stop, the Caves of Milodon, 24 km north of town on gravel roads. In the 1890's the well preserved remains of this enormous ground sloth was discovered here. Twice the height of a human. Apparently it co-existed with the local Paleo Indians although I doubt they shared the cave at the same time. The sloth was a vegetarian. It seem that the Indians weren't and the Milodon is now extinct. The view of the snow capped Andes mountains from the front of the cave is not to be missed. A baby condor circled the van as we pulled out.

We hit a rest stop and 2 people who were already there decided to join our tour. Now it was 11 tourists, 1 driver and 1 guide. Like sardines in a can. A few miles later we stopped the van to watch two guanaco's (look like llamas) fight. They neck wrestled and then one chased the other for 2 miles up and down hills. This stop is note worthy because the van wouldn't start again. Two people decided to walk ahead (five miles to the Ranger Station). A half hour later we were able to hitch a ride to the official park entrance on a large tour bus. US$ 10 park entrance fee. We lost 2 hours before the replacement van arrived. It was smaller than the first. The two walkers caught up.

Lunch was at the lake directly across from Cuernos del Paine (Horns of Paine). The same striking view shown on postcards and in the travel books. A ruggedly stunning sight. We stood and stared at these snow drifted, black granite, sharp edged mountain peaks almost 8,000 feet high.

Lunch was a cold TV dinner with peach drink and cookies. Who cared, we didn't come here for the food.

It's a long drive around the Horns to the glacier on the far side. No sooner that we got out of the van we were hit with gale force winds. If you didn't lean forwards you were sent reeling back. Then we had to cross a wood planked cable bridge in this hurricane. We went one at a time with both hands gripping cable. The path on the other side is tree lined for the downward trail. We can walk upright. At the bottom is ½ mile of black sand and no protection from the in-your-face 50 MPH wind. What a hike, it was like walking through water. At the far end is a 15 foot high sand berm holding back the water and the glacier break off. Dark water, blue ice, moss covered green rolling hills and the black jagged peaks of the Andes in the distance. Just beautiful.

There is a tugboat waiting in the lake. Three hours, US$ 90 for a trip to the glacier itself. If we only had more time. One would think the walk back over the black sand would be easier. It was faster but you still needed glasses for protection from the flying sand.

We were late getting back to town and 3 people missed the last bus back to Punta Arenas. The tour company was nice enough to drive them back for free.

The next morning I got on the wrong boat. Mine was at the next pier down (there are only 2 piers). This was an omen. I trotted to the right one, boarded, and a deck hand brushed my camera. The lens cap popped off and rolled into the black water where it will stay for eternity. There were 5 passengers below deck so there was plenty of room to move about. Off we went into the breeze. The water was choppy but the boat was surprisingly steady. Two hours later we spotted a colony of Cormorants on the left. They made this rocky ledge a permanent home. There are rivers and waterfalls to the right and left feeding this fresh water lake. The water is light blue-green like the Caribbean but opaque. An hour later we slowed, passed Glacier Balmaceda which comes right to the waters edge and docked at the pier for Glacier Serrano. And the rain started. Serious rain. So much for the planned walk to Serrano. Two passengers were using the boat for reasons other than a tour. They hopped into the Zodiac attached to the back of the ship and were dropped off on the edge of the Serrano River a mile away. I assume they brought their own supplies. They weren't going to get anything from this bleak landscape.

Three hours back to town and I caught the bus for Punta Arenas.

The next day was allocated for penguins. Seno Otway is a 1 1/4 hours drive north of town and a one mile walk to the barricade. Obviously the wood for the barricade was imported since there was no vegetation taller than my ankle for as far as I could see. Walking areas are roped off and park guards insure that shortcuts are not taken. There are hundreds of Jackass Penguins (named for their characteristic braying) milling about on the shore. The barricade does not hinder picture taking and the penguins ignored us. They jumped out of the water, into the water, had what looked like meaningful huddles with each other and went about their penguin business. The second viewing area is from a tower, a fifteen minutes walk. I got there just as a fox entered from the left. He walked slowly, head moving from side to side. He spotted a penguin standing in his hole, hesitated, and walked off still looking for food.

I saw a small patch of Antarctic color on the way back. Red leaves on a green thorn bush. I had to take the picture. Even our guide was dressed for summer, wool pull over, gloves and a hood. There is a brisk wind from the water and no wind breaks.

The following day I walked to the edge of town, the Straight of Magellan. The beach is black with small patches of green grass. The sky is nothing but clouds. The dark water is flat and looks cold. I can see land on the distant shore. The same land Magellan and his men saw. This end of South America is a maze of islands and inlets. I have a map so I can see which inlets are dead ends. Magellan didn't and there was nothing here in the way of supplies for the men on board. What courage it must have taken to come through here in a sail boat. This land is not forgiving. I could feel it just standing on the beach.

THE END

## SIDEBAR FOR TORRES DEL PAINE

GETTING THERE - From Santiago, the one stop (in Puerto Montt) airfare to Punta Arenas is approx. $250 RT on Lan Chile. This is also the way to the Falkland Islands but the flights are only once a week ($400 RT from Punta Arenas). Argentina is closer but they still have bad feelings about the Falklands. There are flights to Chilean Antarctic bases from Punta Arenas but arrangements would have to be made in advance.

ACCOMMODATIONS - The best in town is the Hotel Jose Nogueira a half block from the main plaza. Rooms are US$ 150/180 singles/doubles. Tel. 248-840/fax 248-832. Two newer hotels, two blocks north are the Hotel Tierra del Fuego at US$ 100/110 (tel./fax 226-200) and the Hotel Finis Terrae at US$ 130/150 (tel. 228-200/ fax 248-124. The Hostal Calafate, one block north of the square, has rooms for US$ 30/40. Tel. 248-415.

TOURS - Turismo Pali Aike agency is a block south and east of the square and has the full range of tours (tel/fax 223-301). I tried three other agencies and they were closed, possibly for good. The Califante has a travel desk and Internet shop attached and that's where I booked my trips. The 2 nites/2 ½ days to Torres del Paine was approx. US$ 140. That's public bus to and from Puerto Natales, two nites at the Hotel Milodon (tel. 411-727), one days tour of the National Park and one days boat trip through the Patagonian Fjords. Prices increase for a better hotel and a better boat. The Penguin trip was US$ 18 for 4-5 hours.

MISCELLANEOUS - There aren't a lot of fancy places to eat in either Punta Arenas or Puerto Natales. Better stick to your hotel. Chile charges a one time $61 entrance fee at the Santiago Airport in response to the U.S. charging a similar fee for Chileans getting a USA visa.

# VI CHINA

## SELF TOURING IN CHINA AT ONE THIRD THE COST

Or how I stopped worrying and learned to love Beijing

BEIJING, CHINA - We had seen the Great Wall (impressive) and along the way, Ming's Tomb (boring). Spent a day in the shopping district next to the Beijing Hotel. Did Tiananmen Square and all of the Forbidden City. You can't do half the Forbidden City. At the half way point, you can proceed or go back but you can't get out the side. Time was running out and we knew we couldn't see all there should be seen in this big city.

The best way is to read the guide book and decide on what you want to see. Then, couple that information with the tours offered by the various guide services. Tour companies will offer packages to the most popular places and, by and large, the best places to see. Armed with their brochures, we found a nice combination of attractions and decided to do it on our own. The tour price would be US$22 each and we could beat that and have as much time as we like at each place.

### FROM THE HOTEL

Three of us got a taxi in front of the hotel and showed the driver the subway stop we wanted on our map. He didn't get it and the doorman had to interpret. We started at the Landmark Hotel across from the Sheraton Great Wall Hotel and arrived at subway stop #5 in fifteen minutes. The price was agreed on before the trip and we noticed the meter hadn't been turned on. That meant the price would go up after we arrived and, sure enough, it went from $3 to $4. Anticipating this expected price alteration, I gave him the exact change for $3 after we got out of the cab.

This station, typical of others, had thousands of bikes parked in racks surrounding the entrance. We took some time walking through the small park next to the station. It is clearly marked with a large G and a D in the middle. Retired men congregated in small groups practicing their favorite pastime- playing cards. The subway is deep underground and is a link in the air raid shelter plan. It was originally used (1969) by Chinese with special passes but was opened to foreigners in 1980. It's clean, fast, safe and cheap (5 cents). In no time we were at station #6 across from the Yong he gong Temple.

## LAMA TEMPLE

It is the most renowned Tibetan Buddhist Temple in China (outside Tibet). The front door to the temple was locked and it was obviously not open. But, since we were already there, we walked down a side street to look at the neighborhood. Lo and behold, down the street and around the corner, the entrance. The grounds take up most of a long block and the architecture is exquisite. Finely crafted houses in deep red with gold trim. Intricate designs in blue and gold just below the roof line. Green tile walls and lush green gardens. It became a lamasery in 1744 several years after the previous resident was promoted to Emperor and moved to the Forbidden City. The architecture is a mixture of Mongolian, Tibetan and Han and to my untrained eye, looked similar to much of the Forbidden City. This is a popular attraction but pleasant and peaceful even with the crowds. If you plan to see one temple in Beijing, this is it. If you plan on more than one, make this the first and you will probably OD on temples half way through the second.

## THE ZOO

The guide book said the zoo was the pits. None the less, it had pandas and we were going to see them. We took the subway from #5 to #10, across the top of city central for another five cents each. From there, we got a cab for $2 to the zoo. There is an entrance fee for the zoo and for the panda exhibit, as there was for the temple but each was under $1. There are panda t-shirts, panda toys and stuffed pandas at the souvenir stand inside the pavilion. The bears are behind slanted glass with thousands of hand prints and nose prints of the tourists trying to get as close as possible to their childhood teddy bears. The light was low enough to prevent meaningful photography but by chance we saw there was a back yard to the cages.

Outside, the pandas walked the yard and one male was catching a snooze in the Y of a tree. They looked cute, they looked cuddly, they looked big. They are not really bears and you wouldn't want one to get mad at you. But, see the pandas. Relive your childhood.

## THE SUMMER PALACE

Back to the street for a cab. Twenty minutes later we were at the east gate of the Summer Palace, the closest gate to the zoo. It's about 12 KM north west of the city center and is huge. Most of the activity is at the northern side of Kunming Lake. We wove our way through the Hall of Benevolence and Longevity to lakeside. The spot next to the Hall of Jade Ripples is called Fragrance-of-Lotus and is a good place to start. I noticed no fragrance but the view is spectacular. Reportedly the lake was expanded by 100,000 workers and one can only wonder how many hours went into the buildings on Longevity Hill to the right. In the distance, to the left is South Lake Isle, connected by 17-arch bridge. On the lake were row boats, dragon boats and tour boats. We went north a short distance to the east end of the Long Corridor. Aptly named. It is 700 meters long and traverses the length of the hill along the water front. A covered walk with incredible paintings and carvings on the underside. Even while gazing at the nearby houses on the right and the pleasure boats on the left, we were drawn to the Buddhist Temple of the Sea of Wisdom high atop the hill. Impressive. No, Awesome.

We walked by one gorgeous building after another, past the middle - Jade Like Firmament in Bright Clouds - which juts into the lake in a semi circle, and on to the far end of the long corridor. And there it was, the Marble boat. A double deck river boat. Not a toy but a full size boat made of white, green and blue marble parked at the dock. We looked from the front, the side, the back. Stunning.

After refreshments at the concession stands, we were ready to make our way back to the center. Through the Cloud Dispelling Gate and it's associated hall, up we climbed. Stone steps, stone walls, next to pagodas with orange tile roofs.

Too many steps later and another fee, of course, we were at the three story temple. The inside is modest but the view is not. From the front is the entire complex of tiled roofs looking like large stepping stones down to the lake. South Lake Isle connected to the mainland by the 150 meter 17-arch bridge. To the right, the Bronze House separated by sheer cliffs and to the rear, across a chasm, the Hall of Buddhist Tenants with 3 large red arched doors - closed. Not that there was any apparent way to get to there. We took our time and marveled at the view. It was the high spot on the highest ground.

The day was coming to a close and we found a path that led over the hill. Stone steps slick with rain offered several paths and any of them would get us to the North Palace Gate. We were stopped at the Suzhou River, an artificial waterway connecting two parts of the narrow back lake. They wanted a fee to visit the riverside stores accessed by the bridge and it took a while before they understood we just wanted out. The taxi took almost an hour to drive across the top of Beijing. From the northwest corner to the northeast.

## THE RESULTS

A full day and we saw what we wanted and spent as much time as we liked. The tour would have cost $22 each. The total expense for the three of us was less than $20. Three taxi rides, two trips on the subway and countless small entrance fees. Our plane was leaving early the next morning.

## THE END

# GUIDEBOOK FOR BEIJING

GETTING THERE - Northwest, United, Air China, Japan Air Lines and All Nippon Airways serve China, connecting through Tokyo. China Eastern Airlines services Beijing from inside the country. Northwest services Tokyo from both coasts. tel. 1-800-447-4747

If you are going elsewhere in China, it's best to book through the official agency, CITS.

ACCOMMODATIONS - The Great Wall Sheraton, five stars, at around $100 tel. 5005566. Across the street is the Landmark Towers, three stars, $45 (rooms and facilities are very nice) tel. 5006688. Both are northeast of city center, half way to the airport. The most centrally located and most interesting is the five star Beijing Hotel. It is huge and should be visited even if you don't stay there for $100 a night. tel.5137766. Close by are the Peace Hotel, four stars, $75, tel. 5128833 and the Xinqiao Hotel, three stars, $40, tel. 5133366 At the bottom end, the Qiao Yuan Hotel, the Tiantan Sports Hotel and the Beiwei Hotel, from $10 to $15.

FOR MORE INFORMATION - Visas are required. Contact China National Tourist Office, 333 W. Broadway, Suite 201, Glendale, CA 91204 tel. (818)545-7505 and/or China National Tourist Office, 60 E. 42nd St., #3126, New York, NY 10165 tel. (212)867-0271

Something to do if you have a few hours to kill at the
HONG KONG AIRPORT

HONG KONG - And that's exactly what I had. The plane landed at Hong Kong at 6:10 AM and my flight to Sri Lanka didn't leave till that night. It's a brand new airport and I did want to look around so I went through customs even knowing that I'd get burned later for the $ 15 US departure tax. I considered it an admission fee.

I'd bought the Cathay Pacific Airline all pacific air pass and in so doing was destined to spend a lot of time connecting through this airport. The air pass has been very popular with people wanting to see the Orient. In essence, for $ 1200 US you fly to Hong Kong and once there you can fly to any destination Cathay Pacific flies for the next month. That includes Japan, Korea, Taiwan, the Philippines, Viet Nam, Cambodia, Thailand, Sri Lanka - India and Australia are available for an extra charge. The hitch is that the itinerary must be approved beforehand. This may seem to be an inconvenience because you can't make up your mind on the spur of the moment to go elsewhere but it actually turns out to be a benefit. They don't have daily flights on all segments and even when they do, they may leave at an ungodly hour. Every flight must return to the HKG airport, so flight timing is important if you plan to visit several countries and not be stuck with an unwanted over night in Hong Kong.

That said, I wanted a few hours to unwind and look at this Billion dollar facility. The airport was built on Lam Chau Island, directly west of and about the size of Kowloon Peninsula. It's actually a combination of Lam Chau and Chek Lap Kok Islands for 1/4 of the land and the other 3/4 was reclaimed from the sea. From the passenger's view, the terminal is a large rectangle with a tall translucent ceiling (for more light) and gives one a feeling of large open space. The terminal is 1.27 kilometers long, has 48 gates for wide bodied airplanes, 54 moving walkways, 102 elevators, 63 escalators, 288 check in counters and 12 baggage retrieval carousels. The southern runway is 60 meters wide and is 3,800 meters long with 3 parallel taxiways. The northern runway is the same. The on site catering service claims to be the worlds largest flight kitchen with the capacity of handling 80,000 meals a day.

As you might expect, the prices in the airport are no bargain. In the departure area (supposedly tax free) they have clothes and jewelry from every upscale brand name in the world. It's like shopping on Rodeo Drive in Beverly Hills. In the arrivals area, coffee is $ 5 US except for McDonalds ($ 2). There are 2 large restaurants on the second level, Chinese and English Beef and plenty of boutique shops on the first level. There are no check in lockers, only a manual baggage check - in for $ 10 US a day and the bag is x-rayed.

## THE TOUR

You can only drink so much coffee and read a book, so there are 2 alternatives. Directly in front of and attached to the terminal is the Airport Express train station. Traveling at 135 KM/hr, it will get you downtown in 23 minutes for some casual shopping or sightseeing. An alternative is to purchase a tour ticket from Tour Desk 4A on the main level, just to the right of center after you clear customs. The $25 US ticket gets you RT on the train to the Kowloon station and bus transport from the upper level to 3 attractions. The bus leaves at 45 minute intervals which gives ample time to visit and board the next bus.

The train ride was smooth and quiet. I got an iced coffee at the snack stand inside the Kowloon station and waited in the indoor bus section for the bus with the tour marking. 25 minutes later I got off at the first stop and it took a while to figure out I was on the back side of the Wong Tai Sin Taoist Temple. I went left, down 2 flights of stairs and circled around the rear. Then walked through the mid day crowd engulfed in incense smoke to the small ornate Confucian Hall. To the right is a small but pretty garden of miniature trees. Back the other way is the Main Temple and there was a score or so of worshipers on their knees praying in the open area in front of the largest building. The buildings are red with gold roofs and very Chinese (not a real surprise). The legend has it that Wong

Tai Sin was a shepherd boy living in an isolated part of Zhejiang Province when he was taught the art of refining cinnabar into medicine that was supposed to cure all illnesses. He is now worshiped by those worried about their health and those with business problems who come to seek his advice. I hope those I mingled with had business problems.

The first stop is the farthest out and it's about 10 minutes to number 2, Kowloon Walled City. There is an entrance right next to the bus stop but it's not the front. Go left and right at the corner for a ½ block for the main entrance. This park is a square city block and is a pleasant and quiet place to just sit and relax. Just inside the main entrance is the Garden of the Chinese Zodiac with 12 stone sculptures of the rat, ox, tiger, rabbit, dragon, snake, horse, goat, monkey, rooster, dog and boar. The Almshouse, towards the rear, used to be a military office in 1843 but was changed to an old peoples house (hence the name) in 1899. It's the only preserved original structure. This park was opened to the public in DEC 1995.

From the serenity of the park, the last stop is the New World Center on Salisbury Road and the bus stops next to a major shopping center. This is where the action is. Around to the right is the HK Space Museum, the HK Cultural Center and the elegant Clock Tower which is all that remains of the original Kowloon-Canton Railway Terminus built in 1916. The plaza is used for outdoor performing arts and there was a show on when I arrived. The famous Star Ferry Pier is next door and it's a pleasant diversion watching the ferries cross the water to Hong Kong Island. Right across the street is the Peninsula Hotel, often chosen as the finest Hotel in the world. And then back to the shopping mall and decide whether or not to spend another 45 minutes inside the mall. Decisions, decisions. The entire self tour takes 4 hours, airport to airport, unless you go into the mall. Just remember, the last bus leaves the mall at 3:40 PM.

THE END

## SIDEBAR FOR HONG KONG

GETTING THERE - The Cathay Pacific air pass includes 21 days free travel (unless you register online at www.cathay-usa.com as a CyberTraveler to get a total of 31 travel days) from HKG to 15 cities Cathay Pacific flies to in South East Asia. All flights originate in and return to HKG and repeats are not allowed. The itinerary must be agreed on beforehand and tickets will be issued for each segment. Summer departures (May 8 to Aug 21) are $ 200 extra. Upgrades to 1 st class are about double. Premium cities in India, Australia and New Zealand can be added from $ 300-500. Segment changes can be made afterwards for an additional fee.

There is no question that this is a great deal and Cathay Pacific words the agreement very precisely. No departure from the approved plan or the entire trip ticket is void. It's smart to work out the schedule (which will take several hours) in advance to allow time to catch the next flight. Once approved, you're OK. Call Cathay Pacific 1-800-228-4297 or fax at 1-800-617-9470 for free brochures. Book through a travel agent.

FOOD - The airport food is good but it ain't cheap. The prices are better virtually everywhere else in SE Asia, except Japan. There are 2 big restaurants on the upper level, Chinese and British Beef. Lots of small boutique shops on the first level.

LOCAL ARRANGEMENT - Tour desk 4A is in between the customs exit and the train entrance arch. Just to the right of center, in the rear. I got lost and asked. They speak English and are very helpful. Figure on four hours for the complete tour.

HEALTH - There are no vaccinations required for entry into Hong Kong. However, it would be prudent to check on what is needed for the other countries you visit.

MISCELLANEOUS - No visas are required for USA citizens for stays up to 3 months. Departure tax is $ 15 US for each time you clear customs and return. It's not necessary for connecting flights. There are several crossover stations in the departure area. Follow the signs. There is a smoking room in the departure area, center, basement.

SHANGHAI - The most radical city in China

This is where normal rules don't apply

SHANGHAI, CHINA - Gotta admit, there were some pre-conceived ideas about the city before this trip. British sailors with mickey's slipped in their drinks or knocked on the back of the head as they walked along the wharfs of the Thames. They would wake up a day later, well out to sea with a splitting headache as the ship sailed half way around the world. They had been "Shanghaied". This was clearly a port sailors weren't volunteering for. The truth of the matter, however, was something else.

## A NEW CITY

Shanghai is a young city, even by American standards. In the mid 18th Century the population was only 50,000. The first Westerners set foot in the city in 1832. At that time, the population was 300,000 and they lived within a fortified wall as protection from Japanese pirates. The British attempted to obtain rights to establish a trading center and were refused. Ten years later, during the First Opium War, British resolve was shown. They sent warships, bombarded the fortifications and routed the Chinese troops. As part of the Treaty of Nanking, they were given permission to lease land and initiate trade. In 1847 the French followed. The city was divided, on the west bank of the Huangpu River, into the British or International Settlement and the French Concession.

Each of these sections were run independent from Chinese authority. As such, they became a refuge for adventurers, gamblers, bankers, traders, pimps, socialites, drug runners, sailors, and a sanctuary for revolutionaries. The city became known for its garish, luxurious and carnal life style. All forms of vice thrived and the cities name now entered the English language as a synonym for kidnap (Shanghaied).

514

Labor was incredibly cheap because people flooded in to escape war in the outlying provinces. Great textile mills were formed, followed by other light industry and eventually heavy industry. Shanghai became the seaport of China, a dominance which exists today. By 1900 the population reached one million.

By the 1920's, Shanghai was the largest manufacturing city in China. It not only had more cars than any other city but all other cities in China put together. In 1921 the Chinese Communist Party was founded here. Many of the British, French, Americans, Japanese, Italians and Chinese made millions until the forming of the People's Republic of China in 1949. The Communist Party was determined to clean out the prostitution and criminal element. Industrialists were told they could continue to run their factories until taken over by the state.

## SHOPPING

The first place to stop is the friendship store (there are two). They are the official outlet for items sold to foreigners. They, like many of the hotel shops will only take FEC's. That is, Foreign Exchange Certificates, the Chinese money you got in exchange at the airport or the hotel for your dollars or travelers checks. There is another type of money, Renminbi (RMB) or the peoples money. They are equivalent in value and you can tell the difference by turning the bills over. FEC's have English on the back. Another difference, FEC's can be exchanged back to dollars upon your exit. The Friendship stores carry the standard cross section of Chinese commodities and some locally manufactured items. Which means there may be goods in the Shanghai store not available elsewhere in China.

The main Friendship store is at 33 Zhongshan Number One Road East. From the Peace Hotel at the corner of Nanjing Road East and the Huangpu River (the Bund) turn north, or left, walk two blocks and turn west (left again). The store is a half block in, on the north side of the road with signs on the building in Chinese and English. Prices are fixed and a little higher than those on the street but the store caters to foreign tourists (American, European, Japanese) and there will be a selection of familiar

515

brand name merchandise not available elsewhere. There are American and British cigarettes. T-shirts with pictures of Shanghai stenciled across the front are the fourth floor (difficult to find elsewhere). They have sizes large (L) and extra large (XL), an important consideration if you expect them to fit when you get back home. The second Friendship store is the Antiques and Curios branch at 694 Nanjing Road West. It specializes in what the name implies. Credit cards are welcome. A major advantage is that some of the staff speak English.

## INTERNATIONAL SETTLEMENT

Now that you have checked on prices at the Friendship store, you are ready to attack the largest and most congested shopping area in the city. Simply return to the Peace Hotel at Nanjing Road East and the waterfront and walk west. Remember, east is the river. Shanghai has over 24,000 shops and after a few hours, it seems that all of them are here. And most of the population of Shanghai, regardless of the time of day. Workers from the outlying provinces are given staggered days off and use the day to shop in the city. The street is crowded, bustling and energetic. You are entering the arena of real shoppers.

The street runs for over six miles from the waterfront and changes names from East to West. Of note are the two main department stores, Wing On (simply called No. 10) and No. 1 Department Store, a little farther west. Both are huge stores and sell virtually everything from stationary to socks to fur coats to TV sets. No. 1 claims to serve 100,000 people a day and you will no doubt feel that all 100,000 are there with you. Keep in mind that these stores cater to the Chinese and the selection of goods are not unlike those in American department stores except all are locally made. When buying clothes it is important to note that the Chinese do not have the same body build as Americans. Just look around you, the Chinese are very slim. Some are tall, but barely cast a shadow. The clerks don't speak English but there are good buys if you know exactly what you want.

## FRENCH CONCESSION

Shopaholics can catch a taxi from Nanjing Road to Huaihai Road M. (middle) for the minimum fare of $6 US. For those not comfortable in crowds, this shopping district is less congested. There are approximately 200 stores, of which 50 are specialty shops for clothing or shoes.

One can easily spend a day browsing from one interesting shop to another. This is where you can hone your bargaining skills. But take care, these people do it for a living. If you are not interested in shopping or were dragged along against your will, this section of town has some of the most fascinating architecture in all of Shanghai. Old, new, brass, brick, glass and stainless steel.

## WHAT TO DO

The Bund. Start at the bridge over the Wusong River where it intersects the Huangpu and walk south. The boat dock for the river cruise is across the street from the Friendship store. There are restaurants, stores and a park. This is the general meeting area for people to chat or bring the family. Don't be surprised if you are approached by students practicing their English. They are unusually well informed about Chinese politics and current events. Many are self taught from listening to the BBC and American radio. The workers average wage is roughly $1000 a year for a 5 ½ day work week but the rent is only $2 a month.

The Huangpu river cruise is 3 ½ hours, afternoon or evening. The "B" class ticket costs $8 and will get you a deck chair on the top level, in front, and you will be offered free tea or coffee, and ice cream (ice sticks). You're also assigned a seat in an inside compartment with air conditioning and a TV. The ferry goes north to the Yangtse, passing ocean going freighters from all over the world, river steamers, military vessels, a submarine (they are fussy about pictures of the military stuff). A peaceful ride and it gives a different view of the city.

## WHAT TO SEE

Halfway up Nanjing Road, where the name changes from East to West, is Peoples Park. Admission is 4 cents and it's geared primarily for children but it is large, pretty and a pleasant break from the stores of Nanjing. The children play as all children do.

Yuyuan Gardens was built for the Pan family, rich Ming Dynasty officials. It is at the end of the bazaar area of the Old Chinese city. Weaving right and left and right and left through a maze that shows there are pockets of poverty in Shanghai. The gardens took 18 years to build and were finished in 1577. However, in the mid 19th century, they were the home base of the "Society of Small Swords", who inflicted considerably damage on the adjacent French Quarter. The French retaliated with total destruction. They were rebuilt and are magnificent to behold. Warning, there are an average of 100,000 visitors daily.

## JADE BUDDHA

Is an active temple finished in 1918. The center piece is a 6 foot high white jade Buddha on the second floor (no pictures) reported to weigh more than a ton. The temple was inactive from 1949 through 1980 because of the cultural revolution and was saved from destruction by a telegram from a senior state official.

## THE END

## GUIDEBOOK FOR SHANGHAI

GETTING THERE - China Eastern Airlines and Northwest service Shanghai from Tokyo. Northwest Airlines has non stop flights from the west coast to Tokyo where you change planes for Shanghai without carrying your baggage. Northwest also services Tokyo from other parts of the USA on a one stop basis.

ACCOMMODATIONS - There are a plethora of places to stay but, in essence, three distinct arenas. The British/International Settlement, The French Concession and in the sticks. Keep in mind that there are 12 million people in this city, China's largest. No matter where you are, outside the hotel, it will be crowded. Hotels at the top end, in the International Settlement, are The Shanghai Mansions, 20 Suzhou Beilu, next to the junction of the Wusong River and the Huangpu River -The Peace Hotel, at the intersection of Nanjing Road and the Bund (waterfront at the Huangpu River). It reeks of old money, wood, brass and is veddy British. The Overseas China Hotel, 104 Nanjing Xilu, a few miles west of the river on Nanjing Road.

In the French Quarter is the Jingiang Hotel, a huge facility that takes an entire block and the adjacent Jinjiang Tower, 59 Maoming Nanlu, one block north of the district's major shopping street, Huaihai Road. Nixon stayed here in1972. Rooms at the top of the line start at $150 double, suites $400 and penthouse at up to $2500.

From the Bund, the unofficial center of town, there are hotels a taxi ride away (20-40 minutes). To the northeast, the Blue Sky Hotel, to the north, the Haihong Hotel, to the west (towards the airport) are the Shanghai, Hengsan, Hongqiao, Landmark, Cherry Holiday Villa and many others.

The Landmark (old name Qianhe) is a joint venture with Singapore Airlines, is completely modern, 3 star, has western and oriental restaurants (as do the others) and is at 650 Yishan Road. Rooms start at $80. The taxi into town is $15 one way (40 minutes).

FOR MORE INFORMATION - Visas are required. Contact China National Tourist Office, 333 W. Broadway, Suite 201, Glendale, CA 91204 tel. (818)545-7505 and/or China National Tourist Office, 60 E. 42nd St., #3126, New York, NY 10165 tel. (212)867-0271

## SHOPPING IN SHANGHAI

This is the most unChinese city in China

SHANGHAI, CHINA - There are four general areas to shop in the largest city in China (population over 12 million). Two are shopping districts, the British or International Settlement and the French Concession. If you have but a short time because business or travel plans will draw you out of this unique city in a day or so, you can adequately supply your needs with the first and easiest option.

## FAST SHOPPING

The quickest and easiest way to get your shopping done is using the boutiques and/or shops in your hotel. Prices will be 15-20 % higher than the best deals found in the major shopping areas but, time lacking, there should be an adequate selection of jade, ivory (illegal to bring into the USA), wood carvings and jewelry with precious and semi precious stones (jade, quartz, pearls and diamonds, set in silver and gold). There will be men's and women's cashmere sweaters, silk gowns and shirts, silk cloth (plain and heavily embroidered), Chinese paintings and screens, artifacts of stone, chess sets, and even hand engraved furniture.

There are several good reasons to shop at your hotel. First, there is no bargaining. No long negotiations on the price and the never ending doubt that you could have gotten it for less if your bidding skills were better tuned. You know up front you're paying a little more for the convenience of a quick shop. Secondly, the shops are usually open till nine and you can buy those mandatory take home presents after business is done and before the plane leaves in the morning. Third, there is a significantly better chance of getting genuine merchandise in a shop under the roof of a hotel catering to businessmen. The hotel relies on repeat business and will not tolerate a shop selling glass as jade or fake pearls. The better hotels are the ones favored by business people and the ones with the best variety of gift shops.

And lastly, they take the major credit cards. MasterCard, Visa, American Express, Diners. It's advisable to charge your purchases with credit cards since it can give you time to check on the authenticity of gems or other jewelry after returning home and before the bill arrives. Also, some credit card companies give automatic 30 day insurance for merchandise that may be lost, stolen or broken if purchased with their cards (American Express, some Visa and MasterCards).

## FRIENDSHIP STORES

The second place to shop is at the friendship store (there are 2 in Shanghai). Friendship stores are the official outlet for items sold to foreigners. They, like many of the hotel shops will only take FEC's. That is, Foreign Exchange Certificates, the Chinese money you got in exchange at the airport or the hotel for your dollars or travelers checks. There is another type of money, Renbimbi (RMB) or the peoples money. They are equivalent in value and you can tell the difference by turning the bill over, FEC's have English on the back. Another difference, FEC's can be exchanged back to dollars upon your exit. There are Friendship stores in all cities open to foreigners. They carry the standard cross section of Chinese commodities and, in addition, locally manufactured items. Which means there may be goods in the Shanghai store not available anywhere else.

The main Friendship store is at 33 Zhongshan Number One Road East. From the Peace Hotel at the corner of Nanjing Road East and the Huangpu River (the Bund) turn north, or left, walk two blocks and turn west (left again). The store is a half block in, on the north side of the road with signs on the building in Chinese and English. The ground floor has a small market for cookies, sweets and cold drinks, and other sections typical of a drug store. Soap, deodorant, after shave, cigarettes, leather wallets and hand bags. One corner in the rear has furniture and in the other is a small coffee shop. The second floor has Chinese art (paintings, screens), jade, jewelry and an intricately carved five foot long ship, enclosed in glass, with a price tag of $600,000 US. The third floor has carpets, fans, rings and associated jewelry. The fourth has clothes and furs. The fifth is a restaurant. Prices are fixed and a little higher than those on the street but the store caters to foreign tourists (American, European, Japanese) and there will be a selection of familiar brand name merchandise not available elsewhere. There are American and British cigarettes. T-shirts with pictures of Shanghai stenciled across the front are on the fourth floor (difficult to find elsewhere). They have sizes large (L) and extra large (XL), an important consideration if you expect them to fit when you get back home. The second Friendship store is the Antiques and Curios branch at 694 Nanjing Road West. It specializes in what the name implies. Travelers checks and money can be changed for FEC and credit cards are welcome. A major advantage is that some of the staff speak English. This is essential if you want something shipped home. Don't even try to ship anything from any place other than here or at a major hotel. The merchants elsewhere won't understand what you are talking about. At best they will direct you to the Post Office.

## INTERNATIONAL SETTLEMENT

If you have time to shop either of the main shopping districts, it's a good idea to stop at the Friendship store first to check on the prices. With this information as a baseline you are ready to attack the largest and most congested shopping area in the city. Simply return to the Peace Hotel at Nanjing Road East and the waterfront and walk west. Remember, east is the river. Shanghai has over 24,000 shops and after a few hours, it seems that all of them are here. And most of the population of Shanghai, regardless of the time of day. Workers from the outlying provinces are given staggered days off and use the day to shop in the city. The street is crowded, bustling and energetic. You are entering the arena of real shoppers.

There are approximately 400 shops on this street and this is a partial list of the shops you will encounter traveling west from its start. Haida Shirts, Shanghai Typewriters and Duplicators, Laojiefu Woolen & Silk Fabrics, Shanghai Stage Articles Store, Wuliangcai Optician's, Yingfeng Flags & Banners, Youyi Photo Studio, on the south side of the street. Opposite, on the north side are - Shanghai No. 1 Traditional Chinese Musical Instrument - Sales Dept., Penjie Ladies Clothing Store, Shanghai Sports Goods Store, Yuancheng Foodstuff Store, Guanlong Photographic

Equipment Store, Shanghai Stamp Company, Zhonghua Leather Shoes, Hengdali Watch & Clock Shop, Caitongde Chinese Pharmacy. Farther along, there are shops for Electrical appliances, tea, knives, books, embroidery, tobacco, hats, childrens clothes, a beauty parlor, porcelain, bedding, several restaurants and department stores. The street runs for over six miles from the waterfront and changes names from East to West. Of note are the two main department stores, Wing On (simply called No. 10) and No. 1 Department Store, a little farther west. Both are huge stores and sell virtually everything from stationary to socks to fur coats to TV sets. No. 1 claims to serve 100,000 people a day and you will no doubt feel that all 100,000 are there with you. Keep in mind that these stores cater to the Chinese and the selection of goods are not unlike those in American department stores except all are locally made. When buying clothes it is important to note that the Chinese do not have the same body build as mericans. Just look around you, the Chinese are very slim. Some are tall but even they barely cast a shadow. The clerks don't speak English but there are good buys if you know exactly what you want.

## FRENCH CONCESSION

Shopaholics can catch a taxi from Nanjing Road to Huaihai Road M. (middle) for the minimum fare of $6 US. For those not comfortable in crowds, this shopping district is less congested. There are approximately 200 stores, of which 50 are specialty shops for clothing or shoes.

A suggestion for those not interested in marathon shopping. Stop for breakfast or lunch at the Jinjiang Hotel, a magnificent structure, with old and new sections and the centerpiece of the old French Quarter. After a leisurely meal, for about $15 - $20 US, browse the hotel shops, taking notes on the prices and walk off the calories from the meal on Huaihai Rd. Go south for a half block on Maoming Rd. S. and turn left on the main drag (east). In the first few blocks, you will encounter on the north side - A Cinema, Jinlong Cotton & Silk Fabrics, Kaitai General Store, Shanghai Beddings, Meiyi Ladies Shoes, Xinshijie Garments Store, Dafang Cotton & Silk Fabrics, Painting Department of Shanghai Bookstore, Anqi Children's Clothes, Shoes & Caps, Hongxing Optician's. Across the street, on the south - Gujin Women's Articles, Shanghai Western Restaurant, Qimei Leather Shoes, Haiyan Food Products Factory, Xinhua Bookstore, Tianshan Moslem Foodstuff Store, Maoshan Wineshop.

One can easily spend a day browsing from one interesting shop to another. This is where you can hone your bargaining skills. But take care, these people do it for a living. If you are not interested in shopping or were dragged along against your will, this section of town has some of the most fascinating architecture in all of Shanghai. Old, new, brass, brick, glass and stainless steel. Enjoy the sights from outside the shops.

If you can't find what you want in Shanghai, it ain't in China.

THE END

## TIDAL WAVE

### A surprise the guide books left out

HANGZHOU, CHINA - "Who would like to see a tidal wave tomorrow", the guide said as we got out of the van. I was surprised. What tidal wave? The guide book said this city was acclaimed for it's beauty, there was no mention of a tidal wave. Then it dawned on me. I spent the last week in and around Shanghai, without a newspaper or CNN. I did see parts of "Beverly Hills Cop II" and "The Vikings", in Chinese, on the TV in my room, but there had been a virtual news black out for the last seven days.

An island must have blown up, like Krakatoa, and created a giant wave that was on its way to mainland China. Or a cyclone, South East Asia was famous for these devastating storms that could easily create a tidal wave in front. Not so. She continued, "It only happens in two places, here and the Amazon River in Brazil. Tomorrow is the last day we can see it come up the river." Our guide explained that this wave occurred every year for only three days and the last day was tomorrow. I'd never seen a tidal wave. Any kind of tidal wave. I signed up.

It had been a long day. After squeezing in the last bit of sightseeing in Shanghai, we left by train at 5 PM for a four hour, non-stop ride, south west to Hangzhou (Hangchow). It was standing room only in first class - we had reservations and therefore, seats. They were padded and comfortable and there was no livestock sharing the car but the 180 kilometers (110 miles) went rather slowly since the sun had set and the windows showed only the reflections of us, looking out. At Hangzhou, we walked fifteen minutes through the crowded station to the van and slowly fought the busy downtown traffic to our quarters at the Xi Zi Guest House on the outskirts of town. The Xi Zi consisted of a series of buildings in the middle of a mist shrouded, fenced park, patrolled by armed guards. Armed guards? An annual tidal wave? All of this should make sense later.

## BREAKFAST

The phone rang for the morning wake up call. There wasn't a person at the other end but a recording of "Oh Susanna". No words, mind you, just the music. I tried to fill in the lyrics as best I could but it was too early. Breakfast was at the dining hall which we discovered the night before after fifteen minutes of wandering through the fog. It served the entire complex. American or Chinese were the two choices and you needed only to point at your selection on the menu which was in Chinese with the English translation directly below. None of the staff spoke English, so the menu was a must. Toast, butter, plum jam, coffee, heated milk for the coffee, two fried eggs, a piece of ham the size of a postage stamp and half a peach floating in mystery syrup came to a fixed price of roughly $6 US. The milk only comes heated, by the way (don't ask, I don't know). The breakfast was quite nice, actually.

## THE TOUR

It was an overcast day but at least the mist had cleared. We waited outside our bungalow, a crescent shaped, one story, wood building reminiscent of WWII government housing back home. The main exception was the furnishings. Each room was individually suited with similar but unique pieces of what appeared to be antiques. Expensive, custom made desks, beds, drawers and lamps. I later found that this compound, at the foot of Xi-zhao Hill, is in fact an active Army post. It is used by Senior State officials to entertain foreign dignitaries. Mao Tsetung used this retreat to receive guests. During idle times, it's used as a hotel for foreigners with hard cash. That's us.

The bus arrived at 8:30 and $24 US later, we were on our way. All 33 seats were filled and our CITS guide from the night before was our leader. Towards the end of the hour and forty five minute drive, she handed out box lunches. Our bus was among a long line of busses parked in an open field along side a gravel road. I don't know why, but I found all this traffic a surprise. There were literally thousands of people walking alongside the road. The 33 of us stayed close to the guide for the quarter mile walk back

527

along the same road we drove in on. She had the tickets. The first stunning sight (the second actually - the first was when I looked inside the box lunch) was a beautiful six story pagoda off to the left. Four hundred feet away, separated from the road by grass and trees and on the river bank. Mao had seen the tidal wave years ago and I knew where he watched it from.

We followed our guide pass officials, ticket takers, through open areas with chairs, by guards, past stands selling fruit, bottled water, soda, souvenirs, walked down aisles and crawled over chairs to our designated spot. A section of stands covered by an awning, fifty feet from the front row. The chairs were the fold up type and armless and placed for the maximum concentration of people in the least space. The stands had a concrete floor and were stepped so those in the back could see over those in front. I was only five feet from the left side edge of the stands and above those next to us on the left who were in the open and sitting on the grass. The tidal wave was going to come from the left, from the direction of the pagoda, which was still gorgeous to behold. The river bank was lined with guards. There were problems in the past. People committed suicide by throwing themselves in front of the tidal wave. Others tried to surf the wave. The guards were there to prevent any mischief. I didn't see a single surf board among the thousands of spectators so the guard idea was working.

Back to the first surprise - the box lunch. There was time to kill and I took a second look inside the box to see if it was as bad as it first appeared. Originally, it contained bread, some unidentifiable greasy meat, two hard boiled eggs, a can of orange juice and a napkin. However, the box had been bounced around what with crawling over seats and all. The grease was now everywhere. The can of OJ could be saved but the rest was a disaster. I put it under the seat. No more than two percent of the crowd were Westerners and most of the Chinese brought their own food. Good thinking. And what they were eating, looked good.

## THE WAVE

This type of tidal wave is actually called a tidal bore. It happens when a large incoming tide is constrained by a gradually narrowing river channel or by a rise in the river bed or both. A sizable head of water results and moves upstream where a combination of the water friction and downstream river current (beneath) combine to present the greatest resistance to the incoming tide. This results in a solid wall of water that can move as fast as 12 knots and continue upstream until reaching a falls or rapids too strong to overcome. The largest known tidal bore is 24.6 feet high on the Chien Tang Kiang River, here in Hangzhou.

A low throated "Ohhh" rippled through the crowd from left to right like the wave at a football game. All heads in front of me turned towards the Pagoda. Downstream. I had been staring off to the distant shoreline, a mile away. The weather wasn't co-operating. A light, smog-like haze hung in the air obscuring distant viewing. The far shore was a thin line of dark grey separating the grey of the water from the barely lighter grey of the sky.

I followed the heads downstream and saw a faint grey line bisecting the horizon but I couldn't be sure. It was 12 noon and grey on grey is difficult to distinguish. I looked through the telephoto lens on my Nikon but the autofocus was having difficulty finding something concrete to focus on. I turned the camera 90 degrees to the vertical position and the lens locked on the thin grey line in the middle. The approaching tidal wave. The haze extended downstream and my view was grainy but this was the way it was going to be. The line extended across the river and was growing in my viewfinder. I was standing on the step behind my seat and looking over the heads of those next to me and the spectators on the grass. As good a view as one could get without a tripod and a front row seat.

The wave came even with the Pagoda and I could hear the deep rumble. It was churning it's way upstream, overpowering the downstream current. Suddenly, the six foot wave was in front of the stands moving as fast as a man could run. No crash like a wave hitting the beach, just the churn of water sweeping over water. And it swept by in a crescent shape with the middle held back by the faster flowing water in the center. And then it was quiet, we were behind the sound and the crowd was still. The water behind the wave showed turbulence but it was silent chaos.

It wasn't twenty feet high as I'd hoped, but in retrospect it's just as well. I would have been too close to the shore. I don't know how far it continued but I watched it blend into the grey of the upstream horizon. It was time to go and the clouds were starting to look mean. We followed the grass section people towards the Pagoda for a shortcut back to the bus. Just as we hit the road, it started to rain. I thought to bring my clear plastic raincoat and moved like lightening to put it on. It didn't dawn on me that the raincoat was on backwards until it was too late. The heavens opened with a drenching downpour.

The grass field we parked in was now a marsh and the cloud burst didn't help visibility but all 33 found their way back to the bus. The busses had several hours to arrive and park but now we all wanted to get out at the same time and there was only one road.

The rain continued on and off for the rest of the day but I'd seen my first tidal wave. Since I was already half wet, I took a walk around the grounds of the Xi Zi after returning home. The lawns are manicured, the vegetation lush. The mist in the air gave the compound a mystical feeling. A movie set.

## THE END

## GUIDEBOOK FOR HANGZHOU


GETTING THERE - Northwest, United, Air China, Japan Air Lines and All Nippon Airways serve China, mostly through Tokyo. China Eastern Airlines and Northwest service Shanghai from Tokyo. Northwest services Tokyo from both coasts of the United States and planes are changed in Tokyo but the baggage is checked through.

There is an airport in Hangzhou, it was built for President Nixon's visit in 1972. It is easier flying in than flying out unless you are comfortable in the middle of a proverbial Chinese fire drill. Your exit is best arranged with the official Chinese travel agency - CITS.

The train station in Shanghai is clean and modern with all the facilities you might expect. However, train rides are booked in advance, seats are reserved and little or no English is spoken. Getting to the correct platform may be a lot easier than finding the right car or the proper seats. It's safer to use CITS, their guides are multi-lingual. The train ride is five hours and it's better to go in the daylight and enjoy the countryside.

ACCOMMODATIONS - The Xi Zi Guest House, 37 Nanshan Road, Hangzhou, tel. 771614 is several miles from the town but right on West Lake (the main attraction). Twin rooms cost $95-115 US and suites range from $210 to $900 US. A taxi to town is approximately $8 US. The Hangzhou Shangri-La Hotel is on the opposite side of the lake, the north side, tel. 22921 with rates of $140 US for a double. The town, bordering the east side of the lake, has any number of hotels with rates as low as $40 US.

WHEN TO GO - The tidal wave occurs during the autumn equinox, about September 22, the time when the sun crosses the equator making the day and night of equal length all over the world. I saw it on September 24, the third and final day.

*JAY J. STEMMER*

FOR MORE INFORMATION - Visas are required. Contact China National Tourist Office, 333 W. Broadway, Suite 201, Glendale, CA 91204 tel. (818)545-7504 and/or China National Tourist Office, 60 E. 42nd St., #3126, New York, NY 10165

## ABOVE THERE IS HEAVEN, BELOW THERE IS HANGZHOU

A short train ride from Shanghai is
one of the most beautiful lakes in China.


HANGZHOU, CHINA - The phone rang. I picked up the receiver to hear "Oh Susanna" on the other end. No words, mind you, just the music. It was time to get up. The Xi Zi Guest House is China's answer to Camp David and is open to foreign visitors when the government isn't entertaining foreign officials. The reason is simple, hard currency. Our group met at breakfast to plan the days activities.

Three of us would see West Lake, the major attraction in town. The Xi Zi is on the south side of the lake where you can see boats leaving the east and west banks for the island in the middle. We opted to walk to the west. Morning mist continued to hang in the air. The trees were green, the grass wet, the flowers and bushes manicured to perfection. Marco Polo described Hangzhou as one of the finest and most splendid cities in the world.

### WEST LAKE

We followed the foot path along the south bank and continued to the intersection of the western causeway. This causeway runs south to north and separates the larger outer lake (70%) from the western inner lake (20%). There is a northern inner lake formed by another causeway (10%). The causeways are riddled with arched bridges to allow the free flow of boats between lakes and are colorfully named, as is the Chinese fashion. Our causeway had bridges with the following names - Reflecting Ripples, Locking Waves, Viewing Hills, Suppressing Dike, Eastern Lakeside, and at the northern end, Crossing the Rainbows. The lake is about three kilometers long and just shy of three kilometers wide.

Just before the Locking Waves bridge is the Pleasureboat Service Station (the boat dock). One boat had golden dragons atop, big viewing windows on all sides with polished dark wood rails. Another had inside dining service and a bar. They were stunning. They were works of art. We saw a Japanese group board one of the boats. We were impressed and with child like enthusiasm went to the ticket booth and bought our tickets. And went to board one of the boats and was politely denied. The fellow pointed back towards the ticket booth. We walked back and showed our tickets to a group of people standing next to the booth and they pointed towards the path behind the ticket booth, along side the causeway. There was a line of Chinese visitors waiting to board a small, plain, shallow, motor boat. My friend said, "That's why the tickets only cost fifty two cents each!" We got in line and when Diane saw the boat fill to capacity and about to sink from the shear weight of the passengers, she said, "I'm not going." It took time to cajole her and wait for the next boat. Ours had one inch of clearance between the water and the rail. Seven eighths of an inch more than the other boats. They would have boarded more people had there been any more in line.

Slowly we coasted across the lake. The water was calm. The passengers sat very still. Good thing, if two people coughed on the same side of the boat we would have capsized. I saw us approach and continue by Three Pools Mirroring the Moon Island. I turned my head, very slowly, "Isn't that where we are supposed to go?" Little difference at this point, we were going where the boat was going.

## IT'S THE WRONG ISLAND BUT IT'S DRY

There are three islands that can only be reached by boat. Ruan Yuan's Mound, the northern most, with no facilities. For picnics, I suppose. The one we wanted to go to and Midlake Pavilion, where the boat stopped. It took very little time to see the various shops. The only purpose for this stop was to shop since there was little to see and nothing worth a photograph. Now, we watched and waited and boarded a bigger boat and, as luck would have it, got to the Three Pools Island. It was surely built by man since the island is circular and has three lakes inside the island. The interior lakes have more area than does the land, but that's the charm. Mist was still in the air as we walked through an elaborate entrance gate. The trees are beautiful, the lakes filled with spots of green lily pads sprinkled with silver. Light aluminum coins rest on the pads, thrown for good luck. Gardeners are in constant attendance to the flowers. There is a gift shop, dining room and a sitting room filled with singing birds in cages hanging from the ceiling. Outside, a gnarled tree with dense green sitting on top as if it received a bowl-on-the-head haircut. It was in the middle of the lake. Deep violet leaves on the shoulder of the footpath. Circular archways separate one lush green area from another. Serene. On the west side unlit torches stick out from the water. They will have flames at night to guide the boats.

## SHOPPING

The following day I was off to town. My compatriots were off to Xian to see the underground soldiers and I was given a shopping list to fill. T-shirts with scenes of West Lake or Three Pools Mirroring the Moon or the dragon boat we couldn't get on. And the laundry bag that came with the room. Several of us fell in love with the cloth laundry bag embossed with a gorgeous rustic scene. I'd used mine for the designated purpose and was awaiting it's return with my clean laundry. The small "shopping arcade" next to the lobby had none for sale and after several of us expressed an interest at the front desk, they were replaced by plastic ones in each of the rooms. And maps, we wanted a map of the area.

I had the front desk call a cab and noticed the driver turned on the meter. Most cabs don't and a fare dispute comes at trips end. I knew the fare was 20 Yuan and that's what the meter finally read. We followed the east side of the lake to the center of town, turned right and right again. He knew I was there to shop and dropped me in front of the largest department store in town. I knew better but I went into the store anyway. It's a collection of four or five stores that interconnect to offer a full variety of merchandise. Much like J C Penny or the May Company. Men's, women's and children's clothes, radios, TV's, housewares, furniture, record albums, etc. No embossed laundry bags or maps and the t-shirts are plain white. Just like a regular department store. I retraced the path of the cab, looking in store after store to no avail. I walked back to the road that follows the lakeside to see a huge lawn clock tilted at 45 degrees. There is a rearing metal horse atop and the face and sides of the clock are made of grass. And thousands and thousands of bicycles driving by. A few feet further, at the intersection, was what looked like a blue mail box. Like most signs in China, it was in Chinese and English. Stenciled on the side was Supervisory Impeachment Center, Zhejiang People's Government. In large letters, below that was the simple -Impeachment Box. Interesting concept. Hangzhou (pronounced Hahng'-Joh') has a population of 1,310,000 and a voting way to get rid of the Mayor. Several teenagers stared at me looking at the blue box.

I had to be careful of traffic. Not busses or taxis but a constant flow of bikes. The lane closest to the curb on both sides are reserved for bikes and they are often four abreast. The lake side is enchanting. Maybe the mist in the air added to the imagined intrigue. There are lake side stands with the usual trinkets, food, soda, toys and t-shirts. But the T-shirts are for other towns. Rats! Next to the Impeachment box is a large green building that looks colonial. I'm sure it has a story to tell but I'm on the other side of the road now. Then I spotted a small stand with a map hanging from a clothes pin. I tried to engage the young girl into mandatory bargaining but her father took over. She was amazed that I want a map at all and it got confusing when I asked for two. Her father is not confused- business is business and we bargain. Once again I draw a crowd. Obviously, good looks are appreciated the world over. For $2 I get the two maps, mostly in Chinese but the bridges are named in English. There are a variety of boats for hire and you can barely take 10 steps without being approached. The boat men are polite and speak English (as much as is necessary to complete the transaction).

I continue following the taxi's path back towards the hotel because I saw the International House on my way in. A half mile later, I'm at the last chance. Now or never for the T- shirts and laundry bags. The store is for foreigners only and they have T-shirts. For other towns. No laundry bags at all. I bought a chocolate bar for $1 and 2 oz. Nescafe instant coffee for $2.60. There is only tea back in the room. Now I'm too far out of town for a taxi. The ones that go by have passengers and I have to trek back. Half way, I luck out. This driver doesn't turn on his meter and I know what's coming - whatever price he thinks he can get away with. But I get home, give him 20 Yuan and walk away while he tries to ask for more.

I walk to the edge of the lake and just stand. The green, the drizzle, three pools inside an island in the middle. Its quiet. So pleasant. I didn't get any T-shirts or the laundry bags. But I got the maps. The next day my laundry is returned in a plastic bag. They are taking no chance on the real bag leaving with me.

THE END

## ABOVE THERE IS HEAVEN, BELOW THERE IS HANG ZHOU

HANG ZHOU, CHINA - There was an armed guard at the gate to the compound. It was nine o'clock at night and we just completed a five hour train ride from Shanghai. Eight of us on the tour were met at the train station by a CITS guide, an attractive multi lingual young lady. We climbed in the waiting van and maneuvered through congested streets that were slick from a light rain. Left and right and right and left and twenty minutes later we slowed at the gate to the XI ZI Guest House long enough for the guard to recognize the van and wave us through. We exited at one of the several guest lodges and, to our amazement, the luggage was in the foyer (sent ahead by earlier train). We were given keys to the rooms and our guide said the dining room had been kept open for our late arrival. She left and we were on our own.

The room itself was ordinary, typical of Bachelor Officers Quarters with a full bath and space enough to walk around the double bed without having to turn sideways. The furnishings, however, were not ordinary. A golden silk embroidered comforter covered the bed. The desk and dresser were gorgeous pieces of polished mahogany that one would expect to find in an antique store. A huge, ornately painted thermos of hot water adorned the table next to tea bags and cups. It was heavy enough to beat away an attacking tiger and quickly became a piece coveted by every member of the group. A nine inch television set sat at the corner of the desk. No matter, since both stations were in Chinese.

I quickly learned that the two attendants in the foyer smiled at everyone but spoke not a word of English. Venturing outside into what had become a strong drizzle, it was time to find the dining hall. There are pink tinted street lamps every 75 feet and they cast barely enough light to separate the paved road from the grass. Green grass, deep green trees, a halo around the dim street lights and deadly silence. No birds, no traffic, even the sound of my footsteps were muted by the rain. I walked to the first building with lights and found the disco. Roughly one thousand square feet of dance floor with revolving ceiling lights, hard rock music and no customers. I left.

Fog mixed in with the light rain creating a blanket. I couldn't hear the music 20 feet from the front door. As I walked, a large building loomed straight ahead, barely outlined through the fog. The dining room. Behind its foyer was large room with a tall ceiling, much like the high school gym that doubled as the auditorium. The room was filled with empty tables except one, off to the side, chosen to serve the us latecomers. Seven of us came for supper and the waitress brought plates of food. One per minute. I had a beer, West Lake, in a pint size bottle. I couldn't recognize the contents of the plates and as the commercial says, a lion won't eat what he can't smell, I don't eat what I don't recognize. I had another beer and passed on the food. The bill came for each of us, 20 Yuan. I showed the waitress that I didn't eat (empty plate), hence the bill was too high for me. That made no difference to her. I sat at the table, therefore, my bill was the same as the others. Fortunately, one of our group was born in Beijing and entered into a ten minute discussion with the girl. Eventually, the bill was changed.

Next morning we had a menu in English and Chinese. A simple choice really, English breakfast or Chinese breakfast. I had toast, butter, plum jam, coffee, hot milk for the coffee (the Chinese don't believe in anything cold), 2 eggs, ham the size of a postage stamp, and a peach floating in unidentified liquid. The American breakfast for US$6. Pretty good, actually.

## THE COMPOUND

The Xi Zi is not like a hotel. It's the Chinese equivalent of Camp David and entertains senior officials visiting China. There is a full time Army detachment on the fenced grounds, hence the armed guards. The grounds are quite large and the Army stays on the North side away from the collection of buildings that serve as a hotel when not being used by the Government. In this way they can generate hard cash from tourists. The grounds are beautiful. The lawns and bushes are literally manicured. Each day there are teams of workers on their knees looking for weeds.

There is a main lobby in the building past the disco with the only English speaking residents. Safety deposit boxes, a small gift and sweet shop and the only place you can call a taxi. The town of Hang Zhou sits on the east side of West Lake and the Xi Zi is seven miles away on the south side of the lake. You must phone for a cab.

The grounds are so magnificent, you could spend a peaceful day just sitting on one of the ornate benches at the edge of the lake looking at the island in the middle and listening to the water lap the shore. Or walk past fountains, across vast lawns kept as clean as putting greens, or fish in any of several quiet pools. I listened to the breeze sift through the leaves of the willows at lakeside. In the mist, the quiet, I was in a world of my own.

Aside from the waitress on the first night, the attendants are what you might expect. Pleasant, smiling, helpful (even though they don't understand a word that you are saying, they pay polite attention until you are completely finished). One of the young women from our building deserves particular mention. Tall, trim, immaculately dressed in classic Chinese style. If you were to mold a perfect Oriental face, it was her's. Short black hair, snow white teeth, a complexion of cream and features that would turn heads when she entered a room. The women in our group commented on her stunning looks so it wasn't just one fellows opinion. In China it is not customary to tip but there is a need for books, especially English ones. Having finished one of the several novels carried while traveling, I presented it to her as a gift.

## LING YIN TEMPLE

The Lingyin Si or "Temple of Inspired Seclusion" or "Temple of Soul's Retreat", depending on the translation is reported to be the number one attraction in Hangzhou. We called a taxi from the front desk and negotiated a price beforehand. US$30 round trip and he would wait at the temple. It is located north west of the lake at the foot of Northern Peak, a mountain overlooking West lake and the town. There is very little traffic on the north side of the lake and in no time we were parked among a pack of tour busses. Twenty cents admission to the park and another fifty two cents for the temple. In contrast to the Xi Zi, these grounds were filled with tourists.

The Temple was originally built in 326 AD but was partially destroyed and rebuilt at least 16 times, the last of which was 1956. It might have been devastated for good during the Cultural Revolution except for the intervention of Zhou En Lai. He ordered the temple and the rock sculptures on the face of the opposite cliff saved even though the Buddhist Monks were sent to work in the fields. The walking path follows the mountain stream with the cliff of Fei Lai Feng or "Peak Which Flew Here" across the water, to the left, and the temple to the right. The Temple is of classic Chinese design and houses a 60 foot high carved Buddha. The four pillars on either side of the main door date from 969 AD and are the originals. It is an impressive Temple but more memorable is "The Peak That Flew Here" across the stream. The story goes that an Indian Monk, Hui Li, when visiting the temple in the 3rd century said it looked exactly like one in India and asked when it flew to China. The name stuck. The cliff face is chiseled with over 300 sculptures and graffiti from the10th to the 14th centuries. Convenient bridges allow for easy crossing but the narrow stone steps etched into the rock make for treacherous climbing. There is no apparent organized path and the steps are too narrow for passing. Extreme care should be used. All the carvings are religious and each is unique. There are additional carvings inside the caves close to the entrance. The floors in the caves are smooth rock but there is no light. The cliff side is absolutely fascinating and shouldn't be missed. There is an extensive array of gift shops at the parks entrance with some bargains on locally made goods.

The taxi was waiting and, as seems to be the custom, the driver decided to raise the price after he drove back to the hotel. I gave him the agreed upon price, in exact change and we walked into the lobby as he sat and grumbled. Afterwards, I walked across the quiet grounds to a lakeside bench and listened to the birds and the wind and the water rising and falling on the shore.

THE END

NOTE - "Above there is Heaven, below there is Suzhou and Hangzhou" is one of China's oldest tourist sayings. Street signs, Hotel signs and many business signs are in Chinese with English below. Hang Zhou is also shown as Hangzhou and Hangchow, Xi Zi as Xizi, Ling Yin as Lingyin. I was unable to determine a pattern in using one word or two in formal names, so, like the Chinese, I use both.

# VII EUROPE

Mykonos, Greece

If you want to see some of the finest Greek Temples and still enjoy Italian food, try Southern Sicily.

Taormina, Sicily - stone's throw from a volcano

AGRIGENTO, SICILY - To be honest, I stumbled into Agrigento (ah-gree-jen'-toh) by accident when I signed up for a trip for Sicily. I'd been all over Italy but never this far south and the tour price of $1150 for air, hotel and meals was one I couldn't pass up. I'd never heard of this town and had no idea of the world famous Greek ruins that draw visitors the world over.

## HISTORY

The city was founded by the Greeks in 580 BC and named Akragas. It grew to a population of 200,000 and as a trading center became one of the richest cities in the world. In 480 BC they joined forces with Syracuse to throw the Carthinigians (Northern Africa) out and put all of Sicily into the Greek empire. During this period, there was a prolific construction of Doric temples including the temple of Zeus, one of the largest in the Greek world. This prosperity was not to continue. Akragas was sacked by Carthage in 406 BC and many of the temples were damaged or destroyed.

It suffered again during the defeat of Hannibal by the Romans in 262 BC. The Romans renamed the town Agrigentum and found better use of the coliseums that had been built as theaters by the Greeks. The new entertainment would feature Christians and lions. Sicily was taken by the Normans in 1086 and the name changed to Girgenti, a name it kept till 1927 when it officially became Agrigento. It's now a small town of a little more than 50,000 and one might think it deserved some piece and quiet considering it's violent history. However, Patton landed his liberation troops on the beach here during WWII.

## THE TOUR

Our hotel is at the bottom of a long hill below the train station which marks the center of town. It's a long walk going to town but an easy one on the return. The Greek monuments are flood lit at night and this impressive sight of "The Valley of the Temples" is visible from the hotel grounds which is something to be said for the location.

The valley is close enough to walk to, but we paid for a guided tour and the 50 people on this excursion piled on the bus for just that. Our tour guide looked like a Mafia don from central casting. Black shirt, jacket, pants, black hat, black shoes, dark sunglasses and slowly spoken English with a strong Italian flavor. He really looked like a guy you didn't want to mess with. Not that he would do anything himself, although he wore plenty of clothes in which to hide a gun, he undoubtedly knew people who could take care of a problem.

We met him at our first stop, the National Archaeologist Museum and he seemed well versed on the treasures within. Just behind the museum is the amphitheater seemingly undisturbed for the last 2000 years. The Greeks used this open air arena to perform plays for the local population. The Romans decided otherwise when they took over. It was a coliseum for gladiators and Christians and lions. A few lights and a script and this could be used as a movie set.

The next stop is the Temple of Juno (300-500 BC) that commands a hilltop overlooking the Mediterranean Sea. One long side wall contains all the Doric columns and the connecting arch work. The front and other long side just columns and pieces. It's been re-constructed from the original stones and is quite impressive. Walking directly west is what's left of one of the several catacomb sites but these are different because they are stone monuments above ground. They are on a bluff overlooking the sea, clearly meant for people of stature. Holes in the center of the stones are all that remain (of the remains) after centuries of grave robbers.

At the end of this connecting bluff is the Temple of Concord, the only temple in the region to remain intact. Stunning is too mild a word. All the exterior columns and connecting archwork remain including the massive, carved front arch face. This building is as good as any ancient building you will find in Greece. Our guide spent a considerable time explaining the history of this temple which obviously had a place in his heart.

Now to crawl over a collection of rocks to what remains of the temple of Ercole (only the tall columns), down the hill and across the road to the Sleeping Giant. A fifty foot long statue of a man lying on his back on the ground. The two dozen or so rocks, weighting between 5 and 1,000 pounds each are not held together and rely on gravity to keep their shape. He looks like a buffed Michelin tire guy. Our guide continued with an abundance of information about the structures, the walls, the site and the ancient people that once occupied these grounds.

From the edge of this site, we could see, in the far distance, the remains of the Temple of Jupiter, which was immense when it was built. 340 feet by 120 feet with 60 foot columns. Sadly all that remains are a few tall columns.

As it turns out, our guide, instead of being a local Mafia Don, is a PHD in Archaeology with a special interest in the Greek temples of this area. So much for first impressions.

Our hotel has an auditorium in a separate building in the rear and they arranged for a troop of local teenagers to perform a series of regional dances. Men and women in white shorts and white socks, then guys in black pants and vests. The women in red skirts danced in two's and in mass for an enraptured audience. They sang songs of true love and disappointment -I'm guessing here since it is all in Italian - with their own band playing instruments of long ago. They really put their heart in it and some sweat as well.

There are a series of other short tours included in the price - orientation of the town, visit to the house of Luigi Pirandello (Nobel prize writer and local hero because of the Nobel prize), trip to a quiet village atop another mountain (I mean quiet, our arrival is the most exciting thing for the month), optional full day tour of the city of Taormina (optional means more money and in this case it's well worth it) and a trip to the Patton landing site.

Just a few miles from the hotel is a cliff facing south. Patton came north from Africa. Down the dirt path to the ocean and there's a long, curving, shallow beach of amber sand. We had to hustle as the tide was coming in and the few feet of sand would soon disappear. At the end of this water gauntlet is a German pill box set to watch for the coming invasion. We climbed through the sunken entrance one at a time - that's all that could fit - to look out at the sea through the open square holes cut into the concrete.

And imagine the alarm on the faces of the poor guys seeing thousands of troops landing on the beach in front of them.

Considering the history of this island, the feeling of being over powered by invading forces is nothing new. The Carthaginians, the Greeks, the Romans, the Normans, the Germans and finally the Americans. Hopefully they will now have some peace - except for us pesky tourists.

THE END

## AGRIGENTO SIDEBAR

GETTING THERE - Our Alitalia flight to Rome stopped at Milan in both directions. For fuel or passengers or both, I don't know. Follow the signs for a long walk inside the international terminal to change planes and terminals (international to domestic) for the flight to Palermo, Sicily also on Alitalia. Regular airfare is around $1200 RT from the west coast of the U.S..

There is scheduled bus and train service from Palermo to Agrigento for $10 each way. Takes about 3 hours. A taxi would be over $200, it would be more efficient to rent a car.

WHEN TO GO - Spring and Fall are the most pleasant seasons and not crowded with other tourists. Summer is hot and swarmed with vacationers. Winters will be a bit nippy at night and on overcast days.

WHERE TO STAY - Typical is the Hotel Della Valle, Via La Malfa, 3, Agrigento, Sicily 92100. tel. (0922)26966. 4 stars on a European scale equivalent to maybe 3 stars American for $160/room double and $130/meals/person/day. The Hotel caters to tour groups. Rooms in Palermo and Agrigento are small as are the bathrooms.

It is significantly more cost efficient to be part of a group. Our one week tour included air, all ground transport, hotel, meals and four tours with knowledgeable guides for $1150. That's the cost of the regular airfare alone. For tour information - Italiatour S.p.A., 666 Fifth Ave., N.Y., N.Y. tel. (800) 237-0517 // (800) 845-3365

WHERE TO EAT - There are dozens of nice restaurants within 3 blocks of the train station (center of town). $30-50 depending on your beverage.

FOR MORE INFORMATION - Write to the Italian State Tourist Office (ENIT) in New York at 630 Fifth Ave., Suite 1565, NY, NY tel. (212)245-4822 or in L.A. at 12400 Wilshire Blvd., Suite 550, Los Angeles, CA 90025 tel. (310)820-0098 fax (310)820-6357

The Amalfi coast, is it as picturesque as Big Sur ??

Amalfi Coast, Italy

Trevi Fountain, Rome - throw a coin

AMALFI, ITALY - I've driven the incredible coastline between Santa Barbara and San Francisco several times, in a convertible, with the top down. It's been terrific each and every time. The curving mountain roads, treacherous enough that one moment of day dreaming on a sharp curve can find you and the car going over one of the thousands of cliffs to the jagged rocks below. Rocks serrated by million of years of pounding surf ripping the stone apart at its seams. And if the 200 foot fall doesn't kill you the pounding surf at the bottom will. From the highway, you can see the waves crash into this granite and shoot straight up into the air, testing the power of the rock with each incoming assault. All this from inside the car. Since at some point in the drive I usually find myself stuck behind some motor home driving at a snails pace, it's been easy to see all the action below. Which is one of the drawbacks, the narrow road cut into the side of the cliff. The cramped road adds to the charm but the charm is soon lost if your front view is the back end of a slow moving house trailer. But then, I digress.

The fresh sea air, the mountain pines, the battle between sea and land, a stop at Nepenthe for a drink or a quick lunch (made famous in the movie, "The Sandpiper", Richard Burton and Elizabeth Taylor), the Monterey Peninsula, the 17 mile drive and finally, San Francisco, a destination completely opposite in character to that of the drive.

Our guide said the Amalfi coast was comparable to the one through Big Sur. Right. Like I was born yesterday. This is a side trip added to the ones included on the tour through southern Italy. For an extra $100. So what else can she say, it's a crummy drive. Then no one would go. She added that many of people said the Amalfi tour was the best of all the tours. Humm, we already saw the Vatican, the Coliseum, the Trevi fountain in one day. The ruins of Pompei on another day, the stunning Royal Palace at Caserta on yet another day and the Amalfi coast was going to be better? We have a tall order to fill this time, but like they say, "In for a penny, in for a pound". I signed up.

Lets start with some of the similarities of the Amalfi and Big Sur drives. It's a pain in the neck getting to the road at the start of the drive and once your on it, there's no way off except over the cliff. The views are stunning on both coasts. The rocks, the sea, the trees - if you closed your eyes and opened them again, you could be in either place. I was shocked, it really is that beautiful and adding to the charm of Amalfi are little villages along the way built into the cliff side above the road. Now as for the road, it must have been built as a two lane path wide enough for two Fiats to pass one another going in opposite directions. But we were in a 60 seat Mercedes-Benz touring bus that not only hogged all our side of the road but took some of the other side as well. Add to this, the people that live in the houses built into the cliff above have cars. They can hardly drive them straight up the side of the cliff to a garage. For them there is a four foot apron along the inside of the asphalt and they better look twice before opening the car door.

The Amalfi coast was a powerful maritime republic in the 9th century, annexed by Roger II of Sicily in 1131, sacked by the Pisans in 1135 and again in 1137 and gradually declined as a commercial and naval power. The Italian provinces were not unified back then, as we think of them now, and were constantly at war with each other. The coast has returned to its roots and some of the houses look as though they date back to the 9th century.

Then there is the town of Amalfi (yes there actually is one) and we're talking really charming here. Not modern like Monterey, CA, but old, old city charm. Walking through the city gates is like entering a medieval fort (the bus stays outside). A grand old Cathedral, 11th century, is on the right. The group was funneled to the distillery on the left, where they make lemon liquor, to watch the process of extracting the flavor from the lemon skin by soaking it in alcohol and doing something or other (trade secret), to produce the tasty after dinner drink. I no intention of buying any. We tasted several types of finished product for free. Not bad, actually. The bottles containing the liquor are like art pieces, they could be used as gifts when empty. How could I pass up something so useful that I could recycle when I was finished.

One could spend hours wandering through the variety of colorful shops in the town but it was a long drive home. The bus was going to have a tough time of it now. We stopped for lunch at a roadside cafe (a niche cut into the rock to allow for bus parking) and they have a wonderful shop on the first story filled with local wares (2nd story for food). At least it was full of local wares before our bus arrived. Add to that, the souvenirs from the town of Amalfi and the bus must have weighed as much as a locomotive. As for the best tour of the trip, it's like comparing apples to oranges. Better than the Big Sur coast, I don't know, it's a close call. I'll have to go back to Italy and take the Amalfi in a convertible with the top down. My luck, I'll be behind one of those huge Mercedes-Benz busses and I won't be able to see anything.

THE END

## AMALFI SIDEBAR

GETTING THERE - Rome is serviced by Alitalia with excellent rates when booked with any of a large selection of tours. In my case, a week including hotel, meals and countrywide tours was $1300, including RT air. Rome is serviced by virtually all the major airlines in the world. LAX-ROME economy RT is approximately $ 1000. JFK-ROME is $1000.

WHEN TO GO - Italy is hot in the summer and can be very nippy in the winter. The best times to visit are off season, April-June and September-October when the weather is best, prices are most reasonable and it isn't packed with tourists.

FOR MORE INFORMATION- Write to CIT at 242 Madison Ave.,suite 207, NY, NY 10173 tel.(212)697-2497 / or / 6033 Century Blvd. suite 980, Los Angeles, CA 90045 tel. (310)338-8615. CIT is Italy's national tourist agency.

Going to Portugal without going to Europe - sort of.

THE AZORES are a group of nine islands in the middle of the Atlantic Ocean. Each one is the top of a volcano raising from the ocean floor 19,700 feet below. They are on a weak zone of the Atlantic rift, where it meets the African and Eurasian blocks and are among the youngest island chains in the world. They are roughly 1,500 KM from Lisbon (a 2 hour flight) and 3,900 KM from the east coast of America. OK, not exactly the middle, but close enough.

They are a part of Portugal much like Hawaii is American. One of the biggest differences is that Hawaii has beautiful beaches, the Azores have almost none. People didn't move here until the 15 th century even though the islands were known to exist. The Medici Atlas of 1351 AD shows several of the islands. The first Portuguese to discover the islands saw many birds that reminded them of sparrow-hawks, the Portuguese word for which is acor. It was later found that the birds were buzzards, but the name stuck.

Early settlers were Portuguese, Moorish captives and the Flemish. In the 17 th century, the ones that left the islands mostly went to Brazil. In the 19 th century, many Americans moved here and then the reverse happened. Between 1955 and 1974, 130,000 islanders went to North America. The estimated population now is around 245,000. The main livelihood is farming, largely dairy farming, although they do have the only pineapple farm, under glass, in the world. They also grow tea, tobacco, beets, potatoes and bananas.

Tourism is a major source of revenue, so, why do people come here? Peace and quiet. No pollution. A slower life style. Maybe some whale watching. Other than the Portuguese, the largest group of visitors are Germans and Scandinavians. Considering wintertime weather in Northern Europe, the Azores would look like the Garden of Eden for them. Sao

Miguel island (which has the capital, Ponta Delgata and the international airport) is known as the green island.

Sao Miguel formed in three sections. The eastern third came first. Then the middle and, millions of years later, the western third. So, the geography in each is a little different. There are several tour companies that can be booked from your hotel, but Greenzone specializes in jeep tours. That means they can navigate the rough dirt roads of the back country. They offer three, full day tours on alternate days. You guessed it, the eastern third, the middle and the western third. Each for about $75 US. The jeep can hold eight, but six is a lot more comfortable on some of the rough roads.

I did the western tour first. Up into the mountains and weaving down the snake like road to the rugged coast. The two lane roads are paved and very European. That means that your vehicle can stay on the road as oncoming cars pass by, but, if it's a bus or truck, someone has to hit the shoulder.

On the coast, we spotted one of the two lighthouses from the cliff side parking lot. This one was built in 1901, is well kept and surrounded by 1000 feet of grassland. At the other end of the lot is the view of Ponta da Ferraria. Black lava, at the bottom of the cliff, rolling into the sea like spilled pudding. The ocean waves have been battering the lava since the eruption in 1140 AD.

We drove around the mountain to view this western most protrusion from the other side before turning inland. The short cut to the top. A rutted dirt road that only a jeep could handle. And were we bounced around. And then - Sete Cidades. One of the two landmarks of the islands. Two lakes fill the caldera that they believe was formed in 1440 AD. A caldera is formed after a volcano erupts and the center eventually collapses leaving a hole in the middle. Rain water fills the hole. This one is unusual because there two lakes. The northern one is blue and the southern one is green. From our perch, 1000 feet above sea level, we could see both. They are separated by a sliver of land.

Then onto one of the inland villages and lunch. There is a very pretty church at the end of a 200 foot long walkway, lined with trees on either side. Very Portuguese, very Catholic.

Back to the coast for a unique swimming pool. There is a natural pool formed at the ocean edge, surrounded by rocks and fed by an opening between two of them. Waves crash on the rocks and flow in to fill the pool. They built a concrete sun deck at the far end with steps leading down to the water. No chlorine, no cleaning crew. Nature takes care of that. I wonder if a shark ever swam through the opening? We didn't wait to see, it was time to return to town.

The Capitol is quite modern. I t looks like Lisbon. The architecture of the buildings, the restaurants, the parks, the churches, the Euro. You may as well be in Europe. Well, in fact, you are. The western most part. On the eastern edge of town is an amusement park with hamburger stands (trailers). Hot dogs, candy, soda, beer, wine, etc. You know the drill. Santo Cristo church at the north end with a statue of Mother Teresa in front of a white adobe wall. One hundred feet from the south end of the park, is the fort. Thick rock, two story walls, cannons, muskets. All of which was needed in the days of the sailing ship.

A couple of bucks and you can walk around the fort at your leisure. It won't be on the list of "Top 20 forts in the world" but they do a nice job with what they have. Cannons, uniforms, medals, old pistols.

The next tour was to the middle section of the island and the second landmark, boiling geysers. Our lunch, cosido a portuguesa, took advantage of the boiling water. They bury a large pot (big enough to hold food for six) in land undercut with boiling water and let it steam for several hours. The pot contains beef, chicken, pork, cabbage, potatoes and several root vegetables. Close to the town of Furnas (in the middle of the island), we gathered to watch them dig up the pot. Fifty feet away is a steaming pool, then a geyser next to a steaming lake. And more bubbling water, a five foot geyser that lasts ten seconds. And steam, lots of steam.

We carried the pot to a nearby restaurant where it was overturned onto a large tray and we helped ourselves by picking out the pieces we wanted with forks and spoons. A local custom is for restaurants to offer this dish once a week. It's nourishing and different. Then back to the trail.

We walked through a field of streams, boiling water (at 98 deg. C, because of the elevation), smelled sulphur here and there and spotted green mold at the bottom of a hot stream. Actually, it's bacteria and many believe it's the decedent of the first life form on earth. From this bacteria, millions of years ago, all animals evolved.

On to the tea farm. They grow and package both green and black tea. Naturally, there are samples to taste. And then to the swimming pool. A concrete lined pool next to a hot water stream with concrete, one foot, waterfalls. All fed from geyser water. Soap is not allowed.

Then to a beautiful church on the coast overlooking the sea. Atop a hill, hundreds of steps arranged in a pattern of Z's, with a mosaic every ten feet. Next to the church is a large, empty, cross. No steps leading up here. It's atop a hillside of flowers.

The afternoon was almost gone when we got back to town. Enough time to see the pineapple farm. The only one in the world under glass. The seedlings grow and are replanted in the next greenhouse. It takes two years to get a pineapple this way. But, you do what you have to. There is a gift shop showing 200 ways to eat or drink pineapple, plus jewelry, hats, shirts, etc.

I found a nice café in a square away from the waterfront. I sit outside across from a gothic church that looks 400 years old. The sun is out, the weather is nice. I have a cappuccino and a good book to read. This is why people come to the Azores.

## THE END

## SIDEBAR FOR THE AZORES

GETTING THERE - SATA Internationall has red eye flights, daily, from Boston (BOS) to Ponta Delgata (PDL), the Capital of the Azores. $778 RT for mid week- prices go up for weekend flights. They leave just before midnight and arrive just after 8 AM local time. There are frequent flights to and from Lisbon. Flights to the other islands start at PDL.

WHEN TO GO - The islands have a mild climate, year round. Winter can be chilly and require a jacket. Rain falls every month but doesn't last. It's been said that you can experience all four seasons in one day. Whale watching is between May and September. Best time for flowers is June and July, however, July and August are the high season and hotels are usually full. Tours can be viewed at www.greenzoneazores.com

HOTELS - There is a wide variety to choose from. The Hotels Villa Nova (five years old) and the Hotel Ponta Delgata (one of the originals) are two blocks from the edge of town, three stars and have a rack rate of $220/nite, single. Information can be found at www.azores.com. Booking can be made at 1-800-652-9151. I did air and hotel together and got the hotel at half the published rate.

HEALTH - No shots are needed.

MISCELLANEOUS - These are islands in the middle of the Atlantic ocean. Criminals can't escape. It's safe to walk the streets at night. No VISA for USA citizens.

Barging into France

Eiffel Tower from forbidden zone

NICE, FRANCE - I know, barging into anyplace is rude but this is France. So. Anyway, our tour started with three nights in Nice. A city tour, tour of Monaco and an open day we used to catch a train to Cannes. It's pleasant to mingle with rich tourists and pretend we belong. Then the

560

bus took us to Avignon to board our barge. It would be my first time on a barge and it wasn't what I expected. I figured it would be a long, shallow-draft boat where they took out the coal and put in beds for the tourists. I got some of it right.

The boat was waiting on the River Rhone just outside the stone walls of this fortress city whose origins date back to 4000 BC. The MS Viking Burgundy (one of a fleet of Viking barges) is 360 feet long, 38 feet wide and has a draft of only 5.25 feet. The front 1/3 of the boat (above water) has reception, a small library and reading room, an eight seat circular bar and 90 feet of lounge with a piano towards the front. The crews' quarters are below. The lounge is encircled with a 3 foot wide walkway which doubles as the smoking area and has the stairs to get to the top. In the front of the top deck is the Captains wheelhouse which can sink 3 feet into the deck for low slung bridges. In the tented middle are tables and chairs and the rear is an open sun deck and chairs.

The middle 1/3 has three levels of double rooms and the rear 1/3 has the dining room with machinery and crew quarters below. The rooms seem larger that those on a cruise ship although the bathrooms are about the same. The couches flip 180 degrees to make single beds. I didn't find any coal dust - who knew, that would come later.

After a quick unpacking, we walked to the wall of this ancient city. There are permanent openings now that the Romans have made peace. You just have to look to find one. Avignon is an active, modern city with charm written all over it. Each shop is prettier than the last. Even the grocery stores are handsome and colorful. Two blocks in, there is a huge square with tables, chairs, umbrellas and the French enjoying the outdoors and a glass of wine. Two blocks farther is a Cuban Restaurant with a picture of Che Guevara in the window. Fidel Castro's brother killed years ago in terrorist activities. Imagine trying that in Miami.

A total of 7 Popes took up residence in Avignon in the 14th century and this became the center of Christendom. Eventually the papal court returned to Rome but the French didn't accept it. They continued to elect their own Pope. And each Pope excommunicated the other. Regardless of the ancient intrigue, we spent hours walking the streets and were sad to leave the following day.

A bus picked us up at dockside for a trip to Les Baux, the "Eagles Nest" of the province. This castle city is on the top of a cliff (fantastic view) and was an important village during the middle ages. It was destroyed during the 17th century religious wars and is now a tourist haven with streets and alcoves lined with boutique shops. There's a bit of a hike here, but then, Castle's aren't meant for easy access.

The bus dropped us off in Arles for a tour of the town loved by Vincent Van Gogh. They say he produced some of his best works while living here. It was a thriving city way before Vincent. It was the richest city of the Roman empire after Rome. The Amphitheater built by the Romans is still in use, but now, for bull fights. Then we went to Camarque, a nature preserve on the Mediterranean. It would be an interesting walk if you'd never seen a flamingo.

The Burgandy sailed on while we had soup, salad, an entree, desert (choice of two in each category) and coffee. You could order off the menu (limited choice). The food was always good and the portions moderate so I didn't have to diet for 6 months afterwards. There is a midnight buffet but who's awake to eat it?

The Vivarais Railroad connects Lamastre to Tournon, on the Rhone. It took the bus an hour and 15 minutes to get to Lamastre on winding mountainous roads. The 1 meter gauge track was laid in 1891 and closed in 1968 because of lack of use. It was reopened in 1969 by railway enthusiasts. The full journey back is 2 hours and it's a rough ride. Wood benches, coal residue from the steam engine floats through the open cars and the scenery is routine. There is a constant clickety clack of steel wheels not quite matching the track and a constant smell of gunpowder. Not that they use gunpowder, that's just what it smelled like. There's a pit stop at the half way point and the building and surroundings are quite nice. And the bus will take you back from here, if you choose.

Vienne has been occupied from the 4th century BC. It's loyalty to Rome during the Gallic wars earned it the title of Latin Colony and the people had the rights of Roman citizens. It's been eclipsed by Lyon in modern times but a Roman coliseum remains in use as a reminder of things past. A few blocks down from the coliseum is a huge wall painting. A stage that seems to be there for no particular reason. It's beautifully done - I didn't ask - it must be art.

Lyon is a 2000 year old city listed as a UNESCO World Heritage Site. From the banks of the Rhone, you look left, high atop Fourviere Hill and there's a spectacular Basilica and what appears to be a miniature Eiffel Tower. Fortunately, our bus follows the boat each day and is there for city tours included in the boat tour. The city guides change but the driver doesn't. And we got a ride to the top. The Eiffel Tower is actually Tour Metallique and was built in 1893. There is a wonderful view of the city from atop the hill.

One of the blank building walls in Lyon is painted as a lively building wall. With famous Frenchmen (life size) on the balconies, all looking three dimensional from across the road. At a casual glance, it would look like an apartment house with shops on the ground floor. Impressively done.

We got the silk screening tour and a couple of hours to walk the streets in old town, have a beer and just enjoy the city. Back on the boat we had another leisurely cruise through the wine country. The sun, calm waters, a family of swans going upstream ignoring the boat. If you just wanted to unwind, you could forget the tours and just watch the beautiful countryside go by from the sun deck. With a glass and your own bottle of wine. Unlike cruise ships that search your bags for bottles bought in port, the barge people don't. They will even give you glasses and ice - free.

The bus brought us to a Castle in Chalon-sur-Saone for wine tasting. The following day we went to Beaune - the city of wine. The most famous sight is the 15th century Hotel Dieu founded as a hospital. The inside courtyard is stunning, a stark contrast to what the inside must have been to the poor souls that had to sleep 2 to a bed 600 years ago. Most didn't survive. If your illness didn't get you, your bed mates' would. Naturally, there is a church altar inside. From there we went to a wine shop to boost our spirits. One with an actual wine cellar cave (it seemed like it). We each got a small, shallow, silver tasting cup. A nice souvenir and it sure cuts down on the amount of wine you can taste.

Virtually all of the cities we visited are ones not on the beaten track. When people visit France, they usually hit Paris and the French Riviera. Doing the smaller towns means carrying your bag and searching for a hotel in each new town. That's tiresome. The barge is a better way to go. No packing every day, carrying luggage, worrying about meals or where you're going to stay. You can barge around a little and then lie back on the sun deck. The French countryside is beautiful.

# THE END

## SIDEBAR FOR BARGING

GETTING THERE - There are connecting flights to Nice or Marseille from Paris and most capitals in Europe from NYC, Washington, Boston, Chicago and Los Angeles. $900 RT from the east coast, $1150 RT form the west coast (depending on the season), using United, American, Continental, Delta and any number of foreign airlines.

Viking River Cruises offer a seven day cruise for approx. US$1000/ double tel. 0033-688-243-632, depending on the season. All meals are included on the barge. Ours was a 12 day package for $2900 including RT air from the west coast, transfers, 3 nights hotel in Nice, tour of Nice and Monaco and 8 days on the barge. With the package, there is an optional Paris extension for 3 days/nights for $449. All hotels are 4 * or better.

WHEN TO GO - Summer has the best weather and the most tourists and accommodations may not be available. Millions of French people take their vacation in August and that's a month to avoid. Spring and fall would be better choices.

HOTELS - Nice has hundreds of hotels to choose from. 2 * are about US$50, 4 * are $100-200 double.

HEALTH - Much like most of Europe there are no shots necessary nor any health hazards.

MISCELLANEOUS - For additional information contact the French Tourist offices at 444 Madison Ave., NYC, NY 10020, tel. 212-838-7800, email= info @ francetourism.com.

Cagliari, the capital of Sardinia, had no actual start,
it just sort of came to be.

CAGLIARI, SARDINIA - There were storm clouds overhead blocking direct sunlight and filtering what remained of the indirect light. I got the full effect once I turned the corner from Largo Carlo Felice, the main street in town that leads away from the port, onto Via Sardegna, which runs parallel to the waterfront - one block in. Narrow stone streets, tall stone buildings that would block the light, if there were any to block. I'd stepped back in time to the Middle Ages. The buildings oozed character, medieval character. I wove my way through the alleys barely wide enough for a me and a passing cart. Past quiet stores and Trattorias whose interior lights provided more illumination than the noon day sun. A few blocks farther in are houses, with large sturdy doors (which one might need if Huns were actually wandering the streets). Windows and iron grated balconies start at the second floor and continue upward to the third and fourth stories. The balconies have potted plants and wet laundry- both starving for light. And no people in sight. It's a feel more than anything physical. I loved it and took pictures at every corner half expecting to run into a movie crew with a director shouting, "That's a take".

I was headed, in a zig zag fashion, through the silent, virtually empty, mysteriously shadowed streets, to the piazza Constituzione, the main entrance to the walled city five blocks back from the port. That section is called the Castello and is the only section with fortress walls left standing. The other sections, the Marina between the Castello and the port (through which I was walking) and the Stampace to the left (with the Roman Amphitheater) and Villanova, the residential section to the right, all had their walls demolished in 1860 by royal decree. Finally, the King accepted the petition that the Sardinian people be included in the Italian union. And it was a long torturous route to get to there.

## SOME HISTORY

The guide book says that it's impossible to say that Cagliari can trace it's origin to any one civilization. There is evidence that the Phoenicians began trading settlements in the 8th century BC. But no real city. That started with the Carthaginians (from North Africa) years later. The Romans started building when they took over in 238 BC and the Amphitheater they built remains to this day. Then there was a progression of wars, with the Arabs, the Pisans, the Genoese and the Spanish. Even the English gave it a shot. Lots of shots actually and occupied the city in 1708, only to turn control over to Austria which governed until 1717 when the Spanish stepped back in. Sardinia is the second largest island in the Mediterranean and between Italy and Spain so it's logical that these two countries would take turns at power depending on which country had the strongest forces at the time. Eventually, Italy won but they treated Sardinia like an illegitimate child until the King's decree of 1860. As a note, they say the native Sardinian's were never really defeated by any of the invading armies, they merely retreated into the rugged hills.

There are few open spaces in the city but the piazza Constituzione is one of them. It's at the corner of the Castello, Marina and Villanova sections. The busyness of the intersection is overshadowed by the huge four story wall and impressive double wide stone steps that lead to the bastione S. Remy on top. The bastione is an open stone plaza with a breathtaking view of the city. From here the roof tops seem to merge together giving the city a unity of purpose. And then it rained, no poured. Discretion sent me for cover but I'd be back.

The main street along the waterfront is the via Roma and it's feel is completely different from the alleys behind. Upscale shops face the port and their windows are set back fifteen feet from the street to allow the second story to overhang, so the walkway is protected from the elements. Colorful storefronts and trattorias with sidewalk tables dot the walk which is warm and busy with pedestrians. They sell Armani cologne in the tobacco shop for $45. This is the place for a cappuccino or a Heineken draft, better yet both.

The next morning there was occasional sun and I walked uphill on Carlo Felice. Frankly, any street away from the waterfront is uphill. There are classy stores equivalent to those on Via Roma but the etched glass panels in front of the church of S. Agostino caught my eye. They are beautifully out of place on the street, not in a museum where such stunning artwork is usually protected. At the streets end, I turned left onto via Azuni and found two more churches. There seems to be a church on every corner. Looking back, there is an interesting view - framed by the tall buildings and narrow street - a piece of the walled fortress high above the city. A few blocks on and higher, in front of the hospital, is a better view of the walled fortress looming over the town below. It's the best view of the Castello in town.

A few more blocks (uphill) is the Roman Amphitheater built into the hillside of a natural gorge. It dates from the 2nd century AD and is no longer used to feed Christians to the lions, it's for summer concerts. It's a wonder to see how they built the seats of the theater into the natural hillside. From there, it's only a few blocks to the back gate of the Castello and the stone arched entrance to the museum which used to be the entrance to the Arsenal. Its good to have a map to walk inside these walls since the alleys are more narrow than those in town and the windowless walls seem taller. The streets are quiet enough for me to hear the sound of my own footsteps. The most impressive church is the Cathedral and it's dominating cupola is best seen from the bastione S. Remy. There are 4 more churches within the walls and I wonder if there is population enough to fill these and all the other churches.

That night I tried a glass of Candolini, a clear liquor, at my favorite trattoria, the Daisy bar on via Roma. It was like drinking kerosene. A Heineken draft put out the fire and I wandered among the night food and drink carts along the waterfront. In the daytime this section of via Roma is a flea market of local wares. At night, the trucks are there to cook pasta, fish, hamburgers, what have you.

Modern stores, Medieval city streets, a Roman amphitheater, a walled city, churches on every corner, a flea market and great donuts at a sidewalk trattoria (that's breakfast here). Bring your camera.


## THE END

# CAGLIARI SIDEBAR

GETTING THERE - Rome is serviced by Alitalia with excellent rates when booked with any of a large selection of tours. In my case, a week including hotel, meals and countrywide tours was $1300, including RT air. Rome is serviced by virtually all the major airlines in the world. LAX-ROME economy RT is approximately $ 900. JFK-ROME is $970. There are a dozen flights a day from Rome to Cagliari $220 RT.

WHEN TO GO - Sardinia is hot in the summer and can be very nippy in the winter. The best times to visit are spring and fall when the weather is best, prices are most reasonable and the island isn't packed with tourists.

WHERE TO STAY - The 4 star Hotel Regina Margherita is on a street of the same name, #44. US$ 150 for a double. tel.(070) 670342. The Locada Miramire, Via Roma 59 faces the waterfront and is a modest 1 star for $45. tel (070) 664021

WHAT TO DO - Cagliari is worth a few days of just wandering through the narrow streets of the city proper and the fort on the hilltop. Don't miss the Roman amphitheater and the port for daytime shopping and night time snacking. Cagliari is also a stopping off point for the beaches of Alghero to the NW. Alghero is the most popular tourist resort destination on the island and can be reached from Cagliari by air, train and bus.

FOR MORE INFORMATION- Write to CIT at 242 Madison Ave.,suite 207, NY, NY 10173 tel.(212)697-2497 / or / 6033 Century Blvd. suite 980, Los Angeles, CA 90045 tel. (310)338-8615. CIT is Italy's national tourist agency.

The Canary Islands
It didn't start off with a song

PLAYA DE LAS AMERICAS, TENERIFE, CANARY ISLANDS - I don't book hotel rooms in advance. I don't like to be locked in. Anyway, my guide book said the best bet for finding a room was through an apartment agent in the city. So I located one on the book's map next to one of the few hotels they listed in the downtown area and took a cab from the airport, Tenerife Sur. The island has two airports, Sur and Norte (south and north) and Playa de las Americas, in the south, looked like the action spot on the island.

The agents office was 2 flights up and the cab was long gone when I saw the closed sign on the door. So I went to the backup, the hotel next door. It was full. As was the one, up the street, they directed me to. And the one after that, and the next and the next. Hotel lobbies seem to be two flights up from the street and I was beat from lugging my bag up and down the stairs. It was starting to dawn on me. Winter in America is winter in Europe and people all over like to vacation in the sun. It is Saturday night, the sun has set, all the hotels are booked and I'm tired.

Some cab drivers were standing around gabbing and I got one that spoke English. He confirmed that all the hotels were full but he would make a call on his cell phone to see if a place out of town had a room. And that's how I ended up at the Hotel Monica Sur in Isidro next to the airport. That's right, a taxi ride back to the airport. A modest 3 * hotel, the best in town.

I found a travel agent's office the next morning but it's Sunday and they're closed. Oh well, there is a nice bar on the corner and I have a book to read.

I was at the travel office first thing the next morning. All the tours had already left for the day. I asked, "To have a tour today I would have had to book on last Friday - yes?" Answer, "Yes". It figures, I was in the USA on Friday. Oh well, I booked La Gomera (US$46) and the island tour (US$25). Back to the bar and a book. Fortunately, I brought several paperbacks.

The morning pick up was 7 AM at the no name gas station across the bridge on the other side of the highway. 3/4 mile walk and no sidewalks. It is dark at this hour of the morning and I was glad to have made it without becoming a trucks hood ornament. Two donuts and coffee for breakfast (hotel dining room doesn't open till 8) and the bus came. To the pier in Playa after switching busses and off we went. Playa de las Americas is a beautiful sight from the boat at sun rise. No wonder all the rooms were taken.

La Gomera is the least inhabited of the 7 Canary islands. It's round and 1 ½ hours west of Tenerife by boat. Christopher Columbus loaded his 3 boats with food, timber and water and set off on September 6, 1492 to find the West Indies. We all know the rest. The Capital, San Sebastian, wasn't much of a town then. In 1488 the Spanish Governor of Gran Canaria put down an insurrection and in retaliation executed all the males over 15, handed the women to the army and sold the children as slaves. The fortunes of the city improved after Columbus with the subsequent boom in transatlantic trade.

We drove up the hill, through 2 tunnels, into the clouds and back down to the fertile north side. These islands are all the tops of volcanos so it's either up, down or you're on the coast. Our break was at a restaurant featuring a demonstration of the islands whistle language. They switched a hat, glasses and a camera among the crowd of tourists and a girl from the kitchen found what belonged to who from the bartender's whistles alone. Very interesting.

Back to the bus and viewed terraced houses, stone walls, a wind vane on a stone hut atop a hill, a town protected from the wind by steep cliffs and time for lunch. Potato and green leaf soup plus chunks of beef /tuna, a small potato, wine and a banana. There's a national park in the middle of the island and it's the only place with a real grouping of trees.

There was time to walk around the capital and see the Torre del Conde where the wife of the ill fated Governor barricaded herself in 1488 during the insurrection. The only building preserved since that time.

The next morning is the same gauntlet to the no name gas station across the highway. After a gas station/gift shop/donut and coffee stop, we headed to the center of the island and the Roques de Garcia. A desolate place without a blade of grass in sight. The weird shapes are the result of erosion of old volcanic dikes. One of the James Bond movies filmed scenes here. The Roque Cinchado is eroding at the base faster than at the top and should soon topple over. Right now it seems to be giving us all the finger. There is a cable car to the nearby mountain top but we didn't have the time. The bus dropped us off in Puerto de la Cruz, a charming town with a different restaurant every 50 feet. I would have liked to have stayed here but it's too late now.

The next day was a cab north to Santa Cruz de Tenerife (home to the airport north) and a ferry ride east to Gran Canaria Island. It's a short walk from the ferry depot to town but buildings block the view. So I waited 45 minutes for a 5 minute cab ride and he dropped me off at the wrong place. Then my map didn't correspond to the street signs and it started to rain. All ended well when I stumbled upon the Apartmentos Marmoral one block from the beach. A room with a kitchen, big bathroom, enclosed patio and only 1 block from a grocery store. All for US$ 36/nite. Fortune was shining on me even though the sun wasn't. Las Palmas, the capital of this round island sits at 1 o'clock. The airport is around 3 o'clock and the high rollers go to Playa del Ingles which is at 6 o'clock. Las Palmas is the big city and is reminiscent of Miami Beach. Tall buildings (hotels) facing the long curving beach laced with both fancy and fast food restaurants, arcades, gift shops, boardwalk tables with umbrellas, kids running about, women in bikinis and middle aged men in speedos. People are the same the world over. They come here to rest and relax in the sun. The Vegueta section (Las Palmas south) is 20 minutes away by car or bus and is the upscale shopping center of the area. Rodeo Drive with Spanish prices and well worth a visit whether you're buying or just window shopping. Las Palmas is a place to relax. So I did.

# THE END

## SIDEBAR FOR CANARY

GETTING THERE - There are connecting flights through Madrid to Tenerife south or north and Aeropuerto de Grande on Gran Canaria for approx. $950 from the west coast of the US, $500 from the east coast. Iberia has the best schedule from Madrid to the Canaries. Madrid is serviced by all the major US carriers.

WHEN TO GO - The islands are packed during the winter season with Europeans seeking some sun. The Canaries are off the coast of Africa but still a province of Spain, hence Europe.

HOTELS - Both Tenerife and Gran Canaria are packed with hotels and prices range from $30/nite to $3000/nite. The apartment booking agents for Playa de las Americas are Tenerife Holiday rents tel. 922 79 58 18, Custom Holidays tel. 922 79 60 00, and Markus Management tel. 922 75 10 64.

HEALTH - Much like any province of Spain there are no shots necessary nor any health hazards.

MISCELLANEOUS - No visas required. For additional information contact the Spanish tourist offices at 666 Fifth Ave, 35th Fl., NY, NY 10103, tel. 212-265-8822, email= oetny@tourspain.es or 8383 Wilshire Blvd., Ste. 960, Beverly Hills, CA 90211, tel. 323-658-7188, email = oetla@tourspain.es.

Cascais
There's more to Portugal than Lisbon


CASCAIS, PORTUGAL - The transformation of Cascais began in 1870 when the Royal court came for the summer bringing a collection of nobility in it's trail. Now it's the liveliest beach resort on the coast and attracts an international crowd. It's upscale and charming and everything is within easy walking distance since it's a small town with a population of 30,000. This former fishing village is 30 minutes east of Lisbon by train or car. Yes east, since Lisbon, the capital, is inside the port and not on the Atlantic Ocean.

We arrived by bus from Lisbon in the late morning, unpacked and it was time to explore, but first, lunch at one of the many open air squares. I got into a conversation with the waiter about wine. He boasted that Portugese wine was the best in the world and he had a bottle of Portugese wine for 1.5 million escudos. Upon seeing my raised eyebrow he went inside while we browsed the menus. He returned and proudly displayed the US$707 bottle, balancing it on his palm. It was a very nice lunch, even without wine.

The first day trip was to Sintra, about 30 minutes north by car or bus. Another small town (pop. 20,000) but built on a mountain slope. The Sintra National Palace is of Moorish origins is in the center and well worth a visit. There are gardens, parks and other castles if you wanted to spend a day but just walking the cobbled streets and the enjoying the spectacular mountaintop views were enough for me.

We took a cab to the Casino in Estoril (15 minutes west) and watched the high rollers help the local economy. Sunset that night was a stunning crimson. The Royal court couldn't have had it better.

Cabo da Roca is 20 KM northwest of Cascais and is the western most point of continental Europe. A sheer cliff almost 500 feet above a roaring sea and draws every tour bus in the area. Continuing north we stopped at Obidos, a hilltop fortified village entirely enclosed by stone walls. There are 9 churches for a population of 500 and tourist shops line the stone streets. If you're a shopper this is a must stop.

Continuing north we stopped at Nazare for lunch with a seaside view. This town is packed during the summer with tour busses and people trying to get a tan. It's a good place for seafood and best to visit anytime other than summer.

We turned inland to Fatima and if I thought Nazare ever had a tourist problem I was in for an awakening. On May 13, 1917 three shepherd children were tending their flock and said they saw an apparition of the Virgin. The 10 year old, Lucia, claimed the Virgin Mary spoke to her and asked them to return on the 13th of each month for the next 6 months. Naturally, the word spread and by October 13 there were 70,000 devotees gathered. What happened then is called the Miracle of the Sun - intense lights shot from the sun followed by the miraculous cure of disabilities and illnesses suffered by some of the spectators. Apparently the Virgin gave Lucia several messages: one described the hell that resulted from the sins of the flesh and implored the faithful to pray and make sacrifices to secure peace. Another claimed that if her request was heeded Russia would be converted and there would be peace. The third remained secret until 2000, known only by successive Popes. In that year Pope John Paul II revealed the third message before a crowd of a half million. A vision written down by Lucia those many years ago. It had predicted the attempt on the Pope's life in 1981. At the time, the Pope had insisted, mysteriously, that the Lady of Fatima had saved his life and in 2000 he cleared up the mystery. After the recovery, he had the bullet that wounded him welded into the crown on the Virgin's statue in Fatima.

Believe what you wish but Fatima now rivals Lourdes in popularity and is visited by 4 million pilgrims each year. And naturally there are shops for the visitors. There are statues of the Virgin from less than 1 inch to life size. In plaster, wood, painted, unpainted, with the family, with the baby, by herself, praying, not praying, crowned or not, standing, kneeling, sitting, you name it. And each of the hundreds of stands offer similar if not identical, tasteless souvenirs. It's difficult maintaining a feeling of religious reverence after seeing such a gaudy display. Never the less, there are those who do. Around the corner from the displays is a stand where the devoted light candles and it's a virtual bonfire of flames. Some circle a statue of the Virgin at the Capela das Aparicoes (Chapel of the Apparitions), the site where the Virgin appeared, on their knees.

Eight masses a day are held at the huge Basilica, 1953, wherein lie the tombs of two of the three apparition children who later died in the flu epidemic of 1919-20. Lucia entered a convent in 1928 and was 93 in 2000. The Basilica is a stunning monument befitting the devotion of the true worshipers who visit the site and the church the Virgin had asked for in 1917. Whether you believe or not, Fatima is worth a visit and if you said a silent prayer, it couldn't hurt.

THE END

## SIDEBAR FOR CASCAIS

GETTING THERE - There are direct flights to Lisbon from NYC, Washington, Boston and Los Angeles. $900 RT from the east coast, $1150 RT form the west coast, using Continental, Delta and Air Portugal. Cascais is 30 minutes by train from Lisbon. There is hourly service from the Lisbon Airport (50 minute ride).

WHEN TO GO - Temperatures are mild year round equivalent to the coastal regions of North Carolina. Cascais is a resort town and is busy during weekends, holidays, July and August.

HOTELS - Albergaria Valbom, tel 214.865.801, Residencial Solar Dom Carlos, tel 214.828.115 and Hotel Apartamento Ecuador, tel 214.840.524 all go for approx US$80 double. Casa da Pergola, tel 214.840.040 is US$90.

HEALTH - Much like most of Europe there are no shots necessary nor any health hazards.

MISCELLANEOUS - For additional information contact the Portuguese Tourist offices at 590 Fifth Ave, 4th Fl., NYC, NY 10036-4785, tel. 212-354-4403, email= tourism@portugal.org.

Corsica
The birthplace of Napoleon Bonaparte


BASTIA, CORSICA - The taxi ride from the airport to town cost me more than the price of the four hour boat trip from the mainland of France would have. Had I taken the boat, of course. Who knew. Not that the cab driver was taking me for a ride, so to speak. His meter was on and he was driving fast. So fast I figured he was trying to squeeze in another fare after dropping me off, but, after 45 minutes went by, I guessed he just wanted to get home for supper.

Bastia has France's 5th busiest airport and is the business and commercial center of Corsica. But, there isn't a whole lot to see or do and I'm here to catch the train. Specifically, to Corte, a fortified town in the geographical center of the island and on to Ajaccio the birthplace of Napoleon. There isn't much RR track on Corsica so it should be easy. Bastia is located at about 1 o'clock, Corte in the middle and Ajaccio at about 8 o'clock. There is a RR spur just north of Corte but that's it for rail lines. I checked it to the hotel in the middle of town and the clerk gave me directions to the train station, 200 meters west of the town square and I found it before pizza, beer and bed.

Breakfast was French. Bread, butter, OJ, coffee. I talked with some travelers at the next table. Two from the UK and two Canadians. The Canadian fellow had hit the beach at Ajaccio 60 years ago and lost two front teeth. The British Army told him to tough it out but the Americans replaced the teeth for him and he's had warm feelings for Americans ever since. They were taking my trip in reverse and were about to leave for Nice. The Brits said the four get together every year and decided on Corsica because Florida had become too expensive.

The train schedule is posted on the wall of the station and I'd jotted it down the night before so I got there with time to spare. US $10 for the 2 ½ hour ride to Corte. It's a narrow gaged single track going over and through rugged country with scenery that's interesting but not spectacular. The beauty is that there is a railroad at all since the towns along the way are so small you might not see them if the train didn't stop. And sometimes I didn't see the town even after the train did stop. There is a continental divide running down the middle of the island and Corte is on it. With a population of nearly 7,000 it's the biggest city for miles around.

In 1755 Pasquale Paoli led Corsica to independence and made Corte, the Capital. A good choice since it's ringed with mountains and tough for any Army to get to. Never the less, France took over in 1769. Still it's the least touristy town on the island and a good place for hikers.

I had a tight schedule which is why I flew into Bastia from Nice and was scheduled to fly from Ajaccio to Marseille. The boat to Bastia would eat up most of a day and boat from Ajaccio was and overnighter. I had one night in Corte and one in Ajaccio.

From the front of the train station, the fortified town sits atop a hill in the distance to the right. I followed the signs to the left for the HR Hotel. It was close and it advertised. The University, founded in 1769, is directly across the street from the hotel so after checking in, I took the road into the University. It came to a dead end at the back of the campus but there are long steps downhill to the bridge that crosses the river bisecting the town, long steps up the embankment on the far side to narrow stone roads in a city of mortar and rock. It's a beautiful view. Both sides of the river are lined with trees and high above, in the distance, is the 15th century Citadelle overlooking the city and the Chateau (called the Eagle's Nest), the highest part, built in 1419. It looked miles away and if I were a hiker, this is where I'd start. Too much climbing for me.

The Gorges de la Restonica is a deep valley cut through the middle of town by the Reastonica River. The University and business section are on this side, the old town on the other. I returned to the main road, turned right and found the Corsican version of Wal-Mart. Canned food, fresh meat, hats, bicycles, you name it. And entertainment at the entrance. An accordion and violin duo playing the French version of Frank Sinatra's "I did it my way".

Continuing north (sort of) the road curved and a bridge linked the new town to the old without climbing up and down the embankment. On the left is an old, abandoned, stone house on the river's edge. It has vine covered stone walls, missing doorways and a grass covered roof on the sunlit side. The green grass stands out as an bright accessory to the monochromic grey of the walls. It faces the clear water frothing over round stones washed down from the mountains. If these walls could talk, the stories they could tell.

On the far side of the bridge are six story, stone houses on steep hills surrounded by rock walls. Everything was up from here. I followed the road to the left, took the first dirt road on the right and found myself in the rear of the Chateau. The same one that seemed miles away from the University and too far for a leisurely walk. I looked up the steep hill to the top and wondered about the men that must have climbed it with sword and armor. Only to make it half way before the arrows hit.

As I got back to the hotel I noticed a trailer parked off the street directly across from the hotel. The side window was open for the sale of pizza and I glanced in. Ovens on the inside and a menu on the outside. Why not, I ordered one to go. Actually all the pizzas are to go since there are no tables or chairs. During the 20 minute wait, a half dozen cars stopped to pick up their order. Apparently this is a thriving business. Why not, with such low overhead. US $6 is a good size for one person.

The next day, Sunday, the train station was locked. The 8:38 AM train didn't come. People in the bakery attached to the train station didn't have a clue about why not but the man in the nearby magazine store got the information from a customer. In passable English he said the station would open at 9 AM. There are helpful people the world over if you just keep trying. I forgot it was Sunday and the schedule is different on weekends.

Sixteen stops later I got off at noon, thankful there was a train at all. The Hotel Kalliste is located on the main street and there are signs on the street giving directions. It was closed for renovation. Thank you signs. I walked back towards the station thinking I missed a sign for another hotel. That was a mistake, there weren't any. The town looked small on my map and with a population of only 53,000, how long could the main street be. Well, I found out. The first reasonable looking accommodation was 2 blocks off the main street and at the far end. I was wearing down the wheels on my carry on suitcase.

The claim to fame for Ajaccio is that Napoleon was born here. You don't have to be a rocket scientist to figure that out if you walk the main street. Right next to the Café Napoleon sign is another establishment sign - Bonaparte. I was staying at the Hotel Napoleon. Three blocks south is a waterfront park with a fountain statue of, that's right, Napoleon. The harbor has fishing boats, pleasure craft and the overnight cruise ship waiting for boarding. Sandwiched between the main street, Cours Napoleon, and the waterfront, is the most interesting street, rue du Cardinal Fesch. It's a good fifty feet lower and connected by several steep alleys and has real character. The main street has the neon signs and Cartier watches but Cardinal Fesch has restaurants and shops that are more French than flash.

A guest at the hotel helped arrange a 5 AM breakfast and taxi call for my early morning departure. The staff spoke no English. I mention this because in each of the 3 cities I visited in Corsica the local French people went out of their way to help.

The Ajaccio airport is new and modern. On the plane I sat next to a dog. The owner was a very attractive, young French girl. Her poodle was in her lap-held carry-on.

THE END

## SIDEBAR FOR CORSICA

GETTING THERE - There are connecting flights to Nice or Marseille from Paris and most capitals in Europe from NYC, Washington, Boston, Chicago and Los Angeles. $900 RT from the east coast, $1150 RT form the west coast (depending on the season), using United, American, Continental, Delta and any number of foreign airlines. Ferries link Bastia and Ajaccio to Nice and Marseille at least daily. The boat takes 4 hours from Nice to Bastia and overnight from Ajaccio to Marseille. Air France has frequent flights to both Bastia (1 hour) and Ajaccio (1hour 10 minutes). The airfare for Nice - Bastia & Ajaccio - Marseille is approximately US$ 140. The boat price is half that. The train from Bastia to Corte is US$ 10 for a 2 ½ hour ride and the train from Corte to Ajaccio is the same. Train schedules are posted on the wall at the train station.

WHEN TO GO - Although Corsica is in the Mediterranean it can get nippy during the winter months. Especially in the mountainous interior. Summer has the best weather and the most tourists and accommodations may not be available. Millions of French people take their vacation in August and that's a month to avoid.

HOTELS - In Bastia - Hotel Le Riviera tel. 04 95 31 07 16 and Hotel Central tel. 04 95 31 71 12 have basic rooms for US$ 40s/60 double, the Hotel Napoleon tel. 04 95 31 60 30 is US$ 60s/90d. All are centrally located and prices rise in the summer. In Corte - Hotel HR, close to the train station (turn left and follow the signs), tel. 04 95 45 11 11, has simple rooms for US$ 35s/65d, Hotel de la Poste, tel. 04 95 46 01 37, has basic rooms for US$ 45s/65d. In Ajaccio - Hotel Kalliste tel. 04 95 51 34 45 has renovated rooms for US$ 50s/70d and is close to the train station. At the far end of town is the Hotel Napoleon for US$ 60s/90d.

HEALTH - Much like most of Europe there are no shots necessary nor any health hazards.

MISCELLANEOUS - For additional information contact the French Tourist offices at 444 Madison Ave., NYC, NY 10020, tel. 212-838-7800, email= info @ francetourism.com.

Hello Dali, well, hello Dali
The museum is off the beaten path, but then, so is Salvador Dali

Dali Museum, Spain

FIGUERES, SPAIN - I was in my way from Marseille, at the western end of the French Riviera, to Barcelona, on the Costa del Sol, by train. A friend told me that the Dali museum is just north of Barcelona, in a town close to the French border. Since I would be going through the town anyway, I figured why not stop. I did, and that was the easy part. An hour later I was ready to leave.

I used logic and reason instead of proper planning. There are always reasonably priced accommodations around the train station, so I got off the train and started to walk. Diagonally across the park just outside the station. Another block to the dead end and right for ½ a block. I was at the bottom of a rectangular park with a open stall food market in the middle. I walked the long side to the end and had a choice. I picked left and found out later - that was my mistake. I wheeled my suitcase for 45 minutes through a business section with no hotels. None. I circled back to the train station and got a cab. I gave him the one hotel name that I knew. A cheap one. He drove to the same park I walked an hour before but he crossed at the bottom, made a left, then right, then left, another left, a right, drove around the block, up an alley and stopped. I got out not having a clue which way the train station was. Six Euros and off he went. And no one answered the doorbell. That's when I'd had it. Time to get a train to the next town.

I got directions from a bakery a block away. Fifteen minutes later, I was wheeling my bag on a pedestrian only walkway in an upscale shopping area. Two squares later (the town is filled with squares) and a real street and no taxi to be seen. But, across the way, the Hotel Rambla. I didn't know it at the time, but, if I made a right turn an hour and a half ago (at the other square) and walked a block, I would have been 75 feet from the Rambla.

Salvador Dali was born in this town on May 11, 1904, the son of a prosperous notary. He went to art school in Madrid and refused to sit for the final exams. He was expelled and didn't care. His father did and disowned him. Undeterred, he had his first one man show in Barcelona in 1925. International recognition came at the Carnegie International Exhibition in Pittsburgh in 1928. He joined the French Surrealist Group the following year and met Gala, the wife of poet Paul Eluard. Gala stayed with Dali for the rest of her life.

They escaped WWII living in the United States from 1940-48. He returned to Figueres and opened the museum in 1974 living in an apartment next door. He died in 1989 two years after his wife Gala.. He is the only artist to have 2 separate museums dedicated to his works during his lifetime. The other is in Florida.

The museum is 3 blocks from the Rambla and the art exhibit starts outside. Dali was a strange looking man so it comes as no surprise that the castle-like museum is different. The top of the walls are adorned with statues and egg sculptures. The statue in the front courtyard seems to be covered in workman's cloth signifying repair. It's not cloth and it's permanent. Around the corner is a huge head in a glass case with a TV set on it's forehead.

Just inside the front door of the museum is an interior courtyard with a 1941 black Cadillac convertible with a white top and a full size statue of a fat woman perched on the hood. And opera music. Directly ahead, through 2 story plate glass windows is 2 story wall sized mural illuminated by a wire meshed, globe sized, roof mounted skylight. This interior two story room, houses several works of art including the painting that looks like a naked woman up close and President Lincoln from a distance. The rest of the museum is on 2 floors. If there is an explanation for Dali's paintings and statues, I don't have it.

Girona is a big city, half hour south of Figueres by train. A river cuts through the middle and the old town is on the far side. Just follow the street signs from the train station. Narrow medieval streets, a Cathedral atop what seems like 100 steps, stone walls, turrets. The only thing lacking are the cannons. It's a pleasant way to spend a half day and can be done to or from the train Figueres - Barcelona.

I spent another day in Figueres and window shopped with thousands of others. It reminded me of Rodeo Drive in Beverly Hills. Beautiful, well kept shops with the goods from the best of brand names. And across from the Hotel Rambla is the Hotel Paris and it's huge outdoor café. It's a charming town and even though I don't understand Dali's work, I'm glad I stayed and saw it.

THE END

SIDEBAR FOR DALI

GETTING THERE - There are direct flights to Madrid from NYC, Washington, Boston, Atlanta, Chicago and Los Angeles and hourly flights from Madrid to Barcelona. $900 RT from the east coast, $1150 RT form the west coast (depending on the season), using United, American, Continental, Delta and any number of foreign airlines. The train from Barcelona to Figueres is US$ 15 for a 1 ½ hour ride each way. Figueres to Girona is ½ hour. You can get off the train in Girona going to or from Figueres.

WHEN TO GO - Although Barcelona is on the Mediterranean it can get nippy during the winter months. Summer has the best weather and the most tourists but accommodations may not be available.

HOTELS - In Barcelona, there are hundreds of hotels to chose from. In Figueres, there's the Hotel Rambla with nice rooms for US$ 45s/75 double, tel. 34(0)972 676-020, fax 34(0)972 676-019, www.hotelrambla. net, the Hotel Ronda, US$ 35s/45d, tel. 972 503-911, fax 972 501-682, email = info@hotelronda.com, the Hotel Pirineos, US$ 50s/60d, tel. 972 500-312, fax 972 500-766.

HEALTH - Much like most of Europe there are no shots necessary nor any health hazards.

MISCELLANEOUS - For additional information contact the Spanish Tourist offices at 666 Fifth Ave, 35th floor, NYC, NY 10103, tel. 212-265-8822, email= oetny@ tourspain.es

Twelve days on the Danube - from Vienna to Bucharest
and onto Dracula's Castle in Transylvania

Dracula's Castle, Transylvania

Band on Charles Bridge, Prague

VIENNA, AUSTRIA - Three tour groups collected on the MV Carpati, an older ship of Romanian registry, docked on the Danube. One group based in California, another from Virginia and the third from Israel. Two busses were used at each port call for city tours and we were off for our first half day tour in Vienna. The most unusual place in town is Hundertwasserhaus, a collection of buildings originally designed by Friedensreich Hundertwasser to house his own works of art. It's something else now. Colored ceramics, uneven floors, irregular corners and grass on the roof. It looks like a building contractor made every mistake in the book, said that's the way it's supposed to be and the people bought it. I've never seen anything quite like it and, as they say, beauty is in the eye of the beholder.

The tour offered afternoon trips for an extra fee at most of the ports but many of us chose to use the time to explore on our own. On the main shopping street, we saw a group of Indians selling their wares. Leather clothing, handmade trinkets, full feathered hats and books on Indian culture. It was chilly but the men were bare chested. Turns out they are Peruvian Indians, speaking German, selling hand made jewelry and garments on an open mall in Austria. Go figure.

We woke up the next day in Bratislava, Slovakia. A morning walking tour of this upscale, charming port shows what restoration dollars can do. Busses brought us to St. Martin's Cathedral overlooking the city. This was a frontier post for the Roman Empire from the 1st to the 5th centuries. The walk back to the boat is downhill, through Michael's Gate and past the 13th century Michael's Tower, past the building where Mozart had a concert at the age of six and a bronze workman climbing out of a manhole. The boat left this appealing city at 2 PM to arrive at Budapest in 7 AM.

It is, or was, two separate cities. Buda and Pest. Flat lands on one side of the Danube and the hills of Buda on the other. The morning tour started at Hero's Square, a monument to celebrate Hungary's uprising against the Russians. Still in Pest, we drive by the impressive, and huge, neo-Gothic Parliament building next to the Danube. No time to stop and it's across the river to St. Stephen's Church and Fisherman's Bastion high atop the hill in Buda. This view of much of Buda and all of Pest is spectacular. And the Parliament building is just as impressive from across the river.

The next day is Sunday so most shops are closed. Austria, Slovakia, Hungary and the, to be visited, Serbia, Bulgaria and Romania, all have their own currency. They don't want dollars and only Austria uses the Euro, so shopping is difficult. But, today we get a bus trip to Szentendre (St. Andre in English), 14 miles out of town. An artist colony with open shops that will take dollars and Euros. And it's a pretty town to boot.

Next day it's Kalosca, Hungary and the Paprika Museum and one of the prettiest train stations in Europe. And off to Novi Sad, Serbia to walk the streets at our leisure. An attractive but not memorable town. And off to Belgrade the Capital of Serbia and we start at the Kalemegdan Fortress. The moat is now filled with artillery guns and tanks from WWI. The fort has a commanding view of the river and town far below. That afternoon is one of the highlights of the trip, lunch at a farm house, one hours drive from town. The best food on the trip and no end to the bottles of wine. Family members supply live music and even the sober guests dance around the yard. A delightful time.

The following day we pass through the locks of Djerdap, the largest European hydroelectric dam. It's the major supplier of electricity for Romania and Bulgaria. A thirty meter drop for our boat. That afternoon we're at the Turnu Severin Museum of Ancient History. This is the actual site where Emperor Trajan built a one kilometer bridge across the Danube in 153 AD. The museum is on the site of Roman ruins that housed Trajan's armies. The next day the boat docks at Giurgiu, Romania for a bus ride to Bucharest and the famous/infamous "Peoples House", the second largest building in the world. It has 12 stories, 4 underground levels and 1100 rooms. It took 20,000 forced laborers and 700 architects to complete. It almost bankrupted the country and only the death of the Dictator stopped it from becoming the largest.

In the morning we are off to Transylvania with a stop at the absolutely captivating mountain village of Sinaia and the magnificent Peles Castle.

This was the summer residence for Romanian Royalty. Back on the bus for Brasov, home of Dracula's Castle. That's Drrac (roll the r) - u - la. All right, Vlad the Impaler didn't actually live here, but he may have visited. He did live close-by. And yes, he was a bad dude. He lined the roadside with 20,000 impaled bodies of the invading Turkish Army in 1462. Physiological warfare that worked. The Turks were intimidated and withdrew. But then Vlad the conqueror used the same impalement methods on his own people to stay in power. And there really isn't a vampire named Count Dracula. But if there was, this 1377 AD Castle would be his. It was an overcast day. Dark clouds, no sun, trees without leaves and a foreboding castle atop a mountain of rock. Add lightening and this is the movie set.

There is a courtyard in the center, not a big one, but you need it to keep your bearing. Lots of small rooms, furnished with antiques, narrow stone staircases and if it weren't for the arrow signs you would get lost in this maze of connecting rooms. The inside is beautiful, in a scary sort of way. The outside is just - scary.

At the bottom of the hill are Dracula shirts, mugs, tablecloths, dolls, plaques, masks and a collection of knives and swords that would alarm any airport security system. That night is a dinner at the wine cellar in Brasov. Good food and enough wine to assure all a good nights sleep.

Unless you thought about that Castle on the hill and heads on a stake.

THE END

## SIDEBAR FOR DANUBE


GETTING THERE - Arranged through Value World Tours, 17220 Newhope Street, #203, Fountain Valley, CA 92708. www.rivercruises.net tel=800-795-1633

WHEN TO GO - Spring and fall avoids the crowds but the nights can be nippy enough to require four layers of clothing. Summer has the best weather and the most tourists.

BOAT - There are a wide selection of boats that do the Danube, from basic to deluxe. Our boat was considered a 3 star and will not be used by World Tours again. They plan to use a newer boat with more amenities. The selection of what boat can be what you are willing to pay for.

HEALTH - Much like most of Europe there are no shots necessary nor any health hazards.

MISCELLANEOUS - The Dracula Extension for 4 days was an add on to the normal boat trip. The flight out connected in Prague, Czech Republic and several people stayed on in Prague for a few days.

Tallinn, the most charming Capital in Europe

Tallinn, Estonia - is not at all what I expected. Under Communist rule from the end of WWII to 1991, I figured on a country struggling to make it's way up from the third world. Cheap prices, old buildings and a place where the Finnish came for weekend shopping. Well, I got the last part right.

The hydrofoil ride from Helsinki took 1 ½ hours and it took almost as long again to get through passport control. A half hour later and we were at the Tourist Center in Old Town and I was already impressed. Clean, cobble stone streets, well kept, colorful buildings done in Medieval style. If the people then only had it so good. Everything looked so nice, it was a storybook world. I should have known the prices wouldn't be bargain basement and our visit to the tourist center confirmed it.

Hotel prices went down as you moved away from Old Town. We settled for a place within easy walking distance. It looked like 4 blocks on the free map they gave us. However, maps are deceiving, like the side view mirror in the car. Distances may be longer than they appear. And the map didn't show the walk was all uphill.

We freshened up and it was time to go back to Old Town, stopping at Toompea Hill, which used to house Toompea Castle overlooking the town. Actually, it was on the way, downhill. The original 1219 Danish Castle is no more but some walls and towers remain. Just inside the gate is the beautiful, 19th century Russian Orthodox Alexsander Nevski Cathedral on one side of a large plaza. The stone walls of what used to be a fort encircle, gift shops, old stone buildings and classy restaurants. A casual walk through the winding, narrow, stone streets is an absolute delight.

Red tile roofs and clock towers of the town below are visible from the fortress walls. There's a back exit to the town (hole in the wall really). Narrow steps lined with shops declaring their wares with picture signs hanging in front. Common in the Medieval days when most people couldn't read. And handy for those now that don't speak Estonian.

Two blocks from the bottom of the steps is Raekoja Plats, Town Hall Square. It actually has the only surviving Gothic Town Hall (1371-1404) in Northern Europe. The spire is 17$^{th}$ century but the weather vane on top has been there since 1530. The Town Council Pharmacy, on the north side is another institution. There's been an apothecary's shop here since 1422. This, is the actual center of town and it's stunning. Outdoor dining lines the sidewalks. There is a picture in every direction you turn. Charm, nothing but charm. We had lunch on a sunlit afternoon in a beautiful square - pork kabob, cooked tomato, home fries, goat cheese, lettuce, cappuccino and a ½ liter of Saku beer for $21. Couldn't be better.

On a stroll through town we saw an artist in front of a beautiful building. He had a good sized canvas on an easel and I had to look. The stone building had an arched front door with iron grill work and intricate carvings in the concrete facade above and on both sides. Tall, peaked windows on each side framed the doorway. I was curious as to whether he was doing the whole building or just the doorway. And what a shock. His canvas had the profile of a beautiful woman and a couple of bricks. I give up. A few blocks farther there was a 30 foot wood boat on the sidewalk. No sails, no oars and no motor, but, there were 2 tables in the center and an awning above. But no people on board. The people were across the street, under Coca-Cola umbrellas having lunch.

Postcards, calenders and guide books (in English) are on sale on the street. Using beautiful young sales girls, who could resist. An enterprising couple in Medieval garb were making a unique brand of trail mix on a wood cart. Wood pails, a copper pan over a metal cased furnace, a swirl of secret ingredients and wha-laa. The only part of the sign I could read was "sweet almonds". Free samples are on the hanging spoon - it's actually quite good.

We took the bus to Tartu the following day. Busses are just as fast and as cheap and have a better schedule than the train. Two and a half hour express bus for $5. The bus station in Tartu is a little ratty and on the southern end of town. Fortunately, the town is small and there is a nice hotel right at the station.

Four blocks north, along the river bank and turn left. Yes, the former home of Colonel Barclay de Tolly (1761-1818) really is leaning. It's now the Kivisilla Art Gallery. I wonder if they have to hang the paintings crooked so patrons don't have to bend their necks.

Two blocks ahead is Raekoja Plats, town hall square. The beautiful town hall (1782-89) in pink, white and red overlooks a fountain and a cobbled plaza. Like Tallinn, the square has outdoor dining and is the place to eat.

On a nicely restored side street is the Al Capone bar and grill. Inside are black and white pictures of the famous mobster and pictures of Legs Diamond and other criminals of the roaring 20's. Even Chicago doesn't have one of these.

We returned to Tallinn for the last night and chose a hotel close in for only $20 more than the one with the long walk. The McDonalds is on the edge of Old Town, next to a circular stone guard station - from the old days if you don't want to believe it was part of the restoration process that makes this town so delightful. And McDonalds won't take Euros or dollars. Estonian krone only. Oh well, we walked the streets again. Just as charming as before. Some things you never get enough of.

THE END

## SIDEBAR FOR ESTONIA

GETTING THERE - There are connecting flights to Helsinki from the east and west coasts on Lufthansa, Air France, SAS, British Air, KLM, Northwest and American Airlines. We took AA and connected at JFK on Finnair to Helsinki. The best fare is $700 RT from the west coast and $550 from the east coast.

There are 25 ferries and hydrofoils crossing between Helsinki and Tallinn each day. Tallink Express, Lindaline, Eckero Line, Nordic Jet Line and Silja Line operate from the dock in Helsinki. Tickets are $36 RT for the hydrofoil - 1 ½ hours each way. We bought Linda Line from the tourist bureau in Helsinki because departure times could be changed for no additional charge.

WHEN TO GO - Summer and two months on either side is best since the winters are brutal.

HOTELS - The Tourist Bureau has a list of 34 hotels and can book for you. www.tourism.tallinn.ee Nine are in Old Town, 16 in City Center (close to Old Town but with a bigger radius). The following are in Old Town, rates are for a double. Barons - www.baronshotel.ee = $160, Domina City - www.dominahotels.com = $150, Imperial - www.imperial.ee = $175, Old Town Maestro's, www.maestrohotel.ee = $135, Uniquestay, www.uniquestay.com = $100, Vanu Wiru, www.vanawiru.ee - $120.

The Hotel Tartu is next to the bus station - www.tartuhotell.ee = $75 - 10% off for internet booking.

HEALTH - There are no shots necessary.

VISA - None required.

MISCELLANEOUS - For additional information contact the Estonia Tourist Board, 2131 Massachusetts Ave., NW, Washington DC 20008, tel 202-588-0101. Info@estemb.org

Finland, the other Scandinavian Country


Helsinki, Finland - It may be the land of Nokia cell phones now, but it wasn't always that way. There's a lot of ancient history here. Really ancient. They say Moscow started as a trading post established by the Scandinavians in the 9th century. Peter the Great repaid the favor in the 17th century by taking St. Petersburg. OK it was a Finnish swamp, but still. And Finland wasn't a country then, it was a Swedish province. That is, until Russia seized control in 1809 and made it part of Russia. For a while. The 1917 Russian revolution gave Finland an opening and they declared their independence. But that didn't last long. In 1939 Russia invaded again and Finland lost territory. No other country came to their aid so they turned to the Nazi's. Together, they beat back the Russians. And then had to make a treaty with the Russians after the war. With all the fighting behind them, they got their economy together and joined the EU in1995.

All the Scandinavian countries are expensive but Finland gives the biggest bang for the buck. We got our hotel from the visitors desk at the airport. First they said there were no rooms, but we didn't leave. They had to make phone calls and found the Hotel Arthur, two blocks from the train station. We took the 615 bus from the terminal to the outdoor, main bus station in town. Which is right next to the train station. These stations may not be the official center of town but it might as well be. It's certainly the center of transportation. Unlike other European cities where you have to pick a train station depending on the direction you're going, all trains leave from right here. The station has restaurants, a money changer (with better rates than at the airport), a hotel desk and an entrance to the underground. Yes, there is a subway system but it's a limited one. This underground is a complete shopping mall that goes for blocks under the streets in front of the train station. Grocery stores, fast foods, clothes, records and a McDonalds.

Directly in front of the train station are the electric trolleys that run on rails. The #3 goes to the boat docks (next to the outdoor flea market which is 1 block from Senate Square the official center of town).

We took advantage of happy hour prices at the Hotel Arthur for a quick meal. A large sausage (mild), mashed potatoes, tomato and lettuce for $5.65. A ½ liter of dark beer with low carbonation was $4.20. And then set out for the renown (in Finland) Stockmans Department store.

A long block west of the train station is Mannerheiminite, the main street in town. Probably because it's the widest, not the most interesting. A long block south and there it was - on 2 blocks actually. Stockman's is upscale shopping if the prices are any indication. A cup of coffee was $2.40. The slogan says that 'If Stockman's doesn't have it, you don't need it', and after looking around, they are probably right. From there, we walked Pohjoisesplanadi (with a small park running down the center)& Alexanterinkatu streets (both perpendicular to Mannerheiminite & more engaging) and it was like 5<sup>th</sup> Avenue in New York. Clean streets, well dressed shoppers, better dressed mannequins in the store front windows and prices that would require a second mortgage on the house. Concrete buildings showing age and an aura of class.

So we went back to the train station, McDonalds, and had a coffee, hamburger and fudge sundae for $3.40.

The city tour starts a block from the dock on Pohjoisesplanadi. It's an hour and a half for $24 and is money well spent it since it hits the attractions on the outskirts of town. There's nothing anywhere like the Temppeliaukio (Church in the Rock) finished in 1969. A Church in the round, carved into a hill of granite. The 24 meter diameter roof is lined with 22 kilometers of copper stripping. It draws a half million people a year.

Then a pretty park in the midst of which is a collection of vertical, hollow, silvered pipes. I couldn't find a church organ in the middle, so it must be art. A silver head and what appears to be associated shrapnel sits atop a low shelf of granite only fifty feet away.

We returned to Senate square after the tour. Finland was annexed by Russia after the war of 1808-9 with Sweden. In 1808 Helsinki was a small town of 4,000 and just lost 1/3 of their homes in a terrible fire. The Russian Czar Alexander I decided to move the capital from Turku to Helsinki and appointed Johan Ehrenstrom, a former courtier of the King of Sweden, the head of the reconstruction committee. Ehrenstrom found Carl Engel, a Berlin trained architect who had worked in Estonia and Turku and gave him the job of planning an entire city. Engel stayed in Helsinki for the rest of his life and designed 30 public buildings. Some have been lost over time, but the beautiful Senate Building and square remain as the official center of town.

We caught the boat to Soumenlinna Island at the dock ($5.60 RT). Sweden started the building of this fortress island in 1748 because it was worried about the exposure to it's eastern frontier. Thousands of foot soldiers built walls, fortifications, houses and a large dry dock for more than 40 years. The fortress was surrendered to the Russians in 1808 after a blockade. Now it guarded the western frontier. It was because of this fortress that Helsinki was chosen as the new Capital. What was once a military establishment is now an artist colony and 900 people live here. The stone walls remain but the restaurants are quiet and designed for tea and biscuits. There is a majestic Lutheran church (1854) sitting atop a hill. The inside is white, clean and simple. A place for quiet thought.

A modern train connects to Turku for $22 each way. The outside doors open with a push of a button. There's even tea service during the 2 hour ride. The train station is about ½ mile from the center of town and when we got to the huge town square it was filled with flower vendors. Rows of yellow, red, white and orange. The #1 bus goes from the square to the Turku Castle which was prominent in the 16th century since Turku was the capital of Finland. The battered and beleaguered walls still stand even though it's now a museum. Turku is a comfortable town to spend a day. No hustle and bustle.

Naturally we had to return to the flea market at the dock. I bought a pair of super soft, lamb skin gloves for $57. Boats are dockside with their catch of the day. This is the place for fresh fish. And more flowers. Beautiful flowers.

THE END

## SIDEBAR FOR FINLAND

GETTING THERE - There are connecting flights to Helsinki from the east and west coasts on Lufthansa, Air France, SAS, British Air, KLM, Northwest and American Airlines. We took AA and connected at JFK on Finnair to Helsinki. The best fare is $700 RT from the west coast and $550 from the east coast..

WHEN TO GO - Summer and two months on either side is best since the winters are brutal.

HOTELS - Helsinki hotels are in demand during the summer. The Hotel Arthur is centrally located for $130 double, tel 358 (0) 9 173-441. A 20 minute trolley ride from the center is the Hotel Finn Apartments for $100 double, tel 358 (0) 9 774-980, web= www.hotelfenno.fi The Sokos Hotels, downtown, have rates of $130 double weekdays/ $240 weekends.

HEALTH - There are no shots necessary.

VISA - None required.

MISCELLANEOUS - For additional information contact the Finnish Tourist Board, 655 Third Ave, NY, NY 10017, tel 212-885-9700.

GIBRALTAR: home of the Barbary Apes.
Guard your twinkies with your life.


GIBRALTAR - is the northern most pillar of Hercules, 1400 feet high and guards the pinch point between Europe and Africa. All ships from the Mediterranean sea must pass through the Straights of Gibraltar to get to the Atlantic and that has set it's strategic importance through the ages.

In recent history, it was occupied by the Arabs until a surprise attack by the Spanish in 1309. They held the rock until 1333 when it fell again under Moorish control. Finally, the Spanish got it back and kept hold for 240 years. Britain became interested in Gibraltar during the time of Oliver Cromwell but an opportunity to capture it didn't arise until the war of Spanish Succession. It was then seized by a combined Anglo-Dutch fleet and British sovereignty formalized it in 1713 by the Treaty of Utrecht. It was declared a British colony in 1830.

Naturally, this set as well with the Spanish as it would with us if Spain still owned Florida. There have been 15 attempts to recapture it since 1713. The most famous being the Great Siege of 1779, which lasted 3 years, 7 months and 12 days. Recently, Spain has closed the frontier in 1969 and 1985 and shut off their water supply. England has stubbornly hung on. The Spanish are poor losers but then, who can blame them.

Getting there is easy enough if you're vacationing on the Costa del Sol, the south coast of Spain. The entire coast from Malaga to Algeciras is lined with coast view condos and beachfront hotels. The excellent weather and reasonable prices of Spain (compared to other European Countries) make this coast a perfect retirement area for most of Europe. And there are a number of reasonably priced tour packages available from the USA.

From any town on the Costa del Sol, drive south on the coast highway and turn left at the sign. The border check point is a formality but you should have a passport. If the gate is up, you drive across the active runway to the edge of town. Proper planning might get you there at lunchtime, so turn right at the fork towards the waterfront and stop at Gadsby's eating house. Excellent Spanish or English food in an attractive, make that charming, English pub with efficient service and delightful chit-chat that make the experience a delight. Gibraltar has been populated since neolithic times and has become a mixture of cultures from Phoenicians, Romans, Genoese, Carthaginians, Moors, Spanish and of course, the British.

The cable car shuts down at sunset, so the next stop should be at the far side of town. Drive around the town, not through it and look for the fork in the road. Look up for the cables and follow them to the base. There is a parking lot there. US $20 for tickets to the top and entrance to the caves. You change cable cars at the 2/3 point and continue to the top for a stunning view of the surrounding area. The rock's unique position and sub-tropical climate provides a perfect habitat for eagles, lizards, owls, foxes, butterflies and a host of migrating birds flying from northern Europe to Africa. Permanent residents include the Blue Rock Thrush, Peregrine Falcon, Barbary Partridge and the famous Barbary Ape. Over 600 species of wild flowers have been identified, several of which are unique to the rock. If your timing is right there are Apes about. Don't think their casual walk is a lack of alertness. On the top is a concession stand selling food and drink. A woman was sitting at one of the tables and left a chocolate bar several inches from her left hand. An ever aware female ape, forty pounds of muscle and speed, snatched it in a second from the table, moved with her back to the guard rail, peeled off the paper and foil and slowly enjoyed the chocolate. Later, the ape walked from table to table looking for unattended food. She ignored cameras, film, maps and empty cartons. And spotted a plastic shopping bag hanging from the handle of a baby stroller. On the top, in plain view, was a red bag containing peanuts and the ape went for it, startling the life out of the poor mother. The baby wasn't in danger, but little did the mother know, until our thief was walking away with the bag of peanuts.

The ape perched on top of the rail, carefully pulled open the package, slowly shelled the peanuts one at a time and ate in deference to all onlookers.

You can watch birds coasting on the wind to land on the sharp top edge of the rock which extends 300 feet from the concession area. The back side of the mountain is lined with concrete to act as a rain catch basin and 1400 feet below is the Caleta Palace Hotel. Alone, since the town is on the opposite side of the rock. On the cable car side you can look over the straights to the city of Tangiers in Morocco. Legend has it that the Barbary apes travel to and from Morocco by a natural tunnel from St. Michaels cave deep beneath the straights. The caves, located halfway between the top and middle cable car stops, have never been fully explored and their depths are unknown.

The walk down towards the cave and back to the middle cable car stop is longer than it appears on the map, so give yourself lots of time. Don't miss the walk because the wall a favorite sunning spot for families of apes. They are used to people and don't scurry away from clicking cameras.

The town of Gibraltar is a city of shops. All very charming and all very British. The shops take American, Spanish and English money. The best deal is Spanish. Walking through these great shops is a must even if you don't buy a pint of beer, a British flag, a tee shirt of Gibraltar or English teas or jams.

If you leave at night, look back. The rock is lit up by flood lights from below. Impressive, indeed.

## THE END

## SIDEBAR FOR GIBRALTAR

GETTING THERE - Gibraltar is serviced through Heathrow, London by United and British Air and through Gatwick, London by Northwest and Continental. Air fares from the West Coast of the USA are approximately $1100 on BA, UA, NW and on CO (all fares RT). From London, it's served by Gibraltar Airlines. Any airline that gets you to London from anywhere will allow you to connect to Gibraltar Air.

LOCAL TOUR ARRANGEMENT - Tours are easily arranged from any hotel on the south coast of Spain. Typical cost is US $100 RT by bus and should include lunch. There is a public bus that runs from some cities on the Costa del Sol for US$12 RT, once a day. Transportation only. Cars can be rented for about $80 a day and the roads are excellent for the 2 hour drive.

HEALTH - Most of the water is supplied by Spain which has become a first world country. You can eat and drink as safely as in America.

FOR MORE INFORMATION - Contact The British Tourist Authority 350 So. Figueroa St., Suite 450. Los Angeles, CA 90071 tel. (213)628-3525

GOZO - an island without a fort
is an island without people

GOZO, MALTA - In 1551 the Turks invaded this poorly defended island, carried away virtually the entire population and put them into slavery. The next inhabitants didn't make that mistake.

The country of Malta is actually 3 islands. Malta, Gozo to the west and the small island of Comino in between. They are just south of Sicily and 350 KM north of Libya. Strategically placed in the shipping lanes of the Mediterranean which made them a target of the expanding nations in the region. It's been British since the 1800's and the shops are reminiscent of Gibraltar.

If Gozo were round (it's more like a football) Marsalforn would be at 12 O'clock, Mgarr at 3 O'clock and Victoria, the capital, in the center. There is an excellent system of busses all of which start and end in Victoria, like spokes radiating from the hub. The longest ride is 25 minutes.

## HISTORY

Malta was first colonized by the Phoenicians in 800 B.C. Then came the Carthaginians, Romans, Byzantines, Arabs, Normans, Castilians, Knights of St. John, the French and finally the British. The names of the Gozo towns read like a history lesson -Sannat, Munxar, Xabhra, Santa Lucija, Zebug, San Lawrenz, Qala. After the defeat of the Carthaginian General Hannibal by the Romans in 208 B.C. Malta became part of the Roman Empire. In 60 AD St. Paul was a prisoner en route to Rome and was shipwrecked on Malta. He converted the people to Christianity and is the Patron Saint. The Arabs came in 870 AD, tolerated the Christians but were expelled in 1090 by the Norman warlord Count Roger of Sicily. Apt, since Malta is only 93 KM south of Sicily. The official languages are Maltese and English but everyone seems to speak Italian and their English has more of an Italian flavor than British.

# THE KNIGHTS OF ST. JOHN OF JERUSALEM

Or as they are better known, the Knights of Malta, arrived in 1530 after being thrown off the Island of Rhodes by the Turks. These Knights are a story in themselves. Originally formed from aristocratic families in Europe, they provided protection for the Christian pilgrims traveling to the Holy Land. They had become powerful and wealthy but the Turks were now bigger and flexing their muscles in the Mediterranean Sea. The Spanish gave the island to the Knights for the rent of one Maltese Falcon a year. The local inhabitants were given no say in the matter.

The Knights proceeded to fortify Malta for the impending invasion of the Turks which came in the Great Siege of 1565. Gozo had become an early casualty. The Turkish fleet of 200 ships and 40,000 men laid siege to Valletta (capital of the island of Malta) which was defended by 700 Knights and 8,000 Maltese. It lasted for 4 months with enormous bloodshed on both sides until the Turks returned home with ½ their men. The Knights were hailed as the saviors of Europe and money came pouring in. Enormous fortification of the islands began in preparation for the next invasion of the Turks. It never came but the stone walls and buildings remain.

## GOZO

My first sighting of the island was from the ocean liner sized ferry connecting the two islands. Slowly we approached the magnificent Mgarr harbor with sail boats bobbing behind a stone levy. The compact town is nestled against shear cliffs in the shape of a horseshoe that shield it from the rest of the island. From the sea, there appears to be two Gothic Medieval age churches and a Roman ruins atop the cliff. This is an impressive introduction but there is no time to explore, the bus is waiting at the dock and it will fill up before the boat is empty.

The ride to Victoria in the middle of the island is only 12 minutes, the island isn't that big. We pass two towns with unprounceable names, Ghajnsielem and Xewkija, and the heliport but no one gets off or on. The central bus stop is one block south of the main street and has a dozen marked lanes for the busses to park, each with a sign with the name of the destination town so you know where to wait.

I made my first mistake and jumped on the next bus to Xaghra, the town nearest the Ggantija temples. It was a rough go for the old bus, 10 minutes, all uphill. The Arab influence is everywhere and it's easy to forget that these people speak English. Fortunately, the driver knew where most of us were going and stopped. The temples are off the road on the side of a hill and not visible from the street.

I'm not an archaeological buff and did not have a guide to point out the meaning of the various altars, cubby holes and walls. So I missed out on a great deal of the background. But these crude stone structures or what's left of them date back to 3500 B.C., a thousand years before the first pyramids of Egypt. There are several altars where ceremonies were held and an oracle hole through which a priest would announce his predictions. Some of the stone slabs weigh 50 tons and are 20 feet high. The spherical stones lying outside the main entrance were undoubtedly used as rollers to move the stones. The amazing thing about this site, is that these structures were built during cave man times. The builders were wearing animal skins.

I was now one of 6 waiting for the return bus and it's been an hour. Finally we give up and decide to walk back. Fortunately, it's all downhill and I have 45 minutes to wonder why I didn't ask when the return bus would come after I asked when the bus left for Ggantija. No bus passed in either direction during the walk.

## THE RESORT TOWN

I was warned about the lack of accommodations in Victoria and the fact that the sidewalks roll up after 8 o'clock. It was time to head north for the only town with some action, Marsalforn. It is only a 6 minute ride since there are no hills, well hardly any. The busy season is Xmas and July through September when the European tourists flock south to the Mediterranean Sea. Otherwise it's a quiet fishing village with a lot of character.

There is a long, inward curved, stone walled harbor with the giant sized Calypso Hotel at the east end and strange looking cliffs at the west end. There are a smattering of hotels around the square (where the bus stops) but they are only open during high season. Guest houses (small hotels) are one block back from the waterfront. The west end drew my attention and on closer inspection, I found some very nice restaurants. Then a block farther, just as the waterfront ends, a stone cliff with three story apartment houses on top and homes dug into the stone face of the wall. Normal doors, twenty feet apart and rectangular holes drilled in the rock to provide air and a little light. I could only think of the cave people that built Ggantija.

The Calypso is a big hotel with 4 restaurants on the ground floor, a bar/restaurant and a tennis court on the roof. The roof is the place to go for the best view of the entire city and a good drink. Marsalforn is a quiet town, a place to relax, to fish, to dive, to read. The only action in town is the Creek, a bar 2 blocks in from the water.

## THE CITADEL

It's difficult to see this fort from Victoria's main street but it stands out from anywhere outside the city. Atop a hill, this was the answer to the Turks by the Knights of Malta. A stone fort on the highest hill in the center of the island.

The first thing you see inside the main gate is the Cathedral designed by Lorenzo Gafa and finished in 1711. It's a wonderful fort, if you like forts (I do) and gives the best view of virtually the entire island. Narrow stone walled streets, cannons, moats. The medieval houses on the upper most level are gone but the foundations remain as stone lined trenches offering shelter from the bombardments of the Turks. But a little late since, as history shows, the Turks never returned for war. Only now to visit and relax in Marsalforn.

## THE END

Ever wonder where the Maltese Falcon really came from?
That's right, the Island of Malta.

VALLETTA, MALTA - My first view of the city was an impressive one. I walked from the bus stop, over the road (drawbridge) towards a huge stone arch (main gate) and saw the massive, smooth, solid stone walls of a fort. The entire city, the capital, is inside a fort. Continuing through the gate there is a shopping arcade to the right, a sign for McDonalds "Walk 2 blocks ahead" next to stone ruins, a building with shops and a Burger King to the left and buildings of rock and narrow stone streets to the front.

To the left and right of the main drag, Republic Street, are tiny streets, so narrow that the few mini cars that drive inside the city have to park on the sidewalk. Four and five story buildings, all made of limestone, line the streets, shading them from the sun. Talk about atmosphere. But then there is a lot of history here. It seeps from the walls and rises from the stone steps.

## HISTORY

Malta was first colonized by the Phoenicians in 800 B.C. Then came the Carthaginians, Romans, Byzantines, Arabs, Normans, Castilians, Knights of St. John, the French and finally the British. The names of the towns read like a history lesson - Marfa, Zebbiegh, St. Paul's Bay, Mdina, Zebug, Santa Venera, Qrendi, Pieta, Marsaxlokk.

After the defeat of the Carthaginian General Hannibal by the Romans in 208 B.C., it became part of the Roman Empire. In 60 AD St. Paul was a prisoner en route to Rome and was shipwrecked on the island. He converted the people to Christianity and is the Patron Saint of Malta. The Arabs came in 870 AD, tolerated the Christians but were expelled in 1090 by the Norman warlord Count Roger of Sicily. Apt since Malta is only 93 KM south of Sicily. The official languages are Maltese and English but everyone seems to speak Italian and their English has more of an Italian flavor than the crisp British we are used to hearing.

## THE KNIGHTS OF ST. JOHN OF JERUSALEM

Or as they are better known, the Knights of Malta, arrived in 1530 after being thrown off the Island of Rhodes by the Turks. These Knights are a story in themselves. Originally formed from aristocratic families in Europe, they provided protection for the Christian pilgrims traveling to the Holy Land. They had become powerful and wealthy over the years but now the Turks were stronger and were flexing their muscles in the Mediterranean Sea. The Spanish gave the island to the Knights for the rent of one Maltese Falcon a year, thus giving birth to one of the best Bogart movies ever. The local inhabitants were given no say in the matter.

The Knights proceeded to fortify the city for the impending invasion of the Turks which came in the Great Siege of 1565. The Turkish fleet of 200 ships and 40,000 men attacked the city defended by 700 Knights and 8,000 Maltese. It lasted for 4 months with enormous bloodshed on both sides until the Turks returned home with ½ their men. The Knights were hailed as the saviors of Europe and money came pouring in. Enormous fortification of the island began in preparation for the next invasion of the Turks. It never came but the stone walls and buildings remain. That fortification gives the flavor and atmosphere to Malta.

The country is actually 3 islands. Malta, Gozo to the west and the small island of Comino in between. The islands are just south of Sicily and 350 KM north of Libya, strategically placed in the shipping lanes of the Mediterranean and, naturally, piracy is part of their legacy. But that was long ago. It's been British since the 1800's and the shops are reminiscent of Gibraltar. If the main island were round (it's shaped more like a football) Valletta would be at 2 O'clock and the only airport, directly south, in the middle. There is an excellent system of busses all of which start and end in Valletta. The longest ride is a little over an hour and costs 45 cents.

## THE CITY

Is the tip of a peninsula with the gate at the inland side and Fort St. Elmo at the sea end. The main street is lined with shops and restaurants and people of mysterious ethnicity (remember, Arabs, Italians, French, Spanish, English). Malta is famous for lace, silver filigree and blown glass (reportedly learned from the Phoenicians) and there is an ample selection on display in the stores.

## THE WALK

The first great church is four blocks down Republic Street, St. John's Cathedral (1577) in one of the rare open spaces in the city. It was given the status of Co-Cathedral by Pope Pius VII in 1816. Two blocks farther is Republic Square with hundreds of outdoor tables for dinner or a late evening espresso. They fill up at night with people sitting for hours with just a cup of coffee. The National Library is the background building for this setting. Frankly, if you have any shopping instincts, it will take several hours to get these 6 blocks.

One block more on Republic and there's Palace Square on the left and the Grandmasters Palace on the right. Here's where you have to make a decision. Straight ahead is the section of silversmiths leading, seven blocks later to Fort Elmo at the tip, or, turn right for a block, then right again to circle back on Merchants street for the open air market. Not that this simple exercise will cover the shopping opportunities since more shops line the small streets (I take that back, they're all small streets) connecting Merchants and Republic.

If you want to shop later, take Republic or Merchants street to the end of the peninsula to the famous Fort St. Elmo. It was constructed in 1552 to protect the harbors on either side from the Turkish invasion. The walls are massive since they had to take the heavy bombardments of the Turks and held up during heavier bombing during WWII. There is a wonderful view of the city from the upper bastions. The lower part has more recent fame as the site for the shooting of the movie "Midnight Express" about an American held in a Turkish prison.

Turn left after leaving the fort to follow the walls along the Grand Harbor to the Malta Experience. It's a theater built inside the cliff giving a pictorial view of the history of Malta. It's a 45 minute show, in a 280 seat auditorium, on a screen wide enough to hold three simultaneous slides. Put on the headset, dial your language, there are 11 to choose from, and enjoy an outstanding presentation. A bit pricey at $7.50 but worth it.

You must visit the tiny but pretty Upper Barracca Gardens. Walk one block in from the main gate to Ordinance St., the first real street, turn right, weave around St. James Cavalier tower, past the Castillo Hotel on the left (with a wonderful small bar at street level and La Cave Italian restaurant, underground) to the walls edge and there you are. It's like being in Rome. These were originally the private gardens of the Italian Knights and called "Il Belvedere d'Italia". There is a marvelous view of the Grand Harbor and the neighboring islands.

## THE MIAMI BEACH OF MALTA

On the opposite side from the Grand Harbor is Marsamxett Harbor and the ferry to Sliema. A quick 15 minute ride and you are in a modern city with upscale hotels and shops. Steel, concrete and glass buildings that remind me of Miami Beach without the sand. There is only one beach on Malta and that's far to the west. Virtually all the coastlines are rock. Valletta's streets are at right angles and easy to negotiate. Not so in Sliema where you will need a map or a trail of bread crumbs to get back to the ferry. As you can tell, I don't suggest staying in Sliema since it's a long way to travel to be in an American city, but it's worth a visit.

## THE TEMPLES

The bus got me to Qrendi, the closest town, and I followed the signs which pointed me in the right general direction. A half hours downhill stroll, past rolling meadows, brought me to the coast and the first stone temple, Hagar Qim. It was constructed about 3000 B.C. That's 500 years before the Egyptian pyramids at Giza and 1,500 years before Stonehedge. A paved walk leads ½ a mile farther to Mnajdra, a temple located close to the cliffs edge. It's thought to have been built as a solar observatory but that's just a guess. It's closed for restoration and there's a guard on duty to prevent close inspection but it's a mind boggling experience. These heavy stone tablets, many weighing tons, were put here by cave men. But then, all of Malta is a history lesson. Aside from the shopping, that is.


# THE END

## MALTA SIDEBAR

GETTING THERE - Air Malta has regular scheduled flights from 27 European airports. Valletta, the capital, is also served by Alitalia, KLM, Lufthansa and Swissair. Air fare from Palermo, Sicily to Malta is around $200 RT (35 minute flight one way). Air Malta tel. (800)75-MALTA fax (212)245-7758

WHEN TO GO - Malta has good Mediterranean climate throughout the year although summers may get very warm. The light rainfall is between November and February. The big tourist season is June through September when prices are higher.

WHERE TO STAY - The best is the Hotel Phoenicia, just outside the city walls. Rates are $190-230 double. tel. 011-356-225241, fax 011-356-235254. Inside the walls are the 3 star Osborne and the 2 star Hotel British and Hotel Grand Harbour (around $60). In Sliema, across the bay from Valletta, there are more than a dozen 4 star hotels in the midst of upscale shops that remind one of Miami Beach. There is no flavor of Malta here. There is an excellent information office at the airport, it should be a simple matter to book a room from here. After completing customs, turn left and walk to the terminal end. Lots of maps and brochures.

WHERE TO EAT - The main Street in Valletta has more nice restaurants than you can shake a stick at. Maltese workers go to King's Head on the main street (Republic St.) for a full meal, fixed menu for $6.20. Good food, not great, but includes coffee, red wine and desert. For great, go to La Cave (downstairs) at the Castillo Hotel, just inside the wall in the SW corner. Under $10 for Italian Pagliafiendo to kill for. In Sliema, there are 10 restaurants within 100 feet of any hotel. Stop at the Times Square for a drink and great atmosphere. For the homesick, there are Burger Kings and McDonald's. KFC always has a line in front, you may have to get chicken elsewhere.

FOR MORE INFORMATION - Write to the Embassy of Malta, 2017 Connecticut Ave. NW, Washington DC 20008, tel. (202)462-3611 fax (202)387-5470.

MDINA, an ancient city of religion, politics, war, torture,
and a gift store called The Maltese Falcon


MDINA, MALTA - The city's original name was Molina but the
Arabs must have thought the sound didn't roll off the tongue as it should
and renamed it Mdina. That was a long, long time ago but the name sort
of stuck.

## HISTORY

Malta was first colonized by the Phoenicians in 800 B.C. Then came
the Carthaginians, Romans, Byzantines, Arabs, Normans, Castilians,
Knights of St. John, the French and finally the British. The names of the
towns read like a history lesson - Marfa, Zebbiegh, St.Paul's Bay, Mosta,
Zebug, Santa Venera, Qrendi, Pieta, Marsaxlokk.

After the defeat of the Carthaginian General Hannibal by the Romans
in 208 B.C. it became part of the Roman Empire. In 60 AD St. Paul
was a prisoner en route to Rome and was shipwrecked on the island. He
converted them to Christianity and is the Patron Saint of Malta. The Arabs
came in 870 AD, tolerated the Christians but were expelled in 1090 by the
Norman warlord Count Roger of Sicily. Apt, since Malta is only 93 KM
south of Sicily. The official languages are Maltese and English but they
all seems to speak Italian and their English has more of an Italian flavor
than British.

## THE KNIGHTS OF ST. JOHN OF JERUSALEM

Or as they are better known, the Knights of Malta, arrived in 1530
after being thrown off the Island of Rhodes by the Turks. These Knights
are a story in themselves. Originally formed from aristocratic families in
Europe, they provided protection for the Christian pilgrims traveling to
the Holy Land. They had become powerful and wealthy but the Turks
were now bigger and flexing their muscles in the Mediterranean Sea. The

Spanish gave the island to the Knights for the rent of one Maltese Falcon a year. The local inhabitants were given no say in the matter.

The Knights proceeded to fortify for the impending invasion of the Turks which came in the Great Siege of 1565. The Turkish fleet of 200 ships and 40,000 men laid siege to the Valletta, the capital, defended by 700 Knights and 8,000 Maltese. It lasted for 4 months with enormous bloodshed on both sides until the Turks returned home with ½ their men. The Knights were hailed as the saviors of Europe and money came pouring in. Enormous fortification of the island began in preparation for the next invasion of the Turks. It never came but the stone walls and buildings remain. That gives the flavor and atmosphere to Malta.

The country is actually 3 islands. Malta, Gozo to the west and the small island of Comino in between. It's just south of Sicily and 350 KM north of Libya. Strategically placed in the shipping lanes of the Mediterranean. It's been British since the 1800's and the shops are reminiscent of Gibraltar. If the main island were round (it's more like a football) Valletta would be at 2 O'clock and the only airport directly south in the middle. Mdina is west of the airport and right in the center. There is an excellent system of busses all of which start and end in Valletta. The ride to Mdina is 30 minutes, for 30 cents.

## THE FORTRESS MDINA

It's the safest place on the island, on a rock outcrop in the middle surrounded by flat plains. The city has been occupied for almost 3000 years and, considering all the intruders, even the earliest citizens wanted ample warning and the high ground to defend. Hence, most of the Maltese nobility lived here and still do. Not that I expected to see them walking the streets, but then how would I know they weren't. Even Prince Charles doesn't walk around wearing a crown.

I expected a big stone gate at the end of a drawbridge (now a road), a deep moat and sheer rock walls. That's exactly what I got. Once inside I kept my map handy since the streets come in two widths - narrow and narrower. With limestone walls, two and three stories high, often without windows, it's difficult to keep ones bearings without leaving a chalk mark at each turn.

A quick left and a right and there is the ornate Chapel of St. Agatha (1417) which looks like a small stone attachment to the adjacent, and larger, St. Benedict Church (1418). Many of the original buildings were damaged in the earthquake of 1693 and the Chapel was redesigned in 1694 by Lorenzo Gafa. Following the signs, I entered a bicycle width street leading to the Mdina Experience. An outstanding 750 slide, 25 minute show on a screen wide enough for three simultaneous pictures. It shows the fortunes and misfortunes of the cities' long history.

Two blocks farther on Vilegaignon St., the main drag, is the largest open square in the center of the city and the most famous church, The Cathedral. It's situated on the site where St. Paul converted the Roman Governor to Christianity. After the earthquake, it was reconstructed by Lorenzo Gafa and became his masterpiece. It's a classic design with twin towers, three doors with the crest of honor above the center and, naturally, bells in each tower.

A block more is the Maltese Falcon. Not the bird itself but a souvenir shop with Mdina's specialty of blown glass (learned from the Phoenicians), hand sewn lace, silver filigree and Falcon jewelry in all sizes and shapes. There are other shops inside the walls but I had to buy here.

Next door is the Mediaeval Times Adventure, a wax museum depicting normal stores and work shops from the medieval period. It's very well done and costs $3.95 as does the Mdina Experience slide show. Bastion Square is at the very rear of the fort and overlooks the flat countryside surrounding the city. From this height, you can see the Mediterranean Sea and a great deal of the island.

I casually meandered the streets marveling at each ancient, quiet building, wondering of the stories each could tell. The battles, the blood shed at each blind corner, but I was saving the real blood for last - the torture chambers. The Mdina Dungeons is just inside the front gate, next to the marvelous Palazzo Vilhena which was the house of the Grandmaster, then a military hospital under the British and now the Museum of Natural History.

The Dungeons are below ground as dungeons should be. Encased in rock and scream absorbing earth. Cramped and ill lit as it was in the mediaeval days of death and torture. A wax museum not for the faint of heart since the scenes of disfigurement and dismemberment send chills up the spine. It was a period where life had little value and only the fortunate died quickly.

Adjacent the fortress Mdina is the city of Rabat with an equally long history. A 10 minute walk to the center is St. Paul's Church (1592), with catacombs beneath. It's a huge structure with triple arches, three towers, no bells and triple crosses on the roof. At least the people beneath died in their sleep.

## THE END

Normandy, D-Day is not forgotten

D'Orsay Museum, third floor clock, Paris

PARIS, FRANCE is good for a full week or more, I know, but we didn't have the time. Three nights here and three days to see Normandy. We started with a half day city tour of Paris for a quick overview of the tourist sights you can't miss and then one full day to dig deeper. This was a tag-on to a tour of Southern France so we couldn't complain about limited time, we'd been in France for a while. This is what happens when you try to cover too much ground on a vacation. We spotted a flea market from the bus to our hotel and that's where we went in the afternoon, after freshening up. Door knobs, old furniture, paintings, stained glass, even a free concert around the corner. The concept is the same as back home, but, if you buy here you have to carry it 8,000 miles.

Next morning, the tour got us to Notre Dame, past the 60 minute waiting line and right inside. The Gothic exterior has a certain darkness about it and the interior, a definite darkness. It's huge so a flash won't help with pictures of the altars and beautiful stained glass windows. You need high speed film. We got outside just as 50 priests in white robes marched in the front door. A conference?

The next stop was at the Hospital Des Invalides, where Napoleon is buried and onto the Eiffel Tower. The bus stopped at the far end of the long mall and it's the perfect place to take pictures if you want to get the whole tower. There was no time to get close, that would come later. We drove by the Palais de Chaillot, across from the Eiffel, past the Jardin des Tuileries, the Louvre and the Hotel De Ville. We had the bus drop us off 3 blocks from the D'Orsay Museum which specializes in art from 1848 to 1914. Monet, Renoir, Whistler, etc. The best (my opinion) is on the third floor (escalators at the far end). Don't miss the clock that faces Montemarte. It's like a scene from a sci-fi movie and a work of art itself.

We crossed the Seine and walked through the Jardin des Tuileries. Children were sailing boats in the huge fountain. We joined the French at one of the large outdoor patios and had a beer. A beautiful day in a gorgeous setting, what more could you ask for. Two blocks ahead was the Louvre with the impressive glass pyramid in the courtyard. The Louvre was built as a fortress in 1200 AD, later changed to a Palace in the 16th century and became a museum in 1793. But it's too big and the lines too long, so we walked along the Seine and crossed to the Ile de la Cite. It's very pretty and away from the maddening crowds. Notre Dame is at the far end of this island in the middle of the Seine. There are some very attractive restaurants in the middle of the island and a subway stop. We went underground and back to the hotel to freshen up.

Dusk is the time for the Eiffel Tower. The subway stop is a dozen blocks away but it looks closer on the map. The Eiffel was built for the 1889 worlds fair and almost torn down in 1909. It wasn't because it was a good platform for the newfangled transmitting antennae for the radio. Elevators go at an angle to the second level where you switch. The final elevator goes straight to the top and what a view. All of Paris at your feet as the sun goes down and the City of Lights appears. Lights on the barges going up and down the Seine, spot lights on the Palais De Chaillot directly across from the tower. Nothing like it in the world.

The next day we headed for Montemarte and the Sacre Coeur Basilica, the church atop the hill that can be seen from virtually anywhere in the city. The subway stopped in front of the Moulin Rouge. We walked back a full subway stop through Pigalle, the sex shop center of the city. Turn left and walk up. And up. Finally, the funicular to the top. The view is wonderful but the real action is behind the church. The artist colony and the surrounding shops. This is the place for original art. And one charming shop after another. Color in all directions. We spent hours just walking around.

The subway dropped us off at the Arc de Triomphe commissioned by Napoleon in 1806 to honor his military victories. It's the starting place to walk the Champs Elysees. This is the high rent area - the right bank - from the Arc through the Tuileries to the Louvre. We had a snack at the upscale McDonalds on the Champs Elysees and walked the residential side streets to the Seine. You could smell money in the air.

We were told of the strike the day before. French air controllers, trains, busses and subways. The French were upset about the new pension rules the government wanted to put in place. But, we had no choice, it was time to go. Fortunately, this train strike meant 2 trains a day on routes that had 12 a day. And we were going out of the city, not coming in with the commuters. And the strike could be over by the time we were due back. So they said.

Bayeau is 2 hours by train and the closest city of size to the Normandy beaches. It's a charming, small town with one long main street and the train station is a dozen blocks out of town at the far end. The town was there first, so one wonders what the train people were thinking.

Tours of Normandy can be booked at the tourist office next to the bridge crossing the River L'Aure, in the middle of town. US$ 35 for a half day tour. They can book hotels and have maps of the city.

625

The oldest house in the city (still standing) dates from the 14th century. It's on the main street and looks pretty good even now. A block north of the main drag is the Cathedrale Notre-Dame which was consecrated on July 14, 1077 in the presence of William, Duke of Normandy and King of England. This medieval structure has been well preserved. Bayeaux is actually the site of two trans-Channel invasions. The 1066 AD conquest of William the Conqueror and D-day on June 6, 1944. Fortunately, the town was not a bombing target during D-day and the Allied troops passed right by without street fighting.

All the films I've seen showed the invasion from the perspective of the beach and it was interesting to see it from the other side. German artillery guns were in concrete pill boxes, back from the cliff edge (where they would be an easy target). We walked over the, now grassy, cliff tops, pockmarked with craters from the Allies artillery barrage. The Allies couldn't see the German guns so they unleashed thousands of rounds in hopes that some would hit. Our first stop showed the some did. The damaged pill boxes and guns are still in place. Many of the artillery guns that were undamaged were made useless because the communication lines were severed by the bombs. They were too far from the cliffs' edge to see where they were firing.

We stopped at Omaha Beach, the center of the American force and the highest casualties. There are no cliffs here, just a long sandy beach with no cover at all. There are houses here now, but behind them are hills overlooking the beach and that's where the Germans were. It was like shooting ducks in a barrel. No wonder the losses were so high.

The memorial is on a distant cliff overlooking Omaha beach. White crosses and white stars are stone reminders of the 9,286 Americans buried here. There is a memorial for the 1557 whose bodies were never found. Inside the memorial is a wall representation of the entire invasion with colored arrows showing the beaches attacked by each force.

The main museum is at Arromanches, a town intended for tourist souvenirs. The museum has artifacts from the various battles and a film that runs throughout the day. Our guide said the most of the tourists are

British and American with some Canadians and Australians. Very few Germans.

We hoped to spend a day the impressive Mont Saint-Michel, an hours train ride west. The strike was still on and there were no trains going west. We had to go to Cherbourg, the town made famous by the movie about the umbrellas. It's a port city not known for it's charm but it's the jumping off point for crossing the channel to England or a day trip to the Channel Islands. The casino faces the river and the best restaurant in town (for location) is directly behind it. You don't have to walk around the casino, walk through it, out the back door and you're in the restaurant, facing the square. And good hamburgers. After a couple of weeks of formal French meals it was good to drip ketchup on the table.

THE END

## SIDEBAR FOR NORMANDY

GETTING THERE - There are direct and connecting flights to Paris from NYC, Washington, Boston, Chicago and Los Angeles. $900 RT from the east coast, $1150 RT from the west coast (depending on the season), using United, American, Continental, Delta and any number of foreign airlines. French trains are reliable but French strikes are not predictable. Train RT to Bayeux from Paris is approx US$ 65/person. Consolidator air fares, shown in the Sunday travel section of the newspaper, can be ½ of the above air fares.

WHEN TO GO - Paris is best in the spring (April in Paris). Summers can be hot, winters nippy and the February/March school holidays create a surge in tourism. Millions of French people take their vacation in August and that's a month to avoid. Fall is another good choice.

HOTELS - Paris has thousands of hotels to choose from. 2 * are about US$90, 4 * are $200-250 double. In Bayeux, there is the Hotel De Brunville, US$ 78d, tel. 02-31-21-18-00, e-mail = hotel. brunville@ wanadoo.fr + attached and next door is the Grand Hotel Du Luxembourg, US$ 120d, tel. 02-31-92-00-04, e-mail = hotel.luxembourg@wanadoo.fr, both are 3*, Best Western and in the middle of town. On the main street in town are the Churchill, US$ 75d, tel. 02-31-21-31-80, e-mail = hotel-churchill@wanadoo.fr and the Lion D'Or, US$ 90d, tel. 02-31-92-06-90, e-mail = lion.d-or.bayeux@wanadoo.fr, both 3*.

HEALTH - Like most of Europe there are no shots necessary nor any health hazards.

MISCELLANEOUS - For additional information contact the French Tourist offices at 444 Madison Ave., NYC, NY 10020, tel. 212-838-7800, email= info @ francetourism.com.

# VIII  MID EAST

Indiana Jones can stop looking - I know where the Holy Grail is.

Baha'I Shrine, Haifai, Israel - 1400 steps

TEL AVIV is where the plane lands. Just south of the capital is the city of Jaffa, thousands of years old. One hundred years ago, the people there said we should build a new capital for this new country. And, empty desert, just to the north, became Tel Aviv. Unfortunately, there is nothing interesting to see in either city even though we went through the motions. Things really started to happen when we headed north on the bus for the recently uncovered port of Caesarea. About the time of Christ this was one of the great harbors of antiquity. It rivaled the port of Alexandria in Egypt.

Israel is mostly desert. Actually, most of the middle east is desert and deserts have sand dunes. In recent times we have seen sand dunes move on the Sahara. Slowly but surely, blown by the wind, to envelope a thriving town. First the outskirts are covered, then the center and then the town is gone. And that's what happened in Caesarea. The sand moved in, the folks moved out.

Fifteen years ago, kibbutz farmers were tilling the soil and odd bits and pieces come to the surface. Archaeologists followed with shovels and we now have a town as it existed in Herod's time. Roughly 0 AD. The Roman bathes (like swimming pool) are dug into a stone outcrop to the sea. I guess to give people a choice. Next to the baths is the 10,000 seat amphitheater, the oldest in Israel. Tiered stone seats on one side and a long runway in front for the chariot races. They would go back in forth in a flattened oval. During the first Jewish revolt (AD 66-70), thousands of captives where executed, right here. We stand on soil that was once drenched in blood.

The remains of a stone aqueduct runs along the ocean front. From 2,000 years ago. The city was seized by the Arabs in AD 640 and held until the Crusaders came in AD1101. And they discovered a green, hexagonal glass bowl they believed to be the Holy Grail (the glass used by Jesus at the Last Supper). That grail is now at a cathedral in Genoa. By the 14 Th century, the shifting sand moved in, history was buried and people forgot.

From the old, we went north to Haifa, home town for one of the world's youngest religions. Baha'i, formed in 1850. There are 6 million believers worldwide and each is to make a pilgrimage here and walk the 1400 steps to the Baha'i gardens on Mt. Carmel. We viewed the golden dome of the Baha'i Shrine of the Bab from the top. We drove up next is Nazareth (population 64,000) and the Basilicia.of the Annunciation. This is the church built above the home of Mary. Where she lived when the future birth of Jesus was announced to her. Atop a hill, it's the largest church in the middle east and one of Christian's most holy shrines. It's impressively large from the outside but almost vacant on the ground floor inside. Except for the marble lined pit - at the back end. The depression holding an altar and a barred enclave with a statue that people get in line to see. Keep in mind, Jesus and Mary lived thousands of years ago when records weren't kept as they are now. Most of these sites are "believed to be".

After a stop in Safed, an art village, we went to the infamous Golan Heights. This volcanic plateau was captured from Syria during the 6 day war of 1967. It overlooks a vast stretch of land and was the perfect place for Syrian artillery. The bunkers and barbed wire remain but this is now a part of Israel. Farther north, on the same plateau, are Syrian land mines, laid in the 1960's. They are still active.

Around the corner is the tin man's dinosaur collection on a path leading to a mountain top restaurant and gun emplacement (they are separated by 100 feet), on Mt. Ativar.

The following morning we were treated to a boat ride on the Sea of Galilee. This lake is fed by the Jordan River and is the main source of fresh water for Israel. It can get rough sometimes. Some of us sat rail side, the rest on plastic chairs put on the middle of the deck. There is a beautiful view of Tiberias from out in the lake. High rise buildings at sea side and homes climbing up the hill. And then the boat started rocking. The plastic chairs are sliding and soon everyone is rail side and the chairs are stacked and taken away. Our bus met us at Capernaum, the home base for Jesus. We went to the site of the house of Saint Peter. There was a stone church built on top but it's now it's in ruins. Jesus stayed with Saint Peter and this is where he healed the sick and recruited Peter, Andrew, James and John who were local fishermen and Matthew, the tax collector.

Next to the church ruins is a synagogue. Rather, what remains of one. It looks as old as the church but was built 100 years after the crucifixion. Jesus did preach at Synagogues in town, just not this one.

We saw where Mary and Joseph lived. Where Saint Peter and Jesus lived and walked the ground they walked, two thousand years ago. Can't get any closer than that.

## THE END

## SIDEBAR FOR THE HOLY GRAIL

GETTING THERE - Arranged through www.smarTours.com at 501 Fifth Ave, Ste. 1402, NYC, NY 10017, tel 800-337-7773. The basic tour of Israel for 11 days is $2600 each for double occupancy, including side tours. That's from JFK. Adding on Petra extension, airfare from LAX to JFK, taxes, tips, meals, etc. the final cost was $45500.

Airfare JFK to Tel Aviv is roughly $1400 RT, non-stop on El Al. Other airlines fly to Tel Aviv, usually with one stop

WHEN TO GO - Winter can be chilly. Summer blazing hot. Remember, this is a desert. Best to bring layers so you can add and subtract as needed.

HEALTH - No shots are needed.

MISCELLANEOUS - It seemed safe throughout, with a minimum of police presence. The West Bank is done as a group with a local guide. Consulate, tel. 212-499-5400, www.israelemb.org There are consulates in NYC, Wash DC & seven other cities. No VISA for USA citizens.

Jerusalem and Bethlehem - Cities of the birth and death of Christ.


JERUSALEM, ISRAEL, is a city of the ancient world. For the visitor, it's actually two cities. There is greater Jerusalem, the big city with a population of 690,000, and, in the middle, the Old City. As one might suspect, the interesting part is inside the walled confines of the Old. That's what we came to see. The building where Pontius Pilot washed his hands, the streets Jesus walked carrying the cross and the mount he died on.

The Old City is enclosed by a stone wall put up by Suleyman the Magnificent in 1542. It forms a square. Not exactly, but, close enough. In the southeast corner is the Jerusalem Archaeological Park and Davidson Centre. Directly in front of it are the walls surrounding the Temple Mount which takes up approximately 20% of the entire area of the old City. The Mount is the place where Solomon built the first temple (later destroyed, then rebuilt, then destroyed, rebuilt. etc.). It's a holy place for the Muslims. To the north and west of these walls is the Muslim Quarter. Close to the center of the city is the Jewish Quarter. Northwest side is the Christian Quarter, Southwest side is the Armenian Quarter.

We entered by the Dung Gate (south side) to see the exhibits in the Davidson Centre. A wall sign shows a time line - Persians in 500 BC, Hellenistic in 300 BC, Romans from 63 BC, Byzantine from 324 AD, Early Muslim from 638 AD, Crusader 1099 AD. Each conqueror tore down the artifacts of the previous ruler and put up it's own. Which means the streets, temples, churches, buildings and monuments from the time of Christ were gone centuries ago. Now there are buildings atop ruble, atop more ruble. That said, historians have pieced together as best they could, the locations of old. And the religious - Christians, Muslims and Jews - consider them holy places. If the historians are off by a few yards, who knows and who would care.

From the southwest corner of the huge wall of the Temple Mount we can see large stones, lying on the ground. Remnants of Robinson's

Arch that led to the temple. This is the west wall and we head north to it's extension, the Wailing Wall (we have to walk around since there is a blocking perpendicular wall). The west wall was put there 2000 years ago as a retaining wall for the Temple Mount. The Wailing Wall is a small section of the entire west wall. And there is protocol here. Women to the right, men to the left, with a five foot high barricade in between.

The men's side, next to the wall, is busy indeed. Men brought chairs, set up tables, read books, and write notes to push into the wall crevices. Teams of men hold ceremonies next to the women's barricade. The women lean over to cheer them on.

We continue walking through the narrow streets of the Muslim Quarter. Fresh baked pita bread, Fanta orange soda, scarves, shirts, purses, dresses, fresh fruit, you name it. Then we stop at the tiny Church of Flagellation built in 1929. It's on the spot were Jesus first fell. Since it's far too small to hold services, it's probably meant as X marks the spot. Still, it stands out more than the site of his second fall. That's at a doorway with a sign above the door "VII ST".

We have to enter the Christian Quarter to see the huge Church of the Seplucar finished in 335 AD. This is the site where Jesus was buried. Remember, the city has grown in the last 2000 years. Back then, this was outside the city walls. It looks four stories high from the inside. There are many alcoves and several basements. All with poor lighting, large crowds and long lines. The truly devout could easily spend the better part of a day here, but we didn't have that kind of time.

We stopped at an art store in the Jewish Quarter for a change of pace. The brief explanation above may give the impression that the walk (actually a tour) took place in two hours and you could do the same. Not so. There is a line to go through the metal detectors and body search to get to the Wailing Wall, time for lunch and time to go into the major churches. No time for shopping, and still, this visit to the old city started early in the morning and finished in the late afternoon.

Bethlehem is where Jesus was born in a manger. And it's in the West Bank, controlled by the Palestinians. We were told we would be taken to the border and walk to another bus and another guide to enter the city. Someone asked our tour guide what would happen if he came along. He said if the Palestinians found him they would kill him.

After the mandatory stop at the "kick back to the tour guide" jewelry store, we stopped at the Church of the Nativity commissioned by Constantine in 326 AD. It's the marker for the birthplace of Jesus and is the oldest continuously operating church. Some had to bend over to enter the short front door. Clearly meant to exclude soldiers on horseback when it was built. There is a long line on the right of the cavernous inside. That leads to another line to go to the basement and yet another line to look at the small alcove in the wall. Naturally, after waiting hours in line, one isn't apt to look quickly and move on.

Fortunately, our local guide took small groups of us and fed us into the exit, two at a time. Some of the "three hours in line" people complained. We smiled and pretended we didn't hear. Lighting is poor and waiting crowds can be cranky. We were in line for an hour before the shortcut and patience was thinning even among us. If you go alone, bring a lunch.

We walked fifty feet in the dark of night to change busses again. We had stayed together as a group and didn't walk the streets. It felt safe in the bus navigating the narrow streets of Bethlehem. Sort of.

It felt safer the following day when we visited the Israel Museum where the Dead Sea Scrolls are kept. In virtual darkness. With invisible steps on the way in.

There is a beautiful scale model (1:50) of Jerusalem as it was in 66 AD. The fortress walls, buildings with windows, the Temple Mount, streets, courtyards. We could trace the path we had walked the day before from ground level and from an elevated balcony. This would be a good visit before touring the city and again after to put the pieces together.

Then on to the Holocaust Museum. It's not nearly as graphic as some of the WWII presentations on the History channel. From here to the Ben Gurian Institute atop a mountain overlooking miles and miles of empty desert. As far as the eye can see. Nothing green. Nothing moving. Considering what we've seen so far, it's amazing what people can do to make a desert liveable and here and there, an oasis.

THE END

The lowest point on earth - lots of water and not a drop to drink.

TABGHA is the city with the Church of the Loaves and Fishes. Self explanatory name I'd say. Inside, in the center of the altar, is the actual rock upon which Jesus laid five loaves of bread and two fishes that multiplied to feed 5,000 people. A stone table sits above the rock, apparently to keep people from stumbling over it.

From here it is on to the Jordan River and the site where John the Baptist received his own baptism. People celebrate the baptism of Jesus here even though it may have taken place elsewhere. That's just a detail for the Christians that rent a white robe and get into the water to get baptized at the same spot. Naturally, there is a stand that sells water from the Baptismal site. They do note that it's not safe to drink. The Jordan river empties into the Dead Sea and we were headed there for an overnight and a mud bath or a float.

It's the lowest point on earth but didn't feel any different. The water, on the other hand, was very different. The Jordan feeds in but no river leads out so the mineral concentrations build up. The water is 10 times more salty than the ocean. Eleven species of bacteria live in the water, but no fish. This is heavy water and it's apparent as soon as you get in. It's difficult to stand upright when the water hits mid thigh. Before you get to waist level, the water has popped you to the surface. They have installed metal rails that lead into the water. Good thing because the rocky bottom is tough on the feet and you need the rail when the water lifts you up. The water leaves an oily feel to the skin, maybe that's what they're selling in those lotions in the hotel lobby gift shop. The water, the mud and the lotions are suppose to be good for the skin, alleviate arthritis, cure unknown ailments, grow hair on your head and whatever else your willing to believe. Sales are brisk so it must work for some.

The following morning we went to Masada. A stone's throw from the Dead Sea, if you are on top and have a good arm. It's a mountain with a flat top and very steep sides. The ideal place for a castle. It was first fortified between 103 and 76 BC. Herod beefed it up before his death in 4 BC. It's prominence in history came from the Jewish revolt in 66 AD when 967 men, women and children took hold of the fort. There is a way to walk up, it's called the snake path and it's still there. It's wide enough for one, maybe two men at a time. The Roman General was told to quell the revolt and kill the zealots. We can't let them get away with a revolt of any kind or it will spread through out the state. Naturally, the Roman General Flavius Silva sent men up the path first and they were quickly killed. Catapults sent up rocks and fire. Again nothing. So the Romans went about the old technique of laying siege. That means you sit it out and wait for the zealots to run out of water and food.

Unfortunately, the Roman Army was camped out in the middle of the desert where there is no food or water for them. The zealots on top apparently thought ahead and seemed to have plenty of both. The General had to come up with a better idea. This entire drama was made into a wonderful movie with Peter O'Toole playing the Roman General.

We took one of the huge cable cars. Each could hold 40 to 60 people. The car stops just below the top. From the path leading to the top there is a great view of the Snake Path and the Dead Sea in the distance. The flat top is roughly circular with a slanted floor. If you dropped a ball at the north-west corner, it would roll to the south-east corner. The entrance is at the east wall, roughly 3 o'clock. Any wood structures are long gone but pieces of stone walls remain. The center is barren and that's where the Royal Family residence was. The western Palace (9 to 10 O'clock) had the largest building at 4,000 square meters. It had store rooms, a kitchen and underground cisterns to hold water. The Northern wing had the servants quarters. The remains of the Synagogue (10:30) is the oldest in the world. The bath houses (12 to 1 O'clock) had black and red mosaic floors and there was a dressing room with frescoes on the walls and ceiling and a white tiled floor. There was a cold room with a pool and a hot room with a furnace under the floor. Keep in mind, that was 2,000 years ago. Now, we just have stone walls.

Back to the General and his men dropping like flies from heat stroke. The Romans were known for being stubborn. The General was determined to get to the top. He had 8,000 well armed men divided in eight camps, ready to fight but they couldn't get to the top. Roman engineers were the best in the world. They would solve the problem. Build a ramp using Jewish slave labor. And that's what they did. It took time, with dodging incoming arrows and all. But they did it, none the less. When they finally got to the top they found the jews had burned the buildings and committed suicide. Only 2 women and 5 children were left alive. The ramp is still there and can be seen from the top at the western wall (9 O''clock).

Byzantine monks occupied the site during the 5 th and 6 th centuries and then Masada faded into history.

We finished the day in Jerusalem. Atop Mount Olive with a view of the gold plated Dome of the Rock built in the middle of the city in 668-691 AD. It was from this dome that the prophet Mohammed launched himself to heaven to be alongside Allah.

## THE END

Petra, a city carved into rock two thousand years ago.

JORDAN. The guide book says, "If you only go one place in Jordan, make it Petra". What it doesn't say is that when you look at a map, Petra is in the middle of nowhere. There is desert and rough mountains on all sides and it's tough to believe that a thriving city existed here, thousands of years ago. But, it did. Let's look at the area to get some perspective.

Jordan is a country that's almost land locked on the Arabian Peninsula. There is Israel to the west, where they share the Dead Sea. Syria to the north, Iraq to the east and the long southern border is with Saudi Arabia. At the southern tip, there is a tiny opening to the Gulf of Aqaba, in between Israel and Saudi Arabia. Israel's opening here is tiny as well. But it's enough land for both nations to establish ports. Israel's southern (Eliat) and Jordan's only (Aqaba). Petra is about a two hour drive north of Aqaba, through empty desert surrounded by more desert. That's now, but it wasn't always this way.

Petra was built in the third century BC by the Nabateans. They carved temples, palaces, tombs, storerooms and stables into the rocky cliffs. They were located on the direct trade route from Damascus, Syria, to the north and Arabia, to the south. This was the watering hole stop for the caravans carrying spice, silk and slaves. Naturally, they prospered and used the money and their engineering skills to master iron production, hydraulics, copper refining and, of course, stone carving.

There are over 800 registered sites in Petra, 500 of which are tombs. A day trip will only allow us to see the most accessible. An in depth view would take days of climbing the rugged mountains and that's not why we are here.

The easiest way to get there is from Eliat, Israel's port on the gulf. Crossing the border was a song and dance routine. Out of the bus to walk to and through Israel customs and walk to the long line for Jordan immigration. Spending time in line one might wonder if there is a problem with people sneaking into Jordan. If so, why would they use this road when there are hundreds of miles of open desert that's easy to sneak cross.

When we got to the Petra parking lot, the guide was honest with us. It's a long walk in. An hour and a half and all downhill. That means getting back will be all uphill. Then came 3 tips. One, bring a jacket since the desert can get cold suddenly. Two, don't take any pictures on the way down, you'll have plenty of time on the way back. Three, the horse ride out, for the last 800 meters, is included and you only have to tip $5 US. Don't bother, it's not worth it. Walk instead. And off we went.

The path is wide and graveled and it's smart to stay to the right. Two minutes into the walk and horse drawn carriages flew by as though it was the finish line at the Kentucky Derby. Farther along, there were more carriages and an occasional camel. Some going up, others down. So, there is an easy way out, but for how much?

The guide explained the carvings in the stone walls and pointed out the holes (tombs) high up on the cliffs. It was as hot as a sauna and off came the jacket. I had to carry it for the next few hours. Every ten minutes we'd spot a tree. A single piece of green surrounded by reddish brown. While the guide talked, I took pictures.

An hour in, we were at the Sig, the narrow opening in the cliffs leading to the first main monument - The Treasury. It's huge, it's gorgeous and it's considered the best of all the sites. Anyone who has seen pictures of Petra has seen the Treasury. It was featured in "Indiana Jones and the Last Crusade". It was carved out of the sandstone as a tomb for a Nabatean King. So how did it get it's name? It should be called a tomb. Way back when, a rumor started that an Egyptian Pharaoh hid his treasure here while pursuing the Israelites. Some believed it and looked for years - they tried to break open the solid rock urns (to no avail).

There is a large open area in front. Chairs and tables. Time to buy a cup of tea or a bottle of water. There was a film crew working in this large space. They brought their own camels.

I had to climb the Treasury stairs to look inside. Nothing. One large empty room. Smooth rock face on all sides.

The tour continued - path to the right. Tombs and store rooms in the cliff to the left and then, the Amphitheater. Capacity of 8,000. For people to sit on stone seats. Across the way are Bedouins playing a game in the dirt, with small stones and a stick. With the concentration of a chess match. Fifty feet farther, next to the rock face, a couple are having their picture taken (with their own digital camera), with two Bedouins in robes. A small table is set in front with urns sitting on a red table cloth. One of the Arabs and the woman are each wearing a gold crown. I didn't ask.

Next to this area is a huge mountain with carvings and hundreds of holes. The Royal Tombs. The ambitious ones ran over to climb the mountain. I asked the camel driver how much to ride back. $50 US and the price didn't go down. So, walking it was. We had been given 1 ½ hours to get back to the bus and I wouldn't have made it in time if it weren't for the horse ride for the last 800 meters. Walking uphill in the midday sun, carrying my jacket sucked the energy out of me. And the last thing I thought of on the way back, was taking pictures. Oh yes, why did they leave this city? A massive earthquake in AD 555. Mother nature always wins.

Border crossing was quicker on the way back. Just dancing. The next day was for relaxing in this beach town of Eliat, population 35,000. It's unusual in that the airport in the middle. The town (restaurants, bars, shops) are to the east of the runway and the snazzy hotels-on-the-beach, are to the west. Not that there aren't more restaurants and shops around the hotels. There is an iron statue in town celebrating the taking of the town. Israel ground forces fought Jordan troops to take this ground on March 10, 1949. Israel needs a southern port since it's never a given that they will have access to the Suez Canal.

A few miles out of town - not many since the town is only 5 kilometers from the Egyptian border - is the Underwater Observatory Marine Park. You can see fish swimming in the coral reefs from the ocean bottom (13 feet down), snapping turtles and some beautiful fish in tanks with filled with clear water.

The town is the Miami of the Gulf. Beach chairs, boats, sun, first class hotels, an amusement ride that throws you 100 feet into the air, Burger King, jewelry stores, Paddy's Irish bar and some people on the beach wearing bathing suits that you wished were much larger. Just north is 200 KM of desert so I guess it's best to look away from the beach and go have a beer. You don't have to walk very far.

## THE END

From the chaotic heat of Cairo's streets to the bone chilling
cold of the Sinai desert


CAIRO, EGYPT - The tour didn't seem to be jam packed from reading the outline, but, looking back, it certainly was. Thirteen of us, having arrived at various times yesterday and during the night, gathered in the lobby next to the metal detector and armed guard at the door of our hotel. We would get used to metal detectors and armed guards as the days went by. Five men, eight women, median age of 35 and predominantly European. We piled into the van and it was off to the pyramids.

The Great Pyramids are just outside of town. Cheops is the largest in Egypt and dates from 2570 BC. A stones throw away is #2, Chephren and it looks taller because it's built on higher ground. Another stones throw to #3, Mycerinus. For those wishing to see inside, number 2 is the choice and people were lined up to pay the fee, crawl in and see virtually nothing but an empty chamber. We didn't get 10 feet from the van and we were descended on by hawkers trying to sell us something. It was a constant annoyance and at one point I threatened to call the Tourist Police to drive one of them away. Fortunately, there are a lot of uniformed Tourist Police walking around.

A short drive around the corner is the Sphinx, carved from a single block of stone. It's also known as Abu Al-Hol, the father of Terror because the Greeks thought it resembled the mythical winged monster with a woman's head and a lion's body who set riddles and killed anyone unable to answer them. The nose was hammered off between the 11th and 15th centuries. Then, onto the museum for an hours tour. I learned that the statues inside were carved in the form that the Pharaohs wanted to be remembered not as they actually looked.

We were on the road early the next morning. Thirteen of us, Taso, the guide, the van driver, a back up driver and an armed guard wearing a suit to cover the gun (almost cover). The armed guard would stay with us for the entire trip. Drivers would switch off periodically. After stopping at several Police check points, we drove under the Suez Canal onto the Sinai Peninsula. Armed guards could be seen atop the embankments on both sides. Lunch was at the Moon Beach Resort Restaurant, on the Gulf of Suez. Great place to eat and take pictures.

Then, the long drive through featureless desert to Mt. Sinai. It is redundant to mention that the Sinai is a desert with barely a tree or blade of grass because most of Egypt is the same. Things grow and most of the people live on the sides of the Nile. The rest is of the country is desert.

Everyone got up at 2:30 in the morning to drive to the base of Mt. Sinai. Either ride a camel ($12 each way) or walk, half way up in the dark. And then walk the remaining 750 rocky and uneven steps, in the dark, to the top to catch sunrise. The desert gets cold at night. I was shivering with four layers of clothes on. The hotel has a cat that jumps into your lap and insists on being petted, so I chose the cat over the climb.

St. Katherine's Monastery is at the base of the mountain. It was built beside what was believed to be the burning bush from which God spoke to Moses. It's been a place of pilgrimage since 330 AD and is still an active monastery.

That night we made it to the far side of the Sinai, Dahab, on the Gulf of Aquaba. Dahab means gold, in Arabic, and this is Sinai's most popular coastal destination. We had a group supper in town at Friends, on the boardwalk. Six people combined their order to get a huge plate of fish (maybe plate is an understatement). Four waiters delivered it adorned with aluminum foil designed characters around the whole fish and there was lots of yelling and dancing. Along with wine and more than enough fish to eat, their bill came to $20 US each. I had Spicey Macaroni (tasty) and a beer for $6. A good time was had by all.

In the morning we were off to the desert in the back of two enclosed pick ups with bench seats along the sides. But first, a stop at a Bedouin road side stand to buy hand made trinkets. From there it was off road and a bumpy ride it was. Part sand, part soil and part rock, we bounced our way for miles. Then off on foot to find the narrow canyon that leads to nowhere. What better place to rest after a hike, than a Bedouin camp. There are five families that live in the general area, year round. The one chosen has an underground spring and a small oasis of their own. Naturally, they have hand made things to sell and the little kids are the ones doing the selling. And they are very good at it. The men cooked lunch for us over their camp fire. Rice, mixed vegetables, beef and tomato and the biggest piece of bread I've ever seen. We sat inside their long open tent and ate. It was very good.

Onward for the overnight camp out in the Ras Mohammed, Egypt's first National Park. It's located at the bottom of Sinai. Where the Straights of Gubal and Tiran meet (where the Red Sea splits). It's a park without so much as a shrub. The "L" shaped, open sided tent was up when we arrived. It was overcast, windy and cold and it didn't take long for the rebellion. We each had picked a spot, threw down a thin mat and grabbed a blanket. The squat down toilet is 500 yards away. There's no sun and it's cold. Our world is now various shades of brown and grey and we all want to leave. We told Taso, our guide. We'll pay for a hotel, we want out of here. Unfortunately for us, there was no place to go. No hotels close enough.

We decided to build a camp fire and gathered rocks. Three Bedouin helpers (they had their own small tent) gathered wood from who knows where and we lit a fire. Finally some warmth. We had an early supper, around the fire, wrapped in blankets. Rice, mixed vegetables and a mystery meat (I didn't ask). I slept wearing five layers of clothes and three blankets. A bad nights sleep.

Breakfast is worthy of note. Coffee, cookies, a crepe with chocolate syrup and banana and omelette triangles. Very good, actually. Then we drove to the information center to see a film on the diving opportunities in the area and drove to a pebbled beach for snorkeling. It was still grey and overcast but most people donned wet suits and went in the cold water. Then back to the dreaded camp site to get our bags and have lunch. Macaroni& tomatoes with cheese and chicken stew with vegetables and fruit (fresh banana, apples, oranges). At least we eat well.

Onto the port to catch the high speed ferry crossing the Red Sea. There was enough time for a cup of tea before the very rough 2 ½ hour boat ride that sent a lot of people to the bathroom. It's a nice boat, completely enclosed and holds about 150 passengers. And was air borne more than once during the ride. The Hurghada Sea Garden Hotel was a welcome sight after last night and this town, on the mainland, is Egypt's most popular resort destination. Time to rest and shop.

THE END

## SIDEBAR FOR SINAI

GETTING THERE - Arranged through Adventure Center, 1311 63rd St., Ste. 200, Emeryville, CA 94608. tel 800-227-8747. www. adventurecenter.com They are a broker for hundreds of trips run by other tour operators. This tour was done by Explore!, a British company at www.explore.com.uk specializing in low cost, small group trips. The 17 days on the ground is a combination of two trips, Cairo to Sinai and a Nile River cruise. Tour cost of $1400, fees and visa are $85, meals about $300, optional side trips of $400, mandatory insurance of $120. Air fare is extra and prices depend on the time of the year. From the USA, prices range from $1000 to $2000 RT (over the holidays). Adventure Center will book the air fare for you. I went on line to find the best air fare and gave the flight numbers to A.C. to see if they could match the price. They were close enough. Air and tour were paid separately.

WHEN TO GO - Spring and fall avoids the crowds and gives the best weather. Winter is nippy enough to require four layers of clothing at night in the desert. Summer is an oven.

RESTAURANT - In the heart of Cairo, Felfela Downtown, 15 Talaat Harb St., Cairo tel. 3922751. Family style, we had chilled spiced tomatoes, pan bread, several dips, a bowl of steak and egg, eggplant, a mystery plant, a main course of lamb + chicken + steak + chopped beef, 2 thin slices of bread and french fries for $7.50. ½ liter of Stella beer is $2. Recommended.

HEALTH - This is a third world country. See your doctor for shots. Egypt is well known for causing stomach problems. Bring Imodium.

MISCELLANEOUS - You will be hassled by people trying to sell you something from the time you arrive at the airport until you leave the country. Don't count on any of them telling you the truth.

# IX PACIFIC ISLANDS

## CORREGIDOR

An impregnable fortress, they thought.


MANILA, WESTERN LUZON, PHILIPPINES - I didn't know much about Corregidor except it was an island, in the Philippines, one of the last strong holds to fall, and MacArthur said, "I shall return". But I found myself in Manila and the city is worth one day of sight seeing. A tour of Corregidor was $43 and I had the time.

The dock area isn't anything special but the large boat waiting for us is very nice. The 1 hour ride to the mouth of Manila bay was smooth and comfortable. We boarded a bus to climb the first of several long hills. The island is shaped like a sperm. The tail is to the east and has tourist hotels, we stayed to the west. Our first stop was at a large bronze statue of an American helping a wounded Philippine soldier to walk. A very nice piece of artwork. Then on to what remains of the water tanks. There were two, three million gallon water cisterns buried underground. An essential element during a siege. Either age or the Japanese bombs took care of the covers but there is still some water there (green like the surrounding jungle).

Next is the Middle Side barracks, or rather the support beams that remain. Artillery always precedes the landing of troops and the Japanese shelled the island for days. There is a crater for every 25 meters of land. Japanese ships laid down a devastating barrage from miles away in the bay. They needed to blow away as much cover and kill as many soldiers as they could before landing their own troops on the shore. Shelling on Corregidor began on the same day as Pearl Harbor, December 8, 1942. It was scheduled at the same time but on the other side of the date line.

On to the mortar emplacements, there are 2 and the Japanese ships tried their best to knock out both. This was important since either could lob 12" shells onto the beach and that's a big shell by the way. The mortar batteries (4 mortars each) were concealed by walls and jungle overgrowth. Flying overhead for a sighting was a suicide mission. Each gun is bolted to a steel plate which is in turn bolted to the concrete pad. The Japanese did knock one battery out and divots in the barrels remain as evidence of the shrapnel. The doors to the shell bunkers are blown off (that's were they stored the ammo). Then we went to the top of the hill for the 12" long guns. They differ from the mortars because these guys could fire 17 miles. The mortars only lob up and down. The big gun barrel weights 54 tons. Not the biggest in the world, mind you. Big guns on ships have 80 ton barrels. But still, these guns could hit the Japanese ships and were target number one for the Japanese.

Around the bend is the Top Side Barracks, the command center and rightfully on the highest point of the island. Naturally, only a shell of the building remains. This is an open area holding the parade grounds, the light house and now, a souvenir shop. Towards the end of the war, the allied force had to take Corregidor back and this is where the paratroopers landed. The Japanese were caught by surprise since they were convinced the area was too small for paratroopers to land and were unprepared. It saved a lot of lives on both sides.

Our next stop was the Pacific War Memorial. As you walk towards the sea, you enter a large white concrete dome building with a hole in the roof. The hole is placed so the light shines on the white pedestal beneath on June 6, the day of the Treaty noting the end of the war. The walk on the other side to the ocean view is a pretty one marked with an aesthetic statue.

Lunch is included on the tour in the big house overlooking the boat pier. A modern building and a recent addition to the island.

On to the receding or hiding guns. They too are bolted on steel plates that are bolted on concrete. Hidden by walls and beneath the natural jungle growth. But these guys are different. They are bigger than the mortars, smaller than the big guns on top and actually move up and down. Hinges and crossing arms allow the gun to rise above the walls to fire and then retract to ground level for concealment.

The Japanese have a War Memorial for their dead called The Garden of Peace. I'll refrain from comment here.

The Philippine government has an extensive monument with large raised copper plaques imbedded in stone depicting scenes of battle from the Spanish-American war to WWII. Each plate is a work of art. Finally we return to seaside, next to the pier and a large bronze statue of MacArthur with his right hand above his head. The fact of the matter is that he didn't say, "I shall return" until he landed in Australia.

But then, what's the point of putting the statue there.

## THE END

## SIDEBAR FOR CORREGIDOR

GETTING THERE - I got to Manila on the Cathay Pacific air pass. It includes 21 days free travel (unless you register online at www.cathay-usa. com as a CyberTraveler to get a total of 31 travel days) from HKG to 15 cities Cathay Pacific flies to in South East Asia. All flights originate in and return to HKG and repeats are not allowed. The itinerary must be agreed on beforehand and tickets will be issued for each segment. Premium cities in India, Australia and New Zealand can be added from $ 200-500. Segment changes can be made afterwards for an additional fee.

There is no question that this is a great deal and Cathay Pacific words their agreement very precisely. No departure from the approved plan or the entire trip ticket is void. It's smart to work out the schedule (which will take several hours) in advance to allow time to catch the next flight. Also, be flexible since some flights are full and you won't know until after you submit your plan. Once approved, you're OK. Call Cathay Pacific 1-800-228-4297 or fax at 1-800-617- 9470 for free brochures. Book through a travel agent. There are several daily flights from HKG to Manila.

ACCOMMODATIONS - In Manila the choices are as varied as New York City or Los Angeles, from 5 star to no star. There is a hotel desk at the airport and they can book at a discount. Centerpoint Hotel rooms are $50-100, tel 521-2751. Swagman Hotel is in the $80 range. The Palm Plaza (3 stars) is a block from the upscale Robinson's shopping mall, with rooms from $100-200. There should be no need to book in advance, I was there during a International convention and still had a choice of hotels.

LOCAL ARRANGEMENT - This trip can be booked at most any hotel. The boat terminal for Sun Cruises is next to the Cultural Center of the Philippines just south of the center of town and 2 blocks west of the Century Park Sheridan Hotel. tel. 831-8140. Boats leave daily at 8AM and return to Manila at 4PM. Weekends and Holidays have an additional trip from 10AM to 6PM. Price $60 each with an additional charge for the light and sound show.

MISCELLANEOUS - No visas are required for USA citizens.

Guam - Why go there?

Tourism is Guam's biggest industry. They receive more tourists than any Pacific Island other than Hawaii. They have four and five star hotels that line Tumon Bay, less than a half hour from the International Airport. Beaches, pools, fine dining, snorkeling, spas, golf, tennis (yes, I saw people playing in 100 degree heat), and duty free shopping. Guam is a whole lot closer to Japan than Hawaii and it's a little bit cheaper. That's why over 80% of the tourists here are Japanese. Two miles from the strip (Pale San Vitores Road runs along the entire Tumon Bay beach) is the Micronesia Mall, Guam's largest.

Several miles south, at the other end of the bay is Guam Premier Outlets. Both large shopping centers are inland, air conditioned and have free bus service from every large hotel. The Japanese save money on the air fare which they can use to buy an empty duty free suitcase and fill it with duty free designer clothes that are a fraction of the price they would pay back home. They can save more on merchandise than their package trip cost. Naturally, the hotels are geared for Japanese Tour groups and many of the hotels are owned by the Japanese.

That said, Guam has a strong USA military presence. More so now that we are out of the Philippines. Military facilities cover 30% of the land area of the Territory. U.S. citizens can travel here without a passport but it would be foolish to travel without one. Guam is a free port with duties charged only on tobacco, liquor and fuel. The tap water is safe to drink, not so in many of the surrounding islands. Prices here are better than Hawaii but any savings would be eaten up by the additional air fare. So then, why go here unless you're visiting family in the military?

Guam is centrally located. The Pacific Ocean stops here, the Philippine sea is on the west side. After WWII, Continental Air virtually took over all the flights in the area. Continental Micronesia is the regional carrier and flies north, south, east and west to the islands in the area. Saipan, the capital of the Northern Marianas is north. Yap, the Western Carolina Islands, is to the west. Chuuk, to the south, Pohnpei to the east. Continental has non stop service from Hawaii to Guam (7 ½ hours air time). They also have an island hopper - either direction - that goes Guam - Chuuk, Pohnpei, Kosrae, Kwajalein, Majuro, Honolulu. So, if you want to visit any of these other islands, you have to do it from Guam. So if you're going to be here anyway, spend a few days and see the sights.

South of town is Nimitz Hill, War in the Pacific National Park. High atop the bay, it over looks Apra Harbor, the best deep water port west of Hawaii. It's the site of the Allied landing on July 21, 1944. The hill on the right, is Banzai Hill on which the Japanese led a failed charge on July 25, 1944. There is a bronze memorial to the left listing to names of the local people who lost their lives during the occupation. The names are fading through the vagaries of time and weather.

Farther south is Ga'an Point where the Allies landed in July, 1944. The remains of Japanese caves and gun emplacements are still here. Three flags are flown here to honor the dead and it's a disgrace that one of them is for Japanese soldiers who had no business being here in the first place. It's clear what impact the tourist dollar has.

It's easy enough to drive around the island and there is a beautiful bridge at the bottom. Little else to see except run down villages. There is an actual town, Hagatna, south of Tumon Bay, and it has it's own shopping center but little else. Come to think of it, you only have to walk the strip, in front of the hotels, to get designer clothes, watches and what ever. You don't have to go far to shop till you drop.

## THE END

SIDEBAR FOR GUAM

GETTING THERE - There are no direct flights from the mainland USA. From the west coast, you change planes in Honolulu on Continental Air. Fares of $1300 RT. Japan Air Lines and Northwest Air also service Guam. If you want to use the island hopper to visit the Carolina Islands it's easier to book Continental in both directions.

WHEN TO GO - Guam has an average temperature of 80 degrees year round with little variation. The rainiest month is September, followed by the 2 months in either direction.

HOTELS - There are scores of hotels to choose from, all on Tumon Bay. The highest price is the Pacific Island Club starting at $295/D. www. pacificislandsclub.com. The Hyatt Regency is $290/D. www.hyattguam. com. The Guam Marriott Resort is $250/D. www.marriotthotels.com. The Hilton Guam Resort & Spa starts at $175/D. www.guamhilton.com. The Hilton is where you're apt to find more Americans. If they were all the same price, I'd chose the Marriott first and the Hilton second. For the Budget traveler, two blocks up the hill from the Hilton is Hunter's Inn with rooms from $55/D. email: hunters@netpci.com. Rooms have A/C and there is a bar and restaurant on the premises.

HEALTH - No shots necessary. You can drink the tap water.

MISCELLANEOUS - For additional information contact guaminfo@ visitguam.org.

## MOUNT PINATUBO
Ash to Ash, a view from above.

Mt. Pinatubo volcano after the eruption, the Philippines

ANGELES CITY, WESTERN LUZON, PHILIPPINES - I remember seeing on TV, the blizzard of ash settling on buildings and cars, people with umbrellas wading through streets filled with gray powder and mud. Mounds of mush everywhere like the streets of Buffalo after a January storm. But in Buffalo it was clean, it was snow. The snow didn't fill the air and try to take your breath away like it did there. Mount Pinatubo hadn't erupted in 600 years and it was making up for lost time.

That eruption was in 1991 and I was far away at the time. But now I was in Manila and the volcano was only 55 miles northwest. There isn't a whole lot to see in Manila so it would make a good side trip.

I caught the van from the Centerpoint Hotel, $10.50 for a 2 hour ride. One of the other passengers got off in downtown Angeles City which reminded me of the side streets of Juarez where all the action is. The word that comes to mind is seedy. Two miles out of town, the van stopped at it's final destination, the Sunset Garden Inn. As good as anywhere, I checked in. The Sunset Garden looks like a 30 year old, Hollywood, California, apartment house. Two stories, open center, pool in the middle, weight room on the end, pool table and singles and couples hanging about. The difference is the bar and restaurant next to the pool and the guys all seemed ex-military. I fit in fine. A bottle of San Miguel is a buck.

Pictures for the various trips are on the wall next to front desk and I was directed to Rene for information. He spends a bit of time here organizing tours. The on-the-ground walking tour caught my eye for $80. It's a full day. The jeep takes you as far as it can go and from there it's a 2/1/2 hour trek. You have to bring extra socks and shoes since you walk through a stream, plus 2 liters of water, an extra shirt and a backpack. They will supply the backpack. I would have to add my large Nikon, 2 lenses and film. Then there was the airplane ride over the open crater, also for $80. A better view - the mountain is 4,800 feet high -no wet shoes and socks, no schlepping through mud, no five hours of walking through a landscape apparently devoid of features (the pictures on the wall). My fear of flying in small airplanes seemed unimportant. We were to leave at the crack of dawn the following morning.

## THE AIRSTRIP

I was up at 6AM, had breakfast and was ready to go. Rene said the clouds weren't co-operating and we would have to wait. He paid for more coffee.

At 8AM, six of us piled into the van for the short ride to Clark AFB. The guard at the gate gave us a cursory glance and we drove in and parked behind a hanger. It's well kept, big enough for a commercial jet but housing only our tiny silver bird. A three seater plus pilot, single prop and the metal skin shined in the morning light. The pilot is ex-Air Force. A fighter pilot that was stationed here and stayed after retirement. Married locally and lives close by. He was here during the eruption. I'm ex-Air Force myself and we chatted. They had three days notice that the volcano was going to erupt and the Air Force evacuated the base. The wind from the initial eruption blew most of the ash the other way, towards Subic Bay. So the base, only 10 miles away, wasn't hurt that badly. But there was a big push at the time for Philippine independence, in other words, get the Americans out. So the Air Force used this as a good time to leave and not return. The Philippine Government turned the base into a free market zone, whatever that means, since there is virtually no activity now. The Air Force used to fly more sorties in a day than the Philippine Air Force now flies in a month. The base is remarkably well preserved. The terminal building and control tower are within a stones throw from our hanger and appear as well maintained as they would be if there were people about.

As soon as we cleared the immediate grounds of the air field, the effect of the killing ash was apparent. Years later and it still looked like the surface of the moon. The ground was dead. There was a little bit of green here and there, but, just a little. Rolling ridges of bare earth, stream cuts through the crests with no stream water. The eruptions in 1991 produced a column of ash and smoke that went 19 miles high and rock debris fell the same distance from the volcano. It left 100,000 people homeless and 700 dead. To make matters worse, it erupted again in August,1992 killing 72 more.

Clouds were still lingering around the top but we were able to fly around the rim and see into the crater from three sides. It's deceptively peaceful and the center contains an attractive emerald green lake. It's the only part of the blown out mountain top that is green. From this height I could see the Pacific Ocean in the distance and barren earth in every direction.

I took a last look from the hanger and the volcano looks foreboding even from a distance, possibly more so because I know the damage it did and will do again.

The guard at the gate looked into the van on our way out and was disappointed that he didn't find a dismantled control tower in the back seat. I suppose that would have made his day meaningful. I guess he is thankful he has a job, 10,000 jobs vanished when the USAF pulled out.

I checked out the other five motels/hotels within a block of the Sunset after an inexpensive (in relation to Manila) pool side lunch and San Miquel. They are newer, probably more family oriented and priced about the same. They are all far removed from the bustle of downtown which is only 10 minutes by tri-motorcycle, the local taxi. There is an attractive church in the same block as the motels. If you go downtown be sure to visit Margueritaville for food and beverage, it's the best in town. Don't expect the grill at Ritz-Carlton.

THE END

## SIDEBAR FOR MOUNT PINATUBO

GETTING THERE - I got to Manila on the Cathay Pacific air pass. It includes 21 days free travel (unless you register online at www.cathay-usa.com as a CyberTraveler to get a total of 31 travel days) from HKG to 15 cities Cathay Pacific flies to in South East Asia. All flights originate in and return to HKG and repeats are not allowed. The itinerary must be agreed on beforehand and tickets will be issued for each segment. Summer departures (May 8 to Aug 21) are $ 200 extra. Upgrades to 1 st class are about twice the price. Premium cities in India, Australia and New Zealand can be added from $ 200-500. Segment changes can be made afterwards for an additional fee. Book through a travel agent.

There are several daily flights from HKG to Manila. There are daily busses from the Swagman Hotel, A Flores St. and the Centerpoint Hotel, Mabini St., both in Ermita (downtown Manila) to Angeles City for $10.50. They will drop you off where you want.

ACCOMMODATIONS - In Manila the choices are as varied as New York or Los Angeles, from 5 star to no star. There is a hotel desk at the airport and they can book at a discount. Centerpoint Hotel rooms are $70-100, tel 521-2751. Swagman Hotel is in the $90 range. The Palm Plaza is a block from the upscale Robinson's shopping mall, 3 stars and rooms from $100-200. There should be no need to book in advance, I was there during an International convention and still had a choice of hotels.

In Angeles City, the Centerpoint van ends at The Sunset Garden Inn, $40 with A/C and $35 without. Within a block, on the same street, are five similar hotels, some newer, same price range. Some of the others may be more family oriented.

FOOD - Stick to the hotels.

LOCAL ARRANGEMENT - The Sunset has wall brochures advertising the trips and the owner of Sports, Action and Adventure,

Rene M. Wyss (Swiss not German) is often hanging about. He is no hassle, friendly and willing to accommodate. In addition to the airplane rides, they offer trekking, mountain biking, scuba diving (I don't know where but it can't be in Angeles City), windsurfing, ultralight flying, golf, and go-karting. Write to Premiere Hotel, Malabanias Rd., Plaridel I, 2009 Angeles City, Philippines. tel (63)045-892-6239, fax (63)045- 892-6237, e-mail = sportsaa@mozcom.com

MISCELLANEOUS - No visas are required for USA citizens.

Pohnpei, with the ruins of four cultures
Micronesian, Spanish, Germain and Japanese


Pohnpei is the capital of the Federated States of Micronesia. The FSM, from east to west, are the islands of Yap, Chuuk (formerly Truk), Pohnpei (formerly Ponape) and Kosrae. I know, where are they? Well, Pohnpei is 2,024 miles south east of Japan, 2,389 miles north east of Sydney, Australia and 2,685 miles west of Honolulu. Yes, it's in the middle of the Pacific Ocean.

One report puts people on this island in 200 AD. Another has the Saudeleur Dynasty ruling from 1,000 AD to 1,600 AD. Another has Saudeleur rule from 500 AD to 1,450 AD. Much of this is speculation from study of the ruins at Nan Madol. And even today, it's a mystery how the huge stones at these ruins were quarried, transported and assembled.

It is known that individual tribes took care of their own. Clans lived separately, in their own territory and had their own ruler. People worked in groups and food was shared. Children were raised communally. The ruins at Nan Madol do indicate there was a consensus government that connected the various tribes.

Jumping ahead, the Spanish first spotted the island in 1529 but sailed by. They islanders were left alone until whalers arrived in the early 1800's. In 1852 missionaries arrived. That meant the natives were encouraged to wear clothes. In 1854 an American whaler brought smallpox and that wiped out half the population. The Spanish came back only after the Germans laid claim to all the Carolinas (the FSM and other islands). The Spanish then built a town wall and a fort at Kolonia but finally gave up on the island and sold it to Germany in 1899. The Japanese forced the Germans off in 1914 and occupied Pohnpei. The Japanese were on our side during WWI. Japan built up the island and moved in thousands of colonists. In 1941 they outnumbered the Pohnpeians three to one. Naturally, the Japanese fortified the island during WWII but it was never a major base. The Americans launched 200 bombing raids but never landed any troops.

The Budget Rent a car office is in town, Kolonia (the only real town). Across from the Spanish wall (1887) and spitting distance from the Ambrose grocery store. Not much remains of the wall which now is the outside boundary for a baseball field. The Spanish Fort Alfonso XIII disappeared long ago. Close to the store is a statue to commemorate the Japanese that died between 1914 and 1944.

Armed with a car we drove to Sokens island to investigate the Japanese gun emplacements from WWII. The island road is congested with dogs, chickens and children who seemed to resent our driving on their road. A closer read in the guide book shows that Sokens rock is 658 high and it's a two hour climb. It's 80 degrees outside the air conditioned car and the humidity is close to 100 percent. We turned the car around, drove to the airport to confirm our reservations onto Honolulu. The plane coming here was packed. Better safe than sorry.

Since we were close, lunch at the Pwohmaria Beach Resort seemed in order. It's the nicer of the two hotels on the airport island. I had a very nice hamburger with fries for $3 and made the mistake of ordering a bowl of Chicken Soup for $4 (before the hamburger arrived). The soup came in a bowl big enough to feed a family of four. There are spaghetti type noodles, chicken, carrots, cauliflower and cabbage. I asked if we could make it "take out" and they came up with an empty Folgers' coffee can. With the plastic lid. Why not, this would be supper.

The German presence is marked by the burned out ruins of their bell tower located behind the Spanish wall. It's not much, but then the Germans weren't here that long. A new church, Our Lady of Mercy, sits 100 feet away.

The FSM capital complex was built in 1989 and is way out of town. The land must have been free since this location is convenient to absolutely nothing. There is a collection of attractive, low rise buildings, with lawns, surrounded by jungle. The President has his own building as does the

Congress and the Judicial branch. There was no one outside which could mean they were all hard at work.

A mile and a half south of the capital complex is the College of Micronesia. Again, lots of lawn and no one in sight. There are no beer bars or fast food places anywhere in the area. So, the students must be studying.

Our hotel owner said we could see all of the Nan Madol ruins on our own. An hour and a half drive south (25 miles). No need to pay for the boat trip run by the Village Hotel. We could drive there and save a lot of money. We took him at his word. Our first mistake.

An hour out of the city on the only paved road on this side of the island and there is a right turn. At the Ice Maker sign. Straight ahead is a narrow paved road. To the right, a two lane road with a center stripe and that's the one we took. Pohnpei is round. The city, Kolonia, is at 12 o'clock, Nan Madol about 4 o'clock. A half an hour later we stopped for help at one of the many road side stands. We were now at the bottom of the island. 6 o'clock.

Back to the Ice sign and turn right. We went over a causeway, onto a dirt road, back to pavement and stopped a guy walking on the road. "Yes, straight ahead" he said. Finally we were on track. It changed back to a dirt road and it got narrower. Too narrow to turn the car around. Now, we had to keep going forward. We passed two dirt roads on the right and finally came to a stop at the ocean. I got out to look. Water and rock, that's it. Time to pack it in. There have been no road signs for what should be the island's number one attraction. We should have taken the boat tour.

I had a hunch. No particular reason. I looked down both side roads as we passed and saw nothing. We drove 2 ½ hours to get here, so, one more shot. We backed up to the closest side road to turn around and drove to the second. No signs, just jungle. Turn left and lets see what happens.

A half mile in was the sign and two guys standing next to it - waiting to collect $1. Admission fee? Who knows. It's only a buck. We drove down another badly maintained dirt road and stopped at a small jungle clearing 100 feet from someone's house. We walked to the house to ask for directions and found out, we were there. $3 each. Parking fee? Another admission fee? After all this frustration, three bucks is nothing. We paid, they pointed. Walk around the house, cross the lawn and follow the sea shell path.

Nan Madol is the name of the city. It was built on the sea between 500 and 1500 AD. Probably over water to make it more difficult to attack. There are 92 artificial islands for the residence and tombs of the Royal family, servants quarters, guest house, storage houses, religious center, administrative center and coconut oil producing plant. The stone logs used for construction were probably taken from Sokens Island and floated here by raft. The logs vary in diameter from one inch to one foot and in length from three to ten feet. This dimension guess is from the rectangular pile of stacked dark logs seen 50 feet into the jungle, behind the house. The walking path is well marked and made from white sea shells. Stacks of logs are on the right, swamp to the left. The first water crossing has a rickety bridge of loose wood boards. It moves when you walk across, but the fall would only be two feet. Then comes more bridges and additional stacks of logs. Two hundred feet ahead are stone logs, casually discarded next to a stream. Now the moving bridge, with no hand rail, has a six foot fall. This is not the place to break any bones. The best way to see the buildings is from a boat, at high tide. Not from the shore.

The Village is arguably the finest place to stay on the island. Even though it's way out of town, on the road to Nan Madol. A paved road leads from town to the hotel sign and then the adventure begins. There is ½ mile of single lane dirt road on the side of a mountain with a 600 foot drop on the right. A mistake here and they would never find the car or the bodies.

You park on the road. It widens when you get to the facility. Enter at the Deliveries Only sign - the hole in the wall. The Village has 20 thatched huts, with bamboo walls, scattered on the hill side. The lobby/restaurant/ open bar is called the Tattooed Irishman. The food is very good and reasonably priced. The turkey sandwich had real turkey, not processed. The coffee is excellent. The view is the best you will find on the island. The huts have oversized waterbeds, ceilings fans (no air conditioning), private baths and no phones. If you come to Pohnpei with romance in mind, this is the ONLY place to stay.

Pohnpei, if not third world, is close to it and that usually presents a health problem. I ate at many places, all over town, and never got sick. An unusual way to recommend a place but I can't make that same statement for Mexico.

# THE END

## SIDEBAR FOR POHNPEI

GETTING THERE - There are no direct flights from the mainland USA to Guam. From the west coast, you change planes in Honolulu on Continental Air. Fares of $1300 RT. Japan Air Lines and Northwest Air also service Guam. You have to use the island hopper to visit the Carolina Islands and it's easier to book Continental in both directions. Continental Micronesia runs the island hopper three times a week between Guam and Honolulu. From Guam, it stops at Chuuk, Pohnpei, Kosrae, Kwajalein, Majuro, then Honolulu. The same islands in each direction but you can't get off the plane in Kwajalein unless you're military. Stops are free on an unlimited ticket. Only one stop is allowed if you cash in miles.

Flight times are, 6 hours from HNL to Majuro or California, 7 ½ hours HNL to Guam, 16 hours from Guam to HNL on the island hopper (including stops).

WHEN TO GO - Pohnpei has an average temperature of 80 degrees year round with little variation. It rains virtually year round. The 2 driest months are Jan - Feb. and they aren't exactly dry. The coast averages 200 inches of rain a year, the interior gets 400 inches. It may rain every day, but not all day.

HOTELS - There are 13 hotels to choose from. Two are at the airport and the nicer looking one is Pwohmaria Beach Resort, $70/D. tel. (691)320-5941. There is a beach (sort of), don't look for the resort. The highest price is the Ocean View Plaza Hotel - West, $125/D, which is attached to the Ocean View Plaza - East, $110/D. www.fm/oceanview They have a good looking bar and a nice dining area (inside and outside). The nicest hotel is located way out of town and you're isolated without a car. The Village, $105/D. www.theVillageHotel.com Grass huts on the side of a mountain with a great view. First class dining, good bar. On the edge of the island's only town is Cliff Rainbow Hotel, $90/D. email: cliffrainbow@mail.fm Nice dining room, inside and outside. Of the 2 hotel/apartments with kitchens, only one is in town. Yvonne's Hotel, $70/D. Tel. (691)320-5130. email: yneth@hotmail.com Large room, A/C, hot plate, pots, plates and utensils, big frig. The outside view of the other hotels did not tempt me to want to look inside.

PLACES TO EAT - The Village - a very good turkey sandwich, with fries for $4.50 and great coffee. Roast beef also good. Ole Restaurant attached to the Ambrose store has breakfast and lunch only. Cliff Rainbow Hotel - "Across the Street Restaurant" fell into the ocean. Now, the restaurant is attached to the hotel. Ham and egg sandwich with fries and coffee = $6. Very nice. Ocean View Plaza - good pork chops, nice view, recommended. Pwohmaria Hotel (at the airport). Good hamburger with fries = $3, coffee = $1, huge bowl of Chicken Noodle Soup = $4. Angie's Hamburgers = $3, the only fast food looking place on the island. They do a thriving take out business.

HEALTH - No shots necessary. Do not drink the tap water.

MISCELLANEOUS - For additional information contact www.visit-fsm.org/pohnpei.

If you moved Rodeo Drive 5,750 miles west
you would be in Saipan

Saipan is a short hop north of Guam and is the Capital of the Commonwealth of the Northern Marianas. There are 14 islands but only the southern three have a population to speak of and that comes to a total of 69,000. The people, by Covenant, are American citizens. Like those on Guam.

Although there is an active garment industry (made in the USA), the biggest draw is tourism. They have four and five star hotels that line the beach and two star hotels a block in. Beaches, pools, fine dining, snorkeling, spas, golf, tennis, and duty free shopping. You name a designer and they have a shop here. Probably more than one. Saipan is cheaper than Guam and Guam is cheaper than Hawaii. And both islands are a whole lot closer to Japan than Hawaii. That's why 85% of the tourists here are Japanese.

The main town is Garapan and the stores are within easy walking distance. The Japanese save money on air fare which they can use to buy an empty duty free suitcase and fill it with duty free designer clothes that are a fraction of the price they would pay back home. They can save more on merchandise than their package trip cost. Naturally, the hotels are geared for Japanese Tour groups and many of the hotels are owned by the Japanese.

That said, we didn't come here to shop. This island was the center of some fierce fighting during the Second World War and Saipan is where you get the boat to the neighboring island of Tinian and the airfield that the Enola Gay took off from.

Driving north from Garapan, close to the tip is the Okinawa Peace Memorial erected after the war by the Japanese. A beautiful setting with red flower blossoms and green palm trees. And then you look behind to the massive cliffs. A straight drop of 820 feet. Yes indeed, that's suicide cliff. A fitting place for the memorial at it's base.

Right next to the memorial is the Japanese Last Command Post. The round lookout, imbedded in the rock is still there. Flanked by Japanese long guns that look like they cold still work. A shelled Japanese tank sits there as a pile of rubble. There was fierce fighting here in mid-1944. The Japanese had all but lost the war and were desperate as the Allies got closer and closer to their homeland. General Saito ordered his men to take seven lives each for the Emperor, then didn't follow his own orders. He committed seppuku. There is a trail for those who choose to walk up. We drove three miles to get to the top of suicide cliff. Hundreds of Japanese soldiers jumped to their death from here rather than surrender. There are memorials atop to remember them.

Going back down the hill and taking the side road to the right, all the way to the sea, and you're at the Grotto. A pretty, yet scary, sunken pool of water fed by two underground passages to the sea. A favorite place for divers and there are warnings that this place is for experts only. I wasn't the least bit tempted.

Next stop was the northern tip of the island, Banzai Cliff. The Japanese told the locals that the Americans would beat and torture them. Foolishly believing them, entire families lined up here and jumped. Grave markers line the cliff side. Locals claim that the white terns that ride the winds now didn't exist before the war. They bear the souls of the dead.

On the north end of Garapan is a large park and the Saipan American Memorial. It's for the Americans that lost their lives here in WWII.

If there's time to spare, look for IHOP. One block in from the main road. The International House Of Prayer was destroyed in 1944. The Japanese, as a gesture of peace, rebuilt it in 1985. It's not breathtaking but it is peaceful. And quiet.

Back in town, we saw the Hard Rock Café sign and went into the mall. The truth be told, parks are outside and it's over 100 degrees. The mall is air conditioned and it costs nothing to look. We found the Hard Rock Café clothing store but not the café. Humm. Maybe Ralph Lauren is having a sale.

THE END

## SIDEBAR FOR SAIPAN

GETTING THERE - There are no direct flights from the mainland USA. From the west coast, you change planes in Honolulu on Continental Air (fares of $1300 RT) to Guam. RT from Guam to Saipan is $100 on Continental Micronesia. Japan Air Lines and Northwest Air also service Guam. If you want to use the island hopper to visit the Carolina Islands on the way to or from Guam, it's easier to book Continental in both directions. Continental, Northwest and JAL have direct flights from Japan to Saipan.

WHEN TO GO - Saipan has an average temperature of 80 degrees year round with little variation. The rainiest month is September, followed by the 2 months in either direction.

HOTELS - There are many hotels to choose from, most in the main town of Garapan although there are some farther south on the same side of the island. The highest price is the Pacific Island Club starting at $220/D. reservations@picaipan.com. The Hyatt Regency is $160/D. rsv.hrsaipan@saipan.com. For the Budget traveler, Hertz rent a car (at the airport) has a deal with Saipan Ocean View Hotel for $55/day/double and a Toyota for $44/day. A 2 star hotel (email:sovh@itecnmi.com) with a restaurant and one block from the DFS shopping mall.

HEALTH - No shots necessary. It should be safe to drink the tap water, but, better to be safe and stick to bottled.

MISCELLANEOUS - For additional information contact www.mymarianas.com They have a list of hotels and prices. This is an American Territory so passports aren't necessary but it would be foolish to travel without one.

Tinian - the island from which the Enola Gay took off
to drop the Atomic Bomb on Hiroshima

The odds were bad. Eighty five percent of the hotel rooms on Tinian
are at the Dynasty Hotel & Casino. A five star hotel whose lobby, it's said,
is a sight to behold. Before leaving home, I checked for the availability of
rooms at the hotel, on the Internet, and there were none. Apparently lots
of people were going to be beholding while we were in Saipan. That was
then. Now, we were in Saipan and were only a one hour's boat ride away.

The written schedule shows the first boat leaving Saipan at 9:30 AM
and there are returning boats at 8:30 AM (that's if we get to stay the night),
12:30 PM (if we stay the night and want to sleep late before returning) and
5:30 PM (if we can't get a room and look around the island from 10:30
AM to 4:30 PM). We would need a car whether it was 6 hours or a full day.

We got to the dock early and waited. At nine, the ticket booth opened
but the guy inside pointed to the booth across the way. I walked 30 feet and
bought tickets for $3 each. A bargain. Then a Japanese tour group arrived
and we noticed they had 2 tickets each. Back to the first booth to get a boat
ticket. Apparently, the first ticket was a dock fee although neither booth
guys ever said so. With tickets in hand and time to kill I read the posted
sign. Departures from Tinian, 8:30 AM, 12:30 PM. That's it. No 5:30
PM. That means if we couldn't get a room, we'd only have two hours and
that's not enough time to see anything but the lobby of the casino. Time
for a decision. If we knew before hand that the schedule had changed, we
probably wouldn't be at the dock. But we were. Time to roll the dice, we
got on the boat.

A beat up school bus was waiting at the dock in Tinian for a free ride
to the Casino. With nothing but hope and no change of underwear, we
got on. The guide book was right, the outside of the Dynasty is nothing
to write home about.

The attractive, and pleasant, girl behind the counter asked for ID and mentioned the service. Taking the Que, I presented my Military ID and that did the trick. We not only got a room, we got a discount as well. My friend found the car rental place at the hotel and with map of the island in hand, we were on our way. Luck beat skill. This time.

Because Tinian is shaped like Manhattan, the G.I.'s named the roads appropriately. The casino address is 1 Broadway, the bottom end of the road. This two lane road runs up the middle of the island. As it turns out, the single lane on the right is the only lane with consistent asphalt. A mile later, we stopped at the boarded up Japanese Radio Communication building which was used for inter island messages during WWII.

Broadway stops at the circle containing the American Memorial Shrine. It's a modest monument to honor those killed on Tinian. North of here is the top end of the island (about 20 % of the area) and the road splits, on either side, to move close to the ocean. A mile or so later, a dirt road on the right takes us to the blowhole. It's a slippery walk if you want to get close.

Driving back, we crossed the main road and drove into the jungle ending up on Runway Able. The very runway used by the Enola Gay to drop the Atomic Bomb on Hiroshima. There are four parallel runways, all running east to west and Able looks good enough to land a plane on even today. In 1945 this was the largest and busiest airfield in the world. Each runway is 8,500 feet long and 200 feet wide. A total of 19,000 combat missions flew from here. The four runways are connected by damaged, but drive able, asphalt. We weaved south, around patches of jungle that had broken through, to the second runway. It hasn't stood the test of time as well. We went back to drive the length of Able and discovered a road at the half way point leading north to a paved rectangle and the remains of support buildings for the airfield. There's the Japanese Air Operations Building, the shell of the Japanese Air Administrations Building and two, barely damaged, rounded, concrete Air Raid Shelters. Apparently only a direct hit would take these guys out.

A connecting road leads north to a large concrete pad. Separated by 150 feet are two bomb pits. Each held an Atomic bomb and are now glass enclosed with black and white pictures inside from WWII. The bomb, the crew, the plane. One bomb in each storage pit. But if you think about it, if either went off, 150 feet wouldn't mean very much.

We drove out the back end (north) and took the other ocean- side road, south to 8th Ave. It dead ends at the back side of Tinian Airport and it's fenced. A crummy looking dirt road goes to the right. I hate going back. Oh well, in for a penny. We drive to the right, up the hill, into the jungle and the road gets worse. The potholes are big enough to hide a refrigerator. Grass between the ruts in the road are cleaning the underside of the car. The road curves left at the top of the hill. A single lane dirt road and no clearance on either side to turn around. We slowly bump down the road and finally spot an asphalt road at the bottom. Thank goodness it's a rental car.

The coffee shop in the hotel is actually in the casino. The far corner. The reasonably priced club sandwich was big enough that half of it went into a doggy bag for the refrigerator in the room. Now, we had time to look at the hotel lobby and it's gorgeous. The marble is black and pink and white and red. The hotel has 1.5 million square feet of Italian marble. The lobby dome is 8,000 square feet. The huge chandelier took three weeks to assemble. This lobby is stunning, it's a movie set. The hotel's generators produce 10 times the power generated in the rest of the entire island. The outside swimming pool is 8,000 square feet. There are conference rooms (turns out that a Chinese firm has 600 employees at the hotel in training sessions - no wonder the Internet said no rooms). Four restaurants, designer clothes shops, tennis courts, a gym and a total of 412 rooms. Turns out, our room is one of 7 suites with an ocean view.

Back to the car to see the south end of the island. Atop the cliffs is suicide point where Japanese soldiers jumped rather than surrender. There is a memorial that faces the ocean. The cliff is next to the cave lined Carolinas mountain where Japanese soldiers held out for 3 months after Tinian fell.

The main town is San Jose. Our map showed a small town, Carolinas Heights, up in the hills and a Shinto Shrine hidden behind the town. We had a car, so why not. And soon afterwards, we were wondering why. A dirt road led to a smaller dirt road. And higher on the mountain, a left turn, a right turn, a smaller road and lots of jungle. Time to give up on this quest. And suddenly there it was. It looks like it's been abandoned for 200 years. Probably hasn't been, but, it looks very "Indiana Jones".

There were no souvenirs of note in the shops at the hotel and I saw the sign, "Souvenirs - Sale" on an igloo shaped building between San Jose and the Dynasty. Gio Village. They not only had T-shirts for sale but they could make them to order. They had one with a map of Tinian on the back with enough detail to show all four runways, the names of the beaches and mountains and scenic points we stopped at. They printed one for me with the map and my name on the front. $25. Since most of the tourists to this island are Japanese who like to gamble, this shop is hurting for customers.

Supper was easy. We found a market in town for beer and soda to bring back. Add a half a club sandwich and there you go.

We noticed very little activity in the casino during the day and the night. Most of the dealers had empty tables. So, I was surprised to find two active card tables when I went down for breakfast at 7 AM.

At checkout, I asked and got two free tickets for the boat back to Saipan. The car company met us at the boat dock to get their car back (we drove rather than wait for the bus - just an extra precaution) and off we were. This time luck trumped preparation.

## THE END

## SIDEBAR FOR TINIAN

GETTING THERE - There are no direct flights from the mainland USA. From the west coast, you change planes in Honolulu on Continental Air (fares of $1300 RT) to Guam. Japan Air Lines and Northwest also service Guam. RT to Saipan from Guam is $100 on Continental Micronesia. If you want to use the island hopper to visit the Carolina Islands on the way to or from Guam, it's easier to book Continental in both directions. Continental, Northwest and JAL have direct flights from Japan to Saipan.

The one hour ferry from Saipan to Tinian has a dock fee of $3 and ticket price of $10 each way. Buy both, at separate windows, at the dock. Schedules change, check at the dock. or at www.tinian-ferry.8m.com Freedom Air (tel 670/234-8328) and Pacific Island Aviation (tel 671/647-3603) both fly small planes between Guam, Saipan and Tinian.

WHEN TO GO - Tinian has an average temperature of 80 degrees year round with little variation. The rainiest month is September, followed by the 2 months in either direction.

HOTELS - 85% of the islands hotel rooms are at the Dynasty Hotel and Casino. 412 total rooms. tinian.dynasty.@paficica.net A five star hotel with rooms starting at $125/D. Discounts are available in person, none were offered on line. Failing that, there is Lori Lynn's Hotel (tel. 670-433-3256) and the Fleming Hotel (tel. 670-433-0381), both roughly five blocks from the boat dock and charge $40/D

HEALTH - No shots necessary. It should be safe to drink the tap water, but, better to be safe and stick to bottled.

MISCELLANEOUS - For additional information contact www.mymarianas.com Or www.tinian.org This is an American Territory so passports aren't necessary but it would be foolish to travel without one.

# X RUSSIA

## SEA YOU IN SIBERIA

### Lake Baikal, the deepest in the world

IRKUTSK, RUSSIA - Why would anyone in their right mind want to go to Siberia, people asked. I was starting to wonder myself after returning from the airplane bathroom that was so bad I held my breath. I'd been in cleaner Porta Potties. I was on the Aeroflot red eye flight from Moscow to Irkutsk and shoe horned myself back into the smallest space I've ever had on a commercial jet to try to get some sleep. Uncomfortable as it was, I dozed off and woke up for an uneventful landing. There were 16 Americans on this tour to the middle of nowhere and I didn't realize how unique we were until later. I also didn't realize that this ramshackle 1941 terminal I walked into wasn't in Irkutsk until I saw everyone just milling about looking for coffee. Turns out I slept through the announcement that Irkutsk was fogged in and the plane turned north towards the Arctic Circle for the nearest airport. We were 400 KM north in the dreary town of Bratsk.

The 5 ½ hour flight took 10 ½ hours + 5 hours time zone advance. Fortunately, the boat wasn't going to leave without us. The sixteen of us were joined by 2 Dutchmen for a total of 18 passengers on a boat capable of holding 30 with a crew of 14. We learned that this was the only ship to cruise the lake, did 15 trips per year and only one of them had Americans. This year, that was us.

THE BOAT - It was built in 1987 and sailed the Black Sea. They brought it through connecting rivers and lakes (and a little overland) to get it here in the winter of 1999. It was renovated for the lake and has radar and GPS. We won't see the whole lake, it's too big, but we'll do 1000 kilometers in a week.

THE LAKE - Is 400 miles long, 12 to 30 miles wide, and 1 mile deep. It's the deepest lake in the world, the oldest lake in the world and has 20%

of the worlds fresh water. The water is so pure that bottled water on the boat is from 400 meters down in the lake. There are 3500 species of animal and plant life in the area and 2600 exist only here. The lake is frozen from November to April to a depth of 4 ½ feet.

There was enough time for a tour of the town. Irkutsk was founded in 1661 and has a population of 650,000. It's on the Angara River, the only one to flow out of the lake - 365 rivers flow in. A hydroelectric dam on the river supplies the town's electricity. The town is mostly 5 story concrete buildings. Very practical but not attractive. There are some bright spots though. We stopped at the pretty Znamenska Church, the history museum (all about the lake) and the Decabrits house where we got a short concert of classical music.

The next morning was our first adventure on the lake. A morning walk through the forest at Kadilna. Actually, there aren't that many trees here and we were walking through a local family's farm. Our scheduled outdoor barbeque went inside because of the overcast weather. We moved into a big log cabin where the wall logs had bark on the inside as well as out. Food was brought from the boat and cooked on an outside wood fire. Tea was made in an ancient samovar, outside. Shiskabob chunks of beef, slices of fresh tomato and cucumber, black bread, a shot of vodka and one of the crew played a three stringed guitar. Absolutely delightful.

The husband, wife and teenage daughter actually do live here year round. I counted 1 dog, 1 cat, 2 cows, 1 chicken and 1 turkey. The daughter is an artist and sells painted flat rocks with a picture of a seal face for $1.33 and 6" high, fully clothed dolls for $5. There is no pressure to buy and they are really well done. What looked boring at first turned out to be memorable day.

The next day, the sun was out and we went to the fishing village, Huzhir, on Olhan Island. The work here is only part time since other fisheries are doing a better job. It's on it's way to becoming a ghost town. The museum has artifacts from the days when things were better. 10 rubles to take a picture, which you find out after you've taken the picture. We went inside an old woman's house to get a feel for local conditions and inside the local school. They have 300 kids enrolled, no paved roads and 4 hours of electricity at varying times during a day. Teachers get $167 a month.

Three vans took us the Shaman's rock on the far side of the island. The island is the center of the Shaman religion and it's believed that Genghis Khan is buried here. The view is gorgeous and offset the ½ hour of babble from the purple silk robed Shaman who talked and beat a drum to call on, whatever. This section of the island is a resort - room and board for $15 - and that's where we had lunch. Omul fish, potatoes, soup, tomato, cucumber, bread and, of course, a shot of vodka. The Shaman followed us for a free meal. They say a motorcycle was lost in the lake for 2 years. When found, it was left out to dry, gassed and ran perfectly. That's how pure the lake water is.

When we left, we towed a boat from the island that was low on fuel. Apparently, there is no gas station on the island. Stuffed bell pepper for supper, full card bingo afterwards and I didn't win. The sea was rolling, time for Dramamine.

Next morning, the sea was calm, and people were fishing off the back of the boat. We stopped at Gurbulik, a village of 150. Local school goes to the 4th grade and that's about it for most of the children. The sun was out and Emma had her flowered paper parasol to protect her. She had faithfully carried it all the way from America and it was finally getting some use. The kids posed for pictures, there are beautiful summer flowers in the yards of the rustic wood houses. On the far end of town, atop a hill, is the cemetery. Graves are covered with flowers, pictures are on the headstones and the sad part is how young most of them died. A reminder of where we are.

Time for a bath? Apparently the tour thought so. We stopped at the thermal springs at Buht Zmenjnaja. The one closest to the dock is only 100 degrees but we didn't know any better and went to the large one - which isn't all that big when you get there. Two people at a time, max. The temperature here is 115. That'll steam anything off. And the lake is close by if you want to cool down fast. Supper that night was fish and the soup was fish. I guess those efforts from the back of the boat paid off.

The next day started with a totem pole greeting at Buhta Peschanaya, a resort town. Tennis courts, a grand 2 story lodge, lots of trees and fresh air for $10 a day. That's room and board. Afterwards, we took a rather treacherous walk on a narrow path to the Trans-Siberian railroad. After the dam was built, the water level went up and covered the tracks. So, the RR had to be rerouted.

For our last day on the boat (the week went fast) we stopped at Listvjanka. St. Nicholas church (clearly the most popular name for a church) and a bus ride to "the ethnic village". It's a 17th century fortress for a town of 100 and reminds one of what a wild west town would look like if is was built by the Russians. Fortress walls of logs, a tiny church, a school house and outdoor dining among the log cabins. For lunch, they put on a marriage selection play (with the mandatory singing and dancing) for about an hour. There are tables in the complex with local wares, jewelry and fine gemstones, but, no snack shop nor rest rooms.

Dockside they were waiting for us. Rows of tables of gemstones and souvenirs. The best selection for shopping on the entire trip. The sun was out and Emma put her parasol to use. That night was the Captains dinner and when he smiled, the reflected light from all that gold made you reach for sunglasses. Free vodka, wine and cloth napkins (for the first time).

Unexpectedly, every day was different and we saw what few Americans will ever see. A trip of a lifetime for some. For the others, this trip certainly raises the bar. Who would figure you could use sun screen in Siberia, except Emma who came prepared with the paper parasol.

THE END

## SIDEBAR FOR BAIKAL

GETTING THERE - There are direct flights to Moscow from the east coast and connecting flights from the west coast. We connected at JFK to Helsinki and then Moscow on Finnair. Moscow to Irkutsk was on Aeroflot. The best fare to Moscow is $859 RT from the west coast on Aeroflot.

WHEN TO GO - Summer and two months on either side is best. Our visit was part of a tour and that's the best way to see Russia. Although they want tourists they haven't figured out the way to do it efficiently.

ARRANGEMENTS - Lexcorp Cruise & Tour, 3401 Investment Blvd., Ste.#3, Hayward, CA 94545-3819, tel= 800-578-7742, fax=510-784-8989, Email:lexcorp1@pacbell.net, has done hundreds of trips throughout Russia and made the arrangements for this one. Value World Tours is another, 17220 Newhope St., #202, Fountain Valley, CA 92708. Tel= 800-795-1633, Fax= 714-556-6125, http//www.vwtours.com, Email= mail@vwtours.com

HEALTH - There are no shots necessary but don't drink water from the tap.

VISA - Are required. $70 for two months and it may take some time to get on your own. A travel agency (for a tour) can do it faster and easier. There are Info Travel, tel 617-566-2197, Email: infostudy@aol.com, Russia House, tel. 202-986-6010, Email: lozansky@aol.com.

MISCELLANEOUS - For additional information contact the Russian consulate at 2641 Tunlaw Rd., NW, Washington DC 20007, tel 202-939-8907

Moscow on the Hudson (scratch that) Moscow

Moscow Circus - photography is forbidden

RUSSIA - Moscow, the town, is named after Moscow, the river, that snakes through it's center. One might figure it should be the other way around. But then, things are different here. The trip didn't start well. The passport processing line at the airport was slow enough to make me wonder if our plane arrival was a surprise. I found no place at the airport to change dollars for rubles and it was raining as we boarded the bus for town. The road was jammed with trucks and we were lucky to do 10 miles per hour. It felt like rush hour back home except for the girls standing in the rain, every fifty meters, on the other side of the road. They come from the outside provinces looking for work and Moscow has 9 million people. More people than jobs.

We rode past scores of six story concrete buildings devoid of color to the upscale International Hotel built by Armand Hammer for the Russian Olympics. Fortunately, the hotel has an ATM and a full supermarket inside the building. Things were looking up. Before supper, two of the girls in our party ordered rusty nails at the main bar. The bill came to $58 for the two drinks. The yelling and gnashing of teeth that followed could be heard across the large interior atrium. They were certainly sober for supper where a shot of vodka was $1. Lesson learned.

A wedding reception was in progress in the big room next to our small dining room and was the far more interesting place to be. Tables formed a rectangle around a female dancer. Not a strip tease, but close. The vodka flowed and some of the guests joined in to dance with the entertainer. The bride (in a beautiful white gown) and groom (in a black tux) applauded with everyone else. Things are different here.

Moscow became a city in 1147 and the main city of Russia in the 14th century. Our tour guide said it's the second most expensive city in the world, just behind Tokyo. The average wage is $500 a month and the average pension is $60/month.

The morning bus tour crossed the Moscow river several times but the river is in a constant curve and it's impossible to get one's bearings. We looked over the red walls of the Kremlin from across the river. Finally some color - red and gold. Real gold, by the way.

At a split in the river we stopped at an impressive and huge, black statue. It was designed in 1987 as a tribute to Columbus and rejected by local authorities. So as not to waste, the face was changed and it was renamed Peter the Great statue. This, the government accepted. Locals call it Peter the Columbus statue.

We went into the subway, starting at the Victory station for a short ride. It's the deepest at 310 feet and is connected to the surface by one really long escalator. The fare is only 7 rubles (20 cents) even though the real cost is 35 R. The government picks up the difference. Each station is uniquely decorated with paintings and statues. The subway system is an art gallery in itself.

Next was one of the many "fine art" museums. It featured portraits of long dead homely people with too much cheek rouge. However, that night was the famed Moscow circus. An iron car in front (art) drew a crowd. One doesn't think of Moscow having public artwork just for the sake of art, but, there it was. Times are changing. The circus features acrobats and animal acts - bears, monkeys, no big cats - all with a live band and snazzy lighting. It's very well done and the women that used to work for the defunct KGB have found a new job. Enforcing the no picture rule inside the circus.

The Kremlin is in the geographical center of the city, on the banks of the river. It's shaped like a triangle, enclosed in high, red brick walls. Next to the walled complex, just outside the wall, is red square. The entrance to red square is next to a statue of Marshall Zukov, WWII hero of the Soviets. Just inside the gate, to the left is the impressive Kazan Church originally built in the 17th century. It was demolished in 1936 to make more room for the May Day parades and faithfully rebuilt since then. To the right is a huge, red brick, historical museum that forms one end of the square. The far end of the square (actually a rectangle) is Saint Basil's Cathedral. Lenin's Mausoleum is to the right of St. Basil's, but, who cares. St. Basil's is gorgeous. It was finished in 1561, commissioned by Ivan the Terrible to celebrate his victory over the Tartars. The 9 octagonal chapels were originally separate churches. The entire cathedral was named after the holy fool, Vasily, which is Basil in English. There were several wedding parties getting their pictures taken around St. Basil's and Red Square. Must be something in the air. Weddings everyplace we go.

Next to the cathedral, opposite side from Lenin, is Gum department store built in the 19th century. It was designed for 1000 stores and it wasn't long ago that there were 1000 empty store front windows. Not anymore. Prado, Gucci, Armani, you name it, it's here. The 3 story center atrium (one of them) looks like a Victorian train station with water fountains. To me, that's a plus.

The following day we went into the Kremlin. There is the 15th century, 90 CM bore (about 35"), biggest cannon in the world (at the time). It was never fired. It's reported that invaders saw the huge cannon being rolled out

691

for battle and turned tail. Then there's the Annuciation Cathedral that Ivan the Terrible was forbidden to enter by the local Bishop for a 7th wedding. So, Ivan had a side entrance built and was married there. In an adjoining courtyard is the world's largest bell (that's never been rung, of course). The 200 ton bell was forged, crated and put into a pit to age. The wood crate caught fire and people poured river water on it causing a huge chunk to fall off the bell. Like the cannon, the world's biggest and never been used.

Moscow streets are congested with busses, trucks and cars. Real cars made outside the Soviet Union. We saw a red Ferrari cruising Arabat street. The stores are full of merchandise, like most European cities. But the look of the city is distinct, as is the feel. The colorful churches, gold domes, the Kremlin, Red Square, the subway, the circus, the world's biggest - fill in the blank. Things are different here.

THE END

For Pete's Sake, it's the prettiest city in Russia.

Peterhof, outside of St. Petersburg, Russia

St. PETERSBURG, RUSSIA is known for many things, survival being one of them. Peter the Great built this city as a window to the west in 1703. Of all places, atop a Finnish swamp. It was the capital, then it wasn't. It was St. Petersburg, then Leningrad, then St. Petersburg. The Nazi's laid siege for 900 days and couldn't take the city even though nearly 1 million lives were lost. The last couple of hundred years have been rough and yet it's held on to emerge as the most elegant and attractive city in all of Russia.

We didn't have much time, not nearly enough to do this city justice so we hit the ground running with a city tour. St. Nicholas Cathedral is an attractive 18<sup>th</sup> century Baroque style church in blue and gold. The Russian churches are different because the inside walls are lined with pictures. They can't all be Saints, there are too many. The inside icons are gold plated (no pictures can be taken inside).

The city is on the Neva River on the Gulf of Finland, on 44 islands with 50 canals. So it's no surprise that many of the major attractions are next to water. As is the red Rostral columns intended to proclaim the glory of Peter the Great's navy. Unique, for sure. Next to a canal is the Church of Spilled Blood (or Church of the Bleeding Savior) finished in 1907. It was modeled after St. Basil's in Moscow and it's gorgeous. It was built over the site of Tsar Alexsander II's 1881 assassination.

Next to the Admiralty (on the river, of course), is the Bronze Horseman. A statue of Peter the Great on a rearing horse, terrorizing his enemies. Directly across is the 332 foot high glittering gold dome of St. Isaac's Cathedral. 220 pounds of gold coats the dome and 60 laborers died from inhaling the mercury fumes during the gilding process. This church cost five times than of the winter palace and took 40 years to build. To the right is the Astoria Hotel. Hitler printed invitations for a reception here prior to his invasion of St. Petersburg. I guess they're collectors items now. The 1905 Cruiser Aurora is docked on the river and is in very good condition considering it's age - looks like it could go back in service. It's famous for firing a blank at the Winter Palace during the 1917 revolution, scaring the provisional government.

The first of the "big 3" is Catherine's Summer Palace, built in 1756, destroyed by the Nazi's and rebuilt. It's a huge, blue and white building that appears to be a mile long when waiting outside at the gate. We got there early, waited for ½ an hour, at the gate, to get to the inside line for another wait of 1 ½ hours. Clearly, it was too big to see everything, but the opulent rooms, paintings, furnishings, gold outlined windows and doors that we did see is enough to conclude that politics did pay off for some. The amber room has been finished and is a major crowd pleaser (adding to the wait line). The walls of this room are jewels and Russia is borrowing money from the west.

The second of the "big 3" is Pedrodvorets (Peter the Great's Summer Palace) and it's out of town on the Gulf of Finland. The shops and stands just outside have the best selection and best prices for souvenirs in town. Shop here. It's 300 years old and most of the fountains are reconstructions since the Nazi's took the originals and "lost" them. The gardens, the fountains the gold plated Roman statues that light up in the sun - it's absolutely stunning. Sixty four gravity powered fountains empty into the grand canal and take a long trip to the Gulf. Words are inadequate to describe the variety of fountains, statues, flowers and colors. A few hours here are well spent.

The third of the "big 3" is the Hermitage, in town, on the banks of the river. Originally, it was a collection of 225 paintings purchased by Catherine the Great. It now occupies 5 buildings and is the largest art collection in the world. On a par with the Louvre, Prado and the Vatican. Officially, it's the State Hermitage Museum and has 3 million pieces, of which 150,00 are on display at any one time. It has Egyptian, Greek and Roman art, prehistoric artifacts and a full collection of 15th-19th century European art. One could spend days here and not see all the displays. It's one of a kind.

We didn't get to go onboard the Aurora Cruiser or inside St. Isaac's Cathedral which is reported to have fantastic murals and mosaics or see the Vodka Museum, the Chocolate Museum, the Zoological Museum, the Arctic and Antarctic Museum or the Fortress of Peter and Paul, but, we got tickets to The Cossack show. A costumed musical stage play, done in a theater, Russian style. There was a lot of singing and dancing.

I think I would have enjoyed the Chocolate Museum more. I know I would have enjoyed the Vodka Museum more.

THE END